SUCCEEDING ON YOUR OWN
Goals • Resources • Decisions

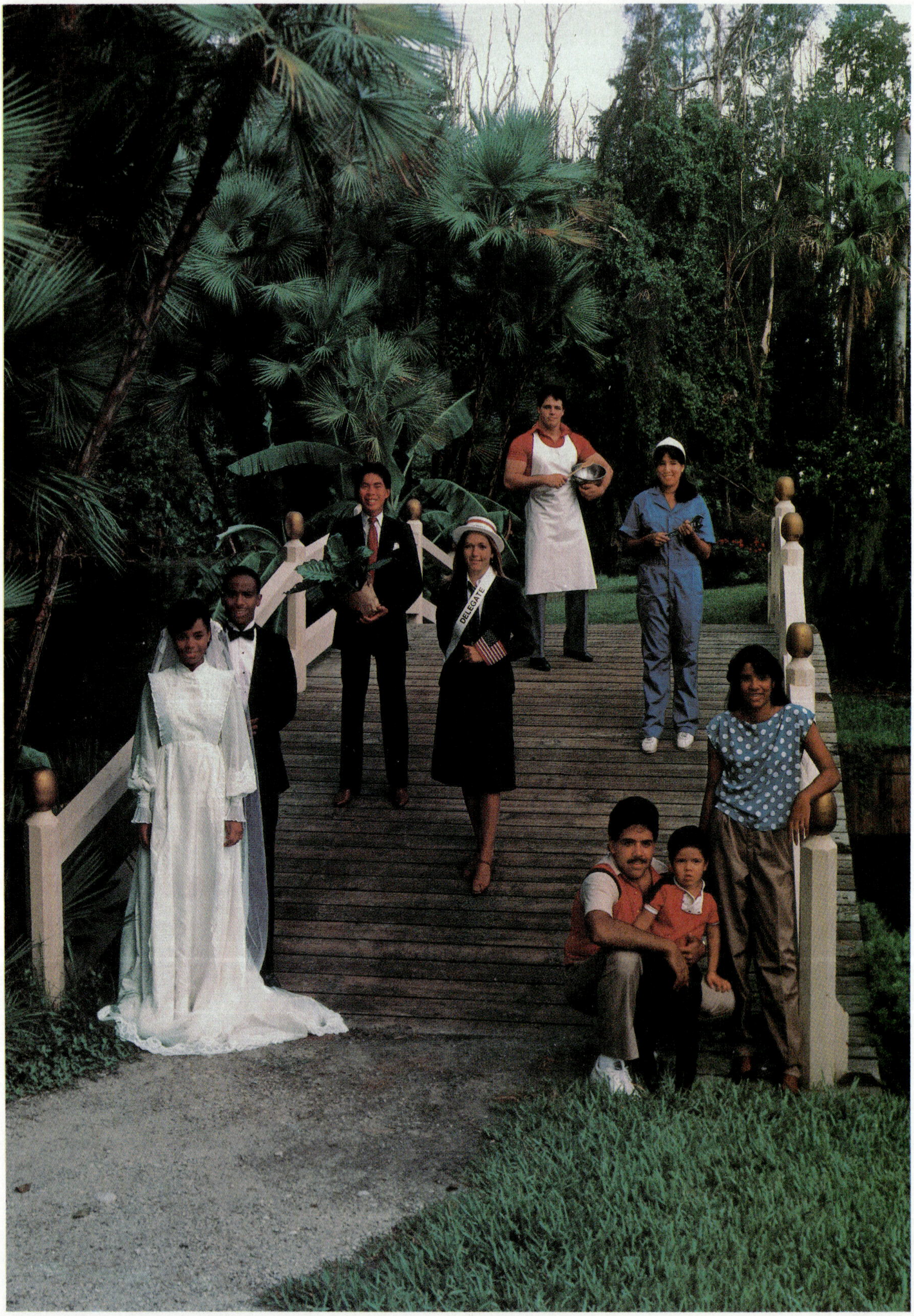
DELEGATE

SUCCEEDING ON YOUR OWN
Goals • Resources • Decisions

Jeri Lyn Rieken **Gail House**
College of Home Economics
Texas Tech University

Harcourt Brace Jovanovich, Publishers
Orlando   San Diego   Chicago   Dallas

ACKNOWLEDGMENTS: Adaptation of charts on pp. 596 and 601, "Phases of Alcoholism and Recovery" and "Effect of Cigarette Smoking on Life Expectancy of 25-Year-Old Persons," from *YOUR HEALTH AND SAFETY for Better Living.* Copyright © 1973 by Harcourt Brace Jovanovich, Inc. Reprinted by permission of Harcourt Brace Jovanovich, Inc. Adaptation of the eight stages of development, according to Erikson, from *Psychology: Its Principles and Applications,* Eighth Edition, by T. L. Engle and Louis Snellgrove. Copyright © 1984 by Harcourt Brace Jovanovich, Inc. Reprinted by permission of Harcourt Brace Jovanovich, Inc.

Copyright © 1986 by Harcourt Brace Jovanovich, Inc.

All rights reserved. No part of this publication may be reproduced or transmitted in any form or by any means, electronic or mechanical, including photocopy, recording, or any information storage and retrieval system, without permission in writing from the publisher.

Request for permission to make copies of any part of the work should be mailed to: Permissions, Harcourt Brace Jovanovich, Publishers, Orlando, Florida 32887

Printed in the United States of America

ISBN 0-15-307000-5

Contributors

Nancy F. Dillon
Phoenix, Arizona

Nancy Proehl Harvey
Home Economics Department
Osceola High School
Seminole, Florida

Mary Anne Symons Brown
New York, New York

Miriam Meyer
Tarrytown, New York

Patricia L. Snyder
Schaumburg, Illinois

Karl Weber
Bronx, New York

Consulting Reviewers

Nancy Bush
Home Economics Department
Franklin High School
Seattle, Washington

Betty Lou Joanos
College of Home Economics
Florida State University
Tallahassee, Florida

Dr. Gwendolyn Newkirk
Department of Consumer
  Science and Education
College of Home Economics
University of Nebraska—
  Lincoln
Lincoln, Nebraska

Kathleen L. Cavanaugh
Registered Dietitian
Orlando, Florida

Jane McEllhiney Stein
Home Economics Department
San Diego High School
San Diego, California

Dr. Diana M. Spillman
Registered Dietitian and
  Professor
College of Home Economics
Florida State University
Tallahassee, Florida

Nancy Clem
Home Economics Department
Pike Central High School
Petersburg, Indiana

Peggy Morrison-Thurston
Home Economics Department
Pinellas Park High School
Largo, Florida

Illustration and Photograph Credits

Illustrations: Graphic Concern, Inc.

Photographs

Key: *(t)* top, *(b)* bottom, *(l)* left, *(r)* right, *(tl)* top left, *(tr)* top right, *(bl)* bottom left, *(bc)* bottom center, *(br)* bottom right.

BLACK AND WHITE PHOTOS (See separate listing below for color photo essay credits.)

Page xvi: HBJ. 2: HBJ. 4: Joan Menschenfreund/Taurus Photos. 6: Karen Rosenthal/Stock, Boston. 9: Laimute E. Druskis/Taurus Photos. 10: Frank Siteman/Taurus Photos. 11: Laimute E. Druskis/Taurus Photos. 12: Erika Stone/Peter Arnold, Inc. 14: Joan Menschenfreund/Taurus Photos. 17: Bob Clay/Jeroboam. 18: HBJ. 19: Leo deWys, Inc. 24: HBJ. 26: courtesy, Florida School for the Deaf and Blind. 27: HBJ. 31: Richard Wood/Taurus Photos. 32: Evan Johnson/Jeroboam. 33: George Roos/Peter Arnold, Inc. 35: (tl) Christopher Brown/Stock, Boston; (tr) Donald Dietz/Stock, Boston; (bl) Peter Vilms/Jeroboam; (br) Doug Wilson/Black Star. 36: Mike Mazzaschi/Stock, Boston. 37: Barbara Rios/Photo Researchers. 38: David Hurn/Magnum Photos. 39: Peter Vilms/Jeroboam. 44: Bettye Lane/Photo Researchers. 46: HBJ. 49: (t and b) HBJ. 51: HBJ. 52: Ann Zane Shanks/Photo Researchers. 53: HBJ. 54: HBJ. 55: HBJ. 56: Mimi Forsyth/Monkmeyer Press Photo Service. 57: Billy E. Barnes/FPG. 62: Hugh Rogers/Monkmeyer Press Photo Service. 63: Sybil Shelton/Peter Arnold, Inc. 68: HBJ. 70: Danilo Nardi/FPG. 72: HBJ. 76: Freda Leinwand. 77: Michelle Vignes/Jeroboam. 78: HBJ. 80: Dave Schaefer/Jeroboam. 82: Guy Gillette/Photo Researchers. 83: Susan Woog Wagner/Photo Researchers. 85: Christopher Morrow/Stock, Boston. 86: Laimute E. Druskis/Taurus Photos. 87: HBJ. 92: HBJ. 97: (l) Laimute E. Druskis/Jeroboam; (r) Willie L. Hill, Jr./FPG. 99: Harry Wilks/Stock, Boston. 103: HBJ. 104: HBJ. 105: HBJ. 107: Nancy

Kaye/Leo deWys, Inc. 110: Joan Menschenfreund/Taurus Photos. 112: Van Bucher/Photo Researchers. 118: HBJ. 121: Paul Conklin/Monkmeyer Press Photo Service. 123: HBJ. 125: Freda Leinwand/Monkmeyer Press Photo Service. 126: HBJ. 127: (l and r) HBJ. 128: F. B. Grunzweig/Photo Researchers. 130: Les Mahon/Monkmeyer Press Photo Service. 134: HBJ. 135: (l) Beckwith Studios/Taurus Photos; (r) Richard Laird/Leo deWys, Inc. 137: Freda Leinwand. 142: HBJ. 145: HBJ. 146: HBJ. 147: HBJ. 150: HBJ. 154: HBJ. 155: Tyrone Hall/Stock, Boston. 156: HBJ. 157: (tl) Bruce Forrester/Jeroboam; (tr) HBJ; (bl) HBJ; (br) Cary Wolinsky/Stock, Boston. 162: David Hurn/Magnum Photos. 165: Laimute E. Druskis/Art Resource. 167: Tim Davis/Photo Researchers. 171: (l) HBJ; (r) Robert Houser/Photo Researchers. 174: Sybil Shelton/Peter Arnold, Inc. 179: HBJ. 184: HBJ. 186: The News World/FPG. 188: (t) Freda Leinwand; (b) HBJ. 192: HBJ. 196: HBJ. 203: Rene Burri/Magnum Photos. 224: HBJ. 226: Ginger Chih/Peter Arnold, Inc. 228: HBJ. 229: Vincent Lisanti/FPG. 230: Imperial Wallcoverings. 233: HBJ. 235: (l) Vincent Lisanti/FPG; (r) Closet Maid Storage Systems, Clairson International. 236: HBJ. 239: HBJ. 241: (l) HBJ; (r) Mimi Forsyth/Monkmeyer Press Photo Service. 246: HBJ. 248: (tl) Freda Leinwand; (tr) Suzanne Szasz/Photo Researchers; (bl) Mimi Forsyth/Monkmeyer Press Photo Service; (br) HBJ. 251: Bill Grimes/Leo deWys, Inc. 252: HBJ/Alan Ulmar. 258: Cary Wolinsky/Stock, Boston. 259: HBJ. 260: HBJ. 266: HBJ. 268: Ann Hagen Griffiths/OMNI Photo Communications. 274: Ann Hagen Griffiths/OMNI Photo Communications. 276: Pfaff American Sales Corporation. 283: HBJ. 284: Hazel Hankin/Stock, Boston. 286: (l and r) Lew Merrim/Monkmeyer Press Photo Service. 287: P & R Associates/Taurus Photos. 292: HBJ. 294: HBJ. 297: HBJ. 298: HBJ. 301: HBJ/Alan Ulmar. 304: Jeffry W. Myers/FPG. 306: Ed Lettau/Photo Researchers. 307: HBJ. 310: (l) HBJ; (r) Kent Reno/Jeroboam. 316: HBJ. 319: Alon Reininger/Leo deWys, Inc. 320: HBJ/Alan Ulmar. 322: Jeffry W. Myers/FPG. 324: (l and c) Laimute E. Druskis/Art Resource; (r) HBJ. 326: HBJ. 329: James Motlow/Jeroboam. 332: HBJ. 335: HBJ/Alan Ulmar. 336: Carolyn A. McKeone/FPG. 342: HBJ. 345: (tl) Frank Siteman/Stock, Boston; (tr) Mimi Forsyth/Monkmeyer Press Photo Service; (bl) Freda Leinwand; (br) Richard Laird/FPG. 347: Chester Higgins, Jr./Photo Researchers. 351: Sybil Shelton/Peter Arnold, Inc. 353: Monkmeyer Press Photo Service. 355: HBJ. 356: HBJ. 357: (l) Peter Vandermark/Stock, Boston; (r) HBJ. 359: Gena Husman/FPG. 361: HBJ. 362: (l and r) HBJ. 368: Michos Tzovaras/Art Resource. 371: (t and b) HBJ. 372: (l) Susan Woog Wagner/Photo Researchers; (r) HBJ. 374: Russ Kinne/Photo Researchers. 375: HBJ. 376: HBJ. 378: Sipa Press/Art Resource. 380: Michael Weisbrot and Family/Stock, Boston. 385: Nancy J. Pierce/Photo Researchers.

COLOR PHOTOS

Page ii: HBJ. 209: Vasarely Center, New York. 210: (tl) Sears, Roebuck & Co.; (tr) Roseline Products; (bl) Cecile Brunswick; (br) J. C. Penney Co., 1985, reproduced by permission. 211: (tl) Simplicity Pattern Co.; (tr) 1001 Home Ideas; (bl) Cecile Brunswick; (br) Simplicity Pattern Co. 212: David Parker/Science Source, Photo Researchers. 214: (t) Sears, Roebuck & Co.; (b) J. C. Penney Co., 1985, reproduced by permission. 215: (t) Sears, Roebuck & Co.; (b) Sunworthy Wallcovering, photo by Photographic House. 216: (tl) Bali Custom Mini Blinds/Marathon Carey-McFall Co.; (tr and bl) HBJ; (br) 1001 Home Ideas. 217: (tl) Cecile Brunswick; (tr) HBJ; (bl) Simplicity Pattern Co.; (br) STAR, Division of Scanmark, Laguna Hills, CA 92653. 218: (t) Conran's Harlequin Kitchen; (b) Conran's Provence Kitchen. 219: (tl and tr) HBJ; (bl) Butterick Co.; (bc and br) courtesy, Spiegel, Chicago, Ill. 220: (l and r) HBJ. 221: (tl) Ron Nicolaysen; (tr) 1001 Home Ideas, photo by Photographic House; (bl) J. C. Penney Co., 1985, reproduced by permission; (br) 1001 Home Ideas. 222: (tl) J. C. Penney Co., 1985, reproduced by permission; (tr) courtesy, Spiegel, Chicago, Ill.; (bl) Cecile Brunswick; (br) Simplicity Pattern Co. 223: (t and b) HBJ.

CONTENTS

CHAPTER 1 Looking Forward to Adulthood — 1

Experiencing Changes and Choices — 2
    Adult Roles — 2
    Adult Responsibilities — 3
    Adult Relationships — 3
    Adult Freedoms — 4
    Adult Choices — 4

Understanding Influences on Your Decisions — 5
    The Influence of Your Heredity — 6
    The Influence of Your Family Environment — 6
    The Influence of Your Community Environment — 9
    The Influence of Important Events in Your Life — 10
    The Influence of Your Self-Concept — 10
    The Influence of Your Self-Esteem — 11

Making the Most of Your Choices — 12
    Understanding Your Needs and Values — 12
    Setting Your Goals — 13
    Recognizing Your Priorities — 15
    Managing Your Resources — 15
    Making Decisions — 17

> *Tips:* **Motivating Yourself to Accept Responsibilities** — 3
> *Tips:* **Ways to Boost Your Self-Esteem** — 11
> *P.S.:* **What Trends Might Affect Your Goals?** — 14
> *How Computers Can Help You:* **Computers as a Resource** — 18
> *Test Your Skills:* **Goal Setting** — 21

CHAPTER 2 Expressing Yourself as an Adult — 25

Gaining Independence Through Communication — 26
    Communication Basics — 26
    Types of Messages — 28
    Sending Messages — 28
    Receiving Messages — 30

Expressing Yourself in the Free Enterprise System — 34
    Principles of the Free Enterprise System — 34

Expressing Yourself in a Democratic Society — 36
    Your New Civic Responsibilities — 37
    Your New Civic Duties — 38

> *How Computers Can Help You:* **Keeping in Touch Through Telecommunications** — 27
> *Tips:* **Getting Your Messages Across** — 29
> *P.S.:* **What Is Your Communication Style?** — 31
> *Tips:* **Becoming a Better Listener** — 33
> *Test Your Skills:* **Decision Making** — 41

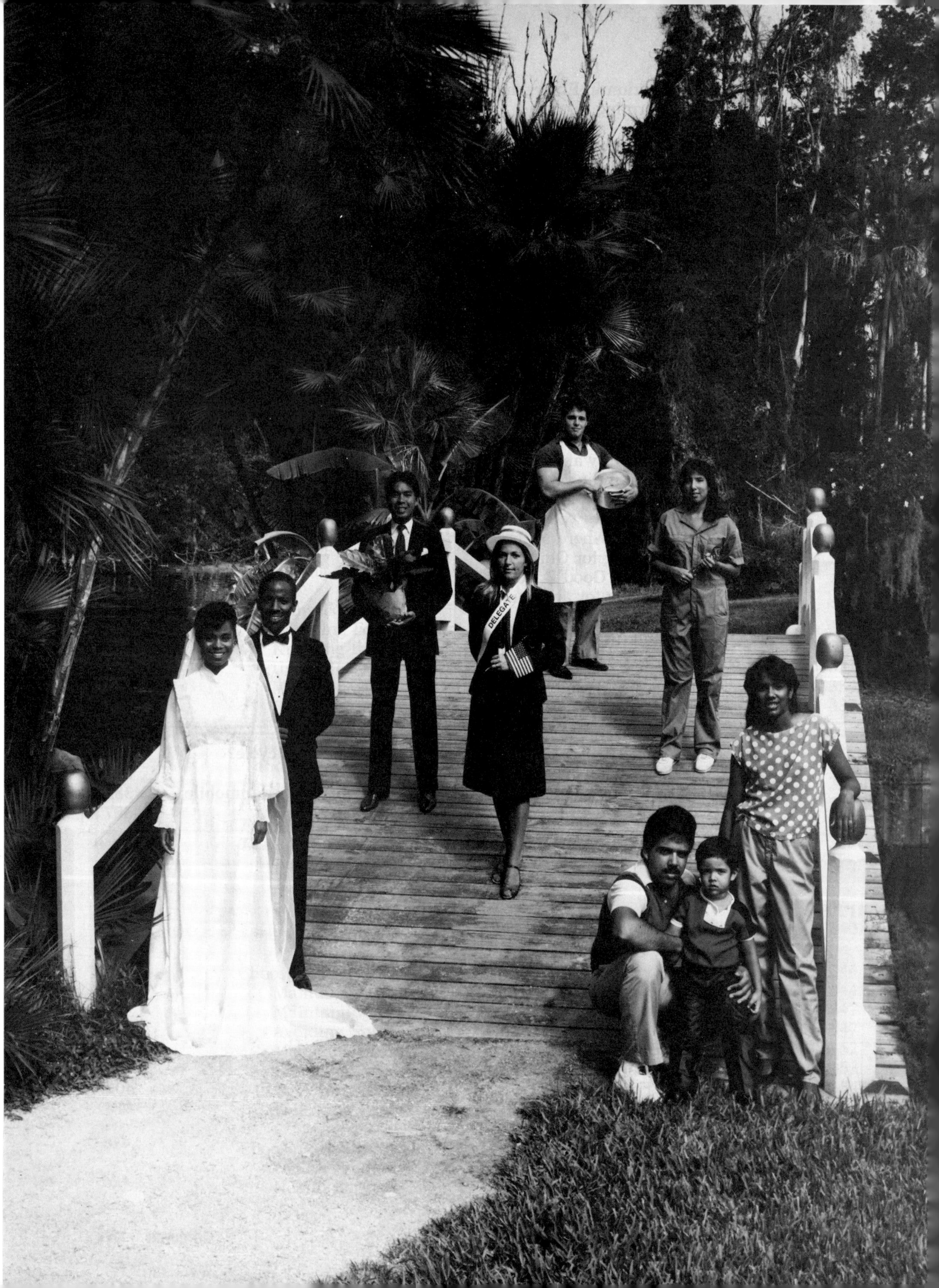
DELEGATE

CHAPTER 1

Looking Forward to Adulthood

Just ahead of you lies adulthood. Now is the time to prepare for this important stage of your life. An important part of getting ready is recognizing the many choices you will have. An even more important part of getting ready is realizing how well prepared you are or can become to make those choices. Being well prepared means understanding who you are and what your values are so you can make sense of the choices you face. It also means being able to set realistic goals and manage your resources so you can make good decisions.

You already make decisions every day. Some of these are more important or more difficult than others. As an adult, you will make even *more* decisions. Your new roles, responsibilities, relationships, and freedoms will bring you many new opportunities for making decisions.

You will also be choosing how to use most of your energy and time. You will probably decide to put a lot of effort into working or preparing to work. Therefore, you will probably decide to get vocational training, go to college, do volunteer work, become an apprentice, join the military, get a civilian job, or a combination of these. You will also probably decide to use a lot of your energy and time to make a home—for yourself and perhaps for others.

Now is a good time to begin thinking about your goals, your resources, and the decisions you will be making.

Discover Through Your Reading

- what it means to have the dual role of homemaker and wage earner
- how you can boost your self-esteem
- how to make sure you are setting a goal that you can reach
- what resources are available to you and how you can manage them
- how you can think through an important decision

Experiencing Changes and Choices

You already have certain roles, responsibilities, relationships, and freedoms. For example, you are a family member, a citizen, and a consumer, a user of products and services. You may also be a wage earner. You probably have accepted responsibility for helping make your family environment a good one for each family member. You probably have also established relationships with many different people, including family members, friends, perhaps an employer, and others. In addition, you probably have the freedom to make many shopping and other decisions.

As you move from adolescence into adulthood, you will experience changes in your roles, responsibilities, relationships, and freedoms. These changes will bring you many new choices.

Adult Roles

When you become an adult, some of the roles you already have will expand. In addition, you will add new roles. The roles you may have as an adult include the following:

- You will be an adult consumer. As such, you will be able to sign contracts by yourself and exercise other rights granted adult consumers.
- You will be an adult citizen. As such, you will be able to vote and exercise other rights granted adult citizens.
- You may marry and become a spouse.
- You may begin a family of your own and become a parent.
- Whether married or single, male or female, you will probably be responsible for making and managing a home for yourself and perhaps for others. You will be a homemaker.

How is this working couple sharing their homemaking duties?

- Whether married or single, male or female, you will probably be a wage earner. Many married couples need or want two incomes. Most single adults, whether or not they have any children, must earn a living.

As a result of your expanded and new roles, you will probably play the dual role of homemaker and wage earner. This double role offers many rewards. It allows each person a say in setting up and running the place he or she calls home. At the same time, it allows each person a chance to have a job that earns some money. This double role also involves many demands. It requires a person to be a good manager—of energy, time, money, and other resources.

You will probably find assuming new roles easier if you do not try to assume too many at once. For example, if you try to add the roles of homemaker, wage earner, and spouse all at one time, you may overextend yourself.

Adding no more than two roles at a time will probably increase your chances for success with each new role. Whenever possible, adding one role at a time may be better.

Adult Responsibilities

Becoming a more independent person at home or on your own means accepting increased responsibilities. If you continue to live at home after high school, you will probably help pay for housing and utilities, in addition to helping care for your family's home. You will also probably cover your personal expenses. If you begin to live on your own, you will probably have all of the responsibilities that come with being independent. This means you will take care of all your needs and wants, not just your housing and personal expenses.

You can gradually prepare for the responsibilities your adult roles will bring by adding a few responsibilities to those you already have. For tips on adding new responsibilities, see below.

Adult Relationships

As you grow toward independence, you will develop new relationships, and your old

---

Tips
Motivating Yourself to Accept Responsibilities

Accepting responsibilities is not always easy. You may need help in maintaining your motivation. If so, try these strategies:

- *Take on new responsibilities a few at a time rather than all at once.* If you take on too many responsibilities, you may become discouraged. If you take on too few, you may become bored.

- *Tackle a new activity when your interest is first sparked or when you feel challenged.* For example, respond to an ad for a job right after the ad captures your attention.

- *Give yourself opportunities to learn and practice new skills.* For example, you might volunteer to cook a roast or another simple main dish for your family. Your feeling of success might motivate you to try other main dishes. Doing this would let you see how easy and satisfying cooking for yourself and others can be.

- *Tell a few people what you are trying to accomplish so they can give you moral support.* For example, if you are trying to improve your study skills, tell other people, such as family members or a teacher, what you are doing. They may then encourage you to keep trying when you sometimes feel like giving up.

- *Let your failures motivate you.* For example, if you decided to save $25 of your income one month and were unable to, find out what happened. By looking back to decide what went wrong, you can learn from your mistakes. Next month, you can try a more workable plan to save $25.

Experiencing Changes and Choices

ones will change. You may see some friends and family members less frequently than you do now. The frequency may not be as important as the quality of the relationships you have with these people.

Your family will probably continue to be a source of support and love. However, your relationship with your family will gradually change to one of increased independence. You will eventually function as an adult rather than as a child. This will require an adjustment for both you and your family.

To help you and your family make the adjustment, you need to show your family that you are trustworthy and dependable. The more trustworthy and dependable you are, the less likely it is that you will feel and be treated like a child. The more you can demonstrate your ability to handle adult responsibilities, the easier it will be for your family to begin to see and treat you as an adult.

Adult Freedoms

As your family has considered you ready, you have probably been given more freedom. Perhaps you have been given the freedom to decide how you will spend much of your time. Maybe you have been given the freedom to select all of your clothing. You probably have several other types of freedom.

Parents, teachers, and others have not only given you more freedom but have also set examples and guidelines for your behavior. As you continue to mature and assume responsibility for your own actions, you will develop your own limits and standards to fit new situations. In this way, you can control your own behavior without supervision.

As an adult, you will have many freedoms that you may not yet have. You will be eligible for a wider range of jobs. You will be the one in charge of your energy, time, money, and other resources. You will be able to vote, serve on a jury, and do much more. Since you will be the one responsible for taking advantage of these freedoms, you will find yourself trying to make good decisions.

Adult Choices

As an adult, you will face many new choices. Among these will be important choices regarding your standard of living and your lifestyle. These elements of your life are often closely related and are often affected by other decisions you make in life.

Within a few years or months, you will be graduating from high school. At that time,

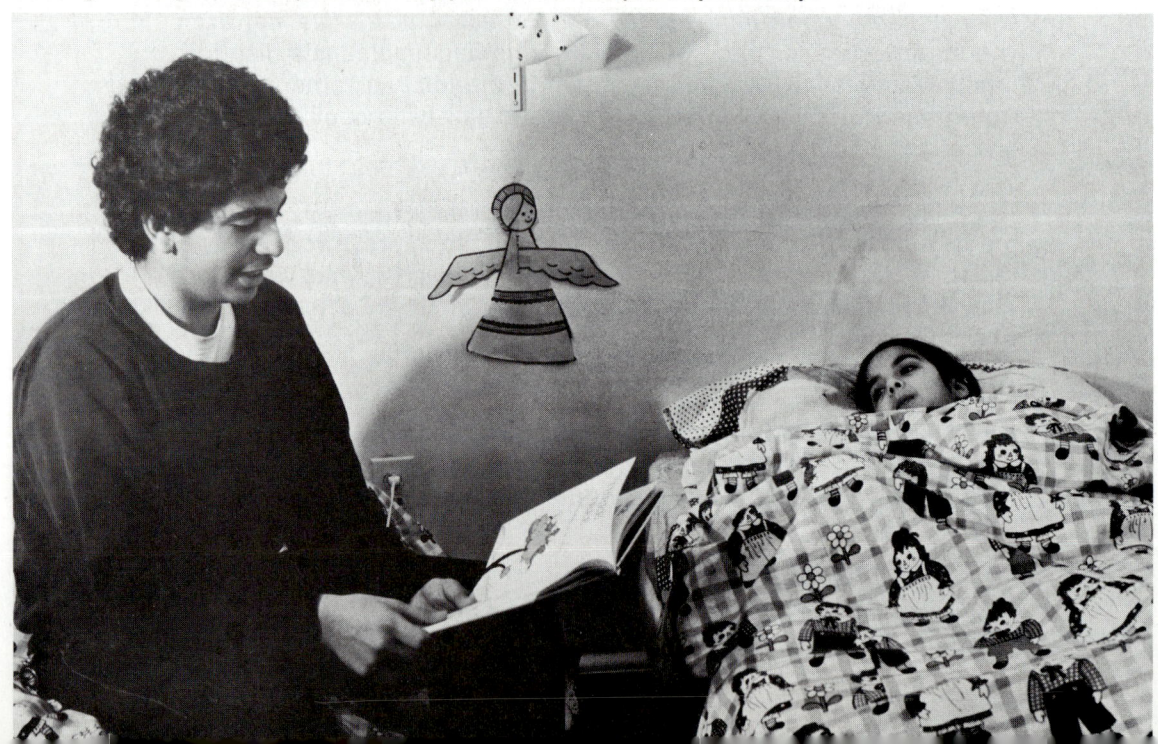

There are many ways to show that you are ready to handle some adult responsibilities. How might caring for a family member help you demonstrate your dependability?

Which of these items do you consider necessities? Which of these items do you consider comforts or luxuries?

your standard of living and your lifestyle are likely to change. A person's **standard of living** is the combination of necessities, comforts, and luxuries the person can afford. A person's **lifestyle** is how that person uses energy and time, with whom, and where. Because of the changes in your life, you will soon have new decisions to make about your standard of living and your lifestyle. Your decisions will probably include how you will cover the cost of necessities and whether you can afford any comforts and luxuries. Your decisions will also probably include how to earn money, how to use your energy and time, where to live, and with whom to spend your leisure hours.

The decisions you make about these matters will have an effect on one another. For example, you may decide to work part-time and continue to live at home. You may decide to work full-time and move into an apartment. You may decide to borrow money and go away to school. Your decisions about how you want to spend your time and where you want to live will affect your decision about what you can afford, and vice versa. These same decisions will affect what kind of jobs you will get, how much leisure time you will have, and what friends you will make, and vice versa.

The decisions you will soon be making will not, however, lock you into one particular standard of living or lifestyle. For example, you may decide to get a full-time job immediately after finishing high school. Later, you may decide that you want to move up at work or try a different type of work. Therefore, you may decide to enter a part-time or a full-time training program. As you make new decisions like these and as other important events occur in your life, your standard of living and your lifestyle will again change.

Understanding Influences on Your Decisions

Several factors that help make you a unique individual already influence the decisions you make. The same factors will also influence decisions you will make as an adult. These factors include your heredity, your family environment, your community environment, and important events in your life. They also include how well you know yourself and how much you like yourself.

The Influence of Your Heredity

The basic blueprint for many aspects of your life was established by your heredity. A person's **heredity** is the combination of characteristics the person got from parents and earlier ancestors. Characteristics you inherited include your physical traits, your general health, and even your special talents.

Your inherited characteristics will sometimes influence your decisions. For example, if you are very short, you may limit your volleyball playing to informal games among friends. If you have inherited the ability to sing, you may practice and perform music with others who have this ability.

While many of your inherited characteristics cannot be changed, some can. If you have a characteristic that can be changed, you may decide that you would like to do so. For example, if you inherited a slender build, you could increase weight and muscle tone through a diet and exercise program.

The Influence of Your Family Environment

Your family members are an important part of your environment, perhaps the most important part. Your family environment is defined by the structure and resources of your family. It is also defined by the life stage of each family member and the life stages of your family as a whole. Like your heredity, your family environment will sometimes influence your decisions.

Structure of Your Family

The structure of a family includes the number of family members, their ages, and their relationships to one another. The structure of your family not only affects decisions you and other family members make now but also decisions you will make as an adult.

The following examples show how your family structure may influence your decisions. If you come from a large family, you may be used to sharing space, activities, and feelings with others. These experiences may influence your decisions about the kind of housing you want or with whom you want to live. If you are the oldest child in your family or an only child, you may be used to handling

How do family members influence one another?

Stages of Family Development

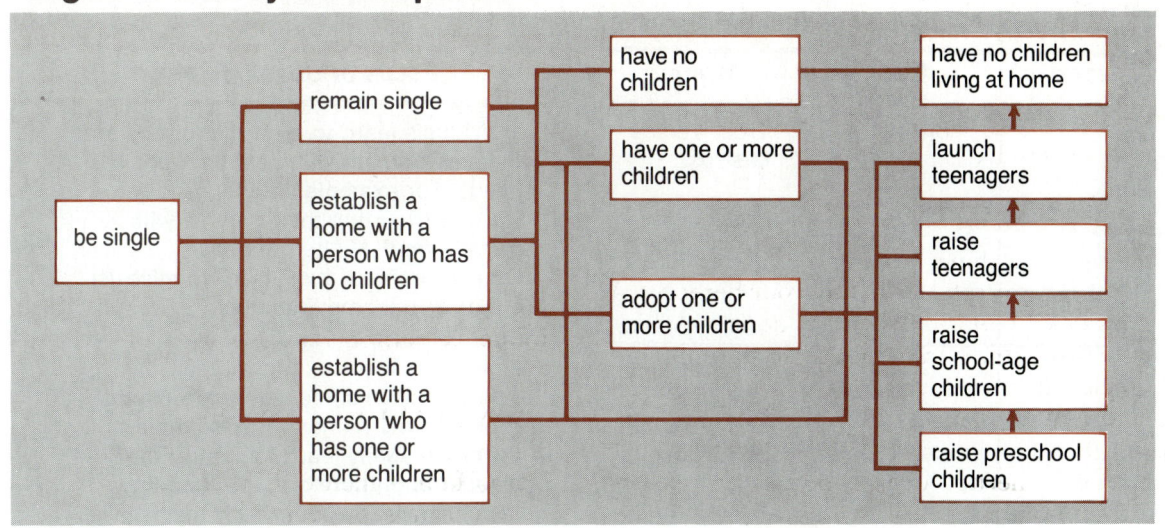

```
be single ─┬─ remain single ──────────────── have no children ──────── have no children living at home
           │
           ├─ establish a home with a         have one or more ──────── launch teenagers
           │  person who has no children      children
           │                                                            raise teenagers
           └─ establish a home with a         adopt one or
              person who has one or           more children             raise school-age children
              more children
                                                                        raise preschool children
```

new situations for yourself. This may make it easy for you to select a doctor or an insurance agent. If you have lived with a grandparent, you may enjoy being with older people and understand their concerns. Because of this, you may decide to work with the elderly or support their stands on public issues.

Resources of Your Family

A family's resources are a combination of those things each family member contributes. These contributions can take the form of knowledge, skills, personal qualities, energy, time, money, or materials.

The resources your family has been able to share with you will sometimes influence your decisions. For example, if your family has made many of its home furnishings, you may decide to make many of your own home furnishings. Maybe your family has set aside some earnings to cover emergencies. You may decide to do the same.

Life Stages of Family Members

Each person goes through various stages of development during childhood and adulthood. On page 8, you will find a list of these stages and a description of each stage.

At any given time, a family will usually consist of members at different stages of development. For example, the parents may be at the stage of intimacy versus isolation while one of their children is at the stage of trust versus mistrust and another is at the stage of initiative versus guilt.

The way your stages of development mesh with those of other family members will sometimes influence your decisions. For example, your parents may be in middle adulthood now, while you are a teenager. If they enjoy their work and feel productive and worthwhile, they will probably communicate this to you. Having them as models may lead you to decide to find or prepare for a demanding but satisfying job.

Life Stages of Your Family

Just as each person goes through a stage of development, so does a family. A family may develop in several different ways. Some families will include children; some will not. Families that include children, however, end up going through many of the same stages of development. Above, you will find a diagram of the various stages of family development.

Your family is currently involved in raising at least one teenager—you. It may also, however, be involved in raising preschool children, raising school-age children, or launching teenagers. Sometimes, families are in two or more stages at the same time.

The number of stages that your family is in will sometimes influence the decisions you make. For example, if your family also has

Understanding Influences on Your Decisions 7

Stages of Individual Development
(as defined by psychologist Erik Erikson)

Stage	Age	Name	Focus of Development
1	Birth–1	Trust Versus Mistrust	Individuals learn to trust that others and the environment will meet their basic needs. For example, infants usually learn to trust that their parents will provide food, shelter, and love. Otherwise, individuals learn to mistrust others and the environment.
2	2–3	Autonomy Versus Shame and Self-Doubt	Individuals learn to control their own actions and in some ways gain control over the environment. For example, children usually learn to control their bladder and, therefore, feel as if they are in some way controlling themselves. Otherwise, they learn shame or self-doubt.
3	4–5	Initiative Versus Guilt	Individuals learn to decide what activities they want to be involved in and with whom they want to do things. Otherwise, they learn guilt.
4	6–11	Industry Versus Inferiority	Individuals learn to work hard and complete tasks. Otherwise, they fail at their tasks and learn to feel inferior.
5	Adolescence	Identity Versus Role Confusion	Individuals learn to see themselves as separate persons, not just part of a family, and, therefore, begin to think about their own future. Otherwise, they develop confusion about who they are.
6	Young Adulthood	Intimacy Versus Isolation	Individuals learn to establish and maintain close relationships with others. Otherwise, individuals are unable to share with and care for others and begin to feel isolated.
7	Middle Adulthood	Generativity Versus Stagnation	Individuals learn to see their part in the meaning of life and feel that what they are doing is worthwhile. For example, people in middle adulthood usually learn to feel responsible for the next generation. Otherwise, they begin to feel that they are not improving their world or making any progress.
8	Late Adulthood	Integrity Versus Despair	Individuals learn to see that they have led a full and rewarding life. Otherwise, they begin to feel that life has been a series of disappointments.

Looking Forward to Adulthood

preschool children, you have probably already had responsibility for some shopping, meal preparation, or child care. If so, you may decide that raising children is something you are familiar with and would enjoy.

The Influence of Your Community Environment

The communities to which you belong are also an important part of your environment. A **community** is any group of related and unrelated people who have something in common. What the members of a community usually have in common is a set of beliefs, feelings, expectations, and ways of behaving that the members consider acceptable. One of the communities to which you already belong is your school. Others may include a neighborhood and religious, civic, or social organizations. Throughout your life you will probably be a member of several types of communities.

Your community environment will sometimes influence your decisions. For example, if you live now in a neighborhood with a crime watch group, you may decide to participate and to set up a similar program if you move to a new neighborhood. If joining a religious, civic, or social group has encouraged you to help others, you may decide to do volunteer work.

Friends

Your friends are members of one or more of the communities to which you belong. Most of your friends are probably people you have met in your own neighborhood, town, or city. Other friends may include people you have met at a statewide, regional, or national conference or contest. They may also include people from other countries.

Your friends will sometimes influence your decisions. For example, if your best friend has convinced you not to smoke, you may continue to be a nonsmoker. If your best friend is always willing to listen to your problems, you may decide to become a better listener. If friends from other regions or

Most people belong to several different communities. If you were a member of your school's newspaper staff, what beliefs, feelings, or expectations might you have in common with other staff members?

countries have taught you how to cook their special dishes, you may decide to fix these dishes for yourself.

The Influence of Important Events in Your Life

Like your family and community, important events during your lifetime are also a part of your total environment. These events may have occurred earlier in your life, be taking place now, or happen in the future. They may happen directly to you or affect a part of your environment rather than you directly.

Important events will sometimes influence your decisions. For example, as a child, you may have experienced a serious illness. As a result, you have probably decided to concentrate on taking good care of yourself. This year, you may have received recognition for your leadership in a schoolwide project. Because of this, you may decide to take on leadership roles in community projects. In a few years, a technological breakthrough may create new jobs. As a result, you may decide to train for a job that does not even exist today.

The Influence of Your Self-Concept

By combining impressions others have of you with your own ideas of who you are, you have formed a self-concept. A person's **self-concept** is the set of ideas that person has about himself or herself. Your self-concept is everything you know about yourself. For example, you probably know something about your heritage, including the race, the nationality, and perhaps the religious views that your family has passed on to you. You also have ideas about how you look, how you think, how you act, and how you feel. In addition, you have information about what you like and what you dislike.

As you grow and change, you will learn more about yourself. This means your self-concept will continue to change somewhat throughout your life. As you mature, you will be able to rely on your own ideas about yourself more than you rely on the impressions of others.

Your self-concept will often influence your decisions. Therefore, it is important to be realistic about yourself. To be realistic, you have to be able to accept your strengths and weaknesses. Everyone has them, including you. If you accept what you cannot change about yourself, you will be likely to make decisions that are right for you. For example, if you realize that you are not comfortable meeting new people, you will probably decide that a career or job in sales would not be a good choice for you. If, on the other hand, you are talented in math and know it, you may decide to choose a career or job that depends on math ability. Again, you will probably have made a good decision for yourself.

How do you think raising a prize-winning calf might contribute to this girl's self-concept and to her self-esteem?

How can trying new activities help you develop a more complete self-concept and more self-esteem?

The Influence of Your Self-Esteem

When you know yourself and accept yourself, you probably have self-esteem. **Self-esteem** is a sense of worth. Having self-esteem is the same thing as liking yourself.

Many different kinds of experiences have helped you like yourself. For example, maybe you have gained recognition or achieved something that was important to you. Perhaps you have received compliments that have made you feel good about yourself. If so, these experiences have helped you increase your self-esteem. On the other hand, you may have experienced criticism or failure. If these experiences have made you question your self-worth, you may need to work on your self-esteem. For tips on building and maintaining your self-esteem, see the suggestions below.

A feeling of self-esteem will often influence your decisions. It will give you the confidence to take on new roles and relationships. It will help you grow into the responsibilities that these will bring. It will also allow you to relax so you can handle your new freedoms and choices.

Tips
Ways to Boost Your Self-Esteem

Sometimes you must consciously work to maintain good feelings about yourself. When you feel discouraged, it may be particularly hard to feel good about yourself. At times like these, give your self-esteem a boost. Try each of the following ideas:

- Remind yourself that it is perfectly normal to go through up-and-down periods.

- Stop yourself when your mind starts going back *over and over* a mistake or shortcoming.

- Picture yourself for a few seconds doing one of the things you do well. Failures and faults can seem bigger than they really are if they are all you choose to see.

- Ask yourself whether you are doing the best you can. If the answer is yes, tell yourself so.

- Remind yourself from time to time that everyone makes mistakes. *No one* is perfect.

Making the Most of Your Choices

Decisions about your standard of living and your lifestyle are just a few of the many decisions you will make as an adult. Your ability to achieve satisfaction from your life will depend largely on how well you learn to make these and other important decisions. Before you make major decisions, you need to understand what your needs and values are and what your wants and goals are. You also need to understand what your priorities are, what resources are available to you, and how to make good decisions. Good decisions are those you feel are right for you.

Understanding Your Needs and Values

To make a good decision, you first have to understand your needs and your values. It is also important to explore how they affect your wants and your goals.

Needs

All people share certain basic needs. **Needs** are the essentials that a person must have to survive. These include physical, emotional, mental, and spiritual needs.

Your physical needs, for example, include the need for air, food, water, and rest. Without these, no one can survive. Other needs include the need to feel safe and secure, the need to love and to be loved and to feel accepted, and the need to feel respected and to feel good about yourself.

When you were a child, most of your needs were probably met without much effort on your part. Your parents or another adult saw that your needs were satisfied. As a young adult, you will be responsible for identifying and meeting your own needs.

Values

A person's **values** are the ideas, beliefs, or qualities that person holds dear. Examples of values are health, freedom, honesty, friendship, courage, creativity, religion, education, adventure, success. *Your* values are what *you* consider important, desirable, or satisfying. They determine what *you* want. Therefore, your values determine what goals you will set, how you will manage your resources, and what decisions you will make.

What is really important to you? As you identify your values, you probably notice that some are similar to those of your family. As a matter of fact, your family has had the first and probably the most powerful influence on your values. The values you have from your family are the result of what family members have taught you and what you have observed. From your family, for example, you have probably learned values related to such things as problem solving, food, housing, clothing, and achievement, to name a few.

Other influences on the development of your values come from the communities to which you belong. Community influences include traditions, customs, and social standards. Ethnic groups, for example, often pass on traditions and customs from generation to

People of all ages need love. Besides love, what are the other basic needs of each of these family members?

12 Looking Forward to Adulthood

generation. Schools and religious organizations encourage specific behavior and objectives. All of these factors—and more—play a role in the development of your values.

At this point, you have a mixture of values from many sources. As you develop greater awareness of your own values, you will probably notice times when some of your values are in conflict. For example, you may value social events with your friends and want to join their party on Thursday evening. You may also value good grades and want to study for Friday's history test. Perhaps you also work evenings and value your job and the income you earn. Being aware of where your values have come from and which values are most important to you will help you set goals.

Setting Your Goals

Although needs and values are often shared by many people, wants and goals are more personal. Your set of wants and goals is unique to you.

Wants and Goals

Wants are the particular items people choose to meet their needs. Each person's wants are different. For example, you may want a ham sandwich to meet your physical need for food. A friend of yours may want a bowl of soup. Many different wants could satisfy a given need. Your values will determine your wants and the goals you set to obtain them.

Goals are what people set to accomplish or get their specific wants. Any goal you set will be as specific as your want is. For example, if you want to know how to operate a camera, learning how to operate a camera will be your goal. How soon you learn and the type of camera are not important. If, however, you want to use your sister's 35 mm camera to take pictures at the party on Saturday night, learning by Saturday will be important. Learning about the specific model your sister has will also be important.

Types of Goals

Goals fall roughly into two categories. These categories are based on the length of time required to reach the goal.

Goals that take a few hours, days, or weeks to reach are often called short-range goals. These goals are what you are currently focusing on. They may, for example, include handling your Saturday routine—laundry, errands, and house cleaning.

Goals that require a long time—months or years—to reach are called long-range goals. These goals focus on the future. Your plans for next summer's vacation belong in this category.

Long-range goals are often accomplished by achieving several short-range goals first. For example, if you plan to work next summer, it might be necessary to write letters to find a job. This would be among your short-range goals. When you reach each short-range goal, you can evaluate your progress toward your long-range goal. Then, you can determine whether to continue as planned, adjust your long-range goal, or even set a new one.

Testing and Revising Your Goals

There are two key questions to ask yourself about each of your goals to make sure it is a goal that you can meet:

- *Is my goal clearly stated?* Each goal you set needs to be well-defined. It is important to express your goal precisely enough that you can keep in mind what you are aiming for. For example, suppose you set the following goal: "I will get ready this week for a job interview." A more clearly expressed goal might be "This week, I will get my coat cleaned for my interview." Keeping a clear statement of your goal in mind will make it easier for you to reach your goal.
- *Is my goal realistic?* Each goal you set needs to be reachable. It is important to set goals that you have a *chance* of accomplishing. If you have never ridden a horse, for example, it might not be realistic for you to set a goal of taking a lengthy trail ride next week. Without conditioning, your body might rebel. You might make your goal more realistic by changing *next week* to something like *next month*.

No matter how clear and realistic the goals you have set are, outside events may make some of your goals hard to reach. You might

P.S.

What Trends Might Affect Your Goals?

Sometimes, new trends in the world around you may cause you and your family to rethink some of your goals. Because of changes in the economy or in society, you may face new obstacles in reaching those goals. However, you may also find new opportunities that you did not have before.

An example of a trend that has affected many people's goals is the gradual increase in people's average life expectancy. This trend has made it more important than ever to provide for financial security during old age. It has also produced many jobs related to health care and other services needed by older people.

This trend and others might affect some of your goals. Other trends that are likely to be important to you include the following:

- the constant rise in the cost of living
- the growing need for most adults to maintain a home and earn a wage
- the growing need for child care services
- changes in the roles males and females have at home, on the job, and elsewhere
- changes in the structure of families
- the increasing number of people who need training or retraining to qualify for new types of jobs
- the rising cost of education and job training programs
- the growing number of people able and ready to be active and productive past age 65

need to rethink some goals or give yourself more time to reach them. For example, one of your long-range goals may be to own a home. When you are ready to buy, however, you may discover that the type of house you want costs too much. At that point, you may have to go back to your basic values and see if there is room for compromise. You might reconsider the size or type of housing you want to buy. You might postpone buying a home. On the other hand, you might decide to rent a home instead of buying one.

If you can be flexible enough to modify your goals sometimes, you will increase your chances for satisfaction. Some of the trends that might affect the goals you or your family might set appear on the opposite page.

Meeting Your Goals

A goal is nothing without a plan to meet it. Planning requires you to consider each of the following factors:

- how soon you want to meet your goal
- what, if any, short-range goals you must meet first
- in what order you need to meet any short-range goals
- whether you already have everything you need to meet your goal
- how you can get whatever you need to meet your goal
- what might get in your way before you can meet your goal
- what alternative ways you could use to meet your goal

Once you have your plan in mind, you are ready to put it into action. To help you plan for future goals, you should take time after meeting a goal to look back over how everything went. It will be unusual if everything went *just* as you planned. Perhaps you will notice that you forgot to break a long-range goal into smaller short-range goals and ran into trouble. Perhaps you will find that you forgot to plan an alternative way to overcome one obstacle. As luck would have it, that was the obstacle you faced. By taking a few minutes to evaluate what worked and what did not work, you gain valuable insights into how you can improve your chances of meeting your future goals.

Recognizing Your Priorities

People set priorities every day. **Priorities** are the relative weights a person gives to needs, values, wants, or goals.

You set priorities among your needs, values, wants, or goals based on the importance you assign to each at any given moment. For example, if, at midnight, your need to eat is more important to you than your need to sleep, you will probably eat. If, at lunch, you value solitude more than the company of friends, you will probably eat alone rather than with friends. If, in the spring, you decide that you want a summer job more than a summer vacation, you will probably set a goal of finding a summer job.

Managing Your Resources

A **resource** is whatever it takes for a person to achieve a goal. Resources include knowledge and skills, personal qualities, energy, time, money, and materials. To understand the relationship between goals and resources, see the chart on page 16. As you can see, every goal requires the use of some energy and time.

Resources are available to everyone in some amount. Although not everyone has the same knowledge, skills, and personal qualities, everyone has some of these resources and will continue to acquire others throughout life. Although not everyone has the same amount of energy, everyone has the same amount of time in a day.

Some resources such as knowledge, skills, and personal qualities cannot be used up. Other resources such as energy, time, money, and materials can. To help you achieve your goals, you will want to use these last four resources carefully. For example, to get the most from your energy, you may want to vary your activities to give your body and mind periods of rest. To get the most from your time, you may want to focus on how you schedule your activities. To get the most from your money, you may want to use a budget. To get the most from materials, you may want to follow use-and-care directions.

Making the Most of Your Choices

Few people have all the resources they need to reach their goals. To achieve your goals, you must figure out which resources you need. Then, you have to separate the resources you need into those you already have and those you must get. **Resource management** is what people do to get the resources they need and then to use those resources to meet their goals. There are three ways to manage resources, and each involves certain costs.

Substituting, Trading, and Sharing Resources

One way to manage resources is to substitute one of your resources for another when necessary. For example, suppose you have to go to your neighborhood store but are short on time. You might substitute some of your energy for some of your time by running to the store instead of walking. Of course, you would need the extra energy running would take. A **resource substitution** is a person's use of one of his or her resources in place of another. It is a way of managing resources that requires no input from others.

A second way to manage your resources is to trade resources with someone else. Suppose again that you are short on time but need something from the store. You might ask a family member or a friend to go for you. In exchange, you might agree to spend some

Resources Needed to Meet Specific Goals

Goal	Resource Needed	Type of Resource
• pass a driver's test	• energy and time to learn and to take test • driver's manual • understanding of information in manual • ability to drive safely	• energy and time • material • knowledge • knowledge and skill
• be a comedian in a talent show	• energy and time to rehearse and to participate • humor and imagination	• energy and time • personal qualities
• qualify for a track meet	• energy and time to practice and to participate • ability to compete in track events	• energy and time • knowledge and skill
• pay the entrance fee for an art show	• energy and time to earn money • $25	• energy and time • money
• type a job application letter	• energy and time to organize thoughts and to type • typewriter • typing paper • ability to type	• energy and time • material • material • knowledge and skill

Looking Forward to Adulthood

In what ways have you shared resources with others?

of your energy and time on another day doing a favor for the person who helped you. A **resource trade** is an exchange of resources between two people.

There is a popular kind of resource trading that can involve any type of resource but money. This kind of exchange is known as bartering. **Bartering** is the exchange of one person's skills, energy, time, or materials for someone else's. Many communities have set up exchange networks so people who want to trade resources can contact one another. You can use these large exchange networks or create your own smaller network—among friends and family members—to extend your resources.

A third way to manage your resources is to combine yours with those of someone else. Suppose, once again, that you are short on time but need something from the store. You might ask a friend or a family member with some time to drive you. By combining resources with this person, you could go to the store more quickly than you could alone. **Resource sharing** is a combining of resources by two or more people.

Opportunity Costs

No matter how you manage your resources, there will be opportunity costs for someone. **Opportunity costs** are those things a person gives up by using resources for something else.

If you decide to spend an entire day at a track meet, you cannot use that same time for any other activity. The other things you had the opportunity to do during that time are your opportunity costs. For example, you may have given up the chance to go to a movie, take advantage of a sale, or get ahead on another project. In this case, you are the one who has paid the opportunity costs of your decision.

When you got a ride to the neighborhood store, you and the person who drove you each paid opportunity costs. Your cost was lower, however, because all you gave up was your energy and time to do other things. Your friend or family member gave up the energy and time to do other things, as well as the use of a car and gasoline.

Every time a resource is used, someone pays opportunity costs. Before you make a decision, consider how great the opportunity costs will be and who will pay them.

Making Decisions

Decisions! Decisions! Should I stay home and study or go to the party? Should I join the softball league or take a part-time job? What will I do after high school? These situations all involve making choices. **Decision making** means choosing from among several alternatives.

Types of Decisions

Some decisions are made every day. For example, you decide each day what to wear, what to eat, and how to use your leisure time. Usually you choose slightly different clothes, foods, and pastimes each day. This makes your life interesting.

Making the Most of Your Choices

How Computers Can Help You

Computers as a Resource

A revolution is going on around you. It began in the 1950s and will undoubtedly continue far into the future. This revolution is a technological revolution, and computers are at its heart. A computer is a machine that helps people store and use information for a variety of purposes. These purposes can range from keeping a simple home budget to sending a spacecraft out to explore the universe.

Look around you. You will find computers in homes, offices, factories, laboratories, hospitals, schools, banks, supermarkets, libraries, and many other places. Ways have been found to put computers to good use in all of these settings. Each day, more and more uses are found for them. As more uses are developed, computers become a highly valuable resource. One thing that makes a computer such a valuable resource is its memory. A computer's memory is the space it has for storing information and programs. Another thing that makes a computer a special resource is its ability to solve increasingly complex problems.

Though computers can help people in many ways, computers are, after all, only machines and cannot think independently. *You* can, however. So, it is up to you to think of new ways to use computers. As a matter of fact, learning how to use computers to gain information and solve problems has become almost as important as knowing how to read and write. Thinking of new ways to use computers is not hard. All you have to do is learn some basics and think of how you might use a computer to make time-consuming tasks faster and easier. As you read each chapter, you will find out several ways in which computers are already a resource at your service.

Sometimes, however, you simplify your decision making by choosing the same things over and over. You establish a habit. Before you establish a habit, however, you need to think through your decision. In this way, you can be sure you are forming a habit you want. Occasionally, you need to look at the habit you have formed to evaluate whether your initial decision still makes sense. It is possible that new information is available to you that makes your original decision—and, therefore, your habit—undesirable.

Most major decisions are made infrequently or only once. Usually, a major decision has more of an impact on your life than an everyday decision has. Many of the choices you will face as a young adult will require you to make important decisions. Understanding who you are, what is important to you, and what you are aiming for will make decision making easier for you. Understanding the basic steps for making good decisions will also help you.

How can establishing a habit make some decision making easy and fast?

Understanding the Decision-Making Process

The decision-making process involves the following six steps:

- *Consider the situation and whether you need to make a decision.* A sound decision is always easier to make when you have a clear understanding of exactly what the situation is.
- *Collect information related to the situation.* Seek as much information as you feel you need. Ask for the opinions and advice of others if you want them.
- *Consider your values, your goals, and your resources.* If some of your values or goals are in conflict, think about which value or goal is most important to you. Think through *all* the resources you have.
- *Identify the choices you have and the consequences of each.* Often, someone who is not involved in the situation can point out alternatives and outcomes that you may have overlooked.
- *Select a course of action.* Usually, the easiest way to make a good decision is to rank your alternatives and select the one highest on your list.
- *Act on your decision, and evaluate the results.* Few decisions cannot be altered in some way. If you have acted on your decision and do not like the results, analyze what has not worked out. Then, look back at your alternatives. Consider trying another alternative—perhaps the one you ranked second.

Following these six steps will help you make effective decisions. To help you keep your thinking straight, you may even want to write down your thoughts step by step. Like any other process, decision making will become easier with practice.

Overcoming Barriers to Decision Making

Uncertainty, fear, and lack of confidence cause people to fail at decision making. Do you recognize anyone you know in the following examples?

- *"I have lots of time to decide."* Some people wait until the last minute to make a decision. They hope that the situation will change or that the need to decide will go away. By putting off decisions, they may make themselves feel nervous and tense.

They may also lose the opportunity to choose the alternative they prefer.
- *"What do you think I should do?"* Many people look to others to decide for them. They want someone else to be responsible for what happens to them. They often blame others for mistakes and use this as an excuse for not reaching their goals.
- *"I have two minutes to decide. Help!"* Some people make impulsive decisions when a quick decision is unnecessary. They may do this to avoid facing a tough decision.
- *"If I bungle this, it could ruin my life."* Some people are unable to tell the difference between an everyday decision and a major decision. These people often feel that every decision is a life-or-death matter. They worry about making a decision. They forget that decisions can usually be reconsidered.

People sometimes avoid making decisions or acting on their decisions. You may feel that not making any decision means not making a wrong decision. By not making a decision, however, you actually do make a decision. The thing to do is to concentrate on making decisions that work for you.

Points to Remember

- As an adult, you can expect to assume new roles, responsibilities, relationships, and freedoms.
- Your family will think of you in more adult terms if you are trustworthy and dependable.
- The decisions you make about your standard of living will affect the decisions you make about your lifestyle, and vice versa.
- Characteristics you have inherited from your family and things you have learned from your family environment influence your decisions.
- The communities to which you belong and events that are important to you influence and will continue to influence your decisions.
- Your self-concept and your self-esteem influence and will continue to influence your decisions.
- Your values influence your wants and, therefore, influence your goals, your management of resources, and your decisions.
- When planning to meet a goal, you need to consider your time, your other resources, possible obstacles, and your alternatives.
- When you manage resources, you get the resources you need and use them to meet your goals.
- Making decisions is easier if you understand who you are, what is important to you, what you are aiming for, and the basic steps in the decision-making process.

Test Your Skills
GOAL SETTING

Imagine yourself in the situation described below. In this situation, a goal needs to be set. As you read, think about what makes a goal reachable. Then, answer the questions that follow. When you need to set goals in the future, remember to ask yourself these questions.

Situation

You sometimes feel a little shy. Often, this stops you from making new friends, even when you would really like to try.

One of the people you would like to get to know is Sam, who is in your English class. From some of his comments in class, you have learned that he has recently moved from an American high school overseas. You have also discovered that, like you, Sam is interested in drawing.

Sam seems easy to talk to, but you are not sure how to get to know him. You have considered waiting for him after class. Then, you could strike up a conversation by asking him whether he made any sketches while he was overseas. You have thought about calling him at home to ask what kind of drawing he likes to do. While you are talking, you could suggest that he bring a couple of his sketches to school. You have thought about catching up with him after school to ask him to join the art club. You have considered waiting a month or two to see if Sam finds out about your interest in drawing and tries to make friends with you.

Questions

1. What is your goal? Make sure it is realistic and clearly stated.
2. Do you think of your goal as short-range or long-range? Why?
3. What plan could you make to meet your goal?
4. What could get in the way of your achieving your goal?
5. What alternative plans could you make to meet your goal?

Terms

On a separate sheet of paper, write a definition for each of the underlined terms below. Base your definition on the clues you find in the sentence(s).

1. Suke's heredity includes the coloring she got from her parents.
2. Bill knows a lot about himself. He has a well-developed self-concept.
3. Sara likes herself. She has self-esteem.
4. Ken's religious beliefs, his family life, and his friendships are three things he holds dear. These three values help him make many decisions.
5. Some of Ellie's wants are different from those of her best friend, Paula. For example, Ellie prefers to try foods from many different ethnic groups. Paula prefers to satisfy her need for food by eating only foods developed by the ethnic group to which her family belongs.
6. Vince wants to help some children get ready for the Special Olympics. He has set a goal of volunteering two hours of his time each Saturday to do this.
7. Jerry is good at resource substitution. For example, when he does not have enough information or skill, he may pay an expert to help him reach one of his goals.
8. Marchelle offered to help Linda with some math problems in exchange for Linda's help with Spanish. Marchelle understands the benefits of resource trading.
9. Theo and John sometimes split the cost of sports equipment that neither of them can afford to buy alone. They use resource sharing.
10. Whenever Nancy decides to do one thing with her time or money, she gives up her chance to do something else with this resource. She pays opportunity costs.
11. Decision making is not new to José. Every day he makes choices from several alternatives. Many of his decisions are not hard to make. A few, however, take a great deal of his time and thought.

Questions

1. Describe what it means to play the dual role of homemaker and wage earner.
2. Name three ways you can help yourself accept new responsibilities.

Looking Forward to Adulthood

3. Identify two new freedoms you will have as an adult.
4. What kinds of decisions does a person make in choosing a standard of living and a lifestyle?
5. What elements of a family environment will influence a family member's decisions?
6. List two ways to increase self-esteem.
7. List two major influences on a person's values.
8. When you are considering whether one of your goals is workable, what questions should you ask yourself?
9. List six types of resources.
10. Describe three ways to manage resources.
11. How can thinking about opportunity costs help you make a decision?
12. List the steps of the decision-making process.
13. What are three ways people sometimes react to their fear, uncertainty, or lack of confidence related to decision making?

Activities

1. Identify a new adult role a young adult might look forward to accepting. Explain why this role might be appealing.
2. Identify a new responsibility that a young adult might accept. Explain how accepting this responsibility might lead to greater independence.
3. Describe a few of the things that make you unique or special.
4. Think of an important event in your life. Describe how it has contributed to your self-concept and your self-esteem.
5. Think of several goals that are important to you now. For each goal, answer the following questions:
   a. Is the goal short-range or long-range?
   b. Do you have all the resources you need to achieve the goal?
   c. How can you obtain the resources you lack?
   d. Why is the goal important to you?
6. Describe a difficult situation that a young adult might face, and describe one decision the young adult might make in that situation. Use the steps in the decision-making process to explain how the decision might be reached.

SUCCEEDING ON YOUR OWN
FOUR-WAY GUIDE TO FITNESS
HOW DO YOU FEEL TODAY?
WHO WILL GET THE JOB?
PLAN-A-MONTH
Special Bell
Welcome Back

CHAPTER 2

Expressing Yourself as an Adult

Your success today depends to a great extent on how well you communicate. Your success as an adult will depend even more on your communication skills. If you communicate well, for example, you will be able to express your own thoughts and feelings. You will also be able to find out how other people think and feel. In short, you will be able to interact and cooperate with other people. You will be the kind of family member, homemaker, wage earner, consumer, and citizen who works well with others to get things done. You will lead a fulfilling life.

In a society that has a free enterprise type of economic system and a democratic form of government, the ability to communicate is especially important. If people in such a society did not express themselves, manufacturers—the makers of products—would not know what to produce. Sellers would not know what products and services to offer. The free enterprise system would fail. Likewise, the government would cease to represent the wishes of its citizens. It would no longer be democratic—governed by the will of the people.

Because communication is essential in this society, your freedom of expression is guaranteed. Now and as an adult, you have not only a right but also a responsibility to communicate well.

Discover Through Your Reading

- how communicating can help you meet your goals
- why a person might place more trust in nonverbal than in verbal messages
- how you can become better at getting your messages across and at listening
- how economic freedom of choice allows you to express your values and preferences
- how being an active citizen allows you to express yourself

Gaining Independence Through Communication

Other people form impressions of you through the way you communicate. They decide what kind of person you are. They also decide whether they have much in common with you and whether they want to spend time with you.

Most of your goals and decisions will involve other people. Therefore, the way you express yourself to others will affect how well you meet the goals you set for yourself. It will also influence how well you implement the decisions you make. If you communicate well, you will probably give those around you an accurate sense of who you are and what your values, goals, and decisions are. Therefore, the ability to communicate is one of the most important keys to your independence and fulfillment as an adult.

Communication Basics

What does it mean to communicate? **Communication** is the two-way process of sending and receiving messages. The message may be in the form of a face-to-face conversation, a telephone conversation, a public speech, or a teleconference. It may be in the form of a comment made in sign language or the way you are standing or sitting. It may be in the form of a message that depends on touch, such as a hug or a passage in Braille. It may be in the form of a written message, such as a letter, a test, a report, or a job application. For more information about teleconferences and other special forms of communication, see page 27.

Whatever form communication takes, it always involves a sender, a message, and a receiver. Communication is effective only when it is complete—when the receiver gets the meaning that the sender intended. When the receiver does not get the meaning that was intended, communication is incomplete and, therefore, fails.

The reasons communication may fail are as follows:

- The sender may be uncertain about the message he or she wants to send.
- The message may not be stated clearly.
- The receiver may be unable to understand the message.

Although it takes skill, time, and energy to make yourself understood and to understand the messages of others, the effort is usually worth it. For example, communicating well helps make your family life and friendships enjoyable. It helps you function as part of a team in the workplace. It helps you make your preferences known in the marketplace, wherever people buy or barter products and services. It helps you make your governmental representatives aware of your wishes.

If you recognize the word hello *when it is expressed with either of these sets of symbols, you know a special way to communicate. What makes such methods of communication special?*

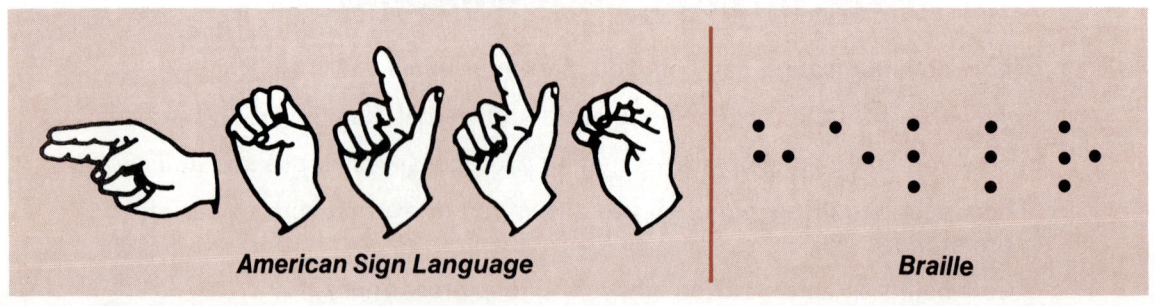

American Sign Language | **Braille**

How Computers Can Help You

Keeping in Touch Through Telecommunications

The Battle of New Orleans, the last battle of the War of 1812, was fought on January 8, 1815. But the treaty that ended the war had already been signed more than two weeks earlier, on December 24, 1814. Unfortunately, communications at that time were so slow that word of the treaty did not reach New Orleans until after the battle was over. Today, however, you can watch and listen to world leaders, for example, at the time they are actually meeting halfway around the world. Telecommunications is helping you see and hear events thousands of miles away as they are happening.

What is telecommunications? It is a form of communication that depends on such technology as a computer, cable, satellite, television, and telephone. You are using telecommunications, for example, when you use a microcomputer (a small personal computer), a telephone line, and a modem (a device that uses telephone lines to connect two computers). You can use these devices to shop from home, bank from home, or look over airline schedules, for example.

In addition, you can use electronic mail and teleconferences. Electronic mail allows you and another person (if you know each other's special number) to leave messages on each other's computer. With this system, you can send letters, forms, reports, and other documents in minutes to people who are far away. A prearranged teleconference enables people in different cities or even countries to hold a meeting or an interview. Although each participant is in a different place, all the participants can hear and see one another. Think of all the time, money, and energy saved.

Telecommunications will continue to help you stay informed and communicate with others in new ways. As a form of communication, it is still in its infancy.

Types of Messages

There are two basic types of messages: verbal and nonverbal. **Verbal messages,** those expressed in words, include the following:

- oral messages, that is, messages that are spoken
- messages expressed in sign language, such as those expressed in American Sign Language, widely used by people with hearing difficulties
- written messages
- messages expressed in raised-dot patterns, such as those expressed in Braille, widely used by people with seeing difficulties

Nonverbal messages, those not expressed in words, include body language. **Body language** is the combination of posture, body movements and gestures, eye contact, and facial expressions that people use as they talk or use sign language.

Sending Messages

No matter what type of message you are sending, you will want to be sure you know what message you want to send. Because your receiver cannot read your mind, you will also want to be sure your message is complete. In addition, you will want to be aware of who is to receive your message. If possible, you will want to consider the receiver's background and communication skills. Above all, you will want to make sure your communication style is effective. To find out what communication style you have, see page 31. Doing these things will help you decrease the chance of misunderstandings.

Talking

When you call your grandparents to tell them about your driving test, you are using oral communication. When you talk with a friend or give a speech, you are, again, using oral communication.

To make sure your listeners understand your oral messages, choose your words carefully. Avoid words that your listeners may not know. Make sure the words you choose are likely to mean the same thing to you and your listeners. Avoid words that suggest more emotion or a more negative attitude than you wish to convey. For example, avoid a word like *hate* when *dislike* better expresses the level of emotion you feel.

In addition, pay attention to your voice. Your success in getting your message across will be affected by how you use your voice. **Inflections,** voice changes that add meaning to words, will help you. You can, for example, vary your pitch, your volume, or your rate of speech. Most of the time you will probably talk at a medium or low pitch, a medium volume, and a medium speed. When you want to emphasize certain words or points, however, you can use inflections. You can use a higher pitch, raise or lower your voice, or talk more slowly or rapidly. For example, to emphasize a major point, you can slow down. When you are covering less important details, you can speed up.

To understand the effect of inflections on a message, look at the sentence "Where do you think you are going?" Spoken softly and without emphasis, it is a simple request for information. If you raise your voice and repeat the sentence quickly, however, the message becomes an urgent plea. If you put more emphasis on *you* than on *where,* the message is no longer a question but a challenge. Inflections can make your spoken messages clearer. To improve your talking and speaking skills, see the tips on page 29.

Body Language

As you talk, use body language to reinforce your message. For example, if you want to express affection, smile and look directly at the faces of your listeners. If you want to express displeasure, avoid smiling or laughing nervously when you speak. Again, look directly at your listeners' faces.

Remember, if your body language contradicts your spoken message, your listeners are likely to ignore your words. People tend to place more trust in nonverbal messages than they do in verbal messages. This is because nonverbal messages are more difficult to control and more revealing than verbal messages. For example, you may be nervous and try to hide that fact with your words.

Tips
Getting Your Messages Across

Think through conversations you have had recently. Did you get your message across each time? If not, some of the following tips may help:

Before You Communicate

- Practice using voice inflections by stressing key words and important ideas as you read aloud to yourself. This will help you add inflections when you are talking to others. Speaking in a monotone, a single tone, is ineffective. It makes listening to your messages difficult. In addition, it may make your listeners wonder whether you are interested in what you have to say.

- Practice using different postures, gestures, and expressions in front of a mirror. Think about the message each conveys, so you understand which will reinforce what you say and which will not.

- Make sure your receivers are ready to listen. You will have more success getting your message across if your listeners are not feeling tired, rushed, or otherwise unable to concentrate on your message. Communicating with your supervisor will be easier, for example, if you pick a relatively quiet time in your supervisor's schedule.

While You Communicate

- Take a little time to think through your message before you start talking. Do not let other people rush you into saying something you do not mean.

- Use the names of the people with whom you are talking. Listeners pay more attention when they are addressed by name.

- Give your listeners opportunities to respond. Do not dictate or talk nonstop. It is hard for listeners to stay interested if they get no chance to participate. They are likely to feel left out of the communication.

- Avoid vagueness. Being vague means not giving a true picture of a situation or leaving out important details. You are being vague, for example, if you respond, "Out," when someone asks, "Where are you going?"

- Ask questions to get feedback from your listeners if they are not responding on their own. Otherwise, you may not be able to tell if they understand your message.

These tips will help you improve not only your conversations but also your ability to speak to a group.

Tapping your foot, however, may give you away. You may say you are not upset, but your forehead may be tense and your hands clenched. Again, your body language will tell the real story. Your communication will be most effective when your verbal and nonverbal messages are the same.

Use the body language of your listeners to gain feedback about whether you are getting your message across. Check your listeners' posture, gestures, and expressions. These will tell you whether your listeners are following your comments. If a listener is slouching, looking away, or frowning, for example, you may not be communicating. You may need to stop and find out what the problem is. If a listener has a relaxed but alert posture, is looking right at you, and occasionally nods to show understanding, you know some communication is probably occurring.

Writing

Talking and writing are similar. They are ways to send messages, and they depend on the use of words. They both assume an audience, one or more receivers.

There are some special differences between speaking and writing, however. For example, a written message usually provides a more permanent record than talking or speaking does. Most of your spoken words, and the body language you use with them, are lost except for your receivers' memories of what you said and did. For those times when you need a record, it is best to write your messages. For example, you might need to take notes on where to find props for an assembly or a play. You might need to make notes about what your supervisor has said to do. You might need to write a letter of complaint to a business or send a letter to one of your governmental representatives.

In addition, a written message often allows you more time to prepare than a spoken message does. Before you write, for example, you usually have plenty of time to consider all of the points you want to make. You also usually have time to create a rough draft and make sure your thoughts are well expressed before your reader sees them. To take advantage of the time you have to get your message just right, do each of the following:

- organize your thoughts
- write down your thoughts in a clear and logical order
- look back over your writing to check your grammar, spelling, and punctuation
- make sure your final copy is neat

Receiving Messages

How well do you understand spoken and written messages? It depends on how clear the message is and on how well you listen and read. Like your speaking and writing skills, your listening and reading skills affect almost everything you do. As a young adult, you will find them essential to your success as a family member, a homemaker, a wage earner, a consumer, and a citizen.

Listening

Hearing is not listening. Hearing requires only that your ears pick up sounds and

Does this written message reflect clear and logical thinking? Why?

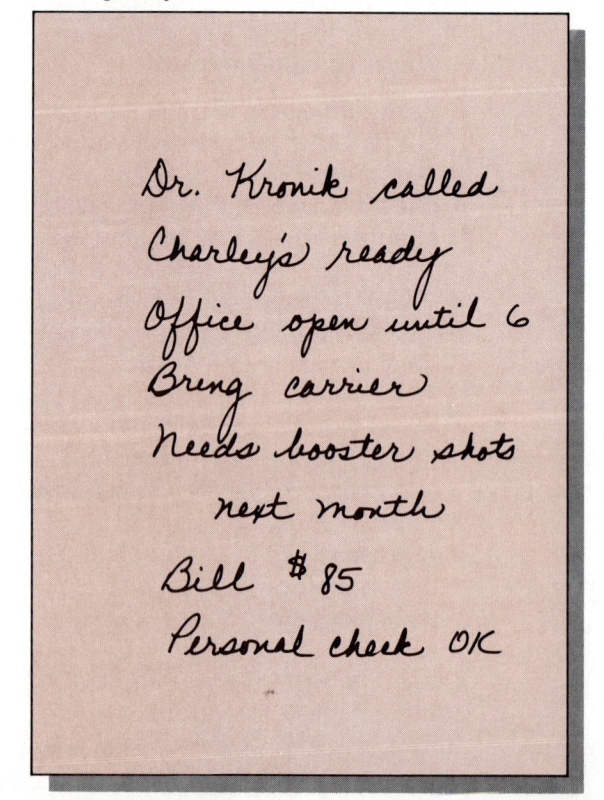

> Dr. Kronik called
> Charley's ready
> Office open until 6
> Bring carrier
> Needs booster shots next month
> Bill $85
> Personal check OK

30 Expressing Yourself as an Adult

P.S. What Is Your Communication Style?

Communication, like many other skills, is first learned at home. Members of your family were probably the first people to talk and listen to you. By the time you got to school, you were communicating with many more people and had begun to make friends. You had probably begun to develop a style of communicating. What is your style? Is it helping you or getting in the way? Being either too passive or too aggressive, for example, will work against you.

If you have a passive communication style, you probably send few messages. Being passive means not taking enough responsibility for your thoughts and feelings to try to express them. For example, if you do not tell a friend that he or she has hurt your feelings, you are being passive. If you pretend you have no problem and end up acting moody, your friend may sense that something is wrong. However, your friend cannot be expected to guess exactly what you are thinking and feeling.

If you have an aggressive communication style, you probably try to send messages, but you fail because your listeners reject them. Being aggressive means trying so hard to express yourself that you do not consider the feelings of the other person. For example, if you yell to let your friend know your feelings have been hurt, you are being aggressive. Usually, an aggressive message hurts the feelings of the other person. It also makes you feel frustrated because you do not get the kind of response you want. Your friend may yell back, start crying, or do other things people do when they feel attacked.

Being assertive, on the other hand, is effective. If you have an assertive communication style, you say what you think or feel. You also avoid attacking the other person or coming on too strong. If you explain your feelings to your friend in a calm, direct way and focus on your feelings—not on what your friend did—you are being assertive. You are probably communicating well.

How does showing empathy help people communicate?

transmit the sounds to your brain. Listening, on the other hand, requires that you make a conscious response to what you are hearing. When you are listening, you are interpreting what you hear. You are really trying to receive the message being sent.

An essential part of understanding the message being sent is showing empathy for the other person. **Empathy** is a willingness to see and feel things from another person's point of view. Showing empathy does not mean agreeing with the other person. It means indicating that, if you were looking at the situation from his or her point of view, you might feel the same way. Trying to see and feel things from the other person's point of view will help you concentrate on the entire message. It will also help you keep an open mind and avoid making a judgment after hearing only part of the other person's message.

Listening well is usually easier if you understand what might get in the way of your receiving a message. Think about how you listen on the telephone, in class, on a date, to a radio or television program, at work, and to a salesperson, for example. Does anything get in the way of your listening? Five reasons people sometimes have difficulty listening are as follows:

- *People can hear faster than they can speak.* This means that you have time to think in between the thoughts conveyed by the person to whom you are listening. During this lag time, you may start making mental notes about how you want to respond. You may start drifting on to unrelated thoughts. When you become too busy with your own thoughts, the other person's message gets lost.
- *Some people think they can listen without putting any effort into it.* They consciously decide to half-listen to the other person. Although these listeners think they will pick up all of the parts of the message that are of interest to them, they often miss the main point. They may also miss important details. Their body language will probably also reveal their lack of attention.
- *Some people think they can almost always anticipate what another person will say.* This leads them to misinterpret the messages they actually receive. Their expectations get in the way of the real message.
- *People often focus on and remember only those parts of the other person's message that support their own point of view.* This means that you are most likely to remember what supports your opinions about the subject and about the speaker. You may tend to ignore or reject information that might change your thinking. Often, this approach can lead you to make inaccurate conclusions about a message.
- *Some people think that how they react to the person talking has no effect on whether the message is conveyed.* They may listen but act as if they are not listening or as if they do not care about the other person's message. By doing either of these things, they will probably disrupt the communication. For example, the person talking may quit

trying to communicate with them. Remember, effective communication involves the active participation of two or more people.

Anything that prevents or blocks communication is an obstacle. When communication is blocked, people do not understand each other. Misunderstandings can lead to conflicts, hurt feelings, and arguments. You can overcome most of the obstacles to good listening if you follow the advice presented in the tips listed on this page.

Reading

In many ways, reading is similar to listening. Both reading and listening are ways to receive messages. Both also depend on the use of words and assume one or more senders. In addition, both help you gain knowledge and understanding.

In certain situations, reading skills are even more important than listening skills.

Learning is a lifelong process. How important a role do you think reading will play in this process?

Tips
Becoming a Better Listener

Listening is a skill. It is something you can improve with practice. To make sure you are on the right track as you practice, consider the following tips:

- Concentrate on the other person's message—the words, voice inflections, and body language. Do not allow your mind to wander. Do not let anything in your surroundings, such as noise or a passerby, distract you.

- Try to identify the other person's main ideas and important details. Do not focus so much on minor details that you lose sight of the main points.

- Tell the other person, if possible, whenever you find yourself unable to concentrate. Avoid letting someone keep talking to you when you are unable to listen carefully. For example, a roommate may try to talk to you when you are too tired to pay attention. In such a situation, it is better to postpone your discussion, if possible, until you feel rested and can concentrate.

- Give the other person some evidence that you are listening and interested in his or her point of view. Establish eye contact, look interested, and nod your understanding from time to time. Nothing stops a conversation faster than a listener who looks or turns away, fidgets, yawns, or gives no response at all.

For example, you need to be able to read legal documents—leases, credit agreements, and other contracts. If you sign such a document without reading and understanding it, you may find yourself in legal and financial difficulty. You also need to be able to read directions and labels related to safety. If you cannot read directions on a fire extinguisher or labels on medicine, for example, you may be unable to care for yourself and others.

Expressing Yourself in the Free Enterprise System

You live in a society that has a free enterprise type of economic system. This means that you already have opportunities every day to express your values and preferences in the marketplace. You communicate your wishes as a consumer, a person who uses products and services.

When you become an adult, your opportunities and responsibility to communicate will increase. You will be an important part of a three-way partnership with business and government. In this partnership, you will play various key roles. You will continue to be a consumer. If you are not already, you will also probably become a wage earner and a taxpayer.

Here is how the three-way partnership between you, business, and government works in a free enterprise system. You are needed by businesses as a consumer and an employee. You, in turn, need businesses because they provide not only products and services but also jobs. You are needed by the government as a taxpayer and an employee. You, in turn, need the government. Like businesses, the government provides you some products and services, as well as jobs. In addition, it helps you provide these same things for others.

Because of your key roles in this partnership, you have more opportunities to express yourself than do individuals in some other economic systems. The free enterprise system is called *free* because it is based on principles that give each individual many opportunities to make choices.

Principles of the Free Enterprise System

Every economic system has to provide answers to the following questions:

- What products and services should be produced?
- How should they be produced?
- How much of each should be produced?
- By whom and for whom should they be produced?

In the free enterprise system, the answers to these questions are made by all three partners. The answers take into consideration five basic principles: economic freedom of choice, private property, the profit motive, supply and demand, and competition.

Economic Freedom of Choice

As a partner in the free enterprise system, you have the freedom to make many economic choices. You can decide how to earn a living, including whether you want to produce or sell certain products or services. You can also decide whether to accept or turn down a job offer. In addition, you can decide which products and services to buy. You can do each of these as long as you obey the laws of the land.

No one, for example, can make you take a job as a salesperson or a mechanic if you want to be a teacher. No one can force you to raise and sell cattle or catfish or to manufacture and sell carpeting or cars. No one can force you to set up a counseling service or to offer any other service. Likewise, no one can make you buy cattle, catfish, carpeting, cars, counseling, or anything else. You have freedom of choice.

How might your decisions as a consumer help determine that products such as these need to be produced?

Private Property

In the free enterprise system, you can own and use property. This includes not only land but also buildings and equipment.

There are several things you can do with any property you own. It is up to you how little or much you use your private property. For example, you can simply hold on to it. Farmers and other businesspeople do this when they leave land idle. Manufacturers do this when they close factories. You are doing this if you keep in your closet clothing that you never wear.

You can also use some of your property to produce a product or a service. Farmers do this when they grow a crop or raise animals. Manufacturers do this when they operate a factory. You are doing this whenever you decide to sell some of your clothing through a secondhand store or a garage sale or at a flea market.

In addition, you can exchange some of your land, buildings, or equipment for other resources. Farmers may rent idle land to other farmers. Manufacturers may sell their factories to factory workers. You may decide to trade clothes with a friend. It is up to you

Expressing Yourself in the Free Enterprise System   35

how much or little you use your private property.

The Profit Motive

A **profit** is the amount of money a business has left after it has covered all of its expenses. If you run a business in the free enterprise system, you are expected to pay your company's bills and to pay any employees you have. The money you have left over is your profit. With this money, you pay yourself and any investors you have. In this way, you reward yourself and anyone else who has taken the risks involved in keeping your business operating. If you do not begin to make a profit at some point, you will probably have to close your business. Therefore, you are motivated to operate your business in such a way that you earn a profit.

How are these consumers expressing their demand for a product?

Supply and Demand

When you buy a product or service, you are showing that there is at least some demand for it. If many other consumers are also trying to buy the item, the demand for it is great. Sometimes, businesses cannot produce enough of a popular item to meet the demand. At this point, the item is in short supply. When an item is in short supply, some consumers are willing to pay more to get the item, and its price rises. When the price rises, fewer consumers can afford the item, so demand for the item decreases. You and other consumers, therefore, help set the price of products and services.

Competition

The free enterprise system works best when several businesses sell the same product or service. This makes the businesses compete for customers. As they compete, each tries to offer the lowest prices and highest quality it can. This benefits you and other consumers. You get better buys than you would if only one business sold the item.

Expressing Yourself in a Democratic Society

You live in a society that has not only a free enterprise economy but also a democratic form of government. You are probably a citizen. A **citizen** is a person who has the full rights and protection of a nation.

In any country with a democratic form of government, the country's citizens—not a ruler or a small group of rulers—govern. In this country, citizens rule themselves by electing representatives to govern on their behalf. This means that each citizen must make his or her values and preferences known. Citizens do this by choosing who will represent them and by communicating with their representatives. Citizens also do this by voting on specific issues and by participating in their government in many other ways.

Most citizens in a democratic society recognize that certain individual rights are basic and cannot be voted away. These rights include the right to protect yourself and your family, the right to speak freely, and the right to lead a fulfilling life. These rights also include equal opportunity and equal treatment under the law. Each of these rights is yours up to the point that it infringes on the rights of another person. For example, you have the right to free speech but not to yell "Fire" in a crowded hall that is not on fire.

Your New Civic Responsibilities

With your civic rights come certain civic responsibilities. A **civic responsibility** is what a person *should* do to contribute to the welfare of the nation.

You already have some civic responsibilities. For example, you have a responsibility to protect the natural environment. People of all ages need to conserve resources and avoid polluting their natural surroundings. You probably already do your part by using electricity, water, and other resources sparingly. You may walk or bicycle sometimes instead of driving. Perhaps you buy items that do not produce a lot of solid waste.

You also have a responsibility to enrich the lives of others. You probably already contribute by being friendly and helpful to neighbors and friends, as well as family members. By using basic courtesy you enrich the lives of others. You may also contribute by doing volunteer work, perhaps with a civic group, a social organization, or a religious group. Volunteering your skills, time, and energy not only gives you the chance to help others. It also helps you learn more about other people and gain valuable work experience.

When you are an adult, you will still have these civic responsibilities. In addition, you will be responsible for being an informed citizen, for voting, and for participating in your government.

How will registering to vote increase your opportunities to express yourself as a citizen?

Being an Informed Citizen

Every adult citizen has a responsibility to be informed. The representatives you elect and the stands they take will affect your life and the lives of others in your immediate area. Your representatives will also affect the lives of others in your state, your nation, and the world. You will need a lot of information to make decisions that will have such a wide impact.

There are many ways to become an informed citizen. For example, you can read newspapers, books, magazines, and government bulletins and reports. You can watch television news and special programs. You can listen to radio news and public affairs programs. You can call government officials and local experts for information. To keep up with local developments, you can also attend public meetings and hearings. In addition, you can attend debates and candidate forums. Local newspapers usually announce the places and times for public events such as these.

Voting

Every citizen who has reached the minimum age for voting has a responsibility to register to vote—and, then, to vote in every

Expressing Yourself in a Democratic Society **37**

election. The alternative—to complain about elected officials or systems and do nothing to make improvements—makes no sense.

To register to vote, contact your county courthouse. The supervisor of elections there will tell you how you can register. Remember, registering to vote is free. Most adult citizens are automatically eligible to register. The only type of citizen who must apply specially for the right to vote is someone who has a criminal record that includes a felony. A felony is a serious crime.

When an election nears, learn about the candidates and issues. After you study the facts, make a decision and vote. In doing so, you contribute to your own welfare and to the welfare of your country.

Participating in Government

Every citizen has a responsibility to make the government work. The only way to do this is to participate in it. In addition to voting, you can participate in many other ways. There are many activities from which you can choose. You can help register other people to vote. You can join a political party. You can lobby your government representatives. **Lobbying** is writing, calling, visiting, or otherwise letting your representatives know your opinions about issues on which they may be voting.

You can join a citizens' group that keeps track of the votes of individual government officials. You can work in a political campaign for a candidate you would like to see elected. You can work in a campaign to get a certain law passed. Campaign work—for a candidate or an issue—can be as high-profile or low-profile as you like. You can volunteer to make public appearances or to stay behind the scenes, perhaps preparing or distributing campaign literature.

When you are an adult citizen, you can also run for public office. If you are interested in running for a public office someday, start preparing now. Get involved in local politics by working in a campaign or assisting as an aide to a governmental representative. In school, participate in debate and speech classes and learn about history and government. Develop your public relations skills, your ability to communicate with the public, one at a time or in groups. Run for one of the offices available at your school. Perhaps you would be a good club or band officer or class representative. Having such a position will help you build leadership skills.

Many people enjoy working in political campaigns. What are some reasons these young campaigners might be working to get a candidate elected?

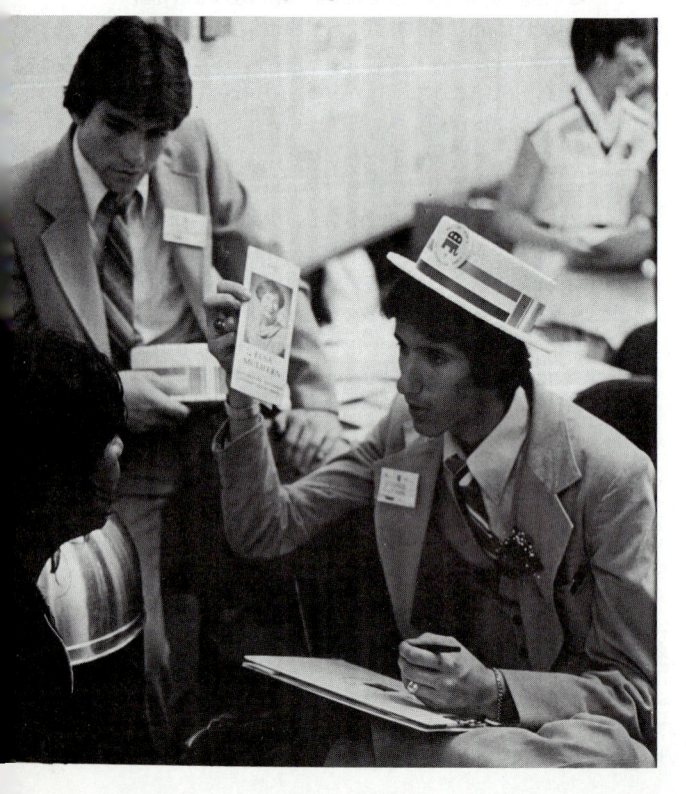

Your New Civic Duties

In addition to civic responsibilities, you have certain civic duties. A **civic duty** is what a person *must* do to contribute to the welfare of the nation.

You already have some civic duties. For example, you have a duty to obey local, state, and national laws. Laws are binding rules designed to provide structure so that people can live together in harmony with other people and with their natural environment. In addition, you already have a duty to appear in court if you are called to testify. With this duty also comes the duty to answer honestly any questions you may be asked in court.

38 Expressing Yourself as an Adult

In what ways will you use your communication skills if you serve on a jury?

When you are an adult, you will be affected by more laws than you are today. You will also face even stricter penalties than you already face for breaking many laws. In addition, you will have a duty to perform jury duty, pay taxes, and defend your country.

Performing Jury Duty

Every adult citizen has the duty to serve on juries. This is a serious matter. The right to a fair trial, judged by a jury of your peers, depends on adult citizens taking their duty seriously.

Taking jury duty seriously means agreeing to serve. Generally, if you are selected for jury duty, you will receive a notice through the mail. There are allowable reasons for not serving, such as having minor children at home or having a personal bias in the case. However, the judicial system works only when citizens participate. Therefore, you are bound to serve whenever you can. If you cannot serve for any reason, you must contact the court.

Taking jury duty seriously also means using good judgment and being fair when you are determining the fate of another person. Serving as a juror, a member of a jury, requires you to listen carefully. It also requires you to express your opinions when you and other jurors are discussing a case.

If you are interested in finding out how jurors are selected in your area, contact your county courthouse. In some areas, jurors are selected from voter or other registration lists. If you are interested in finding out more about legal proceedings, check to see if you can sit in on a trial.

Paying Taxes

Every wage earner, saver and investor, and consumer in this country has a legal obligation to pay federal, state, and local taxes. **Taxes** are the source of money for all services provided by the government. To pay for its activities, the government collects taxes on the money you earn, the money you save and invest, and the money you spend. By paying taxes, you are paying part of the cost of schools, roads, police protection, fire protection, defense, and all the other public services you and other citizens receive.

Many different types of taxes are collected. An **income tax** is a tax collected on money earned and on money received from certain sources, such as any interest received from a savings plan. A **sales tax** is a tax added to the purchase price of a wide variety of different

Expressing Yourself in a Democratic Society

items. An **excise tax** is a tax added to the purchase price of certain products and or services. In Chapter 5 you will find more information about taxes.

Defending the Country

Every citizen has a duty to help if the well-being of the country is threatened. This may mean that you will be required to register for military service when you reach the age specified by law. Military registration involves signing up to indicate your eligibility to be called for service. Military registration is carried out to make sure that individuals who are eligible to serve can be identified quickly. If war or another crisis occurs, registered individuals may be required to report for military training and service.

Some people volunteer for military service. Joining a branch of the military service provides men and women many opportunities. By joining a branch of the military service, you can travel to places that you might otherwise never see. You can meet people from other states and countries. You can develop skills that may help you to get a job when you leave military service. Local recruiting offices are good sources of information about requirements, benefits, and options.

Points to Remember

- Good communication skills are essential to success in many adult roles.
- To avoid misunderstandings during a conversation, consider the effect of your words, your voice, and your body language.
- Your message may be misunderstood if the words you use suggest a more emotional response or a more negative attitude than you have.
- Sometimes, writing is the best way to communicate because it allows you more time to get your message right and allows you to create a record of your message.
- Showing empathy as you listen is as important as concentrating on what the other person is saying.
- You can avoid legal problems and help care for yourself and others by reading legal documents, as well as directions and warning labels on products.
- You will probably participate in the free enterprise system as a wage earner and a taxpayer, as well as a consumer.
- Your civic responsibilities include protecting the natural environment, helping others, staying informed, voting, and helping make the government function well.
- To cast an informed vote, you must study the candidates and issues before making a decision.
- Your civic duties include obeying laws, appearing in court, performing jury duty, paying taxes, and defending your country.

Test Your Skills

DECISION MAKING

Imagine yourself in the situation described below. In this situation, a decision is needed. As you read, think about how to make good decisions. Then, answer the questions that follow. When you make decisions in the future, remember to ask yourself these questions.

Situation

The new house your parents purchased is one mile from your high school. Debbie, who lives next door, offered to drive you to school each day. Since your parents leave the house an hour earlier than you do, you accepted Debbie's offer. Within a few days, however, you discovered that Debbie is a reckless driver. Twice she has run a stop sign.

Recently, your mother mentioned how lucky your family is to have Debbie and her family as neighbors. If you decide to walk to school, you are certain that your parents will ask why. If you explain why, Debbie may get into trouble. If she is grounded, you may risk losing some friends, including Debbie.

Today, in a class you and Debbie both take, someone from a defensive driving school spoke about safe driving. You hope the comments will help Debbie change her driving habits. If she continues to drive carelessly, however, you are not sure what to do. You are wondering whether to talk to her about your concerns, to continue carpooling with her and hope for the best, or to begin walking to school.

Questions

1. What is the problem?
2. What information do you need to help you make a decision?
3. Which of your values, goals, and resources may affect your decision?
4. List three decisions you could make. What are their possible consequences?
5. What is the best decision you could make? Why is it the best for you? What is the next best decision?

Terms

On a separate sheet of paper, write a definition for each of the underlined terms below. Base your definition on the clues you find in the sentence(s).

1. Michelle has decided that she is not as good at sending and receiving messages as she would like to be. Therefore, she has decided to work on her communication skills.
2. When Willie speaks or writes, he uses words well. His verbal messages are clear.
3. By taking acting lessons, Rosalie has become skilled at sending nonverbal messages. She can communicate many messages without words.
4. Joshua usually uses body language that reinforces his words. When refusing to buy from a door-to-door salesperson, for example, he faces the salesperson and says no politely but firmly.
5. The voice inflections Lorene uses make her comments easy to understand. She adds meaning to certain words by varying how high or low, how loud or soft, or how fast or slow she says them.
6. When Matt listens to another person, he tries to see things from that person's point of view. By showing empathy, he is able to communicate well, even when he does not share the other person's opinion.
7. As a consumer, Jill uses many products and services provided by businesses and the government.
8. Chim, who moved to this country from Vietnam, is studying to become a citizen. As a citizen, he will have all the rights and protections this country provides its citizens.
9. Cassandra sometimes expresses her opinions to her governmental representatives. She lobbies her representatives before they vote on a key issue.
10. The taxes Ben pays are used for defense, education, health care, and other public services provided by the government.

Questions

1. Why is it important to be able to communicate well?
2. Name the three basic reasons communication might fail.
3. List five examples of body language that might occur when two people are talking.

4. Name four steps you can take to ensure that your written messages will communicate what you want them to.

5. What is the difference between hearing and listening?

6. Name three ways that you can improve your listening skills.

7. Explain in what ways you are a partner with business and government.

8. What are the principles of the free enterprise system?

9. In what ways can you express your economic freedom of choice?

10. Explain how you can become an informed citizen.

11. How can you find out when and where to register to vote?

12. What must you do if you are called for jury duty when you cannot serve?

13. How does the government pay for the public services it provides?

Activities

1. Think of a specific responsibility you will have as an adult. It might be related to housekeeping, food preparation, shopping, or financial management. Pretend that you can hire someone to do this job for you and that you want the job completed according to your written instructions. Write your message according to the guidelines on page 30.

2. For one week, observe the body language of two of your friends. At the end of the week, think about how each friend's body language has affected your communication with that person. How might you use your observations to improve your own body language?

3. Do you think you are better at sending messages or receiving them? Why? Plan how to improve your weakest communication skill.

4. Think of one product or service you buy. Is the item taxed in any way? What businesses or organizations in your community sell it? In what ways does competition between these sellers affect the product or service? What kinds of jobs do the sellers of this product or service provide in your community? Think of people you know who have such jobs. Might you consider any of these jobs for yourself? How do your findings show the relationship between you, businesses, and the government in your community?

5. Think of an issue at school for which you could be a lobbyist. Who would need to be convinced of your view? How could you communicate your viewpoint?

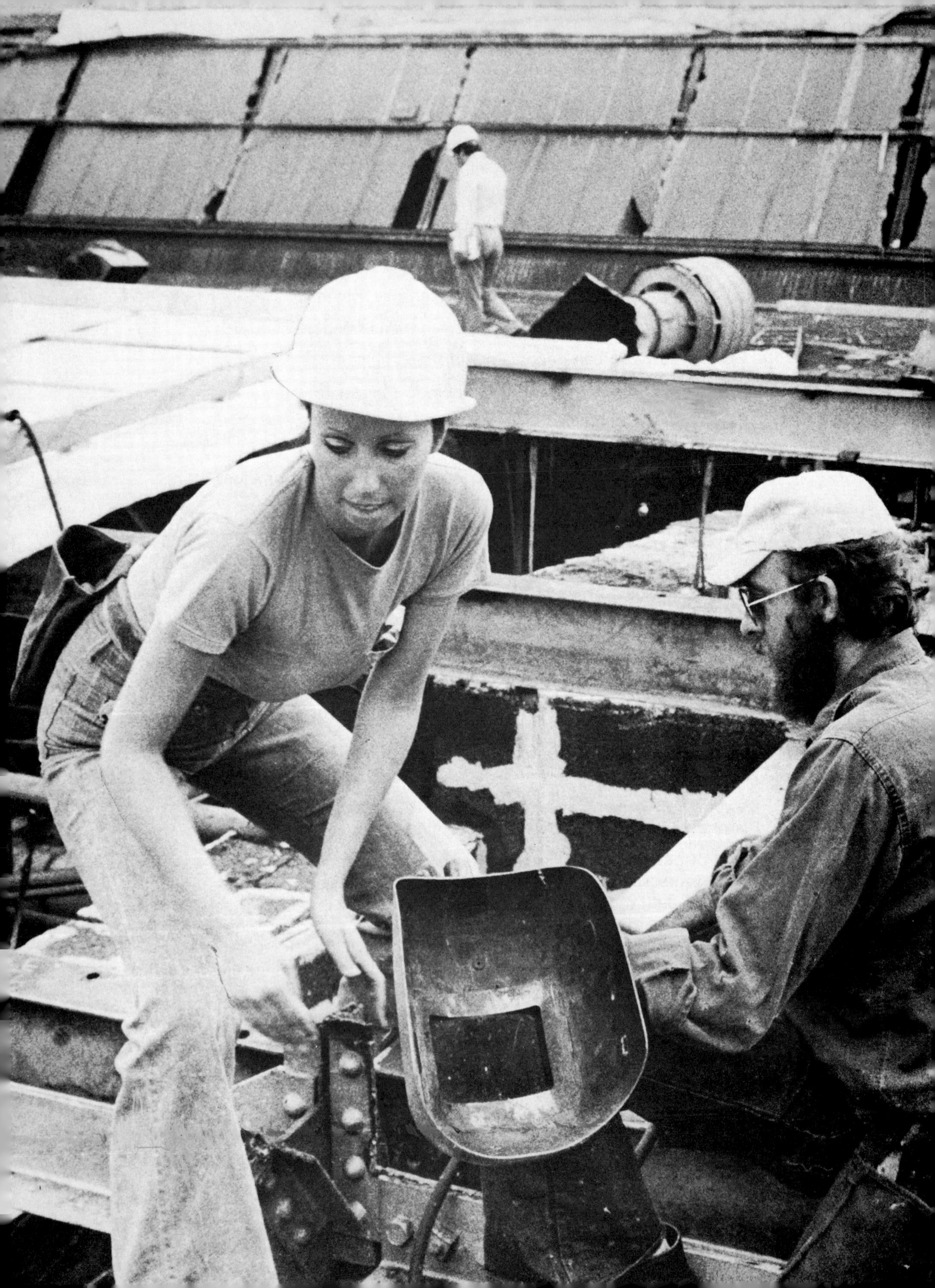

CHAPTER 3

Marketing Your Job Skills

For most young people, the first step toward independence is finding a job and becoming self-supporting. Perhaps you have begun to plan for a summer job or for a job after you graduate. On the other hand, you may already have taken this first step. You may be working part-time or full-time.

Whether or not you are working, several types of work may interest you. Keep in mind that trying more than one kind of job will probably help you select a career. Your on-the-job experiences will give you firsthand information about different lines of work.

You can use your first few jobs to learn which types of work really satisfy you and which do not. Maybe *none* of the first jobs you take will suit you. In spite of this, you will learn something from them. Maybe some part of *each* of your first jobs will suit you. Perhaps you will turn one of them into a career by making a long-term commitment to that type of work.

Whether or not these jobs relate to your future career, it is always best to find jobs that suit you in some way. To do this, you need to discover your special blend of interests and aptitudes, work-style preferences, and knowledge and skills. You need to know how to find out what jobs are available and how to contact employers. You need to know how to make the most of each interview you have. Finally, you need to know how to decide whether to accept a job offer. The jobs you take will affect the skills you gain and the money you make. They will also influence the standard of living you achieve and the people you meet.

Discover Through Your Reading

- what kinds of rewards jobs can offer you
- how to find out what jobs are likely to be available to you
- why some jobs may not be right for you
- how to find out about employers and let them find out about you
- how to make a good impression during an interview

Understanding How Jobs Differ

Jobs are not all alike. They may challenge you physically, mentally, or both. They may pay hundreds or thousands of dollars each year. They may be permanent or temporary, full-time or part-time. Some are available only in certain parts of the country. Others are available only at certain times of the year. Some require you always to work at night. Others require you to work a new set of hours every few weeks. Each job offers a different set of personal and financial rewards. Those rewards that suit you may not suit someone else. Finding a job that satisfies you will be easier if you consider the personal and financial rewards each type of job offers and how available each is.

Why do you think these young people enjoy their work?

Personal Rewards

No two jobs offer the same combination of personal rewards. A job as an emergency medical technician, for example, is a high-pressure position that requires accurate observations and quick decisions. It may require you to work a twenty-four-hour shift and then be off work for a few days. It is a mixture of outdoor and indoor work. It involves dealing with many different kinds of people who are ill, injured, or upset, and who are depending on your skill. It also involves working as part of a team of health professionals. The intensity may be exactly what appeals to you.

A job as a department store salesperson, however, may be a low-pressure position that requires accurate computations but not much hectic decision making. Its hours may be regular or varied. It is indoor work. It involves dealing with many different kinds of people, most of whom are well and not depending on your skills for their survival. It may offer little chance for teamwork with coworkers. In fact, coworkers may compete to help customers. The interaction with customers may be what appeals to you.

Your job duties, your job setting, and the relationships you experience on the job may all be sources of job satisfaction for you. It will be up to you to decide which jobs offer you the best combination of personal rewards.

Job Duties

Duties vary from one job to another. You will enjoy your job more if it includes the kinds of activities you like. For example, if you like to organize and straighten things, choose jobs where you might organize parts or products in a warehouse, sort mail, or file records. If you like to lead others, look for jobs where you can become a supervisor or a manager.

To decide what kinds of job duties might suit you best, you may want to consider which of the following kinds of activities you prefer:

- doing the same work each day
- having variety each day

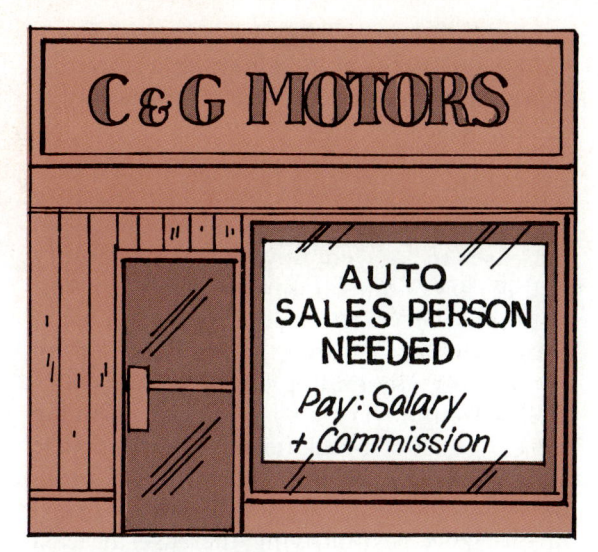

Would you rather be paid a wage, a fixed salary, or a salary plus a commission? Why?

- working with people
- working with machines, animals, or plants
- working with numbers, words, art, or music
- being a follower
- being a leader

Job Setting

Like job duties, job settings also vary. For example, some jobs are always indoors. Others are mostly outdoors. Some are in large settings such as plants, factories, colleges, or hospitals. Others are in smaller settings such as small stores, gasoline stations, doctor's offices, or houses. Some are in cities, while others are in rural areas. Try to picture yourself in different jobs and settings. Think about how you would feel in each.

Personal Relationships

Like job duties and settings, the types of personal relationships you can establish at work vary. What are you looking for in personal relationships on the job? You may like to work with a lot of people. If so, a job that allows you to work with the general public might interest you. You may prefer to work by yourself or with a small team. A job in a research lab might interest you. Do you like working with the same people for a long time? Would you rather work with new people every few months or each year? When you determine the job relationships you want, you are closer to making a job choice.

Financial Rewards

Like personal rewards, financial rewards usually affect a person's job satisfaction. Financial rewards include pay, advancement opportunities, benefits, and job security. Like personal rewards, they differ with each job. Since they will strongly influence your standard of living, consider carefully what financial rewards you want most.

Pay

Some employers pay more than others for a specific job. The amount can vary among employers in one location. It can also vary from one part of the country to another.

Employers also use different payment methods. Many employers pay wages. A **wage** is the amount of money paid to an employee per hour or day, or for each piece of work completed. Other employers pay salaries. A **salary** is a fixed amount of money paid to an employee at fixed intervals throughout a year. Still other employers pay commissions. A **commission** is a percentage of the dollar amount of products or services sold by

Understanding How Jobs Differ

an employee. Although most employees are paid either a wage, a salary, or a commission, some may be paid a combination of these.

Most employers provide for pay increases. A pay increase can come in the form of a promotion or a merit raise. A **promotion** is an increase in an employee's responsibility within an organization. It usually brings with it a new job title and more pay. A **merit raise** is a pay increase that is based on an employee's outstanding job performance.

Some employers also offer cost-of-living raises. A **cost-of-living raise** is a pay increase equal to the percentage that prices of products and services have risen during the previous year. A cost-of-living increase at least assures you of the same buying power year after year.

Sometimes, employers may postpone or eliminate a scheduled pay raise or may ask employees to accept a reduction in pay. These situations usually occur when an employer is faced with a difficult business situation.

Advancement Opportunities

Some employers offer more advancement opportunities than others. Advancement opportunities usually include new responsibilities and new chances to learn. They may also include higher pay or opportunities for promotions. You might want an entry-level job, the lowest-level job in a career field, for example, so you can work your way up to a higher position.

The more opportunities for advancement an employer offers you, the more likely you will be satisfied with your job. Also, the more likely you will be to reach your career goals. If your job offers few opportunities for advancement, you still may be able to achieve your goals. You may be able to use the job as a stepping stone to a better job in another organization.

Benefits

A **job benefit** is a payment or service provided in addition to an employee's wage, salary, or commission. While benefits are as varied as organizations and jobs, some are commonly offered by many employers. For example, you may receive paid vacation time, sick leave, and time off for the birth of a child. You may be offered health, disability, and life insurance free or at a reduced rate. You will probably be entitled to worker's compensation and unemployment insurance benefits. You may even be offered special retirement, savings, and investment plans.

Other benefits may not be as common. For example, you may be entitled to membership in a credit union. You may receive discounts on merchandise or services. You may have the use of a company car. You may have travel or moving expenses paid if they are required by your job.

When investigating a job lead, check on the benefits offered. They can amount to a large percentage, as much as 30 percent, of your annual pay. They can also contribute to your job satisfaction.

Job Security

You will probably feel more secure if you can count on your job being there for as long as you want it. Some jobs, however, offer little **job security,** the likelihood of long-term employment. For example, a temporary job might last only three days or six months. Even a permanent job could be subject to layoffs, depending on the demand for the employer's products or services. A change in management or in the direction of a company could mean a job will be phased out. An employer might move to another part of the state or country or even go out of business. An employer might also have a record of dismissing or firing employees without good reason.

Before taking a job, consider how dependable it will be. Try to find out whether it is likely to be around for as long as you may need it.

Availability

The job market is always changing. A particular job may be available now but not in a few years. Some jobs may continue to be available but never in great numbers. Others may be needed in your community now but not in other parts of your state. These job market possibilities—and more—will affect

Do you think these workers considered the possibility of layoffs at the time they were hired?

you. Before making a job choice, consider what is available now where you live. Also consider what may be available where you want to work in the future.

Today's Jobs

The *Occupational Outlook Handbook*, published by the U.S. Department of Labor, is an excellent job reference. It provides specific information about thousands of jobs available in this country. For each job title it gives a clear description of the work involved. It also indicates the kinds of organizations that offer the job. In addition, it mentions the types of training needed to qualify for the job. You should be able to get a copy of this book from your guidance office, school library, or public library.

Jobs of the Future

Changes in the population, in technology, and in what individual consumers want affect your job opportunities. As these things change, new jobs open up and others become hard to find. For example, use of the computer created a vast new group of jobs—programmers, analysts, and operators. The need for clerks and inventory employees, who used to perform related jobs, decreased. As advances in the computer industry continue, the skills of keypunch operators no longer will be needed.

As you plan for your future, consider changes that might occur in the job market. Most major changes in jobs occur over a period of several years. You can keep up with these changes by making sure that you update your information from time to time.

Again, the *Occupational Outlook Handbook* is a helpful reference. It contains predictions,

What kinds of information about jobs that are of interest to you can you find in the Occupational Outlook Handbook?

Understanding How Jobs Differ **49**

or intelligent guesses, about which jobs and types of jobs will be available. It indicates whether a particular type of job is likely to grow, remain the same, decline, or even disappear. If the outlook for a job that interests you is discouraging, explore alternatives in the handbook. You will undoubtedly find at least one or two job possibilities that appeal to you. For additional information on jobs, read articles in the *Occupational Outlook Quarterly* and the *Monthly Labor Review*. These periodicals are also available in most libraries.

It is important to look carefully at which types of jobs are likely to remain in demand. It is also important to compare the number of jobs predicted to be open and the number of persons predicted to be seeking them. As the number of persons seeking jobs in a particular field increases, so will the skills needed to compete. You will need to be very good at what you choose. You can compete if you are well qualified and can communicate this to employers.

Recognizing Your Job Market Potential

One part of getting a job you want is understanding the job market. Another part is recognizing your potential in it. To do this, think about your interests and aptitudes, your work-style preferences, your knowledge and skills, and your work experiences. Together, these make up your job market potential. Once you know them, you will have a good idea of the kinds of jobs to consider.

Interests and Aptitudes

Selecting jobs that match your interests and aptitudes will help you gain satisfaction from your work. **Interests** are those things that capture a person's attention. **Aptitudes** are natural abilities or talents. If you have mechanical aptitude, for example, you easily and quickly see how machines are made and work.

Several standardized tests are available to help you identify your interests and aptitudes. Your school counselor can tell you about these tests. Free vocational testing is also available if your school counselor refers you to your state employment agency. In addition, job-related testing and counseling services are available at many vocational centers, colleges, and universities. You might even use a computer to help identify jobs and careers for which you are well suited. See more about computer-assisted counseling on page 51.

A simpler way to identify your interests and aptitudes is to list them on a piece of paper. Write down what you like to do, what you do well, and what you would like to do someday. Then, look at your list to see if there are any patterns. Perhaps several items on the list fit into the category of helping others. If so, you may want to consider human-service jobs such as firefighting, day-care work, or nursing. If a lot of items involve problem solving, consider jobs like police work or urban planning. If you seem to be interested in physical activity, look into being a physical fitness expert, coach, or sports instructor. Often, your interests and aptitudes will suggest more than one type of job.

Work-Style Preferences

Everyone has **work-style preferences,** or ways they like to perform job duties. For example, some people work best when they are competing with others. Others work well when they are under great pressure. Still others like to set their own schedules and avoid structured situations. Maybe you dislike competition and really enjoy working at a relaxed pace. Perhaps you accomplish more when you work alone.

Your work-style preferences are important to your overall job satisfaction. Some jobs may demand a type of work style that does

How Computers Can Help You

Identifying Jobs or Careers Suited to You

Have you ever thought of being counseled by a computer? You can be if your state has a computerized career guidance system. Such a system is handy because it relates two important sets of information. One is a set of characteristics that may affect your chance for job success. These personal characteristics include your interests, aptitudes, work-style preferences, and educational level. The other is a set of detailed descriptions of specific occupations. These job characteristics include job duties, working conditions, pay rates, and job security.

Usually, a computerized career guidance system allows you to choose several ways to work with this information. You can ask the computer to list jobs that match certain of your own characteristics. You can ask for information about one or two specific jobs or careers. You can get the computer to quickly compare several characteristics of different jobs or careers. You may be able to get a list of current job openings in your state.

With each request, you will receive a computer printout. This is the information processed by the computer and then printed out on paper. A guidance counselor usually will be available to discuss your printout with you and to answer any follow-up questions you may have. Remember, the computer program itself does not make job choices for you. It does, however, present a variety of choices and appropriate alternatives. You must then evaluate this advice in terms of what is best for you.

If this kind of career counseling program interests you, contact your guidance counselor. Your school may already have such a program. If not, check with the nearest public library, state employment agency, vocational center, community college, or university. Through computer networking, these agencies may be tied into a statewide computerized career guidance system.

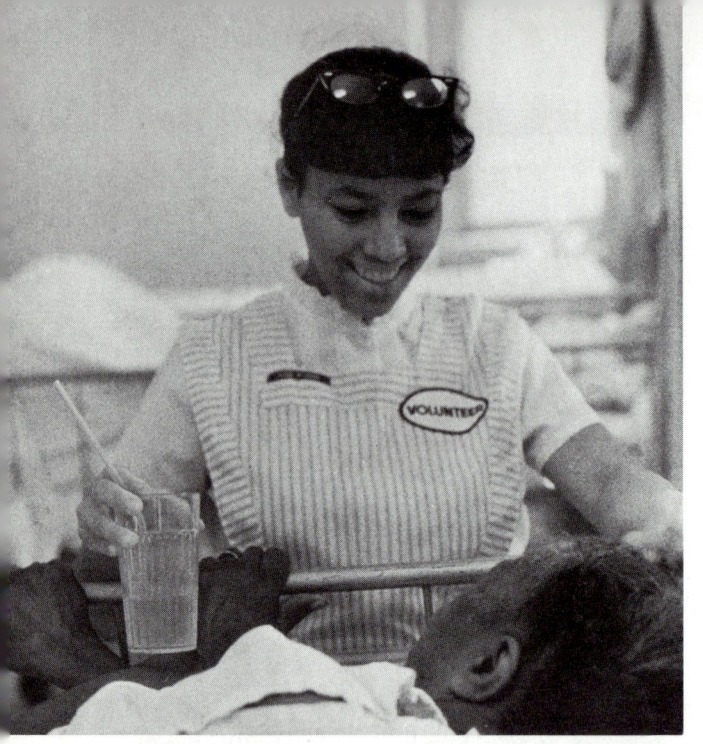

What kinds of volunteer work could you do in your community?

lot about animals or plants? Be honest with yourself. Neither overestimate your knowledge and skills nor sell yourself short. You more than likely already have knowledge and skills that you can use in a job. As you take additional courses, receive on-the-job training, or add to your work experiences, you will learn even more.

Work Experiences

All previous work experience is usually helpful in getting a job. For example, you may have had an afternoon paper route or worked in the ticket booth at your state or county fair. Each summer, you may have volunteered to help teach in your community's swimming program for young children. On weekends, you may have visited patients in the hospital or in a nursing home. Both paid and volunteer activities such as these count as work experience.

not suit you. If you take such a job, you will probably have to change your way of working or change jobs.

Your answers to the following questions may help you understand your work-style preferences:

- Could you be happy working overtime and not being paid for doing so?
- Would you like a job that requires you to travel a lot?
- Is working in pleasant, comfortable surroundings important to you?
- Do you object to being told what to do?
- Does speaking to large groups bother you?
- Could you enjoy your job if your duties were in conflict with your values?

Knowledge and Skills

Think of all the things you have already learned and done. Perhaps you have helped out at a friend's or relative's business. Maybe you are good with tools and have built things. If you have baby-sat, chances are you know something about child care. Have you read a lot in a certain area? Do you know a

Discovering Job Openings

To find a job, you have to be on the lookout for job openings. To get job leads, you can talk to people you know. You can check the classified ads in your newspaper or visit an employment agency. You can learn about job openings through work cooperative programs and apprenticeship programs. To increase your chances of finding a job, try as many job sources as possible.

People You Know

Family members and friends are usually great sources of help in job hunting. They know you and are personally interested in helping you. They know your interests, aptitudes, knowledge, skills, and experience. They also have many contacts. Therefore, be sure to tell them what you are looking for and that you would appreciate their help. You

Marketing Your Job Skills

can accept their help while remaining in charge of your own job search.

Your school is another source of job leads and career advice. Teachers of vocational courses such as agriculture, home economics, industrial arts, and business education often work with employers in helping students find jobs. Guidance counselors are certainly aware of many job openings. They may post notes about these jobs on school bulletin boards. They may also have information on the requirements and application procedures for these jobs. In addition, they may offer group discussions, field trips, and guest speakers related to jobs and careers. By taking advantage of these opportunities you may discover even more job openings.

Employment Ads

Every day or once a week, you can find employment ads in your newspaper's *Help Wanted* section. **Employment ads** are classified ads in which employers and employment agencies announce job openings.

Some newspapers list jobs alphabetically by title. Other newspapers group ads according to specific types of jobs. The types may have labels like *General Employment, Technical, Clubs and Restaurants, Medical, Professional*, and *Secretarial*. Scan all the ads because it is hard to predict under which title a job may be listed. For example, a job in recreation may be called *Counselor, Camp Assistant,* or *Natural Resources Worker*.

If you see an interesting ad, read it carefully. It should include job requirements, the name of the employer, and whom to contact. Be wary of ads that promise quick money or offer once-in-a-lifetime opportunities.

Public Employment Agencies

Many communities have employment agencies. An **employment agency** is an organization that offers professional assistance in locating a job.

Public employment agencies are funded by taxpayers and offer free services. They refer

How can your school guidance counselor help you learn about job training and job openings?

How can employment ads in the newspaper help you find a job?

persons to specific job openings. They also provide some testing services related to specific jobs and job skills. These agencies include state employment agencies, government personnel offices, and armed forces recruiting offices.

State Employment Agencies

Every state has a public employment agency. To find the closest office, check the telephone directory. Look under your state's name, then under *Employment*. If your telephone directory does not list the state employment agency, call for directory assistance.

State employment agencies are often busy places. It is not uncommon to wait an hour or more to see a counselor. If the counselor does not have a job opening that matches your qualifications and needs, you may want to come back in a few days. It is not unusual for an employer's job needs to change quickly.

Government Personnel Offices

All levels of government—local, state, and federal—employ many persons. Each government agency has its own job listings and employment procedures. For some jobs you need to take a job-related test. If you earn the necessary score, your name is placed on a list of eligible applicants. As openings occur, people on this list are contacted for interviews. Many people may be ahead of you on the list, so it is a good idea to become eligible for a job before you actually need it.

To find out about federal job openings, contact the U.S. Office of Personnel Management. You may have to call for directory assistance. To find out about job openings in state or local government, call the appropriate personnel office. Check the telephone directory under the name of your state or your county, city, or other local government agencies.

Armed Forces Recruiting Offices

Recruiting offices for the armed forces are located in every state. There may be an office in your area. To locate one of these federal offices, check your telephone directory under *United States* and then under the branch of the armed forces that interests you. Contacting a recruiting office does not obligate you to join the military. It can, however, provide you with information about job training programs and military careers.

Private Employment Agencies

If you have not found job openings through public employment agencies, consider private employment agencies. These are businesses that specialize in placing people in temporary or permanent jobs. For information on getting work through a temporary help agency, see page 56.

It is a good idea to shop around before deciding on a private employment agency. Be sure to ask about each agency's fee arrangement. Most agencies work with employers who pay a fee if they hire you. This is called a fee-paid agency. Some agencies, however, require you, the job applicant, to pay the fee. If you cannot spend much money on job hunting, you will probably decide that a fee-paid agency is best for you.

Private employment agencies usually require you to sign a contract before you find out about job openings. Do not sign a contract until you have read it carefully and are satisfied that the agency is a good one for you. If you sign a contract, make sure the counselor assigned to you listens and takes into account your job interests. Also, do not let the counselor pressure you to apply for jobs you do not want.

On-the-Job Training

Although most jobs involve at least some on-the-job training, this training is usually provided by the supervisor whenever the need arises, not according to a schedule. Such on-the-job training is informal. Some job openings, however, include special on-the-job training opportunities. These jobs include highly structured training and may allow you to gain a new set of knowledge and skills while you work and earn an income. This type of training usually takes the form of either an apprenticeship program or a work cooperative program.

Apprenticeship Programs

An **apprenticeship program** is a job opportunity designed to teach a profession, trade, or craft through structured, practical experiences. It provides on-the-job training for a particular job. Apprenticeships are required for some professions and for many skilled trades or crafts. For example, teachers must complete practice-teaching experiences. Doctors must go through an internship or residency. Dietitians, hair stylists, and many nonelected government workers also complete apprenticeship programs.

Trades regulated by unions often require formal apprenticeship programs. These programs generally last one to four years and

Many people make use of the services provided by their state employment agency. How might you make use of such services?

Discovering Job Openings

P.S. Why Might You Work for a Temporary Help Agency?

Is it possible to work for an employer that lets you decide *when* you want to work? Can you find an employer that allows you to choose *where* you want to work? Does any employer let you decide *what* job duties you want every few days? If the employer is a temporary help agency, then the answer to all three questions is *yes*.

A temporary help agency contracts your services to employers for a few days, weeks, or months. You work at the employer's location. However, you are usually paid by the temporary help agency.

To become a temp, or temporary worker, you first have to register with a temporary help agency. To find an agency, look under the employment listings in your telephone directory. You will find that some agencies specialize in only one type of job. Others offer many types, including clerical, construction, data processing, and marketing jobs. You may decide to register with several agencies until you find one that offers you the amount and kind of work you want.

As with any job, you must have certain knowledge and skills. Therefore, your education and work experience will be considered. Some temporary help agencies also require you to take a test related to the type of job you want. Once you qualify, your name goes on an eligibility list. When employers contact the agency saying what job skills they need and for how long, the agency may call you. You can always choose whether to accept the offer.

Working as a temporary employee has several advantages. It lets you work part-time, supplement another job, or work between jobs. It lets you try several different employers and types of work. It may even help you land a permanent job. If you really enjoy working as a temp, you may think of the temporary help agency as your permanent employer.

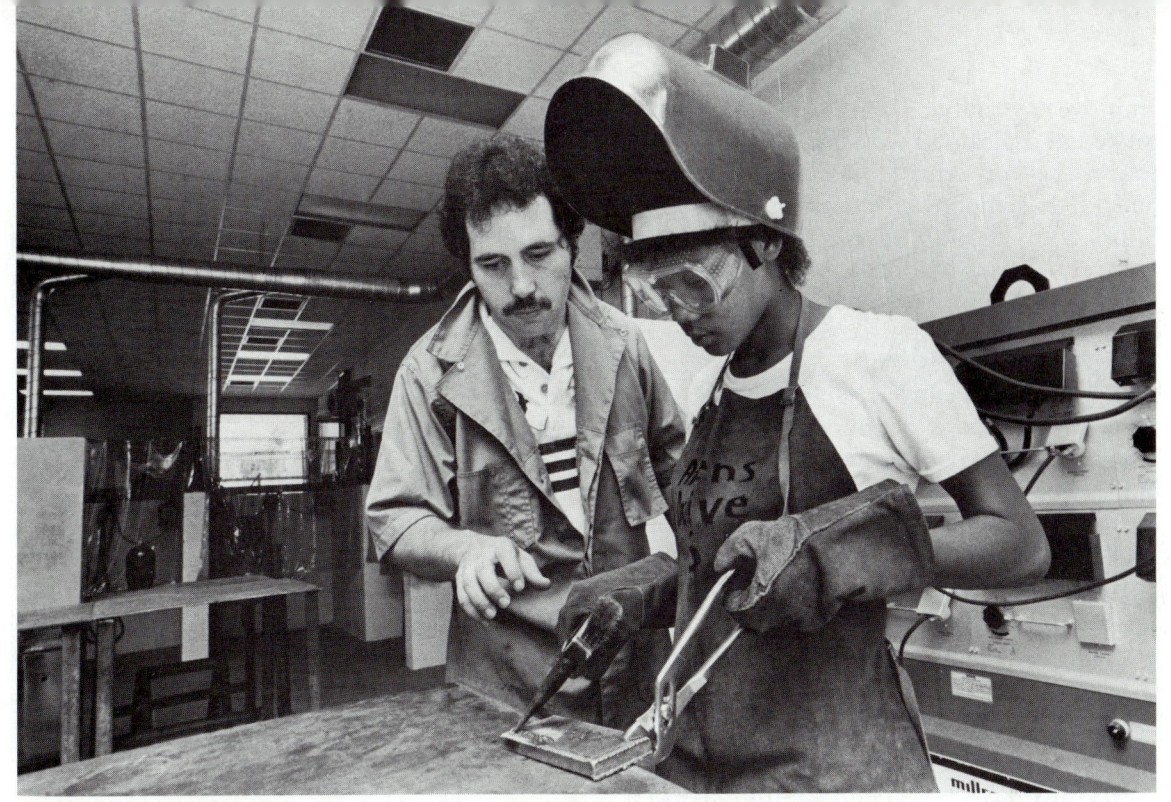

Have you ever known anyone who has served an apprenticeship?

require apprentices to learn and show that they can perform harder and harder tasks. By completing a program, apprentices prove they are skilled in a trade. Many trades that have this type of program are related to the construction industry. These trades train plumbers, electricians, brick layers, and other construction workers.

Some apprenticeships do not offer any pay. Others pay a percentage of the full salary for the job.

Work Cooperative Programs

Another special form of on-the-job training is the work cooperative program. A **work cooperative program** is a job opportunity that allows students to gain paid work experience while completing their schooling. It involves the cooperation of students, parents, teachers, and employers. A student not only learns to perform a specific job but also learns about other job opportunities as well. This type of job experience is available to many high school and college students. Ask your guidance counselor for information about your school's program.

Applying for Jobs

Once you find a job opening that matches your interests, aptitudes, work-style preferences, and qualifications, you will probably want to apply for it. For most jobs, you must have a Social Security card. For some you will also need a personal data sheet. Then, you will be ready to contact the employer and fill out an application.

Getting a Social Security Card

Your Social Security card and the number on it show that you are registered with the Social Security Administration. The Social Security Administration is a federal agency that maintains a permanent record of each employee's contributions to a fund for retired and disabled workers. When workers retire, they are entitled to Social Security benefits based on their contributions.

You may already have a Social Security card. If not, you will probably apply for one in the next few years. To do so, you must be a citizen. When you go to your local Social Security office, take with you at least two types of identification. One of these will probably be a copy of your birth certificate. The other could be a report card or a driver's license. Use the name that appears on these documents, not a nickname. If you change your name, make sure you report the change to the Social Security Administration.

Preparing a Personal Data Sheet

A **personal data sheet**, or a **résumé** (REHZ•uh•may), is a one-page summary of a person's employment qualifications. This summary helps an employer see what knowledge, interests, skills, and other qualities you will bring to a job.

Some employers request that you submit a personal data sheet in addition to your job application. Even if your data sheet is not requested, having one is still helpful. It will have the key information frequently needed for application forms. Therefore, you will not have to try to remember all these facts each time you complete an application.

To see how a personal data sheet might look, refer to the sample on page 59. Remember that the appearance of your personal data sheet is just as important as what it says. It should be neat, error-free, and if possible typed. As you can see, it helps to organize your information by category. These categories might include career goals, work experience, education, special skills, and references. A person's **references** are the people who can vouch for that person's character and ability. Be sure to include the complete address and telephone number for your references and yourself and for any schools and employers you list. As you add to your education and work experience and develop new interests, you will want to update your personal data sheet.

Contacting Employers

Once you learn about a job opening that interests you, you will want to respond as quickly as possible. Otherwise, the position may be filled before you have a chance to apply. Some employers ask for a job application letter and a personal data sheet. Others accept a telephone inquiry. Whether you introduce yourself by letter or telephone, this is the employer's first impression of you.

Job Application Letters

A **job application letter** is a letter expressing an applicant's interest in getting a job interview. It should be typed if possible. Whether typed or handwritten, it should be free of grammatical errors and neat. If you send the employer your letter and do not receive a response within a few days, follow up with a telephone call. This effort shows that you are really interested in the job. See the sample job application letter on page 60.

Telephone Calls

When calling to express interest in a job, be sure to use your best telephone manners. Remember that you are "selling" yourself. Start by stating your name. Be sure to say it clearly and distinctly. State whom you want to speak to and why. Sometimes you may not know the name of the person responsible for hiring. In this case, ask to speak to "the person responsible for hiring new employees." Since some employers may have more than one opening, identify the job that interests you. State what you think you can do to benefit the employer. Close by asking for an interview appointment. Follow through with a letter. In it, restate your interest in the job. Also, thank the employer for talking to you and setting up an appointment.

Filling Out Job Application Forms

For most jobs, you will be asked to fill out a job application form. A **job application form** is a personal data record that employers ask applicants to fill out. Such a form is important because it indicates your qualifications for the job, including how well you follow

PERSONAL DATA

Peter G. Lambrecht
3807 Dunning Street
Milford Lakes, WA 98372
(206) 465-3896

CAREER GOALS

Become a master electrician and work for a manufacturer or retailer of electric machinery

WORK EXPERIENCE

1/86 to present: Valley Electronics Outlet
Milford Lakes, WA 98372
Type of business: Retail sales of home electronic equipment and appliances
Job duties: Selling tape recorders

6/85 to 12/85: Cook's Auto Supply
North Milford, WA 98370
Type of business: Retail sales of new and used auto parts
Job duties: Delivering parts to customers

EDUCATION

9/81 to 6/85: Milford County High School
North Milford, WA 98370

SPECIAL SKILLS

- Knowledge of electrical wiring and machinery
- Experience with common hand and power tools

REFERENCES

Mr. Carl Benson
Sales Manager, Valley Electronics Outlet
Milford Lakes, WA 98372
(206) 461-3809

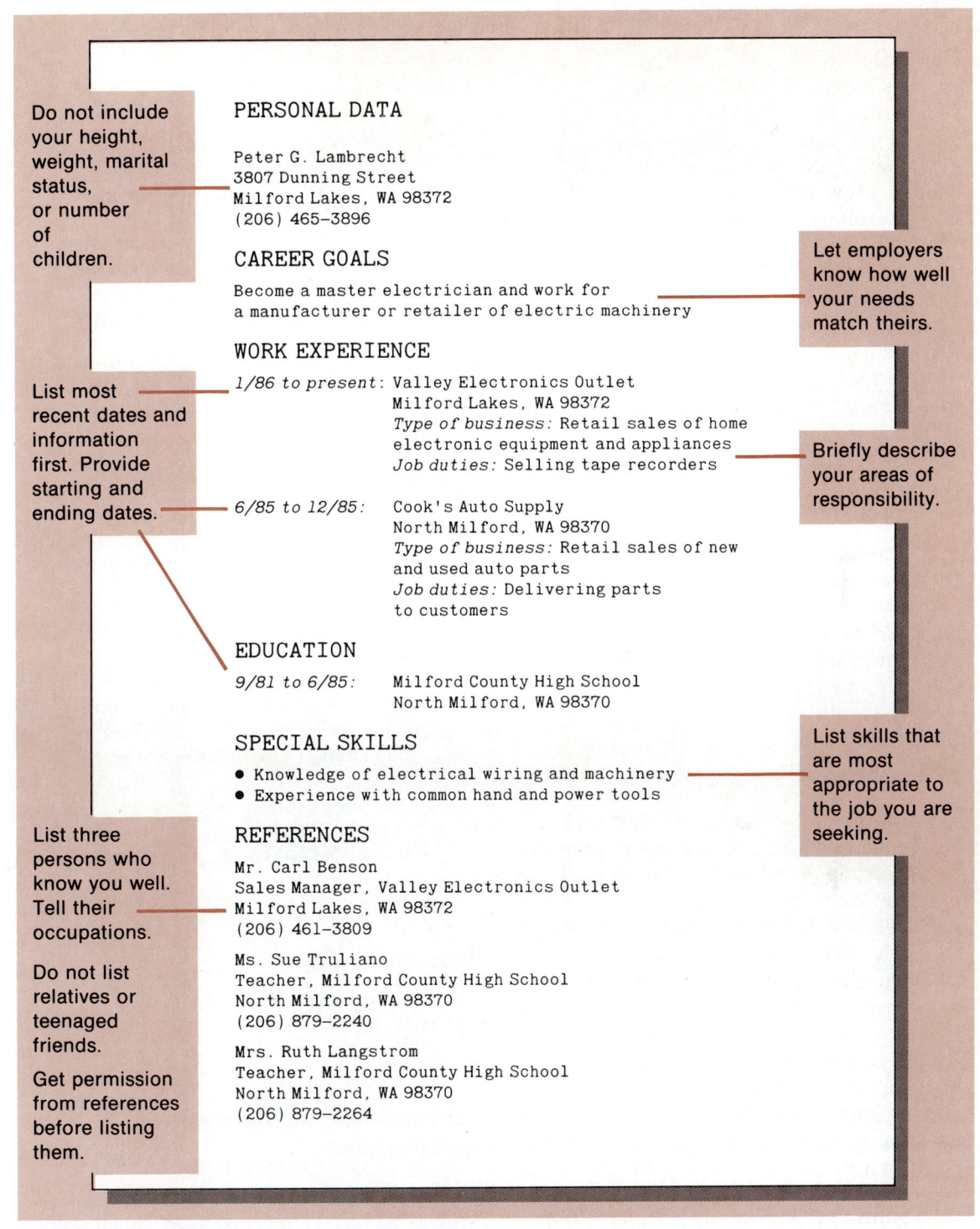

Ms. Sue Truliano
Teacher, Milford County High School
North Milford, WA 98370
(206) 879-2240

Mrs. Ruth Langstrom
Teacher, Milford County High School
North Milford, WA 98370
(206) 879-2264

Callouts:
- Do not include your height, weight, marital status, or number of children.
- Let employers know how well your needs match theirs.
- List most recent dates and information first. Provide starting and ending dates.
- Briefly describe your areas of responsibility.
- List skills that are most appropriate to the job you are seeking.
- List three persons who know you well. Tell their occupations.
- Do not list relatives or teenaged friends.
- Get permission from references before listing them.

For your personal data sheet, whom might you ask to be your references?

directions. It does not, however, guarantee you the job or obligate you to take the job if it is offered.

When completing a job application form, use ink, use good grammar, and be neat. Also, refer to your personal data sheet. It will

Applying for Jobs **59**

>
> 3807 Dunning Street
> Milford Lakes, WA 98372
> Oct. 15, 198–
>
> Mr. Vincent Modugno
> Operations Manager
> Clinton Electric, Inc.
> 6800 Industrial Park Drive
> Renton, WA 98641
>
> Dear Mr. Modugno: ——————————————— Write to a specific person such as a department head or manager.
>
>   I am writing in response to your classified advertisement ——— Tell how you learned about the job opening.
> in Sunday's *Citizen Register* for a maintenance electrician
> trainee. I would like to apply for that position.
>
>   I am very interested in preparing for a career as an
> electrician, and I think that the trainee position with your ——— State why you want to work for the employer.
> company would provide the practical experience I am seeking.
>
>   I am a graduate of Milford County High School, where I
> studied general industrial education and electricity and
> electronics. My education has made me familiar with electrical ——— State how your skills can meet some of the employer's needs.
> machinery and wiring and with many kinds of hand and power tools.
> For the past ten months I have been employed as a salesclerk
> at Valley Electronics Outlet in Milford Lakes. In addition,
> for the six months following my high school graduation, I
> worked as a delivery person for Cook's Auto Supply in North
> Milford. Additional information about my background is
> listed on the enclosed personal data sheet.
>
>   I would like to have an interview with you at your earliest ——— Mention your interest in an interview.
> convenience to discuss this job opportunity. You may telephone
> me during working hours at 645-2284 or evenings at 465-3896.
>
>   Thank you for your consideration.
>
>   Sincerely yours,
>
>   Peter G. Lambrecht
>
> Encl.

What is the most important message to include in your job application letter?

save you time in looking up telephone numbers and addresses.

    Be as complete and accurate as you can with every question on the application form. If there is a question about something you have never done, write *NA* (not applicable) or *none* in the space. If you are asked how much you expect to be paid, write *open*. That gives you a chance to talk later with the employer about your salary. You do not have to fill in blanks that ask for private, personal information such as your religion, age, nationality, and marital status. It is illegal for employers to request such information.

60   Marketing Your Job Skills

Making the Most of Interviews

If an employer is impressed with your job application, you may be asked to come in for a job interview. A **job interview** is a face-to-face discussion about a job opening with an employer. Improve your chances for a successful interview by preparing for the interview, actively participating in the interview, and then following up.

Preparing for an Interview

There are several things you can do to prepare for an interview. Learn what you can about the organization. Find out where the employer is located and about how long it will take you to get there. Look over your personal data sheet so that you are confident of what you are going to say. Practice the interview. Plan something appropriate to wear. Then, when the interview time comes, you will be ready.

When you are interviewing for several jobs, you may want to schedule some of them for the same day. By setting up interviews early in the day for the jobs in which you are least interested, you can practice for later, more crucial interviews.

Learn About the Employer

Whether the employer is a business or a government agency, it is best to know some facts about it before your interview. This will help you talk intelligently about what the employer does. If you are interviewing with a business, check the library for a local business directory. It may provide information about the products or services the company offers. If you know people who work or have worked for the employer, ask them for information. If you request one, some employers will send you a brochure about themselves before your interview.

Review Your Personal Data Sheet

When you are talking with an employer, you probably will discuss information that appears on your personal data sheet. You will make a better impression if you can remember these things. Unless you have just completed your data sheet and remember everything, take a moment to reread it. This simple step will probably make you feel more confident.

Practice the Interview

Prepare yourself for routine interview questions. The interviewer will probably start by saying, "Tell me something about yourself." Respond with a positive statement about yourself. Then, go on to say exactly how your skills, achievements, and goals fit the job you seek. Also, be prepared for the following questions:

- Do you think you can handle this job?
- Why do you want to work for this organization?
- What do you want to be doing in five years?
- What specific experience do you have that will help you succeed in this job?
- Why did you leave your last job?
- What kind of pay are you seeking?

Dress for the Occasion

Your appearance will set the tone for your interview. A neat, conservative look is usually best. It most often leaves an interviewer with a good impression of you.

Clothes should be selected for appropriateness to the job. If you are interviewing for jobs in construction, agriculture, or mechanics, wear a shirt and slacks or jeans, whichever is more appropriate. If the job will demand dressier clothes, a suit or a sports coat and slacks are appropriate for young men, a suit or a dress for young women. Stick with neutral colors like navy, brown, beige, or gray. Whatever you wear should be comfortable, clean, and pressed.

Makeup and jewelry should be kept to a minimum. Make sure your hair is freshly washed and combed and your fingernails clean. Keep in mind that you want to keep

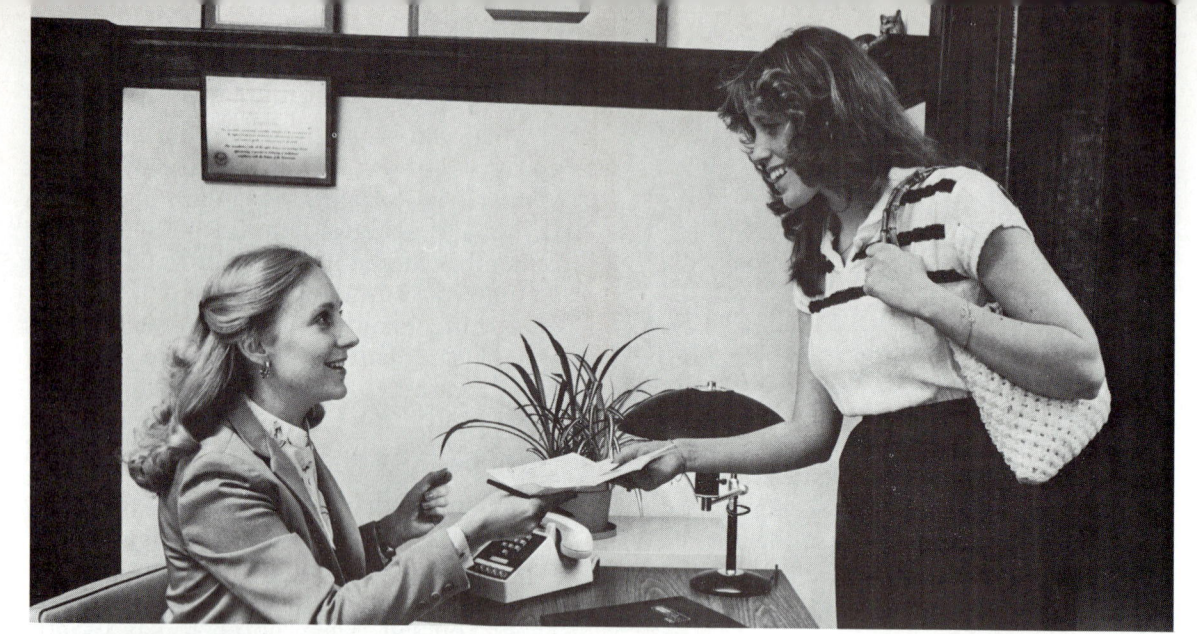

Is this job applicant dressed appropriately for her interview? Why?

the interviewer's attention on your job qualifications. You do not want the interviewer to pay more attention to a poorly groomed appearance than to your knowledge and skills.

Being Interviewed

When you go to the interview, go alone and be on time. Remember that interviewers like to meet courteous, friendly, enthusiastic job seekers. Smile and offer to shake hands with the interviewer when you first meet. Again, remember that you are selling yourself. Ask appropriate questions to show that you are interested in the job.

Be Courteous

Basic good manners are very important during an interview. Unless you really go overboard, it is difficult to be too courteous. Listen attentively and do not interrupt. At the end of the interview, make sure you remember to thank the interviewer for considering you for the job.

Sell Yourself

Try to give the interviewer what you would want if you were in the interviewer's position. The following suggestions can help you do this:

- Be calm, poised, enthusiastic, and confident.
- Maintain eye contact with the interviewer as you talk and listen.
- Avoid yes and no answers since they are conversation stoppers.
- Mention any of your strengths and accomplishments that you feel are related to the job if you feel they have not been covered in the discussion.

Ask Questions

An important part of your interview will be the questions you ask. Ask questions that show you have been listening and that you have an interest in the organization and the position. In addition, get all the information you can about the job. You particularly want to know about those policies that might affect your job satisfaction. If the interviewer does not offer this information, ask the following questions:

- How soon does the employer expect to hire someone for the job?
- What are the responsibilities of the job?
- What specific skills and qualities are needed?
- What are the expected work hours?
- What opportunities for advancement are offered?

Marketing Your Job Skills

Tips

Deciding Whether to Accept a Job Offer

Accepting a job offer is a major decision. Here are some steps that will make this decision easier.

- Consider the job market. Decide how soon you need to start earning money. If jobs are scarce, it may be wise to take the job. If many jobs are available, you may want to wait.

- Consider the employer. Make sure the employer will offer you the job security, pay, benefits, and advancement opportunities you want.

- Think about the job duties and work setting. Consider all their advantages and disadvantages, as well as your feelings about the position. Make sure the job will, in some way, help you meet your work goals.

- Think about your feelings toward the person who would be your supervisor. If you took an immediate dislike to the supervisor, you probably should not accept the job.

- Figure your time, energy, and expense traveling to and from work each day. If getting to work becomes a problem, you may not enjoy the job.

- Talk with others about your decision. Often, the questions they ask will help you think more completely and clearly.

- How often is an employee's job performance evaluated?
- Are employees paid a wage, a salary, or a commission?
- How often are employees eligible for a pay increase?
- What are the job benefits?
- Who will be your supervisor and where will you work?

The answers to questions like these will help you decide if the job and the employer are right for you. If you have more questions than time permits the interviewer to answer, the interviewer may suggest you contact the organization's personnel department after the interview. A **personnel department** is the section of a large organization that handles hiring of new employees and other matters such as employee records and benefits.

Respond to Any Job Offer

Near the end of the interview, the employer usually will indicate whether you qualify for the job. If you qualify, the employer will also tell you how soon you can expect a definite response. In some cases, the employer

If you were offered a job today, what might you think about before accepting? Could anyone in your family help you make your decision?

Making the Most of Interviews

will actually offer you the job at the end of the interview. If you are already sure you do not want the job, say so. The employer wants to consider only those applicants who are really interested. If you are already sure you want the job, feel free to accept the offer before you leave.

If you feel that you need time to decide whether the job is right for you, ask for some time. Many employers will let you respond in a day or two if they feel you are definitely interested in the job. Following the tips on page 63 may help you make a good decision. If you finally decide you do not want the job, let the employer know about your decision as soon as possible.

Following Up After an Interview

Depending on the type of job you have interviewed for, you may want to send a thank-you note after the interview. Such a note is a courtesy that also acts as a reminder of you to the interviewer. Sending it is likely to increase your chances of getting the job.

In addition, you may want to call the interviewer from time to time until you know whether you are being offered the job. This will also remind the interviewer of your interest in the job.

Points to Remember

- A job will be personally rewarding if it includes the duties, the setting, and the personal relationships that you want.
- A job will be financially rewarding if it helps you achieve the standard of living that you want.
- Because the job market is always changing, you need to know what kinds of jobs are available and what qualifications you have to offer.
- You are more likely to find a job if you take advantage of as many job sources as you can.
- Job hunting usually takes both time and patience.
- Some jobs require that you first participate in an apprenticeship program.
- Before applying for your first job, you will probably need to get a Social Security card.
- Filling out a job application form neatly and accurately is an important step in applying for a job.
- During a job interview, you meet the employer and learn more about the job.
- Any decision to accept or turn down a job is one to consider carefully.

Marketing Your Job Skills

Test Your Skills
RESOURCE MANAGEMENT

Imagine yourself in the situation described below. In this situation, resources need managing. As you read, think about the ways that you can manage resources. Then, answer the questions that follow. When you need to manage resources in the future, remember to ask yourself these questions.

Situation

Three days ago, in advanced word processing class, you learned about a great job opportunity. The employment ad read as follows:

"Wanted: Part-time secretary. Flexible hours. Must type 40 wpm and have basic word processing and proofreading skills. One year of work experience required. Apply in person, 10–6, M–F. Hanson's."

Two days ago, you decided to ask your word processing teacher to help you prepare a personal data sheet. Your teacher agreed to also write a letter of recommendation that indicates you type 50 words per minute and earned an A in word processing last year. Your teacher also suggested that, to get the job, you might offer to work weekends. Working after school and on weekends would, however, limit your time for other activities. You are active in the business club and attend an after-school fitness program.

This is exactly the type of job you want. If you could get this part-time job with Hanson's you could probably work there full-time as soon as you graduate. The only thing bothering you is the experience requirement. You have worked only one summer. You wonder if you have a chance for the job.

Questions

1. Which resource do you need to manage most carefully? Why? (Hint: Look for the resource that is in shortest supply.)

2. What are the ways you might manage this resource? (Hint: Be sure to name any resources you could substitute, trade, or share.)

3. What opportunity costs would be involved in each case?

4. Who would pay the opportunity costs in each case?

5. After considering all these opportunity costs, how would you manage your resources in this situation?

Terms

On a separate sheet of paper, write a definition for each of the underlined terms below. Base your definition on the clues you find in the sentence(s).

1. Megan earns a salary of $1,000 a month, or $12,000 a year.
2. In a few weeks, Tony will become a supervisor. He is really looking forward to the promotion, especially because he will get a raise.
3. Keiko has received an Outstanding rating on her job performance. She will soon get a merit raise.
4. Once a week, Dennis checks the employment ads in his newspaper's classified ads section. He is scanning the job openings advertised by employers and employment agencies.
5. Shawna seeks help from an employment agency when she is job hunting. The organization's counselors give her job leads and job-hunting tips.
6. Jeff plans to enroll in an apprenticeship program so that he can learn carpentry from a master, or professional, carpenter.
7. Roberta is in a work cooperative program. In this program, she works closely with her supervisor, her marketing teacher, and her parents. Each morning, she takes classes, including a marketing class. Each afternoon, she goes to her marketing job, for which she earns some income.
8. Cedric was interviewed after he sent an employer a job application letter. In the letter, Cedric briefly explained his qualifications for the job and requested an interview.
9. Lila describes her job qualifications on each job application form an employer asks her to fill out.
10. Tom works in the personnel department for a large organization. He supervises the employees who handle employee benefits and records and hiring.

Questions

1. Why might you think seriously about the kinds of benefits offered by a particular employer before taking a job?
2. Why might a particular job offer little security?
3. List four kinds of job information that you can find in the *Occupational Outlook Handbook*.
4. What contributes to your job market potential?

5. Why is an understanding of your work-style preferences important when you are looking for a job?

6. Does volunteer experience count as work experience?

7. In what ways can your family and school be sources of job leads?

8. When reading employment ads, what kinds of information should you try to find?

9. What is the main difference between the services of public employment agencies and those of private employment agencies?

10. How can a personal data sheet help you when you are applying for a job?

11. Briefly describe how to apply for a job over the telephone.

12. Why does a job application form play an important part in helping you get a job?

13. Identify four things you can do to prepare for an interview.

14. Explain why it is important to ask questions during the interview.

15. Why is it a good idea to follow up after an interview?

Activities

1. Make a list of the five jobs you feel most qualified to do. Beside each one, write a skill you have that would help you perform the job successfully.

2. Ask people you know, including family members and friends, if they have heard of any job openings. Make a list of the openings or job leads as you hear about them. After two weeks, total the number of jobs on your list. Is your total more or less than you expected? How many of these jobs interest you? Which of these jobs are you qualified for now?

3. Write a description of what would make a job rewarding and enjoyable for you. Include such details as work hours, work conditions, location, and size of the organization. Indicate the salary, benefits, and the work-style you would prefer.

4. Choose a career field that interests you. Select a job in this career field that you might like to have in ten or so years. Talk to several people who work in this field. Find out what work experience you might need before you could meet the long-term career goal you have just set.

5. Read the *Help Wanted* section of your local newspaper. Select ads for three job openings that interest you. What kinds of information does each ad provide? What other information would you like to see in the ads?

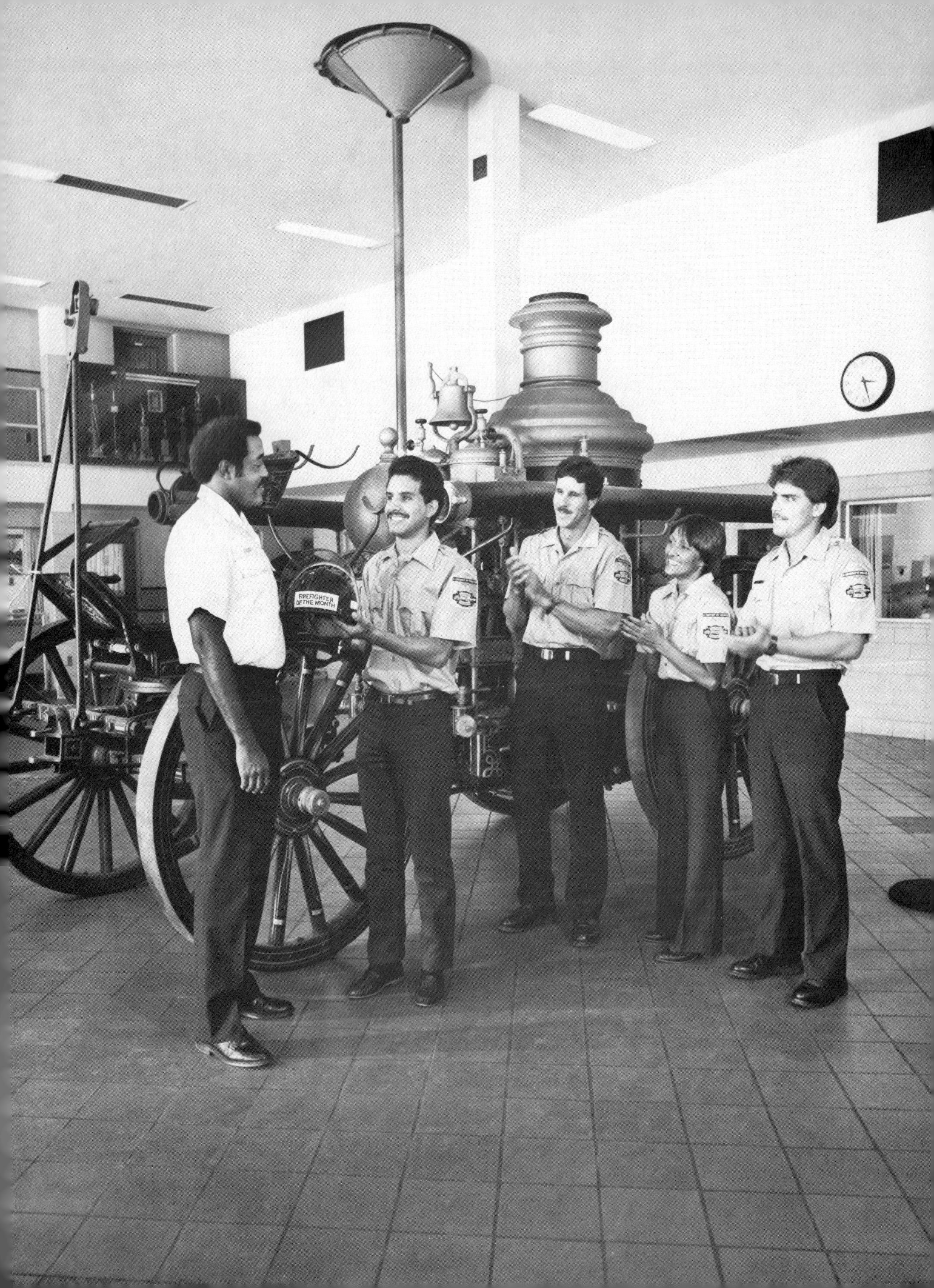
FIREFIGHTER
OF THE MONTH

CHAPTER 4

Succeeding at Work

Even if you work for employers in the same type of business, you will find differences. For example, one food establishment might have you begin work as soon as you arrive the first day. Another might give you time to get acquainted with other workers before you start your first task. One utility company might have an insurance plan that pays the cost of dental checkups. Another might ask you to pay for checkups yourself. One veterinarian might pay you every two weeks. Another might pay you once a month. One newspaper might give you the day off on your birthday. Another might not.

As you can see, certain policies and procedures vary with each employer. You will most likely learn about these kinds of work conditions during your first few days on a job.

There are other rules and regulations, however, that all employers follow. For example, employers are required by law to make certain paycheck deductions. Employers also set certain standards of behavior for employees to follow. These standards for honesty, loyalty, punctuality, and thoroughness almost always reflect the basic values accepted by society. In addition, these standards help employers and employees work together to accomplish the jobs that need to be done.

By learning quickly about your work conditions and by performing according to the standards set, you are likely to experience success on the job.

Discover Through Your Reading

- what to expect your first day on a job
- why you might choose to join your employer's health insurance plan
- why you might not get paid on the first payday after you start working
- how certain legal requirements affect the amount of your paycheck
- how to solve problems that may arise on the job
- how to survive between jobs

Beginning a Job

In some ways, your first day on a job is like your first day at a new school. You will have to get used to new surroundings and may at first have trouble finding your way around. You will meet many new people and may at first have trouble remembering their names. In other ways, your first day at work will be quite different. There will be many forms to complete. You will also find out about your employer's rules and your benefits. Your job duties will be explained more fully and you will begin to perform them. At the end of your first day, you will probably look forward to relaxing and sharing your experiences with family and friends.

Starting Out Right

Knowing what to expect will make your first day on the job easier. When you accept a job, your employer will tell you many things about your first day. It is a good idea to take notes so you can easily remember all the important details later. These details most often concern when and where to report and what to bring with you. It is also a good idea to listen carefully to your employer, as well as to ask questions about anything you do not understand. Doing these things will make you feel more at ease and will help you start out right.

When to Report for Work

You will find out on what day and at what time to report for work. You will also learn how many hours you will be expected to work each day. With some jobs, you may start work the same day you accept the job. For example, you might be offered the job at 9:00 A.M. and be expected to begin at 10:30 A.M. If you work for a temporary help agency, this is often the case. Usually, though, you will have more time to get ready. Remember that not all work takes place during the day. So, it is possible that your first "day" on the job will be a night.

Why do you think this person will make a good first-day impression?

Where to Report for Work

You need to know where to report. Your work place may not be the same place you interviewed. Perhaps your interview was at your employer's personnel office. This office may have been in a different part of the building from where you will work. It may even have been in another part of town. On your first day, you may have to report to the personnel office or you may be asked to go directly to your work area. The person who hires you will usually tell you where and to whom to report.

What to Bring to Work

There are certain things you will take with you on your first day. The most important is probably your Social Security card. This is your ticket to getting your name on the payroll. Perhaps you will also need a uniform, tools, or equipment. If so, your employer will tell you where to get them and whether you need to pay for them yourself.

70 Succeeding at Work

Tips

Getting Ready for Your First Day on the Job

Planning for your first day at work is just as important as planning for your interview. Before you report for work the first day, get ready by making the following plans:

- Make a trial run, or make a high estimate of your travel time if you have never been to your new work location.

- Plan what you are going to wear. Make sure it is clean and neat. Estimate the time you will need for dressing and grooming.

- Plan for your workday meals. Consider how much time you will need to prepare food and eat it before going to work. If you decide to take food to work, be sure to have the food on hand. Estimate the time you will need to prepare it. If you are picking up something on the way instead, estimate this time.

- Total the amounts of time needed for travel, dressing and grooming, food preparation, and eating. Then, add a few minutes more to cover unexpected emergencies. Heavy traffic or a power failure could, for example, cause a delay.

- Give yourself plenty of time for sleep, rest, and relaxation before starting to get ready.

- Subtract the total time you need to prepare for work from the time you are expected at work. Then, set your alarm clock.

Because you will probably eat at least one meal during your work hours, you need to know what your employer provides. Some employers offer facilities for refrigerating and preparing your food at work. Others do not. Some provide a cafeteria or snack bar. Others assume you will make your own eating arrangements. Therefore, you may need to take a meal with you or be sure to have enough money to eat out.

How to Make a Good Impression

On your first day, you will want to make a particularly good impression. This means being on time, well rested, clean, and appropriately dressed. To be all of these, you may need to make some arrangements ahead of time. Following the planning tips on this page should help.

A successful first-day experience is important in two ways. It makes you feel good. It also helps you establish the kind of work record you want.

Getting Oriented

During your first week on the job, you will go through job orientation. **Job orientation** is an employee's introduction to the work setting, policies and benefits, and duties related to a new job.

Employers conduct job orientations in different ways. Some employers hold formal orientation sessions. They may set aside a special time and place for all new employees to meet. Together, you may complete forms, receive a policy handbook, view a film, or even take a tour. Other employers provide informal job orientations. They may have supervisors orient their new employees individually. In this case, you may learn about your workplace in a more personal way and at a more relaxed pace.

Work Setting

Whether you work two or ten hours a day, you will need information about your work setting. Your work setting is more than just the area in which you perform your job duties. It also includes the facilities, equipment, and supplies that help you do the job. Facilities may include restrooms, lounge

Beginning a Job

Beginning a job means meeting new people and learning to do new things. How do employers help new employees feel more at home?

areas, eating places, medical clinics, locker rooms, or telephones.

During orientation, you should learn what facilities, equipment, and supplies are provided. You should also learn where they are and when they can be used.

Work Policies

Every employer has specific work policies that must be observed. **Work policies** are rules and procedures set by an employer to ensure that work is accomplished safely and efficiently. Work policies often focus on the procedures for arriving late, leaving early, or missing a day of work. They specify acceptable reasons for doing so and state whether the time off is paid or unpaid. They also indicate procedures for dealing with accidents on the job. In addition, they may state standards for personal dress and conduct. For example, some employers do not allow smoking on the job. Most state that alcohol and illegal drugs are not permitted at work.

Because satisfied workers are usually more productive, work policies are usually designed to maintain good employer-employee relations. During orientation, you should learn your employer's policies. Be sure to ask questions about any policies you do not understand.

Work Benefits

During your interview, you probably learned about some of your employer's benefits. During orientation, these benefits are explained more fully. For example, you will find out what holidays you get. In addition, you will find out about vacation time. Your employer will tell you how long you must work before becoming eligible for a vacation. For example, you may have to work three months, six months, or perhaps even longer. You may have to schedule your vacation around your employer's work load and perhaps around the vacation schedules of other employees. Usually, the longer you work for an employer, the greater the vacation time you will receive.

Probably the most important benefits of your job are the financial ones. These include group insurance, retirement, and investment plans. They will be easier to understand when you know some basic terms and descriptions. Group insurance plans are discussed later in this chapter. Retirement and investment plans are discussed in Chapter 5.

You may also be entitled to some special benefits. For example, if you work for a food establishment, you may receive free meals at work. If you work in a retail store, you may be able to buy that store's merchandise at reduced cost. Some employers even help provide day care for young children.

Job Responsibilities and Job Performance

During orientation, you will also begin to learn your job responsibilities. The person who explains your job to you will most likely be your supervisor. This person will also explain how your job performance will be evaluated. You should find out who will make the evaluation and when it will be made. You should also ask for a copy of the form that will be used. See the sample

JOB PERFORMANCE EVALUATION

EMPLOYEE: _____ REVIEWER: _____ DATE: _____

	Check one:					Check one:		
	Good	Fair	Poor			Good	Fair	Poor
1. Quality of work					4. Attendance			
2. Productivity					5. Overall performance			
3. Attitude								

Reviewer's Comments: _____

Employee's Comments: _____

Reviewer's Signature: _____ Employee's Signature: _____

In what ways is a job performance evaluation similar to a school report card or a progress report?

evaluation form shown above. By knowing what your supervisor's expectations are, you can definitely improve your chances of being a successful employee.

Important Paperwork

When you start any job, you will have forms to complete and sign. Some of these forms concern work policies. For example, you might need to get a parking permit and be assigned a parking space. You might be given a time sheet and shown how to record the number of hours you work. You might also sign forms related to work benefits, such as insurance and retirement plans.

One of the most important forms you will complete is related to your payment of income tax. This form is called the W-4 form. The **W-4 form** is the paperwork that authorizes an employer to deduct a certain amount of federal income tax from an employee's paycheck each pay period.

Why is it important to think carefully about the number of allowances you will claim on your W-4 form?

Form **W-4** (Rev. January 1984)
Department of the Treasury—Internal Revenue Service
Employee's Withholding Allowance Certificate
OMB No. 1545-0010

1 Type or print your full name

2 Your social security number

Home address (number and street or rural route)

City or town, State, and ZIP code

3 Marital Status
☐ Single ☐ Married
☐ Married, but withhold at higher Single rate
Note: If married, but legally separated, or spouse is a nonresident alien, check the Single box.

4 Total number of allowances you are claiming (from line F of the worksheet on page 2) . . . .

5 Additional amount, if any, you want deducted from each pay . . . . $

6 I claim exemption from withholding because (see instructions and check boxes below that apply):
   a ☐ Last year I did not owe any Federal income tax and had a right to a full refund of **ALL** income tax withheld, **AND**
   b ☐ This year I do not expect to owe any Federal income tax and expect to have a right to a full refund of **ALL** income tax withheld. If both a and b apply, enter the year effective and "EXEMPT" here . . . ▶ Year
   c If you entered "EXEMPT" on line 6b, are you a full-time student? . . . . ☐ Yes ☐ No

Under penalties of perjury, I certify that I am entitled to the number of withholding allowances claimed on this certificate, or if claiming exemption from withholding, that I am entitled to claim the exempt status.

Employee's signature ▶ _____ Date ▶ _____ , 19 ___

7 Employer's name and address (Employer: Complete 7, 8, and 9 only if sending to IRS)

8 Office code

9 Employer identification number

Beginning a Job **73**

As you complete your W-4 form, remember that you can claim a tax exemption for yourself. A **tax exemption,** or **tax allowance,** is an amount of income the Internal Revenue Service (IRS) says does not need to be taxed. If you claim *no* tax exemptions, more money than necessary is withheld from each paycheck. This decision may result in a larger income tax refund, but smaller paychecks than necessary during the year. Decide how you want your tax payments handled before you sign your W-4 form.

Joining Group Insurance Plans

Insurance is a risk-sharing plan that provides protection against financial loss. Individuals do not always have the money available to cover a sudden financial loss. By buying insurance, they contribute to a pool of resources that is available whenever a loss occurs.

If your employer offers group insurance plans, it is usually wise to join them. Your employer may pay the entire cost or share it with you. When you join such a plan, you are protected as long as you work for that employer. In some cases, you can arrange to keep your group insurance even after you leave your job. It will be up to you, however, to pay for the plan. If your employer does not offer group insurance plans, you may be able to get group insurance through an association or union to which you belong. Otherwise, you may decide to purchase some individual insurance policies on your own. The tips on page 75 can help you make wise insurance decisions.

Understanding the Language of Insurance

Before enrolling in any insurance plan, you need to understand what the plan includes. The insurance company, also called the **insurer** or **carrier,** usually provides information about its plans. Employers that offer group plans often provide this information in a special form for their employees. During your job orientation, you may receive a booklet describing your insurance choices. You will also learn how to enroll and whether you will have to pay any costs.

As you read about your employer's insurance program, you may see some special terms commonly used by insurance companies. The following terms are examples:

- An **insurance policy** is a contract by which an insurance company agrees to provide a particular kind of insurance in return for payments.
- A **policyholder** is a person who buys an insurance policy.
- A **provider** is a business from which a policyholder gets services related to an insurance policy. For example, a hospital is a provider.
- **Eligibility** is the set of conditions that a person must meet to become a policyholder. For a group policy, these conditions might include the length of time an employee has worked for an employer. For an individual policy, the conditions might include the age or health of an applicant.
- **Coverage** is the set of circumstances under which an insurance company will pay benefits. The greater the coverage provided by the company, the greater the cost of an insurance policy.
- A **covered charge** is an expense that an insurance company agrees to help pay.
- An **exclusion** is an expense that an insurance company chooses *not* to help pay.
- A **deductible** is the dollar amount a policyholder must pay for some covered charges before an insurance company begins paying any benefits.
- A **co-insurance clause** is a statement that requires a policyholder to pay a certain part of a covered charge. (For example, a medical insurance policy might pay 80 percent of a covered charge. The policyholder would pay the other 20 percent.)
- A **claim** is a policyholder's written notice to the insurance company that benefits are

due. Usually, the policyholder must give notice by submitting to the insurance company a special form called a claim form.
- **Benefits** are the dollar amounts an insurance company pays for covered charges. They may be paid directly to the policyholder, to a provider, or to a beneficiary selected by the policyholder.
- A **beneficiary** is a person who has been named by a policyholder to receive the benefits of the policyholder's insurance policy. Beneficiaries often include depen-

Tips
Buying Insurance

Before buying any insurance, consider the points presented below. Also, ask friends and family members to suggest reputable insurance companies. Most important, compare rates and coverage to find the best coverage for the best price.

Health insurance

- The time to think about medical insurance is before you become ill. If you are uninsured, one illness can create a real financial crisis.

- The cost of dental insurance may be higher than what you would normally pay for dental care without insurance.

Disability income insurance

- The cost of disability income insurance depends on your age, income, and occupation.

- Other income sources that might help you cover the cost of a disability include Social Security and savings. Loans may also be available from family members or friends and should be treated like any other loan.

Life insurance

- The younger you are when you buy life insurance, the lower its cost. As you grow older, you may develop health problems that make it harder or more expensive to get a policy.

- The amount of insurance you need depends on the number and age of your dependents. It also depends on the standard of living you wish to provide for your dependents. You may want to consider coverage equal to twice your yearly income.

- Some policies require you to make payments, called premiums, once a year. Others let you pay twice a year, every quarter, or even every month. Generally, if you make fewer payments per year, the cost will be lower.

- If you choose two or more beneficiaries, you can decide whether they will share benefits equally or inherit them in a particular order. You should let your beneficiaries know about your policy. If you ever decide to change beneficiaries, you must notify your insurance company.

Joining Group Insurance Plans

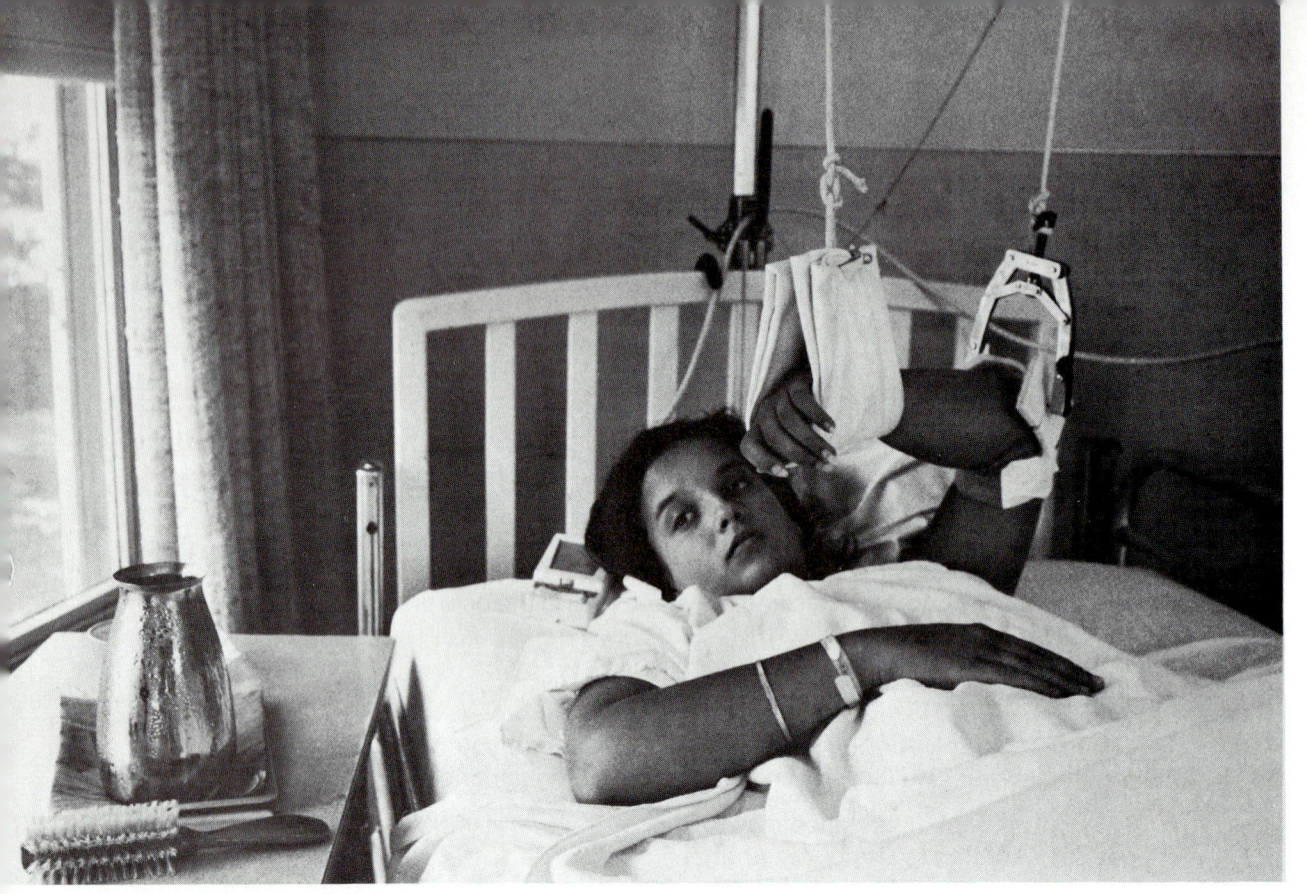

If you had no health insurance, how many days could you afford to stay in the hospital?

dents but may also include other persons.

The types of insurance most often included in a group plan are as follows: health insurance, disability income insurance, and life insurance. Each type has its own specialized coverages.

Health Insurance

Although no one wants to think about getting sick or injured, it does happen. Even people who take good care of themselves can become ill or have an accident. This is when health insurance really helps out. **Health insurance** is a risk-sharing plan that helps pay medical or dental expenses.

Medical Insurance

Many employers offer group medical insurance. The four most common types of medical insurance are as follows:

- *Physician's expense insurance.* Charges for doctors' services not related to surgery are covered by physician's expense insurance. Such services could include office visits, X-rays, and laboratory tests. Usually, there are limits on how often and how much the insurance company will pay for these services.
- *Hospital expense insurance.* Charges for a room, meals, drugs, tests, and nursing care in a hospital are covered by hospital expense insurance. This insurance is particularly important, since the daily cost of a hospital room may be much higher than that of an expensive hotel room.
- *Surgical expense insurance.* Charges for certain operations are covered by surgical expense insurance. This insurance is important because even a minor operation can be expensive. It is also important because the need for an operation is often hard to predict.
- *Major medical expense insurance.* Charges for the lengthy treatment of an injury or illness are covered by major medical expense insurance. This insurance is the most comprehensive. It can include care

76 Succeeding at Work

inside and outside of a hospital, physician's fees, drugs, therapy, and special equipment such as crutches or wheelchairs.

If a group plan combines physician's expense, hospital expense, and surgical expense, the combined form is sometimes called basic protection or basic medical coverage.

Some employers also provide a health maintenance organization (HMO) plan. If you participate in an HMO, you pay a basic fee on a regular basis for a variety of medical services. This form of group health insurance emphasizes preventive measures such as routine checkups, which are not covered by many policies.

Dental Insurance

Some employers offer group dental insurance. This insurance may not cover charges for preventive dentistry services such as routine cleanings and fillings. However, it usually covers major dental work, such as braces and root canals.

Disability Income Insurance

Like health insurance, disability income insurance may be offered by your employer. If so, you may have to pay for it. Because the monthly fee is small and the benefits are great, this insurance may be well worth its cost.

Disability income insurance is a risk-sharing plan that provides an employee some income during a long illness or while injured and unable to work. In this situation, your health insurance policy may not provide enough protection. If you were *not* injured on the job, you will not be covered by **worker's compensation insurance.** This is a type of insurance most employers buy to cover the

Often, the beneficiaries of a life insurance policy are members of the policyholder's family. If you get a life insurance policy, who might you list as your beneficiaries?

Joining Group Insurance Plans **77**

cost of their employees' job-related illnesses and injuries.

With disability income insurance, you receive a fixed monthly amount if you are totally disabled. You receive a portion of that amount if you are partially disabled.

Life Insurance

Another kind of insurance your employer will probably offer is life insurance. **Life insurance** is a risk-sharing plan that provides financial protection for a person's dependents when that person dies. When you first begin to work, you may not have any dependents. In the event of your death, however, you will have funeral expenses and maybe unpaid medical bills, taxes, or loans. A life insurance policy is designed to help cover those costs.

Many employers provide their employees some free life insurance. The amount of coverage varies, however, as does the type. The insurance your employer offers may be term life or whole life.

What makes you think this employee is looking forward to payday?

Term Life Insurance

With a term life insurance policy, the policyholder is protected for a limited term, or period of time. The most common terms are five, ten, or twenty years. A beneficiary receives benefits only if the policyholder dies during the term stated in the policy. Term life insurance is usually inexpensive.

Whole Life Insurance

With a whole life insurance policy, the policyholder gets lifetime protection, savings, and living benefits. Also called ordinary or straight life insurance, whole life insurance covers the policyholder until death. It is more expensive than term insurance because the policy always pays off. It also provides savings because the insurance company invests part of the policyholder's payments. The interest earned on the investments accumulates as savings. Usually, the interest earned on a life insurance policy is less than what could be earned in a savings account.

Living benefits are privileges that policyholders may use during their lifetime. For example, a policyholder could cancel a policy and receive its cash value. This amount of money is based on the interest that the policy has earned. Once the policy is cashed in, the insurance coverage is no longer in effect. A policyholder could borrow an amount of money up to the cash value of the policy. There is no fixed schedule for repayment of the loan or interest. The amount of the loan, however, reduces the insurance coverage of the policy.

Getting Paid

Not all employers pay in the same way or at the same time. Some pay with cash at the end of each working day. Most, however, pay by check at the end of a pay period. A **pay period** is the number of working hours or days between payments. Employers usually establish a regular cycle of pay periods. For

PAY PERIOD		HOURS			EARNINGS				
NO.	DATE	REGULAR	STR. O.T.	1½ O.T.	REGULAR	OVERTIME	CODE*	OTHER	GROSS
23	11/18/8–	70.0			340.00				340.00

DEDUCTIONS									
FED. INC. TAX	FICA	CODE	ST./LOC. TAX	CODE	ST./LOC. TAX	CODE	ST./LOC. TAX	CODE SUI	DISABILITY
55.23	19.89	NY	11.67	NR	1.01				

GROUP INSURANCE	SAVINGS BONDS	CODE*	OTHER	CODE*	OTHER	CODE*	OTHER
.60							

EMPLOYEE NO.	DEPT. NO.	YEAR TO DATE		ADVANCE		CHECK NO.	NET PAY
		GROSS EARNINGS	FED. INC. TAX W.H.	CODE*			
83791	7150	7820.00	1270.29			3230864	251.60

EMPLOYEES PAY STATEMENT
NOTE: RETAIN THIS PERMANENTLY. IT IS A RECORD OF YOUR EARNINGS AND TAX DEDUCTIONS AS REPORTED TO THE FEDERAL, STATE AND LOCAL GOVERNMENTS.

How much money was deducted from this worker's paycheck during this pay period?

example, you might be paid on the first *or* the last day of each month. You might be paid every two weeks, such as every other Friday. You might even be paid every week. During your job orientation, you will learn how and when you will be paid. You will also determine some of your paycheck deductions.

Looking Forward to Payday

As a new employee, you may not be paid at the end of your first regularly scheduled pay period. Instead, you may have to wait until the next one. This delay results from the paperwork that is required to get your records added to the payroll. It is a good idea to plan ahead for such a delay. Until you actually receive your first paycheck, watch your expenses.

Also, know that your paychecks may not have as much money as you may be expecting. When you begin a job, you may be looking forward to earning your gross pay. **Gross pay** is the amount of money earned by an employee—the pay before taxes and other deductions are made. Your paychecks, however, will reflect your take-home or net pay. Your net pay will be less than your gross pay. **Net pay** is the amount of money an employer actually pays a worker after subtracting taxes and other deductions.

When you receive your paycheck, you will also find a check stub attached. This stub shows you exactly how your net pay has been determined. Above you will find an example of a paycheck stub.

Recognizing Required Paycheck Deductions

Certain paycheck deductions are required by law. These are deductions for Social Security and federal income tax. Depending on where you live, your employer may also be required to deduct state and local income taxes.

FICA

On your paycheck stub, you will see the term FICA. This term stands for Federal Insurance Contribution Act. This act was passed to help support retired and disabled workers and other individuals. According to this act, most employees must contribute a portion of their earnings to a special FICA fund, and their employers must contribute a matching amount to the same fund. These contributions are collected and handled by the Social Security Administration, which distributes the money to people covered by the act.

The government determines the minimum amount you must earn before paying into

Getting Paid

FICA. If you earn less than this minimum, you will not see this deduction on your paycheck stub. The government also determines the maximum amount you will be required to contribute.

Federal, State, and Local Income Taxes

A required percentage of your salary is taken out of each paycheck for federal income tax. **Federal income tax** is the amount of money each wage earner must pay to help support the federal government. The amount taken from your paychecks is applied to the tax you must pay by April 15 each year.

In some states, you must also pay a state income tax. **State income tax** is the amount of money each wage earner in a state must pay to help support the state government. This tax money is collected every pay period by the states that have a personal income tax.

In some areas, you must also pay a local income tax. **Local income tax** is the amount of money each wage earner must pay to help support the local government. This tax money is collected every pay period by each city, county, or other local government that has a personal income tax.

On some jobs, you may be required to punch a time clock. How might this practice encourage you to arrive on time?

Recognizing Voluntary Paycheck Deductions

Some deductions are determined by you, the employee. For example, you might have your employer use some of your earnings to pay for a group insurance policy, stock in the company, or a U.S. Savings Bond. You may also have your employer transfer some of your earnings into a savings account or into an account to repay a loan. If you direct your employer to make any of these payments, they will show up on your paycheck stub as paycheck deductions.

Depending on your employer's pay periods, you may not see all your deductions on your first paycheck. Some deductions may be made during one pay period. Others may be made during the next pay period. After your first few paychecks, you will know exactly what to expect.

Keeping a Good Work Record

Your work record begins with your first job and ends with your retirement. It includes your job titles and responsibilities. It also includes your employers and how long you have worked for each. Most importantly, it includes *how* you have worked for each employer. For example, did you perform your job duties well? Were you always on time for work? Were you considerate? Did you give the job your best effort before you moved on?

With a good work record, you are bound to be considered a valued employee in your current job. As such, you will be more likely to receive opportunities for further training, raises, and promotions. In addition, you will

80 Succeeding at Work

be able to count on your employer to give you a good reference for future jobs. To build and keep a good work record, concentrate on the following goals:

- displaying a professional attitude
- being a cooperative worker
- making job changes successfully

Displaying a Professional Attitude

All employers want their employees to display a professional attitude. A **professional attitude** is a concern for doing a job in a way that makes both the employee and employer proud. You can show this concern in several ways. You can be honest and loyal. You can arrive on time and give a full day's work. You can do the work to the best of your ability. You can also ask to take on additional responsibilities and update your knowledge and skills. To learn more about how you can display a professional attitude in this way, see page 82.

Being Honest

One way to be honest is to be truthful with people. In your conversations with supervisors, coworkers, customers, or clients, you need to tell the truth.

Another way to be honest at work is to be careful with your employer's property. This means that you will protect money, merchandise, and equipment that has been entrusted to your care. If you take supplies and materials for your own personal use, you are stealing.

Being Loyal

Besides being an honest employee, you will want to be a loyal employee. You can show loyalty by giving others a good impression of your workplace. For example, you can tell them enjoyable and encouraging events that happen at work and downplay or ignore any unpleasant situations. You might even encourage friends or acquaintances to seek work with your employer. If you ever decide that you do not feel loyal to your employer, it is probably best to look for another employer. You may be able to find an employer whose values are closer to yours.

Managing Time

How well you manage time also contributes to your professional attitude. Because your employer needs you to help accomplish the day's work, you should report every day and be on time. When you are absent, your duties may have to be done by other workers. Sometimes, they cannot be done by others. When you are late, you cannot contribute your full share. You may even cause other workers to wait for you before they can begin to work.

Sometimes, illness and personal or family obligations can prevent you from reporting to work as usual. It is your responsibility, however, to do what you can to keep such situations from occurring too often. By maintaining a healthy lifestyle, for example, you can reduce your chance of getting ill or injured. By planning how to get to and from work you can prevent transportation problems. By taking your work seriously, you will not be tempted to call in sick just because you want the day off.

While on the job, you will want to continue to manage your time. You can do this by taking no more than the allowed time for breaks and meals. You can also make your personal phone calls at home rather than at work. In addition, you can concentrate on your work rather than spending time daydreaming or gossiping.

Doing a Thorough Job

To complete your professional attitude, you will want to show another important quality, perseverance. **Perseverance** is the basic quality that people demonstrate by following through and by not giving up. For example, one assignment could take you more time and effort than you would like to spend. Another assignment could require you to make some changes after you felt it was complete. If you show perseverance, you spend the necessary time and effort to make sure each job you are assigned is done thoroughly and correctly. In other words, you value the quality of your work and want others to think well of it, too.

P.S. How Can You Get Ahead on the Job?

Many employers encourage employees who have mastered the basics of a new job to take on more responsibility. If you work for such an employer, you will probably have many opportunities to assume new job responsibilities. For example, if some of your coworkers are overloaded, you might volunteer to find out what they are doing and help out. If you work especially well with people, you might offer to train a new employee. If you are well-organized and your supervisor is not or is too busy, you might suggest ways to improve the filing system. Before you do anything that involves taking on new responsibilities, be sure you are *not* moving into another worker's territory.

What you learn from your extra work will add experience to your résumé if you decide to look for another job. Your extra experience may give you an advantage over other applicants. It may also get you a better job offer or an advancement in the job you now hold.

Many employers also encourage employees to get job-related training. If your employer helps employees keep up with new trends and technical improvements in their field, you might express interest in a training program. You might suggest that you enroll in workshops or take classes at a nearby school or college. Often, employers will pay some or all of the costs of such training. They may even allow you to train on work time.

Your additional training will help both your employer and you. Your employer will benefit because you will be more skilled and, therefore, able to contribute more to the organization. You will benefit because you will be better equipped to get promotions and raises. You will also be better prepared if you later decide to look for another job.

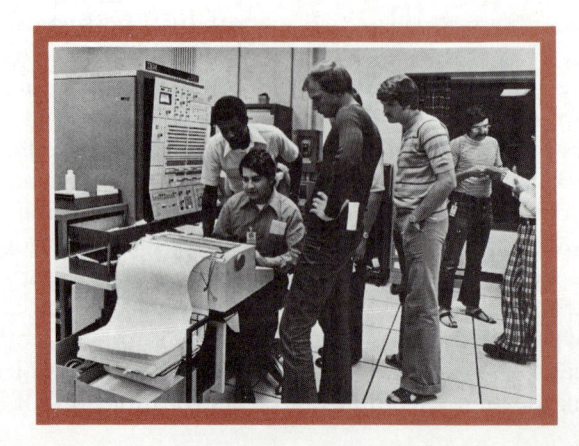

Being a Cooperative Worker

Your work record should reflect not only a professional attitude but also cooperative behavior. How well you get along with others can influence the quality and quantity of work you do. It can also influence whether you enjoy going to work each day.

One of the best ways to cooperate is to show consideration for others. You can do this in the following ways:

- be sure to use good manners and everyday courtesies
- show others that you are friendly, helpful, and interested in them
- practice good communication skills so you can avoid misunderstandings and hurt feelings
- keep your work area neat and clean
- pay attention to special safety rules and report unsafe situations to your employer

Cooperative behavior applies whether you are working with supervisors, coworkers, customers, or clients. It is important regardless of the type of job you have. To learn more about developing good working relationships, see page 84.

Working with Supervisors

In most jobs, employees work under the direction of a supervisor. Supervisors are responsible for seeing that other employees assigned to them do their jobs well.

Your supervisor will most likely be the person who hired you. You may work with your supervisor daily or rarely. Since your supervisor evaluates your work and determines whether you keep your job, however, you will want to work well together. One way you can do this is to understand and adjust to your supervisor's work style. For example, your supervisor might do the following:

- expect a task to be done only one way or remain open to suggestions
- keep a close eye on everything or allow you a lot of freedom
- show no concern for personal problems or be willing to listen and offer help

Whether or not your supervisor's work style is what you would like, try to gain this person's support and interest. Remember, your supervisor is a person, too, and, like you, can have problems and make mistakes.

Working with Coworkers

In some jobs, you may spend a part of each day with coworkers. Some coworkers may share information and offer advice. They will be friendly if you are. Others may be insecure or jealous. They see other employees as a threat to their own position. They may ignore your attempts to be friendly or try to cause problems for you.

To get along with coworkers, take your time in getting to know them. Avoid making snap judgments about them and avoid rushing into friendships. Someone who seems unfriendly may, instead, be very shy. The person who seems to be a "loudmouth" may be covering up for feeling inferior or left out.

The quality of work performed often depends on the working relationship between a supervisor and employees. Does this supervisor's work style seem to contribute to a good working relationship? Why?

Keeping a Good Work Record

Tips
Solving Problems in Your Working Relationships

The following suggestions can help you work more effectively with supervisors, coworkers, and customers or clients:

With your supervisor

- Help solve problems instead of being one. Think of ways to improve situations. Avoid being a complainer or tattler.

- Show that you are willing to learn new tasks.

- Accept critical comments as a form of guidance and help. When you make mistakes, try not to become upset or defensive.

- Apologize when necessary, and ask how you might improve the situation.

- Avoid arguing with your supervisor. Try to understand your supervisor's point of view.

- Ask for a chance to talk over your concerns if you are upset with your supervisor.

With your coworkers

- Accept an offer of help when you really need it. Do not, however, take advantage of such offers because you would rather not do the work yourself.

- Try not to interrupt the work of others. Talking in a loud voice, popping gum, singing, or making repetitive noises can be annoying interruptions. Even wearing noisy jewelry can be distracting.

- Take time to calm down before discussing problems. Recognize that bad feelings, if left unsaid, can grow out of proportion. If you feel that a coworker is upset with you, suggest that you talk about the problem. If the two of you cannot resolve the matter, ask your supervisor for help.

With customers or clients

- Display common sense, patience, and a sense of humor.

- Listen carefully to questions or complaints. Show that you care and want to help. If you cannot help, suggest or offer to find someone who can.

How might spending leisure time with coworkers provide enjoyment, as well as improve on-the-job communications?

Someone who immediately wants to be your friend may only want you to agree to take on more work. If you get to know your coworkers gradually, some may eventually become your personal friends.

Because coworkers often spend so much time together, moods, personalities, and work habits may sometimes clash. When this happens, you can probably solve the problem on your own. However, you and a coworker may clash over a safety or legal matter or a situation that could cost your employer a great deal of money. If so, go immediately to your supervisor, and state the facts clearly. Keep in mind that such an action is in the best interests of everyone.

Working with Customers or Clients

When you work with customers or clients, remember that they are the reason you have your job. Without them, you and your employer would be out of business. Your customers or clients come to you because they want something your employer offers. If their expectations are reasonable and your product or service is good, relations will usually be smooth. Your attitude and actions will also help determine whether a customer or client returns.

In spite of your best efforts, sometimes problems will arise. For example, customers or clients may have complaints. They may even become abusive. When you deal with upset customers or clients, be sure to show empathy. Try as hard as you can to think about how you would feel if you were in their situation.

Getting the Most from Each Job Change

It is very likely that you will change jobs from time to time. It is a good idea, however, to stay with each job at least one or two years. This gives you time to gain new knowledge and skills. It also gives you time to form new friendships. In addition, it gives your employer time to become familiar with your work. Therefore, when you need a reference for future jobs, your employer will have a basis for making such a recommendation. When you do change jobs, you will do so for one of two basic reasons. Either you will decide that you want to get a new job, or some situation will force you into a job change.

Keeping a Good Work Record

Wanting to Change Jobs

You might *want* to change jobs for any of the following reasons:

- You are working in a **dead-end job,** one that offers no possibilities for growth in either job duties or pay.
- You no longer like the kind of work you are doing. You want to try another type of work.
- You have a personality conflict with a supervisor or coworker. You prefer a job that offers a more pleasant environment.
- Your employer's values conflict with yours. You prefer an employer who shares your values.
- Your income does not cover all the things that you want to buy. You prefer a better-paying job.
- You prefer to live in another area of your state or in another region of the country. Your present employer cannot offer you a job where you would like to live.
- You would rather start your own business than work for an employer.

Why is working hard—even on your last day on the job—so important?

Needing to Change Jobs

You may *need* to change jobs for any of the following reasons:

- Your pay does not increase enough to overcome increases in the cost of living. You need a better-paying job.
- You are laid off, or dismissed for lack of a job, because your employer has lost customers or clients.
- Your employer moves out of your employment area, but you do not.
- Your medical doctor indicates that the working conditions with your present employer are damaging your physical or mental health.
- You have school or family obligations that make it difficult or impossible for you to continue working at your present job.
- You are fired for violating a work policy, performing your job poorly, or having a personality conflict with your supervisor.

Changing Jobs Successfully

Whether you want to or need to change jobs, you can take certain steps to make sure that you do so successfully. First, consider your alternatives and choose the one that you feel is best. For example, you might ask for a transfer to another job with your current employer. You might look for a different employer. You might even consider starting a business of your own. On page 87 you can see how the use of computer skills could help you become self-employed.

Second, be sure you have enough money to cover your expenses when making a job change. Should you be unemployed for a while, you will not receive your paychecks and employee benefits. During this time, you may consider using your savings, taking out a loan, or looking for temporary work.

Unless you choose to leave your job or are fired, you may be able to sign up for unemployment compensation. **Unemployment compensation** is money a state offers for a limited number of weeks to persons who have lost their job and are looking for other work. You might also be eligible for severance pay. **Severance pay** is money a few employers give their employees to help cover expenses between jobs.

86 Succeeding at Work

How Computers Can Help You

Starting Your Own Business

If you have a home computer, starting your own business is not as far-fetched as it might sound. One enterprising student ran a profitable babysitting business from her home. However, she herself never did any actual babysitting. She interviewed and screened possible sitters. Then, she fed into the computer information including their ages, telephone numbers, free time, and work experience. Next, she developed a list of people who use the services of a babysitter, including their addresses, telephone numbers, number and ages of their children, and other relevant information. She set up a pay scale for the sitters and hourly or daily rates for the parents. A profit was built into the system, much of which she invested to earn money for a college education.

All of this she accomplished without leaving her home. That meant she could work at any time on any day or night. She did not have to dress in any special way, and she had no transportation expenses. She did not have to worry if busses were late or roads flooded. Even when she had a cold, she could carry on her business. She saved time, money, and energy. All of this meant more profits for her, as well as the satisfaction of running her own business.

As home computers become more common, more and more people will be electing to work at home. Some of them will run their own businesses. Others will work for an employer. This type of work has a special appeal for parents of young children.

Working at home with the help of a computer offers career choices that did not exist even a few years ago. Perhaps this is the career route you might find yourself considering someday.

Third, leave your employer with the best possible impression of you. This is not a difficult thing to do if you follow these basic guidelines:

- Call about job leads, or schedule interviews during your lunch break or after work.
- Be sure you tell your supervisor that you have accepted another job before telling your coworkers.
- Try to give your employer two weeks' notice before leaving your job.
- Maintain good relations with your supervisor and coworkers.
- Continue to give an honest day's work, even on your last day.

Fourth, maintain a positive attitude while looking for another job. Remember, to each new job you take the knowledge and skills gained from an earlier one.

Points to Remember

- Many employers ask you to bring your Social Security card when you report for work the first day. Your Social Security number is needed for payroll purposes.
- Most employers offer new employees some type of job orientation.
- On the job, you will be expected to follow your employer's work policies.
- Work benefits often include vacations, group insurance plans, retirement plans, and investment plans.
- Most workers are evaluated from time to time on how well they do their jobs.
- Important paperwork you must sign when beginning a job includes the W-4 form.
- Your employer may offer low-cost group insurance plans to help you protect yourself and your family in case of illness, injury, or death.
- Employers are required to deduct Social Security contributions and taxes from your paychecks.
- You should have a good work record if you perform your job duties well, act professionally, are cooperative, and change jobs successfully.
- Work cooperatively with your supervisor and coworkers even if their work styles are different from yours.
- No matter why you change jobs, you will want to leave behind the best impression possible.

Test Your Skills

DECISION MAKING

Imagine yourself in the situation described below. In this situation, a decision is needed. As you read, think about how to make good decisions. Then answer the questions that follow. When you make decisions in the future, remember to ask yourself these questions.

Situation

You have a part-time job in a fast-food restaurant. You enjoy your job, and like your work schedule. With hard work, you might get a promotion within six months. Lately, however, your supervisor seems to dislike the way you are handling customers. You have not had a chance to discuss this problem.

A friend of yours owns a landscaping business. She has asked you to consider working for her. While the work would be physically harder, outdoor work appeals to you more than inside work. The hours and the pay would be the same as those of your current job.

You have discussed the situation with your parents and friends. They have pointed out advantages and disadvantages of each job. Several of your friends work with you at the restaurant. They would like you to stay there with them. Your parents would like you to make a good long-term decision.

Within three days, your supervisor will evaluate your work, and the landscaper will need an answer. You need to make your decision soon.

Questions

1. What is the problem?

2. What information do you need to help you make a decision?

3. Which of your values, goals, and resources may affect your decision?

4. List three decisions you could make. What are their possible consequences?

5. What is the best decision you could make? Why is it the best for you? What is the next best decision?

Terms

On a separate sheet of paper, write a definition for each of the underlined terms below. Base your definition on the clues you find in the sentence(s).

1. On his first day at work, Brett learned the work policies his employer had established to make sure employees would work safely and efficiently.

2. Through her employer, Gloria got a group medical insurance policy. When she received her written contract, it stated the cost and benefits of her coverage.

3. Before he joined the Army, Manny named his younger brother, Joel, as his beneficiary. If Manny dies, Joel will receive the benefits from his brother's insurance policy.

4. Tana's insurance company does not pay all of her medical costs. Each year, she has to pay a $150 deductible before the company begins paying any benefits.

5. Roger's health insurance policy has a co-insurance clause that states he will pay a part of the cost of every medicine he buys.

6. Jacinta gets a paycheck every two weeks. Her pay period is ten working days.

7. On each of Jim's paycheck stubs is a statement of his net pay. This amount reflects all of the deductions that have been made for the pay period.

8. The amount of federal income tax Cam pays each pay period is determined by the amount she has earned and by the number of tax exemptions she has claimed on her W-4 form.

9. Lloyd is so good at following through on a project that he is known for his perseverance.

10. Marcia was lucky. When she was laid off, her employer paid her $1,000 in severance pay to help her cover daily expenses until she found a new job.

Questions

1. Name five factors that contribute to your making a good first-day impression on the job.

2. What can you expect to learn during job orientation?

3. Why must you complete the W-4 form?

4. What kinds of insurance are usually offered in group plans?

5. What is the difference between gross pay and net pay?
6. What is a work record?
7. Explain what is meant by displaying a professional attitude.
8. What are four of the things you can do to solve problems in your working relationships with supervisors?
9. If your job involves working with customers or clients, why is it so important to have a good relationship with them?
10. Why is it often a good idea to stay on a job for at least a year or two?
11. What action might your employer take if you use alcohol on the job or violate another work policy?
12. Describe how to leave a good impression when you change jobs.

Activities

1. Ask friends or relatives to share their memories about their very first jobs. What kinds of concerns did they have about their first day? Was their job orientation formal or informal? How long did they work at this job? What did they feel was the most important thing they learned from it?

2. If you were to work for an employer who did not offer a group insurance plan, which kinds of insurance would you probably decide to buy? Why?

3. Imagine that you are an employer. Make a poster or booklet of the work policies and benefits you would establish. Consider these factors:
   a. the type of business you own and the work your employees do
   b. the type of work place—indoors or outdoors
   c. work hours, pay periods, and pay dates
   d. rules for dress, personal conduct, and safety on the job
   e. how often job performance evaluations will be made
   f. leave time—holidays, vacations, personal days
   g. financial benefits—insurance, retirement, and investment plans
   h. family benefits

   Discuss only those work policies and benefits that relate to the type of business you have chosen. Some of the above factors may not apply.

4. Ask family members and friends to describe a conflict they have seen between coworkers. How did the conflict get resolved? If you were in a similar situation, what do you think you would do?

5. Pretend that you have decided to change jobs. Write a letter of resignation. Tell your employer why and when you are quitting your job. Date your letter and give two weeks' notice. Make your letter sound positive and polite.

Chapter Review

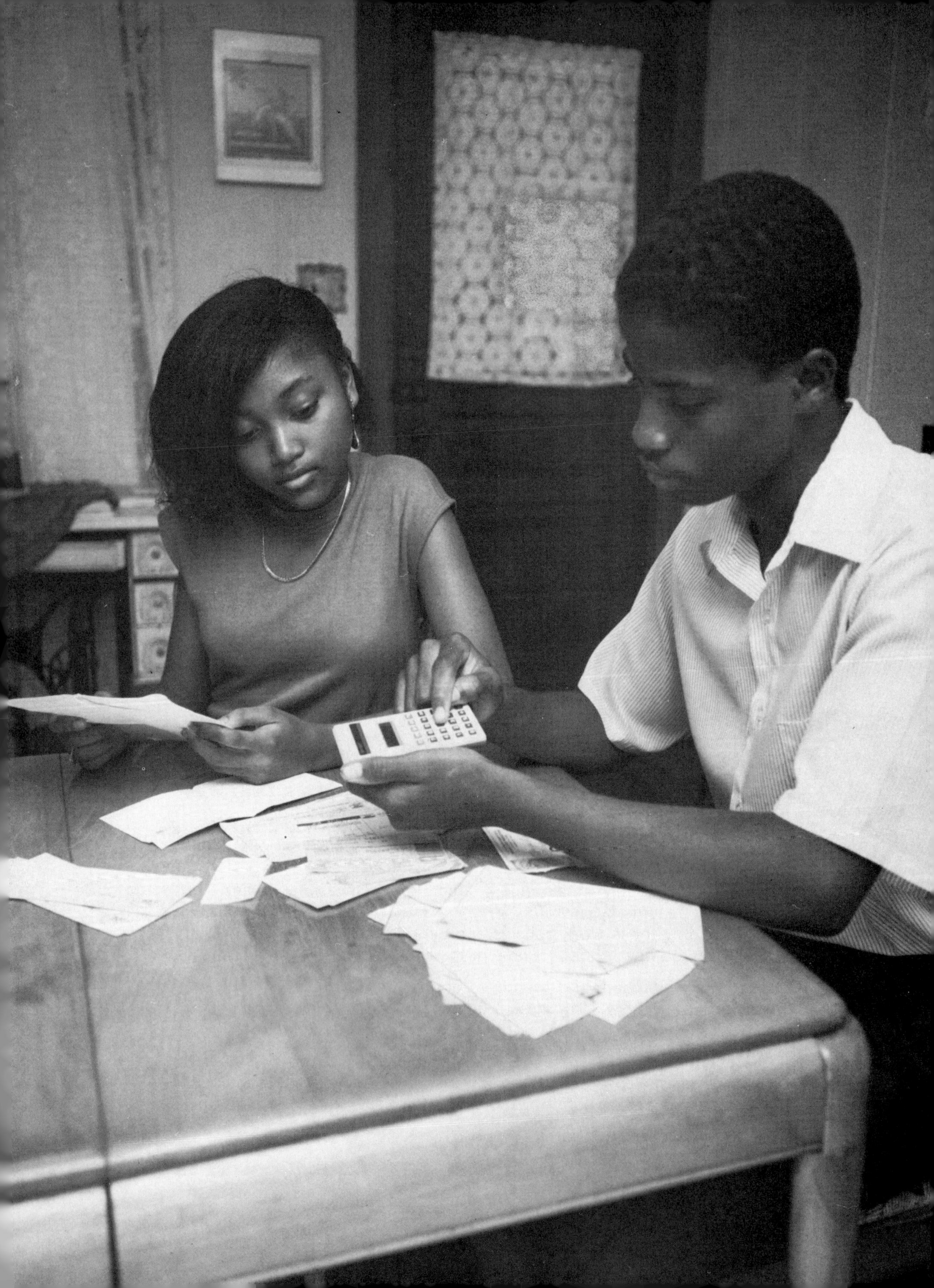

CHAPTER 5

Managing Your Finances

One of the most important tests of your independence will be how well you manage money. Will you be able to meet your day-to-day expenses? Will you succeed in reaching your long-term financial goals, such as affording a home or supporting a family? Achieving these aims will take careful thought and planning.

Now is the time to start developing good money management skills. A useful way to begin is to look closely at your current income and expenses. You need to be sure that you can manage your present financial responsibilities. Then, you can begin planning how to achieve your long-term financial goals. For example, you may wish to start a savings plan to be certain you have money in the future. You will probably also want to start putting money aside to ensure a secure retirement. If your earnings permit it, you might even be able to make investments that could add greatly to your income.

Of course, money management also involves important responsibilities. You need to be sure that your financial goals are realistic. You also have to be able to evaluate the various savings and investment plans that may be presented to you. Finally, you need to learn about paying taxes and about keeping careful financial records.

Money will be one of your most important resources. Start learning now about good money management skills so that you will know how to make the most of every dollar that you earn.

Discover Through Your Reading

- how to make your income cover your expenses
- how to make your savings grow as fast as possible
- how to plan ahead for retirement years free of money worries
- what investments you can make
- how you can file your own tax return
- where to keep financial records and important documents

Planning How to Use Your Money

Already you probably have a few sources of income. They may include allowances, gifts, or paychecks. You probably also have certain ways of using your money. How you use it has most likely been influenced by your family, friends, and others. From them, you may have already started learning how to manage your money.

Money management is developing and following a plan for the use of income. Any plan you develop must cover your day-to-day expenses. It must also meet your other financial goals. For example, you might want to save enough money to buy a house or an automobile. You probably also want to make sure you have money available for emergencies and for your retirement. Your expenses and your financial goals can be different from anyone else's. As a result, your money management plan is likely to be as individual as you.

Recognizing Types of Expenses

Before you can create your money management plan, you must understand the types of expenses you already have or might have. Do some of your expenses seem alike? Perhaps you can see ways to group expenses that are similar.

One way to group expenses is by type of product or service. For example, money spent on suntan lotion or a razor is money spent on personal care. Money spent for gasoline by means of a charge card is money spent on credit. While you are living with your family, your expenses probably fall into only a few groups. When you begin supporting yourself or start your own family, however, you will likely have many of the types of expenses listed on the facing page.

Another way to group expenses is by whether they are fixed or flexible. **Fixed expenses** are payments made at set times and for about the same amount each time. Rent or loan payments are examples. **Flexible expenses** are payments that vary in amount or do not have to be made according to a schedule. Utility bills, grocery bills, and health care payments are examples.

Expenses for which of these items would probably be flexible?

94   Managing Your Finances

Expense Groups

Housing and Utilities

Rent or housing payments
Household insurance
Home furnishings and equipment
Gas, electricity, and fuel oil
Water and sewer
Garbage collection
Telephone
Cable television
Repairs and painting

Food

Groceries
Snacks
Meals eaten away from home

Transportation

Insurance
License and registration fees
Parking fees
Gasoline and oil
Tires and parts
Maintenance and repairs
Fares for public transportation

Savings

Savings accounts
Savings certificates

Investments

Money market funds or accounts
Stocks
Bonds
Real estate
Collectibles

Education and Reading

School expenses
Newspapers, magazines, and books

Health Care

Medical and dental services
Prescription and over-the-counter drugs
Eyeglasses and contact lenses
Health insurance

Clothing

All kinds of clothing
Shoes, belts, and other accessories
Laundering and dry cleaning

Personal Care

Grooming products and services

Credit

Charge accounts
Conditional sales contracts
Loans

Recreation and Entertainment

Vacations and travel
Sports equipment and events
Movies, concerts, and plays
Hobbies, pets, and plants

Other

Gifts and contributions
Life and disability insurance
Miscellaneous

Planning How to Use Your Money

Setting Financial Priorities

Understanding the types of expenses you may have is only a part of money management. Another part is considering what you want your money to do for you. You already know that you want it to cover everyday expenses both now and when you retire. You may even want it to make more money for you in the future. If these are some of your financial goals, then you may plan to use some of your money for savings and investments.

You may find you have so many financial goals, however, that you cannot possibly achieve them all at the same time. This means that you will have to set priorities and, occasionally, adjust them. A person's **financial priorities** are the relative degrees of importance the person gives to each of his or her financial goals.

To set financial priorities, decide how much of your income you wish to spend for each expense group. Follow these steps:

- Choose a period of time, such as a month or year.
- Estimate the income you will have during the same period.
- Estimate the amount of money you plan to spend within each expense group during this period.
- Divide the amount of income into the amount of money you plan to spend within each expense group. Suppose, for example, that you are living on your own and have a monthly income of $500. If you plan to spend $100 on food, you need to divide $100 by $500, as follows:

$$\frac{\$100 \text{ (food)}}{\$500 \text{ (income)}} = \frac{1}{5} = \frac{2}{10} = .20, \text{ or 20 percent}$$

This shows that you plan to spend 20 percent of your income on food.

- If you are not satisfied with the percentages you have figured, adjust your spending plans accordingly.

Look at the illustration below. It shows you how different people's priorities may be. Franklin is paying for his college education.

Examples of How Financial Priorities May Vary

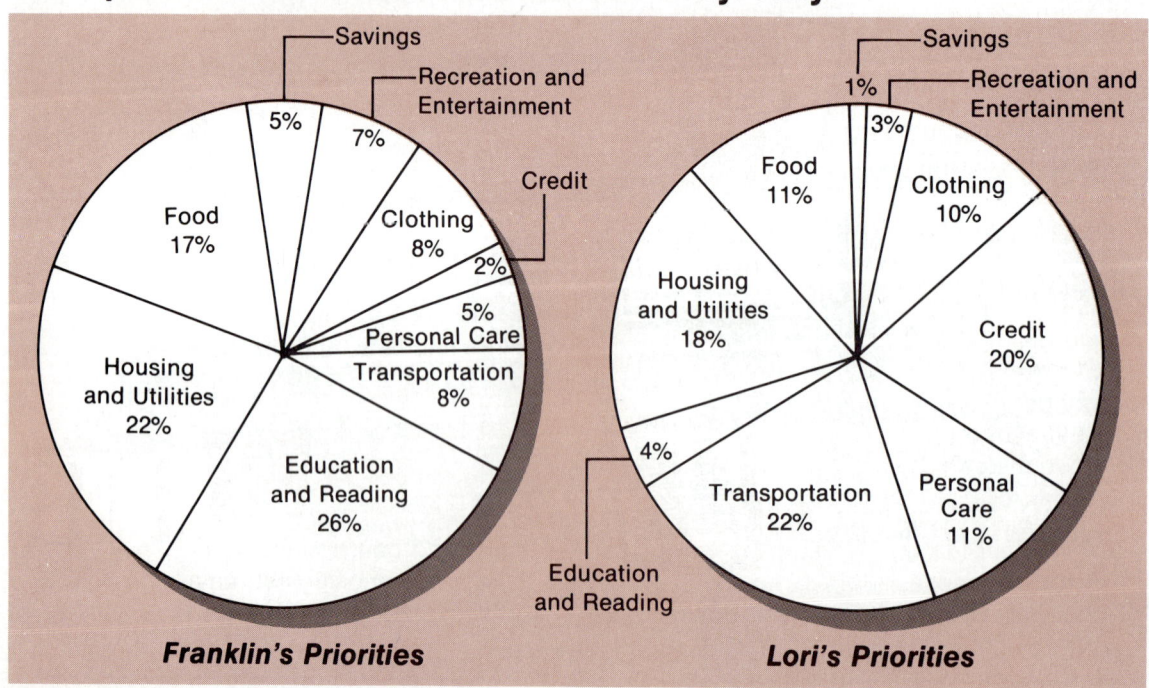

Franklin's Priorities
- Savings 5%
- Recreation and Entertainment 7%
- Food 17%
- Clothing 8%
- Credit 2%
- Personal Care 5%
- Housing and Utilities 22%
- Transportation 8%
- Education and Reading 26%

Lori's Priorities
- Savings 1%
- Recreation and Entertainment 3%
- Food 11%
- Clothing 10%
- Housing and Utilities 18%
- Credit 20%
- Personal Care 11%
- Transportation 22%
- Education and Reading 4%

Recreation comes in many forms and at times may be assigned a high financial priority. What financial priority would you say the young man shown here gives to carving? What financial priority does the young woman seem to give to her interest in music?

He spends much of his income on education and reading, as well as on housing and utilities. Lori, on the other hand, is paying for a new car. She spends much of her income on transportation and credit.

From time to time, your financial goals will change. When this happens, you will need to adjust your financial priorities. This means you will reconsider what percentage of your income to spend within each expense group. Remember, the more you spend within one group, the less you can spend within others. With your financial priorities clearly defined, you are ready to develop a workable plan for using your money.

Creating a Budget

A plan for using income to meet specific goals is a **budget.** To create your budget, choose a time period that is easy to manage. Some people make weekly budgets. Others make monthly or yearly budgets. As a young adult, you will probably have such monthly expenses as rent, utilities, and credit payments. Therefore, a monthly budget may be best for you. The samples that follow show how a young adult might set up and use a budget. While you probably do not yet have all of these expenses, you can use the models to set up a budget that you can use now. The same budgeting principles always apply.

Your Spending Record

Before you create a budget, you need to make a spending record. A **spending record** is a written statement of an individual's or family's expenses for a certain period. Unlike a budget, which shows *expected* expenses, a spending record shows *actual* expenses.

To make a spending record, keep a record of your actual expenses for one month. On a sheet of paper, write down the type and amount of each bill you pay and each pur-

Planning How to Use Your Money 97

Sample Spending Record for One Month

Day of Month	Actual Expense	Housing & Utilities	Food	Transportation	Savings	Clothing	Personal Care	Credit	Recreation and Entertainment
1	Rent	150.00							
	Personal Loan							50.00	
2	Food Items		29.97						
	Personal Supplies						7.50		
4	Bank Credit Card							10.00	
	Dinner for 1		4.98						
	1 Movie Ticket								3.00
5	Gasoline			15.25					
	2 Football Tickets								18.00
7	Laundry					1.25			
9	Telephone	13.52							
12	Slacks					26.25			
15	Laundry					1.25			
16	Gasoline			14.75					
18	Electricity	30.43							
	Savings				25.00				
19	Food Items		33.38						
	Household Supplies	4.24							
21	Dry Cleaning					9.45			
	Haircut						10.00		
25	Laundry					2.25			
	Gasoline and 1 qt. oil			16.15					
30	Car Insurance			100.00					
TOTAL EXPENSES	$576.62	198.19	68.33	146.15	25.00	40.45	17.50	60.00	21.00

98 Managing Your Finances

chase you make. Separate the expenses into columns according to expense group. Also, write down any amounts you save or invest. The easiest way to keep your spending record accurate and complete is to write down your actual expenses each day or so. See the sample spending record that is illustrated to the left of this page.

At the end of the month, figure how much you spent for each expense group. Then add those amounts to figure the total sum you spent during the entire month. Once you have completed your spending record, you can use it to estimate how much you may spend next month and in the months that follow. You are now ready to create a budget for the next month.

Steps in Budgeting

To create a budget, follow these steps:

- Make a realistic estimate of your income for next month. Include your take-home pay if you work, interest you will earn, allowances, and any other income you expect. See the sample income estimate shown on this page.
- Make a realistic estimate of your expenses for the same month. Base your estimate on what you have learned from your spending record. Combined with your estimated income, this estimate of expenses is your

Sample Income Estimate

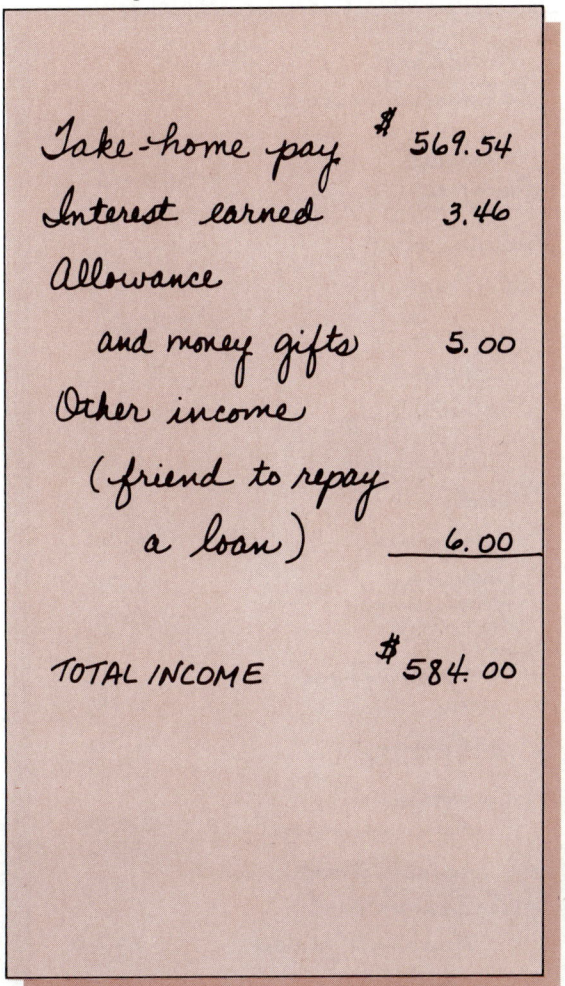

Take-home pay	$569.54
Interest earned	3.46
Allowance and money gifts	5.00
Other income (friend to repay a loan)	6.00
TOTAL INCOME	**$584.00**

Sometimes, the need for health care is difficult to predict. What other kinds of unexpected expenses might make your actual expenses for the month higher than you originally estimated?

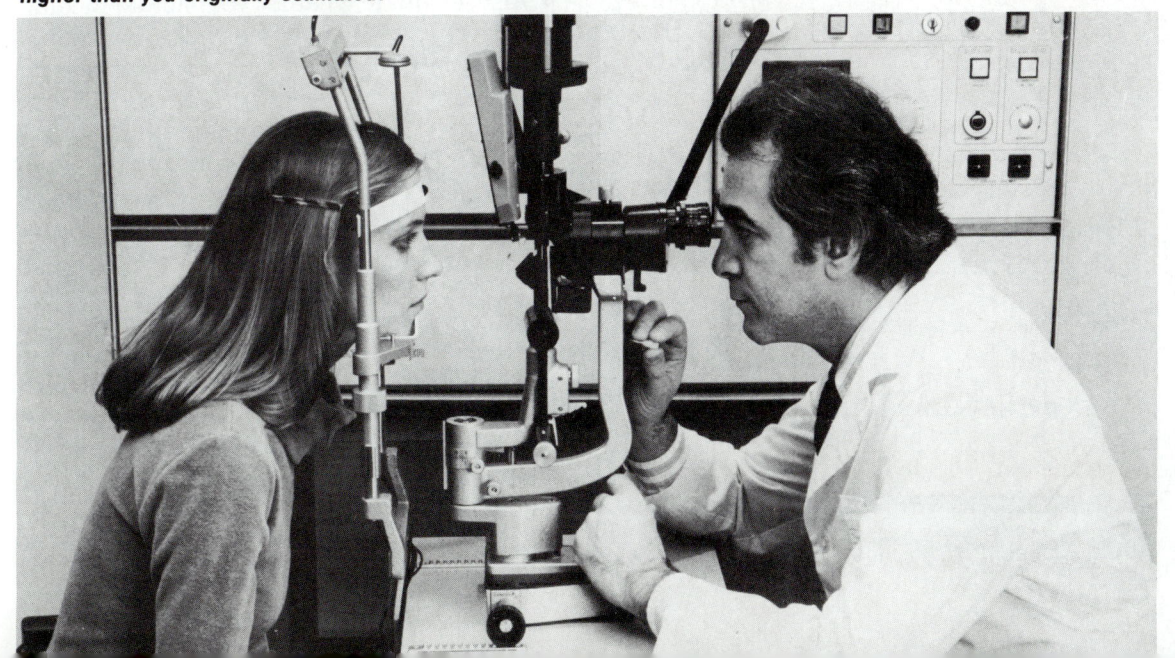

Sample Budget

Month of	May
Estimated Income	$584.00

Planned Expense	Amount
Housing and Utilities	
rent	$250.00
telephone	10.00
electricity	40.00
Food	
groceries	80.00
snacks	10.00
meals away from home	15.00
Transportation	
gas	40.00
oil change	16.00
Savings	
share account	20.00
Recreation and Entertainment	
baseball game	10.00
skating	10.00
concert	15.00
Clothing	
laundry	5.50
shoes	30.00
Personal Care	
basic supplies	15.00
Health Care	
(?)	10.00
Other	
gift	7.50
TOTAL	**$584.00**

budget. See the sample budget shown to the left of this column.

- Check to make sure your estimated income will cover your planned expenses. If it does not, you may want to look for ways to cut some expenses. It is unlikely you will be able to cut your fixed expenses. Your flexible expenses, however, are another matter. For example, maybe you can reduce your spending on clothes by trading outfits with a friend. If cutting expenses is impossible, you need to find ways to increase your income. One way might be to find a job that pays more than you are now earning. Another way might be to take on one or more additional jobs.

Evaluating Your Budget

To make sure your budget is workable, follow these steps:

- Use your budget for one month. As the month goes by, record your actual expenses beside your planned expenses. See the middle column in the illustration on the page to the right. That column shows actual expenses beside the sample budget from the preceding illustration.
- At the end of the month, find the difference between your actual expenses and your planned expenses. Record that difference as shown in the right-hand column in the illustration on the page to the right. Doing this will help you see exactly which types of expenses you underestimated or overestimated when you created your budget.
- Also, evaluate whether your actual income covered your actual expenses. To do this, total your income and total your expenses. Then, subtract your total expenses from your total income. The difference will tell you how well your income covered your expenses. See the totals shown in the illustration on the page to the right.

Once you have created, used, and evaluated a budget, you will find creating the next one easier. You will know the basic steps. Although the steps you take will be the same each time, your budget will change. You will need to revise your budget as your financial goals and priorities or your resources change.

Sample Budget Evaluated

Month of Estimated Income	May $584.00	Actual Income	$584.00	Difference Between Estimated and Actual Income $0
Planned Expense	Amount	Actual Expense	Amount	Difference Between Planned and Actual Expense
Housing and Utilities				
rent	$250.00	✓	$250.00	
telephone	10.00	✓	13.42	$3.42 more
electricity	40.00	✓	35.63	4.37 less
Food				
groceries	80.00	✓	92.13	12.13 more
snacks	10.00	✓	6.50	3.50 less
meals away from home	15.00	✓	11.75	3.25 less
Transportation				
gas	40.00	✓	42.50	2.50 more
oil change	16.00	✓	16.75	.75 more
Savings				
share account	20.00	✓	20.00	
Recreation and Entertainment				
baseball game	10.00			10.00 less
skating	10.00			10.00 less
concert	15.00			15.00 less
		beach weekend	25.00	25.00 more
Clothing				
laundry	5.50	✓	4.25	1.25 less
shoes	30.00			30.00 less
		swimsuit	18.90	18.90 more
Personal Care				
basic supplies	15.00	✓	7.00	8.00 less
Health Care (?)	10.00	dentist	25.00	15.00 more
Other				
gift	7.50	✓	5.08	2.42 less
TOTAL	$584.00	TOTAL	$573.91	TOTAL $10.09 less

Difference Between Actual Income and Actual Expenses $10.09

Planning How to Use Your Money

Changing Financial Goals and Priorities

Expense Group	Approximate Percentage of Income to Spend This Month	Approximate Percentage of Income to Spend Next Month
Housing and utilities	51%	51%
Food	18%	18%
Transportation	10%	10%
Savings	4%	4%
Recreation and entertainment	4%	2%
Clothing	6%	2%
Personal care	3%	1%
Health care	2%	10%
Other	2%	2%
Total	100%	100%

Revising Your Budget

Imagine, for example, that the table shown above illustrates how your financial goals and priorities might change. This month, you have spent more on clothing than you have on health care. For next month, however, one of your goals is to get a tooth filled. So, you have adjusted the amount you plan to spend on health care. In turn, you have decided to spend less within other expense groups. Perhaps, you have decided to spend less on recreation, clothing, and personal care.

On the other hand, imagine that your resources change. Perhaps you receive a raise or get laid off. If so, you will have either more or less money to use. Your budget will reflect this change.

Revising your budget may be even easier if you set it up and maintain it on a computer. For information on budgeting by computer see page 103.

Like other skills, money management will take time to develop. However, it will be time well spent. You will find that you can meet your everyday expenses and still pursue other financial goals. Reaching some of these goals, however, will depend on savings and investments.

Establishing Savings

If you are really managing your money, your savings will be an important part of your budget. You may find it easier to save if you think of savings as a fixed expense. When you are living on your own, you may want to save enough money to be prepared for costly emergencies. Such emergencies might include a car breakdown or an illness. You might want to save for expensive items that you cannot pay for out of your regular paycheck. These items might include a musical instrument or a piece of furniture. In addition, you will probably want to save for your retirement. After all, you will still have to meet your living expenses when you are no longer working.

Apart from allowing you to meet financial goals, saving offers other benefits. For one, it feels good. Collecting your leftover change each day and watching it grow into dollars is satisfying. So is saving a portion of each paycheck after paying your daily expenses.

How Computers Can Help You

Budgeting by Computer

Every family and almost every adult is responsible for a budget of some kind. No matter how simple or complex a budget is, it involves moving numbers around. It probably also involves considering a lot of options. Computers are so well designed for such work that many people turn to computers for budgeting help.

Budgeting by computer can bring you all the same benefits as budgeting by other means. A computer can help you manage your money to afford the items you need. It can also help as you make plans to save some of your money. In addition, it can help as you prepare for large expenses such as a trip, a car, or a vacation. The difference is that budgeting by computer can usually save you time and energy. This is especially true if you use a computer program designed for everyday money management by individuals and by families.

Perhaps your school has a computer and a budgeting program for students to use. Besides using the program to manage your own budget, you might find it useful in managing a budget for a school project. For example, you might be on a committee to raise money for your class yearbook. You could use the budgeting program to determine quickly whether your class might make more by holding a car wash or a talent show.

Perhaps your family already has a computer but has not yet purchased a budgeting program. Before you buy a budgeting program, do some research. You will want a program that is "user friendly"—simple and easy to use. You will also want a program that can be adapted as your goals—and your family's goals—change. As your goals, priorities, or resources change, your program should help you revise your budget. Most important, you will want a program that allows you to consider a variety of options. It should allow you to juggle numbers until you find the ones that suit you best.

Before you decide on a program, try out a few. In addition, talk to people who already use a budgeting program, or read how computer magazines or newsletters rate different budgeting programs.

Saving can also help you to earn extra income through interest. In financial terms, **interest** is income a person earns by lending money to others. For example, when you deposit money as savings in a bank, you are lending the bank that money. In return, the bank will pay you interest for the use of your savings. The more savings you deposit, and the longer you keep your savings in the bank, the more interest you will earn.

Savings Plans

A **savings plan** is a method that allows a person to deposit money with a financial institution, earn interest on it, and withdraw it in a fairly short period of time. When you need cash for a special reason, you can usually withdraw your money immediately or within a few days. Savings plans that specify longer deposit periods are also available.

Maybe you are already saving your money. If so, you may be using a savings plan. Two popular types of savings plans are savings accounts and savings certificates. Both allow you to create a fund for emergencies, for special purchases, and for other purposes.

Savings Accounts

A **savings account** is a savings plan that may not require a minimum deposit and does not specify a deposit period. The only time a minimum deposit may be required is when you open the account. A savings account allows you to deposit or withdraw any amount of your money at any time, without a penalty fee. The money you may withdraw includes the savings you deposited, as well as the interest your savings have earned. In credit unions, a savings account is called a *share account*.

There are three kinds of savings accounts. The passbook savings account and the no-passbook savings account are the two most common. The third type, the interest-bearing account that also offers checking, is discussed in the next chapter.

The main difference between the passbook account and the no-passbook account is in the procedure for using the account. With a passbook account, you are issued a special

How can you tell whether this is a record for a passbook or a no-passbook account?

booklet or passbook. The financial institution must have this passbook whenever you want to deposit or withdraw your money. The transaction is recorded in the passbook and the passbook is returned to you. With a no-passbook account, you may receive a form to help you keep your own record of deposits or withdrawals. The financial institution does not need this form at the time you make a transaction.

Savings Certificates

A **savings certificate** is a savings plan that requires a specified amount and deposit period. It is also called a *certificate of deposit* or, in credit unions, a *share certificate account*. Savings certificates pay higher interest rates than savings accounts.

Savings certificates are different from savings accounts in four other important ways. First, you make only one deposit. Second, your deposit must meet or exceed the minimum deposit requirement established by the financial institution. This minimum may be as low as $100 but is usually higher.

Third, you must state how long you will keep your money deposited. You may decide

104 Managing Your Finances

on any period between one month and ten years. If you withdraw your savings before the end of the period, you will lose at least part of the interest you would otherwise earn. You might also have to pay a penalty fee. Before you buy a savings certificate, find out the consequences of withdrawing your money early.

Fourth, the rate of interest you earn with a savings certificate depends on the length of time you agree to keep your money deposited. For example, if you deposit your money for one month, you will receive interest at one rate. However, if you agree to deposit your money for twelve months, you will get a higher interest rate.

When you purchase a savings certificate, you receive a document. It states the required length of deposit time, as well as the amount of interest you will receive if you do not withdraw your savings early.

Banking and Savings Institutions

Just as there are different ways in which you can save, there are different places where you can save. Most people place their savings in one of four kinds of financial institutions. These are commercial banks, mutual savings banks, savings and loan associations, and credit unions. The different types of banking and savings institutions offer a variety of services. Many of these services are discussed in greater detail in the next chapter.

Commercial Banks

If your community has only one financial institution, that one is likely to be a commercial bank. Commercial banks are the financial institutions you probably see most often. Each commercial bank is owned by a group of stockholders.

How is a savings certificate like this certificate of deposit different from other savings plans? What is its main advantage over other savings plans?

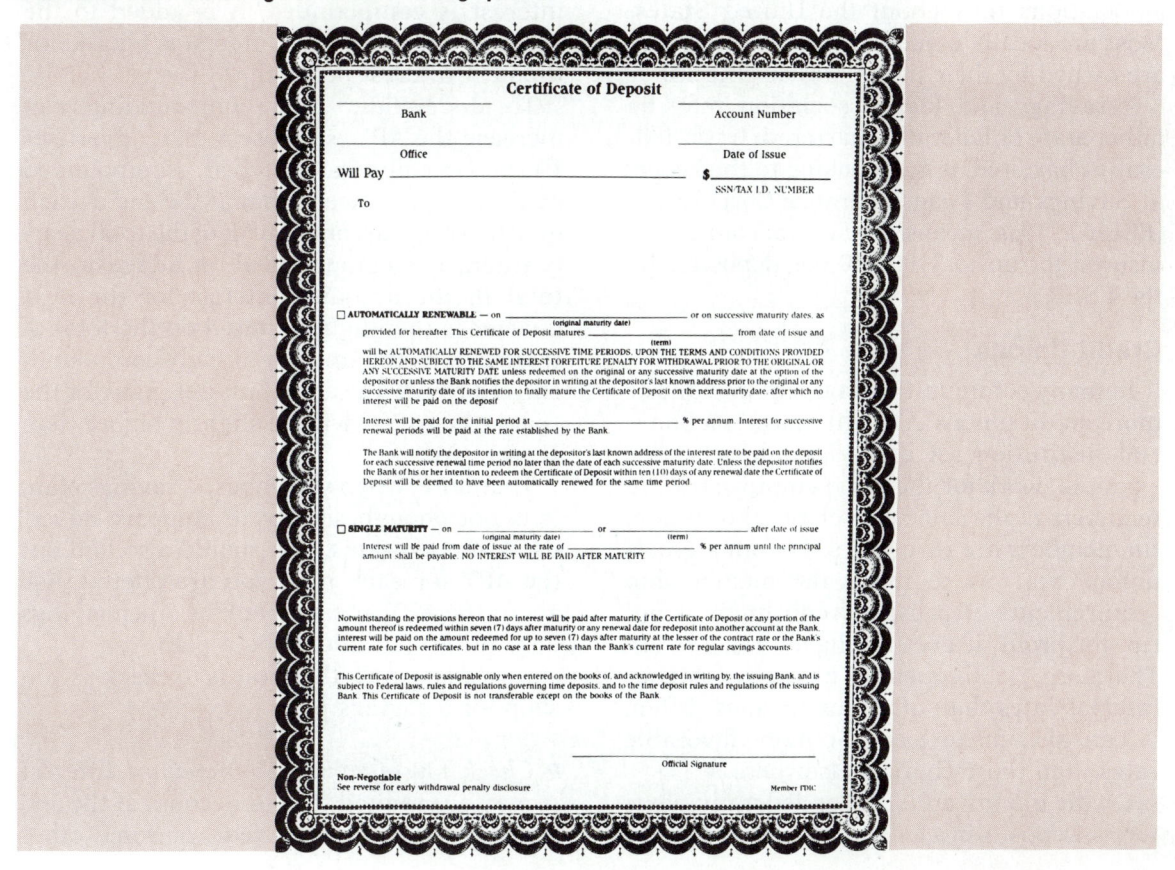

Establishing Savings **105**

The charter, or written contract that outlines how the financial institution will operate, comes from a state or the federal government. For years, commercial banks' charters allowed them to provide more services than other financial institutions. Because of this, commercial banks typically advertise themselves as full-service banks. Up to $100,000 of the money you deposit in a commercial bank is insured by the Federal Deposit Insurance Corporation (FDIC).

Mutual Savings Banks

Most mutual savings banks are located in the Northeast. Some are also located in the Midwest and Northwest. A mutual savings bank is owned by the people who deposit money in it.

The charter for a mutual savings bank comes from a state. Deposits in a mutual savings bank are insured for up to $100,000 per depositor by the FDIC.

Savings and Loan Associations

There are about 5,000 savings and loan associations throughout the United States. Most are locally owned and operated. Some are owned by their depositors or officers.

A savings and loan association may be either state or federally chartered. If it is federally chartered, it must belong to the Federal Savings and Loan Insurance Corporation (FSLIC). This means that its accounts are insured for up to $100,000 per depositor by the FSLIC.

Credit Unions

In many communities, you will find one or more credit unions. A credit union is a financial institution set up by people who, for example, work for the same employer or are members of the same church or labor union. Its members are its owners. To join a credit union, you must meet its membership requirements. Because a credit union is not run for profit, it does not have to pay taxes. Therefore, it frequently can offer higher interest rates than other institutions. Often, it can also make loans at more favorable rates than those charged elsewhere.

Credit unions are state or federally chartered. Deposits in a federally chartered credit union are insured for up to $100,000 per depositor by the National Credit Union Administration (NCUA). Those in a state-chartered credit union are guaranteed up to the same amount.

Selecting a Savings Plan

Before you choose a savings plan at any institution, you will want to compare interest rates. Interest rates vary with the type of plan and the banking or savings institution that offers the plan. You will want a plan that pays the highest annual percentage yield. The **annual percentage yield,** or **APY,** is the rate at which money will actually earn interest in a given savings plan in one year.

The APY may be slightly higher than a plan's advertised interest rate. For example, the plan may advertise an interest rate of 7½ percent, but the APY may be close to 7¾ percent. The reason for this difference lies in how often interest is compounded. When interest is **compounded,** it is added to the account total on which interest is figured for the next interest period.

To understand how compounding can increase the APY, suppose a plan advertises 10 percent annual interest, compounded quarterly. This means that at the end of each quarter of a year, one-fourth of the total yearly interest is compounded, or added to the total in the account. Interest for the next quarter is then figured based on the total of savings plus the interest already compounded. As a result, the actual interest paid for the year—the APY—will be slightly higher than 10 percent.

Therefore, when you choose a savings plan, it is not enough simply to compare advertised interest rates. You should also find out the APY for each plan you are offered. Ask about the APY at each bank or other savings institution that offers you a plan.

Here are some other points to check as you shop for a savings plan.

- *Check how often interest is credited.* Interest may be credited to your account at the end of each day, month, year, or some other period. The more often interest is credited, the more interest you can earn even if you make frequent withdrawals. For example, suppose you withdraw all your money on September 15. If your plan credits interest at the end of each day, you would earn interest right up to September 15. If your plan credits interest only at the end of each month, you would earn no interest for September.

- *Check how interest is figured.* Some plans figure interest based on the smallest amount in your account during a given period. Other plans figure interest based on the average amount in your account during a period. You will probably earn a larger amount if interest is figured on the average amount in your account.
- *Check to see if a grace period is offered.* A grace period allows you to make a deposit after the start of an interest period. It also allows you to make a withdrawal before the end of the period. In either case, you still earn full interest for that period.

Ensuring a Secure Retirement

The day you take your first full-time job is not too soon to start plans for retirement. People used to depend on savings and Social Security for retirement income. As the number of retired people has grown, however, the Social Security system has been overloaded. Also, because prices keep rising, people today can not buy as much with their savings as they once could.

If you are managing your money wisely, you will consider sources of retirement income in addition to savings and Social Security. One source may be a pension plan offered by your employer. Another may be a voluntary individual retirement plan or an annuity, which provides a guaranteed cash income. You might even use a combination of these items.

Social Security

The most widely used retirement plan is the federal government's Social Security program. By law, most of your employers must withhold a portion of your earnings for Social Security. For each sum withheld, the employer must provide a matching sum. The employer then sends both sums in your name to the Social Security Administration. There the money is invested to increase its value.

Once you retire, you or your eligible survivors can receive monthly payments from Social Security. If you become disabled before you retire, you and your eligible dependents can receive monthly benefits. To supplement these benefits, you can use one or more other retirement plans.

How might you plan so you are as well prepared for retirement as this couple?

Ensuring a Secure Retirement **107**

Pension Plans

Employers are not required to offer their employees a pension plan, but many do. A **pension plan** is a benefit whereby an employer regularly pays employees a set sum after they retire. The same benefit may be offered to an employee who is disabled before retirement. It may also be offered to survivors of the employee.

Employers offering pension plans put aside money each year for the benefit of eligible employees. Most employers require that you work for them at least ten years to be vested. Being **vested** means being eligible for pension benefits. Once you are vested, you have a right to your benefits even if you leave that employer. If you move often from employer to employer, you risk never becoming vested in a pension plan. You may work all your life and end up with little or no pension.

Some pension plans require employee contributions. In these cases, the employer withholds a certain amount from each of your paychecks to cover your contribution. If you leave your job before you are vested, you can expect to get back your contributions.

Voluntary Individual Retirement Plans

Only about 65 percent of all eligible workers in this country are covered by employer-sponsored retirement plans. Because of this, the federal government has established two types of voluntary individual retirement plans. These two types are the individual retirement account and the Keogh plan.

An **individual retirement account,** or **IRA,** is a retirement plan for persons who are employees. If you have an IRA, each year you may deposit up to a certain amount of your income in it. Until you reach age 59½, any withdrawal involves a penalty fee. However, as long as your money—and the interest it earns—stays in your account, you pay no income tax on it.

Your benefits can add up fast in an IRA. For example, suppose your IRA paid 12 percent annual interest, compounded at a standard rate. If you contributed $2,000 a year for thirty-six years, you could retire with just over $1 million.

A **Keogh** (KEE·oh) **plan** is a voluntary retirement plan offered by the federal government to self-employed individuals. Keogh plans are similar to IRAs. If you have a Keogh plan, each year you may deposit up to a certain amount of your income in it. Your deposits and interest earnings are not taxable until you withdraw them.

Both IRAs and Keogh plans can be set up relatively easily. IRAs are available through banks and savings institutions, stock brokerage firms, mutual fund companies, and insurance companies. Keogh plans are available through the federal government.

Annuities

Another way to provide money for retirement is to buy an annuity. An **annuity** is a plan by which a life insurance company agrees to provide the purchaser with a certain cash income. You can buy an annuity from a life insurance company. You may also obtain one as an employment benefit.

The advantage of an annuity is that it may provide you with a guaranteed lifetime income once you retire. Also, with a **tax-deferred annuity,** the money you spend to buy it is not taxable until you begin receiving the payments. However, those payments may be less than you could earn from other types of investment. Also, the amount of each payment is fixed, while the prices of goods keep rising.

Making Investments

Investing is a way of trying to increase your income by putting your money to work. Popular investments include stocks, bonds, and real estate. These and other types of investments are described in the chart on the facing page. The chart also tells where to

Types of Investments

Type	Description	Where Available	Advantages	Disadvantages
Stock	A share in the ownership of a company. Ownership makes you a **stockholder,** a person who participates in the company's profits and losses. A group of investors may create a **mutual fund,** a plan to form a company that buys stock in other companies.	• from **stockbrokers,** persons who buy and sell stock for others for a fee • through employee benefit packages • at banking and savings institutions	• pays you a **dividend,** a portion of the company's profits • may increase in value if the company prospers • may be sold quickly for cash • mutual fund shares may be inexpensive	• pays no dividend if the company fails to earn profits • may lose value if the company performs poorly • dividends and profits from stock sales are taxable
Bond	A loan to a company or government agency. At the end of a fixed period the bond **matures;** that is, the borrower repays the loan. Interest is also paid, either during the term of the loan or when the bond matures. The federal government offers Series EE and Series HH savings bonds.	• from stockbrokers • at banking and savings institutions • through payroll savings plans	• less risky than stock • usually earns higher interest than regular savings • interest on state and local government bonds is not subject to federal tax • many types may be sold quickly for cash	• except for savings bonds, may be too expensive for small investors • interest income may not match rises in the cost of living
Money Market Fund or **Account**	A money market *fund* is a plan by which investors pool their funds for a short, specified period to make investments that pay high interest. A money market *account* is a special type of bank savings account. The bank pools deposits in such accounts to make short-term investments on behalf of the depositors.	• *funds* are offered by stockbrokers • *accounts* are offered by banking and savings institutions	• *funds* and *accounts* earn higher interest than regular savings • you may write checks on *accounts* and on some *funds,* subject to restrictions • *account* deposits are insured; there is no risk of losing money	• *fund* and *account* interest rates may decrease over time • interest is taxable • *funds* and *accounts* may require high initial investments • *funds* are not insured
Real Estate	Property—either vacant land, land with buildings on it, or buildings only, including apartments, houses, stores, or any other structures.	• from property owners • from real estate brokers or salespeople	• often may be resold at a higher price • provides tax advantages • may be rented for cash income	• may be damaged or destroyed • may lose value over time • may be difficult to resell

Making Investments

Have You Thought of Investing in Collectibles?

Do you collect rare coins, antiques, or stamps? If so, you are already an investor. What you are investing in are called collectibles. These are physical objects people collect with the hope that the objects will grow in value.

To make money on collectibles, it helps to be able to tell a fake from the real thing. It is also important to know what is and is not a reasonable price to pay. In addition, it is a good idea to keep up with buying trends so you know when to sell. Otherwise, you may end up owning a set of objects for which people are no longer willing to pay much. Finally, it is important to know how much to ask when you are ready to sell.

One way to find out how valuable your collectible may be is to get an estimate from a reputable dealer. The best people to contact are members of a national collectors' association.

When you get ready to sell a coin collection, antique, or other collectible, consider these four methods:

- Sell at a flea market those objects that you have had fun collecting but that are not of great value.

- Look for "Item Wanted" ads in hobby magazines, newspapers, journals published by collectors' associations, and other publications.

- Place an "Item For Sale" ad in any of the above publications.

- Arrange to have valuable objects auctioned. Be prepared to pay the licensed gallery or auctioneer a 10 to 20 percent commission.

If you are considering investing in collectibles for the first time, keep in mind that they are a special kind of investment. Over time, you may become attached to them and decide that you do not want to sell them. If you think that might happen, you may need to rethink your investment plans.

obtain each type and presents some advantages and disadvantages of each type. One additional type of investment is collecting valuable items such as rare coins or stamps. To learn how these collectibles may have already made you an investor, see page 110.

A good way to understand what investing means is to compare it to saving. In both cases you are putting some of your money to work to try to increase your earnings. However, investing your money is often riskier than saving it. In addition, the money you invest is usually less available to you than the money you save. However, investing can offer you the chance to earn more money than you can through most savings plans.

Since investing may be risky, you should have a cushion of savings and a retirement plan before you invest much of your income. If you have enough savings for emergencies and a plan for retirement, you can feel relaxed about investing. You will be sure you are really investing money that you consider "extra."

Before you invest, it is important to determine what you want from your investments. For example, is your aim a quick profit or a steady income over many years? What you want your investments to do can help you decide the type of investment to choose.

Paying Income Taxes

Every wage earner in this country has a legal obligation to pay income taxes. You must pay income taxes on money you earn and on money you receive from certain sources. As a result, you need to know what types of income are taxed. You also need to know which tax forms to use and how to complete and submit those forms. Completing and submitting a tax form is called filing a tax return.

Types of Income That Are Taxed

Income taxes are collected on money you earn. This includes any salaries, wages, and tips you earn. It also includes money you receive as interest (except from some types of bonds), dividends, and certain kinds of benefits. It also includes profits you may make from certain kinds of investments or from operating your own business.

The federal government collects income taxes each year through the Internal Revenue Service, or IRS. Depending on where you live, you may also have to pay state and local income taxes. As you learned in Chapter 4, if you are employed, your employer usually withholds money for income taxes from each of your paychecks. Your employer then forwards that money to the appropriate government agency.

Choosing a Federal Income Tax Form

Every wage earner who earns more than a specified minimum during a year must file a federal income tax return for that year. Although each individual files differently, there is no mystery or trick to this procedure. As long as you keep careful financial records, there is no reason you cannot complete your own tax return.

The IRS mails a form and instructions to all taxpayers who filed the previous year. If this is your first year to file a return, you can find the form you need at your local IRS office, bank, or post office. You may also need state and local forms, which are available where you find the federal forms. Pick up at least two copies of each form so you can keep one copy for your records.

For your federal return, you may choose among three different forms, depending on your personal financial situation. These forms are Form 1040EZ, Form 1040A, and Form 1040.

Forms 1040EZ and 1040A are short forms designed for persons with taxable incomes of less than $50,000 and relatively simple finances. Form 1040, the "long" form, is for persons with higher incomes and more complex finances. It is also used by persons who wish to reduce their taxes by claiming deductions from their income.

If you claim deductions, you can deduct part of your medical and dental expenses; amounts you paid for certain taxes, interest, charitable contributions, and certain financial losses; and some other miscellaneous expenses such as union dues. The deductions you may claim are explained in detail in the instructions accompanying your tax form. You may be required to prove your deductions, so be sure to keep your cancelled checks and receipts.

Filing Tax Returns

Your federal, state, and local tax returns are due each year on April 15. Therefore, well in advance of that date, you should gather all your financial records. If you plan on using Form 1040, you may need bills, sales slips, cancelled checks, stock records, and the like. No matter which tax form you use, you will need all W-2 forms and statements of interest earned.

A W-2 form will be sent to you by each employer you worked for during the tax year. An employee's **W-2 form** is a statement of that employee's gross pay during a year and of the amounts withheld for income taxes and contributed to Social Security during that year. Each W-2 form has three copies—one each for your federal and state returns and one for your records.

A statement of interest earned will be sent to you by each bank or other financial institution where you have an interest-bearing account. On this statement, the institution will note how much interest your account has earned during the year. You must add this interest to your salary and other taxable income listed on your tax form.

Before you start completing your tax form, carefully read all the instructions. Then, complete the form step by step. Take your time and double-check your arithmetic. If you need help completing the form, call or visit your nearest IRS office. You can find the address in your telephone directory. The IRS offers free tax assistance. As an alternative, you may wish to pay an accountant to complete your form.

Once your form is completed, mail it to the tax agency at the address listed in the instruction booklet. Usually, you will be given a preaddressed envelope. If you owe money, enclose a check or money order. If you are due a refund, it will be mailed to you.

Recordkeeping

As you become financially more independent, the number of your receipts, stubs, certificates, and other personal records will grow. On the facing page, you will find a list of what records to keep, as well as where to keep them and for how long.

In general, you will want to keep at home the records you need to refer to often. Your

Filling out income tax returns does not have to be difficult. What steps has this person taken to make the process run smoothly?

112   Managing Your Finances

Storing Your Personal Records

What	Where	How Long
Cancelled checks, bank statements	home	five years
Certificates of birth, adoption, citizenship, education, military service, marriage, divorce	safe-deposit box	lifelong
Health records (including history of vaccinations, allergies)	home	lifelong
Income tax returns	home	five years
Insurance policies	home	lifelong
Lease	safe-deposit box	as long as lease is in effect
List of numbers (credit cards, bank accounts, driver's license, Social Security card)	home	lifelong
List of valuable items in the home	safe-deposit box	lifelong
Loan contracts	safe-deposit box	until loan is paid off
Mortgage	safe-deposit box	until mortgage is paid off
Paycheck stubs	home	one year
Pet records	home	as long as you have the pet
Receipts for major purchases (including home, car, boat)	safe-deposit box	as long as you have the items
Receipts for minor purchases	home	one year
Retirement plan records	home	lifelong
Savings account records	home	five years
Savings certificates	safe-deposit box	until you cash in your certificate
Stock or bond certificates	safe-deposit box	until you cash in your certificate
Titles to major purchases (including home, car, boat)	safe-deposit box	as long as you have the items
Warranties or guarantees, owner's manuals, service contracts for major purchases	home	as long as you have the items
Will	safe-deposit box	lifelong

savings and checking account records are examples of financial records you may want to refer to quickly. So are your paycheck stubs, insurance policies, and income tax returns. You will also want to keep in your home photocopies of some important documents. Examples might include your health records and your lease.

You can put many of your personal records to everyday use. Some—like your records of purchases—will help you plan and revise your budget. Others—like your owner's manuals—will come in handy by answering your questions about items you have purchased.

To make sure you can find your home records with little difficulty, you can set up a filing system. For example, you can keep file folders in something as simple as a large cardboard box. If you prefer, however, you can put them into a metal file box or cabinet.

No matter what container you use, your filing system should be simple and clear. Otherwise, you will be unable to retrieve the records you need. To make retrieval easy, label each file folder. You may also want to file your folders alphabetically by expense group.

To keep your most valuable records safe from fire, theft, or other damage, rent a safe-deposit box. A **safe-deposit box** is a metal container kept locked in a commercial bank or other financial institution. When you rent such a box, you get keys so you can add to or take out your belongings. The annual fee that financial institutions charge for this protection is not high.

Points to Remember

- Setting financial priorities helps you meet your financial goals.
- A good way to manage your money is to use a budget.
- Knowing when interest is credited helps you earn the most from your savings plan.
- A retirement plan other than Social Security is usually needed to cover living expenses when a person no longer works.
- The best time to begin investing in a retirement plan is when you are young.
- Once you have established your savings and retirement plans, you can consider investing.
- Participating in a mutual fund is a good way to begin investing in stocks.
- As a wage earner, you will be required to file income tax returns.
- Some financial records are used often and should be safely and neatly stored at home.
- Renting a safe-deposit box is a smart way to store hard-to-replace personal and financial records.

Test Your Skills
GOAL SETTING

Imagine yourself in the situation described below. In this situation, a goal needs to be set. As you read, think about what makes a goal reachable. Then, answer the questions that follow. When you need to set goals in the future, remember to ask yourself these questions.

Situation

You have worked three months at your first full-time job. You thought the job was permanent. Now, you find out that you may be laid off in three months. Although you have three months to find another job, you may be unable to do so. The job market in your community is limited. As a matter of fact, it took you two months to find the job you have now.

Your current take-home pay is $575 a month. Each month, so far, you have spent $500. Altogether, you have been able to save $225 in three months.

If you do not have another job when your present one ends, you will have trouble covering your living expenses. Your parents, who live in a nearby community, can help some but cannot pay your full living expenses. Your lease lasts for another nine months. If you break it, you will lose your security deposit. Although you really like where you live, you will need $275 more than you have now to stay there one month between jobs. Cutting expenses will help some, but not enough. To get the amount of money you need, you must consider savings plans or investments.

Questions

1. Set your goal. Make sure it is realistic and clearly stated.
2. Do you think of your goal as short-range or long-range? Why?
3. What plan could you make to meet your goal?
4. What could get in the way of your achieving your goal?
5. What alternative plans could you make to meet your goal?

Terms

On a separate sheet of paper, write a definition for each of the underlined terms below. Base your definition on the clues you find in the sentence(s).

1. Mamie's budget helps her figure out whether she can meet all of her financial goals for the month with the income she expects.

2. By depositing money in his savings account, Marv lends to a bank that lends to other people. In return, Marv earns several dollars in interest every three months.

3. Julie has to keep a minimum amount in her savings account. When she opened the account, however, she did not have to agree to keep her money deposited for a certain length of time.

4. To buy a savings certificate, which will pay him a higher interest rate than a savings account, Randy agreed to keep a certain amount of money deposited for a certain number of months.

5. While shopping for a savings plan, Angie always asks what annual percentage yield, or APY, is offered. She knows this is the best way to find out how much income a plan will earn.

6. On his new job, Ramón is covered by a pension plan. It will start paying him a certain percent of his highest salary when he retires.

7. Heather places some of her income in an individual retirement account, or IRA. By doing so, she earns interest and postpones paying taxes on that income.

8. Jesse bought two shares of stock in a company. He gets his portion of the company's profit in the form of a dividend check.

9. Myra decided not to spend a lot of time carefully choosing which stocks to buy. Instead, she bought shares in a mutual fund owned by a group of investors suggested by her brother.

10. The safe-deposit box Yoshi rents at his bank helps him keep many important papers safe from things like fire and theft.

Questions

1. What is the purpose of money management?
2. Explain the difference between fixed and flexible expenses.
3. Describe what it means to set your financial priorities.

Managing Your Finances

4. What kinds of information is it necessary to write down when you are creating a spending record?
5. What steps can you take to make sure your budget is workable?
6. Give four reasons for saving money.
7. How do savings accounts and most savings certificates differ?
8. What are four types of financial institutions that offer savings accounts and savings certificates?
9. If you are eligible to join a credit union, why is it a good idea to do so?
10. Name two points to consider when shopping for a savings plan.
11. Describe three types of retirement programs.
12. In what ways are investments different from savings?
13. Describe three different types of investments.
14. Name three kinds of income that are subject to income tax.
15. Why is it important to keep financial and personal records?

Activities

1. Consider how your financial priorities may change over the next five years. Identify your expense groups and the percentage of income you might spend within each group this year and in five years. You might want to design charts like the ones on page 96.
2. Keep a record of your income and expenses for two weeks. How well do they match? Did you save any of your income? If not, identify expense groups you might be able to cut.
3. Answer the following questions relating to starting a savings plan.
    a. Which of your current financial goals might you reach with the help of a savings plan?
    b. What kind of savings plan might you choose at this time? Why?
    c. Which kind of financial institution might you choose as a place to start saving?
    d. How might being out on your own affect how you save?
4. Interview several retired persons. Find out how they planned for retirement. What recommendations do they have for you? If you do not know any retired persons, consider visiting a center for senior citizens.

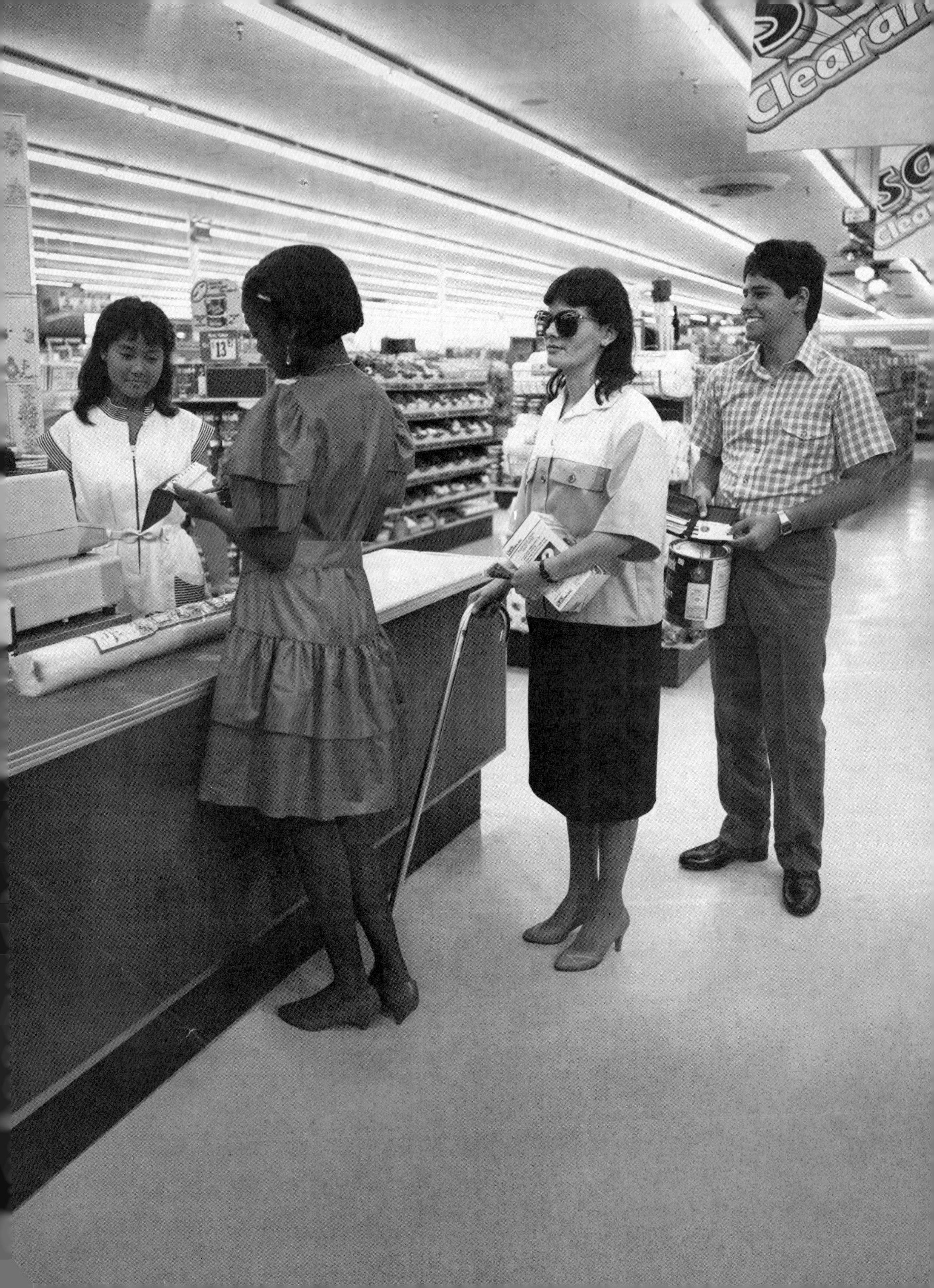

CHAPTER 6

Paying for Your Purchases

Most people carry some coins and paper money, or currency. Often, this is the most convenient form of money to use. For example, suppose your newspaper deliverer knocks at your door and requests payment for this week's newspapers. Perhaps your supermarket has an express lane for persons not paying by check. In situations like these, it is fast and easy to make payments with currency.

Sometimes, however, using currency has its drawbacks. For example, if you pay with currency, you must request a receipt whenever you need one. With most checks, on the other hand, this is not necessary. After paying the amount authorized by your personal check, for example, most financial institutions stamp and return the check. This cancelled check is your receipt. Also, you cannot stop payment on currency, as you can with a check. In addition, carrying large amounts of currency is riskier than carrying checks. Lost or stolen currency can be misused more easily than lost or stolen checks.

Usually, you pay for a product or service—with currency or a check—at the time of purchase. At times, however, you will probably use credit. Using credit allows you to pay for an item over a period of weeks, months, or years.

In the next few years, you will be making more and more purchases. You need to know the different ways that you can make your payments.

Discover Through Your Reading

- how to open your own checking account
- which kinds of checks are the safest to send through the mail
- what to do if your credit card is lost or stolen
- what you are responsible for if you cosign a loan
- what can happen if you do not make your credit payments on time

Having Your Own Checking Account

One of your adult responsibilities will probably be to pay bills. When you think of paying bills, you may think of writing personal checks. To write a personal check, you must have some type of checking account. A checking account is one of the services offered by most banking and savings institutions. Such an account allows you to keep money in a safe place until you are ready to spend it. When you are ready, you let the financial institution know by writing a personal check. The check tells your financial institution how much to pay from your checking account and to whom.

Perhaps you are old enough to use a checking account and already have one. If not, you may wish to open one in the next few years. Before you select a checking account, you will want to consider how you intend to make use of it and the types of accounts available. Then, you will be able to find the best deal on the type of account you want. Once you select and open an account, you will need to understand how to use it.

Choosing a Checking Account

There are different types of checking accounts because people like to use checking accounts in different ways. How are you most likely to use a checking account? Do you plan to write many or a few checks each month? How much money do you plan to keep in your account each month? Do you plan to use your account as a means of earning interest?

Your answers to these questions will probably determine whether you decide to get an account that has a monthly service charge. Such a charge may be a flat monthly fee or a fee based on the number of checks you write within a month. In either case, it is used to pay bookkeeping costs.

Your answers to the questions will also probably determine whether you decide to get an account that requires a minimum balance. A **minimum balance** is the amount of money that must be kept in some checking accounts to avoid a monthly service charge. Remember, not all banking and savings institutions determine a minimum balance in the same way. Some institutions look at the lowest amount in your account. Others look at the average amount in your account. To understand how this difference can affect you, think about the following example.

Banks A and B both require a minimum balance of $500. Bank A considers your minimum to be the *lowest* balance in your account during the month. This month your lowest balance was $428. Since this balance was below $500, you would have to pay a service charge at Bank A. Bank B, on the other hand, considers your minimum to be the *average* balance your account has during the month. This month your average balance was $513. Because this average was above $500, you would not have to pay a service charge at Bank B. As you can see, it may be to your advantage to choose Bank B.

In addition, your answers to the questions raised earlier will probably determine whether you decide to get an account that allows you to earn interest. In this case, it is possible to decrease your paperwork by having one account for savings and checking.

The types of checking accounts available to you fall into three basic categories. These are the special checking account, the regular checking account, and the interest-bearing checking account.

Special Checking Accounts

If you write only a few checks each month and have a small monthly balance, you may want a special checking account. A **special checking account** is an account that requires a monthly service charge but no minimum balance. The service charge may range from a few cents to several dollars. In addition to the service charge, you may have to pay a fee for each check and deposit processed.

Regular Checking Accounts

If you write many checks and have a fairly large monthly balance, you may want a regular checking account. A **regular checking account** is an account that requires a minimum balance but usually no monthly service charge as long as the minimum balance is maintained.

Interest-Bearing Checking Accounts

An **interest-bearing checking account** is one that allows a person to write checks or similar payment orders and to earn interest on the money deposited. Because the account pays interest, it can also be considered a savings account. One such account is called a NOW account (Negotiable Order of Withdrawal). With a NOW account, you write orders of withdrawal, which are similar to personal checks. A NOW account usually requires a higher minimum balance than a regular checking account.

How can this customer service representative help someone choose a type of checking account?

Another account that offers both checking and interest is called an automatic transfer account. It is actually two accounts: a savings account and a checking account. After you write a check, money is transferred from your savings into your checking account. Most of the time, therefore, your checking account has a zero balance.

To help you decide whether an interest-bearing checking account might be right for you, see the tips presented in the lefthand column. As soon as you have decided on a type of checking account, you will be ready to open one.

Opening Your Checking Account

When you open a checking account, you will probably follow each of these steps:

- Sign your name on a special form the way you will sign it when you write or deposit checks.

Tips
Evaluating Checking Accounts That Earn Interest

Before deciding on an interest-bearing checking account, be sure to consider the following factors:

- how much money you must keep in your account to earn interest

- how much more interest you could earn if you put some of your money into a savings plan

- how much of the interest that you earn would be lost to service charges

- what other services you may be offered if you open this type of account

---

Having Your Own Checking Account

- Fill out a deposit slip and make your first deposit.
- Order your checks with either an attached stub or a separate check register. Stubs or registers provide space for you to record how much money you have in your account. While waiting for your checks to be printed, you will receive a temporary supply. After your printed checks arrive, you will be charged for them. The cost will depend on the number and style of the checks you ordered.
- Learn about electronic banking services if they are available to you. For information on electronic banking, see the next page.

Once you have established your account, you can begin using it.

Using Your Checking Account

To use your checking account correctly, you need to follow certain procedures. For example, there are specific ways to write and endorse checks. There are also ways to make deposits and to stop payment on a check.

Writing Checks

Remember to fill out your check stub or check register *before* you write a check. In this way, you can keep your running balance up-to-date. When you write your check, use a pen with permanent ink. If you use a pencil or erasable pen, anyone could easily change the name and amount on your check. Write neatly so there is no mistake about the amount of money or the payee. The payee is the person, business, or agency that you are paying. See the sample check below.

Endorsing Checks

Endorsing a check means signing the back of the check. When you receive a check that you would like to cash, use a blank endorsement. In other words, simply sign your name and add no other message. Remember, *never* use a blank endorsement on a check you plan to cash until you are *actually* cashing it. If

Why should you be careful when writing checks?

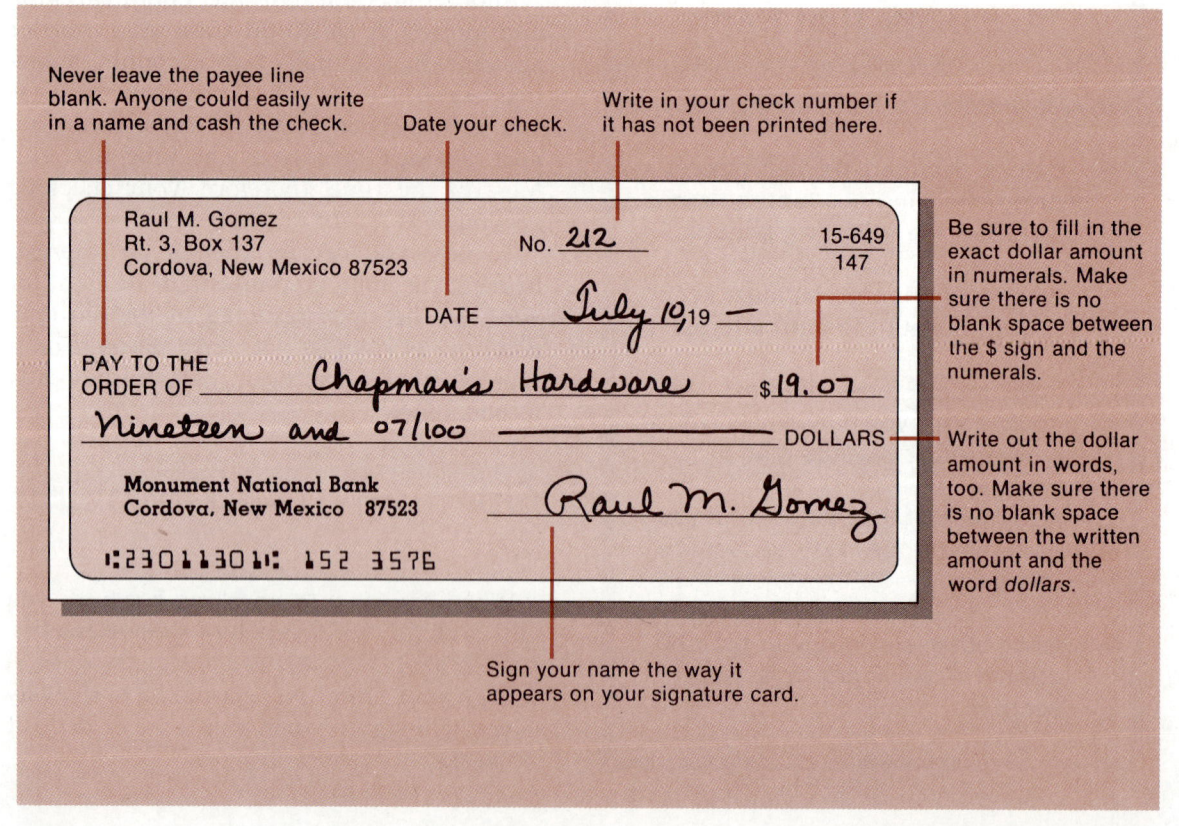

Never leave the payee line blank. Anyone could easily write in a name and cash the check.

Date your check.

Write in your check number if it has not been printed here.

Raul M. Gomez
Rt. 3, Box 137
Cordova, New Mexico 87523

No. 212   15-649/147

DATE July 19, 19—

PAY TO THE ORDER OF Chapman's Hardware $19.07

Nineteen and 07/100 —————— DOLLARS

Monument National Bank
Cordova, New Mexico 87523

Raul M. Gomez

⑈230113011⑈ 152 3576

Be sure to fill in the exact dollar amount in numerals. Make sure there is no blank space between the $ sign and the numerals.

Write out the dollar amount in words, too. Make sure there is no blank space between the written amount and the word *dollars*.

Sign your name the way it appears on your signature card.

122 Paying for Your Purchases

How Computers Can Help You

Electronic Banking

You may already be familiar with one form of electronic banking: automated twenty-four-hour tellers. You can find these machines, which are computer terminals, outside many financial institutions. You can also find them at many supermarkets and shopping malls—perhaps even at your place of work.

To use an automated teller, you must have an electronic funds transfer card. You must also have a personal identification number (PIN). With your card and special number, you can make deposits, withdraw cash, and make many other transactions. In each case, you will receive a receipt. You should use it to record each transaction in your passbook or check register.

Remember, the automated teller will not operate without your card and PIN. This protects you against theft. Be careful not to lose your card or let others know your PIN. If your card is lost or stolen, notify your institution within two business days. If you do this, you are responsible for no more than $50 of charges. If you do not do this, your loss could be as high as $500. To further protect you against theft, financial institutions are developing ways to use fingerprints and voice prints to activate teller machines. The following electronic banking services also may be offered where you live:

- **Direct deposit or withdrawal.** With special deposit and withdrawal forms, you can tell your financial institution to make deposits and pay some of your bills directly. For example, you might have the institution deposit your paycheck or a Social Security check. You might also have the institution pay your utility bills automatically.

- **Point-of-sale transfer.** By using your card, you can pay in full for purchases without using cash or credit. With the card, your money is transferred immediately from your account to the store account.

- **Pay-by-computer.** By using a telephone and personal computer, you can have your financial institution transfer funds between your accounts and pay certain bills.

123

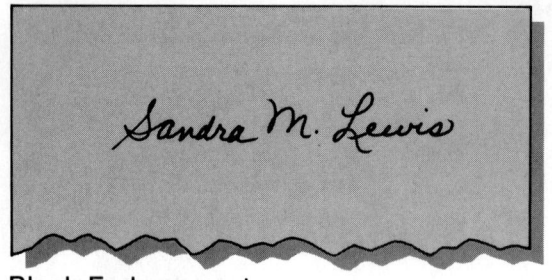

Blank Endorsement

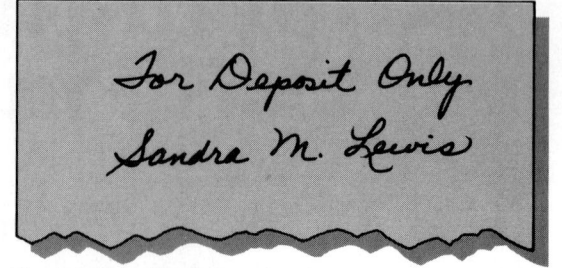

Restrictive Endorsement

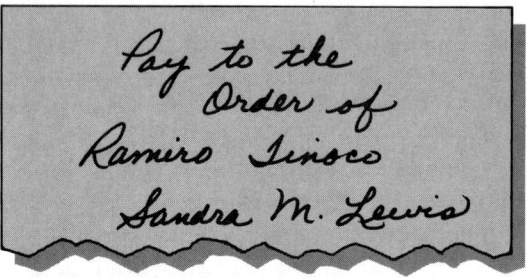

Full, or Special, Endorsement

Which of these endorsements allows you to sign your check over to another individual?

you use a blank endorsement and then lose your check, anyone can cash it.

When you receive a check and want to deposit the entire amount, use a restrictive endorsement. In other words, sign your name and add the message *For deposit only*. If you just sign your name and do not write *For deposit only*, someone could cash your check. Likewise, if you lose your check, someone might try to forge your name and cash your check. With a restrictive endorsement, your check should be safe.

When you receive a check that you would like to sign over to another person, use a full, or special, endorsement. In other words, sign your name and add the message *Pay to the order of* followed by the name of the other person. For an example of each type of endorsement, see above.

Making Deposits

To deposit money into your account, you will probably use a form like the one on the next page. You can use such a deposit slip to add currency or checks to your account. You can safeguard a check as soon as you get it if you use a restrictive endorsement. This step is particularly necessary if you wish to deposit the check by mail.

Stopping Payment on a Check

Occasionally, you may write a check and, then, not want it cashed. This could occur if a check is lost or if a product or service is not delivered. When this happens, you can prevent your financial institution from honoring the check. You will probably be charged for this service.

To stop payment, call or visit the institution and give the following information: the date, the amount and number of the check, and the name of the payee. After you make this call, you must provide the same information in a letter.

Balancing a Checking Account Statement

A **checking account statement** is a report of all checks, deposits, withdrawals, and charges made on the account during a given time. Most financial institutions provide you with a monthly statement. The balance you find on that statement should match the balance on your check stubs or check register.

To keep your account in order, follow these steps to balance your statement:

- Record on your check stubs or check register all deposits and withdrawals when

they are made. Make sure the amounts are correct.
- Look at your statement as soon as it arrives in the mail. Use the step-by-step form that most financial institutions print on the back of the statement. Add and subtract carefully, and go over your arithmetic to avoid mistakes.
- Make sure that you have recorded every transaction that your financial institution has recorded. These may include monthly service charges and fees for new checks. Also make sure you have recorded all of your outstanding checks. An **outstanding check** is a check that has not yet been cashed. It will not appear on your statement.

If an error has been made on your statement, take your records to your financial institution and explain the problem. Together, you will be able to correct it. Be as careful with your checking account as you are with any form of money. Notify your financial institution immediately if you lose a check or do not receive your regular statement.

Some financial institutions do not return cancelled checks for you to keep as records. Instead, these institutions provide checks that allow you to make a copy each time you

When is the best time to balance a checking account statement?

Deposit slips are easy to read and fill out. How much of the money Jeff is depositing is in the form of checks?

Checking Account Deposit Ticket			
First National Bank			
Date: February 2, 19—	CURRENCY	15	00
Name: Jeff Cramer	C H E C K S — BH	202	00
Address: 1040 Mills Street	Cramer	20	00
Sheridan, Wyoming 82801	IRS	141	32
	Total From Other Side		
	TOTAL	378	32
Account Number: 796 428 6	Less Cash Received		
	NET DEPOSIT	378	32

Having Your Own Checking Account

write a check. These copies become your records of the checks you have written.

Insufficient Funds

Suppose you stop by a grocery store to buy a few items that cost about $10. You plan to pay for the items with a check written on your special or regular checking account. However, you do not have $10 left in your account. If you write a $10 check, your financial institution will return it with the notation *NSF*, or *not sufficient funds*.

Having **insufficient funds** means having less money in an account than the amount of a check written on the account. In addition to returning your check, your financial institution will probably charge you a fee. The store owner is also likely to charge you a collection fee. Therefore, you could pay more in fees than the amount of the original check. Such fees are charged to discourage people from writing checks on insufficient funds and to cover the cost of handling these checks.

If you need to make a payment by mail and want an immediate receipt, a money order is the check to use. Have you ever been in this situation?

Using Other Kinds of Checks

Sometimes, it may be better to make payments with other types of checks. Suppose that you have to send money to a mail-order house in another state. Maybe your rent payment is due, and you must make it immediately. Perhaps you are out of town and suddenly need the services of a doctor. In these situations, what kind of check is best? Your personal check may not be acceptable, or you may not have a checking account.

In these instances, there are at least three other kinds of checks you can use: money orders, cashier's checks, or traveler's checks. In deciding which of these to use, consider the following factors:

- the amount of the payment
- where the payment must be made
- how soon the payment must be made

Money Orders

A **money order** is a check for a specified sum of money issued by a financial institution, a post office, an express or telegraph company, or even a grocery store. To get a money order, you pay the amount of the order plus a small service fee. You then fill in the name and address to which you plan to send the money order.

There are a number of advantages to using money orders. They can be cashed more quickly than personal checks. Like personal checks, they can be mailed safely. Unlike many personal checks, they provide an *immediate* receipt of your payment.

Cashier's Checks

A **cashier's check** is a check written on a financial institution's own account and signed by one of its officers. To get a cashier's check, you must go to the financial institution. There, you pay the amount of the check you want plus a small service charge. The institution will then write a check payable to whomever you wish.

Paying for Your Purchases

Why would a person who has a checking account ever use a cashier's check?

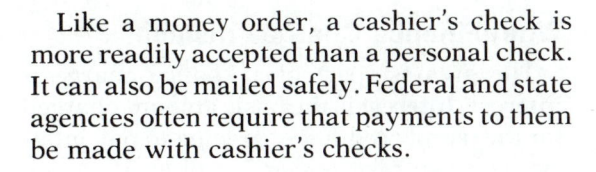

In what ways are traveler's checks different from money orders and cashier's checks?

Like a money order, a cashier's check is more readily accepted than a personal check. It can also be mailed safely. Federal and state agencies often require that payments to them be made with cashier's checks.

Traveler's Checks

Most people buy traveler's checks from banking and savings institutions, express companies, and travel agencies. A **traveler's check** is a check with a set denomination printed on it. Traveler's checks come in denominations of $10, $20, $50, and $100 and are honored all over the world. Depending on where you buy these checks, you may be charged a small service fee. When you buy a traveler's check, you must sign it. When you are ready to cash it, you fill in the name of the payee. Then, you sign the check again. The person taking the check will compare the second signature to the first to make sure that the person who is cashing the check is the person who purchased the check.

Each traveler's check has a number on it so the check can be registered. When you buy traveler's checks, you receive a list of these numbers. You should keep this list separate from your checks. If you lose a check, contact the company that sold it to you and present the list of numbers. The seller will refund or replace your check.

Using Credit

For many purchases you make, the salesperson will ask, "Do you wish to pay by cash, check, or credit?" You need to consider carefully before answering, "Credit."

Credit is an agreement to pay for current purchases some time in the future. It is a method used to buy now and pay later. When you buy on credit, you promise to pay the

Using Credit **127**

It may be better to use credit for expensive items rather than for inexpensive items. Why is this?

money you owe. You must then make payments as promised.

While you may want to use credit for large purchases, such as expensive furniture, appliances, or clothing, you will probably not want to use credit for small purchases, such as your daily expenses. Otherwise, you may end up paying unreasonable amounts for everyday products and services.

Using credit is a privilege, not a right. The privilege of buying on credit costs something. It is not a free service. The cost of buying on credit will be added to the advertised price of each product or service, in the form of a finance charge.

Before you use credit, you need to understand how finance charges are determined. You also need to understand how to apply for credit. In addition, you need to understand what forms of credit are available to you and how to avoid credit problems.

Understanding Finance Charges

Usually, when you use credit, you will have to pay a finance charge. A **finance charge** is the total amount of money paid for a credit purchase. It is important to know what finance charges include and how they are figured.

What Finance Charges Include

The greatest part of a finance charge is interest. **Interest** is the basic amount charged for the use of credit. By agreeing to pay interest, you can take possession of an item you are purchasing before it is paid for. By agreeing to pay interest, you can also borrow a specific amount of money for a set period of time. Interest is usually figured as a percentage of the value of your credit purchase. This percentage is called the interest rate. The interest on, for example, a $500 television bought on credit might be $50 and the interest rate 10 percent.

Another part of the finance charge is the service charge. Some service charges are standard, like the cost of bookkeeping and collection. Others are fees for optional services such as credit insurance.

When you are using certain forms of credit, you may be encouraged to buy credit insurance. **Credit insurance** is a type of insurance that pays credit obligations if a borrower dies or is disabled. It is sold in two forms:

credit life insurance and credit disability insurance. With credit life insurance, the life of the borrower is insured for the amount of the unpaid loan. With credit disability insurance, the insurance company makes payments on the loan if the borrower is disabled. You cannot be denied credit because you do not buy credit insurance.

How Finance Charges Are Figured

The finance charge for any credit purchase is determined by the creditor—the person or business that lends money, products, or services. Because of the Truth in Lending Act, creditors must tell you how they figure their finance charges. For example, they might use the adjusted balance, the average daily balance, or the previous balance method. You will want to understand the differences among these methods because some result in higher finance charges than others.

With the adjusted balance method, the creditor considers *all* payments you have made since the billing period began. This usually results in the lowest finance charge. With the average daily balance method, the creditor adds your daily balances and divides them by the number of days in the billing period. With this method, the finance charge may be higher than that of the adjusted balance method. With the previous balance method, the creditor does *not* consider any payments you make after the billing period begins. The finance charge is usually highest with this method.

Also as a result of the Truth in Lending Act, creditors must state the cost of credit as an annual percentage rate. The **annual percentage rate (APR)** is the rate of interest paid for the yearly use of credit. The APR from one creditor or lender might be 18 percent. The APR from another might be 20 percent. By comparing the percentages, you can determine which creditor is offering credit at a lower price.

Applying for Credit

When you ask for credit, a creditor usually asks you to fill out an application form. Although discrimination in credit matters is prohibited by the Equal Credit Opportunity Act, creditors are not required to accept every person who applies for credit. Some persons may not have a steady income. They may jump from job to job or have jobs that pay low wages. Others may have no savings or personal possessions of any value. Still others may change residences frequently or always be late with their payments.

What is the finance charge on this credit account statement? What is the annual percentage rate?

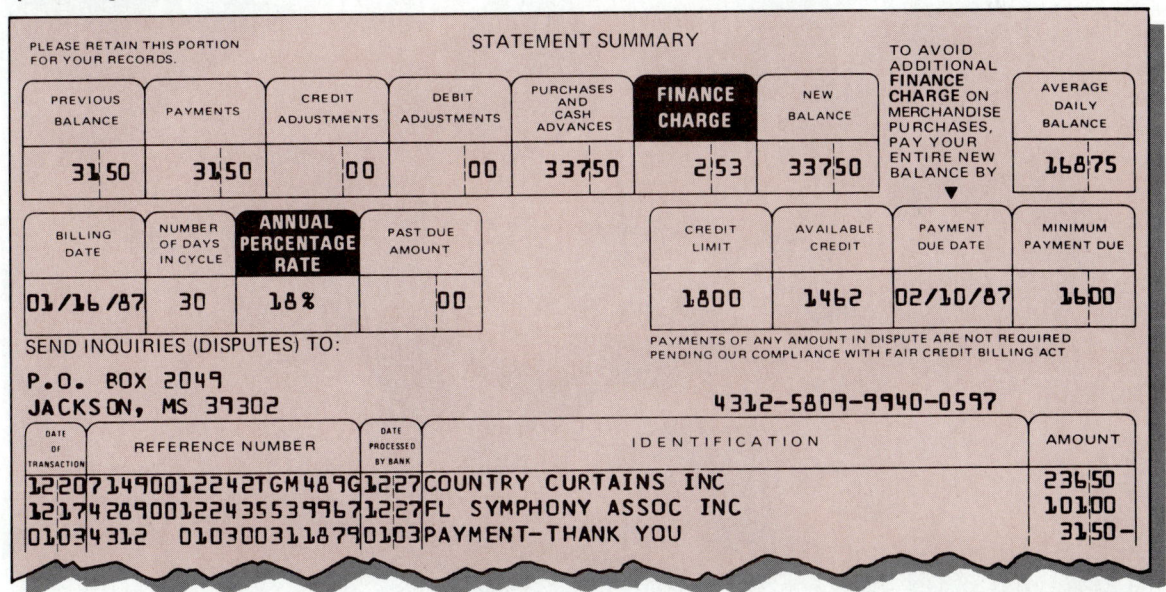

PREVIOUS BALANCE	PAYMENTS	CREDIT ADJUSTMENTS	DEBIT ADJUSTMENTS	PURCHASES AND CASH ADVANCES	FINANCE CHARGE	NEW BALANCE	TO AVOID ADDITIONAL FINANCE CHARGE ON MERCHANDISE PURCHASES, PAY YOUR ENTIRE NEW BALANCE BY ▼	AVERAGE DAILY BALANCE
31.50	31.50	.00	.00	337.50	2.53	337.50		168.75

BILLING DATE	NUMBER OF DAYS IN CYCLE	ANNUAL PERCENTAGE RATE	PAST DUE AMOUNT	CREDIT LIMIT	AVAILABLE CREDIT	PAYMENT DUE DATE	MINIMUM PAYMENT DUE
01/16/87	30	18%	.00	1800	1462	02/10/87	16.00

PAYMENTS OF ANY AMOUNT IN DISPUTE ARE NOT REQUIRED PENDING OUR COMPLIANCE WITH FAIR CREDIT BILLING ACT

SEND INQUIRIES (DISPUTES) TO:
P.O. BOX 2049
JACKSON, MS 39302   4312-5809-9940-0597

DATE OF TRANSACTION	REFERENCE NUMBER	DATE PROCESSED BY BANK	IDENTIFICATION	AMOUNT
1220	71490012242TGM489G	1227	COUNTRY CURTAINS INC	236.50
1217	4289001224355996T	1227	FL SYMPHONY ASSOC INC	101.00
0103	4312 010300311879	0103	PAYMENT—THANK YOU	31.50−

Using Credit

Creditors will probably use the following factors to determine whether to offer you credit:

- *capacity*—your ability to earn enough income to cover payments
- *collateral*—your savings, investments, or possessions that could be used to repay a debt
- *character*—your reputation for being stable and dependable

After reviewing your application, the creditor contacts a credit bureau. A **credit bureau** is a company that gathers credit information on consumers and shares that information with creditors and other credit bureaus. The creditor asks the credit bureau for any information it has on file about your past use of credit—or your credit rating. A person's **credit rating** is a history of that person's credit accounts. It is a report of whether a person has paid bills on time. When the copy of your credit rating comes in, the creditor compares this confidential report with what you have written on your application.

The first time you apply for credit, you will not have a credit rating. The only way to establish a credit rating is to use credit.

Establishing Your Credit Rating

You can establish a credit rating in either of the following ways:

- Ask a parent or someone else with a good credit rating to cosign a small loan with you. By having a **cosigner,** a person who agrees to repay a loan if a borrower cannot, you are more likely to get a loan. The lending institution will be likely to have the confidence it needs to make you the loan. Then, be prompt with your payments. By following this procedure, you will prove yourself a good credit risk.
- Open a credit account at a store where your parents or other family members shop. Some stores have special plans for teenagers.

What step is this young adult taking to establish a credit rating?

It is also usually important to have your own savings and checking accounts when you are ready to establish a credit rating. Having such accounts in good order shows that you know how to handle money carefully.

Maintaining a Good Credit Rating

Although there are many ways to establish a good credit rating, there is only one way to keep it. You must pay your bills on time. Your credit rating, therefore, plays an essential role in determining whether you can keep getting credit.

Understanding Your Credit Application Rights

You can apply for credit as soon as you are old enough to sign a legal contract. A contract is a legally binding agreement between two parties. When you apply for credit, you are guaranteed fair treatment by the Equal Credit Opportunity Act. This law states that you cannot be denied credit because of your sex, race, creed, or marital status.

You also have certain rights related to the credit application process. The creditor has thirty days within which to accept or reject your completed application and notify you of the decision. If your application is rejected, you must receive a written statement from the creditor indicating the reasons. A creditor cannot reject your application without letting you know.

If you are notified that you have been turned down for credit, you may want to check your credit rating. The Fair Credit Reporting Act allows you to contact the credit bureau that reported on your credit history. To find out which credit bureau this was, ask the creditor with whom you are dealing. Then, call or visit that credit bureau and arrange to review your credit file.

If you find incorrect information in your file, the credit bureau is required by law to investigate. Any incorrect information must be removed from your file. The bureau must also resubmit your corrected file, at no cost to you, to any businesses that have received your file. If you do not agree with the results of the investigation, give the bureau a written statement saying so. That statement will be added to your file.

Selecting and Using Charge Accounts

You may want to use a charge account. If so, it is best to be aware of the differences between the two most common types: the regular charge account and the revolving charge account.

The **regular charge account** is a credit account that requires full payment within thirty days for charge purchases. Because of its time limit, it is sometimes called a thirty-day charge account. Oil companies and businesses that sell services, such as utility companies and hospitals, often offer this type of charge account.

A **revolving charge account** is a credit account that allows partial payments on charge purchases but charges interest on the unpaid balances. New purchases can be charged before old ones are paid for, as long as a specific credit limit is not exceeded. Your credit limit is the maximum amount you are allowed to charge. Department stores and other retail stores usually offer revolving charge accounts.

Each month you should receive a statement indicating your charge purchases. Check it carefully to make sure that it is correct. If it is not, take advantage of the Fair Credit Billing Act passed by Congress. This law established procedures for correcting billing errors.

Because of this act, you have sixty days to contact your creditor about any incorrect part of your bill. Also, your creditor must take action on your complaint within thirty days of receiving your letter. In addition, you can withhold payment for the part that you question until the matter is settled. If you are right, your account will be corrected with no additional fees. If the creditor is right, you may have to pay additional finance charges as well as the disputed amount.

Credit Cards

Most charge accounts feature credit cards. A **credit card,** or **charge card,** is a plastic device issued by a creditor to authorize charge purchases. Using a credit card lets you pay for many or all of your purchases with one check. This saves you bank charges

Using Credit

and gives you a permanent record of your expenses. Because there are so many credit cards available, you will need to make some choices.

These are the three basic types of credit cards:

- *Bank cards* are the most popular and the most widely used. These all-purpose cards are available through most commercial banks. Bank cards can be used to charge a variety of products and services. In addition to your unpaid balance, you may have to pay a yearly fee. MasterCard and VISA are two well-known bank cards.

- *Travel and leisure cards* are issued by express companies and credit card companies. These cards are honored at hotels, restaurants, airlines, car-rental agencies, and some department stores. The issuers

Tips
Choosing and Using Credit Cards

Keep these tips in mind when choosing and using credit cards:

- Limit the number of credit cards you have. Then, it will be easier to remember the total amount you have charged each month. It will also be easier to keep track of your cards.

- Be especially careful each time you receive a "preapproved" application form for a credit card. Carefully consider whether you need that charge account. Also, consider whether you want to be responsible for another card.

- Keep a list of your credit card numbers. Immediately call the issuing companies if your cards are lost or stolen. If you do this, you are required to pay only $50 for charges made with your lost or stolen cards. Follow up your call with a letter. Within a few weeks, you should receive replacement cards. If you have several credit cards, you may want to consider credit card protection service. With it, you can call one toll-free number rather than several if your cards are lost or stolen.

- Consider other ways to pay for an item before you charge it. These could include currency, personal checks, or savings.

- Try to pay the full amount due each month on a revolving account. Otherwise, you will have to pay finance charges.

- Avoid reaching your credit limit on all your credit cards at once. Your income should allow for a reasonable percentage of credit expenses, but not for overuse of credit.

of these cards usually require that you have a higher income than a commercial bank requires. They also charge a yearly membership fee. The best-known travel and leisure cards are American Express, Diner's Club, and Carte Blanche.
- *One-company cards* are issued and honored by an individual store or a chain of stores. Examples include oil company cards, department store cards, and individual airline and car-rental company cards. Usually, there is no yearly membership fee.

Credit cards are easy to use, but just as easy to abuse. The tips on the opposite page can help you make the best use of your credit cards.

Understanding Conditional Sales Contracts

When you are making certain major purchases, such as a car, you are likely to use a conditional sales contract. A **conditional sales contract** is a type of installment credit that requires a buyer to completely pay for a product before receiving legal ownership of it. **Installment credit** is any type of credit in which the balance is paid in regular payments at set intervals rather than in one large payment. Whatever you buy on installment credit is yours to use while you are paying for it. You own it, however, only after you have paid the entire amount of the contract.

A conditional sales contract cannot be changed or broken once it is signed unless both you and your creditor agree—with one exception. You *can* cancel a conditional sales contract offered by a door-to-door salesperson. Suppose you buy a piece of equipment from a door-to-door salesperson. After the salesperson leaves, you may change your mind. If so, you can cancel the contract by calling the company within three business days and sending a follow-up letter.

Every conditional sales contract contains a section of basic information. The contract may also contain special clauses or a promissory note.

Standard Information in Conditional Sales Contracts

Before you sign any contract, make sure basic information, including each of the following items, is correct:

- name and address of both you and your creditor (who may also be the seller)
- description of the product you want to buy
- cash price of the item, the amount of your down payment (including any trade-in you make), and the amount being financed
- finance charge and annual percentage rate
- any additional charges not included in the finance charge
- total cost of buying the item on credit (including the cash price, the finance charge, and any additional charges)
- amount, number, and frequency of your payments
- description of any **collateral**—the property pledged as security in case payments are not made

Also, as you should with any contract, make sure that no lines are left blank.

Special Clauses in Conditional Sales Contracts

Before you sign a conditional sales contract, it is important to read and understand any special clauses contained in the contract. Otherwise, you may find that you have agreed to unreasonable conditions.

Clauses you may find are as follows:

- *Prepayment clause.* A prepayment clause outlines what will happen if you make payments before they are due. Some prepayment clauses allow you to benefit by repaying your debt early. Others state that there is a penalty fee for repaying your debt ahead of schedule.
- *Add-on clause.* An add-on clause specifies that any new installment purchases you make will be added to your original contract. The products you have already paid for under the original contract, therefore, become security for your new purchases. With this clause, you do not own *any* of

Using Credit

your purchases until you have paid for *all* of your purchases.
- *Balloon clause.* A balloon clause indicates that your final payment will be much larger than earlier payments. If you cannot make the final, balloon payment when it is due, you will probably lose the merchandise and the money you have already paid for it. In some states, balloon clauses are prohibited.
- *Acceleration clause.* An acceleration clause states that the creditor can demand all remaining payments if you miss a payment. If you cannot pay the balance, the creditor can take back the product. You will no longer have the merchandise. You will also be unable to claim the money that you have already paid.
- *Lien clause.* A lien clause states that the creditor can take the property you have offered as collateral if you cannot make your payments. The creditor can then sell this property to satisfy payment of your debt.
- *Wage-assignment clause.* A wage-assignment clause indicates that your creditor can collect a certain percentage of your salary from your employer if you cannot make your payments. The amount that can be collected is limited by law. To be binding, this clause would have to be stated not only in the contract but also in a separate agreement signed by you and your creditor. In some states, wage-assignment clauses are illegal.

Promissory Notes

A conditional sales contract might also include a promissory note. A **promissory note** is a written promise to repay the total sum owed under the conditions specified. If you are unable to pay as agreed, your creditor can get a court order to force you to make payments.

Considering Cash Loans

Sometimes, you may want to borrow some money. For example, you may want to move into a new home or pay for schooling. In these situations, you may consider getting a cash loan. A **cash loan** is an amount of money borrowed for a specific purpose. Unlike conditional sales agreements, cash loans can be repaid either in installments or in one large payment.

To get a cash loan, you may have to meet special requirements. For example, you may need a cosigner for your loan. A cosigner is a person who, by signing someone else's loan, becomes legally responsible for the loan if the borrower cannot pay. Cosigning a loan is a serious obligation. If you need a cosigner, ask someone who uses credit wisely and knows you well. A family member might be a good choice.

As you can see, cosigning a loan means becoming legally responsible for someone else's contract. If you are ever asked to cosign a loan, think carefully before agreeing. You should not cosign someone's loan unless you are willing and able to pay off the loan by yourself.

To get a cash loan, you may also have to offer collateral. For example, you may decide

To get your first loan, you may need to ask a responsible adult to cosign your loan. Why might this be necessary?

How similar are the cash loans offered by these institutions?

to use your savings or investments, your car, or your home as collateral. If collateral is required, your loan is called a secured loan. If simply your signature—and no collateral—is required, your loan is called an unsecured loan, or signature loan. This type of cash loan allows you to borrow based only on your ability and pledge to repay. To pledge, you sign a promissory note.

There are many types of lending institutions, or creditors who make cash loans. These lenders vary in the following ways:

- their screening of applicants
- the range of loans they offer
- the interest rate they use
- their handling of collateral

Screening of Applicants by Lenders

One type of lender called a pawnbroker will keep some personal item from *any* borrower in exchange for a cash loan. Pawnbrokers do no screening of the borrower. Instead, they look at the item—for example, jewelry, a camera, a musical instrument—that has been offered as collateral. They may reject items that have little value or that they think may have been stolen.

Banking and savings institutions, insurance companies, and finance companies, on the other hand, usually screen applicants. They do not, however, use the same criteria for granting a loan. Commercial banks and savings and loan associations might deny you a loan because you lack experience in managing money. It is also possible, however, that they may consider making a loan to a young borrower like yourself who has a savings or a checking account with them.

Another type of financial institution may consider experience in managing money relatively unimportant. Finance companies, for example, lend to those without an extensive financial history. Credit unions and mutual savings banks are member-owned and are likely to take a chance on a young borrower who is a member. Insurance companies also may lend money to a young borrower who has one of their policies.

Usually, to obtain a loan, you must fill out a financial statement, as well as an application form. A financial statement is a record of your current financial situation. You must also be interviewed by a loan officer. The loan officer reviews your application to determine your ability to repay the loan.

Using Credit

Range of Cash Loans Offered by Lenders

Many financial institutions offer a wide variety of cash loans. Banks, savings and loan associations, and credit unions, for example, make loans ranging from one hundred to several thousand dollars. Such loans may be for items such as a household move, a trip, a car, a mobile home, home improvement, or health care. They may also be for a mortgage to pay for land or a house.

These financial institutions may also offer **automatic overdraft,** a service that allows a person to write a check for an amount greater than the amount in the person's account. The financial institution simply notes your overdraft, treats it as a small loan, and charges you interest on it.

In addition, commercial banks may lend you money through credit cards. Most bank customers who have a bank credit card qualify for "ready credit." If you are eligible, your bank advances you cash or lets you charge over the credit limit on your bank card.

Insurance and finance companies do not offer as broad a range of loans. They should not, however, be overlooked. Life insurance companies, for example, offer some types of insurance against which you can borrow money. Automobile insurance companies may lend you money to buy a motor vehicle if you agree to insure the vehicle with them.

Finance companies offer cash loans. They also offer consolidation loans, which require careful consideration. A **consolidation loan** is a combination of many existing debts into *one* total debt. A **debt** is the amount of money owed to a creditor. The advantage of a consolidation loan is that it stretches your payments over a longer time. Therefore, it makes your monthly payments smaller. It has a drawback, however. Your total debt is greater, because you are using the borrowed money for a longer time.

Rate of Interest Offered by Lenders

The interest rates that lenders use vary. Pawnbrokers use the highest rate of interest. Among financial institutions, credit unions usually offer the lowest and finance companies the highest interest rates. By contacting as many financial institutions as possible, you should find the one that offers the most reasonable interest rate.

Handling of Collateral by Lenders

Although pawnbrokers usually lend less than half the resale value of the collateral they accept, most financial institutions acknowledge the full value of any collateral. In addition, banks, savings and loan associations, and credit unions make loans that require no collateral.

Avoiding and Handling Credit Problems

If you plan to buy on credit, think of it as one of your expense groups. Try to spend no more than 10 to 15 percent of your income on credit payments. If you spend more than this, you may be unable to make your payments. Not making payments when they are due is known as **default.** This is a problem your creditors will not ignore. Instead, they may turn to debt collectors to obtain payment from you.

Should you be contacted by a debt collector, keep in mind that you have certain rights. The Fair Debt Collection Practices Act makes some methods of debt collection illegal. For example, a debt collector cannot advertise your debt or threaten you with violence. The law also states that a debt collector must honor your written request not to be contacted again. The act protects your right not to be abused or harassed. It does not, however, dismiss your obligation to pay a legitimate debt. If you have a problem paying your debts, you should immediately get credit counseling. For more information on how a credit counselor can help you, see the next page. Failure to pay your debts may result in wage garnishment, repossession, or bankruptcy and its alternatives.

Wage Garnishment

In some states, a creditor can get a court order requiring your employer to pay part of your wages directly to the creditor. This is called wage garnishment. In the states where garnishment is permitted, the law limits how much of your wages can be taken for this pur-

Paying for Your Purchases

P.S. How Might Credit Counseling Help You?

If you ever have a problem managing credit payments, you can get help from a reputable credit counseling service. A popular one is the nonprofit agency called Consumer Credit Counseling Service (CCCS). It is located in many communities throughout the country and is supported by local lenders and community leaders. CCCS helps people pay their debts and shows them how to avoid credit problems. These services are usually free.

To provide these services, CCCS employs credit counselors with a wide range of backgrounds. Some are home economists, social workers, or other professionals who have specialized in money matters. Others are nonprofessionals and persons who have had their own serious credit problems.

If you meet with a credit counselor, you will discuss your financial records and spending habits in detail. All information you give will be confidential. You may also be advised to destroy your credit cards.

Your credit counselor will help you make a realistic budget. If necessary, your counselor will work out a new payment schedule with your creditors. In some cases, you will be asked to send part of your paycheck to your counselor, who will pay your creditors.

Most persons who use credit counseling services make an effort to follow their counselor's advice. This advice includes the following guidelines:

- Understand the difference between your gross pay and your net pay.
- Make an accurate estimate of your expenses.
- Set realistic financial goals for yourself.
- Spend only a small percentage of your income on credit payments.

By taking such steps *now,* you will probably be able to avoid credit problems.

pose. It also prevents your employer from firing you after just one garnishment.

Repossession

A creditor can take back and resell products you have purchased on credit if you fail to make the required payments. This is called repossession. The proceeds of the sale are applied to the balance of your debt. If the sale does not pay off your debt, you may have to pay the remaining balance. The U.S. Supreme Court has ruled that no item may be repossessed without the buyer's knowledge. The buyer must have a chance in court to explain the reasons for default.

Bankruptcy and Its Alternatives

If your debts become too great to repay, you have two options. You can declare bankruptcy or enroll in a wage-earner plan. **Bankruptcy** is a procedure that forces a person who is deeply in debt to allow most of his or her assets to be sold at public auction. The money from the sale is then paid to creditors. At that point, the debtor is considered free of most, if not all, debts. The **wage-earner plan** is a procedure that permits a debtor to repay debts over an extended period, usually three years. In the meantime, the debtor is allowed to keep all personal property and real estate.

Points to Remember

- Paying by check is a safe and convenient way to pay for your purchases.
- The main difference between the special and the regular checking account is whether a minimum balance is required.
- If you keep accurate records, you will know about how much money you have in your checking account.
- When your personal check is unacceptable, consider using a money order, a cashier's check, or a traveler's check.
- Buying on credit means that you delay your payment for a particular product or service. Credit is a privilege and usually includes an additional cost.
- Knowing the finance charge and the annual percentage rate will help you compare credit costs.
- Plan to use credit in such a way that you keep a good credit rating.
- Credit cards vary in how much it costs to use them and where they can be used.
- For some credit purchases you may sign a conditional sales contract.
- Whenever you need a cash loan, check with several lending institutions. Then, choose the one that offers you the best terms.
- Although you are legally protected against threats from debt collectors, you still have a responsibility to pay your debts.

Test Your Skills

DECISION MAKING

Imagine yourself in the situation described below. In this situation, a decision is needed. As you read, think about how to make good decisions. Then, answer the questions that follow. When you make decisions in the future, remember to ask yourself these questions.

Situation

At last, your mother agrees to let you buy a car. You agree to check with various sources of cash loans. You discover the following:

- A nearby finance company offers students a five-year loan at 18 percent interest. The company would allow you to be the only signer of the loan.

- Your bank offers a four-year loan at 19 percent interest. The bank would insist that you have a cosigner for the loan.

- Your mother's credit union offers a four-year loan at 17 percent interest. Your mother would have to take out the loan and let you repay her. She would charge you an additional 1 percent interest.

The car you want is a used one costing $3,000. The money you earn from your job will barely cover even the low credit union payments. To make sense of your choices, you have made a chart of your possible sources of credit. You have also listed the income and savings you could put toward the car and its upkeep costs. The decision is not easy. You know, however, that if you borrow from your mother and miss a payment, she will not repossess the car.

Questions

1. What is the problem?
2. What information do you need to help you make a decision?
3. Which of your values, goals, and resources may affect your decision?
4. List three decisions you could make. What are their possible consequences?
5. What is the best decision you could make? Why is it the best for you? What is the next best decision?

Terms

On a separate sheet of paper, write a definition for each of the underlined terms below. Base your definition on the clues you find in the sentence(s).

1. Alonzo opened an <u>interest-bearing checking account</u>. On his first checking account statement, he sees that he has not only avoided paying a service charge but has also earned interest.
2. At the bank, Becky signed her name on the back of her paycheck. After <u>endorsing</u> her check, she asked the cashier to cash it.
3. Once a month, Aaron receives a statement from his bank. It lists the checks he has written, the deposits he has made, and any service charges for his checking account. Aaron then balances his <u>checking account statement</u> to make sure his records and the bank's records match.
4. Kendra discovered that a cash loan from one bank would cost her $500 in interest payments, $25 for service charges, and $15 in special fees. After learning the <u>finance charge</u> at that bank would be $540, she decided to shop around for a cash loan.
5. Sophie asks each creditor what the <u>annual percentage rate</u>, or <u>APR</u>, for credit will be. She has gotten answers ranging from 18 percent interest to 24 percent interest a year.
6. Pete added a $50 charge to his <u>revolving charge account</u>. He can pay off this amount over the next several months.
7. Michelle has almost finished paying for a chair. Once she completes the payments according to her <u>conditional sales contract</u>, the chair will really belong to her and not to the store.
8. To borrow the money he needs for his vocational school program, Miles plans to take out a <u>cash loan</u>.
9. Pam's father has agreed to act as a <u>cosigner</u> on Pam's cash loan. Legally, he must pay off the loan if Pam cannot.
10. Rick's <u>default</u> on his car payments has resulted in a credit problem. His finance company has had a debt collector contact him about the payments he has missed.

Questions

1. What must you consider when choosing a type of checking account?
2. Why is it important to compare the minimum balance required by different financial institutions for a regular checking account?

3. How can you stop payment on a check?
4. What can you do to keep your checking account in balance?
5. Why might you use a money order instead of a personal check?
6. Where must you go to get a cashier's check?
7. Describe two kinds of credit insurance.
8. Which method for figuring a finance charge is usually best for the customer? Why?
9. Define the three factors used to determine eligibility for credit.
10. How does a credit bureau affect whether you will receive credit?
11. What must you do to keep a good credit rating?
12. Explain two special clauses you might find in a conditional sales contract.
13. What is the most you should allow yourself to spend on credit payments?

Activities

1. Call or write several financial institutions. Compare their charges and service fees for checking accounts. Which institution has the lowest charges? Do any of the institutions offer free checking?

2. Buy the lowest denomination of traveler's check ($10) from a bank. What is the fee? Record the check number. Then, cash the check by endorsing it at a local store. If you have any problems cashing the check, describe them.

3. Compare application forms for the following types of credit cards: bank cards, travel and leisure cards, and one-company cards. What kinds of questions are asked?

4. Which types of credit cards do you think you will have as a young adult? Where will you get them? What might influence your selection—for example, television ads, your parents' selection? How often do you think you will use your credit cards? After reviewing your answers to the above questions, which cards could you eliminate? Why?

5. Contact a bank, credit union, finance company, and credit card company. Ask for the APR on a $250 loan to be paid back in a lump sum in one year. Which creditor offers the lowest APR? Which offers the highest?

6. Describe how a person's life would be different if he or she had to declare bankruptcy. How would the person's self-esteem or self-concept be affected? How can you manage your money so that you will not face bankruptcy?

Sale

CHAPTER 7

Using Consumer Information

Imagine an economy in which there was only one kind of every product or service. In such an economy, you as a consumer would have just one choice: either buy an item or do without it. You would not be able to choose an item because it was best for your individual needs. Instead, you would have to buy whatever type of item was offered. You would also have to pay whatever price was asked. Under these circumstances, you would have little need to become well informed about the kinds of items offered for sale. That kind of consumer information would not do you much good because you could not use it to make choices.

Fortunately, however, the free enterprise economy in this country offers you many choices of products and services. Just look around you. Your local shopping malls, neighborhood stores, and mail-order catalogs are filled with hundreds of products and services. The yellow pages of the telephone book are also filled with ads. There seems to be an almost endless variety of businesses offering all kinds of items. Moreover, each business seems to offer a wide variety of types and brands of each item.

With so much to choose from, you are faced with many shopping decisions. How can you be sure that you are making the best shopping decisions possible? A good way to start is by being an informed consumer. This means that you understand your consumer rights and responsibilities. You also know where to find the many different types of consumer information and how to use each type to best advantage.

Discover Through Your Reading

- how many sources of consumer information are available to you
- how you can use the information in commercials and ads to your advantage
- what you should do if you buy a product that turns out to be unsafe
- why some warranties are more useful than others
- whom you can contact to learn about a company's complaint history

Your Consumer Rights and Responsibilities

You have learned that, as a family member and as a citizen, you have certain rights. You have also learned that these rights usually involve responsibilities. For example, as a member of a family, you have the right to be cared for and loved. You also have the responsibility to contribute to your family's well-being. As a citizen, one of your rights is the right to vote in elections. With this right comes the responsibility to learn about the candidates and about the stands they take. Now, as a young adult, you are beginning to see yourself as a consumer in our free enterprise economic system. Being a consumer also involves certain rights and responsibilities. Where did these come from?

Our free enterprise economic system provides a constant flow of new and different products and services. The number of products keeps increasing, and there are constant improvements in quality, style, and usefulness. As new products appear, new stores open to sell them. With new products also come changes in ways of selling and even in people's buying habits. Also, sellers and others often offer buyers new ways of paying for their purchases. Finally, new products also require new advertising to introduce them to the buying public.

As the number and variety of products increase, consumers constantly need more information. They need it to make shopping choices and to understand new ways of selling and buying. They also need it to sort through advertising claims and to find good buys. They especially need it to care for and use complex products properly.

Over time, consumers have become increasingly concerned about their information needs. Beginning more than thirty years ago, consumer groups worked to make the government aware of this and other consumer concerns. In the early 1960s the government responded by defining four consumer rights that it would protect by law. The list of these rights is called the Consumers' Bill of Rights. During the 1970s two more rights were added to the original four.

The Consumers' Bill of Rights is shown in the chart below. As you read the chart, note

Consumer's Bill of Rights

Right	Responsibility	Right	Responsibility
• to be safe	• to use products and services safely	• to be heard	• to express likes and dislikes about products and services
	• to report unsafe products and services	• to seek redress	• to take action after buying a product or service that is defective or was inaccurately described to you
• to be informed	• to seek and use information about products and services		
	• to report misleading information or false claims about products and services	• to receive consumer education	• to learn to be a wise consumer
• to choose	• to select products and services carefully		

144   Using Consumer Information

What warnings might you find on a can of bug spray? In what ways would these warnings be different from the warning label placed on each package of cigarettes?

that, like your rights as a family member and as a citizen, each of your consumer rights carries with it at least one corresponding responsibility.

Your Right to Be Safe

You have the right to safe products and services. To protect you, several government agencies try to make sure items on the market are safe. The Food and Drug Administration (FDA) and the Consumer Product Safety Commission (CPSC) are two such federal agencies. If either agency determines that an item is unsafe, it can have a warning label added or ban the item. State and local governments also set safety standards. Sometimes their standards are even higher than those set at the federal level.

Your Responsibility

With your right to be safe comes your responsibility to use products and services safely. If you buy an aerosol bug spray, for example, you need to read its label. You need to use the spray in the way that it was designed to be used. You need to store it in a safe place, for example, away from children and heat. You also need to throw it away safely.

If an item you buy proves unsafe, you have an additional responsibility. You should notify its seller and manufacturer. Your comments may lead to improvements in the item. Because the item might possibly harm other consumers, you also should let agencies such as the FDA or CPSC know about the problem.

Your Right to Be Informed

You have the right to accurate information about products and services. Much of this information will come from businesses. It may come to you in many forms, including promotional material, product labels, and warranties.

Most businesses will provide you with accurate information. A few, however, are not run honestly and commit fraud. **Fraud** is trickery or dishonesty used to get someone else's money or other resources. Deceptive advertising and selling practices are examples of fraud.

Perhaps you have seen ads that seem too good to be true. They may be ads for losing weight or for earning money at home. Often, such ads contain false claims. You may have also seen ads for merchandise that is supposedly on sale but actually costs as much as or more than usual. For example, a neighborhood store may advertise a portable radio as being "on sale for $20" when $20 is the regular price. This is deceptive advertising and pricing.

Maybe you have also seen an item advertised at a very low price. When you tried to buy it, you were told the item was unavailable or you were shown damaged goods. Then, you were probably urged to buy anoth-

In what ways do you think that this display may be misleading?

er item lower in quality or higher in price. If so, you were seeing bait-and-switch advertising firsthand. **Bait-and-switch advertising** is a deceptive sales practice in which stores deny customers the opportunity to buy the product or service advertised.

Government agencies at all levels try to make sure you get information and to protect you from fraud. They set up consumer affairs departments and consumer hotlines. They insist that products have standard information on their labels. In addition, they try to keep businesses from making false claims or providing misleading information. For example, the Federal Trade Commission watches for deceptive ads or selling practices and takes steps to stop them. The U.S. Postal Service works to stop businesses from sending misleading information through the mail.

Businesses also have watchdog groups. The best known of these is the Council of Better Business Bureaus (BBB). The BBB is described in detail later in this chapter.

Your Responsibility

Although government and other agencies try to protect you, you are still your best and nearest protection. So, it is your responsibility to get enough information to make a good decision. To protect yourself, you should get into the habit of relying on more than one source of consumer information.

If you decide someone is making false or misleading claims for a product or service, you have another responsibility. You should report your discovery to the appropriate agency. By doing so, you help protect other consumers.

Your Right to Choose

You have a right to choices in the marketplace. This means that you have the right to select from among products and services that vary in style, quality, and price. When you can choose from a variety of items, you have a better chance of finding one that meets your needs.

For most items, you have this choice because different businesses are competing to sell you their products and services. You benefit from this competition in two ways. First, you find the variety you want because each business tries to make its product different from those of its competitors. Second, you can shop for good buys because each business tries to offer you better quality and price than its competitors offer you.

All levels of government work to make sure you have many choices. They do this by encouraging competition in business and by trying to prevent monopolies. A **monopoly** is a business that is the only maker or seller of a given product or service. A business that is a monopoly has no competitors to offer you another choice. You must accept whatever product type and price that business offers. There are laws in this country against monopolies.

Your Responsibility

You have a responsibility to choose carefully before buying. You should buy only those items you most need and want and can afford. You also should deal with only the most honest and reliable businesses. This helps you. It also helps the honest businesses survive and the dishonest ones fail.

Your Right to Be Heard

Have you ever felt so pleased with a product or service that you wanted to tell its seller how you felt? Have you ever been so dissatisfied with an item that you wanted to complain to its seller? Perhaps you even felt ready to state your complaint in public—in the newspaper or at a public meeting.

By law you have the right to be heard. You can tell a business, other consumers, and the government what you like and dislike about a product or service. If you have had experience with an item, you may have much to say. You can do this in person, by telephone, or in writing.

Your Responsibility

Again, you have not only a right but also a responsibility. You should let a business and others know when you think a product or service is good. That way, the item is more likely to remain in the marketplace. Likewise, you should let a seller and other consumers know when you think a product or service is bad. In this case, the item is less likely to be on the market a long time.

By speaking up while you shop and after you buy, you can help businesses decide how to improve. You can let other consumers know which businesses seem reliable to you and which do not. At the same time, you can help each level of government set policies related to products and services.

Your Right to Seek Redress

If you have a problem with something you buy, you have the right to seek redress. **Redress** is a remedy or solution to a problem. For example, you can seek redress if an item you bought is defective or was inaccurately described by its manufacturer or seller. An item that is defective is not in good condition or does not work right. If a business uses the term *as is* when it sells you a defective item,

One of the ways that government agencies educate consumers is by publishing helpful booklets. What makes this form of consumer information convenient to use?

Your Consumer Rights and Responsibilities **147**

you cannot go back and seek a remedy. On the other hand, if a business claims to be selling you an item in good condition but does not do so, you have the right to seek redress.

Your Responsibility

To exercise your right to seek redress, you must take responsibility for contacting the business that sold and, possibly, the business that made the item. Because most sellers and manufacturers want satisfied customers, they will try to make sure you are pleased with your purchase. This means that most of the time you can resolve your problem by getting in touch with one or both of them. If you need assistance in seeking a remedy, however, help *is* available. In the next chapter, you will discover guidelines for contacting the seller or manufacturer. You will also learn how to get help from other sources when necessary.

Your Right to Receive Consumer Education

You have the right to consumer education. This means you have the right to learn as much as possible about what it means to be a wise consumer. For example, you have opportunities to learn where to get information about specific products and services. You can learn why you should consider your needs and values, wants and goals, and resources before deciding to make a purchase. You can learn when comparison shopping makes the most sense. You can learn about the many types of businesses that sell products and services. You can also learn how to get good buys and how you can help keep prices down. In addition, you can learn where to get help with a consumer problem. These are things all consumers need to know.

Your opportunities for consumer education come in many forms. The government—at the local, state, and federal levels—has set up offices to provide consumers with information about products and services. In addition, schools at all levels offer courses in consumer education.

Your Responsibility

You have a responsibility to take advantage of your opportunities to become an educated consumer. By reading this chapter, you are already learning some of the basics. Your consumer education should not end here, however. The items offered for sale will keep changing. Your consumer rights and responsibilities will also change. Therefore, you will always need more consumer education.

Sources of Consumer Information

Your experiences may provide you all the information you want before you decide which products or services to buy. The experiences of people you know may also provide you enough information. If you want more information, however, you can get it. Because consumer information is a valuable resource, you will want to manage it effectively. You must know where to find it and how to use it. Consumer information is available from businesses, trade and professional organizations, mass media, nonprofit organizations, and government.

Information from Businesses

The businesses that offer products and services are an important source of consumer information. They send messages to consumers in many ways. They use promotional material like radio and television commercials; telephone directory, newspaper, and magazine ads; billboards; and flyers. They also communicate at the point of purchase. They do this through displays and sales personnel, product labels, seals of approval, and warranties and guarantees.

Promotional Material

A business firm's **promotional material** is the combination of messages it uses to interest consumers in its products or services. No matter what means of communication the business uses, the basic message is always the same: "Buy my product or service." As it tries to get your attention and convince you to buy, however, the business also provides you with information about the product or service.

The messages in promotional material vary in the amount of information provided and the amount of emotional appeal made. They also vary in the accuracy of the information presented. It is up to you to analyze promotional material carefully to decide how useful its information is. For tips on judging the information in promotional material, see page 151.

Some promotional material gives only basic information—what item is available, what special features it has, where it can be purchased, and what special sales and promotions are being held. Other promotional material gives more details. For example, an ad for a product may also tell you how the product is made, how well it performs in tests, and its many uses. An ad about a service may also explain advantages the service has over similar services and the qualifications of the seller. In fact, in some promotional material you will find so much information that you may at first think there is no advertising message. This is likely to be true with posters, booklets, and filmstrips. Businesses often use these to educate people about their products or services.

Some promotional material makes an appeal that is mainly factual. Other promotional material makes an appeal that is mainly emotional.

An **emotional appeal** is an attempt to get you to buy primarily on the basis of feelings. Often, an emotional appeal sneaks up on you. Suppose, for example, you are watching a commercial on television. In it, a popular sports star is endorsing a particular product. Suddenly you stop and think, "What appeal is this commercial making to me? Is it providing factual information upon which to

Which one of these two ads makes a primarily emotional appeal to you? Which provides you more facts?

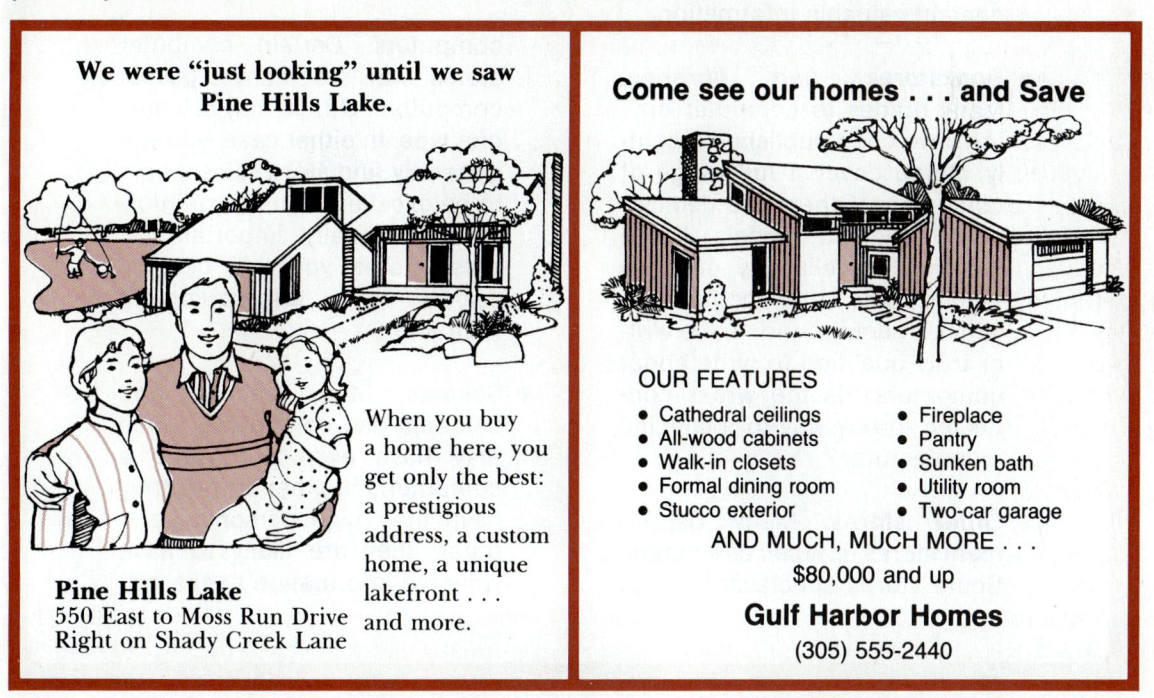

We were "just looking" until we saw Pine Hills Lake.

When you buy a home here, you get only the best: a prestigious address, a custom home, a unique lakefront... and more.

Pine Hills Lake
550 East to Moss Run Drive
Right on Shady Creek Lane

Come see our homes . . . and Save

OUR FEATURES
- Cathedral ceilings
- All-wood cabinets
- Walk-in closets
- Formal dining room
- Stucco exterior
- Fireplace
- Pantry
- Sunken bath
- Utility room
- Two-car garage

AND MUCH, MUCH MORE . . .
$80,000 and up

Gulf Harbor Homes
(305) 555-2440

How Computers Can Help You

Sources of Consumer Information About Computers

You and your family may have decided to look into the purchase of a personal computer. Clearly, the purchase of a computer involves a major expense. Most likely, you and your family will get the greatest value from your money if you check the following sources of information:

- **Magazines.** Many magazines contain information related to computers. Some magazines are devoted solely to computers of a specific manufacturer. A few may, in fact, deal only with a specific model of computer. Many computer magazines, however, examine and rate various brands and models of new equipment. Generally, these are a better place to begin looking for information. In addition, many general-interest consumer magazines offer reliable tips on computers and run ads that contain valuable information.

- **Bookstores and libraries.** Many guides to computer buying have been published recently. Some cover a full range of computers. Others are dedicated to specific models. When judging the reliability of these guides, take into account the writer's background. Is the writer truly qualified to write about computers? Is the writer connected in any way to a specific manufacturer?

- **Other stores.** Many department stores now sell computers. Some stores specialize only in computers. Certain computer stores may sell many types of computers. Others may sell only one type. In either case, you will generally find store salespeople to be excellent sources of information. Equally important, in most stores you will get the opportunity to test equipment firsthand.

- **Schools.** Many teachers and students use computers. Some may have even purchased a computer. Whether or not they have their own personal computer, they are likely to have valuable information to share.

150

base a decision? Or is it making an emotional appeal to my desire to be like someone I admire?" To answer these questions, you may decide to think back through your reasons—factual or emotional—for considering the product. If you decide that you have enough factual information and that you really want the product, you may decide to buy it.

Finally, most promotional material contains only accurate information because most businesses are honest and want satisfied customers. They also try not to make mistakes when they prepare promotional material. Such mistakes can cost them in customer good will and dollars. If, however, you spot a mistake or a statement that may not be true, it is best to do some checking. Contact the business to ask about its message. If necessary, also consult other sources of consumer information.

Tips

Judging the Information in Promotional Material

To judge the information in ads and other promotional material, ask yourself the following questions:

- What is the message? Is it clear?

- Does the information seem complete? Does it seem that important information has been left out?

- Is the appeal mainly factual, or is it mainly emotional? If emotional, what is the particular desire, fear, or emotion to which the message is appealing?

- How accurate and up-to-date is the information? Do any of the claims seem exaggerated?

Displays

The main purpose of most displays is to attract attention. They are designed to create interest in a product or service. Some displays, though, also provide a good deal of consumer information. In self-service stores, for example, displays serve a special role. They offer some of the information that salespeople would otherwise provide. You must judge the completeness and accuracy of the information in any display.

Sales Personnel

Your main contacts with most businesses are through their salespeople. Many salespeople are specially trained to answer questions about what they sell. The information they provide may be complete and accurate enough to help you make a decision. However, their main goal is usually to make a sale. Thus, they will usually avoid suggesting a competing business's products or services—even when those products or services might meet your needs better.

Be particularly wary of salespeople who insist that you buy a certain item. Take your time before making a decision. Do not be afraid to say, "I have to think about it. I'll come back later."

Product Labels

Another source of consumer information is product labels. A **product label** is a piece of paper or cloth that carries a written identification or description of the product to which it is attached. Product labels vary in the amount of information they carry. However, you will almost always find on them the following information:

- the name of the product and the manufacturer's trademark
- the name and address of the manufacturer or producer
- a list of the contents or ingredients of the product
- the quantity (net weight, measure, or count) in the package
- directions for use of the product
- claims for what the product can do
- warning statements
- special care advice

Sources of Consumer Information

When Do You Need a Service Contract?

You have just bought a television set, and the salesperson says, "For $50 more, you can purchase a two-year service contract." What would you do?

There is no simple answer to whether you should buy a service contract. Since most products need service at some time, the question is how you choose to pay for it. You can pay for repairs as they are needed, or you can purchase a service contract. A service contract is an agreement in which you state that you will pay a set amount of money to cover repairs for a certain period of time.

A service contract works a little like insurance. With a service contract, you are betting that the product will need service. The seller of the contract is betting that it will not.

A service contract can be a good buy if the following points apply:

- The price of the contract is lower than the estimated cost of paying for the repairs yourself.

- The backer of the contract is trustworthy. The backer is not always the maker of the product or even the store selling the product. Sometimes the backer is an independent repair shop.

- The contract does not overlap the product warranty.

- The contract will still be honored if you sell the product.

- You can get a refund on the unused portion of the contract if you decide you no longer want the contract.

On the other hand, a service contract can be a waste of money. For example, the contract may be very expensive, or the product itself may be unlikely to require service. In these cases, buying a service contract may be a poor use of your resources.

a defective product or part at no cost to the buyer. Furthermore, the warrantor will return the buyer's money or replace the product or part if the buyer is not satisfied with it.

A **limited warranty** is a guarantee that the warrantor will cover some but not all the costs of repairing or replacing a product. The warranty must clearly state what the warrantor will cover and what you will have to cover. For example, if you have to pay for labor, this fact must be stated in the warranty. If a product's warranty ends once you sell the product, the warranty must say so.

The time to use a warranty as an information source is *before* you make a purchase. By law, if a manufacturer or seller offers a warranty for an item costing $15 or more, the warranty must be available at the point of sale for you to review.

The time to suggest a change in a written warranty is also before you decide to buy. The provider of the warranty may not agree to write in any changes, but you will not know unless you ask.

Although it may not be necessary, it is a good idea to mail in any warranty card provided. It is necessary, however, to keep a copy of the warranty itself, your sales receipt, and a record of the dates you have requested service. This record will be useful if you need to prove that a problem started before the warranty period ended.

Information from Trade and Professional Organizations

Businesses are not alone in informing consumers through promotional material. **Trade and professional organizations** are groups of trade or professional people who spend time, energy, and money promoting their industry or profession. The American Dental Association, for example, is composed of dentists and promotes dental care. Other trade and professional organizations provide consumers with information on such things as appliances, automobiles, furniture, medical care, hotels and motels, and insurance.

The names and addresses of these and other trade and professional organizations are listed in directories found in most libraries.

Information from Mass Media

The **mass media** are the forms of communication that get information to many people simultaneously. Examples include magazines, newspapers, radio, and television.

Consumer-related magazines have been a source of consumer information for years. There are so many that it is often hard to decide which to use as a reference. Two of the most popular, *Consumer Reports* and *Consumers' Research Magazine*, are discussed in the next section of this chapter. Others include *Better Homes and Gardens, Good Housekeeping, Money,* and *Changing Times*. You should be able to find these and more in your local library, bookstores, grocery stores, and elsewhere. By scanning them, you can decide which meet your information needs.

How might an "Action Line" reporter be able to help several consumers at the same time?

Sources of Consumer Information **155**

Your local newspaper may also carry consumer information. In most newspapers, the information will appear in news stories and in regular columns, often called "Action Lines." Large newspapers may devote a whole section to consumer issues.

Most articles in consumer magazines and newspapers are written by individuals who have no ties with the makers or sellers of the products or services discussed. Because of this, the articles are more likely to be free from bias than promotional material. Such articles, therefore, can be extremely helpful.

Other mass media have also begun to report on developments of interest to consumers. For example, on radio and television news programs you can get updates on consumer legislation and hear stories about individual consumers and their concerns. Some stations even have consumer action reporters. Longer programs bring you debates about consumer issues and in-depth coverage of consumer matters. Some networks run public service announcements to keep you and other consumers informed about specific products and services and general consumer issues.

Information from Nonprofit Consumer Organizations

A **nonprofit organization** is an organization that is created to serve a social, charitable, or educational purpose. It does not return a profit to its members. There are many different types of nonprofit organizations.

Two of the nonprofit organizations supported by consumers are Consumers Union and Consumers' Research. Each tests products and publishes its findings in a consumer magazine. Consumers Union publishes *Consumer Reports.* Consumers' Research publishes *Consumers' Research Magazine.*

Each organization reports in its magazine how it rates the products it has tested. Items with the highest quality and lowest price get "best value" ratings.

Another nonprofit organization, the Better Business Bureau (BBB), is set up to serve consumers but is supported by businesses. The BBB is a national organization with bureaus located in cities throughout the country. Each local bureau is funded by membership dues from businesses. The BBB is one of the few consumer information sources that provides information on the reputation of individual businesses.

The local Better Business Bureau keeps a file on each business about which a consumer has made a written complaint. To find out about a particular company's complaint history—how many complaints have been filed and how many settled—you can call your local bureau. For example, you may need to have a room painted and a friend may suggest the name of a painter. From the BBB,

Your local BBB records the complaints that consumers file with them about a business. How can you use such information to avoid a problem?

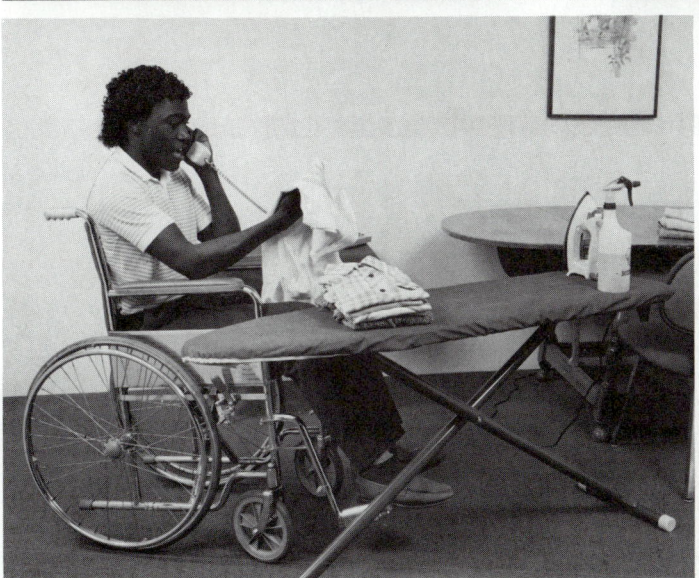

County extension agents can give consumers advice on many different subjects, including how to eat nutritiously, care for plants, and remove stains. What are some other subjects about which you might consult your county extension agent?

you can find out whether any consumers have complained about that painter. The BBB will not, however, recommend any business.

Information from the Government

Many government agencies have public information programs or consumer affairs offices. A federal agency, the Office of Consumer Affairs, reports directly to the President on all types of consumer concerns. These include consumer education, protection, and legislation. To make inquiries, you may write to the U.S. Office of Consumer Affairs, Department of Health and Human Services, 200 Independence Avenue, S.W., Washington, DC 20201. For a free catalog of all federal consumer-related publications and their prices, write to the Consumer Information Center, Pueblo, CO 81009.

State and local governments also have consumer offices. The powers of these vary, but many of these offices work with the state's attorney general to enforce laws designed to protect consumers.

Sources of Consumer Information   **157**

A program run jointly by federal, state, and local government agencies is the U. S. Cooperative Extension Service, often called the *county extension service*. From its home economists, agriculture specialists, and other trained professionals, you can get sound information on a variety of subjects. You can get this information in person, by mail, or by telephone. You will find the county extension service listed in your telephone directory under the name of your county.

Government agencies are listed in books and directories. With the help of a reference librarian, a teacher, or a bookstore salesperson, you can find an appropriate government agency to answer your questions.

Points to Remember

- You can make the most of your consumer rights by accepting your consumer responsibilities.

- The first step you must take to protect yourself from fraud in the marketplace is to recognize it.

- With so many products and services from which to choose, it is important to find, judge, and use consumer information.

- Businesses, trade and professional organizations, mass media, nonprofit organizations, and all levels of government provide consumer information in varying amounts.

- From businesses, you can often learn about products and services through promotional material, displays, sales personnel, product labels, seals of approval, warranties and guarantees.

- Some ads appeal almost entirely to your emotions, while others provide you with factual information.

- Since all product labels must, by law, give certain information, you can easily learn about differences between products.

- Understanding a product's warranty can help you decide whether to buy that particular product.

- You can find out about the reputation of individual businesses by contacting the Better Business Bureau.

Test Your Skills

DECISION MAKING

Imagine yourself in the situation described below. In this situation, a decision is needed. As you read, think about how to make good decisions. Then, answer the questions that follow. When you make decisions in the future, remember to ask yourself these questions.

Situation

Marsh's Hardware has a reputation for honest dealings. For years, its radio commercials have stressed that it sells only new lawn mowers. No one has ever complained about the business to the Better Business Bureau. Two months ago, Marsh's was sold to new owners. However, the old commercials are still being used.

Several weeks ago, you decided to buy a lawn mower. When Marsh's offered lawn mowers on sale last week, you bought one. Because you were familiar with the store's reputation, you assumed that the mower was new.

When you first used the mower, however, the engine did not seem to run as smoothly as a new engine should. After talking with a cousin who works part time at the store, you began to wonder if the mower you bought was really a new one. She told you that, in fact, Marsh's now has an employee whose major responsibility is rebuilding old lawn mower engines. You do not want to place your cousin's job in danger. On the other hand, you do not believe that Marsh's was honest in its dealings with you.

Questions

1. What is the problem?
2. What information do you need to help you make a decision?
3. Which of your values, goals, and resources may affect your decision?
4. List three decisions you could make. What are their possible consequences?
5. What is the best decision you could make? Why is it the best for you? What is the next best decision?

Terms

On a separate sheet of paper, write a definition for each of the underlined terms below. Base your definition on the clues you find in the sentence(s).

1. The Better Business Bureau told Dave that several customers of OK Yard Care had accused the business of fraud. They said that the business charged them for more trimming services than the tree trimmers actually provided.

2. When Todd left the store, he felt he had been a victim of bait-and-switch advertising. He had tried to buy a small appliance he had seen advertised the day before. Instead of showing him the model advertised, the salesperson tried to interest him in a higher-priced model. The salesperson said the advertised model was no longer available.

3. Anya wrote a complaint letter to the manager of the store that sold her a defective hair dryer. In doing so, she was exercising one of her basic consumer responsibilities: to seek redress.

4. Businesses often provide promotional material such as booklets, posters, commercials, and ads.

5. Rodney has decided to buy a certain brand of clothing after viewing a television commercial. In the commercial, the people who wear the advertised clothes seem to be popular and happy. The commercial ends with Rodney's favorite country-western singer endorsing the clothing. By making a strong emotional appeal, the advertiser has convinced Rodney to make the purchase.

6. If you carefully read the information on a product label, you should be able to identify and learn about the product to which the label is attached.

7. Instead of buying generic products, Gina likes to buy products she sees advertised on television and in magazines. She likes their fancy packages and colorful labels.

8. Like other products with a seal of approval, your new toaster has met the performance standards of an independent testing agency.

9. Chuck's new ice chest has an implied warranty. Like all ice chests, his is designed to keep foods cold for a reasonable length of time. The manufacturer's guarantee is not, however, in writing.

10. Before buying a watch, Debra read its written warranty. She found out what the seller or manufacturer guaranteed to repair or replace and under what conditions.

Questions

1. Briefly explain your consumer rights and responsibilities.
2. What kinds of information might you discover in promotional material?
3. Why is it important to evaluate promotional material in terms of its factual and emotional appeal?
4. How are store-brand and national-brand products different?
5. How are a product label and a seal of approval different?
6. Compare and contrast a full warranty and a limited warranty.
7. Why might consumer information from the mass media be more helpful than the information found in promotional material?
8. In what ways are radio and television stations a source of consumer information?
9. How can *Consumer Reports* and *Consumers' Research Magazine* help consumers make shopping decisions?
10. Name two government agencies that provide consumer information.

Activities

1. Identify which of the six consumer rights discussed in the chapter you consider the most important, and explain why.
2. Identify which consumer responsibilities you think are most often ignored, and explain why.
3. Think of a particular product or service you need or would like to buy. Find an advertisement or other form of promotional material relating to this item. Use the tips for "Judging the Information in Promotional Material" on page 151 to evaluate the information. On the basis of your evaluation, would you buy this particular item? Explain your answer.
4. Choose a label from a food, drug, cosmetic, or household cleaning product. Use the list of label information on page 151 to analyze the label as a source of consumer information. Explain how the label might help you make a buying decision.
5. Obtain copies of *Consumer Reports* and *Consumers' Research Magazine*. Read about a product that interests you. Which magazine did you find more helpful? Why?

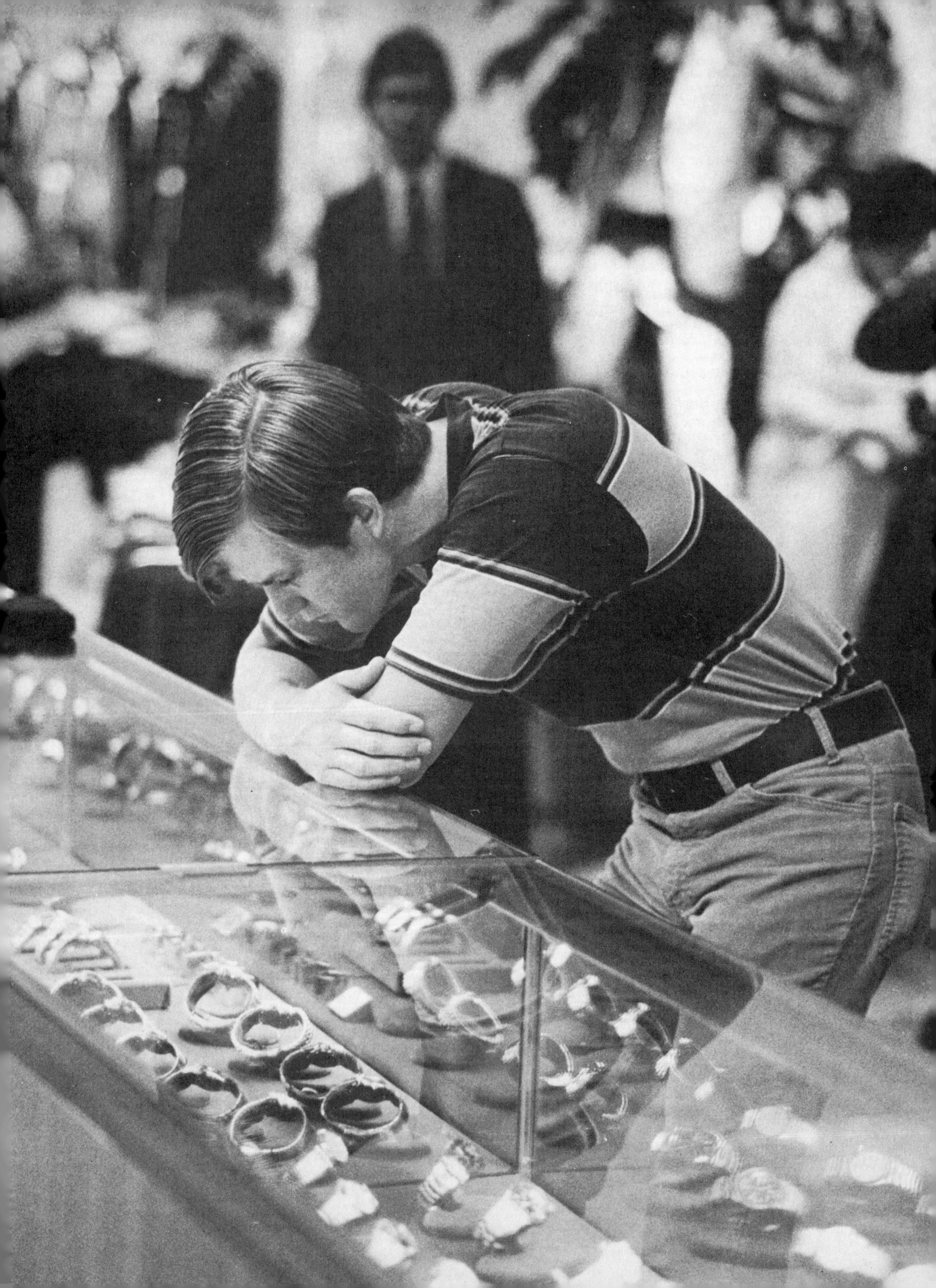

CHAPTER 8

Developing Your Shopping Skills

How old were you the first time you spent money to get something you needed or wanted? You might have been four or five, or even younger. Maybe your parents took you to a fair that had booths where balloons were being sold. One booth had two different colors of round balloons. Another had four different colors of long, skinny balloons. Still another had bright, silver balloons with funny faces on them. Your parents gave you some money and let you decide from which booth to make your purchase.

At that point, you became a shopper. You had a source of money and a specific want that the money could satisfy. You had several types of balloons available and several sellers from which to choose. You had to choose not only where to buy your balloon but also which balloon you wanted.

Now that you are older, your resources have changed. You probably have more money, and your family may no longer be your only source of income. You may have a job or receive interest on a savings account. In addition, although your needs probably remain the same, your wants have been changing.

To satisfy your needs and wants, you may already be doing more of your own shopping. As an adult, you will probably be responsible for doing it all. In fact, some day you may have a family and also have to shop to satisfy the needs and wants of others. You can do this best if you understand how to make good shopping decisions.

Discover Through Your Reading

- what kind of shopper you are
- what to do if you receive unordered merchandise
- some unusual ways to shop
- why it is important to ask for estimates when buying services
- how you can keep from making unplanned purchases
- how a consumer action reporter could help you resolve a shopping problem

163

Making Shopping Decisions

Your success as a shopper depends on your ability to make good shopping decisions. However, these decisions may include more than just choosing which product or service to buy. Especially if the purchase is an important one, you may need to make other decisions as well. Even before you begin shopping for a product or service, you may need to decide

- whether or not to buy it
- where to shop for it

Like any other decisions, shopping decisions are influenced first by your basic needs and values. The choices you make also depend on what resources you have and on what else you might have to give up if you buy the product or service. In addition, your decisions depend on your ability to compare products and services in terms of features such as quality and price.

Needs and Values

Whether or not you realize it, the most basic influences on your shopping decisions are your essential physical, emotional, mental, and spiritual needs. Of course, many products or services are available to help you meet those needs. For example, you could buy a wide variety of products to meet your physical need for food. As in other decisions, however, your values—the ideas, beliefs, and qualities that you hold dear—help you decide on a particular purchase. Depending on your values, you choose the specific product you want to meet your need. For instance, if you value your health, you might want to buy a nutritious apple instead of some less healthy alternative.

Your values also help you set goals. For example, since you value your health, one of your goals might be to play tennis regularly.

You may, therefore, decide that you want to buy a tennis racquet.

Shopping decisions involve more than just needs, values, wants, and goals, however. You must also consider the resources you have to exchange for your purchases.

Resources

If you are like most other people, you have a never-ending supply of wants and goals. For this reason, there will always be products and services you would like to buy. However, for every purchase you make, you have to give up some resource or resources of your own. Most commonly, the resource you give up is money. For most purchases, you use cash or credit. When shopping, however, you may also have to spend some other resources, such as time and energy. One way you spend these resources is in going from store to store to compare merchandise.

No one has an unlimited supply of resources to use for purchases. So, like everyone else, you have to choose how to use your limited supply. One point to remember is that every time you use a resource for one purpose, you give up the chance to use it for something else. In other words, every use of a resource involves opportunity costs.

Opportunity Costs

Like any other decisions, shopping decisions involve opportunity costs. You will recall that opportunity costs are those things a person gives up by deciding to use resources for something else. For example, suppose that you have enough money to buy a tennis racquet or running shoes, but not both. If you decide to buy the tennis racquet to reach your goal of playing tennis regularly, you must give up the opportunity to buy running shoes. In other words, by spending your limited resources to reach one goal, you must give up the opportunity to reach another goal.

It is up to you to decide which goals you can best achieve with your resources. Your values will determine the choices you make in your shopping decisions. Before making those decisions, however, one final point to consider is the use of comparison shopping.

164 Developing Your Shopping Skills

Comparison Shopping

You may wonder just what comparison shopping includes. **Comparison shopping** is using different sources of information before deciding which of several products or services to buy. It may involve comparing the quality and prices of several brands of merchandise or types of service. It may also involve comparing the same brand of merchandise or type of service sold by different businesses. Such careful research takes time, energy, money, and other resources.

Often you will find comparison shopping especially helpful when you plan to buy expensive products and services. If you are buying a typewriter, for example, you will want it to last as long as possible. Therefore, you will be particularly interested in how well it is made. If you need your television repaired, you will want the job done right the first time. So, you will look for a repairperson who is well qualified. By comparing different typewriters or repair services, you will probably find the quality and perhaps the prices you are seeking. Comparison shopping is worthwhile when you gain personal satisfaction with the item or service and also save money.

You may often decide against comparison shopping for many inexpensive items. The opportunity costs might be too great. You might spend more of your time, energy, money, and other resources than you could possibly save by finding the best buy. If, however, the inexpensive item is one you buy over and over again, you may decide that comparison shopping for it once will be worthwhile in the long run. For example, you may want to buy a sauce that contains meat, not just meat flavoring. It may take a few minutes on one shopping trip to read labels on several jars.

How often do you compare ingredients or prices on inexpensive items? What recommendations would you make to other shoppers about doing this?

On later trips, though, you will be able to go immediately to the brand you have found to be the best buy.

Deciding Whether to Buy

Examining your needs, values, resources, and opportunity costs will help you make your first important shopping decision about any new item: whether or not to buy it. For example, you may decide not to buy an expensive new sweater because you value saving. Or you may find that you do not have the resources to afford the sweater. Or you may prefer to spend your money on books. Likewise, by comparison shopping, you may find another sweater that is a better buy.

When you decide not to buy an item, you may plan to do without it permanently or just for the time being. Perhaps, instead, you will look for other ways to get what you want. For example, you might consider buying a lower-cost secondhand item or renting or borrowing an item you will not use often. You might decide to make or grow what you need. You might even swap something you have for the item you want. You can swap not only products but also services. You might, for example, ask a friend to repair your car in return for your services as a babysitter.

However, if you do decide to buy an item, you are ready for your next important shopping decision: deciding where to shop.

Deciding Where to Shop

Before you do any shopping, you need to decide where to shop. There are many kinds of sellers in the marketplace. To choose where to shop, consider what each kind of seller has to offer. Some or all of the following factors will be important to you:

- selection and quality of items sold
- prices and payment methods
- convenience and atmosphere
- types of customer service
- promotional practices
- handling of customer complaints

You determine the importance of these factors according to the specific item you are buying. For example, if you plan to buy a car, you will look for a dealer who offers certain makes and models. You will also want one that sells cars at the price you can afford. When you buy a suit or coat, you may look for a store that provides sales assistance and alteration services. When you buy groceries, you probably want to shop close to your home. Therefore, you are likely to choose a store that is convenient.

Shopping for Products

You are probably familiar with shopping in department and discount stores, supermarkets, and convenience stores. Other places to shop are listed on pages 168–169. Today you can even use a personal computer for shopping, as explained on the facing page. To take advantage of this variety, you need to understand how to shop in some special settings.

Secondhand Stores, Community Sales, Factory Outlets

Some sellers handle mainly secondhand merchandise. They sell it "as is." This means that the product you buy cannot be returned, even if you find it is defective. You will find many such items in a secondhand store or at a community sale such as a garage sale, flea market, or auction. In a factory outlet, you often find new merchandise with flaws. Some of these flaws may affect its use, wear, or look. Other flaws may not. If you examine merchandise carefully before purchasing it, you can improve your chances of getting a bargain.

(continued on page 170)

How Computers Can Help You

Shopping by Computer

A computer can provide a convenient way to shop for many kinds of merchandise. If you have a personal computer and telephone at home, you are almost fully equipped to shop by computer. You need only two more items: a telephone modem and access to a data base that includes a shopping program. A modem is a device that allows your computer to send and receive information over the telephone. A shopping program is software that retrieves data on many available products and services.

You can obtain access to a shopping program by joining any one of several major information network services. When you join one of these services, you pay a membership fee. You are then entitled to connect your own computer to a large central computer that offers the shopping program. All the members of the service share the use of the central computer through a system called computer time-sharing. Each member pays an hourly fee for use of the central computer.

Using a computer shopping program is like visiting an "electronic mall." On your terminal, you can view information from many different types of stores. Simply indicate the type of store, the specific store, and the specific departments from which you want information. Your computer will then find as close a match as possible between what you are looking for and what is available. You can even "window shop" by reading from an electronic list. You cannot see, touch, or try on merchandise when you shop by computer. However, some organizations are trying to develop television-quality pictures that will provide a reasonably accurate likeness of an item.

Shopping by computer can save you time and effort. If you use a computer, you do not have to look at every page of a catalog or walk down every aisle of a store. The computer can do all of the searching for you.

Mail-Order Houses, Buying Clubs, Computer Shopping Services

In many cases it is not necessary to go into a store to shop. Sometimes you will shop without actually dealing with the vendor in person. For example, you may choose items from mail-order catalogs, buying clubs, or computer shopping services.

When you shop from these three types of sellers, you will want to keep in mind the following pointers:

- Check local stores for the same or similar product so you can compare prices.
- Check the company's complaint history with the Better Business Bureau (BBB). If the seller requests a deposit, be especially careful. The seller may keep your "deposit" and never deliver the merchandise you ordered.
- Figure such charges as shipping, handling, postage, tax, and insurance as part of the total price.
- Complete the order form correctly and neatly. Keep a copy for yourself to make sure you receive exactly what you have paid for.
- Pay as directed. The usual forms of payment are personal check, money order, credit card, or cash-on-delivery.
- If you receive unordered merchandise, you have a legal right to keep it and ignore any bill for it.

Telephone and Door-to-Door Salespeople

Not all sellers wait for you to contact them. Some try to sell you products by calling you on the telephone. Others just stop by your door. Remember that the decision whether to deal with these sellers is yours to make. If you do not want to talk with them, you can politely but firmly tell them, "I am not interested."

If you are interested in buying a product from one of these salespeople, you do not have to decide immediately whether to make the purchase. Instead, you can ask the salesperson to contact you at another time. Buying from telephone and door-to-door salespeople can be a good choice if you follow these guidelines:

- Take the time to do some comparison shopping before you decide whether to buy the product.
- Read contracts or purchase agreements carefully. Ask the salesperson to explain unfamiliar terms or phrases to your satisfaction.
- Keep in mind that you have three business days to cancel a door-to-door sales order for any item costing more than $25. Your request to cancel needs to be in writing and must be sent to the salesperson's company. Make a copy of your request for your files, and make sure to send the letter by certified mail.

Shopping for Services

In some ways, buying services is similar to buying products. You still want to compare prices and payment procedures, as well as convenience. You still want to get quality. For example, compare shopping for a hair dryer and shopping for a haircut. You want the hair dryer to be powerful enough to dry your hair quickly. You want the hair stylist to be skilled enough to give a cut you will like.

When you buy a service, you pay for special knowledge or skills. If possible, talk with other customers to learn the seller's reputation. You also pay for the time needed to perform the service. Remember, some businesses charge for missed appointments if you do not give them enough notice to revise their schedules.

Before agreeing to buy, ask for a list of the services the seller is recommending and a price estimate for each service. Suppose, for example, that you want to take an exercise class for one hour a week. When you call a health club, you would ask about its membership plan. You might learn that the plan includes classes you do not want. You might also learn that the classes will take more than one hour a week of your time. As a result, the plan costs more than you want to pay. By asking questions, you can understand exactly what the seller is suggesting you purchase. You may decide that you do not want or cannot afford all of the services offered.

Making Purchases

Shoppers are individuals. Everyone has his or her own style. Some people love crowds and hurrying, while others like to avoid them. Before you start out on a shopping trip, you will want to think about your own feelings and what you prefer. How and when do you like to shop?

Here are some guidelines to help you plan your shopping trips.

- Decide ahead what you intend to buy and how much to spend. Avoid impulse buying. **Impulse buying** is deciding to purchase an item on the spot just because it suddenly seems appealing. This type of buying can put a major dent in your spending plan. Making a shopping list and sticking closely to it will help you resist such purchases.
- Call ahead to make sure the store has the item you want. You may save yourself an unnecessary trip.
- Limit your number of shopping trips. Each time you shop, you increase your chances for impulse buying.
- Watch magazines, the newspaper, or your mail for coupons that let you purchase needed items at a reduced price.
- Pick a good time to make purchases. Consider whether you prefer a quiet or a busy atmosphere. If crowded stores bother you, pick times when fewer people shop. On the other hand, if you want shopping to give you a chance to visit with neighbors and

How would you describe what these shoppers are doing to make sure that their shopping time, energy, and money are well spent?

Making Purchases 171

Tips

How to Make Use of Sales

There are many things you can do to take advantage of sales. Some examples follow:

- Shop early if you want the best selection at a sale.

- Buy an item in quantity while it is on sale if you have enough storage space.

- Ask for a rain check if a store has run out of a sale item by the time you shop. A **rain check** is a record from the store that shows you tried to buy during the sale. It allows you to buy the item at the sale price when the store gets in a new shipment.

- Limit your buying to the loss leaders if a store offers them. **Loss leaders** are items that a store offers at a *very* low price to attract customers. Many customers often buy nonsale items once they are in the store. Therefore, the seller usually more than makes up for the profits it loses on its loss leaders.

- Limit your purchases with coupons to those items you will really use. By doing so, you can create a sale for yourself every day. You can even double your savings in those stores that offer twice the face value of each coupon.

- Pay cash for a sale item whenever possible. Generally, you save more if you pay cash than if you use credit. This is true because interest charges may use up some or all of the money you saved when you bought the item on sale.

- Check for defects before buying a sale item. Consider how much use or wear you can get from it. Often when you buy an item on sale, you cannot return it—even if you find that it is defective.

- Do not buy an item simply because it is on sale.

friends you seldom see, choose a time when you might run into them.
- Allow enough time to shop. It is hard to make good decisions about what to purchase if you are rushed. Being rushed is likely to lead you to make shopping decisions that you may regret later.
- Plan your trip for the best use of your time, energy, and mileage. Think ahead about what order of stops is the most efficient.

172   Developing Your Shopping Skills

Take Advantage of Sales

A great way to get the most for your money is to look for sales. On page 172, you will find tips for taking advantage of sales. Some stores offer sales at a particular time of day, on a particular day, or during a particular part of the week. Many stores hold sales on or around holidays. Certain times of the year are also standard sale times for many items. What better way to save money than by taking advantage of seasonal sales? They offer savings from 20 to 50 percent. To find out which items are usually on sale each month, see page 175.

Be a Responsible Shopper

Remember that as a consumer you have some responsibilities to others in the marketplace. Good manners and honesty in shopping are two of your responsibilities.

Show Respect for People

Use good manners with store employees and fellow shoppers. Salespeople are there to help you. If you do not wish to be helped, express this in a pleasant way and expect that your wishes will be honored. If you are treated discourteously by a salesperson, report it to the manager. Usually this will help correct the situation.

If you do need assistance, though, ask for it. Wait your turn, however. Rudeness will not get you the kind of help you need or want. You probably know how it feels to have someone barge ahead of you in a line. Sales personnel and other customers feel exactly the same way.

Show Respect for Property

Abuse of a business's facilities increases the overall cost of merchandise that you buy. Leave facilities in as good a condition as you find them. For example, avoid taking food or beverages into a store. You may spill them and cause damage.

Avoid damaging merchandise. If you accidentally damage an item, however, tell the salesperson or manager. The damage will usually be corrected without cost to you. In addition, you will help prevent other shoppers from accidentally purchasing the damaged item.

Do not shoplift. **Shoplifting** is stealing. It is a serious crime—one that dishonest customers commit against businesses and other customers. To cover the cost of stolen merchandise, businesses must charge more for each product or service they sell. So, all consumers pay the price of shoplifting.

Because shoplifting is so costly, businesses are using more and more means to prevent it and to catch shoplifters. To do this, they have salespeople watch carefully for shoplifters. Sometimes they also use security guards disguised as shoppers. In addition, many stores use hidden mirrors or cameras.

Some businesses deal with shoplifting by placing special tags on merchandise. When the merchandise is purchased, the salesperson or cashier uses special equipment to remove or cancel the tag. If any merchandise is taken out of the store before its tag is removed or cancelled, an alarm sounds. This alerts the store that a crime may be in progress.

Settling Shopping Problems

There are probably as many different kinds of shopping problems as there are shopping situations. On the one hand, a business may make a minor billing error, or you may have a question about how to use an item after you get it home. A call to the business's accounting office will probably solve the billing problem. A call to a toll-free hotline number on the product's label may solve the second problem. It will put you in touch with the store's consumer service department or the manufacturer. With help from either, you will probably be able to answer your question about how to use the product.

On the other hand, you may buy an item that is defective or does not meet your needs. Suppose you go to a hardware store to buy a screwdriver and a can of white paint. When you get them home, you open the can with your new screwdriver. At about the same moment, two things happen. The top of your screwdriver breaks off and you see that the paint is light blue, not white!

Before you decide whether to take the screwdriver and paint back, you need to consider whether you have lived up to your responsibilities. Since a screwdriver is not designed for opening cans, you cannot blame the seller or manufacturer for its breaking. When you recheck the paint can, however, you notice that its label *does* read *white*. In this case, you have a shopping problem that needs resolving. Because the product does not reflect the claim made on its label, you will probably decide to return the paint.

When shopping problems arise that lead you to make a return, you will want to contact the seller or manufacturer. If you are unable to settle your problem with either of these businesses, you can seek assistance from others.

Contact the Seller or Manufacturer

Returning an item is often, but not always, a simple matter. Businesses are required by law to accept a return if the item they sold

Why is it a good idea to contact the seller first when you are trying to resolve a shopping problem?

174   Developing Your Shopping Skills

Monthly Sales Calendar

JANUARY	FEBRUARY	MARCH	APRIL

Dishes
Furniture
Housewares
Radios
Rugs, carpets
Sheets, towels
Small appliances
Stereo equipment
Tape recorders
	Air conditioners
	Bedding
	Bicycles
	Curtains, drapes
	Radios
	Rugs, carpets
	Shoes
	Televisions
	Used cars
		Bedding
		Dishes
		Garden tools
		Laundry
		  appliances
		Shoes
		Luggage
			Dresses
			Fabrics
			Laundry
			  appliances
			Men's suits
			Rugs, carpets
			Sheets, towels
			Televisions

MAY	JUNE	JULY	AUGUST

Blankets, quilts
Camping
  equipment
Dishwashers
Housewares
Summer
  sportswear
Televisions
	Bedding
	Coats
	Fabrics
	Furniture
		Air conditioners
		Coats
		Radios
		Rugs, carpets
		Sheets, towels
		Shoes
		Sports equipment
		Stereo equipment
		Summer
		  sportswear
			Air conditioners
			Bedding
			Curtains, drapes
			Electric fans
			Furniture
			Lamps
			New cars
			Rugs, carpets
			Sheets, towels
			Sports equipment
			Curtains, draperies

SEPTEMBER	OCTOBER	NOVEMBER	DECEMBER

Bicycles
Dishes
Furniture
Gardening
  equipment
Housewares
Laundry
  appliances
New cars
Rugs, carpets
	Bicycles
	Boats
	Cars
	Dishes
	Glassware
	Lawn furniture
	Silverware
	Sports equipment
		Blankets, quilts
		Dresses
		Fabrics
		Men's suits
		Shoes
		Used cars
			Blankets, quilts
			Dishwashers
			Microwave
			  ovens
			Holiday cards,
			  ornaments
			  (after holidays)
			Party goods
			Televisions

Settling Shopping Problems

was defective or inaccurately described to you. Generally, though, businesses are so interested in having satisfied customers that they establish quite generous return policies. Such policies cover more than the law requires.

There are three types of return policies. Some businesses make exchanges. They have an **exchange policy,** which allows a customer to return an item and get a replacement or an item that costs the same.

Some businesses make refunds. They have a **refund policy,** which allows a customer to return an item and get the purchase money back. If the customer paid in cash, the refund is made at once. A customer who paid by personal check, however, may have to wait until the bank clears the check. Then, the business will refund the money in cash.

Some businesses adjust the customer's credit. They have a **return for credit policy,** which allows the customer to return an item and either get credit for future purchases or have the charge removed from the customer's charge account.

Be aware that a seller's return policy may not be the same for all of its items. Often the return policy applies only to items not bought on sale. Before you make a purchase, find out the seller's return policy. In some states, each seller is required by law to post its return policy.

You will save time and other resources if you can avoid making returns of merchandise. If you need to make a return, however, it helps to be aware of each of the following points:

- The item you are returning must be in its original condition.
- Usually, the item must be unused.
- You must have the sales receipt.

Personal Visits

When you return an item, go expecting to be helped. Keep a positive attitude as you tell the salesperson what is wrong and what you want. Be calm but firm.

If the first answer you get is not satisfactory, go to the manager or someone in a higher position and follow the same procedure. In any event, note the name of each person with whom you discuss the problem.

Letters

Sometimes, you cannot resolve a shopping problem in person. For example, the manufacturer of an item may be located out of town. In such cases, you may need to write a letter. For an example, see the sample letter of complaint on the opposite page. Like that sample, your letter should be positive, clear, and to the point. Keep copies of your letter and related records. Mail your letter certified, with a return receipt requested.

Seek Assistance from Others

In those instances when you are unable to get your problem settled by contacting the seller or manufacturer, you may have to seek assistance. You can get it from the sources shown in the illustration on page 178. If all else fails, you may even need the help of a lawyer. To learn where you might find that kind of legal assistance, see page 179.

Trade and Professional Organizations

Sometimes, trade and professional organizations can help you. Such organizations usually want their trade or profession to have a good public image. Therefore, they want customers to be satisfied. As a group, organization members may be able to put some pressure on the seller. To request assistance, either call or write to the organization that represents the seller's trade or profession.

Consumer Action Reporters

You may decide to call a consumer action reporter at a local radio station, television station, or newspaper for help. After you explain your problem, the reporter may contact the seller or manufacturer to get an explanation. Often, by merely requesting such an explanation, the reporter will get action. To avoid bad publicity, the seller or manufacturer may agree to settle the matter at once.

Better Business Bureaus

You can seek assistance from your local Better Business Bureau (BBB). To do so, you need to file a complaint. In your letter of complaint, be sure to mention the steps you have taken in trying to reach a settlement with the seller or manufacturer. Enclose copies of all letters, including the names and addresses of all concerned.

Your local BBB will investigate your complaint by writing to the company. The BBB

What are the key elements of every letter of complaint?

- Describe your purchase.
- State product and serial or model number, or type of service performed.
- Include date and location of purchase and other details.
- State problem in a calm and businesslike way.
- Give history of problem.
- Ask for specific action.
- Enclose copies of documents.
- State reasonable time for action.
- Include telephone numbers and address.
- Sign the letter.

```
                         Your Address
                         Your City, State, and Zip Code
                         Date

Appropriate Person
Company Name
Street Address
City, State, and Zip Code

Dear Company President:

    Last week I purchased (or had repaired) a (give
the name of the product complete with the serial or
model number, or the service performed). I made
this purchase at (state the store's name, location,
date, and other important details of the
transaction).

    Unfortunately, your product (or service) has not
performed satisfactorily (or the service was
inadequate) because _____.
Therefore, to solve the problem, I would appreciate
your (here state the specific action you want).
Enclosed are copies (copies—NOT originals) of my
records (receipts, guarantees, warranties,
cancelled checks, contracts, model and serial
numbers, and any other documents).

    I am looking forward to your reply and resolution
of my problem and will wait three weeks before
seeking third-party assistance. Contact me at the
above address or by phone at (home and office
numbers here).

                         Sincerely,


                         Your Name
```

Settling Shopping Problems

Seller
- Salesperson
- Manager/Owner

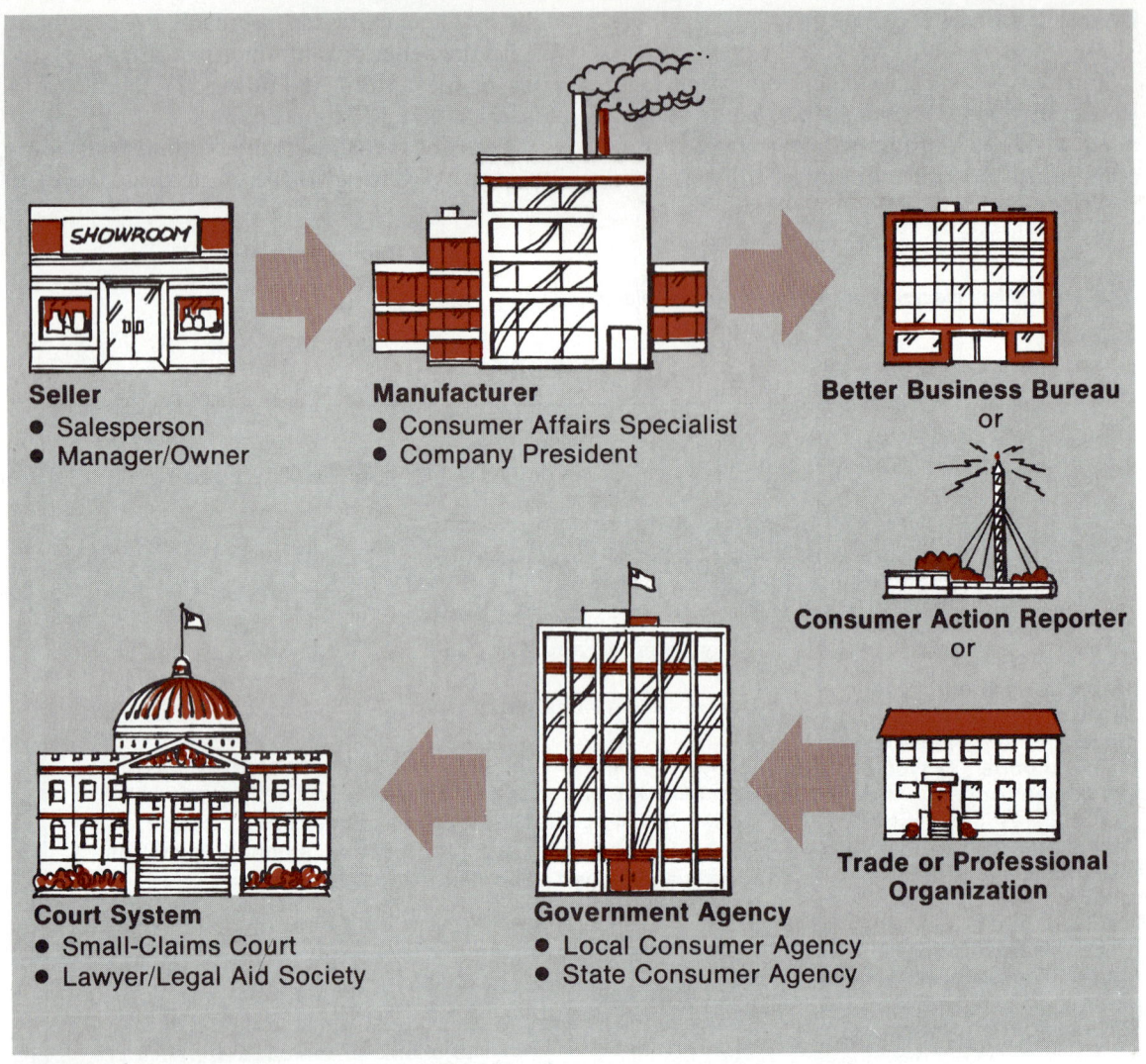

Manufacturer
- Consumer Affairs Specialist
- Company President

Better Business Bureau
or

Consumer Action Reporter
or

Trade or Professional Organization

Government Agency
- Local Consumer Agency
- State Consumer Agency

Court System
- Small-Claims Court
- Lawyer/Legal Aid Society

To settle a shopping problem, contact the seller first. If necessary, contact the manufacturer next. If you need assistance, you can seek it from others in the order shown here. At what point does it make sense to get legal assistance?

will not only report your complaint but also request a response. If you are not satisfied with the company's response, you can ask the BBB to hear your case. If the company agrees to this process, the BBB will arrange for a trained, unbiased individual or group to judge your case. If you think the decision is fair, you will sign a statement that says you agree to be bound by this decision. By signing this statement, you will be giving up the right to appeal your case in court. Usually, this is a quick and effective way to resolve a consumer complaint.

Government Agencies

Another way to try to settle your problem is to write to state and local government agencies. All states and many cities and counties have a central department or agency that deals with consumer problems. It may be part of the state attorney general's office or a separate consumer affairs bureau or consumer protection agency. Check your telephone directory or call your city or county government if you have trouble locating the appropriate agency.

178 Developing Your Shopping Skills

P.S. Where Can You Get Legal Assistance?

Have you ever thought you might need legal advice and wondered where you could get it? Like most people, you may find yourself in situations where such advice may be helpful. Here are some typical situations:

- You are about to sign a legal document such as a contract or lease.
- You want to write a will.
- You want to start a business.
- You want to bring a suit against someone.
- You need to protect your rights because someone is bringing a suit against you.

You may also need legal advice about consumer complaints, traffic violations, civil rights protection, or employment disagreements.

Lawyers in private practice are good sources of legal assistance. A private attorney can also help point you to other sources for help if he or she understands your circumstances. To find a lawyer, call the local, county, or state bar association for a referral. The fee for a half-hour consultation with a lawyer is usually small.

Sometimes, however, lawyers in private practice prove more costly than most young people can afford. In this case, your needs may be met just as well by a legal aid society. Check your telephone book for the legal aid society in your area and for other sources of legal assistance. For example, many universities also have legal aid offices and can supply students with information and leads on seeking further help.

Small-Claims Court

You may decide to take your problem to **small-claims court.** These are courts established to handle minor legal problems and thus relieve an overburdened legal system. They have some advantages over the regular court system. They give faster responses and cost less to operate and use. At the same time, they offer final, legally binding, and enforceable answers to disputes.

Some small-claims courts offer handbooks or guides on procedures. Others have presentations, training sessions, or individuals who counsel you. These services not only help you understand the procedures better but also eliminate some uncertainty and fear so you can represent yourself successfully.

Although the procedures and regulations for use of small-claims courts vary among states, the following general guidelines apply in most instances:

- You should plan to represent yourself.
- You should plan to file a simple statement and pay very low fees.
- You need to let the court know if you want your case decided by a jury. Otherwise, the trial will be heard by a judge.

At the hearing, you and the seller will present your testimony, evidence, and any witnesses you have. A decision will then be reached. If you are dissatisfied with it, you can appeal to a higher court—usually the county or municipal court.

Points to Remember

- Your needs, values, goals, and resources determine which products and services you will buy.
- How you use your resources depends on the opportunity costs you are willing to accept.
- In deciding on places to shop, you should compare the advantages and disadvantages of buying from different kinds of sellers.
- Before buying a service, check on the seller's reputation and ask for a price estimate.
- You can take advantage of sales by watching for special sale times, knowing the regular prices, and being able to identify merchandise that will be acceptable to you.
- Courteous shoppers add to the enjoyment of shopping and help keep prices down.
- Shoplifters not only break the law but also cause prices to rise.
- Settling consumer problems takes time, patience, and in some cases, the assistance of others.

Test Your Skills

RESOURCE MANAGEMENT

Imagine yourself in the situation described below. In this situation, resources need managing. As you read, think about the ways that you can manage resources. Then, answer the questions that follow. When you need to manage resources in the future, remember to ask yourself these questions.

Situation

Saturday was turning out even busier than you had planned. You promised to help your dad tear down a shed in the afternoon. First, however, you helped your younger sister sand an antique chest she was refinishing. Then, just before noon you drove to town to deposit your paycheck and buy a jacket on sale at the western wear store. You wanted to wear it on a date that night. In your rush to get back home and help with the shed, you picked up the wrong-sized jacket.

You have a problem: It will take all afternoon to take down the shed if you and your dad do the work by yourselves. Yet, you need almost an hour of the afternoon to get back to town and exchange the jacket before the store closes. One thing you are *not* worried about is making the exchange. You kept your receipt and know that the store will allow you to exchange one size for another. You checked on the store's return policy before you made your first purchase there a few months ago. One thing you *are* worried about is letting your dad down after promising to work with him on the shed.

Questions

1. Which resource do you need to manage most carefully? Why? (Hint: Look for the resource that is in shortest supply.)

2. What are the ways you might manage this resource? (Hint: Be sure to name the resource(s) you could substitute, trade, or share.)

3. What opportunity costs would be involved in each case?

4. Who would pay the opportunity costs in each case?

5. After considering all these opportunity costs, how would you manage your resources in this situation?

Terms

On a separate sheet of paper, write a definition for each of the underlined terms below. Base your definition on the clues you find in the sentence(s).

1. Tanya used comparison shopping to find the best buy on water skis. Now she has skis that have the features she wants. They also cost less than she had planned to pay and have a good warranty.
2. A shoe repair service and an ice cream parlor are both specialty shops.
3. Mike likes to buy from consumer cooperatives. He buys from a food co-op and a book co-op. One of them charges a membership fee. Both offer him lower prices than he finds elsewhere.
4. Carlos could never be accused of impulse buying. He buys only what is on his shopping lists.
5. When Mia arrived at the store, the advertised sale-priced perfume had sold out. The cashier gave Mia a special ticket called a rain check. The next week the store got a new shipment of the perfume. Mia used her rain check to buy the perfume at the sale price.
6. Some drugstores may use facial tissue, vitamins, and batteries as loss leaders. Many customers will be attracted to the sale-priced items and then may buy nonsale items as well.
7. Peggy was arrested for shoplifting when she walked out of the store with a bracelet for which she had not paid.
8. The concert was cancelled because the star performer had laryngitis. Tran, who had paid $15 for a ticket, received a $15 refund.
9. Going to small-claims court is sometimes the best way to resolve a consumer complaint. This kind of court handles minor legal problems.

Questions

1. How do your values, goals, and resources determine what you buy?
2. Why must you consider opportunity costs before you buy a product or service?
3. Under what circumstances might you decide against doing comparison shopping?
4. What factors do you need to consider as you decide where to shop?
5. Why would you want to select items carefully that are sold "as is"?
6. Name two ways to make good decisions when buying items over the telephone or from door-to-door salespeople.

7. Why is it important to consider a seller's reputation?
8. Why is it a good idea to get an estimate before buying a service?
9. Describe how you can resist impulse buying.
10. How can you be a responsible shopper?
11. List three conditions that most return policies require you to meet.
12. How can the Better Business Bureau help you resolve a complaint?
13. When might you want to use the services of a small-claims court?

Activities

1. Think of a product you would like or need to buy. Evaluate your plan to buy this item on the basis of the following:
    a. Will you need to gather much information about the product? Why or why not?
    b. Do you have the time and other resources to get the amount of information you will need?
    c. Where could you buy this item? List as many types of businesses as possible.
    d. Of the businesses you listed, which do you think will probably give you the best buy? Why?

2. Make a poster of the types of businesses you buy from most often. Identify them according to their type, the selection of merchandise, and the services they offer. Also include the prices they charge and the reasons you do or do not like shopping with the businesses.

3. Describe your shopping style. Your answers to the following questions can help you write your description:
    a. Are you an impulse buyer? If so, for what items and how often?
    b. For what items have you used comparison shopping?
    c. Do you like shopping at busy or quiet times?
    d. In what ways have you taken advantage of sales?
    e. How do you usually treat people and property while you shop?
    f. How would you rate yourself as a shopper? If you could improve your style, how would you do it?

4. Of the three types of return policies, which do you prefer and why? When would a store's policy influence your decision to buy?

5. Imagine that you ask a business to repair or replace a faulty product or refund your money. The business does not do what you ask. Write a complaint letter to one of the following: the manufacturer, the Better Business Bureau, or a local government agency.

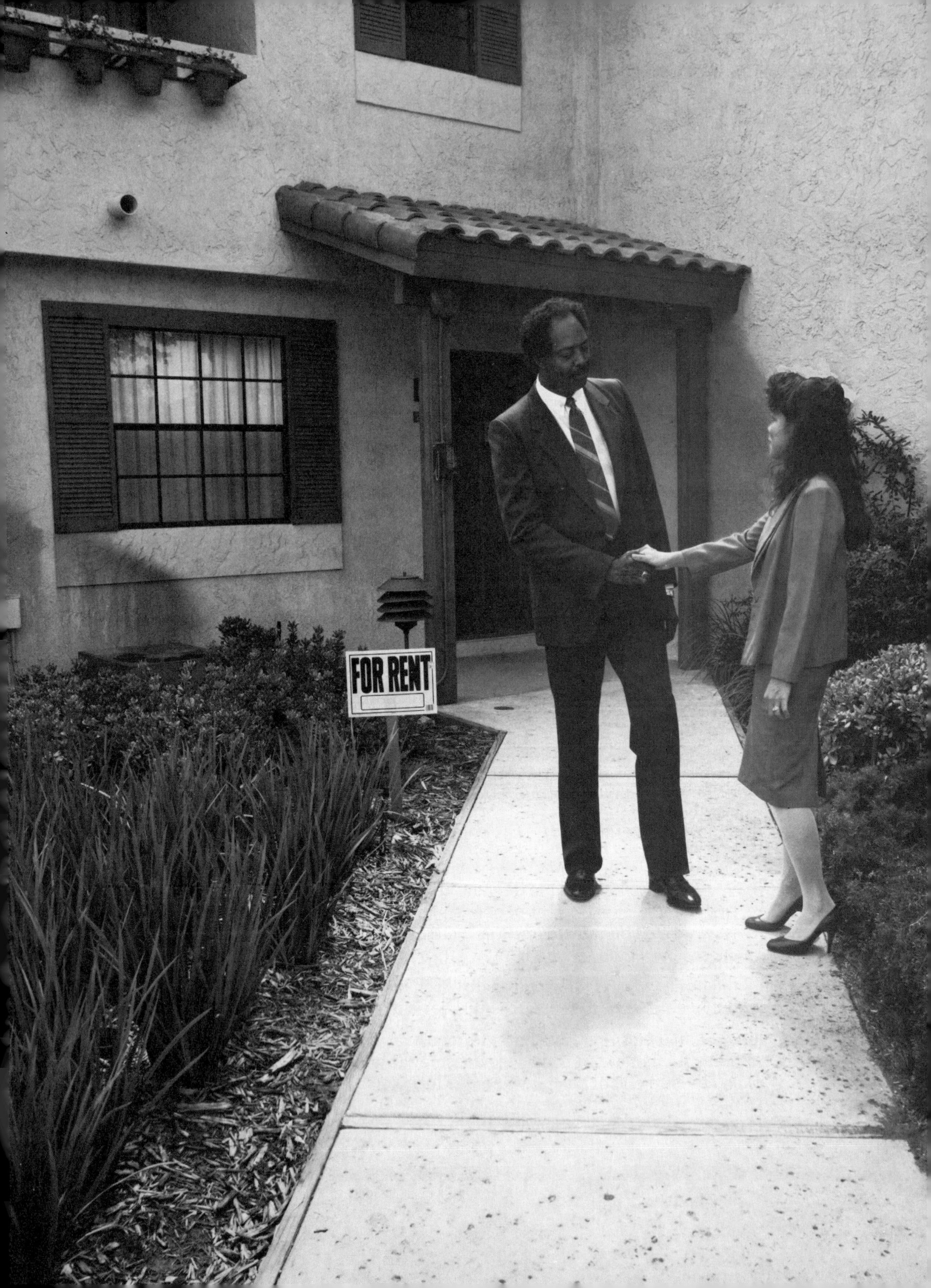
FOR RENT

CHAPTER 9

Arranging for Housing

Many young people look forward to graduating from high school and having a place of their own. They are eager to be independent and make decisions about housing, furnishings, and decorating.

Other young people prefer to live at home for some time after graduation. They think that the security, comfort, and savings of living with their families for a few more years will better prepare them for setting up a home of their own.

Right now, you may have opinions about moving out on your own or continuing to stay at home. However, before you make a decision, consider all the facts about your choices. Ask yourself questions like these: How much does it really cost to set up a home for yourself? Can you afford it? Is that how you want to spend your money? Would you like living alone? Can you find roommates who are easy to get along with and reliable about paying bills? Is there housing available at reasonable rates in your community? What are the typical rental deposits and utility bills that will add to the basic cost of a housing unit in your area?

Perhaps you think these details are not important, but they definitely are. Moving out on your own can be a great experience or a big, expensive mistake. The difference depends on planning. To plan, you need to know the answers to all these questions, and more. Being informed about your choices can help you make a housing decision that is right for you.

Discover Through Your Reading

- what kinds of housing expenses you will have when you get a place of your own
- what furnishings and equipment you will need to live on your own
- how to decide whether you want to continue living at home, live with roommates, or live alone
- how to determine whether a neighborhood is right for you
- why it is important to understand a lease

Thinking About Housing Costs

You will probably make several moves during your adult life. For example, your work may require you to move to a new community, perhaps in another state or region. A change in the size of your family or in the amount of your income may make a move likely or desirable. Because housing and utilities will be among your biggest expenses, you will want to learn about these expenses before you move.

Whenever you establish a residence in your name, you must consider the costs of security deposits and connection fees required by utility companies. If you are renting, you must also consider the cost of any security deposits required by the landlord. You must also think about regular housing expenses such as rent or mortgage payments, utilities, and insurance. Finally, you must consider the costs of any furnishings and equipment that you will need for your home. By totaling all of these costs, you will have a fairly realistic tally of probable housing costs.

Security Deposits

One of your first housing expenses will be the payment of security deposits. A **security deposit** is money a person pays to guarantee that he or she will take care of property and pay bills promptly. Usually, you pay a security deposit when you sign a rental agreement and when you arrange for a utility service.

A rental security deposit may be the amount of one month's rent or more. However, it may be two or even three months' rent. Pet owners are often required to make an additional security deposit to cover any damages caused by a pet and any special cleaning procedures. Each security deposit is kept until your rental agreement ends. If you complete the agreement and do not damage the property, your security deposit will usually be returned. Your rental agreement will indicate whether your deposit will be returned, how soon it will be returned, and whether it will earn interest. Often, security deposits are returned within thirty to sixty days after you move out. Do not forget to ask for return of your security deposits when you move. If you move before your rental agreement ends or if you damage the property, you may lose all or part of your deposits.

Security deposits for utilities vary. A deposit for electricity, gas, or telephone service might equal one or two months' use or might be a flat fee. This deposit must be paid before service can begin. It is usually returned to you after a certain period of time, sometimes with interest. Once you have established a utility service in your name, you begin to build a credit reference. When you move to another community, your new utility company may accept this credit reference instead of a security deposit. In addition to a security deposit, most utilities charge a connection fee. This fee usually appears on your first bill.

It is not always easy to find a rental unit that will accept a renter with a large pet. If you find a place that does, what must you be prepared to do?

186 Arranging for Housing

Regular Housing Expenses

Your regular housing expenses include rent or mortgage payments, utilities, and insurance. While rent or mortgage payments and utilities are usually paid monthly, insurance may be paid quarterly, semiannually, or annually.

As a young adult, you will probably rent rather than own your own home. Therefore, you will have rent payments rather than mortgage payments. To get a rough estimate of your regular housing expenses, if you rent, do some investigating. Contact several landlords to find out the range of rents in your community. Call your local utility companies to get information with which to estimate a typical monthly bill. Estimate the value of your most important possessions and contact several insurance companies to get an idea of insurance costs. These estimates will be your major housing expenses.

Rent

Most financial experts suggest that you spend no more for rent than the amount of one week's paycheck. You may, however, find that there is little or no housing available at rents that allow you to stay within this limit. Instead, you may find yourself paying almost two weeks' take-home pay for rent each month. In this situation, there is little money left for food, clothing, automobile payments and expenses, medical needs, and entertainment. Remember, the more you spend for rent, the less you have available for everything else in your life.

Utilities

Utilities may include electricity, gas, fuel oil, water and sewer service, garbage pickup, telephone service, and cable television. The amount of money you need for utilities depends on which ones you have and how much you use them. For example, your electric bill may be quite high if you run your air conditioner twenty-four hours a day at 70°F (21°C). Your telephone bill may be low if you make few long-distance calls or keep your long-distance calls brief.

Insurance

When you first get out on your own, you may have only a few valuable items such as a stereo, a television, or a musical instrument. If these items were stolen or accidentally damaged, you would probably find it difficult to replace them. Household insurance could protect you in such a situation.

The cost of household insurance will vary with the particular company, the specific items you want insured, and the deductible. For example, the higher the deductible you are willing to pay, the lower the cost of insurance. To keep down the cost of your household insurance, insure only your most valuable items. Otherwise, your insurance policy might cost you more than the cost of replacing the items without insurance.

Furnishings and Equipment

In addition to security deposits and regular housing expenses, you need to consider how much it will cost you to furnish and equip a home. Perhaps your parents, relatives, or neighbors can lend or give you some of the items you will need. Maybe you can take something and adapt it for a new purpose. For example, you might paint an old sewing machine cabinet or turn a packing crate into a practical end table. For those items you do need to buy, you may be able to cut costs by shopping in secondhand stores and at garage sales.

Selecting Home Furnishings and Equipment

Some of the items you may need to select for your home include furniture, kitchen equipment, household textiles, accessories,

Sometimes, a good way to save money on furnishings is to make your own. Do you already know how or know someone who could show you how to make basic furnishings?

and household maintenance equipment. Selecting these items can be a challenge, and even fun. If you buy these things, you will want to get the most for your money. Therefore, you need to be aware of the different types of furnishings and equipment available to you. You also need to identify the factors associated with quality in furnishings and equipment.

Furniture

Before buying any piece of furniture, you need to decide how and where you want to use it. You also need to decide how long you want to keep it. These decisions will influence your choice of style, color, material, and quality of construction. These decisions will also influence the amount of money you spend and where you shop for the item.

You may, for example, live in a small apartment without space for a bed. If you plan to stay in the apartment for several years, you might buy a sofa bed. If you decide to invest in a sofa bed, you will want a style and color that you really like. You will also want a type of material and quality of construction that will last. For tips to help you identify quality furniture, see page 189. To find what you want, you will probably do comparison shopping in department stores, discount stores, and specialty shops. On the other hand, if you plan to move to a place

What are some reasons knockdown furniture might be a good buy for someone who rents rather than owns a home?

with a separate bedroom in a few months, you might buy a small cot, instead. You will probably not be too concerned with its style or color. You are not likely to do comparison shopping and may shop flea markets and secondhand stores.

If you plan to move often, you may want to consider renting furniture for short periods or buying knockdown furniture. Rental furniture is available in many communities. Knockdown furniture comes in pieces that you put together or take apart as necessary. It is usually inexpensive and sturdy and will often fit into a box for easy moving.

Beds

Like most furniture pieces, beds come in various styles and are made of different materials. Maybe you would like a conventional bed with a headboard and a footboard made of wood or metal. Perhaps you prefer a set of box springs and a mattress on the floor. Maybe you really want a water bed. When buying a bed, remember that it is likely to be one of your largest and heaviest pieces of furniture. Its weight, its cost, the size of your bedroom, and the number of moves you anticipate will influence your selection of a bed.

If you buy a conventional bed, you will want to choose the best quality springs and mattress that you can afford. To determine quality, consider the number of coils or springs used, the amount of padding over the coils, and the type and durability of the cover fabric. Box springs are usually considered to be the best type of springs you can buy. Mattresses are available in extra-firm, firm, medium, and soft styles. For the best back support during sleep, you may want to choose a firm or extra-firm style. If you suffer from asthma or allergies, you may want to select a foam mattress instead of a spring mattress. If your budget is tight, you might want to consider an inflatable air mattress like the ones used for camping.

If you buy a water bed, you will need special equipment. For example, you will need devices for filling and emptying the bed, patching the bed if necessary, heating the water, and preventing bacterial growth in the water. The total cost of upkeep for a water bed is worth considering before you make your decision. It is also important to know that some landlords do not allow water beds.

Couches and Chairs

An upholstered piece of furniture is one that is made more comfortable and attractive by the use of padding and a fabric cover-

---

Tips

Judging the Quality of Furniture

To identify the quality of construction for a piece of furniture, check for each of the following characteristics:

- The joints, legs, and other areas where two pieces connect should be solid and sturdy.

- The wood, metal, plastic, or other material should be strong enough to support weight and withstand use.

- Drawers and doors should open and close smoothly.

- Corners of the drawers and other sections should be dovetailed, formed from sturdy, interlocking pieces.

- The surfaces should be even and unwarped.

- The edges should be free of splinters and cracks.

- Fabric coverings should be easy to clean. Most are now made of fabrics that have a finish that helps them resist stains.

ing. While couches are usually upholstered, chairs may or may not be upholstered. For example, you would probably want an upholstered chair in your living area and maybe in a formal dining area. You might not, however, want upholstered chairs for use with a kitchen table or desk. Some couches and chairs are completely upholstered in that you see little, if any, of the frame. Other pieces have cushions but also have much of the frame showing. These pieces may offer greater versatility and also be lighter in weight.

Tables and Storage Pieces

Of all the furniture pieces, tables and storage pieces probably offer the greatest flexibility in style, material, color, and use. You can choose, for example, from card tables, drop-leaf tables, and dining room tables with extensions. You can select either open tables or enclosed tables that double as storage for records, magazines, books, or other items. You can choose shelves that hang from walls or stand alone and are designed for storage of a wide variety of items. You can buy these pieces of furniture as part of a set or as single pieces. You can buy unpainted furniture and, then, finish it yourself. You can even create furniture from concrete blocks or bricks and plywood.

Kitchen Equipment

Even if you plan to do little cooking at home, you will probably want your kitchen to include the basics. You will need some equipment for cooking on top of the range and in the oven. You may want a few small appliances to make food preparation easier and faster. You will certainly need dishware, flatware, and glassware for eating and equipment and supplies for storing food and cleaning up after you eat.

Before choosing kitchen equipment, you need to consider the kind of food preparation you will be doing and how often you will do it. Once you decide on the items you need, think about their characteristics. Then, you can choose the specific items that will be best for you.

Kitchen Utensils

The small items that help you prepare food are called kitchen utensils. For example, bottle and can openers and kitchen scissors are needed to open or prepare many foods. Measuring spoons and measuring cups are needed for ensuring accurate amounts of ingredients. Chef's knives, carving knives, paring knives, peelers, and graters/shredders are used for cutting, chopping, or peeling many foods. Cutting boards are needed to protect kitchen counter surfaces. Mixing bowls, wooden spoons, mashers, and rotary beaters are used to combine ingredients. Cooking spoons, turners, meat forks, tongs, and ladles are used for stirring, lifting, or turning foods. Strainers and colanders are used for draining foods. These commonly used kitchen utensils are shown on page 191.

Cookware

Skillets, saucepans, and saucepots are all types of cookware because they are usually used to cook foods on top of the range. Cookware is often sold in sets. Some sets may include only one type of cookware, such as saucepans. Others may include a combination of skillets, saucepans, and saucepots. Cookware may also be bought by the individual piece.

When buying cookware, remember that it is available in many sizes. Skillets can be 8 inches, 10 inches, or 12 inches in diameter. Saucepans, which have one long handle, are usually made in 1-quart, 1½-quart, 2-quart, and 3-quart sizes. Saucepots, which have two short handles, may be made in 3-quart, 4-quart, or 5-quart sizes. Plan to buy the sizes that you will use most often. Look for cookware with heat-resistant, easy-to-hold handles; flat bottoms; and snugly fitting lids. Also, look for cookware made of material that is a good conductor, or distributor, of heat.

Bakeware

Muffin pans, cookie sheets, cake pans, pie plates, roasting pans, and some casserole dishes are all types of bakeware. These items are most often used in the oven to bake or broil foods. Because bakeware comes in many sizes and shapes, you will want to select items that best meet your needs. Popular sizes of cake pans are the 8-inch and 9-inch round pans and the 8-inch by 8-inch square pan. Common sizes of casserole dishes are the 1-quart, 1½-quart, 2-quart, 2½-quart, and 3-quart casseroles.

Small Appliances

When choosing small appliances, consider only those that you will use most often. Any small appliance that is not used at least one to three hours weekly is probably unnecessary to own. It is possible that you will want an electric can opener, a toaster, and possibly an electric mixer and a coffee maker. You might also find at least one multipurpose appliance helpful. A toaster oven, a slow cooker, an electric skillet, and a blender are examples of multipurpose appliances. In addition, you might want special-purpose appliances. An electric wok, a yogurt maker, a popcorn popper, and a deep fryer are examples of these kinds of appliances. Remember to look for appliances with heat-resistant

Kitchen Utensils

Bottle Opener Can Opener Kitchen Scissors Measuring Spoons Measuring Cups

Chef's Knife Carving Knife Paring Knife Parer Grater/Shredder

Cutting Board Mixing Bowls Wooden Spoon Masher Rotary Beater

Cooking Spoons Turner Meat Fork Tongs Ladle

Strainer Colander

Selecting Home Furnishings and Equipment

This table has been set with the pieces from two starter sets, one of dinnerware and one of flatware, and four water glasses. What other dinnerware might be needed to serve four people?

handles and a UL (Underwriters' Laboratories) seal of approval.

Dinnerware and Flatware

Plates, cups, saucers, bowls, and platters are called dinnerware. Dinner knives, forks, and spoons are called flatware. When you buy dinnerware or flatware, you will probably buy a certain number of place settings. A **place setting** is the set of basic items used by a person for eating. A place setting of dinnerware includes a dinner plate, a salad plate, a cup, and a saucer. Sometimes, a cereal bowl, a fruit dish, or a dessert plate is also included. A place setting of flatware includes a dinner knife, a dinner fork, a salad fork, and a teaspoon.

You can also buy many patterns, or designs, of dinnerware in starter sets or from open stock. A **starter set** is usually the group of items that four persons will use when eating. **Open stock** is the dinnerware, flatware, and glassware available for purchase as individual pieces.

Glassware

A complete glassware set includes six or eight glasses in 4-ounce, 8-ounce, and 10-ounce or 12-ounce sizes. The smallest sizes are usually used for serving juices and the largest for serving the main beverage during a meal. While you will probably use tumblers, drinking glasses without stems, each day, you may occasionally use stemware for water and other beverages.

Food Storage and Clean-Up Equipment

To complete your kitchen equipment, you will need containers for storing leftover foods. Your best choices are multipurpose containers. They can be used in the freezer, in the refrigerator, and in conventional and microwave ovens and are dishwasher-safe. Other containers are more limited in their use or may even be disposable. In addition to storage containers, you will also need some items for cleaning up after food preparation and eating. These items might include a dish drainer and tray.

Household Textiles

Any fabric item that is used as a home furnishing is called a household textile. From time to time, you will need to buy some of these items. For example, you will want to have dish towels, dishcloths, and pot holders

192 Arranging for Housing

to use in your kitchen. You may need a tablecloth, placemats, or even cloth napkins for dining. You will need bed and bath linens. You may even need to provide your own window and floor coverings. Household textiles that are durable and easy to care for will be your best buys.

Bed and Bath Linens

Perhaps your family can give you pillows, a mattress cover or pad, a bedspread or comforter, sheets, pillowcases, blankets, bath towels, and washcloths. If you must buy these furnishings, remember the following facts:

- Both percale and muslin sheets and pillowcases are available in "no iron" styles.
- Because percale bed linens have high thread counts, they are more durable than other bed linens. Likewise, percale sheets and pillowcases are usually more expensive than other bed linens.
- Polyester fiberfill pillows and foam pillows are usually moderately priced. Down pillows and feather pillows are the most expensive.
- Electric blankets are more expensive than regular blankets.
- Towels made of cotton are usually the most absorbent.

Window and Floor Coverings

Depending on your housing arrangement, you may have to buy your own window and floor coverings. For window coverings, you might choose shades, mini or vertical blinds, curtains, or draperies. Your choice of a window covering will determine the type of curtain rod, if any, that you need. For example, traverse rods are usually needed for draw draperies. These rods are more expensive than tension rods, which are appropriate for cafe curtains set into a window.

For floor coverings, you might choose rugs, area carpets, or wall-to-wall carpeting. Of

Window Coverings

Shades

Venetian Blinds

Mini Blinds

Curtains

Draperies

Regular Curtain Rod

Tension Rod

Traverse Rod

Selecting Home Furnishings and Equipment

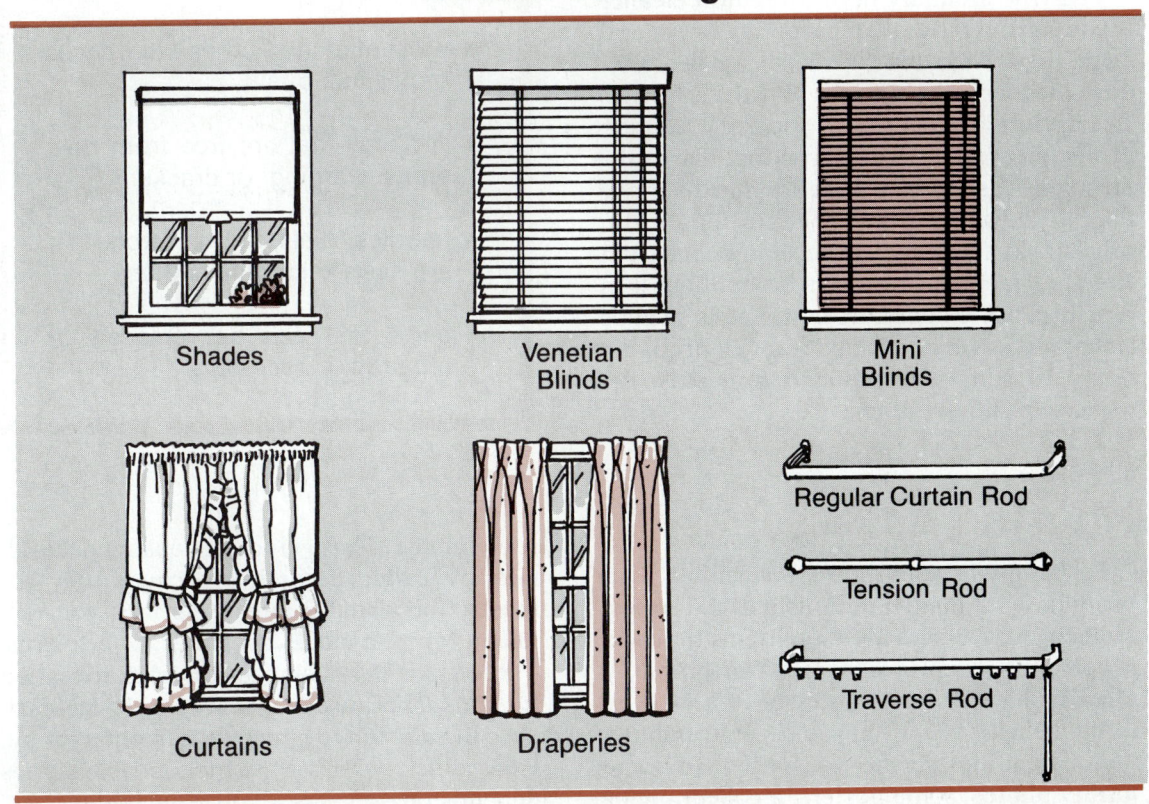

these, rugs will be the least expensive. You usually find rugs in standard sizes such as 2 feet by 3 feet or 12 feet by 15 feet. The smaller ones often have nonskid backings to make them safer.

Household Maintenance Equipment

Certain kinds of equipment are needed to maintain a comfortable place to live. For example, you may need to provide your own fan or air conditioner, space heater, and humidifier or dehumidifier. Because these items can be quite expensive, you will want to shop carefully. The tips on this page may help you.

In addition to maintaining a comfortable home, you will want to keep your home clean. Your basic cleaning equipment such as wastebaskets, a broom, a dust pan, a dust mop, a sponge mop, a scrub brush, a bucket, and dust cloths may be relatively inexpensive. A vacuum cleaner, however, can be a major expense.

You will probably need a vacuum cleaner if you have wall-to-wall carpeting or several large rugs. There are two basic styles of vacuum cleaners, the upright and the canister. The upright cleaner usually does the best job of cleaning wall-to-wall carpeting. The canister model is usually best for hard-surface floors and above-the-floor cleaning. You might also need an electric shampooer from time to time. However, it is probably best to rent expensive floor-care equipment such as a shampooer or a polisher. You will probably not use them often enough to justify the expense of buying them.

Tips
Buying Household Maintenance Equipment

A fan, an air conditioner, a space heater, a vacuum cleaner, and other appliances are important purchases. Be sure that those you buy are safe and in good working condition. Look for the following features:

- a UL seal that indicates an electrical product has been designed to be safe when used according to manufacturer directions

- plugs and cords in excellent condition, not frayed, broken, or damaged in any way

- use-and-care booklets that provide clear and thorough instructions

- warranties and other assurances of product quality

- surfaces that are free from rust, dents, warping, or cracks

- handles, dials, and controls that are easy to identify and use

- parts that can be replaced or repaired, if necessary

Housing Accessories

To complete your home furnishings list, you will want to include housing accessories. **Housing accessories** are those items that add a personal touch to a home. You probably already have several accessories that you will take with you when you become an independent adult. Maybe you will take some family photos, some posters, a collection, or some plants. These kinds of housing accessories are called *decorative* because they are mostly for visual interest. Perhaps you will take a lamp, a clock, bookends, or a mirror. These kinds of housing accessories are called *functional* because they serve a practical purpose in addition to being visually interesting. How much you will spend on accessories depends on your taste and your budget.

Comparing Living Arrangements

By now you have a good idea of what it will cost to cover the many kinds of housing expenses. When you are deciding on a place to live, be as realistic as possible about your choices. For example, you might find it best to continue to live at home for a while. You might, however, choose to rent a place and live either with roommates or by yourself. Before making your decision, discuss the situation with your family. Maybe the experiences of older relatives or friends can be of help.

Living at Home

There are several advantages to both you and your family if you continue to live at home. Even if you pay for room and board or meals, you almost certainly cannot live anywhere more reasonably. You may feel safer and more secure at home than in a rental place. You will have the company of family members to keep you from feeling lonely. Your family, in turn, may appreciate your help with housework, with caring for younger brothers and sisters or older relatives, and with expenses.

There are also disadvantages if you continue to live at home. You will not have complete privacy. You may still have to follow family rules for curfews, parties, and other matters. Your family may continue to feel a great deal of responsibility for you. Therefore, you may find that it will take you a little longer to finally establish your independence than it would if you were living away from home.

Before deciding to continue living at home, discuss your concerns with your family. Maybe you can make some compromises so that all of you are comfortable with the standards established.

Living with Roommates

If you want to rent a place to live and cannot afford or do not want to live alone, you may want roommates. Roommates can help share expenses and household work and provide companionship. On the other hand, they may have different values from yours.

Depending on where you live, you may first think about asking friends to be your roommates. Before acting on this decision, remember that friends can be either great roommates or poor ones. The great ones are usually financially reliable and considerate. They are able to give and take and contribute their fair share. If you decide not to ask a friend, there are other ways to find roommates. The information on page 196 may help.

To make a good decision about a particular roommate, talk with the person about your expectations. Maybe you expect the place to be neat and clean all the time. Perhaps you plan to have your friends over every weekend. You may want to buy groceries together and split the bills evenly or you may want to buy groceries separately. Once each of you knows what the other expects, you have a better chance of having a successful living arrangement. If you both feel that the situation will work, you might want to put your guidelines in writing. This will help each of you make sure you understand the agreements you are reaching. If you cannot agree on a living arrangement and you decide the situation would not work out, you can continue to look for a roommate.

Living Alone

If you can afford it and not feel too lonely by yourself, then, living alone may be just for you. When you live alone, you can set your own schedules. You can invite friends over whenever you like. You can listen to the radio stations you prefer. You can prepare only the foods you like. On the other hand, you must pay the total rent and utilities. You must also take care of all household tasks yourself. In other words, living alone, like living at home or with roommates, has its advantages and disadvantages.

How Might You Find a Roommate?

P.S.

Sometimes, you already know a person whom you can ask to be your roommate. At other times, you need to find someone. Here are some ideas:

- **Ask around.** Often, people you know will have a friend who needs a roommate. They may give you some good leads.

- **Contact colleges and clubs that serve young people.** Colleges and clubs frequently provide roommate referrals. You might add your name to their lists of available roommates and contact people already listed.

- **Put up a notice on a bulletin board.** Supermarkets, schools, laundromats, and other places have bulletin boards for roommate notices. A typical notice might read, "Male, 21, wants to share apartment. Willing to pay $150; prefers own room. References on request. Phone 555-5498." It is best not to include your name or address.

- **Read classified ads.** Check newspaper "Roommates Wanted" or "Apartments to Share" listings. Ask someone who knows the area whether the apartments are in good neighborhoods. Ask for personal references so that you know the person looking for roommates is reliable. Take a friend so you have someone for a second opinion and for safety.

- **Use a roommate agency.** Roommate agencies match people who are looking for an apartment with people who have one to share. In some cities, using such an agency is the most efficient way to find a roommate. Reliable agencies require all applicants to list references. There is a fee—sometimes high—for the service.

Renting

When you first get a place of your own, you will probably rent. Renting provides a great deal of convenience with a minimum of responsibility. For example, you may not need to take care of the lawn or handle repairs. Instead, the **landlord,** the person who owns the property and offers it for rent, may assume this responsibility. In addition, renting is almost always less expensive than buying.

Like job hunting and beginning a job, renting is a process you may go through several times. It will be easier if you understand the various steps. You already know that you must decide how much rent you can afford. In addition, you need to know where to look for vacancies. You should consider whether you want a furnished or unfurnished place. You need to think about the type of housing unit you want and the kind of neighborhood you want to live in. Finally, you must make preparations to move and, then, move.

Identifying Sources of Rental Information

There are several ways to find out about housing vacancies. You can talk to your family and friends. You can check for rental notices on bulletin boards at schools, supermarkets, laundromats, community centers, and libraries. You can look for rental signs in windows or front lawns.

You can also skim the classified ad section of your newspaper. You will probably find the most ads in the Sunday edition. In these ads, you are likely to see many abbreviations. To understand what they may mean, see page 198. Be aware that some ads offer to locate apartments for a fee. Before paying such a fee, you might want to contact the Chamber of Commerce, Better Business Bureau, or local realty board. By doing this, you can find out whether any complaints have been filed against the rental agency.

You might also want to contact a real estate agency. Such an agency often employs rental agents, persons who represent both landlords and renters. There is usually a fee for this service, often equal to one month's rent or even more. Check to see whether you or the landlord will pay this fee. Perhaps you and the landlord will split the fee.

Considering Furnished or Unfurnished Places

A **furnished rental** is one that is equipped with many basic home furnishings. These usually include living-dining area furniture, bedroom furniture, kitchen equipment, and household textiles. As a rule, the more furnishings provided, the higher the rent.

An **unfurnished rental** is usually one that is equipped with a range and refrigerator but no other furnishings or equipment. Sometimes, air conditioning, wall-to-wall carpeting, a dishwasher, or a ceiling fan are also included. In general, the more equipment provided, the higher the rent. Therefore, an unfurnished rental is often less expensive than a furnished one.

Choosing a Type of Housing Unit

No matter where you live or want to live, you will probably find several types of housing units available for rent. You may find rooms and efficiency, or studio, apartments. You may also find apartments with one, two, or even more bedrooms and town, or row, houses. In addition, you may find mobile homes and houses for rent. You may even be able to find furnished and unfurnished places of each type. For more information on each type of housing unit, see pages 200–201.

It will be up to you to decide which type of housing unit offers the features you want and can afford. For example, you may want a home with a great deal of space or with many rooms. In general, the more space or rooms you get, the higher the rent. You may want a home that has a yard, a balcony, a garage, or a fireplace. You may want a home that

Tips

Understanding Housing Ads

Furn studio apt, pnld, cptg, a/c, mod BA, appl, util incl, pkg avail, res, immed, ref req, sec dep, short/long term.   Call 555-4402.

Would this apartment be right for you? The only way to know is to understand what the abbreviations used in classified housing ads mean. Here are some typical abbreviations and the meaning of each:

a/c	air-conditioned
appl	appliances (usually means a range and refrigerator are provided)
apt	apartment
BA	bath
bsmt	basement
cptg	carpeting
DR	dining room
elec	electricity (may describe the type of heat or indicate that this utility is included in the rent)
exc	excellent
fac	facilities
furn	furnished
gar	garage
immed	immediate occupancy (the apartment is available now)
kit priv	kitchen privileges (you can use the kitchen)
LR	living room
ldry	laundry
lg	large
loc	location
mo rates	monthly rates
mod	modern
nr trnsp	near transportation
newly dec	newly decorated
pkg avail	parking available
pnld	panelled
pvt	private
ref req	references required
res	residential neighborhood
sec dep	security deposit
short/long term	both short-term and long-term leases available
unfurn	unfurnished
util incl	utilities included (heat, water, electricity are included in the rent)

198   Arranging for Housing

includes a recreational facility such as a swimming pool, a weight room, a sauna, a clubhouse, a tennis or racquetball court, or a golf course. Usually, the more such features you want, the more you can expect to pay for rent. You may want to keep a large dog or another pet. In general, the more space the rental unit has, the more likely it is that you will be allowed to keep a pet, especially a large one. Also, the older the housing unit, the more likely it is that you will be able to keep a pet.

You may want neighbors close by. In general, the closer your neighbors, the more chances you will have for companionship. Living close to neighbors provides you opportunities for casual conversations and planned social events. Some housing developments schedule regular get-togethers for all their tenants. Also, the closer your neighbors, the safer you may feel and the greater the chance that your neighbors will notice a threat to you or your property. In addition, the closer your neighbors, the more sources of help you will have in an emergency.

You may want privacy and quiet. In general, the more walls and the more ceiling or floor space you share with neighbors, the less privacy you will have. Also, the more walls and the more ceiling or floor space you share with neighbors, the noisier your home will probably be.

Looking at Neighborhoods

What do you like about the neighborhood where you live now? Is it safe and attractive? Are the people friendly? When selecting a place to live, take the time to consider not only the convenience of its location but also the character of the neighborhood. If you choose a neighborhood you like, you can enjoy your home more.

The character of a neighborhood depends on its safety, appearance, and friendliness. A neighborhood may have streets, lawns, and buildings that are clean and well kept. It may, on the other hand, have poorly kept roads, deteriorating buildings, and litter. A neighborhood may have excellent police and fire protection services. It may even have a **crime watch program,** a cooperative effort by neighbors to stay alert to and report any suspicious activities occurring within their neighborhood. On the other hand, a neighborhood may have inadequate security services and be a high-crime area. The residents of a neighborhood may often get together for parties or community projects. On the other hand, they may seldom visit, work together, or even say hello to each other.

Evaluating Housing Units

What matters most to you about the specific housing unit you want? It might be the overall size, the number of rooms, or the amount of storage space. It could be the temperature and humidity of the place. It might be the amount of sunlight coming into a room or the degree of soundproofing between walls. It could be the types of appliances and fixtures available and the safety features and maintenance provided.

Size, Number of Rooms, and Storage Space

Housing units come in various sizes, with different numbers of rooms and amounts of storage space. To evaluate how well a housing unit's size, number of rooms, and storage space match your needs, look carefully at the unit. As you do this, think about your activities, furnishings, and equipment. For example, if you want to invite friends to dinner, you may want a kitchen, a dining area, and ample parking. If you have exercise equipment, you will want space to use and store this equipment. If you have many clothes, you will want a large closet. If you have a bicycle or a barbecue grill, you may want an outside storage area.

Heating, Cooling, and Lighting

Housing units also vary in the heating, cooling, and lighting they provide. Most rental units supply some type of heat, but not all places supply air conditioning. Ceiling lights are usually provided in kitchens and bath-

Rental Housing Units

Type	Description	Where Available	Special Features
Room	• a housing unit that has a multi-purpose room with closet space but no kitchen or bathroom area	• in a house • in a residential hotel	• inside and outside maintenance is provided • recreational facilities may be provided • neighbors live nearby • a private entrance may be provided
Efficiency, or Studio, Apartment	• a housing unit that has a multi-purpose room with closet space and a small kitchen area and a bathroom and that can be a part of many different types of rental structures	• in a house • in a **duplex,** a set of two connected apartments • in a **triplex,** a set of three connected apartments • in a **quadruplex,** a set of four connected apartments • in a **one-story apartment building,** a rental structure with five or more apartments, with only one floor • in a **walk-up apartment building,** a rental structure with five or more apartments, two or three floors, and no elevator • in a **high-rise apartment building,** a rental structure with five or more apartments, four or more floors, and an elevator • in an **apartment complex,** a group of one-story or walk-up apartment buildings	• inside and outside maintenance is provided • yard may be provided • patio, porch, balcony, or deck may be provided • recreational facilities may be provided • pets may be allowed • neighbors live nearby • social events may be organized • a security guard may be provided • a private entrance will probably be provided
One- or More Bedroom Apartment	• a housing unit that has several rooms and that can be a part of many different types of rental structures	• in a house • in a duplex, a triplex, or a quadruplex • in a one-story, walk-up, or high-rise apartment building • in an apartment complex	• inside and outside maintenance is provided • yard may be provided • patio, porch, balcony, or deck may be provided • fireplace may be provided • recreational facilities may be provided • pets may be allowed • neighbors live nearby • organized social events may be offered • a security guard may be provided • a private entrance is provided

rooms but may not be available in other rooms. Some housing units have many windows, while others have few. A place with windows that face directly east or west will provide plenty of morning or afternoon light. This means that your heating bill could amount to less in the winter, while your air conditioning bill could amount to more in the summer.

Although it is usually possible to check the lighting of a housing unit, it is sometimes difficult to check its heating and cooling. If possible, test the heating and cooling systems by turning them on. If they do not seem ade-

200 Arranging for Housing

Type	Description	Where Available	Special Features
Town, or Row, House	• a housing unit that has several rooms, that is erected in a row with similar two- or three-floor housing units, and that shares at least one or two sidewalls with neighboring units	• on a small lot in a city or a town	• inside maintenance is provided • outside maintenance may be provided • yard may be provided • patio, porch, or deck may be provided • garage may be provided • fireplace may be provided • pets may be allowed • neighbors live nearby • a private entrance is provided
Mobile Home	• a housing unit that has several rooms, that is unattached to other housing units, and that is designed to be placed on a foundation and attached to sewer and water lines and, then, detached and moved easily whenever necessary	• on a small lot in a mobile home park in or near a city or a town • on a piece of land of any size in the country	• inside maintenance is provided • yard is provided • patio, porch, or deck may be provided • carpet may be provided • recreational facilities may be provided • pets may be allowed • neighbors may be nearby • organized social events may be offered • security guard may be provided • a private entrance is provided
House	• a housing unit that has several rooms, that is unattached to other housing units, and that is designed to be permanently located where it was erected	• on a lot of any size in or near a city or a town • on a piece of land of any size in the country	• inside maintenance is provided • outside maintenance may be provided • yard is provided • patio, porch, or deck may be provided • garage or carport may be provided • fireplace may be provided • recreational facilities may be provided • pets may be allowed • neighbors may be nearby • a private entrance is provided

quate, ask whether repairs are scheduled or whether you can add a space heater, a fan, or an air conditioner of your own.

Noise Levels

Housing units differ in their noise levels. Some are more soundproof or are located in a quieter neighborhood than others. Noise may not bother you at all, or you may be sensitive to it. If noise does bother you, you will want a place that has a good deal of soundproofing and is located in a quiet neighborhood.

To evaluate a housing unit's noise level, listen for sounds of neighbors through any

Renting

shared walls, floors, or ceilings. Also, check the noise level of the neighborhood. If possible, check the noise level several times during the day and evening.

Appliances and Fixtures, Safety Features, and Maintenance

Basic appliances and fixtures are provided in most rental units. Appliances include a range, a refrigerator, and a water heater. Standard plumbing fixtures are sinks, a bathtub or shower stall, a toilet, and running water. Standard electrical fixtures are sufficient electrical outlets for room lighting and a smoke alarm. Most landlords also provide window screens. Some supply screen doors, drapery rods, draperies, and carpeting. Many landlords provide some safety features. They also usually agree to handle maintenance of the basic appliances and fixtures they are renting to you.

To find out whether you are satisfied with the appliances and fixtures in a housing unit, check each one. Make sure it works. Remember to flush the toilet and run some water to make sure the water pressure is sufficient and the plumbing is sound. Also, run through a checklist in your mind to make sure important security features are present. Ask yourself the following questions:

- Is there a fire escape, a fire extinguisher, a smoke alarm?
- Are there locks and viewers on each outside door? Remember, a chain latch offers the least security, while a double-cylinder deadbolt offers the most. Outside doors should have a wide-angle viewer to allow you to see visitors.
- Are the windows secure?
- Is there a security guard on duty either in the building or on the premises?

For more information about home safety features, see the next page.

Before you agree to rent, make sure the landlord agrees to add any items you find missing. Also, make sure the landlord agrees to fix any basic feature that seems to be in poor condition. Find out what maintenance services you are responsible for once you move in and which ones will be provided.

Preparing to Move

Once you have decided where to move, you will need to take care of certain details. You will probably need to sign a lease. In addition, you will need to pay deposits and report your change of address. Then, you can pack your belongings.

Signing a Lease

Although it is sometimes possible to rent a housing unit without the protection of a lease, this arrangement means you can be asked to move with less than one month's notice. A **lease** is a written contract between a landlord and a tenant that explains the rights and responsibilities of each. A **tenant** is a person who pays rent and lives in a housing unit.

If you sign a lease, you are making a financial and legal commitment that is binding. If you will be the only tenant, you will sign the lease. If you will have one or more roommates, you will have to decide who will sign. Whoever signs the lease is responsible for the rent.

Anyone who does not meet the obligations as described in the lease can be evicted. Being **evicted** means being legally forced by the landlord to move from a housing unit. Such a situation might cause you to have difficulty convincing others to rent to you.

If you choose to move before your lease has ended, you may still be responsible for paying the remaining rent agreed to in the lease. Even if your lease does not require this rent payment, your lease may require you to pay a penalty fee and forfeit your security deposit.

You may have a lease that includes a sublet clause. A **sublet clause** is a part of those leases that allow a tenant to rent his or her rental unit to another person. If the new renter fails to pay the rent, the original holder of the lease will be responsible for the rent.

Paying Deposits and Reporting Address Changes

When you sign a lease or otherwise agree to rent, you will pay your rental deposits. Then, you can arrange for utility services and pay any deposits they require. Next, you will want to notify the post office and any other agencies that have your address on file.

How Computers Can Help You

Securing Your Home by Computer

Picture a duplex a short distance from town and out of the sight of neighbors. No one is at home. The scream of a smoke alarm echoes through the building. Soon, flames leap from the windows. When the occupants return, the house is a smoldering wreck. Even though there were smoke alarms in all the right places, the building is a total loss. Although this fire was not caught in time, others could be, with the help of a computerized smoke-alarm system.

A computerized smoke-alarm system takes the place of a person. If, when a smoke alarm goes off, the cancel button is not pushed within thirty seconds, the computer automatically dials an emergency number. The number is probably that of the nearest fire department. The computer transmits information about the location of the house. If, for some reason, that call is not answered, the computer will dial a second number. The computer will alternate between the two numbers until one of them answers or someone signals the machine to shut down.

There are computerized burglar alarm systems that work in a similar way. When an unauthorized person attempts to enter a house that has such a system, the computer places a call to the local police station or to a security company. Information about the location of the house is flashed on a screen there. If the information about the attempted break-in is received by a security company, the company calls the home to make sure that the system was not accidentally set off. Then, the security company phones the police and relays the necessary information.

How do *you* fit into all of this? Sometime in the future, you will be looking for your own housing. By being aware of what computerized safety features are available, you will be in a better position to make sure that your housing is adequately protected. Right now, you can help your family do as much as they can to ensure the safety of their, and your, home.

Packing Your Belongings

Choose your moving day. Count on at least one full day to pack and a minimum of one day to move if you are moving locally. For short moves, you will probably want to do your own packing. Number every carton and keep a master list. For example, you might write, "Kitchen equipment: flatware, glassware, salad bowls." Try to move when traffic is light. If you are moving a long distance and have many furnishings and equipment to move, you might consider using a professional mover. If so, you may want the mover to pack your belongings.

Enjoying the Move

Before you move, make sure your new home is clean and ready for you. Then, get a good night's sleep. Pack a picnic lunch for yourself and everyone who will be helping you. Be prepared for a busy and challenging moving day.

As you unload each carton, you may want to put it into the room where its contents belong. You may, however, want to put all cartons in a central place, with a separate pile of cartons for each room. Try to unpack cartons as soon as possible. Later, you can sort things into their final place.

Points to Remember

- Housing expenses include security deposits, rent, utilities, insurance, and furnishings and equipment.
- It is important to understand what features make particular furnishings and equipment good choices.
- There are advantages, disadvantages, and compromises involved in living with your family, living alone, or living with roommates.
- Renting is the most convenient and reasonable housing choice for most young people who want to live on their own.
- The rent for an unfurnished apartment may be lower than that for a furnished apartment, but the actual cost of living in a furnished apartment may be less.
- Rental housing units include rooms, apartments, town houses, mobile homes, and houses at many different price levels.
- The location and character of the neighborhood in which it is located will probably influence how much you like a particular housing unit.
- When comparing housing units, you should consider what you want and what each offers in terms of size, number of rooms, storage space, heating, cooling, lighting, noise, safety, and maintenance.
- A lease is a binding legal agreement that must be complete, clear, and carefully read before signing.
- Preparing to move involves signing a lease, paying deposits, reporting your change of address, and packing your belongings efficiently.

Test Your Skills

DECISION MAKING

Imagine yourself in the situation described below. In this situation, a decision is needed. As you read, think about how to make good decisions. Then, answer the questions that follow. When you make decisions in the future, remember to ask yourself these questions.

Situation

Graduation is only two months away. The bank at which you work half time has offered you a full-time job as a bank teller. Your net pay would be $550 a month. You would like to find a place of your own as soon as possible. In the classified rental ads, you find the following possibilities:

- a one-bedroom unfurnished apartment in town for $350 a month
- a two-bedroom unfurnished apartment just outside of town for $400 a month
- a two-bedroom furnished mobile home about ten miles (16 kilometers) outside of town for $350 a month
- a two-bedroom unfurnished beach house four miles (6.4 kilometers) from town for $600 a month

You have a friend who has offered to share costs and move in with you. However, you value your privacy and are not sure you want a roommate. You have always wanted to live on the beach, but living in town would save you transportation costs. Whatever you decide, you need money for furnishings and equipment and security deposits in addition to enough money for rent.

Questions

1. What is the problem?
2. What information do you need to help you make a decision?
3. Which of your values, goals, and resources may affect your decision?
4. List three decisions you could make. What are their possible consequences?
5. What is the best decision you could make? Why is it the best for you? What is the next best decision?

Terms

On a separate sheet of paper, write a definition for each of the underlined terms below. Base your definition on the clues you find in the sentence(s).

1. Chen was surprised when he had to pay a <u>security deposit</u> equal to two months' rent. The apartment manager explained, however, that the entire amount would be refunded if Chen made all his rent payments and damaged no rental property.

2. In trying to find a place to rent, Dolores spoke with the owners of several older houses. Each <u>landlord</u> told her that lawn care would be her responsibility.

3. Nick's new <u>furnished apartment</u> has all the furnishings he needs. It has not only living room, dining room, and bedroom furniture but also kitchen equipment and household textiles.

4. Cindy has agreed to rent an <u>unfurnished apartment</u>. Her landlord will supply a range and refrigerator. Cindy will borrow or buy everything else she needs.

5. Jeremy has decided that he would like to rent an <u>efficiency, or studio, apartment</u>. He thinks that a combination living-dining-sleeping room with some closet and kitchen space and a private bathroom are all he wants at this time.

6. Ginger grew up in a <u>town, or row, house</u> and wants to rent one someday. She likes the long and narrow two-story design and does not mind sharing sidewalls with neighbors.

7. Calvin participates in the <u>crime watch program</u> his neighborhood sponsors. If he notices any suspicious activity in the neighborhood, he reports it to the police and, then, alerts another member of the crime watch.

8. Before Tina signed her <u>lease</u>, she made sure she understood each statement in it, both her rights and responsibilities and those of her landlord.

9. Larry has been a <u>tenant</u> since March, when he began to rent and live in his first apartment.

10. Dawn thinks being <u>evicted</u> would be a real problem. To make sure her landlord has no reason to legally force her to move out of her apartment, Dawn plans to meet each obligation stated in her lease.

11. Glen's lease includes a <u>sublet clause</u>, but Glen does not plan to use the clause. He realizes that, if he were to decide to move before his lease is up and then rent to a new tenant, he would be responsible if the new tenant missed a payment or damaged the property.

Questions

1. Why is it necessary to pay special attention to the cost of housing before deciding to move out on your own?
2. What security deposits will you probably be asked to make before you can move into a rental housing unit?
3. What three decisions should you make before you shop for furniture?
4. Which two types of furniture probably offer the greatest flexibility in style, material, color, and use?
5. What characteristics should you look for when selecting cookware?
6. Describe the difference between a place setting and a starter set.
7. What are two advantages and two disadvantages of having roommates?
8. What are three sources of rental information?
9. What are the main differences in facilities and cost between furnished and unfurnished units of rental housing?
10. What are one advantage and one disadvantage of using a sublet clause?

Activities

1. Collect classified rental ads for places that might be right for you. What is the typical rent? What security deposit, if any, is required?
2. Contact utility companies to find out what they charge for establishing service. Would you have to pay an installation fee or security deposit? What conditions must you meet to have the deposit returned?
3. Visit department and discount stores to compare the prices and availability of cookware, bakeware, dinnerware, flatware, and glassware. Which stores offer starter sets? Which sell from open stock?
4. Visit a discount store or a supermarket, and make a list of all the cleaning supplies and equipment you would need for a place of your own. Record the price of each item. What is the total cost?
5. Talk with some young people who have graduated from high school and are living at home and with others who are renting a place to live. What advice do they give?

Chapter Review 207

Understanding Design

Design is the arrangement of objects and their parts to create an interesting and appealing effect. It is a visual art. Because design must be seen to be enjoyed and understood, this section contains several illustrations and photographs. Look at them carefully. Each one will show you an important fact about design.

Looking Closely at Design Elements

Understanding design can be helpful to you. With it, you can make your home, your wardrobe, and other parts of your surroundings attractive and comfortable. You can use design to create around you the effects you like. Your tools will be the elements and principles of design.

The **elements of design** include line, color, texture, and shape. Learning to use these elements is a two-step process.

The first step is to understand that the elements of design can be used to improve the looks of objects by creating optical illusions. An **optical illusion** is what a person "sees" when the line, color, texture, or shape of an object makes that object look different from the way it really is. Some optical illusions can make you see things that seem quite incredible. For example, if you look at the sculpture in Figure 1, you can see two sections that sometimes seem to float in thin air and sometimes seem missing altogether. The optical illusions used in everyday designing—of rooms, clothing, or even meals, for example—are not quite so spectacular. They are used mainly to create artful improvements in the way everyday objects appear. For example, such optical illusions may make an object look a little longer, shorter, larger, or smaller than it is. When you are making design decisions about rooms, clothing, or meals, remember that optical illusions can help you.

The second step in using the elements of design is to learn the characteristics of each element. Once you learn those characteristics, you will be able to recognize the specific effect each element can have. You will also be more aware of how to use line, color, texture, and shape to help you create optical illusions.

Figure 1 This sculpture by Victor Vasarely is entitled "Spring." Hand painted on wood and completed in 1985, this sculpture creates optical illusions. What optical illusions do you see? How does the outer shape of the sculpture differ from the other shapes you can see in the sculpture? Which elements of design do you think the artist used to create the illusions of these other shapes?

Looking Closely at Design Elements **209**

Line

The two-dimensional frame or skeleton of design that always has greater length than width is **line.** There are four types of lines: vertical, horizontal, diagonal, and curved. Each has a different effect on the eye. To understand the kind of optical illusion each type of line creates, see Figures 2, 3, 4, and 5.

SEARS, ROEBUCK & CO.

Figure 2 Vertical lines make the eye move up and down. They give the illusion of height. The vertical stripes on this dress [left] make its wearer look taller and slimmer. In this kitchen [above], vertical stripes on the cabinets make the ceiling look higher.

J. C. PENNEY CO.

Figure 3 Horizontal lines make the eye move from side to side. They make things look wider. The horizontal lines of the furnishings in this bedroom [above] make the wall whose lines they parallel look longer. This shirt with its horizontal lines [right] makes its wearer look heavier.

210   Understanding Design

Figure 4 Diagonal lines slant and attract special attention. Look at the effect of diagonal lines on this shirt [below] and in this living room [right]. Notice how dramatic lines can be on furnishings and on clothes.

Figure 5 Curved lines give the illusion of softness. The curved lines of the sink, soap holders, and vase add a graceful and appealing look to this bathroom [above]. A curved neckline softens a square or pointed jawline [right].

Color

Like line, color influences the images your eyes see. What is color? **Color** is light reflected into your eyes. When light shines onto an object, some rays of the light are absorbed by the object. The rays that are not absorbed bounce off the object and into your eyes. These rays create the color that your eyes identify. You can see the different-colored rays that make up light if you look at light shining through a prism. See Figure 6.

Now, look at the color wheel in Figure 7. A **color wheel** is a circle used to show the relationships between the colors in the rainbow. Three colors on the color wheel are the basis for all colors. These are the **primary colors:** red, yellow, and blue. Every other color is made by combining red and yellow, yellow and blue, or red and blue. **Secondary colors** are those made by mixing two primary colors. Orange, for example, is the secondary color made from red and yellow. **Intermediate colors** are those made by combining a primary and a secondary color. Yellow-orange, for example, is the intermediate color made by combining yellow and orange.

Figure 6 When light passes through a prism, the color within the light is divided into the many colors of the rainbow.

Hue

Each color on the color wheel is a **hue.** For example, red is a hue. So is red-orange. Because each hue can have different values and intensities, each hue represents a whole family of colors.

Value

The **value** of a hue is its lightness or darkness. A lighter version of a hue is a **tint.** It is made by adding white to the hue. A darker version of a hue is a **shade.** It is made by adding black to the hue. Every blue from the lightest to the darkest is a different value of blue.

Different values of the same hue can affect the way an object looks. Tints make things look larger. Shades make things look smaller. For example, light paint makes a room look larger than dark paint does. A coat in a dark color looks smaller than the same coat in a lighter color.

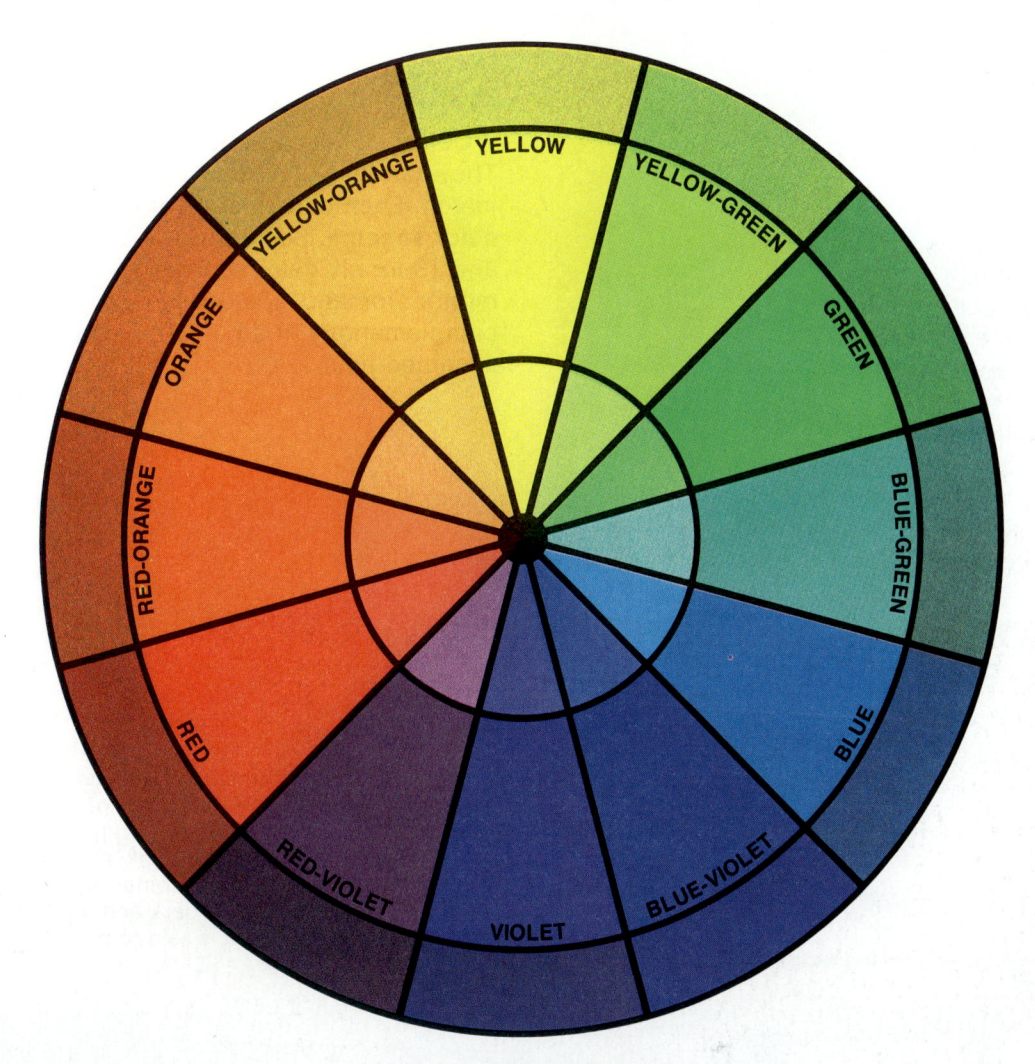

Figure 7 Look at the middle circle in this color wheel. The middle circle contains the primary, secondary, and intermediate colors. See if you can find the three primary, three secondary, and six intermediate colors. What primary and secondary color is used to make each intermediate color?

Intensity

The **intensity** of a hue is its brightness or dullness. Look at the red on the color wheel. This strong, bright color is the red with the highest intensity. To decrease the intensity of the hues on the color wheel, you can do one of two things. You can add some of the hue's complement, the hue directly across the color wheel. Or you can add some black or white to the hue. Adding black or white, however, changes the value, as well as the intensity, of the hue.

Different intensities of the same hue can affect the way an object looks. Bright colors can make things look larger. Dull colors can make things look smaller. For example, a chair covered in a bright color will look bigger than the same chair covered in a dull color of the same cloth. In the same way, a bright yellow belt will make a thick waist look even larger. A dull yellow belt will make a slim waist look even smaller.

Looking Closely at Design Elements

Color Schemes

Colors can work together in several ways. They can blend, contrast, complement, or match. Each combination of colors is a **color scheme.** See Figures 8, 9, 10, 11, 12, and 13 for six color schemes: monochromatic, analogous or adjacent, complementary, triad, neutral, and accented neutral.

Figure 8 A monochromatic color scheme is one that uses values and intensities of the same hue. This outfit [left] combines a bright pink sweater and pants with a pale pink and white blouse. This nook [below] combines light blue wallpaper and blinds with a dark and light blue rug. Such a color scheme is said to be restful and relaxing to the eye.

SEARS, ROEBUCK & CO.

Figure 9 An analogous or adjacent color scheme is one that uses hues that are next to each other on the color wheel. This outfit [right], which combines blue-violet and blue, has an analogous color scheme. This bedroom [below], which combines orange, yellow-orange, yellow, and yellow-green, also has an analogous color scheme. Such a color scheme is said to be interesting but not startling.

Looking Closely at Design Elements   **215**

Figure 10 A complementary color scheme is one that uses hues that are opposite each other on the color wheel. This living room [left], with its orange and blue furnishings, has a complementary color scheme. This red and green outfit [below] also has a complementary color scheme. Such a color scheme is said to be dramatic and eye-catching.

Figure 11 A triad color scheme is one that includes three colors that are the same distance from one another on the color wheel. This red, yellow, and blue tennis wear [above] and bedroom [right] show the use of a triad color scheme. Such a color scheme is considered very colorful and imaginative.

1001 HOME IDEAS

216 Understanding Design

Figure 12 A neutral color scheme is one that uses tints and shades of black and white. These tints and shades are grays, and do not appear on the color wheel. They do, however, blend with all the colors on the color wheel. This gray, white, and black dining room [above] has a neutral color scheme. This black, gray, and white outfit [right] also has a neutral color scheme. Such a color scheme is thought to create a functional and businesslike look.

Figure 13 An accented neutral color scheme is one that uses tints and shades of black and white highlighted by a hue. This gray and yellow outfit [left] has an accented neutral color scheme. This wall unit with its black and yellow objects [above] also has an accented neutral color scheme. Such a color scheme can be quite sophisticated looking.

Looking Closely at Design Elements   **217**

Texture

An object's **texture** is its surface characteristics. These determine how the object feels. For example, plastic objects often feel smooth, while wooden objects often feel rough. Satin feels smooth, while terry cloth feels somewhat rough.

An object's texture also influences how the object looks. Smooth textures give a formal look. Rough textures give a more informal look. See Figures 14 and 15.

In addition, smoother fabrics make objects look smaller. Nubby fabrics make them look larger. For example, a chair upholstered in vinyl will appear smaller than the same chair upholstered in corduroy. Likewise, a person wearing a smooth fabric will look thinner than the same person in otherwise identical clothes made from a nubby fabric.

Figure 14 This room with its smooth white cabinets and dining furniture [left] looks more formal than this room with its knotty pine cabinets and dining furniture [below].

Figure 15 This shirt with its smooth surface [below] looks more formal than this knit shirt with its rougher surface [left].

Shape

The outline or silhouette of an object is its **shape.** Standard shapes include the square, rectangle, circle, and triangle. You will find these and other shapes used in furnishings and clothing. See Figure 16.

Figure 16 How many different shapes can you see in this room [right]? What are they? Can you see the square and triangle formed by the necklines on these outfits [above]? What shapes do the straight-legged shorts have?

Looking Closely at Design Elements   **219**

Putting Design Principles into Action

The **principles of design** include proportion, rhythm, balance, emphasis, and harmony. Following is a definition of each principle and some examples of how each contributes to the total effect of a design.

Proportion

When something is well proportioned, its parts usually are not the same size and shape, yet they make up a pleasing whole. **Proportion** is the relationship among the parts of something and between each part and the whole, based on the way space is divided. For example, a well-proportioned set of furniture has pieces that vary in size and shape but look good together. A well-proportioned suit has a jacket and a skirt or pants that are not the same length yet make a pleasing whole. See Figure 17 for examples of what can happen if too little attention is given to proportion.

Figure 17 In this dining room set [above], the table and chairs and the narrow cupboard are the right size for each other, but the wide cupboard is out of proportion to the other pieces. This outfit [right] also lacks a pleasing proportion. The jacket and skirt seem to be almost exactly the same length. The outfit would be well proportioned if the jacket were shorter or if the skirt were longer.

Understanding Design

Rhythm

When a design element is repeated, your eyes follow it. Repeating an element to create a flow is **rhythm.** See Figure 18.

Figure 18 In this room [above], rhythm is created by the blocks of color in the rug, pillows, shade, wall paint, and couch/bed cover. In this outfit [left], rhythm is created by the color repeated in the sweater, shirt, socks, and shoes.

Balance

If all the parts of a design appear to balance one another, you feel at rest. Coordinating all the parts to provide a feeling of equal weight between them is balance. There are two types of balance. **Formal balance** is a mirror-image arrangement. That means both halves are essentially the same. **Informal balance** is an uneven arrangement around the center. With informal balance, the items on one side of the center differ from those on the other side. See examples of formal and informal balance in Figures 19 and 20.

Figure 19 The living room [above] has formal balance. Its left and right sides are almost identical. The living room [left] has informal balance. Its end table and lamp divide its chairs unevenly. Its coffee table is not centered on the rug.

Figure 20 The outfit [left] has informal balance. It has a well-proportioned but different treatment of its left and right sides. The outfit [above] has formal balance. It has exactly the same features on each side of its center.

Emphasis

When one part of a design is made the center of attention, your eyes will focus on that part. Accenting one part of a whole is **emphasis.** Emphasis is like an exclamation mark. It adds a bit of excitement to a room or a piece of clothing. See the use of emphasis in Figure 21.

Figure 21 This room [left] has earth tones and neutral colors. Its design downplays the inside of the room and emphasizes the view through the skylight and windows. This outfit [above] includes red accessories. The red earrings, bracelet, and belt focus attention on their wearer's face, wrist, and waistline.

Harmony

When all the parts of a design seem to fit together, you get a feeling of unity. Blending a variety of parts into a unified whole is **harmony.** See Figure 22 for an outfit that lacks harmony and Figure 23 for an outfit that has harmony. Harmony is not to be confused with sameness. In a room or outfit, variety is what adds interest. Harmony is what pulls it all together.

Think about a well-designed room. Every piece in the room fits together. The lines, colors, textures, and shapes all seem to fit the space and to blend together right. They all seem to have a place in the room.

Think about a designer's collection of clothes for a season. Every outfit is distinctive, yet all of the lines, colors, textures, and shapes used are in harmony. They all look as though they belong to the same collection of clothes.

Figure 22 What contributes to the lack of harmony in this outfit [above]?

Figure 23 Do you see variety yet harmony in the lines, colors, textures, and shapes of this outfit [left]?

The Basics Are Just the Beginning

Now that you know some basics about design elements and principles, see how often you can use them.

Consider line, color, texture, shape, and space when you choose accessories for your home or plan your wardrobe or your meals. Experiment with proportion, rhythm, balance, emphasis, and harmony. Together, these design elements and principles can help you make the most of your creativity and talent.

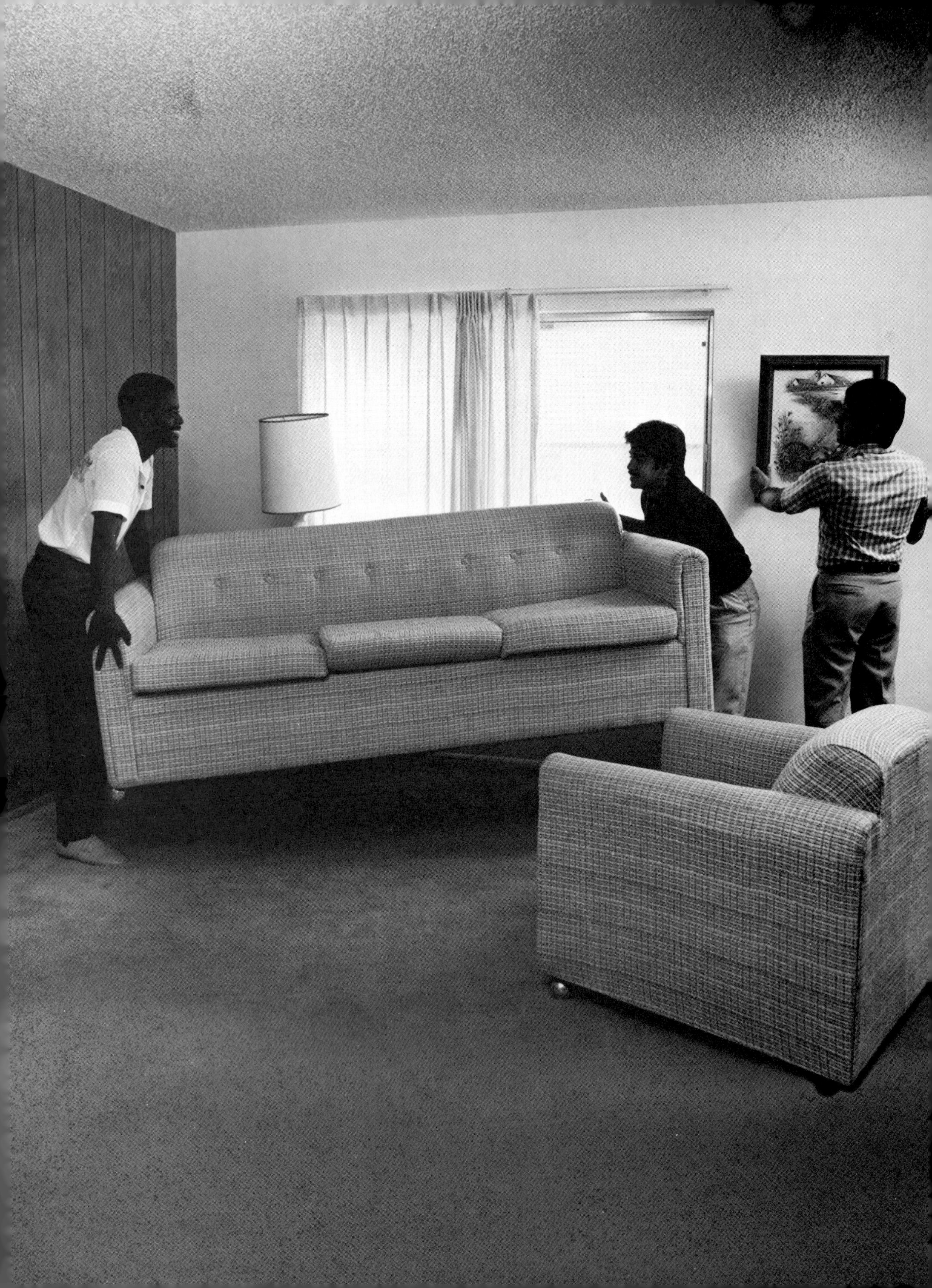

CHAPTER 10

Decorating and Caring for Your Home

Have you ever visited someplace and felt right at home? What made you feel so comfortable? Most likely, the furniture was conveniently arranged, the decorating was attractive, and everything was neat and clean.

When you get a place of your own, you may want it to be just as comfortable and enjoyable. It can be, if you decorate and organize household tasks with your lifestyle in mind. For example, you may be going to college, working part-time or full-time, or combining school and work. You may want certain parts of your home arranged for studying and hobbies and other parts arranged for entertaining friends. You may be involved in so many activities that you feel there is little time for cleaning. For such an active lifestyle, you will want to set up a simple system for accomplishing household tasks.

Depending on where you live, you may have much freedom to decorate. You may be allowed to paint or wallpaper walls or even to build in bookshelves. On the other hand, your decorating may be limited to your imaginative use of accessories. Either way, it will be up to you to decide on a decorating plan. For example, maybe you like to have lots of plants around you. Perhaps you like your walls covered with posters. Whatever your personal preferences, you will want to use the elements and principles of design to make your plan work.

Discover Through Your Reading

- how you can make a home comfortable and attractive
- what makes certain furniture arrangements more convenient than others
- how to decorate easily and inexpensively
- how well-planned storage can eliminate extra work for you
- where to store the many items you will use in a kitchen
- how to plan a reasonable cleaning schedule for your home
- how to handle minor household maintenance problems

Arranging Furniture

One of the most challenging parts of moving into a place of your own is arranging furniture. Before moving the first piece, consider what will make one arrangement more convenient than another. Consider how you want to use each room and what furniture you will be arranging. Think about what effects you want to achieve. Many arrangements may achieve the effects you want. Therefore, you will probably have the opportunity to experiment and occasionally to rearrange your furnishings.

Arranging Furniture for Convenience

Convenience should be your first goal when you arrange furniture. If you place furnishings where they are easy to use, you will enjoy using them more often. To decide what is most convenient, you will want to consider furniture groupings and traffic flow. You will also want to consider special requirements of furniture pieces.

Planning Furniture Groupings

How many rooms will your place have? What kinds of activities will you do in each? What furniture will help you carry out these activities? The answers to these questions will help you plan the furniture groupings you want in each room.

A **furniture grouping** is the arrangement of furniture to serve a particular activity in a certain part of a room. Examples of furniture groupings include conversation areas, sleeping areas, dressing areas, reading areas, and work areas. Each room of your home will include one or more furniture groupings. For example, a bedroom will include a sleeping area, a dressing area, and maybe a reading area. It may also include a work area for studying, sewing, or ironing.

How has the furniture in this room been organized to accommodate a favorite hobby?

Analyze each of your rooms to determine the furniture groupings you want in it. The living room is a good place to start. Suppose you will be studying, reading, and watching television in it. You will want two furniture groupings. One will be a work area for studying. The other will be a reading or television area. For your study area, you will want to arrange a desk or a table and a straight-back chair near a source of light. If you will do all of your studying during the day, you might place these furnishings near a window. Otherwise, you will need a study lamp on or near the desk. For your reading or television area, you will want to have a floor or table lamp and an end table near an easy chair. You will want to arrange these pieces a comfortable distance from the television.

There are many ways to create a furniture grouping. You can make a conversation area with a couch and two or three chairs. You can make a reading area with an easy chair and a lamp. You can make a hobby area with bookshelves, a table, and a stool or a straight-back chair.

Determining Traffic Flow Through and Between Rooms

Knowing which furniture groupings you want in a room is the first part of arranging furniture for convenience. The second part is determining how you want people to move through the room. **Traffic flow** is the pattern that people follow as they walk through and between rooms. Your placement of furniture can make a traffic flow very convenient or very inconvenient. See the examples at the bottom of this page.

Generally, a straight line of traffic flow is the most convenient. Sometimes, however, you may not want a straight line of traffic flow. For example, maybe you are planning a conversation area and need to route traffic around it. In this way, you will make sure that persons walking through the room are not likely to disturb those who are talking.

Recognizing Special Requirements of Furniture Pieces

As you arrange your furniture, remember that some pieces have special requirements. For example, some are designed to look good from all sides. You can use these as room dividers. Others are unfinished on the back. They will look best if placed against a wall. A bed is best arranged so that it can be easily reached from both sides. This arrangement will allow you to make the bed easily.

Items such as televisions, stereos, radios, and lamps usually have electrical cords. Therefore, these furnishings need to be placed near electrical outlets. When placing televisions, stereos, and radios, remember that their noise levels might be disturbing to neighbors. Therefore, you may not want to put them against a wall that you share with another apartment. Also, you may not want to arrange those items in front of radiators or windows.

Using a Floor Plan

Even if you really enjoy arranging furniture, moving heavy pieces of furniture is hard work. You can make this job easier by looking at several furniture arrangements before actually trying them out. To get started, you must know the size of the rooms and the size of your furniture.

You need to know the dimensions of the rooms so that you can draw floor plans to scale. A **floor plan** is an outline of a room or rooms that shows the location of walls, doors, windows, hallways, closets, and electrical outlets. It is usually drawn to the following scale: ¼ inch equals 1 foot. You must know the dimensions of your furniture so that you can draw or select furniture templates of the right size. A **furniture template** is a two-dimensional form that shows the amount of floor space a particular piece of furniture will occupy. Like a floor plan, a furniture template is generally drawn to the following scale: ¼ inch equals 1 foot.

Which of these furniture arrangements provides the most convenient traffic flow? Why?

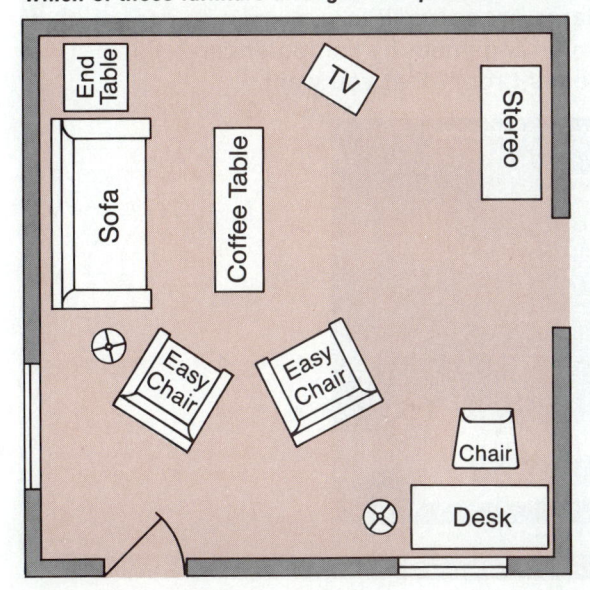

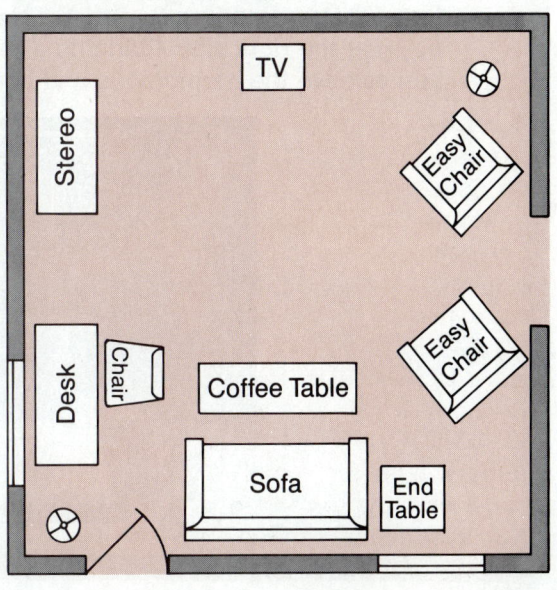

Arranging Furniture 227

How Computers Can Help You

Planning Room Arrangements by Computer

The next time you decide to rearrange furniture in a room, relax. You do not have to shove around heavy sofas, tables, and chairs. You do not have to wonder if a new piece of furniture will actually fit in the room and have the correct proportion. Instead, all you have to do is turn on a computer.

If you do not have a computer, maybe you can use a friend's or use one at school. The mechanical drawing, industrial arts, home economics, or art department is likely to have a computer. The department may also have the necessary attachment or program to help you create a pleasing furniture arrangement. What you will need is a computer that has a graphics tablet. This device hooks into the computer and allows you to produce computer graphics. In other words, you can use the computer to help you make drawings or designs.

With a graphics tablet, you can draw a floor plan of a room to scale. You can include doorways and windows to help you determine how much wall space is actually available. Next, you can draw furniture templates of items you already have or plan to buy. Then, you can move your furniture templates around on your floor plan. With the computer, you can "see" how furniture will look not only in various places but also in various sizes. You can experiment with many arrangements until you find one that gives you the proportion, balance, and traffic flow you want.

Once you have created a satisfactory arrangement, you can have the computer print a copy for you. By following your plan, you can save energy and time when moving furniture into position. You can also save money by knowing whether a particular piece of furniture will fit with your room dimensions. Instead of buying furniture that is too large or too small for a room, you can buy just the right size. Planning a room arrangement by computer can help you achieve the harmonious and convenient room that you want.

You can work with a floor plan and furniture templates in either of two ways. Probably the newest way is to use a computer. On page 228, you will find more information about using computers to help arrange furniture. If you do not have such a computer program available, you can use a paper floor plan and furniture templates. You can buy the graph paper to draw your floor plan and may be able to buy ready-made templates. If you cannot locate ready-made templates in the decorating section of a store, you can buy graph paper and make your own.

As you arrange your furniture templates on your floor plan, allow enough space for people to walk. Generally, you will need 1½ to 2 feet (.5 to .6 m) of space between furniture pieces. With a scaled floor plan and furniture templates, you can easily compare different furniture arrangements. After you decide on an arrangement, you need only move your actual furniture into the positions indicated on the plan.

How have the elements and principles of design been used in this room to create an interesting furniture arrangement?

Creating an Interesting Room Arrangement

Your rooms will have a more interesting look if they reflect the basic elements and principles of design. These elements and principles are illustrated on pages 208–223.

You can apply design basics to your furniture arrangements in several ways. The following strategies are some examples:

- First, position any items that you want to emphasize.
- Place the largest pieces of furniture against walls to give a feeling of space.
- Use a large picture or grouping of pictures over a large sofa to create a feeling of proportion.
- Distribute colors throughout the room so that no one area is overemphasized.
- Group furniture pieces that have vertical lines to increase the feeling of height in a room with a low ceiling.
- Make a small room appear larger by using only a few pieces of furniture or furniture that is fairly small.
- Use natural light when you can.

Decorating Your Living Space

Once you have your basic furniture arrangement in mind, you will want to think about a decorating plan. Perhaps the easiest way to begin is to look at the furnishings you already own. What do they tell you about your decorating preferences? For example, what are the predominant colors? Can you identify any specific color scheme? Are the predominant materials wood, metal, fabric, or plastic? What kind of mood or atmosphere do they give to a room? If you like what you have, you may want to keep the same decorating plan for a while. If not, you may want some other ideas.

Decorating magazines can give you many suggestions for matching colors, arranging furnishings, and planning a comfortable and attractive place. You may want to keep a clipping file of certain articles and pictures. Then, when you are ready to decorate a particular room, you will have many ideas to consider. To make your place interesting and unique, collect decorating ideas that make use of walls, floors, windows, and housing accessories.

Walls

If you are renting, check your lease for rules about decorating walls. In some rentals, you cannot paint, make nail holes, or change the walls in any way. If you change the walls even though your lease forbids it, you may have to pay repair fees or lose your security deposit when you move. In other rentals, you can decorate the walls as you like.

Wall decorating can be divided into two general categories. Some decorations change only the look of the wall. Other decorations change the look and the function of the wall.

Have you ever wallpapered a room? If not, would you like to try this kind of decorating project when you get a place of your own? Why?

For example, painting changes only the look. Adding shelves or a stereo rack changes not only the look but also the function.

There are many ways to decorate that make use of walls. Some of the more popular ways include the following:

- adding wall hangings, such as prints, paintings, posters, quilts, mirrors, or clocks
- adding wallpaper or a vinyl covering
- painting
- adding shelves or shelving systems

To find out more about do-it-yourself decorating projects such as these, see page 231.

Floors

In many rental units, floor coverings are provided. If, however, you can choose your own floor coverings, you can use them as part of your decorating plan. You can use them to help set a mood. For example, if your furniture reflects a country look, you might choose braided rugs. If your furniture is tropical-looking in material or design, you might want an area carpet with a similar pattern. If you have very modern furniture, you might like to put down vinyl tiles.

Windows

If you are renting, check with your landlord before you make any decisions about window coverings. In some situations, you cannot change the window coverings that are provided. In other instances, you can decorate windows in any way that does not change their structure.

Window coverings can do more than just provide privacy and control the amount of natural light in a room. They can muffle traffic sounds or voices from an adjoining apartment. They can keep out unwanted heat during the summer and cold during the winter. They can provide additional insulation by preventing air conditioning or heat from escaping. Depending on their material, construction, and style, some window coverings serve these purposes better than others.

Do-It-Yourself Home Decorating

Project	Supplies	Procedures
Preparing surfaces for painting or wallpapering	• a cleaning solution of soap or detergent and water • drop cloths • a scraper • sandpaper • spackling • masking tape • a ladder or a stool	• Place drop cloths over furnishings and floors. • Rinse or scrub walls and woodwork. • Sand rough spots. • Use spackling according to package directions to fix cracks or bumps. • Put masking tape around window panes and other edges that need protection from paint or wallpaper glue.
Painting	• appropriate paint for surface • rollers, paint pads, or a paint-spraying device • brushes in various narrow and wide sizes • a stirring stick • a small disposable paint bucket or pan	• Describe your painting project to a salesperson in a paint store. Ask for advice about suitable paints, rollers, or brushes. • Use long, smooth strokes. • Be careful when working from a stool or a ladder.
Wallpapering	• wallpaper • chalk, string, and a weight to make a plumb line • a wetting tray for prepasted paper • paste and a wide brush for unpasted paper • a smooth, wide brush for applying paper • a single-edge razor-knife or a sharp cutting tool and scissors • a yard stick, a pin, and a damp cloth	• Carefully select a pattern. Avoid detailed, fine patterns and plain, light colors until you become experienced. Also avoid patterns that require matching. • Cut paper about 1 inch longer than the wall area you are covering. Apply paste to the paper, if necessary. • Start 1/2 inch from a corner. Attach the top of the paper to the wall. Gradually smooth the rest of the paper length onto the wall. Use a plumb line to help you determine a straight, vertical line. • Smooth out wrinkles with a dry brush. Make a tiny hole with a pin to release air bubbles. Smooth paper again and again. • Wipe off excess paste with a damp cloth. • Trim excess paper with a razor-knife.
Hanging pictures or plants	• a hammer • a pencil • small nails or picture hooks • wire, sturdy cords, or chains	• Use a hammer to find the studs, or supports for the wall. Tap the wall lightly until you hear a solid sound that indicates a stud is behind the surface. • Decide where you want the picture or plant to hang. Make a light mark with a pencil. • Hammer a nail or hook into the wall. For pictures, use two nails, each one a few inches off center. This will make it easier to level the picture. • Position plants so that they are easy to water. Do not place them so that water can drip onto furniture, electrical cords, or sockets.

Window coverings can also give you plenty of decorating opportunities. For example, you might choose mini blinds or shades to accent a color scheme. You might hang a curtain or drapery to make a room appear to have windows where there are none. You might hang a drapery from ceiling to floor to give a room a feeling of elegance or height.

Decorating Your Living Space

Housing Accessories

How many accessories are enough? The answer to this question is a matter of personal taste. Generally, too many accessories make a place look cluttered. Too few make it look lifeless or boring.

There are several ways to decorate with accessories. You might want to use some of the following ideas:

- Set plants in window sills or hang them from the walls or ceiling.
- Hang different sizes, shapes, and styles of baskets from walls.
- Use vases, emptied coffee cans, or other containers to hold shells, rocks, feathers, pinecones, dried or silk flowers, coins, or matchbooks.
- Stick magnetic items on metal furnishings such as file cabinets or the refrigerator.
- Set fishbowls or aquariums on coffee tables or end tables.
- Set glass objects where they can catch and reflect rays of sunlight.

Storing Household and Personal Belongings

Think of all the items you now have stored in your bedroom. When you move to a place of your own, you will probably take many of these things with you. You will have to find new places not only for these items but also for many other furnishings and equipment. For example, you will need to set up your kitchen and put away bathroom furnishings and supplies. You will also have to find places for living-dining area accessories. In addition, you will need to store some items that you use only occasionally, perhaps only once a year.

Well-planned use of storage is the key to comfort, convenience, and easy care. You can store items effectively by putting them as close as possible to where they are needed. You can do this with storage devices that are either seen or hidden. On the one hand, you might place a plastic or wood rack where it can be seen. On the other hand, you might fit low, wide boxes under the bed—out of sight but within easy reach. Storage devices are available in a wide range of prices, styles, and sizes. Choose the ones that will serve you best.

Setting Up Your Kitchen

The kitchen in your new place may be very different from what you are used to. A few adjustments, however, may help you make it more comfortable and convenient. For example, your kitchen drawers may be extremely deep. You can make each drawer more usable by adding drawer dividers and creating several deep sections. On the bottom layer of each section, you can put the items that you seldom use. On the top layer of each section, you can place items that you use frequently.

You may also have little cabinet space or cabinets that are too deep. By adding a narrow shelf to a room, you could have the storage you need. A shelf 4 inches wide, for example, will hold a single row of cans or jars. To make such a shelf, you would only need to nail a few 2-inch by 4-inch boards horizontally to the wall. You might attach the shelf to a closet wall or to the back of a door.

Setting up your kitchen is one of the biggest jobs of moving into a place of your own. This is because so many items need to be stored in the kitchen. You can make the job easier, however, by thinking of the kitchen as three basic work centers. One center is the area for food storage and preparation. Another is the area for cooking and serving foods. Still another is the area for cleaning up after meal preparation and dining. To work most efficiently in the kitchen, you will want to store different types of items in each of these areas. The tips on page 234 can give you some ideas for storing specific items of kitchen equipment.

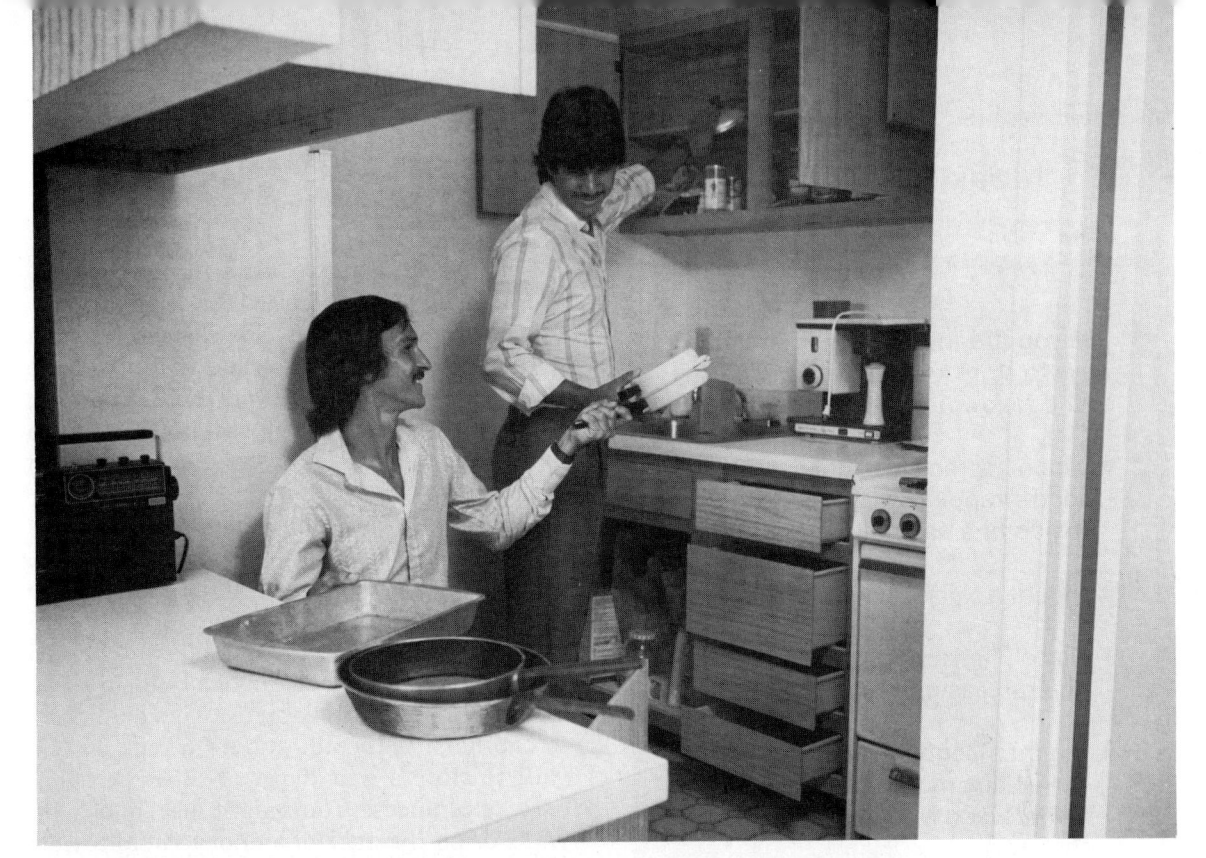

These roommates are setting up their kitchen. Which work center are they organizing?

Food Storage and Preparation Center

The area where foods are kept and first prepared in some form is known as the **food storage and preparation center.** This center includes the refrigerator and sink. It usually also includes some cabinets, drawers, and counter space. In this center, you will probably store these items:

- canned, packaged, fresh, and frozen foods
- bottle and can openers
- kitchen scissors
- food-wrapping supplies such as waxed paper, aluminum foil, plastic bags, and paper towels
- knives, a peeler, a grater/shredder, and a cutting board
- measuring spoons and cups
- mixing bowls in several sizes, a wooden spoon, and a rotary beater
- small appliances such as an electric can opener, an electric mixer, a blender, and a yogurt maker
- glassware and pitchers
- multipurpose food-storage containers

Cooking and Serving Center

Many types of equipment need to be within reach for cooking and serving foods. The **cooking and serving center** is the area where food preparation is completed and foods are made ready for serving. This center includes the range. It usually also includes some cabinets, drawers, and counter space. It may also include a microwave oven. In this center, you will probably store the following items:

- cooking spoons, a turner, a meat fork, tongs, and a ladle
- a strainer and a colander
- skillets, saucepans, saucepots, and lids
- a muffin pan, a cookie sheet, cake pans, a pie plate, and casserole dishes
- small appliances such as a toaster, a coffee maker, a toaster oven, a slow cooker, an electric skillet, an electric wok, and a popcorn popper
- dinnerware
- flatware
- pot holders, tablecloths, and placemats

Storing Household and Personal Belongings

> **Tips**
>
> **Ideas for Storing Kitchen Equipment**
>
> If you are looking for interesting ways to store kitchen items, consider the following possibilities:
>
> - Mount a rack designed to hold food-wrapping supplies on the inside of a cabinet door.
>
> - Mount a knife rack on a wall.
>
> - Place measuring spoons inside liquid-measuring cups.
>
> - Mount a pegboard on a wall and, then, hang muffin tins, cake pans, turners, and wooden spoons from the pegs.
>
> - Nail thin pieces of wood inside a cabinet to form vertical dividers for storing lids, trays, and cookie sheets.
>
> - Store dishcloths and towels in a basket on a counter.

Organizing Bathroom Furnishings and Supplies

You are likely to have many household textiles and supplies to store in or near the bathroom. You will have towels, washcloths, bath mats, and possibly rugs. You will also have tissues, soaps, and other personal grooming supplies. In addition, you will probably keep medicines and some cleaning equipment in this area.

While most bathrooms have built-in cabinets or shelves, they may not offer the amount of storage you need. You may need to look for other forms of storage for your supplies. For example, you could buy and hang a wire shelf from the bottom of a built-in shelf. You could attach stick-on drawers or shelves to cabinets. You could mount a rack on one wall to store a hair dryer or other personal care appliances. You might use hooks on walls or on the back of a door to hold towels or robes.

There are cabinets or shelves on flexible poles that can be placed over the back of the toilet. Other cabinets can be placed above the sink. In the shower, a rack that sticks to the wall or slips over the shower head can be used. Sometimes, washcloths and towels can be stored neatly folded on the countertop or in a basket.

Remember that many household cleaning and personal care products in the bathroom are poisonous. If small children visit you often, make sure that these items are stored out of their way. If possible, store such supplies in a cabinet that can be locked.

Finding Space for Living-Dining Area Accessories

The accessories you use in your living-dining area will need some type of storage. Some of these items will fit best in special furniture intended for storage. Examples of storage pieces are a china cabinet or hutch, a large trunk, a stereo cabinet, and a cedar chest. Some of these items can do double

Clean-Up Center

The area where kitchen equipment is scraped, washed, and dried is called the **clean-up center.** This center includes the sink. It usually also includes some cabinets and counter space. It may also include some drawers, a dishwasher, a garbage disposal, and a trash compactor. In this center, you will probably store the following items:

- a dish drainer and tray
- dishcloths and towels
- scouring pads, sponges, detergents, and cleansers
- a garbage pail and trash bags

duty. A large trunk could be used as an end table. A cedar chest could be topped with a cushion and pillows and used for informal seating.

Serving trays, pitchers, bowls, platters, and serving baskets also are often attractive on display. You might want to put these on a mantle, a bookshelf, an end table, the dining room table, or on top of the refrigerator.

As you think about storing accessories, consider the trade-offs. If everything in a room is put inside something, there is little clutter. The room takes on a structured or more formal look. If nothing in a room is put away, there is too much clutter. The room appears messy and takes on a disorganized or more informal look. Your aim should be to provide just enough storage, not too much or too little.

Organizing Bed Linens, Clothes, and Clothing Accessories

There are many ways to store bed linens. Bedspreads/comforters, sheets, pillowcases, and blankets can be stored on closet shelves or in a chest of drawers. They can be stored in a suitcase that is not used often. They can even be stored in a special storage box that fits under the bed.

You will want to use a closet storage system for your clothes and clothing accessories. Some closet storage systems are designed around rods and poles. Others are made from plastic-covered wire. You can either buy a closet system or make one of your own.

The principle behind any closet storage system is to arrange items of similar size together. For example, you can hang rods low for shirts and shorts and high for pants, dresses, and coats. You can place shoes, handbags, ties, scarves, and belts on special racks. In addition, you may want to display some clothing accessories while storing them. For example, you can hang hats, caps, or jewelry from hooks on the wall.

Storing Household Maintenance and Laundry Equipment

You will need to have some closet space set aside for the purpose of storing household maintenance and laundry equipment.

How can you tell that the people who live here understand that items must be stored in a convenient location to be stored well?

Storing Household and Personal Belongings

In that space, you can store the following items:

- cleaning equipment such as a vacuum cleaner, a broom, a dustpan, a dust mop, dust cloths, a sponge mop, and a bucket
- personal comfort equipment such as a fan, a space heater, and a humidifier or a dehumidifier
- laundry equipment such as an ironing board, an iron, and a laundry basket

Storing Occasional-Use Items

If you are like most people, you have some things that you use only occasionally. Some occasional-use items, such as board games and cookie cutters, are used from time to time throughout the year. Others, such as camping equipment and holiday decorations, are used only at certain times of the year. When not in use, these items will need to be stored.

Things you seldom use should be stored up high or down low. You might put them at the back of a top shelf in a closet. You might store them in a box that could fit under the bed. You might even disguise them in some way and use them as part of your regular furnishings. For example, you could use a patio table indoors by covering it with a floor-length tablecloth. You could hang a bike on a bedroom wall by using heavy-duty hooks. You could hang a kite from the ceiling.

Taking Charge of Cleaning

Getting furnishings arranged and organized is only the beginning of maintaining a place of your own. Another very important part is housekeeping. While you might hire someone to do your cleaning, you will prob-

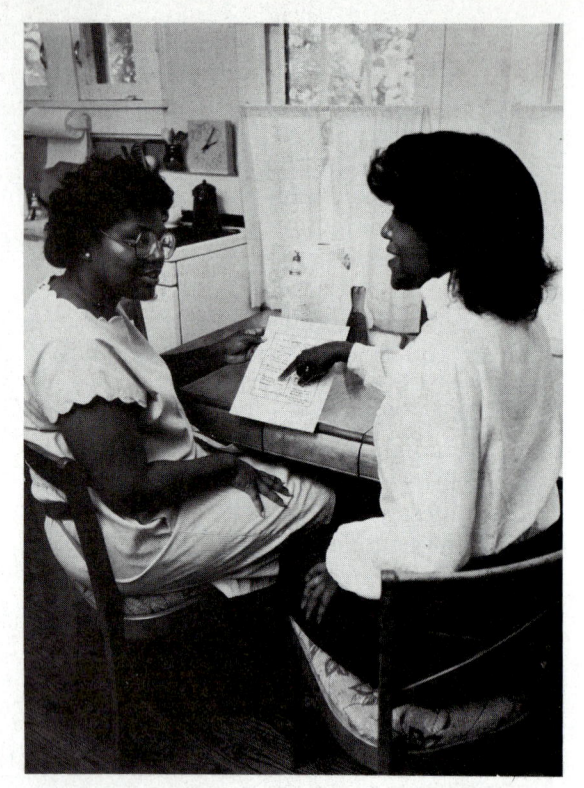

How can agreeing on a cleaning schedule help roommates get along well together?

ably assume this responsibility yourself. Housekeeping will be easier if you set up a schedule that is convenient for you. It will be more effective if you use suitable cleaning products and techniques.

Setting Up a Cleaning Schedule

An effective cleaning schedule requires some organization. The first step of organizing a cleaning schedule is to know what needs to be done. Some cleaning jobs involve specific furniture pieces and household textiles. For example, you may have a wood table that requires polishing or a shower curtain and a tub mat that need cleaning. Other cleaning jobs involve entire rooms, such as the living-dining area, the bathroom, and the kitchen.

The second step of organizing a cleaning schedule is to know how often a job needs to be done. While some cleaning jobs need to be done every day, others can be done less often. These might be done weekly, monthly, or only seasonally. For example, kitchen equipment should be washed, or rinsed and placed in the dishwasher, after every meal. Carpets may need to be vacuumed every week, and the refrigerator may need to be cleaned once a month. Draperies may need to be cleaned once a year.

Try to set up a cleaning schedule to fit your lifestyle. Start with a plan that seems workable. Be prepared, however, to make adjustments. Suppose, for example, that you decide to vacuum the living room carpet, mop the kitchen floor, and clean the bathroom once a week. You might find that trying to do all of these tasks on the same day is difficult. Instead, you might want to do one of the tasks each day.

Cleaning Furniture, Household Textiles, and Floors

How you care for a piece of furniture depends on the materials used in its construction. To clean wood furniture, dust often and use wax sparingly. Remove excess or old wax about once a year. If you have glass or plastic furniture, clean with a glass cleaner or an all-purpose cleaner. Buff to remove streaks or excess soil. Clean with special metal cleaners any chrome, brass, or metal handles or trims.

Upholstered furniture should be thoroughly cleaned about twice a year. Using a dry shampoo product or a shampoo foam is usually a suitable cleaning method. Before using either, however, read its product label, as well as the care information you received with the furniture. Also, test a small hidden section on the back or underside of the piece of furniture. Then, you will be sure that the product is suitable for the fabric. Between thorough cleanings, use a stiff-bristle brush or a vacuum cleaner to remove dust. You might also place small pieces of fabric on the arms and headrest to protect against heavy soiling. You should clean or treat spots immediately to avoid letting stains set and thereby cause permanent damage.

Major household textiles that need cleaning include rugs, carpets, curtains, and draperies. Perhaps your landlord will take care of these cleaning responsibilities. If not, you will need to do so. The following suggestions may help:

- Vacuum rugs and carpets often, using long, even strokes. Empty or change the vacuum cleaner bag frequently to improve the suction.
- Shampoo carpeting at least every six months. Test a small area first. Make sure that the dyes do not run and the cleaning product or equipment does not harm the carpet. Do not soak the carpet, as you might damage its backing.
- Gently shake or vacuum curtains and draperies often to remove dust. Wipe off stains, and clean spots as soon as you discover them. Follow the manufacturer's directions for cleaning.

You can keep floors looking good if you clean them regularly. A wood floor should be waxed or, if it has a no-wax finish, dry-mopped regularly. The wax, if needed, should be applied sparingly. Remove old wax once a year. Other types of floors should be mopped regularly with a nonabrasive, all-purpose cleaner. Later, wax may be applied unless the floor is made of a material that never needs waxing.

Cleaning Bathroom Fixtures

There are several different materials used for bathroom fixtures. Each material has special care requirements. For example, glass should not be cleaned with an abrasive cleaner. An **abrasive cleaner** is one that contains fine particles that help scour or break up heavy soil. Cleanser is one type of abrasive cleaner. When an abrasive cleaner is used, it can make tiny scratches in the surface of some materials. After many cleanings, these scratches can become apparent and ruin the beauty and durability of the material. To choose products that are suitable for cleaning bathroom fixtures, consider the care requirements of each of the following materials:

- Glass and porcelain surfaces require a nonabrasive cleaner.
- Chrome surfaces require a cleaner that is nonabrasive, will polish metal, and will remove soil buildup.
- Stainless steel surfaces can take either an abrasive or a nonabrasive cleaner.
- Plastic surfaces need a nonabrasive all-purpose cleaner, detergent, or soap.
- Ceramic-tile surfaces require a nonabrasive cleaner that will clean the tiles and the grouting between the tiles and will kill mildew.

After choosing the appropriate cleaning product, use the proper technique. For example, do not exert heavy pressure when scrubbing. Doing so may scratch the surface or cause pitted marks. Do not mix ammonia with bleach, or mix products containing these substances. The result could be a poisonous gas.

Cleaning Kitchen Appliances

All appliances last longer and work better if you keep them in good condition. Whether you own or rent them, you have a responsibility to take care of the appliances in your kitchen. These include the range and refrigerator. They may also include a microwave oven, a dishwasher, a garbage disposal, and a trash compactor. The clean-up appliances do not require any special cleaning. However, the range, microwave oven, and refrigerator do require it.

Cleaning a Range

A good way to keep your range clean is to wipe off spills and greasy soil after each use. You can use a solution made of an all-purpose cleaner and water. As you clean the range, follow these guidelines:

- Make sure that the range is not hot.
- Make sure that no pilot lights or other heat sources are directly exposed to the cleaning product.
- Do not use abrasive cleaners on porcelain surfaces.
- Clean the drip bowls under the surface heating elements or burners, as well as the oven and oven racks.
- Clean the oven according to the type of cleaning system it has. This system may be either conventional, continuous-cleaning, or self-cleaning.

If you have an oven with a conventional cleaning system, you must clean the oven by hand, with or without an oven cleaner. If you have an oven with a continuous-cleaning system or a self-cleaning system, you should use an oven cleaner. A **continuous-cleaning oven** is an oven in which regular cooking heat interacts with a special coating on the interior to prevent burned-on food splatters. You can usually easily recognize a continuous-cleaning oven by the dark, rough surface of its interior. A **self-cleaning oven** is an oven in which a special cycle seals the oven shut, heats the interior to a very high temperature, and so burns off any food splatters. You can recognize this type of oven by its special locking device. For more information about self-cleaning ovens, see page 239.

Cleaning a Microwave Oven

The interior of a microwave oven is usually made of plastic. Therefore, you should not use an abrasive cleaner on it. Instead, use a mild solution of all-purpose cleaner and water. Remember to clean racks and turntables used in the oven, as well as the oven itself. Then, rinse and wipe everything dry. If you wipe the interior after each use, cleaning will be easy.

Cleaning a Refrigerator

Nonabrasive all-purpose cleaners can be used to clean the exterior of a refrigerator. A baking soda solution can be used to clean its interior. It is always best to clean the interior whenever a food spill occurs and according to a regular schedule.

Some refrigerators, called frost-free, defrost automatically. To learn more about these refrigerators, see page 239. Others must be defrosted manually. If you must defrost your refrigerator, do so when the ice

P.S.

What Special Features Help Ranges, Refrigerators, and You?

Of the major kitchen appliances, the range and refrigerator require the most care. To make your job easier, manufacturers have designed some very special features for the two appliances. These features are a self-cleaning oven and a frost-free cooling unit. How do these features work?

A self-cleaning oven works by actually cooking or burning food spills and splatters off the oven walls and racks. All you do is set the controls according to directions printed on the control panel of the range. Then, you set a timer, lock the door, and wait from one to three hours. While the oven is cleaning itself, you cannot open its door. Many self-cleaning ovens have a special light to let you know when cleaning is in progress and when it has ended. When the cleaning process is over, you simply wipe away the ashes.

A frost-free cooling unit works by removing moisture from the air inside the refrigerator. A special process causes the moisture to evaporate. The drying effect of this process keeps frost from forming on the cooling unit. Therefore, there is no ice to remove from the appliance.

In addition to these advantages of using appliances outfitted with such convenience features, there are a few disadvantages. For example, during the cleaning process, the self-cleaning oven will noticeably increase the temperature in your kitchen. The frost-free refrigerator will dry out foods that are not carefully packaged. In addition, although a self-cleaning oven will not add greatly to your electricity bill, a frost-free refrigerator will.

buildup is no more than ¼ inch (6 mm) thick. To defrost, follow these steps:

- Turn the refrigerator off or set it to "defrost" until the ice in its freezer melts. Do not try to hurry up the process by removing ice with a knife or an ice pick. These tools can damage the interior.
- Use a sponge to absorb the melted ice.
- Keep the freezer door open to allow the remaining moisture to dry.

Handling Maintenance

If you own your own place, you will have total responsibility for home maintenance. If you rent, your landlord will probably provide some but not all maintenance services. For example, you will need to replace light bulbs and may need to replace fluorescent lamps. These tasks are easy. You may also need to reset a circuit breaker or a smoke alarm or replace a fuse or a battery. In addition, you may have to make simple plumbing repairs, handle pest control, or do yard work. These tasks are easy, too, if you know what to do and what equipment to use.

Making Minor Household Repairs

Before beginning any repair job, make sure you have all the equipment and materials you need. It is a good idea to keep some basic "fix-it" tools and supplies on hand. These might include a flashlight, a hammer, various sizes of nails, a screwdriver, pliers, a wrench, and masking tape or electrical tape. When you run into a problem, ask a salesperson in a hardware store what additional supplies you will need for the specific repair. Then, read and follow any directions that are provided with these supplies. Take the time to do the job safely and correctly.

Taking Care of Electrical Maintenance

To prevent fires, the electricity flow through the wires, or circuits, in a house is generally monitored by devices called circuit breakers. If a circuit becomes overloaded—perhaps because too many appliances are connected to the same outlet—the circuit breaker will trip, or cut off the electricity. When this happens, you need to identify which circuit is overloaded, correct the situation, and reset the circuit breaker. Often, you can correct the situation by turning off or removing some of the electrical items connected to the overloaded circuit. If the circuit breaker continues to trip, you may have an appliance that needs repairing.

Each time you move, you need to locate the circuit breaker box in your new residence. It may be located in a hallway or in a closet. It may include a list that identifies the rooms that are on each circuit. If not, you will want to make such a list. By turning each breaker switch off one at a time, you can find out which switch controls which circuit.

Some homes have a fuse box rather than a circuit breaker box. A fuse box also stops the flow of electricity into a home. It does so by blowing one of its fuses. If a fuse blows, replace it with another one of the same size and strength. When you replace a fuse, twist it firmly to be sure it is secure.

If your place has a smoke alarm, you will need to test the alarm at least once a month to make certain that it can detect smoke. Most smoke alarms have a tiny red light or a test button that you can use to see if the battery is working. If the battery has gone dead, you will need to replace it. To replace the battery, remove the alarm cover or take the alarm off the wall. Inside the cover or on the back of the alarm, you may find directions for replacing the battery. If not, check to see how the dead battery is positioned. Then, insert the new battery in the same way. The top of the new battery should face the same direction as the top of the old one. Once the new battery is in position, replace the alarm cover or reattach the alarm to the wall. Test the smoke alarm again. Make sure it creates a sound that is loud enough to alert you in case of emergency.

240 Decorating and Caring for Your Home

Why might you want to know how to make minor household repairs such as these?

Taking Care of Plumbing Maintenance

If a faucet drips or cannot be turned off completely, you probably need to replace its washer. Before doing so, turn off the water by turning the knob under the sink. Then, replace the old washer with one of *exactly* the same size. Otherwise, you will still have drips, or the faucet will not turn on and off correctly. Next, test the faucet by turning it on and off several times. It should move smoothly but turn off securely. When you are sure the faucet is working well, turn the water back on.

If a toilet will not stop running, you can probably also solve this problem yourself. First, remove the top of the tank. Then, flush the toilet and watch how the flushing mechanism works. As the water flows into the tank, you should see a float, or ball, rise to a certain point. At this point, the water flow should stop. If the flow does not stop, the problem may be the result of one of the following situations:

- The rubber stopper at the bottom of the tank is worn out and needs to be replaced.
- The float is not moving to the top of the tank as the tank fills with water. If this is the case, the float needs to be adjusted or replaced.
- The tank is full of rust or other debris and needs to be cleaned.

If the rubber stopper or the float must be replaced, you can buy a replacement at a hardware store or department. The package directions will tell you how to install it. If the float needs adjusting, you may be able to bend it slightly so that it rides higher in the water. If the tank needs to be cleaned, you should pour some ammonia *or* bleach—never both—into the water in the tank. After you allow the mixture to stand for two or three minutes, flush the toilet. Keep repeating this procedure until the inside of the tank is completely clean.

Handling Pest Control and Yard Work

If you are responsible for pest control in your home, you may want to contact a pest control service. Between visits, however, you

Handling Maintenance **241**

can take the following measures to keep pests under control:

- Take out garbage and newspapers daily.
- Keep floors and cabinets clean.
- Seal cracks or openings around doors and windows.
- Use pesticides with caution. A **pesticide** is a strong poison that is sprayed on or fed to insects to kill them. If small children or animals are in your home, avoid the use of harsh poisons.

If you are responsible for yard care, you can hire someone to handle it or take care of the yard yourself. If you decide to handle your own yard care, you will need to buy, rent, or borrow certain equipment. Basic items include a lawn mower, a hoe, an edge-trimmer, clippers, a hose, and a sprinkler. You may also need special supplies like fertilizer. The best way to find out how to care for your yard is to ask and watch other renters or homeowners who have had practice in caring for their yards.

Points to Remember

- Using floor plans and furniture templates can help you plan convenient, interesting arrangements before actually moving your furniture.
- To walk comfortably between furniture pieces or furniture and walls, allow 1½ to 2 feet (.5 to .6 m) of walk space.
- Sometimes a wall decoration changes both the appearance and the function of a wall.
- When decorating windows, consider the effect of the material, construction, and style of the window covering.
- Storing items close to their point of use is desirable.
- Storing kitchen equipment is easier if it is organized around the three kitchen work centers.
- To make housekeeping easy, set up a convenient cleaning schedule and use appropriate cleaning products and techniques.
- Glass, porcelain, chrome, plastic, and ceramic-tile surfaces all require non-abrasive cleaners.
- Ranges and refrigerators must be cleaned regularly.
- As a renter, you may have to handle minor electrical and plumbing repairs. You may also need to provide your own pest control and yard care services.

Test Your Skills
RESOURCE MANAGEMENT

Imagine yourself in the situation described below. In this situation, resources need managing. As you read, think about the ways that you can manage resources. Then, answer the questions that follow. When you need to manage resources in the future, remember to ask yourself these questions.

Situation

You and your roommate have moved into a large, old apartment. Your landlord says that you can decorate however you please. You know that you want some rooms painted and others wallpapered. You also want certain styles of window coverings in each room. In addition, you want to include some unusual plants.

Both of you are busy with jobs and school. The amount of money you can spend on decorating is limited and so are some of your skills. You have no experience in painting or wallpapering a room. You have never made curtains, draperies, or slip-covered cushions. You want to decorate as soon as possible but are not sure of the best way to do it.

You could try a professional decorating service but are afraid it would cost too much. You could try to do the work yourselves but are not sure you could spend enough time to get the results you want. You could offer your services through a bartering network. After all, the two of you enjoy running errands and shopping for others and could easily work such activities into your schedules.

Questions

1. Which resource do you need to manage most carefully. Why? (Hint: Look for the resource that is in shortest supply.)

2. What are the ways you might manage this resource? (Hint: Be sure to name any resources you could substitute, trade, or share.)

3. What opportunity costs would be involved in each case?

4. Who would pay the opportunity costs in each case?

5. After considering all these opportunity costs, how would you manage your resources in this situation?

Terms

On a separate sheet of paper, write a definition for each of the underlined terms below. Base your definition on the clues you find in the statement(s).

1. Trent considered what the traffic flow in each room would be before he arranged his furniture. He wanted to make sure people would have pathways for walking easily through and between rooms.

2. LaShonda looked at the floor plan for the one-bedroom apartments in an apartment complex. The outline showed where such features as doors, windows, and closets were.

3. Chang considers different room arrangements by using homemade furniture templates. He draws the width and length of each piece of his furniture to the following scale: ¼ inch equals 1 foot. He then cuts out his scale drawings and arranges them on a scale drawing of his room.

4. The food storage and preparation center in Tiffany's kitchen includes a sink, a refrigerator, cabinets, and some counter space.

5. Alan's apartment has a kitchen with a large cooking and serving center. The center's range and spacious cabinet and counter space are exactly what he wants.

6. Kaulana uses her kitchen's clean-up center to scrape off, wash, and dry the kitchen equipment she has used.

7. Sherman avoids using an abrasive cleaner on a plastic surface. He knows that such a cleaner might not only clean but also scratch the plastic.

8. When Cristina's parents chose a continuous-cleaning oven, they knew that its special interior would react with heat to keep food from burning onto the oven.

9. Roosevelt is in charge of oven cleaning in his home. It is his duty to set the self-cleaning oven so it seals shut and heats up to an extremely high temperature. This procedure burns off any food spatters.

10. Lisa is careful when she uses a pesticide. Although she sometimes sprays it on an insect in the kitchen, she does not spray it near food.

Questions

1. What factors help you plan the furniture groupings you want?
2. Name two strategies for creating interesting furniture arrangements.
3. As a renter, why might you not be able to decorate walls, windows, and floors the way you would like?

4. How can window coverings change the look of a room?
5. List three items that should be stored in each of the three kitchen work centers.
6. What should you remember about storing household cleaning and personal care products?
7. What are two general guidelines to follow when you store occasional-use items?
8. Briefly describe how to set up a cleaning schedule.
9. What factor most often helps you decide how to clean furniture, floors, and bathroom fixtures?
10. Identify four parts of a range that need to be cleaned.
11. What should you avoid doing when defrosting a refrigerator?
12. Name two typical electrical and two typical plumbing maintenance tasks you may need to perform.
13. List two things you can do to help keep pests under control.

Activities

1. Collect magazine pictures of various room arrangements. Evaluate each example according to any or all of the following factors:
   a. furniture groupings—purpose or type
   b. traffic flow—convenient or inconvenient
   c. design elements—line, color, texture, shape
   d. design principles—proportion, rhythm, balance, emphasis, harmony
   e. storage—hidden or displayed, adequate or inadequate, convenient or inconvenient
2. Make a decorating plan. Include your preferences for colors, lighting, privacy, storage, furniture materials and styles, furniture groupings, and accessories.
3. List the housing accessories that young people might take with them when they move to a place of their own. How might they create different moods or atmospheres with these accessories?
4. Make a list of the cleaning tasks that you now have. Indicate whether each cleaning task is a daily, weekly, monthly, or seasonal task and about how long it takes to complete. What additional cleaning jobs will you probably have total responsibility for as a young adult? How much more time each week will these require, and how might you schedule them?
5. Read pesticide labels and describe the kinds of precautions they list.

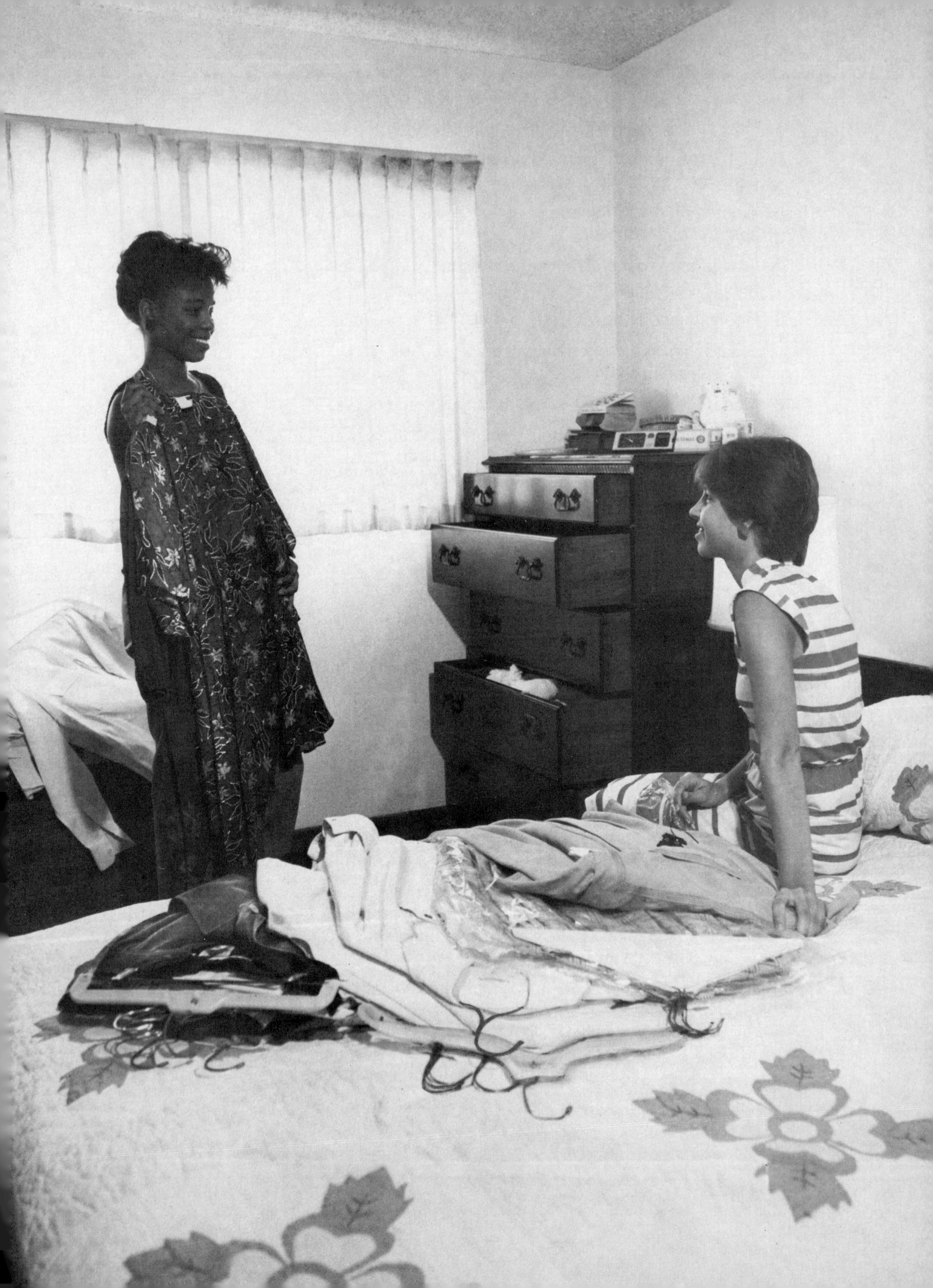

CHAPTER 11

Updating Your Wardrobe

What you wear helps to create an impression of you in the minds of others. It gives clues about the type of work you do, your interests, and your lifestyle. Selecting what you wear is one way you express yourself.

Right now, you are a student, and your lifestyle includes school activities and perhaps a job, sports, and other outside interests. In a few months or years, you will be graduating. Then, you will probably start a full-time job, get vocational training, begin an apprentice program, enter the service, attend college, or a combination of these. As you become involved in new activities, your wardrobe needs will change.

Adding to your wardrobe or building a new one has many challenges. You want to select clothes and accessories that are suitable for your activities. You will probably want a combination of items that are in style—some classics and some fads. You will want items that are well suited to you and make you look attractive. You will also want items that fit you, last as long as you need them, and fit your budget.

Clothes and accessories that do all of these things should reflect the real you. They should also make you feel confident, knowing that you look your best.

Discover Through Your Reading

- how changes in your lifestyle influence the types of clothes and accessories you wear
- why you may want to include both classics and fads in your wardrobe
- why some lines, colors, textures, and shapes might look better on you than on someone else
- how fit, fabrics, and finishes affect how often you wear each item in your wardrobe
- how you can add to your wardrobe without always having to buy new clothing and accessories

Looking at Your Wardrobe Needs

As you become more independent, your lifestyle and the clothes and accessories you need will probably change. Most likely, you will either be starting your career or continuing your education. In any case, you probably will be making new friends and getting involved in new activities. Some of your clothes and accessories will probably continue to serve you well. Others, however, will need to be replaced. You will want to update your wardrobe with items better suited to your new lifestyle. A person's **wardrobe,** or **apparel,** is all the clothes and clothing accessories that person owns. Clothing accessories include such items as shoes, belts, ties, scarves, and jewelry.

As you update your wardrobe, you will want to consider which type of apparel will be appropriate for each of your activities: work, school, leisure, and special occasions.

Any wardrobe you create needs to contain items suited to your many activities. What special characteristics do you want for school clothes, for work clothes, for leisure clothes, and for special-occasion clothes?

If you make sure your wardrobe includes items for each of these activities, you will probably feel confident that you are making a good impression.

Apparel for Work or School

The apparel you need for work will depend on your job. For example, some employers provide uniforms or costumes and may provide free or low-cost laundry or dry-cleaning services for them. Such jobs allow you to save time and money you would otherwise spend buying and caring for a variety of clothes and accessories.

Other jobs do not require uniforms but do have more or less formal dress codes that all employees are expected to follow. To find out if there is a written dress code or if certain apparel is recommended, ask during an interview. Also, watch what other employees are wearing, and choose similar apparel.

The same principle applies if you are attending vocational school or college. You can look around and choose clothes and accessories that are as casual or as tailored as those that other students are wearing.

Apparel for Leisure Time

Meeting new friends and getting involved in new activities is one of the most rewarding parts of life after high school. The apparel you wear for these leisure activities should be attractive, practical, and durable.

Today, leisure apparel is available in many different styles. For example, there are special clothes and accessories designed for many sports. You may choose certain apparel for tennis, jogging, softball, or basketball, swimming, hiking, or skiing. Many items designed for a sport can also be worn for other activities such as shopping, housework, or relaxing. This is especially true for leisure apparel made from stretchy, color-coordinated fabrics that are easy to launder. Such items are usually comfortable, attractive, and practical.

Apparel for Special Occasions

A special occasion such as a business dinner, a wedding, a party, or a banquet occurs from time to time. Sometimes, a printed invitation or announcement to such a special event will specify the appropriate type of dress. The following phrases are typically used to indicate what should be worn:

- *Formal dress.* Men wear a tuxedo. Women wear a gown or wear a very fancy skirt or pants with a fancy top.
- *Dress clothes.* Men wear a dark business suit, a shirt, and a tie. Women wear a suit with a shirt or wear a dress.
- *Informal dress.* Men wear pants with a sports coat, a jacket, or a sweater and a shirt. Women wear a dress or wear a skirt or pants with a jacket or a sweater and a shirt.
- *Casual dress.* Men and women wear pants or shorts with a shirt or a leisure top or wear swimsuits or other active wear.

If there is no printed invitation or announcement for a special event, ask other people who will be going what they plan to wear. This will give you a good idea of what types of apparel are suitable.

Considering What Makes a Wardrobe Wearable

Before you start updating your wardrobe, think about what makes a wardrobe wearable. Many people buy some clothes and accessories that they never wear. Perhaps you have noticed a few such items in your closet. For example, you may have shirts that match nothing else you own. You may have shoes that looked great in the store but have never felt comfortable. Everyone has made some poor wardrobe choices. If you learn why you made yours, you can make better choices in the future.

In general, you will probably wear the clothes and accessories you buy if they are in style and make you look attractive. You will also probably get more wear from them if they fit comfortably and are well made.

A Look That Is in Style

Because what you wear influences how people on the job, at school, and elsewhere react to you, it is important to be alert to fashion trends. There are several interesting ways to learn what is in style, or popular with a great number of people. You can look at the ads in newspapers or magazines or look at fashion displays in stores. You can also read articles or books about fashion. In addition, you can ask for advice about fashion from friends or salespeople.

Some of the clothes and clothing accessories that are in style are classics. Others are fashion fads. For a flexible, attractive wardrobe, you will probably want to include some of each.

Wardrobe Classics

Styles of clothing and accessories that have been popular for many years and change only slightly from season to season are called **wardrobe classics.** A classic item usually works well with many other wardrobe items you own. For example, men can combine a navy blazer with gray pants one year and with plaid the next year. Women can wear a navy blazer with a pleated skirt, with a straight skirt, or with pants.

Two characteristics of classic styles are the use of certain colors and the use of certain prints. Standard colors for classic clothes and clothing accessories are gray, black, white, brown, tan, navy, and red. Traditional prints include solids, plaids, and stripes.

Because you can wear a classic item for several years, you will want to buy the best quality that you can afford. Some classic clothes that you may want in your wardrobe include the following basic items:

- shirts that button up the front and have medium-length collars
- shirts in ever-popular solids and prints
- pants with straight legs and no pleats
- skirts and dresses hemmed to hit just below the knee
- jackets or blazers with medium-width lapels

Wardrobe Fads

Styles of clothes and accessories that are popular for only a few weeks or months are **wardrobe fads.** They are usually fun, lively, and imaginative, but short-lived. For example, this month, blazing, brightly colored socks might be popular. Next month, plaid socks might take their place.

Fad items can give your wardrobe an interesting look. You can combine them with classics or wear them instead of classics, especially for leisure activities and special events. However, your budget will probably lead you to buy fewer fad items than classic items. It may also lead you to buy inexpensive fad items. After all, if you spend a great deal of money on one fad, you may not have money for basics or for a later fad item.

A Look That Is Attractive for You

Most likely, the clothes and accessories you wear often are the ones that make you look your best. They accent your best features, while automatically taking attention away from any less attractive features. For example, they may make you look taller or shorter, thinner or heavier. They can make you look healthy or pale, happy or sad, silly or serious, younger or older.

Clothing and accessories do the most for you if they reflect the basic elements and principles of design. For an illustration of these elements and principles, see pages 208–223. To apply these design basics to your selection of wardrobe items, you need to identify your build and coloring.

People with different builds can look attractive. How would you describe your build?

Determining Your Build

How would you describe your build? A person's **build** is that person's combination of bone structure, muscle development, height, weight, and proportions. You may have large bones or small bones, for example. You may have well-developed muscles or undeveloped ones. You may be short or tall, thin or heavy. Your arms, legs, and neck may be long or short. The shape of your face may be round, square, oval, diamond, or heart. Your shoulders may be broad or sloping. You may be short-waisted or long-waisted.

Whatever your features, decide which add to your attractiveness and which detract from your appearance. Then, use the elements and principles of design as you select clothes and accessories.

Understanding Your Coloring

A person's **coloring** is that person's combination of eye color, hair color, and skin color. Depending on the combination, a person's coloring is either cool or warm. Of the three color factors, skin color plays the biggest part in determining whether a person has cool or warm coloring. A person with *cool* coloring usually has skin with blue undertones. A person with *warm* coloring usually has skin with yellow undertones.

Whether you have cool or warm coloring, you will probably look good in at least one shade or tint of each color. A person's coloring will, however, determine which shades and tints are most flattering to that person. For example, a person with cool coloring will probably look best in many variations of cool colors and in fewer variations of warm colors. A person with warm coloring will probably look best in many variations of warm colors and in fewer variations of cool colors. The cool colors are blue, violet, and green. The warm colors are red, yellow, and orange.

What is your coloring? You can find out by either consulting a professional color analyst or doing your own color analysis. If you are thinking about getting a professional color analysis, the information on page 252 may be of interest. If you want to analyze your own coloring, start by looking at your current wardrobe.

Under natural lighting, hold up to your face fabrics or garments of different colors. Use as many values and intensities of each color as you have available. Remember that *value* means the darkness or lightness of a color. *Intensity* means the dullness or brightness of a color. Some colors will look better on you than others. The colors that highlight your skin, hair, and eyes are your best colors. If your best colors are mostly cool colors, you probably have cool coloring. If your best colors are mostly warm colors, you probably have warm coloring. Knowing your best colors and your coloring can help you select clothing and accessories that you will wear and enjoy wearing.

A Comfortable Fit

Clothes and accessories must fit comfortably or you will not wear them often. For a clothing item to fit, it must be the right size. Fortunately, clothing manufacturers make clothes in many different sizes, including tall, short, large, husky, full figure, and petite. Because of the range of sizes offered,

Considering What Makes a Wardrobe Wearable

P.S. How Can a Color Analyst Benefit You?

Some people clearly have cool or warm coloring. They can tell right away which they have. Other people have more difficulty figuring out their coloring. Even a professional color analyst may have difficulty determining whether the client's coloring is cool or warm. In fact, the color analyst may have to hold different colors near the client's face *several times* before deciding.

Most color analysts are trained to accurately determine the skin, hair, and eye coloring of any man or woman. Most analysts do more, however. They also check to see whether a hue itself, its shade, or its tint is most attractive near a client's face. On the one hand, certain hues and their shades may overpower a client's coloring. Tints of those same hues, on the other hand, may be just right. The analyst can look at a client under natural lighting and tell which hues, shades, and tints look best on that person. After determining a client's "best colors," the analyst will give the client a sample of those colors to carry while shopping.

If you decide to use the services of a professional color analyst, the analyst may come to your home to make the analysis. You may also attend a group session led by the analyst. By watching in a mirror as the analyst holds colored paper or cloth near your face, you can see for yourself how you look in various colors. If the color analyst encourages you to invite friends in to watch the analysis, your friends can give you feedback, too.

Only you can decide whether you need to rely on a professional to determine your coloring. Whether you analyze your coloring or have a professional do it, you are likely to feel afterwards that shopping for clothing is more rewarding and easier. You will find yourself spending the money you have budgeted for clothing on items whose colors look great on you. You will also find yourself saving time you used to waste trying on items whose color did not enhance yours.

Fitting Details

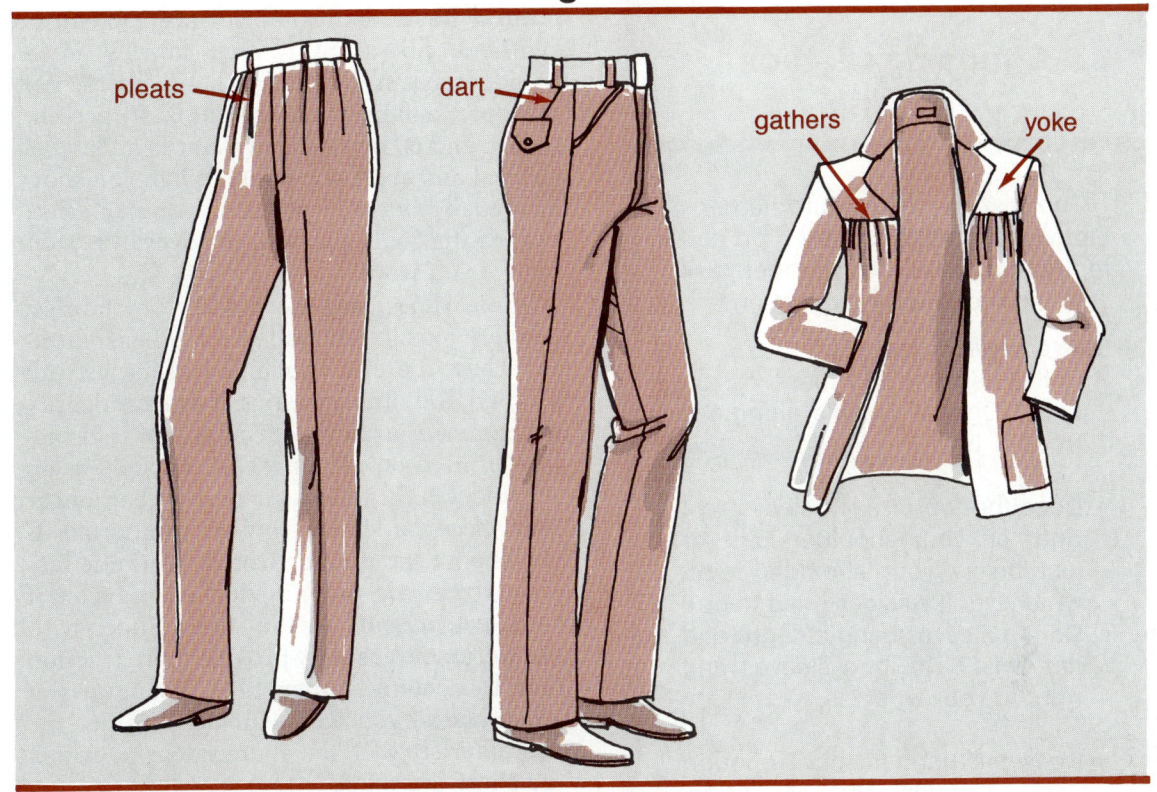

chances are good that you will find a size that is right for you.

For a clothing item to fit, it must also have enough **ease,** or room for free movement. While some styles are loosely fitted, others are more closely fitted. Fitted styles often have pleats, yokes, gathers, or darts. These construction details make the garment smaller where the body is smaller and larger where the body is larger. For tips on choosing clothes that fit, see page 254.

A Satisfactory Performance

Another factor that determines how often you will wear a wardrobe item is how long it will last. When selecting a wardrobe item, consider how you want it to perform. The performance of any such item will depend on several factors. These include the fabric or material content, the finish, the care requirements, and the quality of construction.

Fabric or Material Content

Many items in a wardrobe are made from **fabric,** cloth made by knitting or weaving yarns. Yarns result from the twisting or pulling together of fibers. **Fibers** are threadlike strands of a natural or synthetic substance. **Natural fibers** are fibers produced by plants and animals. Cotton and linen are examples of plant fibers. Wool and silk are examples of animal fibers. **Synthetic fibers** are fibers developed in a laboratory. Polyester, nylon, acrylic, modacrylic, and acetate are examples of synthetic fibers.

Each type of fiber has characteristics that affect the performance of fabric made from it. Therefore, it is important to recognize fiber names and their characteristics. The chart on page 255 shows you what to expect from fabrics made from different natural and synthetic fibers.

Some clothes and accessories are made from only one fiber. An example is a 100 percent cotton T-shirt. Other clothes and accessories are made from two or more fibers.

Considering What Makes a Wardrobe Wearable

> ## Tips
> ### Choosing Clothes That Fit
>
> The best way to find out whether a clothing item fits is to try it on and look in the mirror. As you look, ask yourself the following questions:
>
> **Shirts, tops, or jackets**
> - Is the neckline too loose or too tight? Does it wrinkle along the front or back?
>
> - Does the top of each sleeve rest right on your shoulder joint or just below your shoulder joint, whichever it was designed to do? Do the sleeves hang straight and not twist? Do long sleeves end right at your wrist?
>
> - Does the garment have enough room through the shoulders, across the chest, and at the waist for you to be comfortable?
>
> - Does the garment close without pulling or straining?
>
> - Are yokes, gathers, pleats, or darts positioned where you need the most fullness?
>
> **Pants, shorts, or skirts**
> - Is the waist too tight?
>
> - Do the seams pull when you stand, sit, walk, or move?
>
> - Is the garment hemmed too short or too long for you?

When fibers are combined, they usually produce fabrics with the best characteristics of each fiber. If a combination of fibers is used to make the yarn in a fabric, the fabric is called a **blend**. Some fabrics are a blend of natural fibers. Other fabrics are a blend of synthetic fibers. Still other fabrics are a blend of natural and synthetic fibers. For example, a fabric that contains 40 percent cotton and 60 percent polyester is a blend of natural and synthetic fibers. When you know how each fiber will perform, you can select fabrics that will give you the overall performance you want.

While shoes may be made from fabrics, they are most often made from other materials. These materials include leather, as well as vinyl and other plastics. You can identify the material used by checking the information printed on the inside of the shoe or on the sole. Leather shoes generally wear longer than those made from synthetic materials. If you choose shoes made from a synthetic material, be aware that an odor may develop if your feet perspire in the shoes. Shoes with synthetic soles usually provide more traction than those with leather soles. Whenever you select shoes, you will want to consider the characteristics of the material from which the shoes are made.

Fabric Finish

Perhaps you have a pair of jeans that has been "preshrunk." Maybe you have a swimsuit that is "colorfast." Maybe you have suede boots that are "soil-resistant." If so, you have clothes and accessories with some type of fabric finish.

A **fabric finish** is any treatment of a fabric that either changes its appearance or improves its performance. A fabric finish may be chemical or physical. For example, apparel that is "water-repellent," "soil-resistant," "fire-retardant," or "wrinkle-resistant" has been treated chemically. Clothes that have a glossy surface may be made from a fabric treated with heat and pressure.

If a garment has a fabric finish, the finish may be described on the clothing label. If the terms *wrinkle-resistant* and *colorfast* do not appear on the label, you can test the fabric for these finishes yourself. To test for wrinkle-resistance, squeeze a small piece of the fabric in your hand. If the fabric wrinkles, you will need to iron the garment to keep it looking nice. To test for colorfastness, rub a

Fibers Used in Fabrics: A Guide to Characteristics and Care

Fiber	Characteristics	Typical Garments	Care
NATURAL Cotton	• is very absorbent • is durable • wrinkles easily • is comfortable to wear	• shirts • sportswear • T-shirts • jeans	• machine-wash and tumble-dry • iron unless treated to be wrinkle-resistant
Linen	• is durable • wrinkles easily	• suits • dresses	• wash in cool water • iron
Silk	• is soft and lustrous • drapes well • wrinkles • may fade	• shirts • suits • dresses	• usually, dry-clean • may be hand-washed • do not use chlorine bleach
Wool	• is warm and comfortable • is very absorbent • sheds wrinkles • may shrink • may **pill**, mat into little balls	• suits • sweaters • sportswear • dresses • socks	• usually, dry-clean • may be hand-washed and drip-dried
SYNTHETIC Acetate	• has a silk-like look • drapes well • is subject to abrasion • is heat-sensitive • loses strength when wet	• shirts • formal dresses	• usually, machine-wash gently • do not wring or twist • iron on a low setting
Acrylic/ modacrylic	• resembles wool • is wrinkle-resistant • is soft, fluffy, and bulky • may have static electricity • may pill	• sweaters • sportswear • sleepwear • synthetic furs	• machine-wash with warm water and tumble-dry • use fabric softener to reduce static electricity • iron on a low setting
Nylon	• is very strong • is durable • is subject to abrasion • does not shrink or stretch • is not very absorbent • tends to pick up soil and dye during washing	• shirts • sweaters • jackets • sportswear • pants • dresses • underwear	• machine-wash and tumble-dry • use fabric softener to reduce static electricity • use a warm iron
Polyester	• is very wrinkle-resistant • is strong • does not shrink or stretch • may pill • attracts and holds oily stains • picks up soil and dye when washed	• suits • sweaters • pants • dresses • fiberfill for jackets and comforters	• pretreat greasy stains • machine-wash and tumble-dry • use fabric softener to reduce static electricity • use a warm iron
Rayon	• is absorbent • has a high shine • may lose strength when wet	• shirts • suits • jackets • dresses • linings	• machine-wash gently and tumble-dry on low setting • may require dry-cleaning
Spandex	• is stretchy • is lightweight • may weaken or yellow over time	• children's clothes • swimsuits • exercise clothes • underwear	• machine-wash and tumble-dry on low setting • do not use chlorine bleach

Considering What Makes a Wardrobe Wearable

small piece of an inside seam or hem on white paper. If the color rubs off, the fabric is not colorfast and may fade when washed.

Care Requirements

Part of your satisfaction with a clothing item will depend on how easy the item is to care for. The type of care required is usually determined by the amount of each fiber used and by the fabric construction. For example, clothes made entirely or mostly from silk or wool need to be dry-cleaned or perhaps hand-washed. Clothes made from a small amount of silk or wool in combination with much polyester can probably be machine-washed. A knitted nylon sweater may need to be hand-washed. A woven nylon shirt can probably be machine-washed.

A good way to select clothes with the care requirements you want is to read clothing labels. By law, each clothing item must have some type of labeling to indicate fiber content and recommended care. You will find the fiber content stated either on a removable label called a hang tag or on a permanent clothing label. A **hang tag** is a *removable* label that may provide information concerning the manufacturer, fiber content, care, and other characteristics of the garment. You will find the recommended care described on a *permanent* clothing label called a care label and perhaps repeated on the hang tag. A **care label** is a sewn-in tag describing the care the garment will need.

Part of your satisfaction with shoes and other accessories will depend on how easy they are to take care of. The type of care required will usually be determined by the kind of materials used. For example, shoes made of vinyl or other plastics or made of smooth leather are easier to care for than suede shoes.

Quality of Construction

To get the most from your clothes and accessories, you will want them to be well constructed. After all, the quality of construction not only affects an item's durability, but also its fit and appearance.

Before selecting any wardrobe item, you will want to examine certain construction details. To determine whether the construc-

Hang Tag

Designer Looks, Inc.
Permanent Press
100% Polyester

This easy-care knit sportshirt makes a great addition to your wardrobe.

Care Instructions on Reverse

Care Label

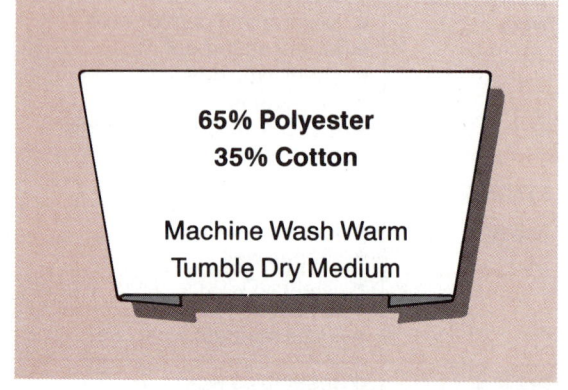

65% Polyester
35% Cotton

Machine Wash Warm
Tumble Dry Medium

tion details of a clothing item reflect quality, do each of the following:

- Make sure that the thread used is not frayed or broken.
- Make sure there are no gaps between stitches. Pay special attention to the stitching on seams, zippers, and buttonholes. A **seam** is a set of stitches that holds together two pieces of material.
- Check for double rows of stitching or other reinforcement at areas of stress, such as at armholes.
- Check to see that seams lie flat and do not pucker.
- Make sure that seams are finished in such a way that the fabric will not ravel or fray easily. Make sure that hems are secure, that is, not coming loose. A **hem** is the set of stitches where an edge of a garment is folded up and attached to the inside of the garment.

- Fasten and unfasten closings such as zippers, buttons, snaps, and hooks and eyes to make sure they work properly.
- Look at the positioning of plaids, stripes, and other fabric designs to see if they match at the item's seams.
- Make sure that all parts of the garment require the same type of care. For example, if the fabric is machine-washable, the lining, buttons, and zipper should be machine-washable, too.

To make sure the construction details of shoes reflect quality, check for each of the following:

- sturdy stitching
- no evidence of glue at any seam
- firmly attached eyelets or other closings
- firmly attached heels and innersoles

Seams and Hems

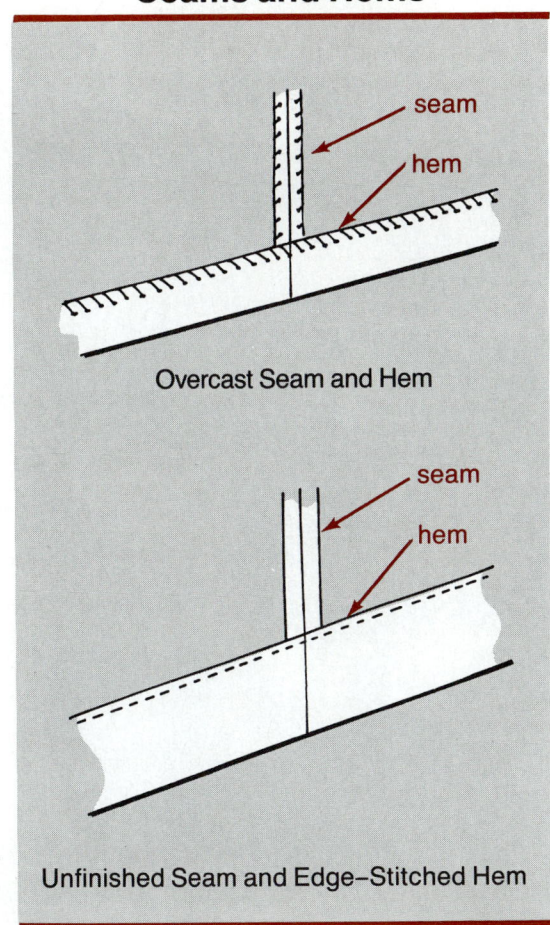

Overcast Seam and Hem

Unfinished Seam and Edge–Stitched Hem

Getting the Apparel You Need

Before you make any additions to your current wardrobe, take a good look at the apparel you already own. You may find that some of the items are perfect in every way. They are appropriate for one or more occasions. They are in style and make you look your best. They are comfortable, durable, easy to care for, and well made. You will probably find that some items meet part of your needs but not all. For example, they may be suitable for certain activities. They may not, however, be in style or be comfortable. You will most likely find that some items really do not belong in your wardrobe. They may not be your best colors or may be too worn-out.

One of the best ways to evaluate your wardrobe is to take a wardrobe inventory. Just follow the tips on page 258. Then, use the results to help you determine your future wardrobe needs. Your needs and resources will help you decide when to buy ready-to-wear apparel, when to exchange or recycle items, and when to sew your own apparel.

Buying Clothes and Accessories

You may already buy many of your own clothes and accessories. Many of these are probably either new or used ready-to-wear items. **Ready-to-wear apparel** is clothes and accessories that are mass-produced. Buying ready-to-wear items usually allows you to find the styles, sizes, and colors you need. However, it also increases your chances of selecting the same items as those worn by people you know. Also, there are other, less expensive ways to add to your wardrobe. Depending on where you shop, you can buy either new or used ready-to-wear apparel.

Tips

Taking Inventory of Your Wardrobe

Taking a wardrobe inventory is easy when you follow each of these steps:

- Take all of your clothes and accessories out of your closet and dresser drawers.

- Try on each item, even if you have not worn it in a while. Check each item for style, color, fit, cleaning, mending, and altering.

- Separate out all items that require some care or repair.

- Now, try on each garment with every other one. You may be amazed to see how many shirts look good with different pants, for example.

- Make note of the outfits you have. You may want to list each outfit on an index card. Note which clothes and accessories go together well.

- Then, prepare a list of the wardrobe items that you need to get. As often as possible, list those items that you can easily coordinate with each other and with items you already own.

- Consider all the ways you can get apparel, and decide which is best for each item.

- Exchange, sell, or give away items you do not use. Otherwise, they will continue to clutter your closet when someone else could be using them.

New Ready-to-Wear Apparel

Buying new ready-to-wear apparel, if you can afford it, may be a good choice when any of the following factors apply:

- you want an item that is in style
- you want an item that will last
- you want the most detailed information about an item's care requirements

You can buy new ready-to-wear items in department stores, discount stores, specialty shops, and factory outlets. You might even order through a catalog. In that case, however, you must order without seeing or trying on the actual item.

New ready-to-wear items may sometimes need to be altered. For example, the sleeves

You can pay a professional to alter your clothing or you can make your own alterations. Which do you prefer?

258 Updating Your Wardrobe

of a jacket may be too long or the waistband on a pair of slacks may be too loose. If you purchase an item that needs to be altered, the place where you shop may provide an alteration service. The store may employ an **alterationist,** a person who changes the fit of clothing. If the store does not provide this service and you cannot make the alteration yourself, you will need to contact someone who can. For example, you might try a dry-cleaning service.

Used Ready-to-Wear Apparel

If you need a jacket for an occasional camping trip, you may want to buy a used one. Buying used ready-to-wear items may be a good choice when any of the following factors apply:

- you do not need the latest style or a particular color
- you will wear the item only occasionally
- you do not need the item to last a long time
- you do not need to know the item's special care requirements
- you cannot or do not want to spend the money for a new item

When you buy used ready-to-wear items, you can shop at garage sales, flea markets, and secondhand stores. Keep in mind that you may not find the sizes you need or the quality of construction you want, and you may not have the chance to try on items for fit. In addition, you may need to have some items cleaned or altered.

Exchanging Clothes and Accessories

A popular way to add to your wardrobe is to exchange wardrobe items with family members or friends. Perhaps you and your cousin wear the same shoe size. Maybe you and your older brother or sister like the same colors and styles. Maybe your friend is tired of a tan jacket and you would like it. Perhaps your friend has always admired some of your shirts. You might trade two shirts you never wear for the jacket. Then, each of you would

What are some of the advantages and some of the disadvantages of buying used ready-to-wear items?

have something "almost new" to round out your wardrobe.

Recycling Clothes and Accessories

When you recycle a wardrobe item, you change its appearance and possibly its use. There are several ways to change only the appearance of apparel. For example, you could use different buttons on a shirt or on a jacket. You could add trim to collars, sleeves, or cuffs. You could dye a vest. To learn how a computer can help you design recycled clothes, see page 260.

There are also ways to change the use of clothes and accessories as well as their appearance. You might want to recycle a pair of pants into a pair of shorts. You might want to turn a long-sleeve shirt into a short-sleeve shirt. You might remove the sleeves from a jacket and make it into a vest. You

Getting the Apparel You Need **259**

How Computers Can Help You

Using Computer Designs to Recycle Clothes

So you are tired of some of your clothes. That jacket has seen four seasons. True, it is not torn or especially worn. You just do not like it anymore. Since it still fits you, you know your family would not be pleased if you gave it away. Besides, a new jacket would cost a lot, and neither you nor they are prepared to replace a perfectly good jacket. What can you do?

All you need is a computer and a program that lets you create all kinds of designs. The home economics, industrial arts, or art department of your school is likely to have such a program. If not, it may be well worth it for you and your friends to chip in and buy such a program. The savings you could make by recycling some clothes would pay for the cost of the program many times over.

Using such a computer graphics program, you can create hundreds of beautiful designs and patterns in a never-ending series of colors. These patterns appear on the computer screen at the touch of a key. They can be expanded, contracted, or rotated. The patterns may resemble the designs found in beautiful old tapestries, mosaic tiles, or modern art. You can change the colors in a variety of ways.

When you have created patterns and designs you like and think are suitable for certain pieces of clothing, you can have the computer print copies of those designs. Then, you can stencil one or more designs onto the article of clothing you want to recycle and personalize. Next, you can go over the stenciled designs with paints especially designed for use on fabrics, or with colored threads.

Thus, instead of burying your old but still good clothes at the bottom of your closet, you can recycle and personalize them with computer designs. You can use these designs to give new life, color, and style to jackets, shirts, gloves, jeans, and even bookbags. Each item will be one of a kind.

could cover a pair of shoes with fabric to match an outfit you have made. You could even cut fabric from a skirt, dress, or tunic and turn it into a tie or a scarf.

Sewing Clothes and Accessories

Maybe you know someone who sews a part or all of his or her wardrobe. Perhaps you have already made some clothes or accessories for yourself. Sewing your own apparel gives you the chance to have clothing items that may fit better than ready-to-wear items. It also allows you to create a more original wardrobe than you may be able to buy ready-to-wear. You will not be as likely to see your friends or coworkers wearing items that are exactly the same. In addition, sewing may cut your wardrobe costs in half. Sewing does, however, take time, knowledge, skill, and equipment. Therefore, it may not be the fastest way to add to your wardrobe.

Sewing your own clothes and accessories may be a good choice when any of the following factors apply:

- you have trouble finding ready-to-wear items in styles or colors you like
- you have trouble finding ready-to-wear items in sizes that fit
- you enjoy the opportunity to work on creative projects
- you want your wardrobe to be more original than you feel it would be with ready-to-wear items

If you are interested in learning to sew or want to gain additional sewing skills, there are several ways to do so. You may have the chance to take a clothing construction course as one of your school subjects. You may have an opportunity to learn from a family member or a friend who sews well. You may be able to take a course offered by a fabric store, a sewing machine company, a recreation center, or a community college. Sewing some of your wardrobe means that you will need a sewing machine. It also means that you will need to learn how to find the patterns and fabrics that you want.

Choosing a Sewing Machine

When you first begin sewing, you might want to rent a sewing machine. Then, if you decide that you really enjoy sewing, you may want to buy your own. You can buy a new or used machine. While a used machine will be less expensive, it probably will not have a warranty. Before making your purchase, try to compare at least three different brands. Find out about the repairs, maintenance, and life expectancy of the machine. Ask for a demonstration and, then, try the machine yourself.

Sewing machines are available in various styles and price ranges. For example, you can buy a portable machine or one that is installed in a cabinet. You can buy one with a foot control or a knee control.

It is a good idea to buy the best sewing machine that you can afford, but do not buy one with more features than you will use. For example, if you plan to sew many shirts and jackets, you may need a machine with a buttonhole attachment. If you do not plan to sew knit fabrics, you may not need a machine with stretch-stitching.

Buying Patterns and Fabrics

To find patterns and fabrics for home sewing, you can shop several places. There are specialty shops for patterns and fabrics just as there are for clothes. Some of these stores carry a wide range of fabrics, including those used for home furnishings. Other stores sell fabrics used only for clothing and accessories. In addition to special fabric stores, you may find patterns and fabrics in discount stores and some department stores.

If you like designing, you may want to create your own patterns. When you first begin sewing, however, you will probably use patterns from a pattern company. These companies publish pattern catalogs several times a year. A pattern catalog shows you exactly which styles go together. It also identifies the patterns that are very easy and those that are more advanced. Each pattern then recommends appropriate fabrics, the amount of fabric needed, and other necessary supplies, such as thread, zippers, or buttons. The pattern also includes step-by-step instructions for making the item.

Getting the Apparel You Need **261**

Just like ready-to-wear garments, fabrics for home sewing carry labeling. You will usually find this labeling on the end of the carton around which the fabric is rolled. The label information includes the name and address of the manufacturer, the fiber content, the width of the fabric, and the care requirements. You might want to write down this information and keep it for reference. Or, you can ask the salesperson for the care label that accompanies the fabric. If you sew this label into your new garment, your garment will have permanent care instructions like those in ready-to-wear garments.

Points to Remember

- Your clothing needs will change as your lifestyle changes.
- Most jobs have definite clothing requirements, either as described in a formal dress code or as understood by employees after observing others on the job.
- Clothes that are in style, look good on you, fit you well, and are durable are an excellent investment.
- A wardrobe usually includes many classic items and some fad items.
- An understanding of the elements and principles of design can help you plan a wardrobe that is flattering.
- To be comfortable, clothes and accessories need enough ease to allow you to move freely.
- The characteristics of fibers and fabrics influence how a garment will look, feel, and wear.
- Clothing labels describe the fiber content and care requirements of every garment.
- You can build a wardrobe by buying new and used ready-to-wear items, exchanging clothes and accessories with others, recycling old items, and sewing your own apparel.

Test Your Skills

GOAL SETTING

Imagine yourself in the situation described below. In this situation, a goal needs to be set. As you read, think about what makes a goal reachable. Then, answer the questions that follow. When you need to set goals in the future, remember to ask yourself these questions.

Situation

You are so proud of yourself! You have just lost twenty pounds. The diet was rough to stick to but worth the effort. Now, your clothes are all too large and baggy. Since you have every intention of keeping off this weight, you need to make some changes in your wardrobe.

You have also just gotten a job as a child care aide in the local day-care center. This job will require you to have a neat and clean appearance and to wear clothes that are soil-resistant and easily laundered. Since preschoolers are so active, you will also want clothing that is comfortable, with plenty of room to move around in.

Some of your clothing can be altered to fit your new measurements. Most of it, however, needs to be replaced. If you spend even $65 a month to buy and care for your wardrobe, your $300 a month paycheck will not cover any miscellaneous or emergency expenses. Until now, your parents have paid for your clothes. They have agreed to help out with a part of your wardrobe expenses until you can assume complete responsibility for these costs.

Questions

1. What is your goal? Make sure it is realistic and clearly stated.
2. Do you think of your goal as short-range or long-range? Why?
3. What plan could you make to meet your goal?
4. What could get in the way of your achieving your goal?
5. What alternative plans could you make to meet your goal?

Terms

On a separate sheet of paper, write a definition for each of the underlined terms below. Base your definition on the clues you find in the statement(s).

1. Holly just bought a tan suit that should be in style for years. This <u>wardrobe classic</u> has medium-width lapels and a hem that comes to just below her knees.

2. Tim went shopping for a pair of shoes just like those all his friends wear. He knows the shoes will not be popular for long, but he likes to spend a little money on <u>wardrobe fads</u> from time to time.

3. Miyoko has learned from her grandmother how to weave yarn into <u>fabric</u>. Someday, Miyoko would like to learn how to make fabric the other way—by knitting yarn into cloth.

4. Phil has cool <u>coloring</u>. He has dark brown hair, medium-blue eyes, and dark skin with blue undertones.

5. Audrey's clothes always have enough <u>ease</u>. They allow her to move freely.

6. Reggie has a shirt that is made from a <u>blend</u> of cotton and polyester. The fabric has some characteristics of each type of fiber.

7. Laura wants to buy a pair of pants with a wrinkle-resistant <u>fabric finish</u>. Therefore, she is looking for pants whose care label indicates the fabric has been chemically treated to resist wrinkles.

8. While shopping for a new sweater, Kevin read the <u>hang tag</u> pinned to each one to find out who made the sweater and what kind of fiber was used.

9. Amy checks the <u>care labels</u> sewn into any ready-to-wear clothes she buys so that she can tell how to clean the items.

10. Luis knows how to look at each <u>seam</u> before he buys a ready-to-wear item. He makes sure there are no gaps or broken stitches wherever two separate pieces of material were sewn together.

Questions

1. Give an advantage of having to wear a uniform to work.
2. How should people dress for special occasions that require formal dress?
3. Name two characteristics of classic styles.

4. How will an understanding of your build and coloring help you put together an attractive wardrobe?

5. List two ways to check for fit in shirts, tops, or jackets. List two ways to check for fit in pants, shorts, or skirts.

6. Why is it important to consider the fiber content of clothes and clothing accessories?

7. How can clothing labels help you select items for your wardrobe?

8. Name four ways you can check for quality construction in a clothing item.

9. What is the purpose of a wardrobe inventory?

10. What are three factors that make shopping for new ready-to-wear apparel a good choice?

11. How do pattern companies and fabric manufacturers help consumers make satisfactory clothing choices?

Activities

1. Imagine a lifestyle that a young adult might have. Which specific clothes and clothing accessories would this person probably consider the most important? Why?

2. Think about three very different occupations. What clothes and accessories seem appropriate for each occupation? Which, if any, of the occupations would require uniforms? In what ways would your current wardrobe be appropriate for each of these occupations?

3. Would you describe yourself as having cool or warm coloring? Why? Name the colors you wear most often. Are these your best colors? Why?

4. Think about two clothing selections you have made—one satisfactory and one unsatisfactory. Describe the performance characteristics of each clothing item. What made you happy or unhappy with your selection?

5. Describe a garment that might require dry-cleaning. Call to determine the cost of cleaning the garment. Estimate the cost of wearing and cleaning the garment for a year. Would the cost of dry-cleaning influence your decision about whether to own the item?

6. Comparison shop for a specific wardrobe item that you might sew yourself. Price the item if purchased new at several different stores. Price the item if bought used. Then, figure the price of making the item yourself. Which alternative is the least expensive?

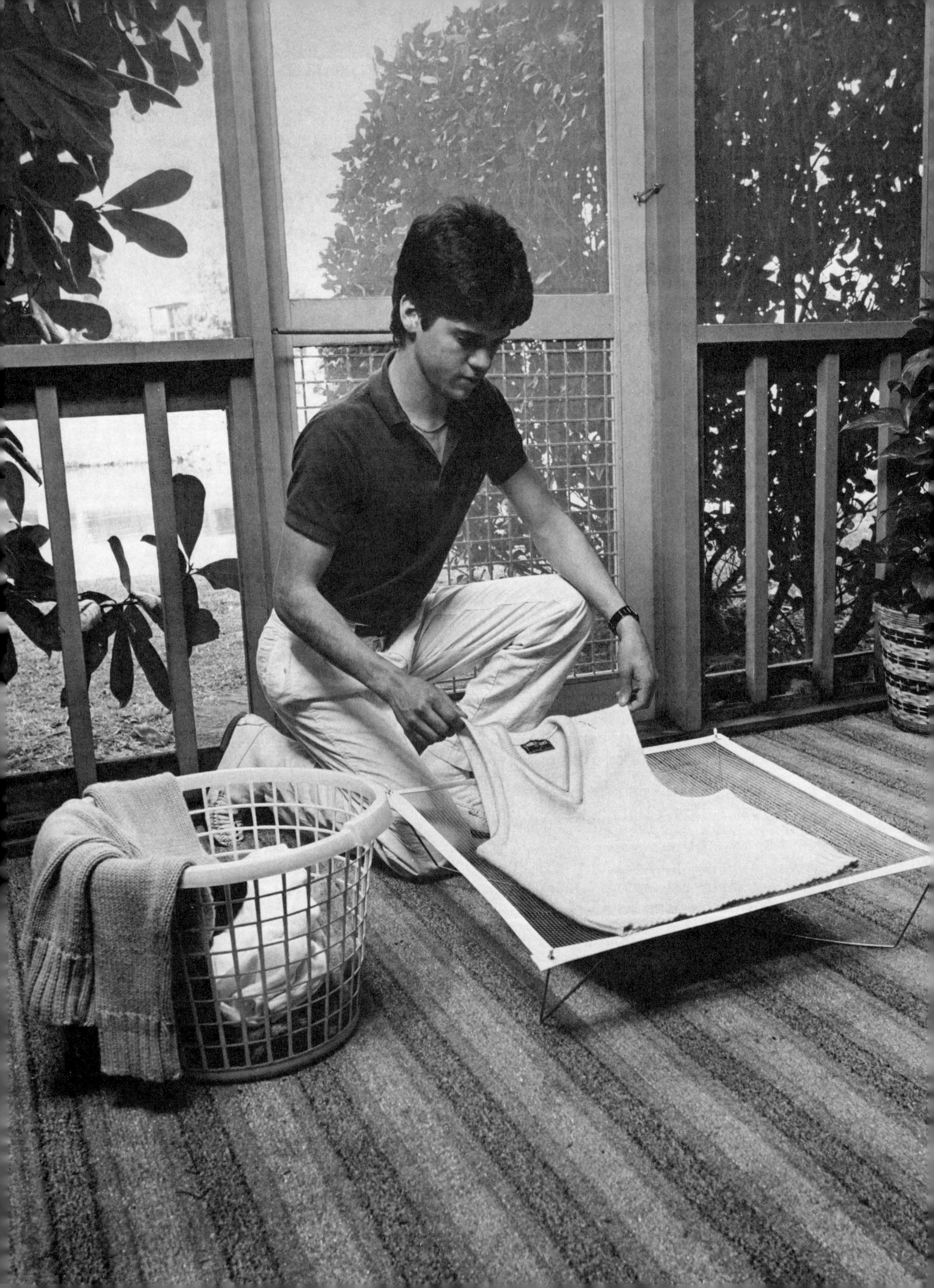

CHAPTER 12

Looking Well Groomed

Looking good depends partly on your careful planning and selection of a wardrobe. It also depends on how you take care of your clothes, your clothing accessories, and yourself.

As a young adult, you will be responsible for all aspects of your grooming. You will be in charge of dry-cleaning your clothes or selecting dry-cleaning services. You will also be responsible for doing your own laundry. To keep your clothes clean, you will need to know which laundry aids are best for each item. You will also need to know how to remove stains. To keep your clothes wearable, you may need to make minor clothing repairs. For example, you may need to sew a button onto a jacket or restitch a seam in a pair of pants. To keep your clothes looking good, you will always need to store them properly. From time to time, you may also need to iron some of them.

In addition to caring for your wardrobe, you will need to maintain a personal grooming routine. You already know the importance of bathing, brushing your teeth, and washing your hair. You probably use some grooming appliances and services; however, you may not yet be familiar with others.

Remember, good grooming has many benefits. It helps you look your best. It also encourages people to think of you in a positive way. In addition, it contributes to your feelings of self-confidence.

Discover Through Your Reading

- how to choose the correct cleaning methods for your clothes
- how to remove some common clothing stains
- why you might want to keep basic sewing supplies on hand
- how to store your clothes so they last longer and are ready to wear at a moment's notice
- what to consider before buying personal care products and grooming appliances

Wearing Clean Clothing

Whether going to school, to work, or on a date, you will always want to wear clean clothes. Keeping your clothes clean is easier when you know the basics. Sorting clothes according to the cleaning method they require is your first step. For those clothes that must be dry-cleaned, the next step is dry-cleaning them yourself or selecting a reliable dry cleaner. For clothes that you can wash, the next step is using the correct laundry aids and techniques.

Sorting Your Laundry

If all clothes required the same cleaning method, there would be no need to sort clothes before cleaning them. Different fabrics, however, require different cleaning methods. Some of your clothes, for example, may be made of fabrics that must be dry-cleaned. Being **dry-cleaned** means being rinsed in a solution of fluids that dissolve grease and dirt. The rest of your clothes are probably made of fabrics that can be laundered. Being **laundered** means being washed with soap or detergent and water.

Before you clean a garment, you need to find out which cleaning method is recommended for it. Your first sorting guide, therefore, is the permanent care label found in your clothing. Every clothing item must have a permanent care label attached. This label indicates what cleaning method is best for the garment.

The instructions on the care label will be specific. For example, if a garment can be washed, but only by hand in cool water, the label will read "Hand-wash, cold." If a specific laundering product or procedure could harm the garment, the care label will provide a warning such as "Do not bleach." If a care label does not specify that a laundering or drying method be avoided, you can use the method. For example, if the care label does not say "Warm water," or "Cold wash," you can safely use hot water. If you fail to follow care instructions and thereby damage a garment, you are responsible for the damage. For a description of terms used on permanent care labels, see pages 270–271.

Clothes That Require Dry-Cleaning

Clothes that should be dry-cleaned are those that might be damaged by soap, detergent, or water. Tailored suits, jackets, or blazers and garments made from 100 percent wool or silk, for example, may have a care label that says to dry-clean. Clothes that require dry-cleaning should be cleaned regularly. Otherwise, perspiration, grease, and dust may collect in the fabric and affect the garment's appearance and durability.

Many communities have coin-operated dry-cleaning machines, as well as professional dry-cleaning services. Coin-operated dry-cleaning machines are inexpensive to use and effective for some garments. For other garments, using a professional dry cleaner is best. To determine whether to dry-clean the garment yourself, check its care label. If the label does not say "Professionally dry-clean," you can do the job yourself.

How can you find out which of your clothing items can be cleaned in a coin-operated dry-cleaning machine?

268 Looking Well Groomed

Clothes That Can Be Washed

After you have separated out your dry-cleaning, you are ready to use your second sorting guide. You are ready to sort your washable items according to the following four characteristics:

- how soiled the item is
- what fabric the item is made of
- how colorfast the item is
- how much lint the item produces

These characteristics will determine the wash load into which you put each item.

Lightly soiled items, for example, do not need long soaking or washing cycles. By contrast, heavily soiled items may need pretreating, soaking, and extended washing or rinsing. **Pretreating** means applying a cleaning agent directly to a heavily soiled or stained area before washing the item.

Loosely knit or woven garments and very sheer or delicate fabrics must usually be hand-washed. If they are machine-washed, a gentle cycle must be used.

Colorfast clothing can be washed together. Items that are not colorfast should be washed separately or with items of the same color. Before washing new clothes or household textiles, you will want to test them for colorfastness. To test the colorfastness of an item before washing it, dip a small part of the inside of the garment into hot water. If dye runs into the water, the item is not colorfast.

In general, it is a good idea to wash similar colors together. Remember, however, that some fibers are color scavengers. A **color scavenger** is a fiber that has a tendency to pick up soil and loose dyes from the wash water. Nylon is a color scavenger, as is some polyester. Clothing made from these fabrics should be washed separately.

It is also a good idea to launder all lint-producing fabrics together, separately from other fabrics. Fabrics such as terry cloth make lint. Acrylic fabrics and polyester fabrics can collect lint.

In addition, as you sort your laundry, take the following steps:

- Make sure each wash load has a mixture of small, medium, and large items. This helps items circulate freely during washing and, therefore, get cleaner.
- Empty pockets. Then, turn them inside out and brush away lint and crumbs. This helps prevent stains and makes certain that money, pens, or other items do not get washed by mistake.
- Close all zippers and hooks.
- Loosely tie washable belts to prevent their tangling or tearing during washing.
- Mend tears or loose hems, and refasten buttons before washing garments.
- Look for spots, stains, or heavily soiled areas that need to be pretreated before washing garments.

Washing Your Clothes

You will probably wash most of your clothing in an automatic washer. You may have your own washer, or you may use a coin-operated washer in a public laundromat or in a laundromat operated by your landlord. To ensure that your clothing gets as clean as possible, you will want to use the appropriate wash cycle, water temperature, and laundry product. You will also want to load the machine correctly.

Choosing a Wash Cycle

The action of an automatic washer is called agitation. **Agitation** is the force used to move the water and circulate the clothes during laundering. Generally, the more agitation, the cleaner the clothes become. However, sheer or delicate fabrics can be damaged with regular agitation. Therefore, most washers have different wash cycles to provide differences in agitation.

A **wash cycle** is a series of cleaning actions used to clean a single load of laundry. For example, a wash cycle may include a pre-soak, a regular wash, a warm rinse, a second wash, and a cold rinse. Both care labels and laundry product labels can help you choose a wash cycle for your laundry needs.

Selecting the Water Temperature

Most automatic washers allow you to select either hot, warm, or cold water for the wash cycle. Again, both permanent care labels and laundry product labels can help you determine which temperature is best.

Wearing Clean Clothing **269**

Permanent Care Labels

Label	Meaning
Dry-Cleaning	
Dry-clean only	Take the item to a professional dry cleaner or dry-clean the item yourself in a coin-operated machine.
Professionally dry-clean	Take the item to a professional dry cleaner. Do not dry-clean the item yourself.
No dry-cleaning	Use recommended care instructions only. Do not take the item to a professional dry cleaner or dry-clean the item yourself.
Washing, Machine Methods	
Machine-wash	Clean by any customary method, including commercial laundering and dry-cleaning. When no temperature is specified, hot water up to 150° F (60° C) can be used.
Warm wash	Use an initial water temperature setting of 90 to 110° F (32 to 43° C)—a temperature comfortable to the hand.
Cold wash	Use an initial water temperature setting up to 85° F (29° C)—the temperature of cold tap water.
Do not have commercially laundered/Home launder only	Do not use a commercial, industrial, or institutional laundry. Launder the item at home or at a laundromat.
Delicate cycle/Gentle cycle	Use the appropriate machine cycle. It will have slower than usual agitation and a shorter than usual washing time.
Durable press cycle/Permanent press cycle	Use the appropriate machine setting. It will have a cool-down or cold rinse and a shorter than usual spinning time.
Wash separately	Wash the item by itself.
Wash with like colors	Wash the item with other items of similar hue and intensity.
No chlorine bleach	Do not use a chlorine bleach. An oxygen bleach may be used.
Warm rinse	Use an initial water temperature setting of 90 to 110° F (32 to 43° C)—a temperature comfortable to the hand.
Cold rinse	Use an initial water temperature setting up to 85° F (29° C)—the temperature of cold tap water.
Rinse thoroughly	Rinse the item several times to remove any detergent, soap, or bleach.
No spin/Do not spin	Remove the item before the final spin cycle starts.
No wring/Do not wring	Do not use a roller wringer or wring the item by hand.

Hot water does the quickest and most thorough cleaning job. You can use hot water on sturdy whites, as well as on colorfast items and heavily soiled garments unless their care label recommends otherwise.

Using warm or cold water reduces fading and wrinkling. You can use warm water on moderately soiled clothes, noncolorfast garments, and items with a permanent press finish unless their care label recommends cold water or dry-cleaning. You can use cold water on any garments, including jeans, that are not heavily or moderately soiled.

Most automatic washers use cold water for the final rinse. Cold water rinses effectively, prevents shrinkage, and is less expensive than hot or warm water.

Using Laundry Products

Many different laundry products are available. These include detergents and soaps,

Label	Meaning
Washing, Hand Methods	
Hand-wash	Launder only by hand in lukewarm water—water with a temperature comfortable to the hand. Dry-cleaning is permitted.
Cold wash	Use cold tap water instead of lukewarm or hot water.
Wash separately	Wash the item by itself.
Wash with like colors	Wash the item with other items of similar hue and intensity.
No wring or twist	Handle the item in such a way that wrinkles and distortions are not added to the fabric.
Rinse thoroughly	Rinse the item several times to remove any detergent, soap, or bleach.
Damp-wipe only	Use a damp cloth or a sponge to clean the surface of the item.
Drying, All Methods	
Tumble-dry	Use an automatic clothes dryer. When no temperature setting is specified, a high-heat setting may be used.
Medium heat	Set the clothes dryer on medium heat.
Low heat	Set the clothes dryer on low heat.
Durable press/ Permanent press	Use the clothes dryer's permanent press cycle, if the dryer has one.
No heat	Use the clothes dryer's no-heat cycle, if the dryer has one; if not, air-dry.
Remove promptly	When an item is dry, remove it immediately from the dryer to prevent wrinkles.
Drip-dry	Hang the item while it is dripping wet. You can hand-shape and smooth it.
Line-dry	Hang the item in or out of doors while the item is still damp but is not dripping wet.
Dry flat	Lay the item on a flat surface to dry.
Block to dry	Hand-shape the item on a flat surface so that the item will maintain its original size and shape while it dries.
Ironing or Pressing	
Cool iron	Set iron on a low setting.
Warm iron	Set iron on a medium setting.
Hot iron	Set iron on a high setting.
Iron damp	Dampen the item or a press cloth before ironing or pressing the item.

pretreatment products, bleaches, fabric softeners, water softeners, and fabric finishes. Your laundry needs will determine which products you will want to use.

To clean many of your clothes, you will probably use a detergent. You have a choice between an all-purpose detergent and a cold-water detergent. An **all-purpose detergent** is one that can be used to clean any washable fabric. It will clean best in hot water but will also clean in warm or cold water. It can be used for hand-washing or machine-washing of delicate, regular, or sturdy clothes. An extra amount of all-purpose detergent may be needed in areas with especially hard water or for clothes that are very heavily soiled. A **cold-water detergent** is one that is specially formulated to clean effectively in cold water. It can be used for hand-washing or machine-washing of lightly soiled items.

Occasionally, you may brush against a freshly painted wall, or notice a spot on your shirt. At times like these, you may need to remove a stain. There are a few common stain removal methods. Some methods require the use of an all-purpose liquid detergent or a pretreatment product. A **pretreatment product** is a laundry aid that is sold separately as a spray or a liquid to work on spots, stains, and heavily soiled areas. Other methods require the use of a **solvent**, a substance capable of dissolving other substances. Solvents used to remove stains from clothing include dry-cleaning fluid, rubbing alcohol, and turpentine.

On page 273, you will find procedures for treating common stains. In general, it is best to treat stains immediately. Old or dry stains may be impossible to remove. Also, it is essential to read carefully the directions for using and storing laundry aids used for stain removal. It is equally important to follow stain-removal procedures exactly and to avoid mixing stain removers. Finally, it is best to test the stain-removal method on a seam or other hidden area. Make sure that the method will not change the fabric's color, appearance, or texture.

When you want to remove dullness, dinginess, or mildew from your clothes, you may want to use a bleach. A **bleach** is a whitening agent. You can use a detergent that contains bleach or a liquid or powder bleach.

The two types of bleach are chlorine and oxygen. Chlorine bleach is a liquid. It is the strongest form of bleach and can be used not only to whiten and clean but also to disinfect clothes. It can, however, damage certain fabrics. Oxygen bleach is a powder and is milder than chlorine bleach. It is suggested for many fabrics that are too sensitive for chlorine bleach. When using either type of bleach, never pour the bleach directly onto fabrics. Instead, thoroughly dilute or dissolve the bleach in the wash water before adding your clothes. Follow package directions.

If you want to use a fabric softener, you can find it in several forms. A **fabric softener** is a laundry product that reduces static and helps fabrics feel soft, smell nice, and remain free of wrinkles. Some fabric softeners are added to detergents. Others are sold separately as liquids to be added to the final rinse cycle. Still others are sold separately on specially treated paper or foam sheets to be used in clothes dryers. Each type is effective.

You may live in an area that has hard water. To check, wash your hands with a bar of soap and rinse them in a basin of water. If you have soft water, you will see suds. If you have hard water, you will see a soapy scum. This scum means that the active ingredients in the soap are bound together and the soap cannot work. In an area that has hard water, you may need to use a water softener to get your clothes really clean.

A **water softener** is a chemical that ties up the minerals in hard water and allows soaps to work and detergents to work more efficiently. You can use a detergent that contains a water softener, or you can add a powdered water-softening agent to each wash load. You might even find a laundromat that has automatic water-softening machines. These machines put chemicals into every wash or rinse cycle.

Finally, you may want to use starches and other fabric finishes. Although starch is sold in liquid and powder form, it is most often sold as a spray-on finish. Starch or a similar finish designed for use on synthetics can be sprayed onto clothes just before they are ironed. These fabric finishes help the clothes keep their crisp, new appearance. Another type of fabric finish can be used to protect clothes and their wearer from moisture. A water-repellent finish can be sprayed onto jackets and all-weather coats, for example, to keep them from absorbing water. Other types of fabric finishes are also available.

Loading the Washer

The best guidelines for loading the washer are the directions found on the machine. With a front-loading machine, put the clothes inside and shut the door. Start the machine and, then, add your laundry products. With a top-loading machine, place each item next to the center post, or the agitator. Do not wind large items such as sheets or towels around the agitator. This will clog the machine and prevent it from cleaning thoroughly. Start the washer and add your laundry products *after* the water starts to flow in.

When the machine begins washing, check to see that the clothes are circulating freely.

Removing Stains

Stain	Step-by-Step Method to Get It Out
Adhesive tape Chewing gum	If adhesive or gum is soft, rub with ice to harden. Scrape off what you can with a dull knife. Use dry-cleaning fluid to remove rest.
Alcoholic drinks Perfumes Soft drinks	Sponge with cool water and glycerine. Soak 30 minutes. Sponge with rubbing alcohol if safe for fabric.
Butter, cream, milk, margarine Chocolate Gravy, sauces Mayonnaise, oil Smoke, soot Vomit	Pretreat with an all-purpose liquid detergent or a pretreatment product. Launder. For heavy stains, place stained area face down on white paper towels. Apply dry-cleaning fluid to back side of stain. Replace towels often. Let dry. Treat with liquid detergent, rinse, and launder.
Candy (nonchocolate) Coffee, tea (no milk) Egg Vegetables, catsup	Sponge with cold water. Soak 30 minutes. Launder.
Collar ring Perspiration	Pretreat with an all-purpose liquid detergent or a pretreatment product. Launder. Repeat, as necessary.
Nail polish	Place stain face down on white paper towels. Sponge back of stain with nail polish remover. Replace paper towels often. Repeat until stain disappears. Launder. Do not use nail polish remover on acetate.
Paint, varnish	If possible, treat before stain dries. Flush cool water through the back of a stain made by paint with a water base. Launder. For a stain made by paint with an oil base, sponge with a solvent such as turpentine, as recommended on the paint label. Rinse. Launder.
Scorch	Pretreat with a heavy-duty liquid detergent or a pretreatment product. Launder. Severe scorching may have harmed the fabric permanently.
Shoe polish	Since there are several types of shoe polish, read the stain-removal information on the label of the particular polish used. Otherwise, pretreat with an all-purpose liquid detergent or a pretreatment product. Launder if stain seems to be loosened. If no instructions are available, rub with rubbing alcohol or dry-cleaning fluid. Then launder.
Carbon paper (duplicating) Ink (ballpoint)	Sponge with rubbing alcohol. If stain remains, sponge with dry-cleaning fluid. Launder.
Fruits, berries Fruit juices	Sponge immediately with cool water. If fabric can withstand high heat, pour boiling water through the back. Treat with an all-purpose liquid detergent or a pretreatment product. Launder.
Mildew	Launder, using chlorine bleach if it is safe for the fabric. Otherwise, dampen with oxygen bleach and water, a solution of lemon juice and salt, or hydrogen peroxide. Allow to dry. Launder.
Mustard	Work an all-purpose liquid detergent or a pretreatment product into the stain. Rinse. Launder. Soaking and several treatments may be needed.

Wearing Clean Clothing **273**

If they are not, the washer is too full. As a result, the machine can be damaged and the clothes left uncleaned. To prevent this, stop the washer and remove some items.

Drying Your Clothes

How you dry clothes will depend on the particular items you have, on the types of drying equipment available to you, and on how much energy and time you want to spend. For example, items such as some sweaters need to be dried on a flat surface. They should be placed on top of a towel or another absorbent surface and allowed to air-dry. Other garments can be dried on a clothesline or a clothesrack or in an automatic clothes dryer if either is available. If you have a clothesline, you can let the air and sun dry your clothes. The air removes odors and helps the clothes smell fresh. The sun helps bleach out stains and keep colors bright. If you have no outdoor clothesline or want to dry your clothes no matter what the weather, you may prefer to use an automatic clothes dryer. If so, you need to be familiar with automatic dryer cycles and proper loading of the dryer.

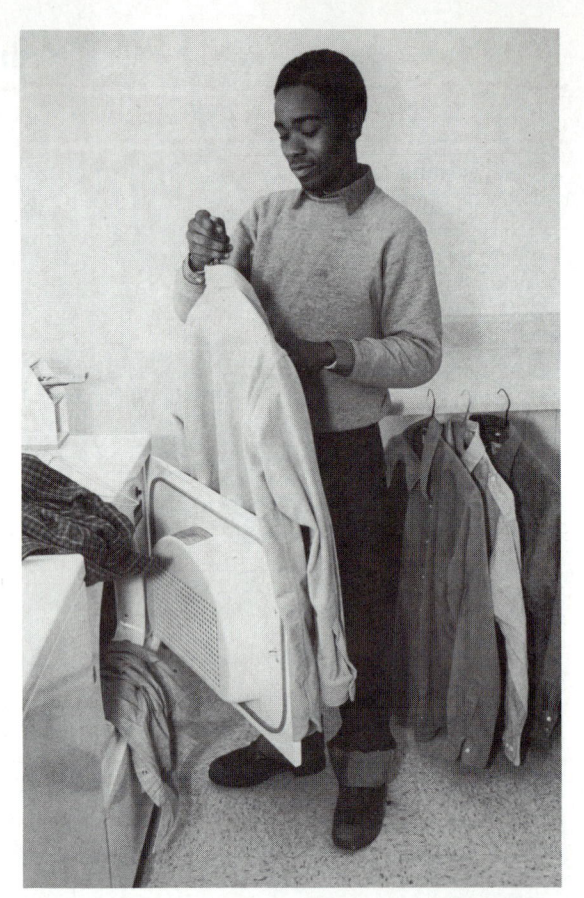

What clothes are best removed from the dryer and hung up while damp?

Choosing a Drying Cycle or a Drying Time

Like automatic washers, automatic dryers also have certain cycles. A **drying cycle** is a temperature and time setting designed to dry certain types of fabrics.

The cycles you will find on dryers used in laundromats and dryers used in homes are likely to differ. The dryers in laundromats will probably have only two cycles. One cycle will probably supply high heat for a certain number of minutes. The other cycle will probably supply low heat for the same length of time. The high-heat cycle, often labelled "regular," should work well for sturdy and heavy clothes like jeans and towels. The low-heat cycle should work well for permanent press and more delicate items.

When you are using a laundromat dryer, you can vary the length of time you dry a load in one of two ways. On the one hand, you can take items out of the dryer before the cycle is finished. On the other hand, you can run your clothes through a cycle more than once. The number of times will depend on how large the load is and how dry you want the items to be. The number of times will also depend on how much time and money you want to spend at the laundromat.

The typical dryer used in a home offers several cycles. Often, it has a no-heat cycle in addition to a low-heat cycle and a high-heat cycle. If you have a dryer at home, you need to know what each cycle is designed to do.

As you read the following descriptions, think about your wardrobe and decide which cycle would be best for each item in it.

- *No heat.* This is the coolest setting. Use it for clothes you want dry enough to iron but still damp. Also, use it for clothes made from heat-sensitive fibers that could be scorched at other settings and for fabrics coated with rubber, plastic, or other materials easily damaged by heat.

- *Low heat.* This setting provides more heat than a no-heat setting but not enough to wrinkle fabrics. Use it for knits and delicate garments, clothes with spandex or modacrylic fibers, and permanent press items unless your home dryer has separate settings for these items.
- *High heat.* This is the hottest setting. Use it for sturdy clothing.

In addition to several cycles, many home dryers have special features designed to provide flexibility and convenience. For example, the dryer's design may allow you to select more or less drying time than the preset cycles provide. You merely set a timer for the number of minutes you want. In addition, the dryer may have a dampness sensor, a device that can detect how much moisture clothing has. The sensor causes the dryer to turn off as soon as clothes are suitably dry. With permanent press fabrics, such a device will shut off the machine when the items are still slightly damp. This way, the clothing can be hung on hangers to dry wrinkle-free in moments. With heavy fabrics, the sensor will shut off the dryer only after the items are completely dry.

Loading the Dryer

For best drying results, read the care labels in your clothing and follow the directions on the machine. In addition, take each of the following measures:

- Wring or blot hand-washed clothes to remove as much moisture as possible before putting them into the dryer. An automatic clothes washer will usually spin out the excess water for you.
- Avoid placing very wet and almost dry items in the same load. The items that are almost dry will get too dry before the others get damp dry.
- Shake clothes to open them up and prevent wrinkling during the drying cycle.
- Do not underload or overload the dryer. Otherwise, the clothes will not tumble freely. They may wrinkle and take longer to dry.
- Remove clothes as soon as the drying cycle is complete. Then, hang or fold them immediately to reduce wrinkling.

Wearing Neat Clothing

Day in and day out, your wardrobe gets a good deal of wear. Sometimes this wear shows. It may take the form of missing buttons, small tears, a loose hem, or wrinkled clothes. Whether or not you keep your clothing in good repair, as well as clean, will affect the impressions others have of you.

Maybe you already know how to make your own clothing repairs either with a sewing machine or by hand. Perhaps you know how to iron and press your clothes. If not, you might want to start learning and practicing these skills now. Then, when you are fully responsible for these tasks, you can do them quickly and well. Remember that basic mending, ironing, and pressing skills will help you keep your clothing—and you—looking good.

Having Sewing Equipment and Supplies on Hand

You may not feel that a sewing machine is necessary. After all, many repairs can be made by hand. If, however, you already have a sewing machine or plan to buy one, it will probably prove helpful. You might even consider using one that is computerized. For more information about this latest development in sewing machines, see page 276.

Whether you intend to make sewing repairs by machine or by hand, you will want a few sewing tools and supplies. While there are many that you could buy, start with the basics. In such places as fabric stores, discount stores, and sometimes drugstores, you can find the following items:

- *Needles in several sizes.* Embroidery needles are a good choice. They have easy-to-thread eyes and do not make big holes in fabric.

How Computers Can Help You

Making Repairs with a Computerized Sewing Machine

Repairing your clothing can be fun, especially when you use a computerized sewing machine. Maybe you have already seen such a sewing machine demonstrated in your school's home economics department or in stores. If so, you know that it can do things that earlier models cannot begin to do.

With a computerized sewing machine, you merely push buttons to select the features you need. You can adjust the length of a stitch with the touch of a finger. This is a handy feature to have when you need a smaller stitch to reinforce a certain area. For example, if the sleeve of one of your shirts rips, you can restitch most of the seam with one stitch length. Then, at the underarm, where more reinforcement is needed, you can switch easily to a smaller stitch. On a computerized machine, you can also use a darning program to mend or programs designed specifically to replace a buttonhole or to reattach a belt loop. Some features on a computerized sewing machine come in handy whether you are creating a new item or repairing an old one. One such feature is the machine's bobbin thread monitor. If the bobbin thread gets low, a light comes on to alert you.

Computerized sewing machines are usually more expensive to buy than other models. However, because computerized machines have fewer moving parts, you are likely to have fewer repair bills. Therefore, a computerized sewing machine may be less expensive to maintain.

If you think that you will use a computerized sewing machine for minor clothing repairs only, think again. You will probably find it so much fun that you will begin to create original items, not only for yourself but also perhaps for others. With regular use, a computerized sewing machine will more than pay for itself.

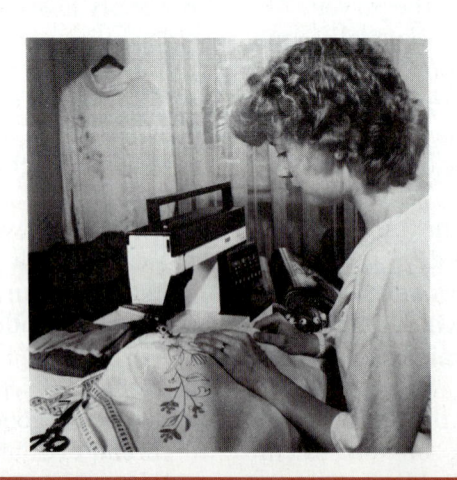

- *Thread.* It is a good idea to have thread to match the colors you tend to wear.
- *Scissors.* A pair of small scissors will help you snip threads. A pair of shears will help you cut fabric.
- *Pins and a pin cushion.* It is a good idea to have safety pins, as well as straight pins and a pin cushion for them.
- *Snaps, hooks and eyes, and other fasteners.* All standard fasteners can come in handy.
- *A tape measure and a gauge.* A tape measure will help you take your measurements. A gauge will help you measure fabric as you sew.
- *A sewing kit.* You may want to make your own sewing kit. All you need is a box, basket, or similar container with a firmly closing lid. If you plan to travel or move often, keep your sewing kit compact. For example, a 4-inch × 6-inch kit is more convenient than a huge sewing box.

Items that you may not consider basic but may want on hand include a thimble and iron-on tapes. A thimble can protect your finger from needle punctures. Iron-on mending tape and iron-on hem tape can save you time as you make clothing repairs.

Using a Sewing Machine

There are several clothing repairs that you can make on a sewing machine. The two that you are likely to make most often are repairing ripped seams and replacing hems.

While every sewing machine is a little different, most have many of the same parts. By looking at the illustration on page 278, you can get an idea of how a sewing machine works. For directions specific to your machine, always refer to your machine's use-and-care booklet. For tips to help you successfully use any sewing machine, see page 279.

Sewing a Ripped Seam by Machine

What if a seam in your pants splits or your jacket rips along the armhole? Do you know what to do? To make this kind of repair with a sewing machine, you can follow these steps:

- Press the garment, so the fabric is smooth.
- Line up the seam allowances as they were originally sewn, as shown on page 280.
- Set the stitch-width regulator to sew a straight stitch. Practice the stitch on fabric that is similar to the garment fabric. Make sure your stitches are smooth.
- Position the garment under the needle so that the rip is about ½ inch ahead of the needle. Then, lower the presser foot.
- Begin with a reverse stitch or two and, then, sew forward to close the ripped seam, as shown on page 280. Sew about ½ inch beyond the rip and, then, make one or two reverse stitches.
- Raise the presser foot, remove the garment, and snip off the threads.

Sewing a Hem by Machine

What if you want to repair the hem on pants or a skirt? If you have never used a machine stitch for hemming, practice on a scrap of fabric and, then, follow these steps:

- Fold the hem allowance toward the wrong side of the garment and, then, press the hem allowance in this position.
- Pin the hem allowance in the pressed position. Place pins about 2 to 3 inches apart, about ¼ inch from the cut edge of the hem, as shown on page 280.
- Fold the hem back toward the garment so that the hem allowance is resting on the slide plate of the machine. The ¼-inch edge of the hem allowance should be extended, as shown on page 280.
- To sew the hem, use the machine's special hem stitch or a zigzag stitch.

Repairing Clothes by Hand

There are several clothing repairs that you can make by hand. Those that you are likely to make most often are replacing hems and fasteners. To make these repairs, you will need thread. You will also need a needle that is thin and sharp. In addition, you will need scissors to cut the thread.

To thread the needle, hold the cut end of the thread securely between your thumb and

Wearing Neat Clothing 277

Basic Parts of a Sewing Machine

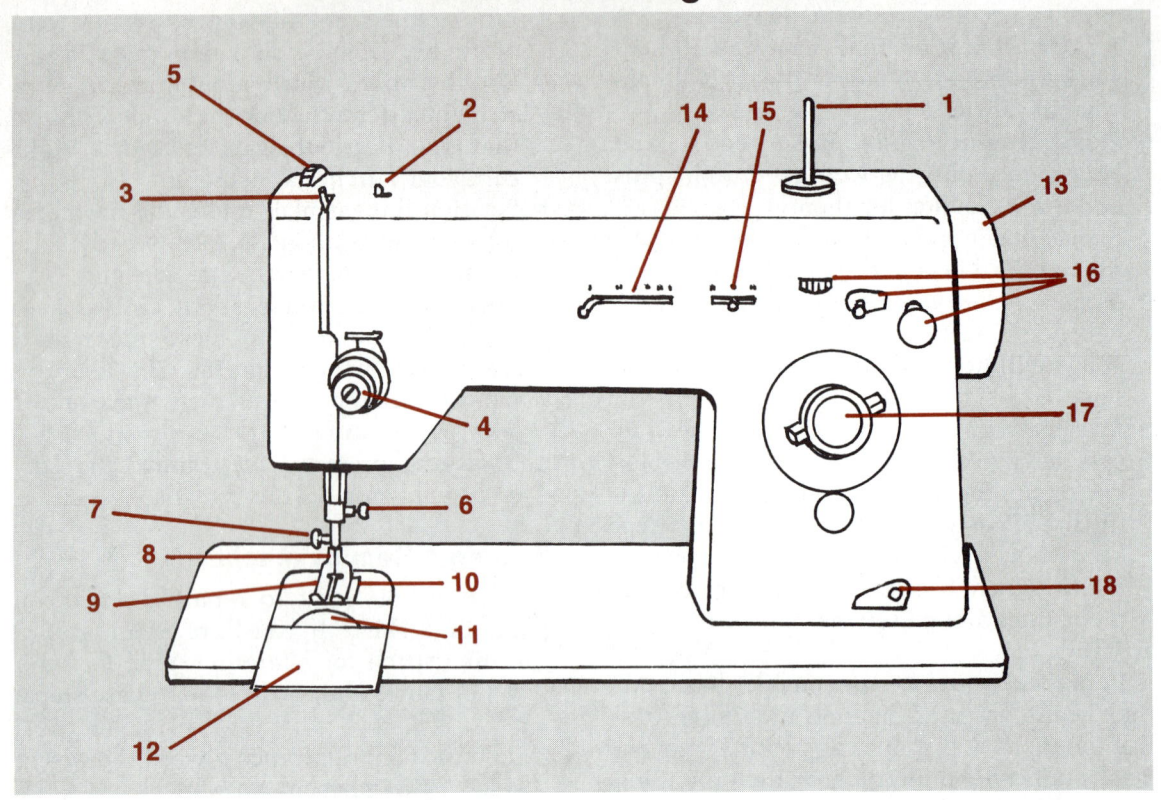

1. **Spool pin** (may be located on the back of the machine) holds the spool of thread
2. **Thread guides** hold the thread in place
3. **Take-up lever** pulls thread from the spool and feeds it through the needle
4. **Tension regulator** controls the tension on the upper thread
5. **Pressure regulator** controls pressure on the fabric being fed through the machine
6. **Needle clamp** opens for insertion or removal of the needle
7. **Presser foot clamp** holds the presser foot in place
8. **Needle** feeds the upper thread and forms the upper half of each stitch
9. **Presser foot** holds the fabric in place
10. **Feed dog** feeds the fabric through the machine for stitching
11. **Bobbin** holds the bottom thread and forms the bottom half of each stitch
12. **Slide plate** opens for insertion or removal of the bobbin
13. **Handwheel** is used to start stitching and to closely control the stitching speed
14. **Stitch-width regulator** controls the width of a stitch, including zigzag stitches
15. **Needle-position selector** adjusts the left-to-right position of the needle
16. **Bobbin-winding assembly** feeds thread from the spool to the bobbin
17. **Stitch-length regulator** controls the length of each stitch
18. **Bobbin-winding tension spring** guides thread onto the bobbin from the spool to ensure even winding
19. (not shown) **Foot or knee pedal** controls power to the machine

278 Looking Well Groomed

Tips

How to Use Any Sewing Machine

To use a sewing machine correctly, follow these guidelines:

- Thread the machine according to the manufacturer's directions. These directions are often found not only in the use-and-care booklet but also illustrated on the machine itself. Remember, even models that look alike may require different threading techniques.

- Raise the presser foot and bring the take-up lever to its highest point before beginning to thread the machine.

- Make sure that the thread passes between the tension disks in the tension regulator when you thread the machine.

- Use the size of needle specified in the use-and-care booklet.

- Thread the needle from front to back *if* the last thread guide is in front of the needle. The position of the last thread guide indicates the direction that the thread goes through the needle.

- Use the correct size and style of bobbin. Do not wind the bobbin too full. Check to see that the thread is smooth—without knots or tangles.

- Turn the handwheel to lower the needle and pick up the bobbin thread.

- Hold both needle and bobbin threads back when you lower the needle into the fabric.

- Use 10 to 12 stitches per inch for heavy fabrics. Use 12 to 15 stitches per inch for fabrics of average weight. Use 16 to 20 stitches per inch for light or sheer fabrics.

- Adjust the pressure according to the type of fabric. Thick fabrics require more pressure; thin fabrics require less.

- Let the fabric feed under the presser foot at its own speed. Do not push or pull the fabric.

- Cover the machine or return it to its case between sewing sessions.

---

index finger. Guide the thread through the needle's eye, and pull the end of the thread through about 6 inches. For most hand-sewing, you should use a single thread. A single thread gives a neater seam and does not tangle as easily as a double thread. To tie a knot in the end of the thread, follow the diagram on page 281.

Wearing Neat Clothing   **279**

Machine-Sewing Techniques

Repairing a Ripped Seam

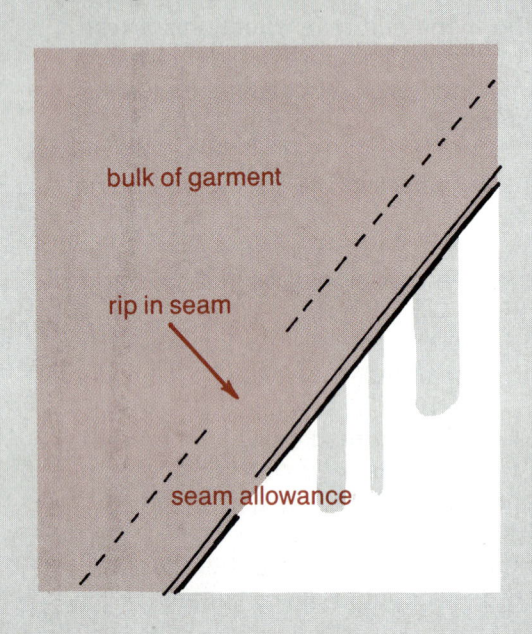

- bulk of garment
- rip in seam
- seam allowance

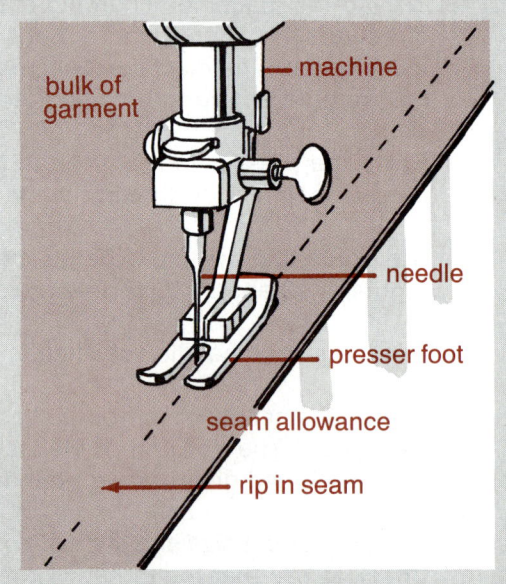

- bulk of garment
- machine
- needle
- presser foot
- seam allowance
- rip in seam

Replacing a Hem

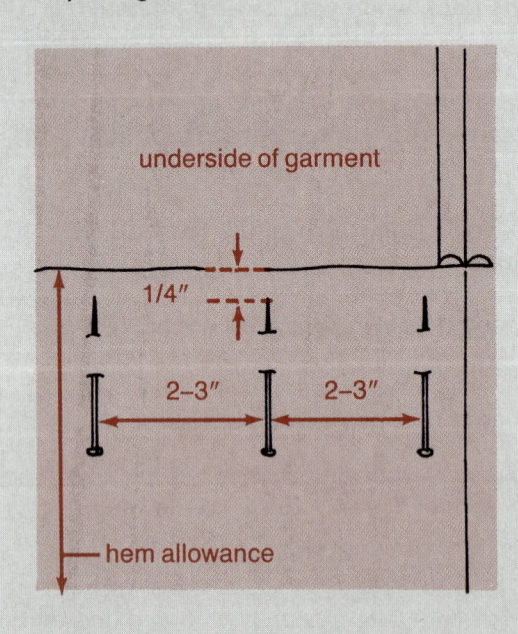

- underside of garment
- 1/4"
- 2–3"
- 2–3"
- hem allowance

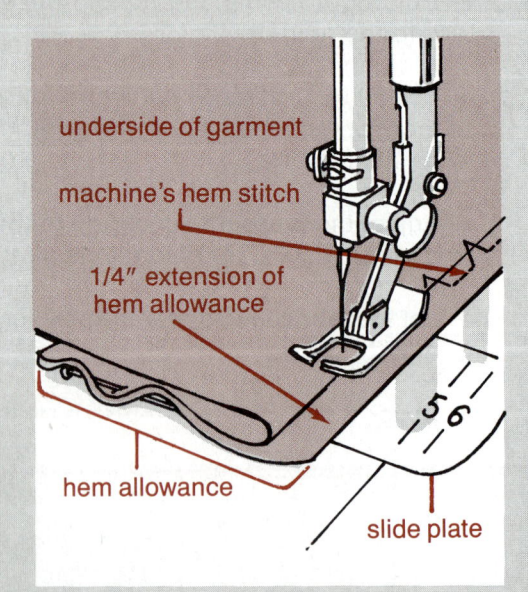

- underside of garment
- machine's hem stitch
- 1/4" extension of hem allowance
- hem allowance
- slide plate

280 Looking Well Groomed

Hand-Sewing Techniques

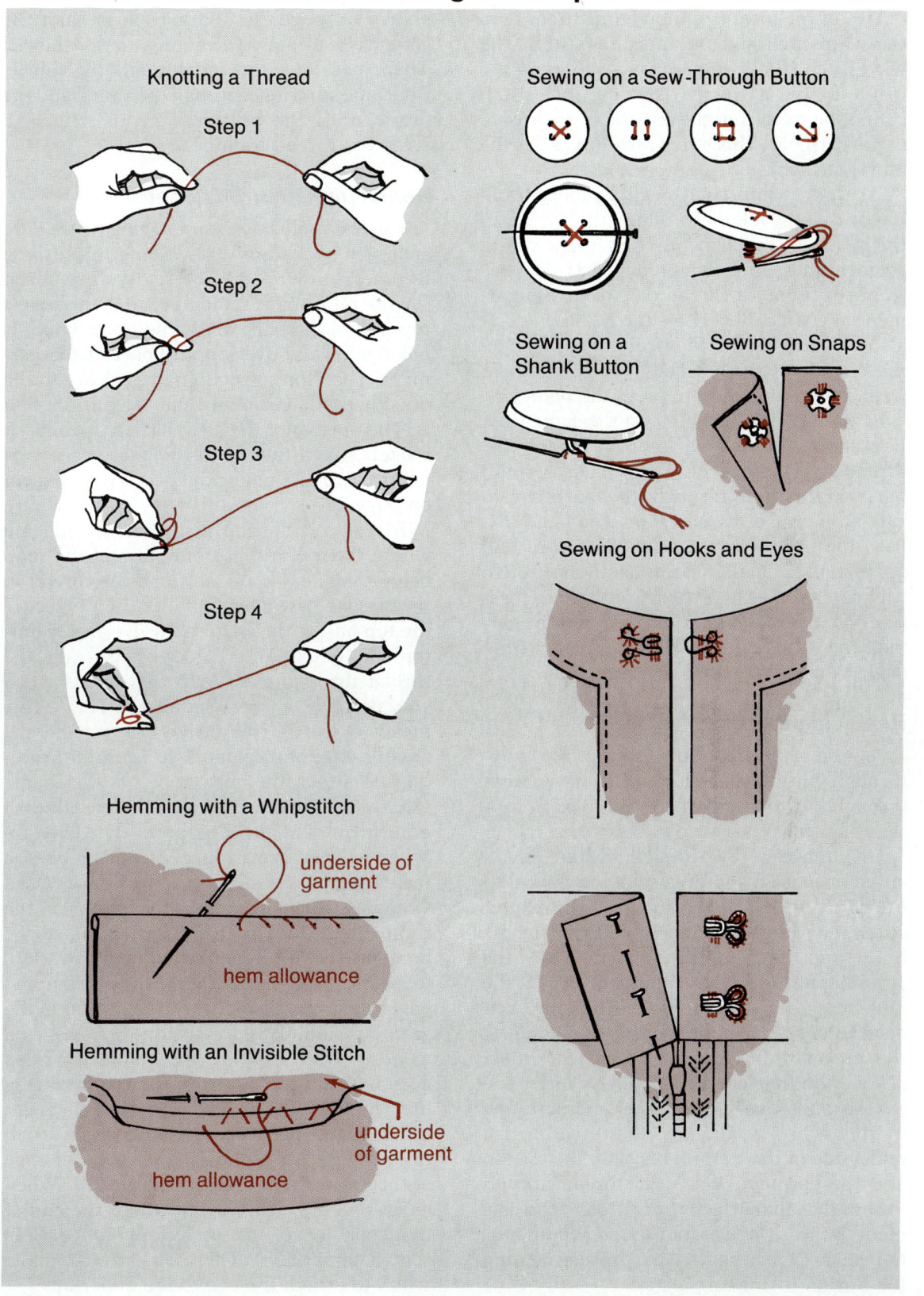

Knotting a Thread

Step 1

Step 2

Step 3

Step 4

Hemming with a Whipstitch

underside of garment

hem allowance

Hemming with an Invisible Stitch

hem allowance

underside of garment

Sewing on a Sew-Through Button

Sewing on a Shank Button

Sewing on Snaps

Sewing on Hooks and Eyes

Wearing Neat Clothing **281**

Replacing Hems

Two of the most common hem stitches are the whipstitch and the invisible stitch. The whipstitch is fast and easy but shows on the inside of the garment. The invisible stitch cannot be seen from the outside or the inside of the garment. This stitch also "gives" as the fabric stretches during wear.

To use the whipstitch, begin by backstitching or making a knot to attach the thread to the inside of the garment. Then, make small, even stitches, as shown on page 281. Be sure to pick up only a thread or two of the garment at a time. This helps the hem lie flat. It also prevents the stitches from being seen on the outside of the garment. Finish the hem with a backstitch. Then, press the hem.

Begin the invisible stitch in the same way. Backstitch or make a knot to attach the thread to the garment. Then, make a small horizontal stitch through the garment to catch a thread or two, as shown on page 281. Pass the needle to the hem allowance and again make a small horizontal stitch through it to catch a thread or two. Continue to form a very narrow, zigzag stitch between the garment and the hem allowance. Finish with a backstitch or knot, and press the hem.

Replacing Buttons

Popular styles of buttons are the sew-through button and shank button. A sew-through button has two or four holes in it. A shank button has a loop on its back.

To replace a sew-through button, backstitch or make a knot to attach the thread to the garment. Put the button in position, and stitch it to the garment by sewing through its holes and through the garment. See the stitching patterns shown on page 281. If the button is to go through a buttonhole, you need to create a shank, or stem, as you sew the button to the garment. To make a shank, place a toothpick or a thick pin on top of the button and sew over it. Then, remove the toothpick or pin, and pass the thread to the underside of the button, between the button and the garment. Wrap the thread around the stitches that attach the button to the garment. Do this three or four times. Whether or not you are creating a shank, finish attaching the button by making a knot.

To replace a shank button like the one shown on page 281, backstitch or knot the thread to attach it securely to the fabric. Then, pass the thread through the fabric. Continue stitching through the shank and the fabric until the button is firmly attached. Knot the thread to finish.

Replacing Other Fasteners

You probably have some garments that use snaps or hooks and eyes. Sometimes, these fasteners may need to be reattached. When sewing on a snap, remember that the snap's top half is the part with a bump or knob. It belongs on the overlapping part of the garment. Therefore, the top half is closer to the outside of the garment than the bottom half is. The bottom of the snap has an opening or socket. It is attached to the part of the garment that rests under the overlap, as shown on page 281.

To sew on a snap, use pins to indicate where the top and bottom parts of the snap belong. Make a knot to attach the thread to the overlap. Use a buttonhole stitch to secure the top half of the snap to the overlap. A buttonhole stitch is created by passing the thread through each loop that forms when you stitch over the edge of the snap. This makes a sturdy row of stitches around the outside edge of the snap. Use a similar procedure to attach the bottom half of the snap.

A hook and eye can be attached to edges of a garment that meet or parts that overlap. When edges meet, place the hook on the inside of the garment near one edge. On a woman's garment, place the hook on the right edge. On a man's garment, place the hook on the left edge. When edges overlap, place the hook on the edge of the overlapping part. Make a knot to attach the thread to the garment, and, then, use the buttonhole stitch to attach the hook. To make sure the hook does not move away from the fabric during use, whipstitch its neck to the garment. When edges meet, use the buttonhole stitch to attach the eye of the hook to the other edge of the garment, as shown on page 281. When edges overlap, place a pin where the end of the hook meets the underlapping part, as shown on page 281. Then, use the buttonhole stitch to attach the eye to the underlap.

Storing Clothes Properly

No matter how busy your lifestyle as a young adult, you will probably want a good-looking wardrobe. Some basic principles of daily and seasonal clothing storage can help you meet this goal. One of the most important principles is one you can put into action everyday. That is to neatly fold or hang up your clothes. Clothes that are stored in this way need less frequent ironing and last longer. They also are ready to wear at a moment's notice.

Daily Storage

There are several ways to keep your closet in order and your clothes in shape. Investing in high-quality hangers is one way. Other ways include the following strategies:

- Close top buttons, zippers, and other fasteners before putting clothes away. Remove accessories from clothing before storing it.
- Spot-treat minor stains and make repairs before storing an item of clothing.
- Hang pants by the cuffs from spring-clip or tension hangers, or neatly hang them across hangers. Hang skirts from spring-clip hangers by the waistband.
- Hang shirts and dresses so that their shoulder seams rest on the hanger. Use shaped and padded hangers for blazers, suit jackets, and other tailored clothes.
- Brush clothes to remove lint or surface dust after you hang them up. Steam clothes to remove wrinkles.
- Place similar items side by side. This makes selection easier.
- Allow clothes to air. Keep the closet door open during the day, or let the clothes hang outside for an hour or so before putting them in a closed closet.

Seasonal Storage

Depending on where you live, you may need to put away one wardrobe and get out another as the seasons change. The way you store clothes for any long period will affect how good they look. Therefore, you might want to consider the following advice related to long-term storage of clothing:

- Clean garments before storing them.
- Fold clothes neatly to avoid wrinkling them.
- Use moth-repellent and other treatments to prevent insects from damaging the clothes during storage.
- Store clothing in a container that can be sealed to prevent damage. Place the container away from extreme moisture, heat, direct sun, grease, or fumes.
- Polish leather items *long* before storing them, so the polish has time to dry.

Ironing Your Clothes

Even with the permanent press fabrics available, you will probably have some clothes that need ironing. Therefore, you will need to have an iron and know how to use it.

With some fabrics, such as wool, you will also need to use a press cloth. Otherwise, the

When you change clothes after school and perhaps after work, do you care for your clothes the way this person is doing?

P.S. How Might You Pack for a Trip?

If you pack right, you will have what you want with you—in wearable condition. Before you throw everything you own into a suitcase, ask yourself a few questions. Will you be gone just overnight, for a weekend, or for a week or longer? Will you be going to a warmer or a cooler climate? What will you be doing? Which of your clothes travel well? Then, plan to pack at least one outfit for each day and a change of clothes for evening. Plan to take more than one pair of shoes to give your feet relief. Check to see what weather is predicted for your destination. In addition, plan to take items that will protect you in case of rain or unexpected weather changes. Make sure that everything you think about taking matches the activities you have in mind. Finally, plan to take clothes that do not wrinkle or that need little or no ironing.

Now, you are ready to start packing. Roll, fold, or hang clothes with as few creases as possible, and put them in a suitcase or a travel bag. Stuff small items into shoes and other empty spaces. To prevent accidents, put breakables in plastic bags or pouches. Place these in the *center* of your suitcase or travel bag, where they will be protected from rough handling. Try to pack only what you can carry. For a long trip, you may need to pack several bags and check them in. If so, pack a carry-on bag so that you will have the basics even if your bags arrive later than you do. Include a change of clothes, shoes, and basic grooming aids.

However you travel, you will probably be sitting for several hours. Therefore, wear comfortable clothes for your trip. By following these suggestions, you will be ready to go.

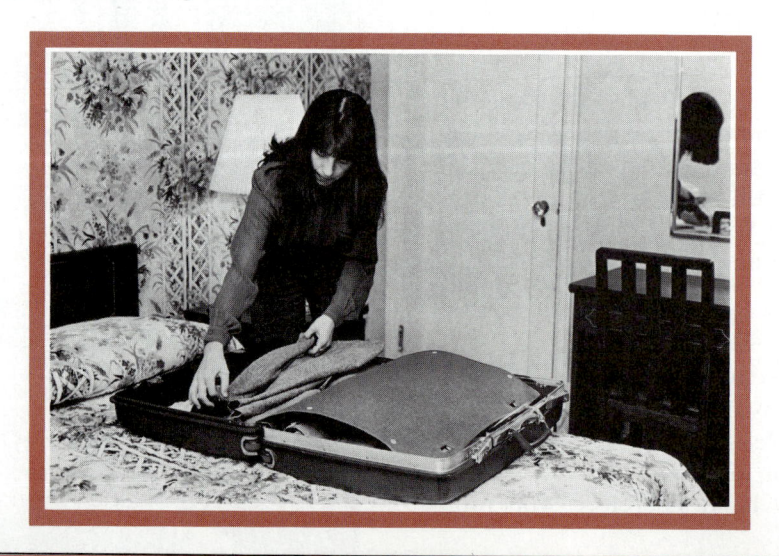

iron may create an unattractive shine or even damage the fabric's fibers. **A press cloth** is a piece of fabric, placed on top of the garment, to keep the iron from directly touching the garment. The press cloth should be made from fibers that do not produce lint.

Selecting an Iron

You can choose either a dry iron or a steam iron. A dry iron is best for ironing garments that moisture might spot or stain, because it does not depend on moisture to help remove wrinkles. A dry iron can also be used, however, with a damp press cloth.

A steam iron is best for ironing moisture-tolerant garments and is recommended for permanent press fabrics. It has a container for water and creates steam as the iron heats. Its underside has holes to allow the steam to escape. The more steam vents or holes the iron has, the better its steam coverage. Without water, the iron can also be used as a dry iron.

If you take many trips during which your clothes may be packed all day or longer, you may want to have a travel iron. **A travel iron** is a small, lightweight, and sometimes folding iron that is designed more for touch-up ironing than for heavy-duty ironing. It may be either a dry iron or a steam iron and can be a welcome companion on a trip. To find out how to pack for a trip, see the opposite page.

Using an Iron

Every iron has settings for different levels of heat. The standard settings are "Low—delicate fabrics," "Medium—wool or permanent press fabrics," and "High—fabrics not sensitive to heat." The best guide to heat setting is the care label in your clothing or the iron manufacturer's recommendations. If you have a steam iron and live in an area with hard water, you may need to use distilled water in your iron. This will prevent mineral buildups that can clog the steam vents or create marks on your clothes.

To iron, you will need a sturdy ironing board or a table. Cover it with padding and a heat-resistant, nonfading fabric. Next, spread across the board the garment you want to iron. If you are ironing jeans, for example, place them so you can iron one whole leg at a time. Remember, ironing is fastest when you use the entire width and length of the board as often as possible. Then, move the iron in long, smooth strokes to iron as much of the garment as you can. Be sure to use the pointed end of the iron for narrow areas or curved areas such as at shoulders.

Be very careful how and where you set up your ironing board. Make sure that your work area will not cause someone to trip over the iron cord and pull a hot iron down. In addition, make sure you turn the iron off and unplug it whenever you walk away from it. A surprising number of home fires begin with an iron that has been forgotten. Never risk such an accident. You may even want to use an iron with an automatic shut-off device.

Keeping Yourself Neat and Clean

A well-groomed look depends not only on your clothes but also on other aspects of your appearance. As a young adult, you may find that changes in your lifestyle have an effect on your personal grooming. For example, a new job may cause you to decide on a different hairstyle. A new school or work schedule may mean less time for optional grooming routines. Grooming products, appliances, and services that you have never used before may begin to appeal to you.

Using Personal Care Products

You can choose from a wide variety of national-brand, store-brand, and generic personal care products. These items are found in various kinds of stores and can even be bought through party plans.

Some personal care products do not cost much; others are extremely expensive. Many inexpensive products work as well, however, as the expensive ones. Often, the price of a product relates more to the cost of perfumes it contains and to advertising costs than to the product's effectiveness.

The number of personal care products that you use is up to you. Whether you decide to spend a lot or a little on personal care products, be sure to shop for the basics you need. These will probably include products for skin, hair, nail, and dental care.

Some people also consider cosmetics basic. If you use cosmetics, be sure to buy only the amount that you can use in a reasonable time. An extra-large container is no bargain if it takes five years to use. When cosmetics are exposed to air, heat, or moisture, they can become contaminated with bacteria. To reduce this risk, store cosmetics in closed containers. To avoid using a contaminated product, use clean swabs or other applicators—especially when "testing" a cosmetic. In addition, never use another person's cosmetics or lend yours to anyone. If you are sensitive to certain ingredients, you can try cosmetics labelled "nonallergenic" or "hypoallergenic." These cosmetics are made especially for people with allergies.

Skin Care Products

A daily shower or bath removes the natural oils and perspiration produced by normal activity and exercise. Daily bathing also removes dead skin cells, dust, and other debris. To clean your skin, you need not only water but also some type of soap. If you perspire very heavily, you may find that a deodorant soap is a good choice. If you have sensitive or dry skin, you may need a mild soap.

To help prevent chapping or dryness, you may need to use oil, skin cream or lotion, or even talcum or baby powder. Many doctors who treat skin conditions recommend using a moisturizer to protect your skin. A moisturizer can protect your skin from extreme heat, sunlight, and cold air.

Daily use of a deodorant or an antiperspirant can help keep body odors under control. A **deodorant** is a substance designed to de-

A little effort goes a long way when it comes to keeping your hands clean and your nails smooth. In what ways do these hands look well groomed?

stroy or mask body odors. An **antiperspirant** is a substance that helps reduce perspiration by covering the skin with astringents that close some sweat glands. Antiperspirants are *not* recommended for persons who *need* to perspire heavily to maintain normal body temperature. Persons in this category include workers who do heavy manual labor and athletes. Most deodorants and antiperspirants are available as a cream, lotion, roll-on, or spray.

Hair Care Products

Some people shampoo their hair daily, others less often. Clean, shining hair is essential to a well-groomed look. Only you can decide how often you need to wash your hair to keep it looking its best. To clean your hair, you will need to use a shampoo. In addition to shampoo, you may want to use other products. These might include the following:

- conditioners, to keep hair from tangling, relax curls, or add body
- rinses or tints, to add temporary color
- dyes, to add permanent color
- permanent waves or hair straighteners, to change the texture of hair
- hair sprays or gels, to set and style hair

Nail Care Products

Your hands and nails do hard work. They are exposed to the weather, household cleaning chemicals, and everyday tasks such as driving, writing, and cooking. To keep your hands looking good, scrub them several times each day. Use a small brush to remove dirt from under and around the nails. Use a towel or a soft cuticle stick if you push back your cuticles. A person's **cuticles** are the soft edges of skin around the nails. After pushing back cuticles, apply a light touch of skin cream or oil to soften them.

About once a week, trim your fingernails with nail scissors or clippers. Then, file away any uneven edges with an emery board. An **emery board** is a cardboard nail file covered with abrasive powder.

At least once a month, trim, file, and clean your toenails. After soaking your feet, use a pumice stone to remove callouses. A **pumice stone** is a piece of volcanic glass that is great for smoothing rough areas of skin. Using a stone is safer than cutting callouses. Cutting them might result in a serious infection. If you like, push back your toenail cuticles.

Dental Care Products

Each day, you need to brush and floss to protect your teeth and gums. You should brush your teeth after each meal. To do this, you need a toothbrush that is firm but not too tough. You may also want to use a fluoride toothpaste to help prevent cavities. As you brush, be sure to use up-and-down strokes on the vertical surfaces and crosswise strokes on the horizontal surfaces of your teeth. You should also clean your teeth at least once each day with dental floss to protect your gums from disease.

While most mouthwash is designed to "cleanse" breath, there is no strong evidence

Good grooming is an important part of your appearance. How much time do you devote to your grooming routine each day?

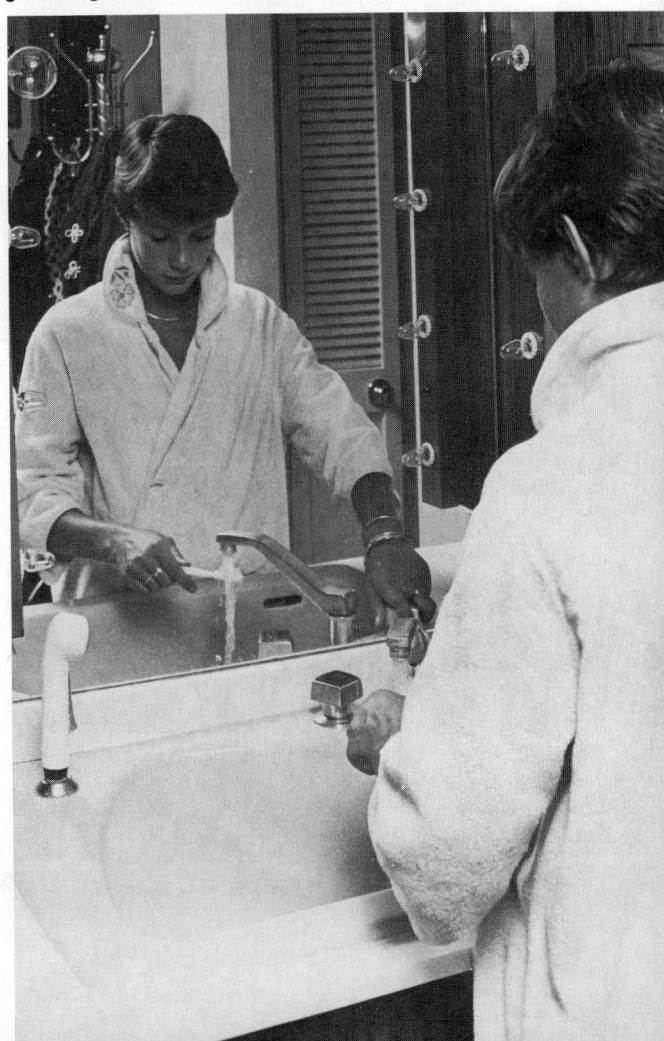

to date that it provides a significant health benefit. Consider mouthwash an optional personal care product, not an essential one.

Using Grooming Appliances and Services

Most grooming appliances are more of a convenience than a necessity. Choose only the ones that you feel you really need, can afford, and have space to store. For example, maybe you have a hairstyle that looks great when blown dry. If so, a hair dryer may be a necessity for you. On the other hand, you may consider an electric toothbrush too expensive for your budget. Maybe you would like a lighted mirror but really have no place to put it. Remember that some grooming appliances take up a good deal of space.

The most popular grooming service is probably hair styling. If you get your hair styled often, you will want to carefully choose a stylist. You need not only someone you can afford but also someone who can really help your hair look well groomed.

Points to Remember

- The best way to clean most clothing items is to follow the directions on the permanent care label.
- Some washable items may not be colorfast, and others may be color scavengers.
- Heavily soiled items may need pretreating, soaking, and extended washing or rinsing.
- Empty pockets, close zippers and hooks, and tie belts as you get clothes ready for washing.
- Unlike soaps, detergents clean clothes well in hard water.
- Permanent press fabrics require less heat or time to dry than sturdy clothes like jeans and towels.
- Basic sewing equipment, supplies, and knowledge can help you take care of minor clothing repairs.
- Your clothes will probably last longer if they are cared for on a daily basis.
- When pressing some garments, you may need to use a press cloth to avoid creating a shiny surface and to protect the fibers.
- Taking care of your skin, hair, nails, and teeth helps you look well groomed.
- Many grooming appliances are more of a luxury than a necessity, so you will want to select carefully from among them.

Test Your Skills

RESOURCE MANAGEMENT

Imagine yourself in the situation described below. In this situation, resources need managing. As you read, think about the ways that you can manage resources. Then, answer the questions that follow. When you need to manage resources in the future, remember to ask yourself these questions.

Situation

On your first day of spring break, you spend all morning horseback riding. After lunch, you start working in the garden. Late in the afternoon, you get a call from Jim, a good friend. His cousin is visiting from out of town. Jim wants you to be his cousin's date for a dinner and a movie that night. You had planned to spend the evening catching up on reading your favorite magazine, but you agree to go.

You had planned to take a long shower when you finished in the garden. Now, you realize that you do not have much time to get ready. The clothes you prefer to wear need to be dry-cleaned. You do not have the time or money to get them cleaned. The only other clothes you would like to wear need a seam restitched and a button replaced. You have never sewn before and are not sure how long this mending would take or how well you could do it. You could, however, ask your neighbor to help with the mending. Although you do not blow-dry your hair, you could borrow a hair dryer from your neighbor to dry your hair faster. You definitely want to look your best for the date.

Questions

1. Which resource do you need to manage most carefully? Why? (Hint: Look for the resource that is in shortest supply.)

2. What are the ways you might manage this resource? (Hint: Be sure to name any resources you could substitute, trade, or share.)

3. What opportunity costs would be involved in each case?

4. Who would pay the opportunity costs in each case?

5. After considering all these opportunity costs, how would you manage your resources in this situation?

Terms

On a separate sheet of paper, write a definition for each of the underlined terms below. Base your definition on the clues you find in the statement(s).

1. Jonathan has to have some of his clothes dry-cleaned. He takes them to a dry cleaner, who rinses them in fluids to remove any dirt or grease.

2. Most of the clothes Miriam has can be laundered. Before Miriam washes them with soap or detergent and water, she sorts them into two or three wash loads.

3. Instead of buying several different soaps and detergents to clean his clothes, Gene buys one all-purpose detergent.

4. When Tammy discovers a spot, stain, or heavily soiled area on a washable garment, she uses a pretreatment product and, then, washes the item.

5. Neil found a paint stain on his corduroy pants. On a stain removal chart, he read that using a solvent is the best way to remove that kind of paint.

6. Dominique has one shirt that she must whiten with bleach each time she washes clothes.

7. Saburo knows which temperature and time setting on his automatic clothes dryer is best for his permanent press clothes. He has read carefully about his washer's drying cycles.

8. Brenda always uses a press cloth when she presses her wool clothing. She does this to avoid giving the fabric a shiny surface or damaging its fiber.

9. Reed is careful to keep his nails clean and strong and his cuticles pushed back from his nails.

10. Carla evens the edges of her fingernails about once a week with an emery board. She can buy emery boards cheaply because they are made of cardboard and an inexpensive abrasive powder.

Questions

1. What major characteristics should you consider when sorting washable items?

2. What items are best washed in hot water? What items are best washed in warm water?

3. Why is it important to treat stains immediately?

4. What happens when too many clothes are put in a wash load?
5. Describe how to load an automatic dryer.
6. List some basic sewing tools and supplies for repairing clothing.
7. Give three tips for correctly using any sewing machine.
8. Name three things you can do each day to take care of your clothes.
9. What should you remember to do before storing seasonal clothing?
10. What safety precautions should you take when ironing?
11. Why is it important to floss your teeth at least once a day?
12. What are three factors you should consider before buying personal grooming appliances?

Activities

1. Read the care label instructions for different types of items in your wardrobe. You might choose a shirt, a swimsuit, a winter coat, a sweater, and a tie or a scarf. In what ways do the care instructions for these items differ? If there are any similarities, what are they?

2. Make a chart showing how you could sort your washable items according to color. Include sheets and towels. Use the following headings: "whites," "solid pastels and light prints," "medium and bright colors," and "dark colors." List specific items under the appropriate headings. Which color category would produce your largest wash load? What water temperature would you probably use for this load? Why?

3. Collect labels of laundry products that you think you will want to use. For each product, briefly describe the directions for use and any precautions. Also, give the approximate number of wash or dryer loads that size package will handle. Determine how often you may need to buy each laundry product, based on your estimate of the number of laundry loads that you might do in one month.

4. Rate your current clothing care practices according to the suggestions given in the chapter. Which of your garments show signs of proper care? Which show signs of improper care? What, if any, type of clothing care might you concentrate on more—cleaning, repairs, storage?

5. Check stores or newspaper or catalog advertisements for information about irons. Decide which iron you would select. Describe why you would select it.

6. Check to see how much the price varies for one grooming product, appliance, or service sold in your area.

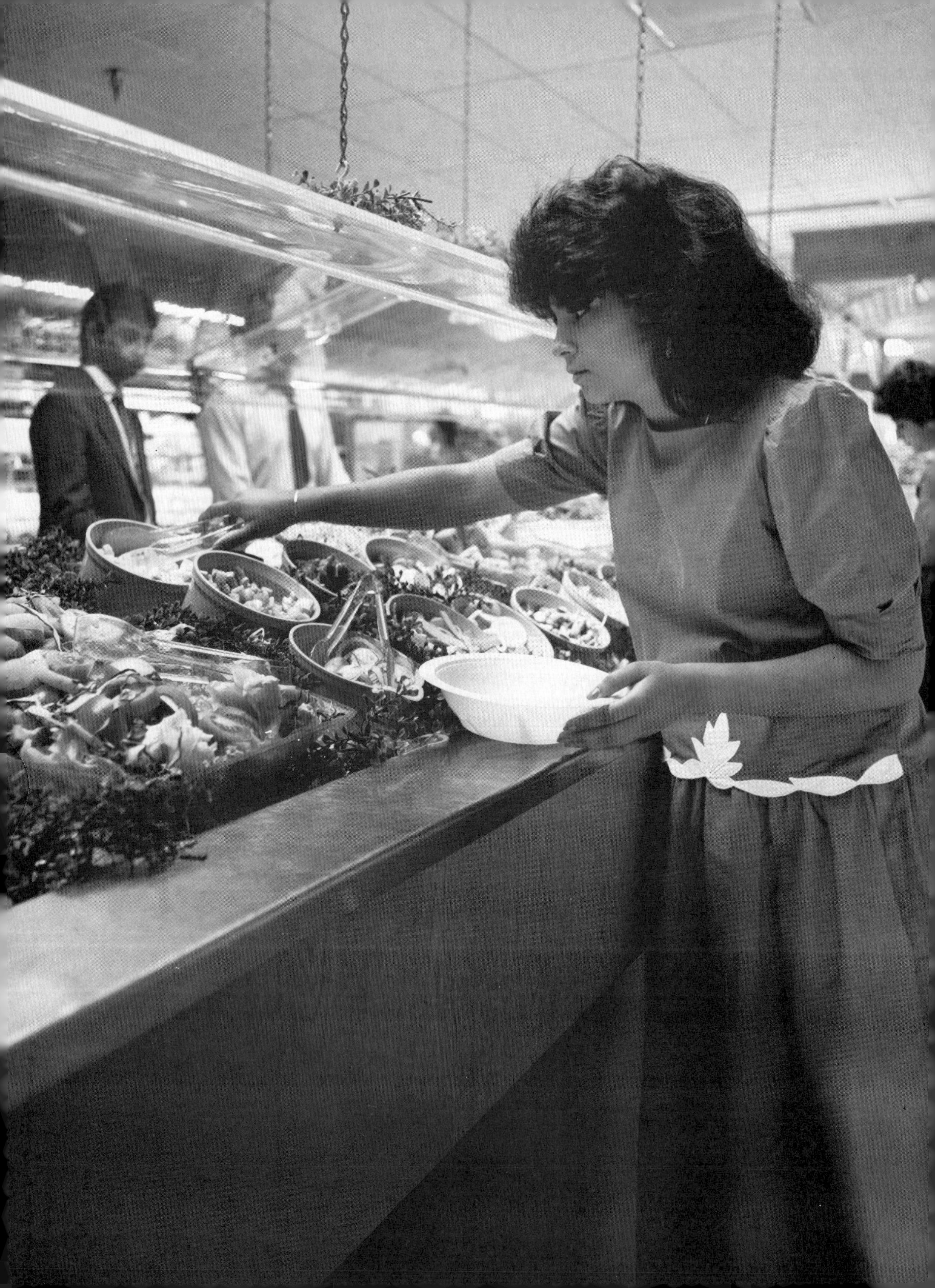

CHAPTER 13

Planning for Nutritious Meals

Do you know why it might be a good idea to choose the salad bar at a fast-food restaurant? Do you know the meaning of terms commonly used on restaurant menus? Your answers to these questions give you clues about what kind of meal planner you are right now.

When you are completely on your own, what kind of meal planner will you be? You can plan the best meals if you think nutrition first. After all, your energy level, health, and appearance depend to a great extent on what and how much you eat. In other words, you need specific nutrients in certain amounts. Without the right amounts of these nutrients, your energy level, health, and appearance suffer. With the right amounts of these nutrients, you feel and look your best.

In addition to creating nutritious meals, you can plan meals that provide a variety of dining experiences. Your time, budget, and skills will help you decide when to eat away from home and when to eat at home. Being familiar with menu terms, types of meal service, table settings, table manners, and check-paying customs will help you feel confident and relaxed when you eat out. Understanding ways to use convenience foods, recipes, and ingredients will encourage you to try new and interesting food combinations when you dine at home.

Discover Through Your Reading

- how nutrients contribute to your health
- what foods contain the nutrients you need every day
- how to maintain the right weight for you
- what unfamiliar words or phrases often found on menus mean
- what foods to have on hand to make convenient, nutritious meals at home

Planning What to Eat

When you plan meals, you of course want them to include foods that look and taste good. You should also want them to contain all the nutrients you need. **Nutrients** are chemical compounds that provide the body with energy, regulate its functions, and help it maintain tissue and grow. You should also know how much of each nutrient you need each day and which foods supply it. To make the planning of nutritious meals quick and easy, you can rely on four of the basic food groups.

Thinking About Nutrients

Everyone needs six major types of nutrients: proteins, fats, carbohydrates, vitamins, minerals, and water. Each type of nutrient has a different chemical makeup and serves a major function. For example, carbohydrates, fats, and proteins provide energy. Vitamins, minerals, and water help regulate various body processes, including the release of energy from carbohydrates, fats, and proteins.

While all foods contain nutrients, some foods are better sources of particular nutrients than are others. By looking at Appendix 8 on pages 404–413, you can see for yourself which foods are good sources of which important nutrients.

Proteins

The primary function of proteins is to provide for the maintenance and repair of your body cells and for growth. In addition, proteins help you fight off infections by being the basic units in your body's immune system. Any proteins that are not needed for maintenance, repair, or defense are available to provide your body with energy.

When your body digests proteins, the proteins are broken down into amino acids, their

Which of these menu choices are good sources of complete proteins? Are any of the items on this menu made of foods that offer a combination of incomplete proteins?

basic building blocks. This is the form in which your body's cells can use the proteins available to it.

Of the twenty-two amino acids that make up proteins, ten must come from the foods that you eat. Because these amino acids cannot be made by your body, they are called essential. The other twelve amino acids can be made by your body and, therefore, are not essential to your diet.

There is more than one way to get the essential amino acids. One way is to eat foods that contain complete proteins. Complete proteins are those that contain *all* the essential amino acids. Meat, poultry, fish, dairy products, and eggs are good sources of complete proteins. Dried beans and peas and nuts also contain complete proteins.

A second way to get the essential amino acids is to eat foods from plant sources whose

Planning for Nutritious Meals

incomplete proteins, when combined, offer all the amino acids needed to make up complete proteins. Examples of such combinations include kidney beans and rice, corn and lima beans, and peanut butter and bread.

Fats

Fats provide the most concentrated source of energy. They also aid in your body's absorption of nutrients. In addition, they insulate your body and protect your vital organs by cushioning them.

Fats are made of smaller compounds called fatty acids. Not all fatty acids are alike. Differences in their chemical structure make some fatty acids saturated and others unsaturated. Saturated fats contain more hydrogen than unsaturated fats. Eaten in too great a quantity, saturated fats have been linked to heart disease in some studies. Although not all the evidence is in, limiting the amount of saturated fats you eat may be wise.

Fats come from both animal and plant sources. Fats from animal sources are saturated. Fats from plant sources may be saturated or unsaturated. Even without knowing its source, you can tell whether a fat is saturated or unsaturated. Only saturated fats are solid at room temperature.

When you eat saturated fats from animal sources, you also take in cholesterol. Your body also makes cholesterol, a fatlike compound necessary for the manufacture of hormones and Vitamin D. Although recent studies point out that certain individuals may need to limit their intake of cholesterol, methods for identifying those individuals have not been perfected.

If, as research continues, you wish to reduce your intake of saturated fats and cholesterol, you can do so in any of several ways. For tips on how to reduce your intake of these two substances, see the next page.

Carbohydrates

Carbohydrates are a good source of energy. As a matter of fact, your body depends most heavily on carbohydrates for energy. Only if you eat too few carbohydrates to meet your body's need for energy does your body begin to use fats or proteins for the energy it needs.

Your body also depends on a type of carbohydrate for aid in the elimination of wastes.

Depending on their chemical structure, carbohydrates are simple or quite complex. They occur in three basic forms: as sugars, as starches, or as fiber.

The simplest form of carbohydrates is sugar. The sugars include glucose and fructose. Glucose is present in some fruits and vegetables. It is also created when your body digests more complex sugars like sucrose (table sugar) and lactose (a sugar present in milk) and when your body digests starches. Like glucose, fructose is present in fruits. It is also created when your body digests sucrose and thereby breaks sucrose into glucose and fructose. Glucose and fructose play an important role in your body. All carbohydrates must become glucose or fructose for your body to use them as a source of energy.

Starch is the most complex form of carbohydrates. It is made of many different units of sugar and is broken down into those individual units when your body digests the starches you have eaten. Starch is present in foods such as cereal, rice, potatoes, pasta, and dried beans and peas.

Fiber is also a complex form of carbohydrate. Unlike starch, however, fiber does not completely break down when your body digests it. The tough part of fiber passes through your system—undigested. In doing so, it helps your body get rid of wastes. Fiber is present in bran, whole-grain foods, raw fruits and vegetables, dried beans and peas, nuts and seeds, and popcorn.

Carbohydrates make up the largest part of the human diet and are present in every food from plant sources. Therefore, it is easy to get plenty of carbohydrates—in each form.

Vitamins

Vitamins are substances that are required in small amounts to regulate body processes and contribute to the performance of other nutrients. Although vitamins do not provide energy, they do help your body use the energy it gets from other nutrients.

Vitamins are present in the foods you eat. Although they can be destroyed by overcooking, this is not usually the case in normal

Tips

Reducing Your Intake of Saturated Fats and Cholesterol

Here are some easy ways to cut down the amount of saturated fats and cholesterol you take in:

- Choose margarine made from polyunsaturated vegetable oils instead of butter.

- Buy a liquid or tub margarine whose ingredients list begins with an unsaturated vegetable oil like safflower, sunflower, corn, or soybean oil.

- Cook with vegetable oils like safflower, sunflower, corn, or soybean.

- Use low-fat, skim, or nonfat milk and other dairy products.

- Select chicken, turkey, fish, and lean red meat rather than fatty red meat.

- Use dried beans and peas and other meat alternatives that contain neither saturated fats nor cholesterol.

- Remove the skin from poultry, and remove the visible fat from both poultry and red meat.

- Cook meat in such a way that the fat that you have been unable to trim off runs off.

- Avoid cooking meat and other foods in deep fat.

- Read nutrition labels to find out whether a food contains any saturated fats or cholesterol and how much. You may be surprised. Many packaged foods contain inexpensive coconut or palm oil or even lard. All three fats are more saturated than safflower, sunflower, corn, or soybean oil. Because lard is an animal fat, it also contains cholesterol.

- Consider how much saturated fat and cholesterol a recipe or a menu item is likely to have before you decide on it.

food preparation. Therefore, a well-balanced diet usually provides all the vitamins most young people need. Because of this, it is unlikely that you need a vitamin supplement. Vitamin supplements are a type of **nutrient supplement,** that is, a single nutrient or a combination of nutrients prepared and sold commercially to help people get the total number of nutrients they need each day.

There are two categories of vitamins. Some are water-soluble, and others are fat-soluble.

You do have some muscle storage of all water-soluble vitamins, but your body eliminates a small proportion of these water-soluble vitamins each day. Therefore, you need to eat foods containing water-soluble vitamins often. Fat-soluble vitamins can be stored in your body. Because of this storage, it is not absolutely necessary that you eat foods containing these vitamins each day. It is, however, recommended by the Nutrition Board of the National Academy of Sciences.

The water-soluble vitamins include Vitamin C and the B vitamins. Vitamin C, or ascorbic acid, performs many functions. For example, it helps form cells and helps your body heal. It also helps your body absorb minerals such as iron and calcium. Orange juice is well known for its Vitamin C content, but it is not the only food source of ascorbic acid. When you eat a potato, cabbage, or any berries, for example, you are also getting this vitamin.

The B vitamins include thiamine (B-1), riboflavin (B-2), niacin, pyridoxine (B-6), B-12, and folacin (folic acid). Together, the B vitamins are instrumental in your body's production of energy from foods. Breads and cereals, meats, and dark green leafy vegetables are good sources of the B vitamins.

The fat-soluble vitamins are A, D, E, and K. Vitamin A contributes to healthy eyes, skin, hair, and mucous membranes. Vitamin D helps the minerals calcium and phosphorus build strong bones and teeth. Vitamin E helps protect Vitamin A and your body's red blood cells from damage by oxygen. Vitamin K, made by your body, helps your blood to clot. Because Vitamins A, D, and E are found in many popular foods, it is easy to plan meals to include them. For example, a certain amount of each of these vitamins is supplied by the following meal:

Scrambled Eggs (Vitamins A and E)
Hot Pumpkin Bread with Margarine
(Vitamins A and E)
Milk (Vitamins A, D, and E)

The absence or severe lack of any vitamin can cause vitamin deficiency diseases. Too much of certain vitamins can also be harmful. Getting too much of a vitamin is called hypervitaminosis. The way to avoid this problem is to rely on foods to provide your nutrients and to plan your meals to include a well-balanced variety of foods.

Minerals

Minerals are substances that are required in small amounts to help regulate body processes and maintain body tissues. Unlike vitamins, minerals are elements and cannot be destroyed by overcooking food. If you eat a balanced diet, you will get the approximately twenty minerals you need. By concentrating on getting six major minerals each day, you will probably ensure that you are, in fact, getting all twenty minerals. These six minerals are calcium, phosphorus, iron, iodine, magnesium, and zinc.

Calcium and phosphorus work together to build strong bones and teeth. In addition,

These foods represent the many foods from which a person can create a well-balanced diet. What foods would be good sources of the B vitamins?

Planning What to Eat

calcium is required for your nerves to function, regulates your heart beat, and helps your blood to clot. Iron helps make hemoglobin, the part of your red blood cells that carries oxygen. Iodine is used by your thyroid gland to make a compound that helps control the rate at which your body uses energy. Magnesium promotes growth and helps keep nerves and muscles healthy. Zinc helps promote healing and growth and is important for a normal sense of taste.

You must get the minerals you need through the foods you eat. This is easy to do when you plan meals to include milk and milk products, meats, fish, poultry, dried beans and peas, breads, cereals, and dark green leafy vegetables. For example, a meal like this one supplies many of the necessary minerals:

Roast Beef
Broccoli   Carrots
Tossed Salad
Bread Pudding
Low-fat Milk

What is a better way to get the vitamins you need each day?

Water

You may not think of water as a nutrient, but it definitely is. You need water, for example, to carry other nutrients to every cell in your body, to help regulate your body processes, and to give your body form. While you could survive for some time without a single bite of food, you would die within a few days without water, and you need a regular and generous intake of water each day.

To replace the water you lose through elimination and normal perspiration, you probably need about eight glasses of fluid each day. If you engage in strenuous exercise or are ill with a fever, diarrhea, or vomiting, however, the water level in your body can become dangerously low quite quickly. To overcome this excess water loss, you may need to take in more than eight glasses per day. When you add up the fluid you get in one day, you can count anything you drink, including milk, clear soups, fruit juices, tea, and coffee, for example. In addition, you can count any water in the foods you eat. All foods contain some water. Some foods contain a lot. Cantaloupe, for example, has a great deal of water. In fact, 8 ounces of cantaloupe contains more water than 8 ounces of orange juice.

Identifying the Amounts of Nutrients You Need

While everyone needs some amount of most nutrients each day, not everyone needs the same amount. The amount of a nutrient that a person needs depends on the particular nutrient. For example, people need much more protein each day than they do Vitamin C. The amount of a nutrient that a person needs also depends on such characteristics as the person's age. For example, a child who is growing rapidly needs more protein per pound of body weight than an adult who has finished growing.

How can you find out the amounts of nutrients that you need each day? One way is to use the RDAs. The abbreviation *RDA* stands for Recommended Dietary Allowance. The RDAs are scientifically reached estimates of the greatest amounts of basic nutrients that a healthy person might need each day. Because the needs of *all* people are considered, these estimates are higher than what most individuals need.

The chart below lists the RDAs for nine nutrients. As you can see, not only do the amounts vary for the different nutrients, but so do the units of measure. For example, the amount of protein needed is measured in grams. However, the amount of Vitamin C is measured in milligrams, and the amount of Vitamin A is measured in International Units. A **gram** is a unit of measure that is equal to approximately one-twenty-eighth of an ounce. A milligram is one-thousandth of a gram, and an International Unit is one-millionth of a gram. Therefore, nutrients measured in milligrams or International Units are needed in much smaller amounts than those needed in grams.

Recognizing the Amounts of Nutrients in Foods

Just as your need for particular nutrients varies, so do the amounts of nutrients supplied by different foods. For example, steak provides a significant amount of proteins, along with fats, vitamins, and minerals but no carbohydrates at all. Corn flakes provide many carbohydrates, vitamins, and minerals but almost no proteins or fats.

Using the RDAs and Nutrition Charts

How can you know whether the foods you select will help you meet the RDAs? After all, not all foods are marked with nutrition information. It is possible, however, to use package labels and nutrition charts to determine

Recommended Dietary Allowances (RDAs)

Adapted from *Recommended Dietary Allowances*, 9th ed., published in 1980 by the National Academy of Sciences—National Research Council, Washington, DC 20418.

Person		Protein	Vitamin A	Thiamine	Riboflavin	Niacin	Ascorbic Acid	Calcium	Phosphorus	Iron
Sex or Condition	Age	Grams	International Units	Milligrams	Milligrams	Milligrams	Milligrams	Milligrams	Milligrams	Milligrams
Males	15–18	54	5,000	1.5	1.8	20	45	1,200	1,200	18
	19–22	54	5,000	1.5	1.8	20	45	800	800	10
	23–50	56	5,000	1.4	1.6	18	45	800	800	10
Females	15–18	48	4,000	1.1	1.4	14	45	1,200	1,200	18
	19–22	46	4,000	1.1	1.4	14	45	800	800	18
	23–50	46	4,000	1.0	1.2	13	45	800	800	18
Pregnant		+30	5,000	+.3	+.3	+2	60	1,200	1,200	+18*
Lactating		+20	6,000	+.3	+.5	+4	80	1,200	1,200	18

*This requirement can only be met with the use of a dietary supplement. Ordinary diets do not contain this much iron.

Planning What to Eat

how much of specific nutrients are contained in a serving size of a food. For a list of the amounts of nutrients in serving sizes of foods you might select, refer to Appendix 8 on pages 404–413. To find out how you can use a computer to determine whether you are getting enough nutrients, see page 301.

Using the U.S. RDAs and Nutrition Labels

The U.S. RDAs (Recommended Daily Allowances) are a simplified form of the RDAs (Recommended Dietary Allowances). Like the RDAs, the U.S. RDAs specify the greatest amounts of several nutrients suggested for *any* person. Therefore, they recommend amounts that are probably greater than those *you* actually need.

The U.S. RDAs are used by manufacturers of many packaged foods to report what percentages of the recommended amounts of eight key nutrients are contained in a particular food. You have probably noticed such use of the U.S. RDAs on many packaged foods. Any food that has a nutrient added to it or is advertised on the basis of nutrition must have a nutrition label. A **nutrition label** is a written statement of the amounts of energy and basic nutrients supplied by an individual serving of a food.

All nutrition labels must present information in the same way. The top half of the label shows the serving size; the number of servings per container; the number of calories, or units of food energy, per serving; and the amounts of proteins, carbohydrates, and fats per serving. The bottom half of the label lists the percentages of the U.S. RDAs for proteins and for several vitamins and minerals present per serving.

The vitamins listed on a nutrition label always include Vitamin A, Vitamin C, and the B vitamins thiamine, riboflavin, and niacin. The minerals listed always include calcium and iron. Manufacturers must also list certain other nutrients if these nutrients have been added to the product. These nutrients include Vitamin D, Vitamin E, Vitamin B-6, Vitamin B-12, folacin, phosphorus, iodine, magnesium, zinc, and copper. Manufacturers can list other nutrients on the label if they wish. For example, many labels now

NUTRITION INFORMATION PER SERVING

Serving Size: ½ cup (1 oz.)
Servings per Container: 16

BRAN

	1 oz.	With ½ Cup Whole Milk
Calories	70	150
Protein	3 g	7 g
Carbohydrate	21 g	27 g
Fat	2 g	6 g

PERCENTAGE OF U.S. RECOMMENDED DAILY ALLOWANCES (U.S. RDAs)

Protein	4	10
Vitamin A	*	2
Vitamin C	45	45
Thiamine	45	45
Riboflavin	45	60
Niacin	45	45
Calcium	2	15
Iron	15	15
Vitamin B$_6$	45	45
Vitamin B$_{12}$	45	50
Phosphorus	30	45
Magnesium	30	35
Zinc	10	15
Copper	15	15

*Contains less than 2% of the U.S. RDA of these nutrients.

INGREDIENTS: 100% Wheat Bran, Sugar, Malted Barley Flour, Salt, Fig Juice, Prune Juice, Ascorbic Acid (Vitamin C), Niacinamide, Pyridoxine Hydrochloride (Vitamin B$_6$), Thiamine Mononitrate (Vitamin B$_1$), Riboflavin (Vitamin B$_2$), Vitamin B$_{12}$

Which nutrient does this nutrition label say you would get in the greatest amount if you eat one serving of this food?

give information about saturated fats, cholesterol, and sodium because people are concerned about the amount of these nutrients contained in foods.

How Computers Can Help You

Nutritional Analysis by Computer

You may have wished for a fast and accurate way to figure out how nutritiously you are eating. If so, you may be just the person to try a computer program created to help you do this. There are now available computer programs designed to collect information from you and analyze what and how much you have eaten (or plan to eat) over a twenty-four-hour period. Some of these programs ask your age, sex, height, and weight, as well as your activity level for the same period. After adding in this information, you can get feedback that is fairly specific to your individual needs.

Such a program will analyze the soundness of your diet, based on the RDAs for key nutrients. It will then offer you suggestions on how to improve your diet. For example, this message might appear on the computer screen: "Your food choices supply less than 10% of the RDA for iron." The screen would then show a list of foods and the amount of each you could eat to get the iron you need. After reading the list, you could decide which iron source(s) to add during the day to get the other 90 percent of the RDA.

Such a program can also help you eat nutritiously as you lose or gain weight. If, for example, your food choices for one day contain 100 more calories than recommended, you could have the computer list the number of calories contained in each food. By omitting one high-calorie food, you might be able to bring your calories for that day down to where they should be. By choosing carefully, you could still get the proper amount of each of the nutrients you need.

Planning Meals Around Basic Food Groups

A meal is not just a blend of proteins, carbohydrates, fats, vitamins, minerals, and water. Instead, it is a combination of different foods that supply these nutrients. To help you choose foods that make nutritious meals, use the basic food groups as a guide.

A **basic food group** is a group of many foods that supply many of the same types of nutrients. For example, fruits and vegetables form one basic food group because they are excellent sources of fiber, vitamins, and minerals. One fruit or vegetable may provide more or less of a particular nutrient than another fruit or vegetable does. Still, all the foods in the group offer the same types of nutrients.

No one food has all the nutrients you need. When you eat a variety of foods from four of the food groups, however, you can get the nutrients you need. The chart below lists five food groups. It also shows the number of servings that it is recommended you get each day from the food groups known as the Basic Four. The Basic Four Food Groups are as follows: fruits and vegetables; breads and cereals; milk and selected dairy products; and meats and meat alternatives. These four

The Basic Food Groups

Food Group	Number of Servings Recommended Each Day	Sample Foods	Main Nutrients Provided
Fruits and Vegetables	4 or more	apples, bananas, beans, carrots, grapes, mangoes, oranges, peaches, pears, peas, pumpkin squash, zucchini	Vitamin A, Vitamin C, carbohydrates
Breads and Cereals	4	bran, bread, corn, grits, hot or cold cereal, oats, pasta, rice	thiamine, niacin, iron, carbohydrates
Milk and Selected Dairy Products	4	buttermilk, cheese, custard or flan, milk, yogurt	calcium, riboflavin, proteins
Meats and Meat Alternatives	2	beef, chicken, dried beans and peas, eggs, fish, peanut butter, pork	proteins, thiamine, niacin, iron
Extra Foods	No recommendation	candy, cake, pie, chips and dip, soda, pretzels, jelly, most salty or fatty snacks and rich desserts	calories, not many nutrients

How Much Is a Serving?

Food Group	What Is a Serving?	How Much Is It?
Fruits and Vegetables	1 average piece of fruit	a medium-sized apple, pear, or orange
	½ of a large fruit	half of a cantaloupe or banana
	4 ounces of juice	a small glass
	½ cup of cooked fruit	a custard-cup dish of apple-sauce or crushed pineapple
Breads and Cereals	1 slice of bread	a slice of white or whole grain bread, 1 biscuit, a hamburger or hotdog roll, an English muffin
	¾ to 1 cup of uncooked cereal	an individual box or medium bowl of corn flakes or other ready-to-eat cereal
	½ to ¾ cup of cooked cereal	a scoop of rice the size of an ice-cream dipper; a small bowl of grits, oatmeal, or noodles
Milk and Selected Dairy Products	8 ounces of liquid	a large glass of buttermilk, skim milk, or whole milk; a 1-cup container of yogurt
	1½ ounces of hard cheese	1 slice of American, Swiss, provolone, or mozzarella cheese; a 1-inch cube of cheddar or other block cheese
	2 cups of cottage cheese	four large scoops
Meats and Meat Alternatives	2 to 3 ounces of cooked meat, fish, or poultry	a small hamburger, an individual-size can of tuna or salmon, a chicken thigh
	2 eggs	2 eggs
	1 cup of peas or beans	a large bowl of chili
	½ cup of nuts	a sandwich with four tablespoons of peanut butter; a half cup of chopped walnuts or cashews

groups provide foods that contribute to nutritious meals. The Extra Foods Group includes foods that offer few nutrients.

You can take advantage of the food group system by planning meals to include the recommended servings. For example, you might have orange juice before school, a stuffed potato at lunch, and broccoli and strawberries at dinner. If so, you will have eaten four servings from the fruits and vegetables group during the day. The chart above gives you an idea of serving sizes for different kinds of foods. Only after you plan meals that include the appropriate number of servings from the Basic Four should you consider foods from the Extra Foods Group.

Planning What to Eat

Planning Meals with Variety in Mind

You could plan to eat the same meals every week and get all of the nutrients you need. You would probably not want to do this, however. Variety can make life very enjoyable, and one way you can add variety to your life is to vary your meal plans. Many possible combinations of foods will provide the nutrients you need. Therefore, you have much room to experiment. You can try many different foods—both when you eat away from home and when you cook for yourself.

As you try different combinations of foods in different settings, you will probably notice how pleasing it is to eat a plateful of food that has some variety. The variety can be in colors, textures, tastes, and temperatures. Perhaps you have already noticed the effect of planning a meal with little variety. For example, you may already realize that a meal of cottage cheese with tomatoes, baked chicken breast, lima beans, rice pudding, and milk would be quite bland. You may also realize that a meal of sweet and sour chicken, fried rice, carrot sticks, cucumber salad, and milk would be more interesting.

Knowing How Much to Eat

One part of meal planning is to choose foods that give you the necessary nutrients. Another part is to make sure that you are eating these foods in the amounts needed to supply you with the appropriate level of energy. When you do not get enough energy from the foods you eat, you tend to be underweight. When you get more than you need, you become overweight. An understanding of calories can help you judge the amount of specific foods to eat each day to maintain a weight that is desirable for you.

Understanding Calories

Foods are fuel for your body, just as gasoline is fuel for a car. Just as a gasoline engine converts fuel into energy, your body converts food into energy. From the food you eat, you get energy—measured in calories—to stay

Do you think these individuals need more or less than the average number of calories for their age group? Why?

alive, be active, and grow. A **calorie** is a measure of the energy a person gets from food.

Some calories are available to you in foods that also provide many of the nutrients you need. Other calories are available in foods with few nutrients. This means that some foods have greater nutrient density than others. **Nutrient density** is the amount of a nutrient that one serving of a food provides per calorie. A serving of food that provides a great amount of a nutrient and few calories is said to have a high nutrient density. For example, a serving of squash is an excellent source of nutrients and has very few calories. It has a high nutrient density. By comparison, many snack or dessert foods are high in calories but low in nutrients. These foods have a low nutrient density. To make the most of the calories you eat, select foods with a high nutrient density.

The number of calories a food contains depends on which nutrients it contains. The only nutrients that produce calories are proteins, fats, and carbohydrates. Every gram of fat yields 9 calories. Every gram of protein or carbohydrate yields 4 calories. This means that one cup of canned chili con carne and beans, for example, contains 344 calories. The following calculations show why:

	Carbohydrates	Proteins	Fats	Total
Number of grams	31	19	16	
Calories per gram	× 4	× 4	× 9	
Number of calories	124	+ 76	+ 144	= 344

As you plan meals, think about the calories each food supplies. Then, try to balance the number of calories you take in with the number you use up.

Taking In and Using Up Calories

It is best to take in only the number of calories that you need. The number of calories an average person 15 to 18 years old might need each day is as follows:

	Females	Males
Average number	2,100	2,800

Because of differences among individuals, you may need fewer or more than the average number of calories for your sex. The number of calories you need each day is usually determined by two major factors. These factors are your basal metabolism and the amount of physical activity you get.

Basal metabolism is the amount of energy needed by the body when it is at rest. The main factors that determine your basal metabolism are your age, your sex, and the surface area of your body. For example, your basal metabolism will be faster if you are younger rather than older. It will also be faster if you are male rather than female. In addition, it will be faster the greater the surface area of your body.

The amount of physical activity you get may be above or below average. If you are involved in sports or other demanding physical activities, you need more calories than if you do not exercise.

Just as it is important to consider the number of calories you need, it is also important to think about *when* you need them. During the day you are probably walking, running, studying, and using up energy at peak levels. As you sleep, you will not be as physically active. Therefore, eating a heavy meal just before bedtime may make less sense than eating a heavy meal at breakfast or lunch would.

Looking at Your Weight

Think about how you look to yourself in the mirror. Also, think about how you feel. Do you think you would look or feel better if you gained or lost some weight? Do you think you are about the right weight? In general, being **underweight** is defined as being 10 percent or more below one's desirable weight. Being **overweight** is defined as being 10 percent or more above one's desirable weight. Being **obese** is defined as being 20 percent or more above one's desirable weight. The chart on page 306 gives you a rough idea of a weight that may be right for you based on your age, height, and sex.

If, according to the chart on page 306, you are underweight, overweight, or obese or if you can pinch more than 1 inch of flesh on

Knowing How Much to Eat **305**

the back of your upper arm, you will probably want to adjust your eating patterns. Do not do so, however, before discussing the matter with your medical doctor. As you will read on the next page, not all diets are healthy and safe. By checking with your doctor, you can find out whether you really need to gain or to lose. You can also get a weight-gain or weight-loss plan that is specific to your needs. Such a plan will probably incorporate guidelines like the ones that follow.

Gaining Weight

It is possible to gain weight and be healthy by taking steps like these:

- Eat three regular-size meals or several smaller meals each day.
- Eat at mealtime even if you are not hungry.
- Eat second servings of some of your favorite nutrient-dense foods.
- Substitute fluids with calories for water or low-calorie fluids.
- Snack often, as long as it does not decrease your appetite for meals. Nutritious high-calorie snacks include peanuts and custard.
- Exercise to make sure you add weight in the form of muscle not fat.

Losing Weight

It is possible to lose weight and be healthy by taking steps like these:

- Try to lose no more than 1 or 2 pounds a week.
- Cook or order the amount you plan to eat. Resist second helpings.

Some people can eat whatever they like without gaining weight. Why must others choose very small portions to simply maintain their weight?

- Serve yourself smaller portions, and use smaller plates.
- Season foods with herbs and spices, not sauces or salt.
- Choose lean meats or meat alternatives rather than fatty meats.
- Broil or bake meats or order them cooked in these ways as often as possible. Avoid frying meats or ordering fried meats.
- Include high-fiber foods in meals and snacks. Lettuce, celery, cauliflower, mushrooms, apples, and pears are examples.
- Use low-fat dairy foods such as skim milk and low-fat yogurt.
- Eat slowly, chew carefully, and give yourself time to digest your food.

Average Heights and Weights of Females and Males, Ages 14–17

		Females				Males		
		HEIGHT		WEIGHT		HEIGHT		WEIGHT	
AGE		Inches	Centimeters	Pounds	Kilograms	Inches	Centimeters	Pounds	Kilograms
14		63.15	160.4	110.87	50.28	64.21	163.1	111.95	50.77
15		63.70	161.8	118.36	53.68	66.54	169.0	125.05	56.71
16		63.94	162.4	123.24	55.89	68.31	173.5	136.93	62.10
17		64.21	163.1	125.00	56.69	69.37	176.2	146.21	66.31

Planning for Nutritious Meals

P.S.

What Is the Truth About Weight-Loss Diets?

Do the claims in some ads sound incredible? They are.

How do you know when a diet will work? How can a diet be downright dangerous? This is a list of typical diets, with an explanation of why most of them cannot deliver as much as they promise.

- **High fat, extra-low carbohydrate diet.** Red meat, fish, bacon, butter, and other fats and oils are recommended. Breads, cereals, fruits, and vegetables are not recommended. *Disadvantages:* The diet does not include foods that would provide Vitamins B and C. The number of calories can be high.

- **Very low fat and protein diet.** A single grain, fruit, or vegetable is used for the entire diet. Often, the dieter goes to a clinic or a resort. Typically, the same food is served for every meal. *Disadvantages:* The dieter cannot lead a normal life; food becomes the focus of everything. The diet is monotonous and expensive and provides inadequate amounts of Vitamin A, riboflavin, calcium, iron, and protein.

- **Liquid-protein diet.** A powder or liquid "protein" mixture is used instead of food. *Disadvantages:* The calorie level is dangerously low. The liquid protein meal is boring, because the dieter only gets to drink a single glass of flavored liquid morning, noon, and night. Vitamin and mineral supplements, if provided, may be inadequate. Some research shows that this type of diet can trigger underlying medical problems.

- **Herbal blends and other mysterious-formula diets.** Often, secret combinations of herbs and plants are used. *Disadvantages:* The powder or other diet "food" is expensive. The ingredients are "secret," so you do not know what you are buying or eating.

After you lose weight, try not to "yo-yo" your weight. Studies show that the cycle of losing, then gaining, then losing weight can be hard on the body. It can strain the heart and other organs. Actually, it is far less strenuous to maintain a reasonable amount of extra weight than to diet severely, and then gain weight rapidly over and over.

Deciding Where to Eat

Right now, you may like to eat many meals in fast-food restaurants. While these kinds of restaurants are certainly popular, they often offer limited selections. More than likely, when you are out on your own, you will want your meals to reflect a greater variety. You may begin to choose other kinds of restaurants and even prepare many of your meals at home. For example, you and your date may want to dine at a very special restaurant. You and your coworkers may want to get together to share a home-cooked meal. If you understand nutrition and dining basics, you can make dining anywhere not only nutritious but also more relaxing.

Planning to Eat Away from Home

Good food is available everywhere. You can buy it from vending machines, fast-food restaurants, cafeterias, or elegant clubs. Wherever you buy a meal or snack, you will want to keep good nutrition in mind. This means that you will want to take the same care in planning a meal from a menu as you would in planning a meal to prepare at home. Even in a fast-food restaurant, you may be able to create a meal that has most or all of the various nutrients that your body needs.

Depending on the type of restaurant you select, the menu, the meal service, the table setting, and even the procedure for paying the check may vary. One thing, however, that does not vary is the need for customers to use good table manners. If you know what to expect in different kinds of restaurants, you can dine with ease in them. By trying many kinds of restaurants, you can enjoy a variety of dining experiences.

Ordering from a Menu

Choosing food from a menu can be fun and sometimes challenging. It offers you a chance to experiment by trying new flavors or ordering interesting combinations. It may also bring you face to face with interesting food terms that are unfamiliar to you. When this happens, ask the person who is taking your order to describe the food and the way it is prepared. Never be shy about asking. A chef would much rather have you ask than have you ignore a restaurant specialty. For a description of some of the more common menu terms, see the next page.

Understanding a Variety of Services and Settings

You are probably already familiar with several types of meal service. **Meal service** is the way in which foods are served. Some restaurants serve foods family style, or the way many families do. Platters and bowls of food are placed on the table so that you can help yourself to a serving or more. Often, the main dish is put on your plate and, then, the side dishes such as vegetables and salads are served in bowls.

Some restaurants and all cafeterias serve foods buffet style. With buffet-style meal service, foods are displayed on a table. You can help yourself to various salads, vegetables, and desserts. You can help yourself or you may be assisted with main dishes.

Other restaurants serve foods American style. If your plate is completely prepared in the restaurant kitchen before being brought to you, you are being served American style. Your meat and vegetables will be on the same plate. You may have a separate salad plate and a separate bread plate.

Still other restaurants serve food continental style. With this type of meal service, your food is placed on your plate at the table by

Menu Terms

Term	Description
A la carte	A French phrase meaning "by the card or list." On a menu, it indicates that every part of the meal is priced separately. For example, you would pay extra for a salad or a dessert.
A la mode	A French phrase meaning "in the manner." Often desserts are served "a la mode," which means topped with ice cream.
Antipasto	A platter of sardines, tuna, salami, celery, onions, pickled mushrooms, olives, and pimentos. It can be hot or cold. Antipasto is a traditional Italian specialty.
Appetizer	A "first course" such as juice, soup, or a small portion of meat or vegetables to start the meal.
Au gratin	A French phrase for "with cheese." Potatoes and other vegetables often are prepared au gratin.
Au jus	A French phrase for "with juice." It often is used to describe meat, such as "roast beef au jus."
Compote	A stewed, boiled, or fresh combination of fruit.
Creole	A tangy sauce made from tomato, onion, and green pepper. Creole sauce often is used on seafood, meat, and vegetables.
Demitasse	A French phrase meaning "half cup." A demitasse is a small cup of strong black coffee served at the end of a meal. Turkish coffee, espresso, or filtered coffee can be served in a demitasse.
Entree	The main course of a meal.
Fillet	A boneless cut of meat, fish, or poultry.
Gumbo	A soup made with the vegetable okra. Often it also contains tomato, onion, green pepper, and fish.
Jardinière	A French phrase for "of the garden." The phrase is used to describe a blend of mixed cut vegetables.
Lyonnaise	A French term meaning that food has been prepared with sliced and lightly fried onions.
Parfait	A layered dessert served in tall, narrow glasses. Generally, the term is used to describe a syrup and ice cream combination.
Petit fours	Small, assorted fancy cakes, often with pastel or chocolate icing and cream fillings.
Potage	The French word for "soup."
Ragout	A French term that describes a thick, well-seasoned meat stew.
Table d'hôte	A French phrase meaning "host's table." It is used to describe a meal that includes an appetizer, a main course, a beverage, and a dessert for a set price.

your waiter. For example, if you order broiled fish, the waiter will bring the fish on a platter and transfer the fish to your plate. The waiter may then ask if you want sauce or seasoning on your fish. If you do, the waiter will prepare the fish the way you ask and will then set your plate in front of you.

The more formal the service, the more flatware you are likely to find at your place setting. As a general rule, use the flatware farthest from your plate first. If you have two forks to the left of your plate, the outer fork is for your appetizer or salad. The fork closer to your plate is for your main course.

Displaying Good Table Manners

Table manners definitely make a difference. Whether you are eating away from home or at home, the following table manners are appropriate:

Deciding Where to Eat **309**

Which two types of meal service are shown here?

- Take small bites, only what you can fit comfortably onto a fork or spoon. Keep your mouth closed as you chew.
- Wipe your mouth with your napkin after you take a sip of water or any other beverage.
- Break bread rather than cutting it.
- Rest your knife or fork across the edge of the plate when you pause to talk or take a sip. Place them across the center of the plate, parallel to the edge of the table, when you have finished eating.
- Remove something from your mouth in the most dignified way possible. For example, if you are eating fish, remove the fish bones with your fork, if possible. If this is not possible, use your fingers. If you are eating grapes, put your grape seeds in your napkin to remove them from your mouth.
- Do not chase small bites of food around your plate with your fingers or a utensil.

When eating in a restaurant, try to decide promptly what you want to order. Be prepared to tell the waiter exactly what you want.

Taking Care of the Check

Unless you are being treated to a meal, you will receive the check when you finish your meal. Review the check carefully to be certain that everything you had was recorded accurately. Also, make sure that the addition was correct. If you will be dividing the check with other people, decide in advance how you want to split it. For example, you may decide to divide it evenly, regardless of the specific prices of each main course. You may choose to give one person in your group some money before you enter the restaurant. That person can pay and you can settle up later. If, however, you want separate checks, tell the waiter before you order. Usually, you will pay the cashier as you leave the restaurant. In some restaurants, however, you will pay the waiter, who will then return with your change. Ask if you are not certain which payment method is used.

Sometimes, you will see the phrase *Gratuity not included* on your check. A **gratuity** means a tip. A tip is almost always required. Although a tip was originally for outstanding service, today it is usually part of the waiter's salary. If you find that the service is poor, still tip, but consider not returning to that particular restaurant. A standard tip is 15 percent of the total bill (not including the tax). A 20 percent tip is generous. A still larger tip is in order if the service and meal are outstanding. If a large group of people eat out together or if special services are provided, the restaurant may figure the gratuity into its check.

310 Planning for Nutritious Meals

Planning to Eat at Home

As a young adult, you may soon find that eating out all the time costs more than you can afford. You may begin planning to eat more meals at home. When you use your imagination and creativity, eating at home can be just as enjoyable as eating out. All you need are some convenience foods, some recipes, and a good supply of basic ingredients. In addition, it may help to have some ideas about how to plan meals for only one or two persons.

Considering Convenience Foods

Convenience foods are no longer only foods to be served straight from the can or package. Instead, they can be combined with other convenience foods or fresh ingredients to make interesting meals. For example, you can add your favorite cheeses and toppings to a frozen pizza or pizza mix. You can combine canned, frozen, or dry soup mixes with vegetables or meat cubes to make tasty main dishes. You can make appetizing casseroles from still other combinations of canned or packaged ingredients. Once made, these casseroles can be divided into smaller portions and frozen for later use. In other words, you can make your own delicious "convenience" foods.

You might also consider planning meals around ready-to-go main dishes, salads, and specialty items found in delicatessen or take-out stores. Just remember that convenience does have its cost, not only in money but sometimes in nutrition. When you can, choose those convenience foods that are on sale and are low in calories, salt, and fat.

Choosing Recipes

If you are an experienced cook, you may have the knack of mixing this and that to make a wonderful dish. This is a true talent. However, it still pays to stay alert for recipes. You can find them in newspapers, cookbooks, and magazines. You can also learn about new recipes from friends and family members. You may even want to ask members of your family for some of their favorite recipes before you get out on your own. Maybe you can get someone to help you learn the special ways to prepare them.

A good recipe can give its ingredients a whole new flavor. It can also help you make good use of your food budget. When you look at a recipe, be sure that it is complete and easy to follow. Check to see how long it will take to prepare. For it to turn out right, you will need to allow the amount of preparation time indicated. Also, check the amount of food the recipe will yield. Some recipes can be either divided or doubled to yield either less or more food. Others cannot. In addition, some recipes provide good leftovers, while others do not.

Maintaining Basic Ingredients

Always keep on hand a supply of basic ingredients. You will certainly need them to make your own meals. You will also find them useful for preparing foods quickly in case family members or friends drop by unexpectedly.

Some basic ingredients that you will probably want to keep on hand are foods that can usually be stored up to a year and do not require refrigeration. The following are some examples:

- flour, rice, cereals, and pasta
- salt, pepper, baking soda, and baking powder
- dry or canned milk
- sugar, syrup, and molasses
- shortening, cooking oils, and vinegar
- dried or canned soups, canned meats and fish
- canned juices, vegetables, and fruits

Other basic ingredients that you will probably want to have on hand are perishables. **Perishables** are foods that can be stored for only a few weeks or less and must be refrigerated. Examples include fresh meat and fish, milk and cheeses, and fresh fruits and vegetables. These perishables should keep about a week. Other examples include eggs, butter or margarine, salad dressing, frankfurters, bacon, and cold cuts in sealed packages. These perishables should keep for two to three weeks.

Planning Meals for One or Two Persons

Making meals for yourself or for yourself and one other person is not difficult. However, it may require some planning to get the nutrition and variety you want within a limited budget. Here are some ideas to try:

- Buy for several meals at a time. For example, buy a ham and bake it for dinner. Then, use the leftovers as cubed ham in a casserole, as ground ham in a ham loaf, and as slices in sandwiches. Buy a whole chicken and separate it into several packages—such as a package for each breast half, a package for each drumstick and thigh, a package for the wings, and a package for the remaining parts. The last package can be the basis of a wonderful soup or stew.
- Divide a recipe in half. Just use half as much of every ingredient, but keep the cooking time the same.
- Shop for foods sold in individual portions. Baked chicken, chops, and sausages are examples of such foods.

Points to Remember

- All foods are combinations of two or more of the following nutrients: proteins, fats, carbohydrates, vitamins, minerals, and water.
- Because different foods contain different nutrients, you need to eat a variety of foods each day.
- Two ways to select nutritious foods are using the RDAs and the U.S. RDAs and using the basic food groups.
- The nutrient that provides the most calories per gram is fat.
- Your daily need for a particular nutrient depends on the nutrient itself, as well as on your age, sex, basal metabolism, and the amount of physical activity you get.
- You maintain a particular weight when you balance the number of calories you take in with those you use up.
- Your body uses calories more quickly when you are active than when you are inactive.
- Eating out can mean eating nutritiously if you consider the nutritive value of the foods before you order.
- An understanding of menu terms, types of meal service, and good table manners can make eating out more enjoyable.
- Preparing meals at home depends on maintaining a supply of basic foods.

Test Your Skills

DECISION MAKING

Imagine yourself in the situation described below. In this situation, a decision is needed. As you read, think about how to make good decisions. Then, answer the questions that follow. When you make decisions in the future, remember to ask yourself these questions.

Situation

After a recent routine medical examination, your roommate was told to lose 20 pounds. You have no reason to lose weight. Your weight is within 10 percent of your desirable weight. However, you are aware that your roommate will lose weight better if you help out. In fact, you are in a perfect position to help out, since you and your roommate agreed when you moved in together that you would be in charge of meal planning.

For one week, your roommate ate small servings of the nutritious meals you planned. This week, however, you have noticed that your roommate has begun to eat larger servings. You are concerned about this change for several reasons. You know that overeating is not good for your roommate. You feel frustrated because you are no longer sure what meal size to plan for the two of you. If you do not make an adjustment soon, you will keep getting servings that are too small for you. You are worried that if you do not start serving larger portions, your roommate may start eating low-nutrient snack foods and take in even more calories.

Questions

1. What is the problem?
2. What information do you need to help you make a decision?
3. Which of your values, goals, and resources may affect your decision?
4. List three decisions you could make. What are their possible consequences?
5. What is the best decision you could make? Why is it the best for you? What is the next best decision?

Terms

On a separate sheet of paper, write a definition for each of the underlined terms below. Base your definition on the clues you find in the statement(s).

1. Jacqueline eats a variety of foods so that she will get all the <u>nutrients</u> she needs. She knows that no one can stay alive without proteins, fats, carbohydrates, vitamins, minerals, and water.

2. Ian uses <u>nutrition labels</u> to help him decide which brands of cereal supply the most nutrients and the most energy per serving.

3. Leah plans her meals by relying on four of the <u>basic food groups</u>. From each of these food groups she gets a particular combination of nutrients to round out her diet.

4. The <u>nutrient density</u> of the foods Arturo eats is usually high. He tries to eat as many foods as possible that give him a lot of nutrients per calorie.

5. The number of calories Channing uses up when she is resting is greater than the number of calories her friend Rachel uses up when resting. They have different rates of <u>basal metabolism</u>.

6. Bay is sure that he is not <u>underweight</u>. The last time he weighed himself, his weight was within 10 percent of his desirable weight.

7. Amanda takes in just enough calories to balance those she uses up. She has no intention of weighing more than 10 percent above her desirable weight. She realizes that being <u>overweight</u> causes health problems.

8. Ulysses has tried restaurants with all types of <u>meal service</u>. He has decided that he prefers food to be served to him family style.

9. Because they never last very long in the refrigerator, Steve is careful to eat within a week many of the <u>perishables</u> he buys.

Questions

1. List two ways to get all of the essential amino acids in your meals.

2. What is a possible advantage of choosing foods that have more unsaturated than saturated fats?

3. Name the three forms in which foods may supply carbohydrates.

4. What is the best way to get the vitamins you need?

5. Which six minerals should you concentrate on getting each day?

6. In what types of situations might you need to increase your daily intake of fluids?

7. What information can you find on a nutrition label?

8. Is it easier to use RDAs or the basic food group system to plan nutritious meals? Why?

9. Why is it important to consider nutrient density when choosing foods?

10. What two major factors contribute to the number of calories you need each day?

11. If a table is set with many pieces of flatware, what basic rule helps you know which piece to use first?

12. How much should you usually tip a waiter in a restaurant?

13. Name an advantage and a disadvantage of using convenience foods.

Activities

1. List snack items that are often sold in vending machines. Rate each in terms of high or low nutritive value and indicate why you gave the rating. Name alternative snacks that might replace items that are low in nutritive value.

2. How would you recommend that a male and a female, age 15 to 18, meet the RDAs for calcium, iron, and Vitamin A? Use the RDA chart on page 299 and Appendix 8 on pages 404–413 to help select specific foods.

3. Make an illustrated chart, poster, or bulletin board called "What 100 Calories Look Like." Use Appendix 8 on pages 404–413 to identify portion sizes that equal 100 calories.

4. Record everything you eat on one weekday and on one day of a weekend. For each day, total the number of servings from each food group represented. On which day did you eat a more nutritious diet? What conclusions can you make about your eating habits?

5. After eating at a restaurant, describe the type of meal service that was used. List any unfamiliar menu terms you saw. Then, use the chart on page 309 to describe them. Write down the menu of the meal you ordered, using the format of the menu shown on page 298. Analyze your meal in terms of nutritive value, price, and variety of colors, temperatures, textures, shapes, and flavors.

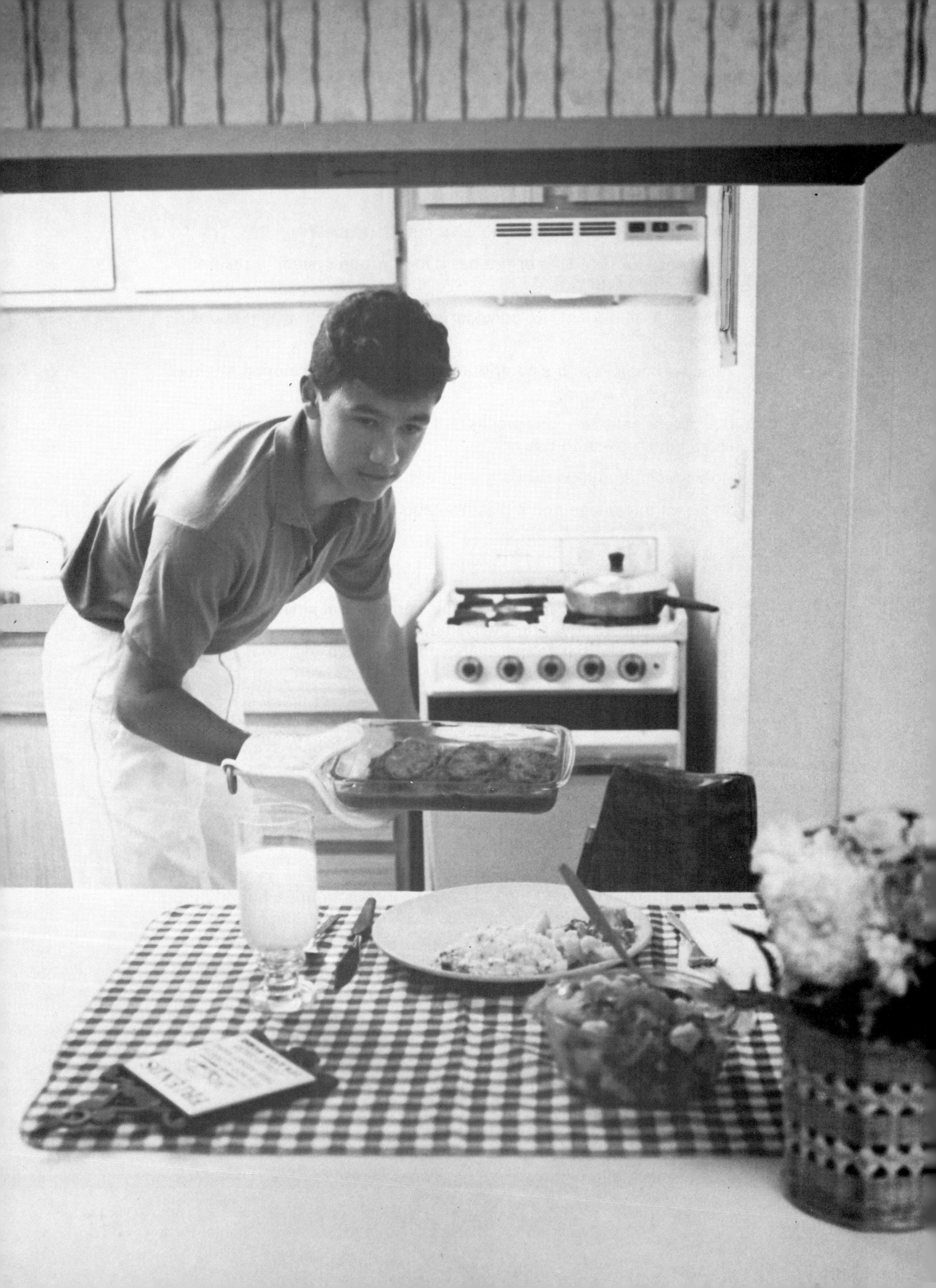

CHAPTER 14

Buying and Preparing Food

Living on your own requires you to be more than a meal planner. It also requires you to be a meal manager. As a young adult, you will probably find that both your time and money for meals are limited. To conserve both of these resources, you will want to practice meal management. Meal management will help you with both shopping for and preparing meals.

At the grocery store, you can depend on many shopping skills that you already have and make use of several new ones. For example, you might use a shopping list to organize your trip through the store. You might also use a shopping list to help you guarantee that you will get the items you must have before you spend money on optional foods. You might use unit prices and other information to compare prices carefully so that you can get the best buy. You might pay attention to nutrition and other food labels so that you get just the combination of ingredients you prefer. You might check carefully for freshness in all the different types of foods you buy so that you reject low-quality foods.

At home, you can make light work of meals by following recipes and package directions and using kitchen equipment efficiently. Even making a ham and cheese omelet, lasagna, or a Greek salad will seem easy. All it takes to be a successful meal manager is a little know-how and some practice.

Discover Through Your Reading

- how to decide where to shop for food
- how to plan a food shopping list
- why food additives play an important role in many foods
- what cooking methods you can use to prepare different kinds of foods
- what to remember when cooking with a microwave oven
- how to plan all parts of a meal so that they are ready at the same time

Getting Ready to Shop for Food

With a little planning, food shopping can be easy. You already know that you must plan meals around nutritious foods. Before you shop for these foods, you need to consider which markets give you the selections you need and can afford. You also need to know the layout of the store so that you can organize your shopping list and shop easily and quickly. With an organized list, you have a head start on making the most of your food-shopping time and money.

Choosing Food Markets

You can buy food just about anywhere. There are giant supermarkets, some open all night long. There are convenience stores and specialty food shops. Wherever you shop, the store should be clean, the food fresh and wholesome, and the employees courteous.

Several factors will influence where you decide to shop. These factors include your budget, the selection of foods you need, and convenience. The factors that are most important to you will probably determine the places you shop most often. Sometimes, however, you may have to make trade-offs. For example, you may value both convenience and a wide selection of fruits. The most convenient store may carry few fruits. A store several miles away may have a great fruit selection. One trade-off you might make is to plan meals around fewer varieties of fruits. Another is to drive the extra miles.

Markets That Fit Your Budget

Because where you buy can have a major impact on your budget, you may choose certain markets simply because of the prices they offer. Comparison shopping will help you identify the less-expensive stores. Remember that the price of the same item can be much higher in some stores than in others. For example, the same 1-quart jar of mayonnaise might be $1.59 in a supermarket, $2.25 in a neighborhood store, and $3.45 in a gourmet food store. Also, keep in mind that some stores may double or triple the value of food coupons and help you pay an even lower price. Other stores might not accept coupons at all.

Markets That Offer Selections You Need

Not all stores offer the same selections. For this reason, you may decide to shop for some items at one store and other items at another. For example, you may buy convenience foods at a supermarket, but fresh fruits and vegetables at a neighborhood stand. If you need special foods or ingredients, you may find that some stores offer better selections than others. Again, comparison shopping can help you find what you need.

Maybe you are a vegetarian. If so, you may want to look for a store that sells several types of **tofu,** a soybean product, and sprouts. The same food store will probably sell many different fresh fruits and vegetables as well. Perhaps you want **kosher foods,** foods specially prepared according to Jewish dietary laws. Then, you will want to find a store that sells these foods. You can recognize kosher foods by the letter *U* inside a circle or by the letter *K* marked on them. Maybe you prefer to make many ethnic dishes and need stores that offer a wide variety of Oriental, Mexican, Scandinavian, or other ethnic foods. Perhaps you like to pick up deli sandwiches for parties or picnics. The delicatessen section of a supermarket might have just what you need.

Markets That Offer Convenience

Some stores will be more convenient for you to use than others. Perhaps the stores with good prices and selections are located close to where you live or work. They may be open during the hours when you need to shop. In addition, they may offer you check-cashing privileges, adequate parking, and speedy checkout service.

If a store offers fast checkout service, it may be using a computerized checkout system that relies on the Universal Product

318   Buying and Preparing Food

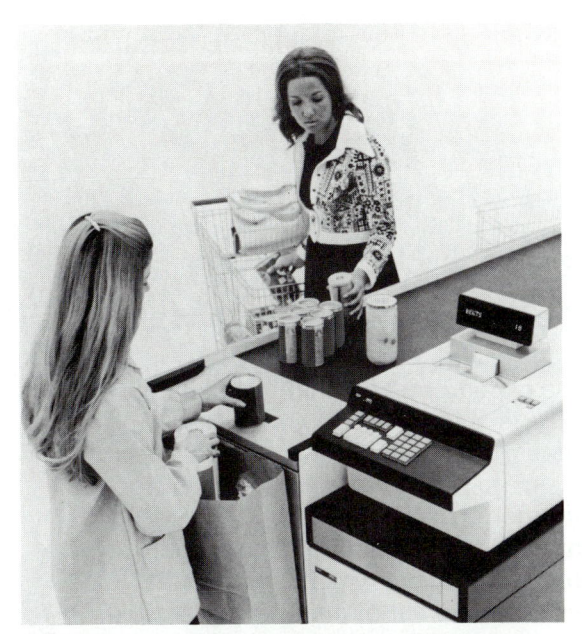

A checkout clerk with a UPC scanner can do three things at once. The clerk can ring up a purchase, update the store's inventory, and record the purchase on the register tape. How does a scanner benefit you, the customer?

Organizing Your Food Shopping List

To make sure that you remember all the food items you need, you can keep a running list of items you have already or are about to run out of. For information on how a computer might help you create a shopping list for food, see page 320.

There are many nonfood items that can also be bought at food markets. However, you may want to list these items separately because they can often be purchased less expensively elsewhere. These items include hardware, clothing, school supplies, and personal grooming products. Also, be sure not to use the money you have budgeted for food on nonfood items like these.

You can shop more quickly and keep track of your spending if you organize your list. One way is to group items according to where they are found in the store. For example, as you walk into the store, you will find a particular category of foods along the nearest wall. Perhaps this category will be **produce**, fresh fruits and vegetables. If so, you may decide to put these foods first on your shopping list. You can continue to develop your list by writing down the categories of food you need, in the order in which they are found in the store. For example, you might list produce first, canned foods second, meats third, and frozen foods last.

Another effective method of organizing is to list foods from the most important—the ones that you must have—to the least important—the ones that you could do without. For example, you might want to list foods you need for specific meals first, followed by staples and, then, snack items. This system helps you to buy the important main course foods first and also save money.

As you make your list, consider how much of each food item you need. The amount of an item you put on your list will depend on several factors. One factor is the number of servings you need. If you are not sure how much meat, fish, or poultry to buy, the following guidelines may help:

- Allow 3/4 pound of bony meat, poultry, or fish per serving.

Code. The **Universal Product Code**, or **UPC**, is the set of vertical lines and numbers that appears on product labels. Such a system allows a checkout clerk to pass each product over an electronic scanner attached to a computerized register. The register prints out a tape with the name and price of the item. Because the UPC system relies on electronic scanners, it is usually fast and accurate. Therefore, stores that use the UPC system not only ring up fewer wrong prices on the average, but they also generally allow you to complete your shopping in a shorter amount of time.

Perhaps the places with the best prices and selections are inconveniently located. Maybe they are open only during the hours that you are in school or at work. They may not offer you the check-cashing or parking services that you need. Their checkout service may be slow and sometimes even inaccurate. Even the best prices and selections cannot always make up for a store's lack of convenience. Only you can decide whether low prices and wide selection are more important to you than convenient location.

Getting Ready to Shop for Food

How Computers Can Help You

Working with Recipes and Creating Shopping Lists

Within a few months or years, you will be in charge of planning, shopping for, and preparing your own meals. If you have children, you will be responsible for seeing to it that they have nutritious, varied, and appealing meals, too. And, if you have not already done so, you are bound to be asked to assist in arranging a meal for a school, club, or other group event.

If your home economics department or your family has a computer, you may want to investigate some of the computer programs that offer assistance in meal planning, shopping, and preparation. Some of these programs include a variety of delicious recipes, to which you can add your own favorites. Other programs depend on your typing recipes into a computer, which can be a time-consuming task. The benefits of being able to work with the recipes you have stored, however, may make your efforts worthwhile.

Here are some of the benefits. Some programs allow you to cross-index recipes. For example, a recipe for an apple salad would be indexed under "apple" and "salad." Whenever you get a good buy on apples, you can have the computer call up every recipe indexed under "apples." Whenever you want to consider all types of salads or all salads with a particular ingredient, your computer will call up the recipes for you.

Once you have selected a recipe or a group of recipes, some computer programs will help you adapt each recipe to the number of people you are serving. Some of these same programs will then create a shopping list based on the recipes. If the computer has a printer, you can print the list, cross off any ingredients you know you have enough of, and take the list along to the store.

- Allow 1/3 to 1/2 pound of less bony cuts such as steaks, chops, fillets, or slices of roast per serving.
- Allow 1 pound of boneless meat such as ground meat or chicken breasts when you are making a casserole that serves four people.
- Allow one Cornish hen or one-half of a duck per serving.
- Allow 1 pound of turkey per serving if the turkey weighs 12 pounds or less. Allow 1/2 pound of turkey per serving if the turkey weighs more.

Another factor that will influence the amount of an item you will put on your list is the price advertised for the item. Still another factor is the amount of storage space you have. For example, maybe your refrigerator does not have a large freezer or has a freezer that freezes no lower than 20°F (−6°C). If so, you may not be able to buy many frozen foods at a time, or you may not be able to buy specific kinds of frozen foods such as ice cream.

Keep your list flexible. If the price of steak is higher than you can afford, consider ground beef and make tacos or Swedish meatballs instead. If you see a special price break on canned products that you really like, buy them in place of other items on your list. If an item you need is on sale, you may want to buy more than the amount indicated on your list. Buying a sale item in quantity is an especially good idea if the item is not perishable.

Shopping for Food

Once you have found your favorite food stores, find out on which days they offer the best buys. Many stores, for example, begin special sales on Thursdays. To make choices that will satisfy your budget, nutritional requirements, and appetite, plan to rely on the basic food-shopping techniques. These techniques involve an understanding of unit pricing, food labels, and food quality and form.

Taking Advantage of Unit Pricing

How can you tell if one size or brand of a product is a better buy than another? For example, is an 8-ounce jar of peanut butter a better buy than a 4-ounce or 15-ounce jar? Is one brand of dishwasher detergent a better buy than another brand of the same size? Is one manufacturer's 6 1/2-ounce can of tuna fish a better buy than another manufacturer's 8-ounce can? These may seem like difficult comparisons, but unit pricing can make them simple.

Unit pricing is a system of marking items to show how much they cost according to a particular measurement, such as an ounce or a pound. There are several ways you can use unit pricing to identify the most economical choice. For example, you can compare *different sizes of the same brand.* Suppose your favorite brand of spaghetti sauce is packaged in 8-ounce and 44-ounce jars. The unit price for the 8-ounce jar may be 90 cents per pound. The unit price for the 44-ounce jar may be 56 cents per pound. In this case, the larger size jar is the better buy if you can use the whole amount conveniently. With unit pricing, you can also compare *different brands of the same size.* Furthermore, with unit pricing you can also compare *different sizes of different brands.*

Unit pricing also helps you recognize the true price of packaging. It helps you learn, for example, how much the tumbler-style jar adds to the cost of jelly. It helps you figure out whether your favorite margarine is more expensive when packaged in a plastic tub or in sticks.

Unit pricing is no longer used just for food items. You can now find it for many different types of products. In most stores that use unit pricing, you will find the unit price on a small label attached to the shelf where the items are displayed.

Using Food Labels

As you may recall, the food label on each item must include certain information. This information includes the name of the product, the net contents or weight, and the name and address of the manufacturer, packer, or distributor. In addition, the food label lists the ingredients in descending order according to weight.

There are several ways that reading food labels can help you make good food choices. The labels help you compare ingredients. For example, you might see the following list of ingredients on a jar of tomato sauce:

>   water, tomatoes, tomato puree, peanut oil, salt, romano cheese, olive oil, onion, black pepper, garlic, basil

This sauce contains more water, by weight, than it contains tomatoes or tomato puree. Therefore, if you select this sauce, you may be paying a high price for flavored water. Sauce with tomato puree listed first would be thicker and more flavorful.

Food labels also help you compare the nutritive value of different food items. Suppose you are trying to decide between two fruit juices. The nutrition label on one juice may show that a serving provides 100 percent of the RDA for Vitamin C. The nutrition label on the other may show that a serving provides only 25 percent of this vitamin. If you plan to use fruit juices as your major source of Vitamin C each day, the juice supplying 100 percent may be your best buy.

As you look at food labels, see how much information you can find. Are there additives listed as ingredients? Does the product have a freshness date? Are there any government or industry seals or marks to indicate quality? Such information can also be helpful.

Identifying Food Additives

As you read food labels, you will probably notice that some of the ingredients are food additives. A **food additive** is a natural or synthetic substance that affects a particular characteristic of a food. Some food additives are used to improve freshness, appearance, or texture. For example, a **preservative** is a type of food additive that helps protect a food from browning, mold, or other damage from oxygen or bacteria. A loaf of bread, for example, would mold much faster when preservatives were not used. Common preservatives that you may see on food labels include sodium benzoate and nitrites. An **emulsifier** is a type of food additive that helps maintain or improve the texture and consistency of foods. Peanut butter, for example, would be tough and sticky if emulsifiers were not used. Monoglycerides and diglycerides are typical emulsifiers.

Other food additives are, for example, used to improve the nutritional value of foods. You know that a food has these additives when you see the term *enriched* or *fortified* on the label. An **enriched food** is one that has lost certain nutrients during processing and then had those same nutrients added back. The nutrients that are usually lost and then replaced are riboflavin, thiamine, niacin, and iron. The enriched food may contain

How can reading nutrition labels help you get the most food value for your money?

Ingredients

Crust: Enriched flour (flour, niacin, reduced iron, thiamine mononitrate, riboflavin), water, hydrogenated soybean oil, yeast, salt.

Sauce: Tomato puree, water, sugar, hydrogenated vegetable oil (soybean and cottonseed), modified corn starch, salt, spice and coloring, natural flavor, beet powder, hydrolyzed vegetable protein.

Topping: Mozzarella cheese substitute (water, casein, hydrogenated soybean oil, salt, sodium aluminum phosphate, lactic acid, natural flavor, modified corn starch, sodium citrate, sorbic acid [a preservative], sodium phosphate, artificial color, guar gum, magnesium oxide, ferric orthophosphate, zinc oxide, riboflavin [Vitamin B-2], Vitamin B-12, folic acid, Vitamin B-6 hydrochloride, niacinamide, thiamine mononitrate [Vitamin B-1], Vitamin A palmitate), cooked pork sausage (pork, salt, garlic powder, spice), pepperoni (pork and beef, salt, dextrose, spice and color, natural flavor, lactic acid starter culture, garlic powder, sodium nitrite with BHA, BHT and citric acid added to help protect flavor), low-moisture part-skim mozzarella cheese, textured vegetable protein (soy flour, caramel color).

Many foods contain additives. How many additives can you identify on this list of ingredients for pizza?

higher levels of these nutrients than did the original. A **fortified food** is one that has had certain nutrients added that it either lacked or contained in only small amounts. You are likely to see enriched or fortified products when you buy breads and cereals and milk and dairy foods.

Food additives must pass rigid safety tests. Some, such as salt and sugar, have been used for years and are included on the Generally Recognized as Safe list. This list, which is registered with the Food and Drug Administration, includes more than 650 additives. Manufacturers can use these additives without further study. However, many manufacturers and government agencies constantly monitor additives for safety. To protect yourself from an unsafe additive as studies continue, eat a lot of different foods. In this way, you will avoid eating too much of any additive that may later be found to be unsafe.

A few people seem to have an allergic reaction, or sensitivity, to some food additives. For example, a person might get a headache after eating food that contains monosodium glutamate (MSG). If you suspect that you are allergic to some additives, eliminate them from your diet for a few days. Then, slowly add one additive at a time to your diet. If you notice feelings of nervousness, headache, or stomach upset, you may be allergic to the additive. Though the allergy may not cause you serious problems, you may choose to eliminate that particular additive from your diet permanently, just to be sure.

Recognizing Open Dates

On many food labels, you will see special dates. These dates are part of an open dating system used by manufacturers. Manufacturers use the system to help consumers judge the freshness of certain food products. For example, pack dates refer to when the food was packed. Pull or sell dates tell you when the store should remove the product from the shelves or sell it. Expiration dates tell you how long a product will be safe to eat. Freshness dates indicate how long a product will be flavorful. If you see a food label with the statement "Use by Sept. 1990," you know that the food will be fresh until then.

You can use open dating information when you know the kind of date that is given. If you buy a loaf of bread that was packed several days ago, it could be stale. If you buy a container of yogurt with a pull or sell date of the next day, you need to eat it soon. If you know that you cannot use cold cuts before their expiration date, you might decide not to buy them. On the other hand, if a pizza mix has a freshness date that is several months away, you might buy it on sale and use it later.

Shopping for Food   **323**

What do government marks and open dates such as these tell you about the products they are on?

Understanding Government Marks

There are two kinds of government marks that you may see on food labels. One is a government grade mark, the other a government inspection stamp. Both provide information that you can use when shopping for food.

A **government grade mark** is a symbol, established by a U.S. government agency, that indicates a specific level of taste, texture, and appearance for certain kinds of foods. Because the U.S. Department of Agriculture (USDA) has set standards for the grading of many foods, USDA grades are commonly seen. You may want to consider grades when buying the following foods:

- *Beef, veal, and lamb—U.S. Prime, U.S. Choice, or U.S. Good.* Prime meats are the most tender, flavorful, and expensive. Choice meats are less expensive but acceptable for many uses. U.S. Good meats are less tender but excellent for stews.
- *Pork—U.S. 1, U.S. 2, or U.S. 3.* Grade 1 is the most tender and expensive. The lower grades are just as good if cooked slowly.
- *Chicken, turkey, duck, and Cornish hen— U.S. Grade A.* Although other grades are used by canners and other commercial buyers, the only grade of poultry you see in the grocery store is Grade A.
- *Eggs—U.S. Grade AA or Grade A.* Grade AA eggs have smooth shells with no cracks. Grade A eggs have slight bumps on the shell and an occasional hairline crack or very thin chip. Both grades may be Extra Large, Large, Medium, or Small.
- *Canned fruits—Grade A, Grade B, or Grade C.* Grades B or C are acceptable when the fruit's size and uniformity of shape are not important to you.
- *Canned vegetables—Grade A, Grade B, Grade C.* Like fruits, Grade A vegetables are the largest and the most uniform in shape.

Although grading is voluntary for all kinds of foods, inspection is required for some but not others. Meats and poultry sold commercially must be inspected, but fish may not be. Foods that meet inspection standards will carry a government inspection stamp. A **government inspection stamp** is a symbol, established by a U.S. government agency, that indicates that a food is wholesome and safe to eat. When you buy meats and poultry, you may see the USDA inspection stamp in purple dye. Foods with this stamp will have come from healthy animals and have been processed under sanitary conditions. Canned fish that has met similar requirements may carry an inspection seal from the U.S. Department of Commerce.

Buying the Quality of Food You Need

In addition to using unit pricing and food labels, you will want to recognize differences in food quality and form. Remember that many foods may not have open dates, government marks, or other detailed label information to help you judge their quality. Bananas, onions, fish, and other fresh foods are typical examples. To judge the quality of many types of foods, follow the tips opposite.

Buying and Preparing Food

Tips

Judging Food Quality and Freshness

Identifying fresh, high-quality food is easy. Just look closely and keep the following guidelines in mind:

Whatever you buy

- Look for packages that are firmly sealed, with no tears or punctures.

- Select cans that are normal in size and not dented, wrinkled, or puffy. The food in damaged cans could cause severe food poisoning.

Meat

- Select beef or lamb that is bright or deep red and has creamy white fat.

- Select pork that is light pink or rose-colored.

- Avoid meat that looks dried around the edges or that has a gray cast, a strong off-odor, or deep yellow fat.

Poultry

- Select poultry with firm and moist-looking flesh. Some poultry has a natural yellow color. Other poultry is more white. The color difference depends on the type of feed used. It does not affect the poultry's quality or flavor.

- Avoid poultry with bruises, broken bones, torn flesh, or mottled skin.

Fish

- Select a whole fish that has firm flesh, bright eyes, and shiny scales.

- Make sure frozen fish is frozen solid, with no signs of leakage or moisture.

- Avoid any fish that has a strong, unpleasant odor.

Eggs

- Look for eggs with shells that are well shaped and uncracked.

- Avoid buying eggs that look damp or dirty.

Produce

- Select fruits and vegetables that are fresh, well shaped, and free of bruises, nicks, discolorations, and mold.

- Buy produce in season and only in the quantities you can use. If necessary, ask the manager to open prepackaged items and sell you a small portion.

Shopping for Food

Preparing Foods

After you get your nutritious, high-quality food home, you will want to prepare it efficiently and attractively. With a little practice, you can be just as skillful in the kitchen as you are in the store. Maybe you already help with the meal preparation in your family. If so, you may be aware of the value of storing foods properly and following recipes carefully. You may also use kitchen appliances to their greatest advantage. If you are a real meal manager, you also time food preparation so that all of the meal is ready at the same time.

Handling Foods Safely

Food safety begins while you are doing your shopping. For example, it is usually best to pick up frozen, refrigerated, or hot foods on your way to the checkout cashier. It is also best to go straight home and put away your food immediately. If the checkout clerk has packed together foods of the same type, such as cold or frozen foods, then unpacking and storing them will be easy.

Unpacking the Grocery Bag

When you get home from the store, first put frozen foods into the freezer. Then, put away items that need refrigeration. The following suggestions can help you store perishable foods properly:

- Remove meats, poultry, and fish from store wrappings and loosely rewrap them in plastic wrap or wax paper. Place them in the meat compartment of the refrigerator to preserve their appearance, flavor, and nutrients. If these foods are to be frozen, wrap them tightly in aluminum foil or other freezer wrap, and add the food name and purchase date.
- Store dairy foods in their original containers in the back of the refrigerator shelves rather than on the inside of the refrigerator door.

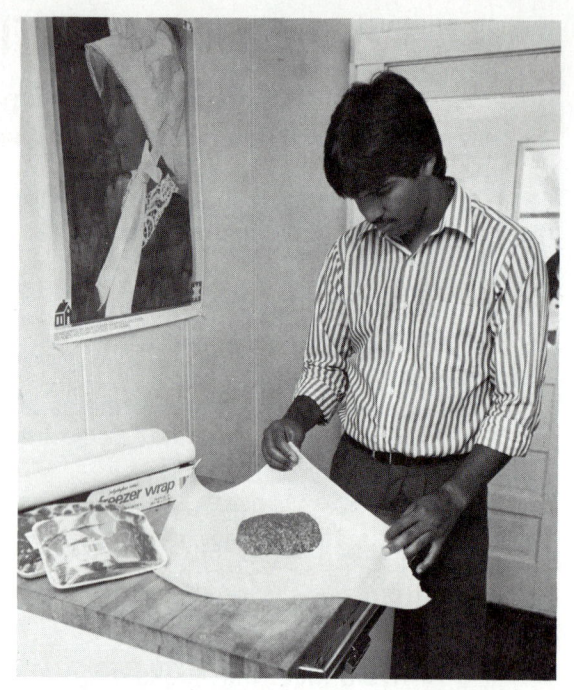

Knowing how to store foods correctly is one way to help you get the most from your food budget. What are some other ways foods can be stored?

- Store eggs, covered or in their original container, with the large end up to maintain their quality and to keep their yolks centered.
- Store most fresh vegetables and some fruits in the crisper drawers of the refrigerator to keep them moist and fresh longer.
- Store potatoes and onions in a cool, dark place, but never in the same bin. Store bananas and tomatoes at room temperature.
- Store bread at room temperature or in the refrigerator. If you do not eat bread often, store it in the freezer.

Storing Prepared Foods

Preparing foods in advance and using leftovers are important parts of meal management. When you do this, however, you need to be aware that certain prepared foods need to be stored more carefully than others. Potato salad, custard pie, turkey, and broccoli, for example, need special attention. If not stored carefully, they can cause food poisoning.

Food poisoning is a physical condition caused by food that has molded or is otherwise contaminated. Most food poisoning is mild, resulting in unpleasant nausea or headaches. However, some is very serious, even deadly. The best way to avoid food poisoning is to use safe handling and storage methods. For example, keep kitchen counters and utensils clean. Rather than cut foods directly on countertops, cut them on plastic or laminated cutting boards that can be washed easily. If you are slicing meats and vegetables for the same meal, use different knives or wash the knife and board in between uses. Once foods are prepared, store them as follows:

- Cover foods with plastic wrap or aluminum foil, or store them in glass or plastic food storage containers.
- Allow very hot foods to cool slightly before refrigerating them. Refrigerate all foods within an hour or two of preparing them.

Use prepared foods or leftovers within two or three days.

Packing Prepared Foods

Your busy lifestyle may mean that you take meals or snacks to school, work, and picnics or other social gatherings. The foods you take will be flavorful and safe to eat if you follow these suggestions:

- Pack hot foods and cold foods in separate containers.
- Use insulated containers to help keep hot foods hot and cold foods cold. When using a thermos bottle for hot foods or beverages, rinse the container with boiling water before adding the food or beverage. Special liquid-filled cubes can be frozen and used over and over to keep foods cold.
- Place sandwiches and other foods in plastic containers, or wrap them firmly with aluminum foil or plastic wrap to seal out moisture.
- Avoid combination salads such as tuna, chicken, and egg salad in warm weather when you know that you cannot keep them chilled. Instead, use cheese, raw fruits and vegetables, and other foods that will not spoil at room temperature.
- Always keep food storage containers clean. Wash and dry them thoroughly as soon as you get home.

Knowing the Best Way to Prepare Foods

Which would you rather eat—a broiled steak or a steamed steak? Which do you prefer—stir-fried peppers and onions or boiled peppers and onions? Knowing how to use various cooking methods has many advantages. It lets you enjoy the best flavor and texture and the highest nutritional value of foods. It helps you choose the correct form of a food and, therefore, saves you money. In addition, it lets you save calories or add them to your diet. For example, a typical *baked* potato has about 145 calories. To get the same number of calories in *french fries*, you could use a potato only half the size.

The chart on page 328 shows you many of the cooking methods you will see in recipes and package instructions. Some cooking methods use moist heat while others use dry heat. **Moist-heat cooking** is a cooking method that uses liquid to help tenderize and add flavor to a food. Braising, boiling, and stewing are examples. **Dry-heat cooking** is a cooking method that uses no additional liquid to tenderize or flavor a food. Broiling, baking, and roasting are examples.

Just as some foods are best cooked by moist or dry heat, some are best cooked by direct or indirect heat. In direct-heat cooking, the food is exposed directly to the heat one side at a time. For example, when you broil chicken or panfry pork chops, you are cooking with direct heat. In indirect-heat cooking, heat surrounds the food so that no one part cooks much faster than others. When you poach an egg or bake cornbread, you are cooking with indirect heat.

Fruits and vegetables, breads and cereals, milk and dairy products, and meats, fish, poultry, and eggs all have certain characteristics that make them different. Therefore, a cooking method that is great for one type of food may not be good for another. When you know which methods are best for which foods, you will have a head start on becoming a successful cook.

Preparing Fruits and Vegetables

Most fruits and vegetables are tender and do not require long cooking. They also con-

Often-Used Cooking Methods

Term	Description
Cooking Methods Using Moist Heat	
Boil	To cook in bubbling liquid that has reached the point of 212°F (100°C)
Braise	To brown in a small amount of fat and, then, cook in a small amount of liquid in a covered container
Parboil	To boil until partly cooked
Poach	To cook in enough liquid to cover the food and at a low temperature
Scald	To heat a liquid, usually milk, to just under the boiling point
Simmer	To cook in liquid just below the boiling point
Steam	To cook on a rack or tray over boiling water in a tightly covered container
Stew	To cook in liquid, in a covered container, for a long time to tenderize the food or blend flavors
Cooking Methods Using Dry Heat	
Bake	To cook in an oven
Barbecue	To cook over a direct heat source such as charcoal or a flame
Broil or grill	To cook over or under direct heat
Roast	To cook meats or poultry in an uncovered container in an oven
Sear	To quickly brown the surface of a food by using high heat to seal in juices
Cooking Methods Using Fat	
Brown	To cook with direct heat in fat until food has a brown color
Deep-fry	To cook in enough hot oil to cover the food completely
Pan-broil	To cook in an open skillet over direct heat and with no other fat than what is present in the food
Panfry or sauté	To cook in a skillet over direct heat and with a small amount of fat
Stir-fry	To quickly cook small amounts of food in a small amount of hot oil in an open skillet or a wok

tain water-soluble nutrients that can be lost when cut surfaces are exposed to air, large amounts of water, or heat. Therefore, avoid cutting these foods into tiny pieces, cooking them in more liquid than necessary, or overcooking them. Fruits and vegetables can be nutritious, flavorful, and attractive if steamed, sautéed, baked, or broiled.

Preparing Breads and Cereals

Many cooking methods are used to prepare bread and cereal products. Muffins, biscuits, pies, and cookies are usually baked. Pancakes are panfried, and hush puppies are deep-fried. Macaroni, spaghetti, and other pasta products are usually boiled and then

Buying and Preparing Food

drained. It is not necessary to rinse these foods after draining them. Oatmeal, grits, and rice are usually added to boiling water and then allowed to simmer for a specified number of minutes.

Preparing Milk and Dairy Products

Gentle cooking methods are used to prepare such milk and dairy foods as hot cocoa, puddings, and cheese sauces. The protein in these foods requires low cooking temperatures. To allow the protein to cook evenly and to achieve the best flavor and texture, use low heat and stir constantly.

High temperatures usually scorch or curdle these foods. You know that a food is scorched if it has a burnt appearance and flavor. You know that it is curdled if it appears lumpy. Extremely high heat will make cheese stringy and will melt sour cream into fat.

Preparing Meats, Poultry, Fish, and Eggs

Meats, poultry, fish, and eggs are also high in protein and require medium to low cooking temperatures. In general, tender cuts of meat can be cooked by either moist-heat or dry-heat methods. Often, tender cuts of meat such as beef sirloin, pork loin, or leg of lamb are broiled, roasted, or sautéed. Less tender cuts are best prepared with moist-heat methods. Usually, when you need to cook less tender cuts of meat such as chuck or flank, your best choice is to either braise or pot roast them.

Tender cuts of poultry such as fryers or broilers can be prepared according to the method their name indicates. Hens and stewing chickens are less tender. These types of poultry should be cooked with moist-heat methods.

Fish and eggs usually require shorter cooking times than do meats or poultry. Fish can be prepared in many ways, including deep-frying and panfrying, broiling, steaming, poaching, and baking. Eggs are usually pan-fried, hard-cooked in the shell, poached, or are sometimes baked. However you prepare fish and eggs, remember that if you cook them for too long a time, they may turn out tough or rubbery.

Why are some foods best cooked at low temperatures?

Food Preparation Terms

Term	Description
Baste	To keep food moist during cooking by pouring liquid over it every so often
Beat	To mix vigorously to add air as ingredients are blended
Blend	To mix ingredients thoroughly
Bone	To remove bones from meat, fish, or poultry by cutting around them with a sharp knife
Bread	To cover with crumbs or a similar flour or cracker coating
Brush	To cover lightly with melted fat, egg yolk or white, using a pastry brush
Chop	To cut into small pieces
Cream	To stir ingredients such as sugar and butter until smooth and creamy in texture
Cube	To cut into squares
Cut in	To thoroughly mix shortening into flour, using a pastry blender, two dinner knives, or a fork
Dice	To cut into small cubes
Dot	To cover the surface with small pieces of margarine, butter, or fat to promote browning and add flavor
Dredge	To cover with flour or another dry ingredient before frying
Dust	To cover lightly with flour or sugar
Fold in	To gently blend two ingredients by using an under-and-over folding motion
Garnish	To decorate food
Grate	To rub a hard food against a sharp grid to break the food into tiny particles
Grease	To lightly coat with shortening, cooking oil, or other fat
Grind	To put through a series of blades to cut into fine pieces
Julienne	To cut into thin, long strips
Knead	To repeatedly press, fold, and turn a dough mixture with your hands to make it smooth and elastic
Marinate	To soak in a mixture of oil, seasonings, and vinegar to tenderize or add flavor
Mince	To cut into very tiny pieces
Pare or peel	To remove the skin, rind, or outer covering of a food
Preheat	To heat the oven to the recommended temperature before putting the food in
Puree	To make a smooth paste
Score	To cut the surface of a food with a sharp knife either as a decorative effect or to allow excess fat or liquid to escape during cooking
Shred	To cut into slivers
Sift	To add air to flour or other dry ingredients by passing them through a sieve or sifter
Toss	To mix lightly
Truss	To tie the wings and legs of poultry in place before cooking, to prevent them from burning or losing their natural shape
Whip	To beat rapidly to add air

Using Recipes and Package Instructions

When preparing certain foods, you will need to follow a recipe. A recipe explains how to prepare a particular dish. A recipe gives you not only a set of instructions but also a list of the ingredients you need. It also indicates the amounts of each ingredient to use. A set of instructions on a packaged food is similar to a recipe but less complicated. A sample recipe is shown on this page.

There is a whole dictionary of words and phrases used in recipes and package instructions. For example, a recipe for pot roast may say to *marinate* the beef. A recipe for a vegetable dish may say to *mince* onion or *julienne* carrots. If you understand these food preparation terms and those listed on the facing page, you will be more successful in making foods that taste and look good.

When using a recipe or package instructions, you will want to follow each of these steps:

- Read the recipe or package instructions *before* beginning to prepare the food.
- Make sure that you have all the ingredients you need *before* you begin to prepare the food.
- Measure all ingredients accurately.
- Follow directions in the order listed in the recipe.
- Use the correct time and temperature.

Assembling Ingredients

To make the most of your time in the kitchen, get organized before starting any food preparation. Check to see that you have all the necessary ingredients. If you are missing some, you might be able to make some substitutions. Common substitutions include the following:

- stale bread or crackers, crumbled and oven-toasted, *instead of* packaged bread crumbs
- vinegar *instead of* lemon juice
- honey or corn syrup *instead of* maple or cane pancake syrup
- margarine *instead of* butter, unless your recipe indicates no substitutions
- cooking oil *instead of* melted butter
- 3 tablespoons of baking cocoa plus 1 tablespoon of margarine or butter *instead of* one square of baking chocolate
- 1/8 teaspoon of garlic powder *instead of* one clove of fresh garlic. A clove of garlic is one of several wedges that form the larger garlic bulb
- 1/3 to 1/2 teaspoon of dried herbs or spices *instead of* 1 tablespoon of fresh. Herbs and spices are flavorings made from plant parts

Once you are sure that you have what you need, put all ingredients out on a counter or

Sample Recipe

Great Little Sausage Balls

1/2 lb. ground pork sausage, hot/mild/or sage flavor

1 c. grated cheese, Cheddar or Monterey Jack

1 small package or 3/4 c. biscuit baking mix

Preheat oven to 325° F.

1. For easier handling, remove sausage from refrigerator a few minutes before beginning preparation.
2. Grate cheese if not already grated.
3. In a medium to large mixing bowl, combine sausage and cheese.
4. Add biscuit mix to sausage mixture, and blend thoroughly.
5. With hands, shape mixture into small balls, and place the balls about 1 inch apart on an ungreased cookie sheet.
6. Bake 30 minutes at 325° F. Remove from oven and transfer to a cooling rack. Serve hot or allow to cool slightly before storing in refrigerator or freezer.
7. Yield: Approximately 3 doz.

Serving Suggestions

- Heat and eat with cereal for a quick breakfast.
- Serve with a fruit salad of apples, peaches, and strawberries for lunch.
- Add as a topping for homemade or frozen pizza at dinner.
- Insert a toothpick into each ball and serve with taco sauce or sweet and sour sauce at a party.

Preparing Foods **331**

Do you know how to use each of the measuring devices shown here?

table. You might even want to arrange them in the order that you will use them.

Measuring Ingredients

Of the many factors that contribute to food preparation success, accurate measurement of ingredients is one of the most important. A dash of hot sauce may be just what your favorite chili needs. On the other hand, two dashes may make it too hot to enjoy.

When measuring ingredients, read the recipe or package instructions carefully. If you decide to make more or less than the amount the recipe usually makes, you will need to change each measurement in the same way. The chart on page 333 lists the common types of measurements, their equivalents, and their abbreviations. When you use the correct measuring utensils and techniques, you will get the correct measurement.

Measuring utensils are designed to measure different kinds of ingredients. There are liquid measuring cups for such ingredients as milk, water, and oil. These cups are usually glass or clear plastic so that you can see through them. They also have a rim ¼ to ½ inch above the final measure to keep you from spilling the ingredient. There are dry measuring cups for such ingredients as flour, sugar, shortening, and peanut butter. These cups may be metal or plastic, and their final measure is the rim. There are also measuring spoons in various sizes for flavorings and other ingredients used in small amounts.

When you measure liquid ingredients, place the cup on a flat surface. Fill the cup so that, when you look at it from eye level, the liquid *covers* the line that indicates the measurement. When you measure dry ingredients, use a cup of the size indicated. When you measure flour, white sugar, or powdered sugar, lightly spoon the ingredient into the cup. Do not pat down the ingredient or pack it firmly. (The only time you should do this is when measuring brown sugar.) Then, slide the blade of a knife across the top of the cup to smooth off any excess ingredient.

Other ingredients that you may measure include margarine and eggs. Tub margarine must be pushed into the measuring cup carefully, because it is easy to leave pockets of air. Stick margarine is easier to measure. A standard stick of margarine contains 8 tablespoons, or one-half of a cup. The wrapper around each stick often shows where to cut to get a tablespoon measure. A whole egg is easy to measure. If you need less than a whole egg, however, remember that one egg equals about 3 tablespoons.

Using Correct Utensils and Equipment

Food preparation will be faster and safer when you use utensils in the correct way. For example, there are many times you might want to strain liquid from something. Which utensil should you use? A slotted spoon would be ideal if you are lifting small pieces of food from water, broth, or another liquid.

332 Buying and Preparing Food

Measurements and Abbreviations Used in Recipes and Package Directions

Measurement	Conventional Amount	Approximate Metric Equivalent
dash	8 drops	8 drops
1 teaspoon	60 drops	5 milliliters
1 tablespoon	3 teaspoons	15 milliliters
1 fluid ounce	2 tablespoons	30 milliliters
1/4 cup	4 tablespoons	60 milliliters
1/2 cup	8 tablespoons; 1 stick butter	120 milliliters
1 cup	16 tablespoons; 8 fluid ounces	240 milliliters
1 pint	2 cups	475 milliliters
1 quart	2 pints; 4 cups	.95 liter
1 gallon	4 quarts; 8 pints; 16 cups	3.80 liters
1/4 pound	4 ounces	115 grams
1/2 pound	8 ounces	225 grams
1 pound	16 ounces	450 grams
2.2 pounds	35 ounces	1 kilogram

Abbreviation	Meaning	Abbreviation	Meaning
t. or tsp.	teaspoon	l	liter
T. or Tbs.	tablespoon	ml	milliliter
c.	cup	g	gram
oz.	ounce	kg	kilogram
pt.	pint	m	meter
qt.	quart	cm	centimeter
lb.	pound		

A sieve would be fine if draining water from a small saucepan of peas. For large quantities of food or items cooked in large saucepots, a collander would be best.

Often, one utensil can be used for several purposes. For example, a wooden spoon could be used to stir cheese sauce, soup, or even vegetables being stir-fried in a skillet. At other times, a specific piece of equipment is needed. To bake muffins, for example, you must use a muffin pan or paper-lined custard cups. A cake pan will not give the same results.

For some kinds of food preparation, a piece of flatware may serve the purpose. For others, it may not do the job well or safely. For example, you could use a dinner knife to cut a measure of margarine. However, you would need to use a utility or paring knife to cut vegetables or fruits. An iced-tea spoon is fine for stirring beverages but not for stirring scrambled eggs. A dinner fork might be used to transfer broccoli spears to a serving dish. However, it should not be used to turn foods that are being fried. The food could easily fall back into the hot fat and splatter onto you.

Preparing Foods **333**

Making Good Use of Kitchen Appliances

As you prepare foods, make the most of the appliances you have. For example, think of your refrigerator-freezer as an appliance to help you prepare salads or other chilled or frozen dishes. Also, think of your refrigerator-freezer as an appliance designed to help you prepare foods before they are needed. You could, for example, make a four-serving casserole and then freeze individual portions to eat later. You could prepare and freeze the main course, bread or rolls, and dessert for a party weeks ahead and then just thaw them. For more ideas on entertaining, see page 335.

Because the range will probably play the biggest part in food preparation, you will want to use it efficiently and safely. If you have a microwave oven, small appliances, and clean-up appliances, you will also want to use them correctly.

Using a Range

You can use a range for top-of-range cooking, baking, and broiling. Before you use a range, however, it helps to read the manufacturer's booklet to find out what specific features the range has. On some ranges, you must set both a temperature dial and a bake or broil dial for the oven or broiler unit to operate. On others, you have only one dial to set. On an electric range, you are to leave the oven door slightly ajar while broiling. On a gas range, this is not necessary. If the range has a minute timer, you can use it to ensure that foods will be cooked the right amount of time. In any range, you should place foods in the center of the oven.

Plan to use your range safely. For example, on a gas range, make sure the flame adjusts from a low setting to a high one without going out, flickering, or shooting into large flames. If any of these problems occur, have the range inspected. Whether cooking on a gas or electric range, turn pot handles toward the center to avoid accidents. When removing foods from the oven or handling hot cookware on top of the range, always use pot holders. In addition, take the following precautions to avoid grease fires:

- Use no more than the amount of fat or oil indicated in a recipe.
- Carefully watch foods being cooked at high temperatures.
- Keep range surfaces clean.

If you have a grease fire, turn off the range. Then, throw baking soda on the fire, or cover the utensil with a lid. Do not use water or pick up the flaming utensil to take it outside. If you receive a burn, treat it with ice water or an ice cube, not butter.

Using a Microwave Oven

If you have a microwave oven, you can use it to help you prepare many kinds of foods quickly, safely, and nutritiously. Like any appliance, microwave ovens should be used according to the manufacturer's instructions. For example, utensils containing metal cannot be used because they interfere with the cooking process. They also interfere with the operation of the oven. On the other hand, ceramic, glass, and some plastic utensils and wax paper, plastic wrap, and paper towels and plates can be used. Microwave ovens can heat leftovers and do much more, but sometimes another appliance might serve your purpose better. For tips on using a microwave oven, see page 336.

Using Small Appliances

You can also use small appliances to save yourself energy and time. The manufacturer's booklet will give you many ideas for doing so. In fact, it is likely to suggest uses that you have never thought of for the appliance. For example, you can use a blender to mix the batter for banana bread. You can also use a blender to make coleslaw or prepare lemonade and other beverages. You can use a slow cooker to make a dinner of franks and beans or vegetable soup. You can use a toaster oven to bake a potato stuffed with broccoli and cheese. You can also use it to make cinnamon toast, as well as to heat frozen dinners. You can even use an electric skillet to make shrimp creole.

Plan to use your small appliances safely. Make sure any cord attached to the appliance is away from the sink and other sources of water. Also, follow the cleaning instructions

P.S.

How Can You Entertain Easily?

You can have great parties with a minimum of effort if you understand the art of entertaining. All you need to do is consider the following steps:

- **Focus on your goal.** Do what you can to ensure that people have a good time. Arrange the room to encourage conversation yet still allow space for other activities. Invite friendly people with common interests.

- **Plan your preparations.** Make a list of all the preparations you need to make. Your list might include planning a place to hang coats, getting tables and chairs, choosing entertainment, and taking care of cleanup.

- **Borrow or rent items if necessary.** If you do not entertain often, consider borrowing or renting some party equipment. Such items might include tables, chairs, serving trays, punch bowls, and decorations.

- **Simplify your work.** You can shop for food, get ice, prepare most foods, clean the house, and arrange the furniture all well in advance. If you ask a friend to help give the party, the two of you can split the work.

- **Keep your menu simple, attractive, and nutritious.** Often, party guests are standing as food is served. They may also be holding a beverage. Avoid foods that must be cut, peeled, or served in sauces that can drip. Use a variety of colors, flavors, and textures, and include foods high in nutritive value. Fresh fruits and vegetables with yogurt dips and a cheese platter with whole grain crackers are always good choices.

- **Clean up as you can.** If the crowd is large, wash items as you are finished with them, or use disposable plates, glasses, and flatware.

- **Plan on having a good time.** If you relax, your guests will, too.

Tips

Cooking with Microwaves

To get the most from your microwave oven, remember the following tips:

- Use pot holders to remove foods that have been microwaved for more than just a few minutes. While the oven may be only warm, the utensil will be hot wherever the food touches it.

- Remove plastic wrap from microwaved foods *away* from you to avoid the possibility of steam burns.

- Use the microwave oven to defrost foods right from the freezer and then cook them.

- Use a special browning unit or a dish supplied by the manufacturer to give meats and other foods a crispy, browned surface.

- Marinate or pound less tender cuts of meat to tenderize them before microwaving them. This is necessary because the cooking action of the microwave oven is so quick.

- Use the microwave oven to help with minor preparation tasks, such as melting butter or chocolate or heating water or milk.

cords. Blender containers and the blades of electric knives are immersible, but their electric bases are not. Some appliances are even dishwasher safe.

Using Clean-Up Appliances

The one part of meal and snack preparation that few people like to do is to clean up. To make this task easier, plan to clean up as you go. In other words, while one food is cooking, clean the utensils used to prepare it. Then, when the meal is over, you will have glassware, flatware, dinnerware, and only a minimum of cookware or bakeware to wash.

If you wash dishes by hand, start with the glasses and flatware first, because these will be the least dirty. Wash the dinnerware and greasy utensils last.

If you have a dishwasher and wish to use it, follow the manufacturer's directions for

How might using a small appliance such as an electric skillet help you manage meal preparation?

included in the manufacturer's booklet and perhaps stamped on the appliance itself. They will indicate whether the appliance is **immersible**, capable of being put completely into water. For example, many electric skillets are immersible and have detachable

336   Buying and Preparing Food

loading. Always use an automatic dishwashing detergent and only in the amount indicated by the detergent dispenser in the dishwasher. For maximum efficiency, run the dishwasher only when you have a full load. To save energy, air-dry the dishes rather than using the drying cycle.

If your kitchen is equipped with a garbage disposal, you will want to make good use of this appliance. Remember, a garbage disposal is designed to grind up food wastes, not food packaging. Whenever you are operating the disposal, you need to run cold water into it. If the disposal should jam, turn it off. Next, you should use a broom handle to dislodge the object that is causing the problem. Then, reset the safety switch located on the disposal unit and try again. To clean the disposal, periodically let it grind up ice cubes or some lemon peel.

If your kitchen has a trash compactor, you can put this appliance to good use, too. Remember, a compactor is designed to dispose of food packaging, not food wastes. The only type of container that you should not put into this appliance is an aerosol can.

Getting Meals Ready on Time

The menu below, like many menus, includes items that take different times to prepare. For example, the chicken will take longer than the beans. Preparing this meal will take careful timing.

To prepare meals like this one, you may need a time schedule like the one shown at the bottom of this page. To create this kind

Sample Dinner Menu

Baked Chicken

Potatoes au Gratin

Fresh Green Beans

Peach Gelatin Salad

Baked Cinnamon Apple

Milk

Meal-Time Schedule for "Dinner at 6:00 p.m."

How Much Time Will You Need?

Menu Item	To Assemble, Prepare, Measure, and Combine Ingredients	To Chill or Cook Menu Item	TOTAL TIME	WHEN TO START
Baked chicken	15 minutes	1 hour to bake	1¼ hours	4:45 p.m. or earlier
Potatoes au gratin	30 minutes	1 hour to bake	1½ hours	4:30 p.m. or earlier
Fresh green beans	30 minutes	15–20 minutes to steam	¾ hour	5:15 p.m. or earlier
Peach gelatin salad	15 minutes	at least 3 hours to chill	3¼ hours	2:45 p.m. or earlier (possibly the day before)
Baked cinnamon apple	15 minutes	8 hours to bake in a slow cooker	8¼ hours	9:45 a.m. or earlier
Milk	5 minutes	—	5 minutes	5:55 p.m.

Preparing Foods 337

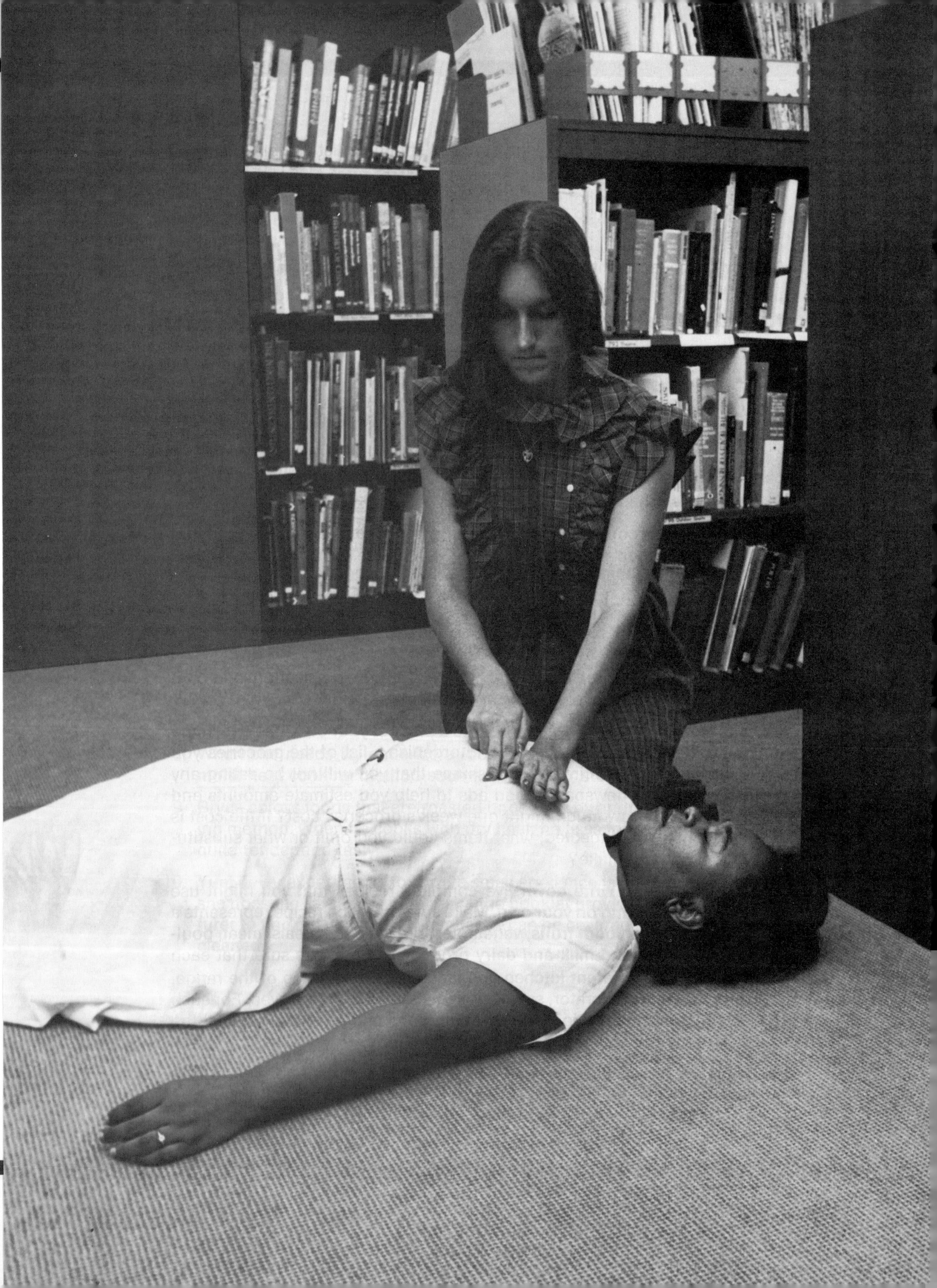

CHAPTER 15

Ensuring Your Health and Safety

Thinking about how to maintain a healthy and safe lifestyle may seem unimportant to you now. However, it is at this time in your life that establishing habits that contribute to a healthy and safe lifestyle is most critical. The habits—good and bad—that you establish now are likely to remain with you when you are on your own. For example, if you decide now not to smoke or to quit smoking, you will be more likely to live your adult life as a nonsmoker. If you wear seat belts now, you may have learned firsthand that they can save your life. If so, you are even more likely to wear them in the future.

Ensuring your health and safety involves making wise health and safety decisions. One area in which these decisions are critical is that of lifestyle. Another area in which making wise health and safety decisions is critical is that of selecting health products and services. Still another area is that of taking action in an emergency.

Discover Through Your Reading

- what a healthy and safe lifestyle is
- why you should avoid substance abuse
- why the use of some drugs is controlled by the government
- why it is important to monitor your physical and emotional health
- where to get routine and special medical and dental care
- how to seek help for emotional problems
- how you can be a help in an emergency situation

Choosing a Healthy and Safe Lifestyle

Probably the most effective way to ensure your health and safety is to choose a healthy and safe lifestyle. Your lifestyle is how you use energy and time, with whom, and where. What you choose to eat also helps make up your lifestyle. How you choose to think about or to act toward your family, your friends, and strangers also helps make up your lifestyle. Exercising regularly may be a part of your lifestyle. You already make many choices about your lifestyle. When you are on your own, you will make even more. What kind of a lifestyle do you have now? Will you choose a healthy and safe lifestyle when you are an adult?

To choose a healthy and safe lifestyle, you first need to know what such a lifestyle involves. A healthy and safe lifestyle involves eating, exercising, resting, and sleeping for fitness. It also involves maintaining good emotional and social health, avoiding substance abuse, managing stress, and detecting potential physical and emotional problems. In addition, it involves following recommended safety practices.

Maintaining Fitness

Your body requires a daily balance of nutritious foods, adequate exercise, rest, and sleep. Your body needs these to carry out its activities at the highest level possible, or to be fit. If you do not make wise choices involving any *one* of these areas—food, exercise, rest, and sleep—you will not be fit.

Eating for Fitness

There is only one way to eat for fitness. That way is to eat a well-balanced diet of nutritious food. To review the nutrients you need for a balanced diet, see Chapter 13.

Some young people choose not to eat a balanced diet of nutritious foods daily. These young people make this choice because they think they cannot eat a variety of foods and maintain their body image. **Body image** is how people appear physically to themselves and to others. Today many people seem obsessed with body image. Many people your age, in particular, seem to think that being thin is the same thing as being healthy. However, these two concepts—thinness and healthiness—are not the same. In fact, being too thin can be as harmful to health as being overweight.

Two very serious health problems can develop from the obsession with body image. One of these problems is anorexia nervosa. **Anorexia nervosa** (an·o·REK·see·uh ner·VO·sah) is a problem experienced by people who constantly see themselves as overweight even though they are usually of normal weight or less. To achieve the body image they feel they do not have, anorexics severely limit the amount of food they eat. They often refuse to eat anything. In time, anorexics, if not successfully treated, starve to death. Anorexia nervosa is found most often among females in their teens and twenties.

The second serious health problem that can result from an obsession with body image is bulimia. **Bulimia** (byu LIM ee uh) is a health problem experienced by people who are obsessed with fear of becoming overweight and yet crave food. Bulimics binge-eat and then induce vomiting and abuse laxatives. This behavior results in food not being digested. The behavior also results in severe malnutrition and other serious health problems. Malnutrition results when a person does not take in all the nutrients the body needs to carry out its activities.

Eating a balanced diet that helps you maintain your desirable weight is important. Equally important, however, is choosing to eat certain foods and avoiding overeating certain others. Recent scientific evidence indicates that eating some foods tends to increase people's chances of developing certain diseases. For example, eating foods high in saturated fats may cause heart disease. Eating foods high in salt content can contribute to high blood pressure in people who have a tendency to develop high blood pressure. Eating foods high in sugar content can contribute to a person's becoming overweight and developing dental cavities.

Exercising for Fitness

Besides requiring nutritious foods daily, your body also requires regular exercise to be fit. As you think about exercise, you may have some questions about it. For example, what does exercising regularly do for your body, and what does the term *regular exercise* mean?

Regular exercise has many benefits. One benefit is **cardiovascular fitness,** or having a strong heart and blood vessels that are able to circulate blood easily. A second benefit of regular exercise is firm, strong muscles. Having firm, strong muscles enables you to carry on your daily activities without undue tiredness. A third benefit of regular exercise is weight control. The more active your body is, the greater the number of calories your body uses. A fourth benefit of regular exercise is simply a feeling of fitness. People who are physically active just seem to feel happier and healthier than people who do not exercise regularly.

Based on the benefits of regular exercise, it would seem logical that you would want to choose to exercise regularly. Like many people, however, you may wonder how often you need to exercise. You may not know what kind of exercise you need. Physical fitness experts recommend that you exercise at least twenty to thirty minutes each day, at least three or four days each week. They also recommend that you do different kinds of exercises. Some kinds of exercises help you give your heart and blood vessels a good workout.

How would you describe the role of nutrition, exercise, rest, and sleep in maintaining a healthy lifestyle?

They may also help you build strong muscles and help you maintain your desirable weight. Aerobic dancing, swimming, and other exercises that can keep you moving constantly for twenty minutes or more are examples. Other exercises do little to keep your heart and blood vessels in good condition but do help you build strong, firm muscles. They may also help you maintain your desirable weight. Start-and-stop sports like racquetball and golf are such exercises.

While you are in school, you may have many chances to get regular exercise. After you finish school, however, you will have to set up your own opportunities to exercise. Fortunately, you can always choose to exercise on your own by bicycling, jogging, dancing, or other such activities. In addition, your community may have an inexpensive exercise center or teams sponsored by the town or city or by religious or social organizations. Perhaps your place of work will also sponsor teams or a fitness program.

Exercise clubs and health spas also are available in many communities. If you choose to get your regular exercise through an exercise club or spa, be sure to check out carefully the program it offers. Does the club or spa require the payment of a long-term membership fee? Does it offer a safe exercise program? Are the instructors competent? Can you afford the price of membership? Will membership help you be regular in your exercise routine? These are important questions. If you do not consider the answers carefully, you may find yourself out of some money, unhappy, and even injured if the program was not a safe one.

Whatever form of exercise you select needs to be appropriate for you. If you are having trouble setting aside special times to exercise, consider adding exercise to your daily routine. You can add exercise to your schedule, for example, simply by walking to school or to work instead of driving or taking a bus. You can use stairs rather than elevators.

Remember, the kind of exercise you get is not nearly as important as how often you exercise and for how long. Try to set up a plan to exercise daily for at least twenty minutes. After you have set up your plan, stick to it.

Resting for Fitness

The next time you are at a shopping mall or near a busy street, stop for a moment and "people-watch." If you watch closely, you will see that most people are in a hurry. This "hurry-up" attitude often prevents people from achieving another important part of fitness, namely, getting adequate daily rest.

Getting adequate daily rest means spending some time doing things that give the mind and body relief from daily routines. For example, such rest for an office worker might be to take an hour's walk. A truck driver, on the other hand, might want to read. Most people find that rest helps them relieve their mind and body of daily tensions.

Many people find it difficult, however, to put aside their "hurry-up" attitude. They want to rest but do not know how. Therefore, they hamper their overall fitness.

For a moment, think through *your* daily routine. Is something preventing you from getting the relaxing moments you need each day? Are you involved in too many extracurricular activities to have time to rest? Do you manage your time well, or do you seem to lose time and not know where the time went? Are you working too many hours of overtime at your job? Now, think through your daily routine in a new way. Within it, try to find an hour or so for rest. Then, make a commitment to use that time for resting. Try it for a week to see if you feel better.

Sleeping for Fitness

In addition to eating nutritious foods, getting regular exercise, and getting adequate rest, you also need adequate sleep. Your body needs a certain amount of sleep to function at its best. The amount needed varies from person to person. For example, you may need eight hours of sleep daily. Your best friend may need only five hours.

One good way to determine the amount of sleep you need is to allow yourself to sleep until you wake up naturally. Do this for several nights in a row. How many hours of sleep per night did you average? This average number of hours is probably your ideal number. Try sleeping this number of hours nightly for one week to see if at the end of the week you feel rested.

Maintaining Good Emotional and Social Health

Maintaining good emotional and social health are also essentials of a healthy lifestyle. People who are emotionally healthy have certain characteristics in common. Some of these characteristics are a well-developed self-concept and realistic goals. Other characteristics include the feelings of self-acceptance and self-esteem as well as a sense of humor.

No one is born with these characteristics. They are developed throughout your lifetime. The degree to which you develop these characteristics depends upon the decisions you make as you grow and mature. For example, you can decide to—rather than *not* to—do things and think thoughts that help you understand who you are. You can set and pursue reachable rather than unreachable goals. You can accept rather than reject your strengths and your weaknesses. You can dwell on your strengths rather than on your weaknesses. You can see the humor in some of the things you say and do rather than taking yourself too seriously. With effort, you can develop the characteristics common to people who are emotionally healthy.

People who are socially healthy also have certain characteristics. Some of these characteristics are an interest in people and the ability to communicate well with others. Other characteristics include the ability to get along with others and respect for the thoughts, feelings, and property of others.

As is true with developing the characteristics of emotional health, you develop the characteristics of social health through decisions you make as you grow and develop. For example, you can decide to focus on resolving rather than maintaining conflicts with others. You can express your thoughts and feelings in an assertive rather than in an aggressive or passive way. You can make an effort to get along with others rather than not make that effort. You can show others respect rather than disrespect. If you try, you can develop the characteristics shared by people who are socially healthy.

What signs do you see that this person has good emotional health?

Avoiding Substance Abuse

Having a healthy lifestyle also means avoiding substance abuse. **Substance abuse** is using any drug—including alcohol and tobacco—in heavy, repeated amounts that may damage health and also cause other problems. Substance abuse also includes the misuse of controlled drugs and the use of any illegal drugs.

Avoiding substance abuse is a responsibility you have now and will continue to have as an adult. You may already be aware of some of the dangers of substance abuse. The more you learn about how substance abuse can harm you, the better prepared you will be to avoid becoming a substance abuser.

The effects of substance abuse vary, depending on the substance being abused. The ways people become substance abusers may also vary. Alcohol, tobacco, and controlled drugs are the substances most often subject to abuse.

Alcohol

To understand alcohol's effects on people, it helps to realize that alcohol is actually a kind of drug. Like other drugs, it changes how the body works. At first, it makes the

Effects of Increasing Blood Alcohol Levels

Number of Drinks per Hour	Blood Alcohol Content	Effects
1 drink*	.02–.03%	slight feeling of relaxation and warmth
2 drinks	.05–.06%	increased feeling of relaxation, slight lack of coordination
3 drinks	.08–.09%	loss of balance and coordination; feeling of lightheadedness and excitement; slight trouble seeing, hearing, talking, thinking
4 drinks	.11–.12%	lack of coordination and balance; decreased reaction time; lack of judgment and other mental abilities; legally intoxicated in most states
5 drinks	.14–.15%	slurred speech; blurred vision; lack of motor control; impaired judgment, thinking; legally intoxicated in all states
7 drinks	.20%	mental confusion; loss of all motor control
10 drinks	.30%	severe intoxication; little control of mind and body
14 drinks	.40%	unconsciousness
17 drinks	.50%	deep coma likely
20 drinks	.60%	breathing may stop; death likely

*1 drink = ¾ ounce (22.1 ml) of alcohol
Based upon data from the National Highway Traffic Safety Administration

heart beat faster. Soon, however, it slows down the nervous system. As a result, it is classified as a depressant.

Alcohol weakens the brain's control over behavior. People who drink just a small amount of alcohol may feel mildly relaxed. After drinking more alcohol, however, their reactions start to slow down. They also begin losing the ability to think clearly and to make sound judgments. After still more drinking, they may develop problems with muscle coordination. They may lose their balance or be unable to speak clearly. At this point, they are said to be drunk, or intoxicated. The amount of alcohol needed for intoxication varies from person to person. After still more drinking, a person may lose consciousness. Drinking very large amounts of alcohol may even cause death. To learn how the effects of alcohol relate to the level of alcohol in a person's blood (blood alcohol content, or BAC), see the chart above.

Drinking even small amounts of alcohol can be deadly when combined with driving. Almost 50 percent of all automobile accidents involve drivers who have been drinking. When people drink and drive, they endanger themselves and others.

People can develop a tolerance for alcohol. A **tolerance** is a need to consume more and more of a substance to feel the same effect. People who develop a high tolerance for alcohol may become heavy drinkers. They may also develop a dependence on alcohol. A **dependence** is a need to continue consuming a substance in order to keep feeling a certain way. For example, people who drink to relieve tension may develop a dependence on alcohol.

Long-term, heavy drinking has additional harmful effects. It can damage the stomach and liver. It can damage the brain and nervous system. Drinking alcohol while pregnant can damage the unborn baby.

People who cannot control their drinking are called alcoholics. They suffer from a disease called alcoholism. **Alcoholism** is a psychological and physical dependence on alcohol. It can affect people of all ages, including teenagers and even children. It can start slowly and develop step by step into a serious problem. Besides causing physical damage,

Phases of Alcoholism and Recovery

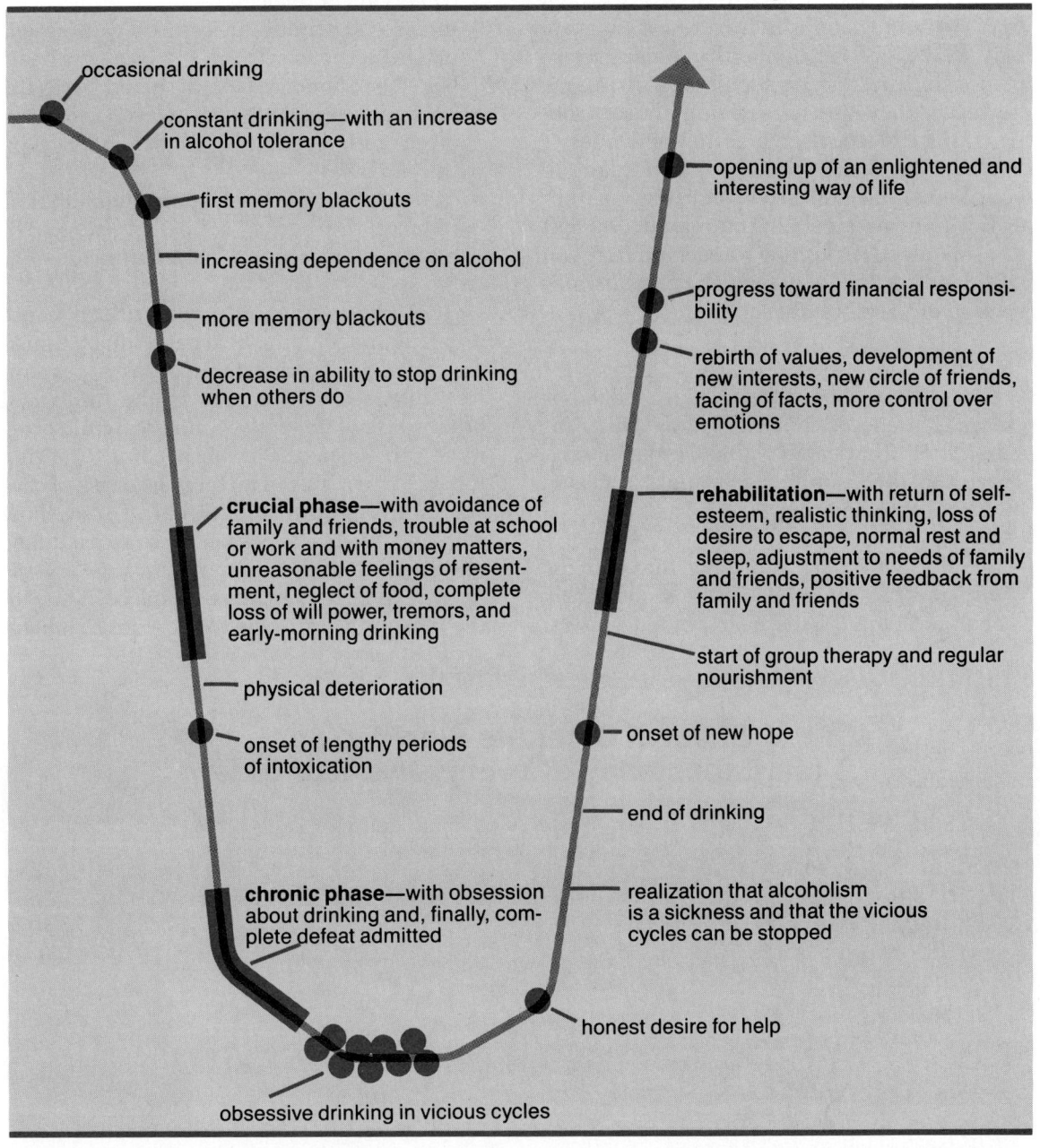

- occasional drinking
- constant drinking—with an increase in alcohol tolerance
- first memory blackouts
- increasing dependence on alcohol
- more memory blackouts
- decrease in ability to stop drinking when others do
- **crucial phase**—with avoidance of family and friends, trouble at school or work and with money matters, unreasonable feelings of resentment, neglect of food, complete loss of will power, tremors, and early-morning drinking
- physical deterioration
- onset of lengthy periods of intoxication
- **chronic phase**—with obsession about drinking and, finally, complete defeat admitted
- obsessive drinking in vicious cycles

- honest desire for help
- realization that alcoholism is a sickness and that the vicious cycles can be stopped
- end of drinking
- onset of new hope
- start of group therapy and regular nourishment
- **rehabilitation**—with return of self-esteem, realistic thinking, loss of desire to escape, normal rest and sleep, adjustment to needs of family and friends, positive feedback from family and friends
- rebirth of values, development of new interests, new circle of friends, facing of facts, more control over emotions
- progress toward financial responsibility
- opening up of an enlightened and interesting way of life

it can also cause other kinds of problems. Alcoholics may not be able to function normally at school or at work. They may not be able to maintain normal personal relationships. They may do or say things that hurt others. As a result, family and friends may also be affected. Hospitals and other health care centers offer help to alcoholics and their families. Telephone numbers for these health centers are usually listed in the telephone directory. For information on the phases of alcoholism and recovery, see the chart above.

If drinking can lead to so many problems, why do people drink? Some people drink because it may be customary at social gatherings or because they like the way it makes them feel. Others may be influenced by peer

Choosing a Healthy and Safe Lifestyle

pressure and by advertisements that make drinking look like a way to appear "grown up." For some people, however, drinking is a way to relieve tension or to escape from responsibilities or problems. By drinking, however, they are not solving those problems. Instead, they are creating new ones.

When you reach the legal drinking age in your state, you will need to decide whether or not to drink alcohol. You may decide not to drink alcohol at all. If you decide that you will drink alcohol, you have the responsibility to avoid alcohol abuse.

Tobacco

Like alcohol, tobacco is a drug. Smoked or chewed, tobacco contains many different substances that affect the human body. Three substances in tobacco smoke that can be harmful to health are:

- *tar*, a brown, sticky substance that collects on smokers' lungs. It contains chemicals that can damage the heart, blood vessels, and lungs. Some of these chemicals can cause cancer, especially in the lungs.
- *nicotine*, a stimulant, or drug that speeds up the nervous system. It makes the heart beat faster and raises the blood pressure. Tobacco users develop a tolerance for nicotine and, eventually, a dependence on this drug.
- *carbon monoxide*, a gas that, when inhaled, reduces the body's supply of oxygen. It makes tobacco users feel breathless.

Over time, smoking tobacco can cause severe damage to the heart and lungs. Smokers can suffer heart attacks, strokes, respiratory diseases, and cancer of the lungs and other parts of the body. Smoking while pregnant can harm the unborn baby. Chewing tobacco can result in an increased risk of cancer of the mouth and throat. To see how smoking affects a person's life expectancy, see the chart below.

Why, then, do people use tobacco? Many of the reasons are similar to those for drinking.

Effect of Cigarette Smoking on Life Expectancy of Twenty-five Year Olds

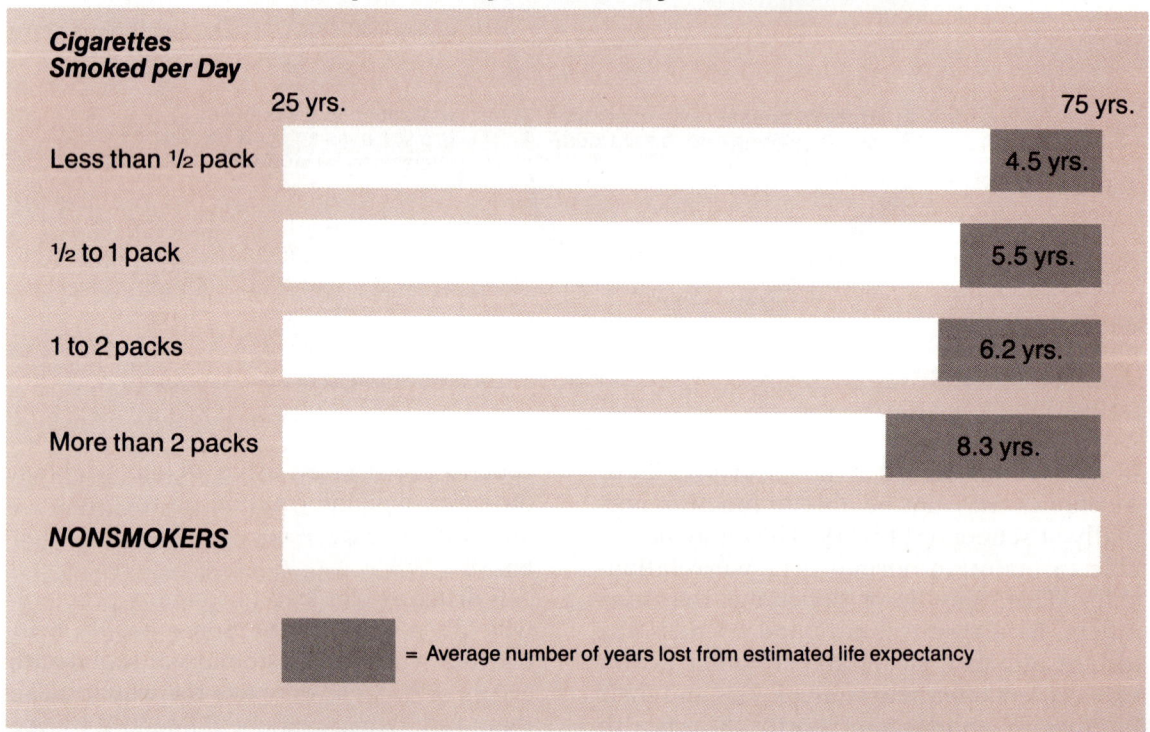

Cigarettes Smoked per Day	Years lost (25 yrs. – 75 yrs.)
Less than ½ pack	4.5 yrs.
½ to 1 pack	5.5 yrs.
1 to 2 packs	6.2 yrs.
More than 2 packs	8.3 yrs.
NONSMOKERS	

= Average number of years lost from estimated life expectancy

The smoking habit is hard to kick. How are the three smokers shown here going about it? What other help might be available to them?

Young people often start smoking because they want to feel or appear "grown up." They may also be influenced by cigarette advertisements. Once they start smoking, they quickly develop a dependence. Stopping smoking becomes very difficult.

As you assume adult responsibilities, you will need to decide whether or not to use tobacco. As you make your decision, keep in mind that it is much easier not to start using it than it is to stop.

Controlled Drugs

The third kind of substance abuse involves controlled drugs. Any kind of drug can be dangerous if misused. People who take a drug they do not need or take one without following directions risk damaging their health. If they continue abusing the drug in this way, they also risk developing a tolerance for it. Eventually they may develop a dependence on it. A person who has a drug tolerance may take such a large amount that serious physical damage results. An amount of this size is called an overdose. The actual amount necessary for an overdose varies from person to person. Another hazard of drug abuse is withdrawal sickness. Withdrawal sickness results when people with a drug dependency stop taking the drug.

The drugs that are most commonly abused in this way are those that change the ways people think and feel. Most affect the nervous system in different ways. People who abuse them may risk damage to the heart, lungs, and other organs. These drugs may also prevent people from thinking clearly. As a result, people who take them may have problems at school or on the job. They may also endanger themselves and others, especially if they attempt to drive a motor vehicle. For all of these reasons, most of these drugs are controlled by the government. Some controlled drugs are available only with a prescription. A prescription is a written order from a physician or a dentist for a specific drug. Other controlled drugs are not legally available under any circumstances.

Commonly abused controlled drugs include tranquilizers and barbiturates, which are both depressants. Other dangerous controlled drugs include amphetamines and cocaine, which are stimulants. Also controlled are narcotics, drugs that numb the senses. Heroin, one type of narcotic, is extremely dangerous and not legally available for any reason. Hallucinogens, drugs that distort what people see and feel, are another type of dangerous controlled drug. A powerful hallucinogen is lysergic acid dieth-

Choosing a Healthy and Safe Lifestyle

ylamide, or LSD. Another is PCP, or "angel dust." Two other commonly abused drugs are marijuana and hashish, which can be both stimulants and depressants.

Because these drugs are controlled, abusers may face additional consequences besides those already listed. Abusers may be arrested on drug-related charges and fined or jailed. They may have to pay very high prices to illegal drug dealers. In addition, they may be sold impure drugs that can cause additional harmful effects and even death.

Why, then, do some people abuse controlled drugs? The reasons are similar to those for other kinds of substance abuse. Some people like the way drugs make them feel. Others take drugs to escape personal problems, to reduce tension, or to relieve boredom. Like other forms of substance abuse, however, drug abuse does not solve any of these problems. It simply creates more problems. To help drug abusers, many health care centers offer special programs.

How can you make sure that you never become a victim of drug abuse? The best way is to know the facts about what controlled drugs can do to health. This knowledge will help you say no if someone tries to persuade you to take one of these drugs.

Managing Stress

Another part of having a healthy lifestyle is learning to manage stress. **Stress** is any force or influence that upsets a person or makes that person's body work harder than usual. In small amounts, stress can be a healthy stimulus that makes you more active or productive. However, when stress becomes excessive and your ability to cope with the stress is exhausted, stress can become harmful. Most people can manage stress if they learn its causes, its results, and ways to manage it.

Causes of Stress

Stress is a normal part of everyday living. It may result from something pleasurable, such as accepting an award or promotion. It may also result from a high-pressure situation such as competition, a problem, or a change in your life such as moving or starting a new job. More serious stress-causing events may include illness or a death in your family. Emotional stress is stress that upsets you mentally or emotionally. Physical stress is stress that results from a strain on your body.

Results of Stress

Your mind and body work to cope with stress in various ways. Your mind may react by feeling excited, tense, nervous, or anxious. Both your mind and body may also feel fatigue, a strong feeling of tiredness and lack of energy. Fatigue is often a signal that you are under more stress than your mind or body can handle.

Sometimes, people reach a point where they can no longer cope with stress. Then, they become depressed or frightened or angry. They may develop physical symptoms of stress, such as ulcers, high blood pressure, and lowered resistance to certain diseases.

Ways to Manage Stress

The first step in managing stress is to establish a positive attitude about it. Understand that stress is a natural part of life. Recognize that mild stress can be a healthy stimulus to new achievements. Next, try to develop a sensitivity to stress. Learn to recognize when you are under too much stress.

If you find that you are under too much stress, try to identify the source of the stress. Examine the events in your life. Does the fatigue you feel result from working for too long? Or is it caused by boredom? Correctly identifying the source of stress will help you find the right way to relieve it.

Strategies for coping with stress vary widely. The ones you choose will depend on what works best for you. A good way to start is to describe your feelings to a sympathetic family member or a friend. Keeping your feelings to yourself may increase stress. Also, be sure you are getting enough sleep and eating nutritious meals. When you are not in good physical shape, your ability to handle stress is reduced.

Emotional stress can often be relieved by physical activity. Reading, listening to music, or just daydreaming can also relieve tension and help you relax. A good laugh or good cry is sometimes the best way to release pent-up anxieties. It may also be helpful to take a break from your normal routine. Back off from a stressful situation for a while, and return to it when you feel relaxed.

Detecting Physical Problems

Even people who are in the best physical condition are likely to be ill at times. Sometimes, you can treat your illness by yourself. At other times, the illness requires the care of a physician, a medical doctor. It is important to know when to seek a physician's help. It is also important to be able to detect physical problems early in their development. Early detection will enable you to seek medical treatment before a physical problem becomes more serious.

To be able to detect a physical problem, you need to pay attention to physical symptoms. **Symptoms** are signals that the body gives to indicate a disorder. Any time a symptom appears, ask yourself when and where it first occurred. Then, determine if it had a minor cause that you can identify and treat by yourself. For example, is your cough a symptom of a minor sore throat that you can treat with an over-the-counter medicine? (An **over-the-counter medicine** can be bought without a prescription.)

If you are not sure what is causing a symptom, ask yourself whether you have had the symptom for more than a few days. Also, ask whether you have had the symptom before and whether you are worried about it. If you answer yes to any of these questions, seek a physician's help. A physician can observe the symptom and make a professional diagnosis. A **diagnosis** is an identification of a disorder based on an analysis of symptoms.

When you consult a physician, be that physician's partner in your care. Help the physician by being a good observer and reporter. Follow instructions carefully. Ask questions if there is anything you do not understand about your treatment or medication. For serious problems, get a second opinion from a different physician. A second opinion can help you feel confident about the diagnosis and prescribed treatment.

One important symptom to watch for is a fever, or body temperature that is higher than normal. A fever is one of the body's ways of protecting itself. A low or moderate fever, for example, can help your body kill the germs that cause certain diseases. If a fever is high or persistent, however, you should seek a physician's help immediately.

Pain is another symptom to watch for. If you have pain and cannot identify its cause, check with a physician.

Another way to detect physical problems is to learn a few simple health check procedures. Learn to take your temperature. Most people's normal temperature is approximately 98.6°F (37°C). Learn to take your own pulse. You can take your pulse by counting the number of beats per minute at a pulse spot, such as on your wrist. Learn to take your blood pressure. You can purchase a blood pressure kit or visit agencies that offer free blood pressure checks. Women should learn to do breast self-examinations, and men should learn to do testicular self-examinations. Both these procedures are important in the early detection of cancer. The

Keeping tabs on your blood pressure is one way to monitor your physical condition. What are other ways?

Choosing a Healthy and Safe Lifestyle

> # Tips
> ## Recognizing Warning Signs of Cancer
>
> To protect against cancer, consult a physician if you notice any of these warning signs:
>
> - A change in bowel or bladder habits
> - A sore that does not heal
> - Unusual bleeding or discharges
> - A thickening or lump in a breast or elsewhere
> - Indigestion or difficulty in swallowing
> - An obvious change in a wart or a mole
> - A nagging cough or hoarseness

American Cancer Society offers free self-examination information upon request. For tips on recognizing the warning signs of cancer, see above.

Detecting Emotional Problems

Emotional problems may be as serious as physical ones. However, their symptoms are often less easy to see. To avoid emotional illness, you will want to be able to recognize these problems if they occur. It is important to know when to seek professional treatment for an emotional problem and when to urge others to seek such treatment.

Depression

One of the most common emotional problems is depression. **Depression** is a condition characterized by feelings of deep sadness and hopelessness. It can have a variety of causes. Its symptoms include lack of appetite and sleep difficulties. Without treatment, depression may make a person unable to function normally at home, at school, or on the job. People suffering from depression should seek professional treatment.

Suicide

Sometimes, people's emotional problems cause them to consider suicide. Suicide is killing oneself. Many different kinds of emotional problems may lead people to attempt suicide. Sometimes the cause is depression, or it may be an inability to deal with stress. Even teenagers may attempt suicide when they cannot handle the pressures they face or crises in their lives. Sometimes, too, they may use a suicide attempt to express feelings of rebellion or anger.

People who are considering suicide often give signals of their intentions. They may threaten suicide. They may also seem depressed, moody, or withdrawn. They may even make "final arrangements," such as giving away prized possessions.

Counselors who work to prevent suicide warn that all suicide threats should be taken extremely seriously. They advise that if someone is threatening suicide, you should speak openly with that person about the problem. You should show understanding and sympathy. You should also make sure the person gets professional help from a counselor or psychiatrist. In many places there are "suicide hotline" telephone numbers that a person who is considering suicide may call to speak with a counselor.

Physical Abuse

Sometimes people who have emotional problems physically harm members of their own families. This physical abuse may involve parents and children, husbands and wives, or other family members.

Since people who commit physical abuse risk criminal charges, victims may be unwilling to tell about abuse by a family member. However, abuse seldom stops unless someone reports it. Children and teenagers who are abused may discuss the problem with an

What are some of the counseling services available near you?

adult they trust. The adult may be a family member, a teacher, or a physician. Although physicians and sometimes teachers are required by law to report the abuse officially, often the next step is counseling for the victim and also for the abuser.

Abuse victims may also call the national "hotline" number listed under "Abuse Registry" in the front of the telephone directory. Following the call, the proper local agency will be asked to resolve the problem. In addition, many organizations operate shelters for abuse victims.

Following Recommended Safety Practices

Accidents are the leading cause of death in the United States for persons age 14 to 24. You will want to make special efforts to prevent accidents in your home, on the job, and in between.

Safety Practices at Home

The types of accidents that occur most often in the home are falls, poisonings, electric shocks, drownings, suffocation, and fires. To prevent these accidents, you can take the following precautions:

- To prevent falls, clean up spills immediately. Use nonslip strips in the bathtub or shower. Use nonskid wax and rugs on floors. Clear walkways of obstructions. Make sure lighting is adequate in walkways. Make sure any stairs have handrails. Use a gate or other barrier to keep small children away from stairways.
- To prevent poisonings, keep all of the following products out of the reach of small children and properly labelled: bleach, ammonia, aspirin and other medicines, gasoline and other fuels, furniture polish and other household cleaners, paint thinners and removers, lighter fluid, insect sprays, and weed killers. Never place any of these substances in containers used for food or drink. Store them separate from foods.
- To prevent electric shocks, never mix water and electricity. Touch electrical appliances—including electric toothbrushes and hair dryers—with dry hands only. Disconnect an appliance to dry off any water spilled on it. Avoid using electrical appliances when you are standing on a

Choosing a Healthy and Safe Lifestyle **355**

damp surface. Insert electrical plugs firmly and completely into wall sockets. Unplug appliances by pulling on the plug, not on the cord. Keep power tools and appliances unplugged when they are not in use, so that they cannot be turned on accidentally. Protect small children by using snap-in plastic safety covers on wall outlets. Unplug, check, and if necessary have repaired any appliance that is hot or shocks you when you touch it.
- To prevent drowning, never leave children unsupervised near water—including the bathtub and toilet.
- To prevent suffocation, store unused refrigerators and freezers locked or turned against a wall or with their doors removed. Store plastic bags away from small children. Tie knots in plastic wrap or bags before discarding them.
- To prevent fires, store matches in metal containers out of the reach of children. Never smoke lying down, or empty live ashes into the garbage. Do not leave cooking food unattended or leave grease spilled. Store oily rags in covered metal containers until you can dispose of them. Store flammable liquids in approved containers. Avoid accumulating rubbish.

Safety Practices at Work

Some and perhaps many of the safety practices you follow at home will also apply to your work setting. In addition, however, you may have special safety guidelines to follow related to your specific occupation. For example, there may be certain protective clothing and equipment that you must use. Whatever you wear, your clothes should, for the sake of your safety, allow you to move around easily—and quickly if necessary.

If you see a condition at work that looks unsafe to you, do not ignore it. Report any unsafe condition you spot to your supervisor as soon as possible.

Safety Practices on the Road

A few safety practices will go a long way toward ensuring your safety when you are driving on the road. These safety practices include the following:

What other safety precautions should you take when driving?

- Drive within the speed limit.
- Obey all traffic laws.
- Stay alert when driving.
- Keep your vehicle in good condition.
- Use the safety equipment recommended for use with the vehicle. In cars, vans, and trucks, for example, wear a safety belt. On motorcycles, motorbikes, and motorized and regular bicycles, use any safety helmet or other safety gear recommended.

Choosing Health Products and Services

A basic part of ensuring your health and safety is choosing high-quality health products and services. A health product is a product that people use to help maintain or improve their level of health. An example of a health product is cough syrup. A health service is a service people use to help maintain or improve their level of health. An example of a health service is the care you get from your physician or your dentist.

You need to be especially careful when shopping for health products and services. As usual, you will be looking for high quality at reasonable prices. However, you will also be making important choices that can greatly affect your health and safety.

Health Products

The health products that you will probably buy most often are prescription drugs and over-the-counter drugs. **Prescription drugs** are drugs that can be obtained only with a prescription. Prescription drugs are more powerful than over-the-counter drugs, which are sold without a prescription. Examples of over-the-counter drugs include aspirin, some cough syrups, cold symptom remedies, laxatives, remedies for upset stomach, and some antibiotics for cuts or burns.

When you shop for a prescription drug, you will be following a physician's or dentist's instructions about what to buy and how to use it. When choosing and using over-the-counter drugs, however, you will need to read the labels on drug packages very carefully. You may also ask your pharmacist for advice.

Government regulations require all over-the-counter drugs to be "safe and effective" and "properly labeled." The labels should tell you exactly how to use the drug. For example, a label may say, "Adults: Take two tablets every four hours. Do not take more than twelve tablets in twenty-four hours." The label will probably also give a warning such as "If relief does not occur within three days, discontinue use and consult a physician." The label should also warn of any possible dangers. For example, it may say, "Do not use if high blood pressure, heart disease, diabetes, or heart condition is present."

Finally, the label should warn of any possible side effects. **Side effects** are unwanted, harmful reactions that some people have to a given drug. For example, a label may warn, "This medication may cause drowsiness. Do

How might you go about selecting the people from whom you want health care and advice?

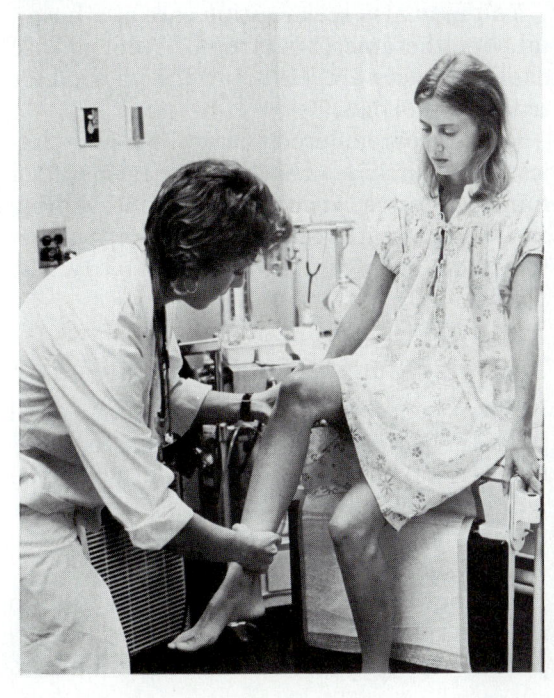

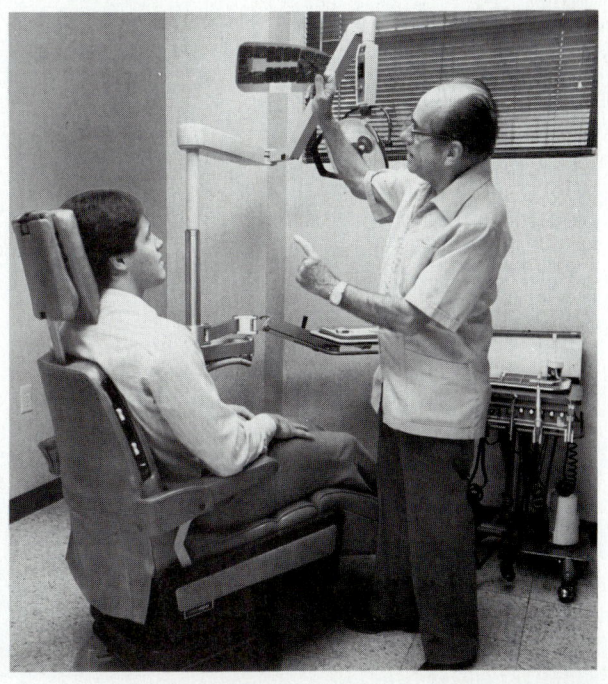

Choosing Health Products and Services **357**

not drive or operate machinery while taking this medication." Another typical warning is "Alcohol may intensify the effect of this medication." It is up to the user to be aware of these warnings and to follow directions.

Sometimes, when you need to buy a drug, you will find it sold in two ways. One way is under a brand name created by the manufacturer. The other way is under its generic name, the medical name for the drug. In either case, the drug must meet the same standards for purity and safety. However, often a drug will cost less when sold under its generic name. Ask your pharmacist for advice about generic drugs.

Health Services

Health services can be divided into two main types. The first type is routine care, such as regular checkups. This care helps prevent illnesses from occurring. It also helps detect illnesses before they become serious. In addition, it includes treatment for occasional minor illnesses, such as colds. The second type of care is designed for treating serious medical problems and handling medical emergencies. Physicians and dentists provide both types of health services. Professional counselors provide care for emotional problems.

Routine Medical Care

For routine medical care, it is important to have a physician whom you can consult regularly. It is also usually wise to seek all your routine care from the same physician. That way, over time the physician will learn all about your general medical condition. The physician can, then, provide care that meets your individual needs. To find out how some physicians are using computers to collect information about your medical condition, see page 359.

In most cases, routine medical care is provided by physicians called general practitioners (GPs) or family practitioners. A general practitioner provides a variety of medical services and treats many different illnesses. A family practitioner provides a broad range of medical services to families.

Often, routine care is provided in the physician's office. Physicians who offer care in their own offices are said to have a private practice. Routine care may also be provided in the offices of a group practice, a group of physicians sharing offices. Group practices may offer extra services such as x-rays.

If you move to a new community, you may need to choose a new physician for routine care. You will want to choose very carefully. The wisest course usually is to ask your previous physician to recommend a physician in your new community. You may also ask at the local hospital for names of physicians who practice nearby. Before deciding on a physician, you will want to find out whether that physician's office is conveniently located, what kinds of care are provided, and when the physician normally receives patients. You also need to find out about the physician's fees. Finally, you will want to know whether the physician is approved for treating patients in nearby hospitals.

Many kinds of routine medical care are also offered at clinics. A clinic is a health care center where patients are treated but usually do not stay overnight, as they might at a hospital. Also, patients at a clinic usually do not expect to see a particular physician. Instead, they are treated by whichever staff physician is on duty.

You may also seek routine care at a hospital, but the emergency room is not a wise choice. Its fees are high, and it is needed for true emergencies.

Routine care offered at hospitals and clinics may include checkups, treatment of minor illnesses, vision and hearing testing, and immunizations. An **immunization** is a treatment for protection against a particular disease.

Treatment for Medical Problems

When you need care for a serious medical problem, if possible, seek help from your regular physician. In some cases, your physician will be able to provide the proper treatment. Sometimes, the treatment can be provided in the physician's own office.

At other times, it will be necessary to go to a hospital or other health care center. A hospital is equipped to care for major illnesses

How Computers Can Help You

Using Computers to Detect Medical Problems

These days when you need medical care, you are likely to find that even your family physician is using a computer. Today computers are used in medicine for everything from routine examinations to the most advanced surgical procedures. The impact on health services has been dramatic.

One of the most important medical uses of computers is to detect medical problems. A good example is the use of computers in blood tests. A computer is first used in the process that separates the blood sample into the precise amounts required for each part of the test. Afterwards, the computer uses the test data to calculate a wide range of information, including the red and white blood cell count, the kinds and amounts of fats in the blood, and so forth. This information can quickly alert the physician to many types of disorders.

Another medical test in which computers are widely used is the electrocardiogram (EKG). An electrocardiogram gives information about the action of the heart. A computer can analyze that information quickly and accurately to tell whether the heart is beating normally.

An important medical test that depends entirely on computers is the CAT scan. CAT stands for "computerized axial tomography." In a CAT scan, the computer "reads" the information from x-rays and displays it in images on a video screen. Using those images, a physician can "see" inside the patient's body to detect hidden disorders.

Computer programs have been created that will analyze information about a patient's symptoms and identify the disease that might be responsible. The computer will even suggest a possible course of treatment. With techniques like these, computers are able to help health professionals save many people's lives.

and injuries. Surgery is performed at hospitals. Hospitals also provide care during delivery of babies.

Sometimes the care you need requires the services of a specialist. A specialist is a physician who concentrates on treating a single health problem or body area. Your regular physician can usually recommend a specialist. If your physician is part of a group practice, the group may include specialists who can help you. Many specialists are on staff at hospitals and at clinics.

For serious medical problems requiring immediate treatment, it is wisest to go directly to a hospital emergency room. Physicians will be on duty there to help you. They will have the equipment needed to cope with major emergencies.

Certain problems are less serious but still require quick treatment. Examples include a broken bone or a minor burn. For these problems, care is available at other types of health centers besides hospitals. In recent years, emergency centers have been created in many communities. An emergency center is a health care center equipped to deal with minor emergencies. Emergency centers often charge lower fees than hospitals for the same type of care.

Dental Care

For dental care, like routine medical care, it is important to have a dentist whom you can consult regularly. You should visit your dentist at least every six months to have your teeth cleaned professionally and your teeth and gums checked.

Different types of dentists offer different services. Some practice general dentistry and provide a range of services like filling, pulling, capping, and cleaning teeth. These dentists will refer you to a specialist if you need other kinds of treatment. Dental specialists perform treatments such as oral surgery, orthodontic work (straightening teeth), or periodontic work (treating diseases of the gums and other mouth tissues).

If you move to a new community, you may need to choose a new dentist. Finding a new dentist is an important responsibility. Try asking your previous dentist to recommend a dentist in your new community.

In many communities, dental clinics offer a wide range of dental services. A clinic may offer walk-in or emergency services or both. The services may cost less than those of a dentist with a private practice. However, you may not see the same dentist each time you visit the clinic.

Care for Emotional Problems

For emotional problems, it is a good idea to seek help from your regular physician. Your physician can refer you if necessary to the proper specialists for treatment.

For emergencies, such as extreme depression or suicide threats, help is offered in many communities through telephone "hotlines." A caller can speak about the problem with a trained counselor. The counselor can tell the caller where to find help.

In many communities there are also community counseling centers that help with emotional or mental problems. These centers are sponsored by city or county governments, religious groups, schools, universities, and other organizations. The fees charged at these centers may vary. City or county counseling services are often the least expensive. Some counseling services may charge you only in proportion to your income.

Taking Action in Emergencies

No matter what a person does to avoid emergencies, sometimes accidents and other emergencies do occur. Although you may never be completely prepared for them, you can take some precautions.

One general way in which you and others in your community can prepare for emergencies is to donate blood to your local hospital or blood bank. For more information on how you can become a blood or organ donor, see page 361.

P.S. How Can You Become a Blood or Organ Donor?

According to current statistics, between 80 and 90 percent of Americans will require a blood donation during their lifetime. Often, the situation is an emergency. Blood is available in the event of emergencies when healthy people are willing to donate it. Because whole blood lasts only 35 days and some blood components last only 72 hours, a continuous supply is needed. As a matter of fact, all blood types are needed all the time in most areas.

In general, you can donate blood if you are healthy, are 17 years old or older, weigh at least 110 pounds, and have waited a minimum of 8 weeks since your last donation.

If you would like to donate blood, you can do so through one of several organizations. You can go to a nonprofit community blood bank or to a for-profit blood donation center that pays you to "donate." You can also participate in blood drives sponsored by the American Red Cross, employee groups, religious organizations, clubs, and other groups.

Also, according to current statistics, each year only 40 percent of the Americans who need an organ transplant receive one. If more of the approximately 20,000 people who die each year were to become organ donors, many more people could survive the life-threatening emergencies they face. You can indicate your willingness to be an organ donor in the event of your death by adding this message to your driver's license or by carrying or wearing a card that indicates your desire to donate.

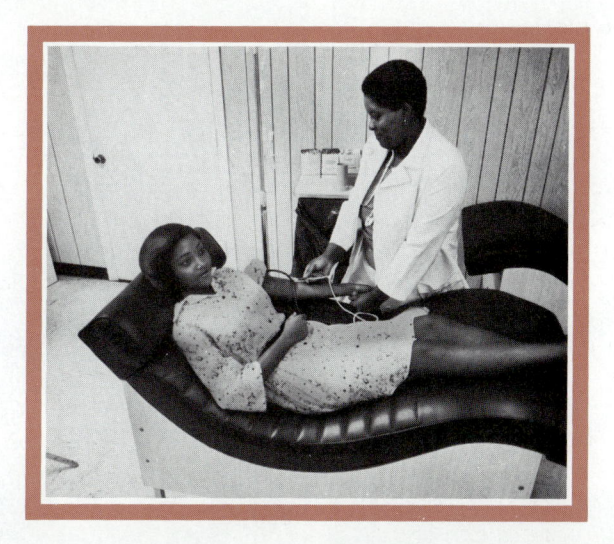

As an individual, the first precaution you can take for emergencies is to stay alert to what is happening around you. By doing this, you are more likely to avoid accidents. You also are more likely to hear or see warnings of natural disasters.

A second precaution you can take is to know basic first-aid procedures so that you can help yourself and others in case of an emergency. Even if you know only a few procedures, you may be able to make the difference between life and death—your own or someone else's.

A third precaution you can take is to learn whether your community has a short emergency telephone number that will immediately connect you with a network of emergency services. Such a network would usually include the police and fire departments, ambulance and rescue services, and perhaps the nearest Civil Defense office. Memorize that number or keep it posted by the telephone.

A fourth precaution you can take is to wear a medical alert. A medical alert is a tag that lists the wearer's medical problems and allergies. This tag can help a medical professional treat you in case you are unconscious in an emergency.

Performing First Aid

Knowing a few basic first-aid procedures will help you keep yourself and others as healthy as possible until medical help can be secured. Learning these basics should never, however, be considered a substitute for first-aid training. Community organizations such as the American Red Cross can offer you thorough first-aid training.

Choking

One medical emergency you may witness is choking. Most choking is related to eating. Therefore, choking often occurs during meals at home or away from home. In either setting, it is often mistaken for a heart attack. Unlike the victim of a heart attack, however, most choking victims grasp their throats and cannot talk.

Choking requires that you quickly use the **Heimlich maneuver,** a set of procedures that rely on force to unblock the airway of a choking victim. To do this, stand behind the victim and strike the victim four times between the shoulder blades. Then, place your arms around the victim's waist, with the side of your fist against the victim's abdomen, under the ribs, as shown below, left. Grasp

To perform many first-aid procedures, you need to know exactly what position to be in or to have the victim in. Can you demonstrate the correct hand positions for the Heimlich maneuver and for keeping a victim's blood flowing through the use of CPR?

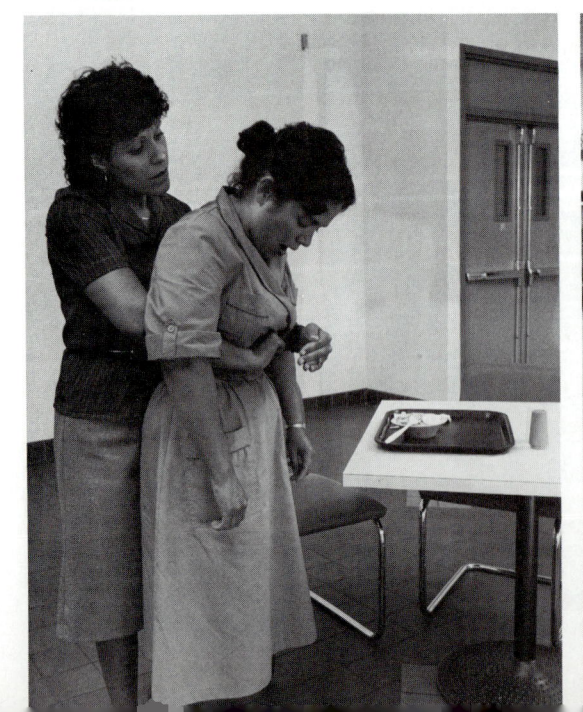

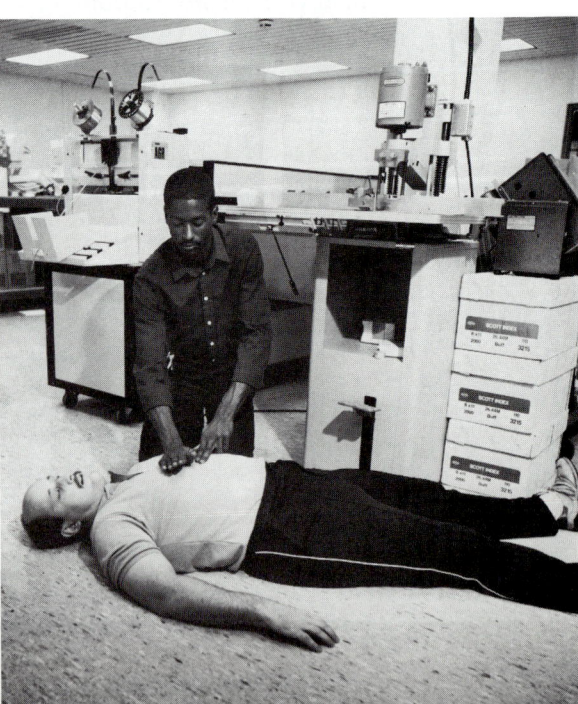

your fist with your other hand, and make four quick upward thrusts. The force of air should push the material out of the victim's windpipe. If the material is not forced out, repeat the back blows and thrusts to the victim's abdomen.

Respiratory Failure

A second medical emergency you may face is **respiratory failure,** or stopped breathing. In this situation, you need to try to restore breathing through the use of mouth-to-mouth resuscitation.

Place the victim on his or her back. Open the victim's airway. To do so, you may have to use your fingers to clear the victim's mouth. With one hand, push the victim's forehead back, and hold the victim's nose closed. With the other hand, pull the victim's jaw forward, and seal your mouth over the victim's. Blow four quick breaths into the victim's mouth. Then, breathe into the victim's mouth at twelve breaths per minute. When the victim's chest is expanded, stop and see if the victim is beginning to breathe. If not, check the victim's carotid pulse in the main artery of the neck.

If the victim has no pulse and you are trained to, begin artificial circulation, the second step of cardiopulmonary resuscitation. **Cardiopulmonary resuscitation,** or **CPR,** is a set of procedures to help a victim breathe and keep blood circulating. To begin, locate the victim's sternum, or breast bone. Place one hand flat on the sternum, two finger widths up from the tip of the sternum, as shown on page 362. Then, place your other hand flat on top of the one already in place. Pressing down with both hands, depress the sternum 1½ to 2 inches. Do this 60 to 80 times per minute, alternated with your artificial respiration efforts until the victim begins to breathe or help arrives. If you are not yet trained for CPR, you can get training from the American Red Cross or from anyone certified by the Red Cross to teach this technique.

Bleeding

For massive bleeding from a severed blood vessel or deep cut, apply direct pressure to the wound to help control the bleeding.

If the cut is in an arm or leg and you do not think a bone is broken, elevate the limb while applying firm pressure on the wound. To apply pressure, use a sterile gauze or clean cloth. If neither is available, use your bare hand to stop the bleeding. Blood loss is more dangerous than the risk of infection.

After you have controlled the bleeding, do not remove the gauze or cloth. Its removal may start the bleeding again.

If direct pressure on the wound does not stop the bleeding or if the wound is caused by a broken bone or by an imbedded object, you will need to try another technique. This technique involves the use of pressure points. A **pressure point** is a point on the body where an artery passes over a bone. Pressing an artery here causes the blood to slow.

The final choice for stopping bleeding is a tourniquet, which usually causes loss of the injured limb. A **tourniquet** is a piece of cloth or other material tied tightly around an injured limb to stop the flow of blood. A tourniquet should be used only if all other methods have failed and blood loss seems to threaten the victim's life.

To make a tourniquet, tie a band of cloth 2 inches wide around the injured limb between the wound and the heart. Use a belt, tie, stocking, scarf, or strip of cloth. Do not use a wire, a rope, or a cord. Wrap the tourniquet around the limb twice, and tie a half knot. Tie a short, strong stick on top of the knot, and twist the stick just until the bleeding stops. Never loosen the tourniquet. Always indicate somewhere near the tourniquet the time that it was applied.

Burns

Burns can be light, moderate, or severe. Light burns cause redness, mild swelling, and pain. You can treat such burns by putting cold water but not ice on them and, then, covering them with clean bandages. Moderate burns cause redness, more long-lasting swelling, blisters, oozing, and pain. You can treat such burns as you would light burns and, then, elevate the victim's arms and legs and seek medical assistance. Severe burns result in white, charred, or destroyed skin but little pain. For a victim of severe burns, there is little the average person can do except treat the victim for shock and seek medical help.

Shock

Shock can result from any injury or illness and, if not treated, can result in death. **Shock** is a condition in which the victim's body processes are severely depressed. Symptoms of shock include a rapid but weak pulse, shallow and irregular breathing, a pale face, weakness, chills, thirst, nausea, cold skin with clammy perspiration, and, eventually, low blood pressure.

To treat a person for shock, keep the victim lying down. Clear the victim's breathing passage and keep it clear. Elevate the victim's legs and loosen tight clothing, particularly around the victim's neck and waist. Cover the victim to keep him or her warm. Seek immediate medical attention.

Poisoning

Poisoning requires quick action. Call the poison control center in your area immediately. If you do not have a poison control center in your area, call a doctor, hospital, or rescue unit or the fire department, police, or sheriff. Keep these telephone numbers posted in a handy place. When reporting a poisoning, it is important to tell exactly what substance is involved.

Fractures

In general, do not move a person who may have a fracture. Keep the person calm, treat him or her for shock, and call for medical assistance. If you must move the person, immobilize the suspected fracture. A splint can be used on a limb for this purpose. This will prevent further damage to tissues and blood vessels or vital organs.

Points to Remember

- Each day, your body needs a certain amount of nutritious foods, as well as exercise, rest, and sleep.
- Regular exercise means exercise lasting at least twenty to thirty minutes at least three or four days a week.
- Avoiding substance abuse is one of your responsibilities now and will remain an important responsibility throughout your life.
- Stress can be a healthy stimulus to new achievements, but unrelieved stress can lead to physical and emotional problems.
- You need to monitor your physical and emotional health to detect problems and seek treatment before any problem becomes serious.
- The most common types of accidents in the home are falls, poisonings, electric shocks, drownings, suffocation, and fires.
- It is important to get health care on a routine basis and whenever you have a special physical or emotional health problem.
- You can help save a life if you know basic procedures for handling the victims of choking, respiratory failure, bleeding, burns, shock, poisoning, and even fractures.

Test Your Skills
RESOURCE MANAGEMENT

Imagine yourself in the situation described below. In this situation, resources need managing. As you read, think about the ways that you can manage resources. Then, answer the questions that follow. When you need to manage resources in the future, remember to ask yourself these questions.

Situation

This year you are planning to try out for a sport. You know that eligibility depends on academic, physical, and emotional fitness. Although your counselor cautioned you against taking very demanding courses this semester, you thought you could handle them. Now, you are not so sure. Two courses seem very hard, although your classmates think they are easy. Sports practice is taking a great deal of time and energy. Your family has changed your household responsibilities, and your new tasks are more time-consuming and difficult than your old ones.

For weeks now, you have skipped meals or eaten foods with little nutritive value. You have stayed up late, slept little, and worried a lot. Because you are unable to concentrate, your grades are slipping. You are performing poorly at practice and getting pressure from the coach to work harder or quit. Your poor grades and neglect of household tasks are causing family arguments.

Your health is suffering, but you are determined to make the tryouts. If your total health continues to fail, however, you have little chance of succeeding in sports, schoolwork, or relationships with family members and friends.

Questions

1. Which resource do you need to manage most carefully? Why? (Hint: Look for the resource that is in shortest supply.)

2. What are the ways you might manage this resource? (Hint: Be sure to name any resources you could substitute, trade, or share.)

3. What opportunity costs would be involved in each case?

4. Who would pay the opportunity costs in each case?

5. After considering all these opportunity costs, how would you manage your resources in this situation?

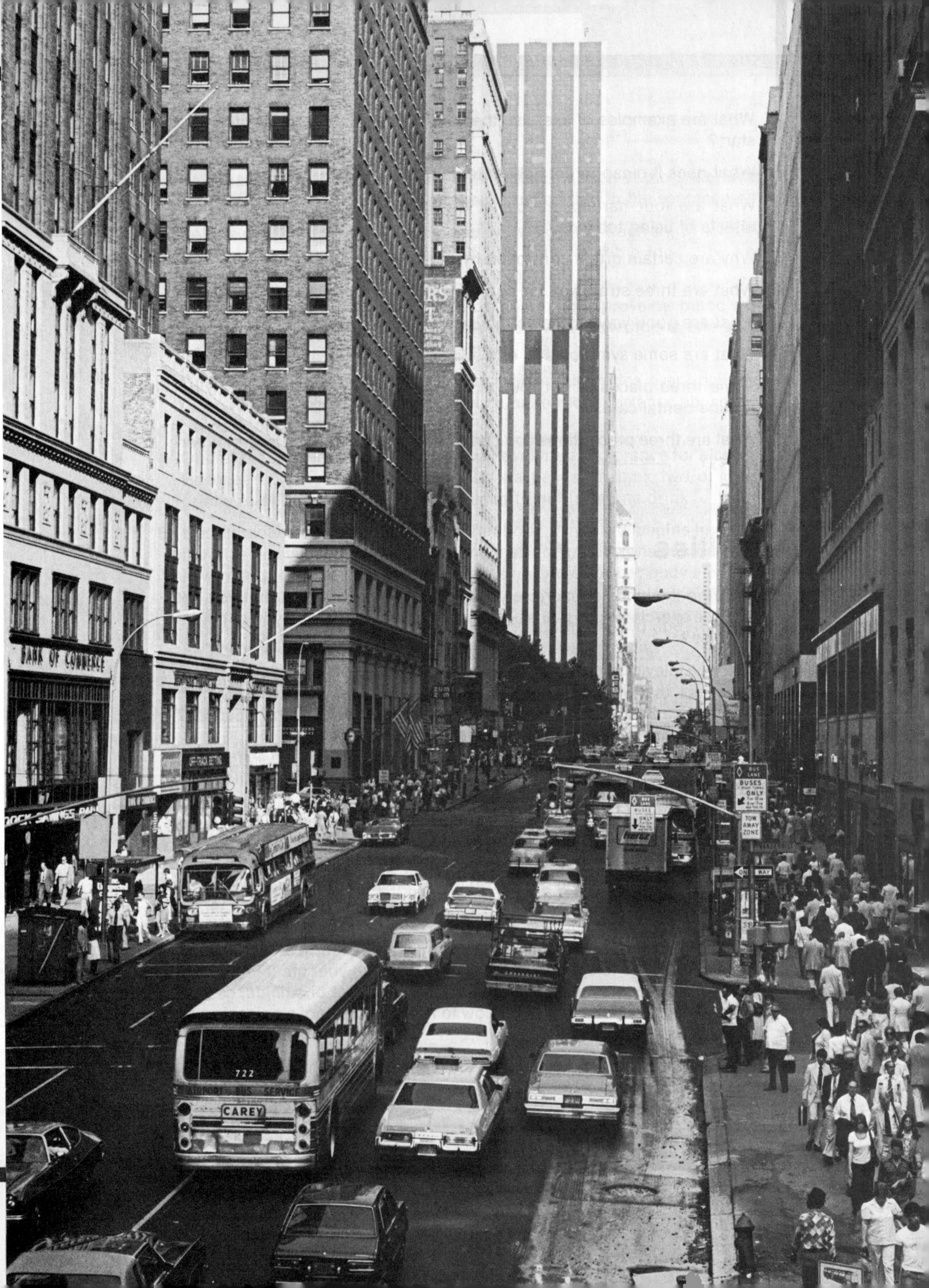

BANK OF COMMERCE
722
CAREY
BUSES ONLY
TOW AWAY ZONE
ONE WAY

CHAPTER 16

Arranging for Transportation

You probably already spend a large part of your time getting from one place to another. Perhaps a family member or friend drives you. Perhaps you take a bus. Maybe you own an automobile and drive places by yourself. As you assume more and more adult responsibilities, your need for transportation is likely to grow. You may need transportation to get to work, to provide for the needs of a family, and for special purposes such as vacations. A very important part of succeeding on your own will be learning how to meet your transportation needs.

Like other adult responsibilities, arranging for transportation involves making decisions and managing resources. You will have to decide which form of transportation best suits your needs. If you are considering buying an automobile, you will have to decide if you can afford to own one. You will also have to manage your resources carefully in order to pay the purchase, insurance, and upkeep costs. In addition, you will need to shop wisely as you consider different automobile makes and models.

Start thinking now about your future transportation needs. Having reliable, affordable transportation will help you achieve your goals. It can also help you take advantage of opportunities. Knowing how to arrange transportation will be an important step toward gaining your independence.

Discover Through Your Reading

- what to consider when choosing a form of transportation
- how to decide whether to own an automobile
- what is included in the full cost of automobile ownership
- how to shop for an automobile

Choosing a Form of Transportation

Think about how you get to school each day. If your school is close to your home, you may walk or ride your bicycle. If your school is farther away, you may walk to a bus stop to catch a school bus or a city bus. You may drive your own automobile or be driven by a family member. Perhaps a family member drives you to a friend's home so that you can get a ride. Whatever form of transportation you use, you probably count on getting to school in the same way every day. On some days, however, you may need to choose a different form of transportation. In certain circumstances, your usual method of travel may not be as convenient or safe as some other method.

As you become more independent, you will have more and more places to go. Whether you are going to school, to work, to a store, or to a friend's home, you will want to choose the form of transportation that best matches your needs. This may mean that you will use several different forms of transportation instead of just one. There are many different forms of transportation, and each form has its advantages and disadvantages. To help you decide what form of transportation to use, think about how well each one meets your needs for safety, convenience, and conservation of resources.

Considering Safety

The first point to consider when choosing a form of transportation should be safety. No matter how you travel, you will want to arrive safely. Whether or not a particular form of transportation is safe can depend on the circumstances. These circumstances may include weather conditions, conditions along the route, the use of special safety equipment, the skill and alertness of the driver, and other factors. Depending on the circumstances, walking, bicycling, riding a motorcycle or a motorized bike, driving, and taking buses, trains, subways, and taxis can all be safe ways to travel.

Travel Conditions

Under certain conditions, one form of transportation may be safer than another. For example, suppose you need to travel to a nearby city on a day when the roads are icy. If you have an automobile, you might use it for your trip. However, if you can take a bus or train, that might be a much safer way of traveling on that particular day. Driving your automobile might be more convenient or less expensive than taking the bus or train. However, no possible saving of your energy or time or your money is worth taking chances with your safety.

Skills and Equipment

Special skills and safety equipment can be especially important to safe driving. A most important piece of safety equipment is your seatbelt. Keep it fastened whenever you are in an automobile. For an example of safe driving skills, suppose you lived in a region where winter driving is often hazardous. You would need to know techniques for driving in snow and ice. You might also need snow tires and tire chains. If you lacked these resources, it might be safer to ride with someone who had them. That way, you could protect yourself and others and prevent damage to your automobile.

Alertness

Alertness is also especially important to safe driving. If alertness is reduced by alcohol, drugs, fatigue, or anything else, driving is very dangerous. If you are less than fully alert, you should not drive. Likewise, when any person is intoxicated, whether from alcohol or from drugs, that person should not be permitted to drive. This is important not just for the safety of the intoxicated person, but also for the protection of the other drivers on the road. Also, never accept a ride from an intoxicated person. Instead, take a bus, train, or subway, if possible, or call a family member or a taxi for a ride. These alternatives may be costly or inconvenient, but they are certainly much safer.

People in all walks of life use public transportation. When might you use it?

Considering Convenience

A second point to consider when choosing a form of transportation is convenience. What is convenient for you will depend on where you live, what type of work you do, your lifestyle, and the availability of different forms of transportation. For example, driving your own automobile is convenient if you live in a place where there is little traffic congestion and ample parking. It is also convenient if you need to set your own schedule. Under some circumstances, having an automobile may be a necessity as well as a convenience. You may have a job that requires a great deal of automobile travel. You may live in a neighborhood where there are no buses and no other people who travel to the same places you do each day.

On the other hand, if you live in a large city with heavy traffic and few parking places, you may decide that public transportation is more convenient. **Public transportation** is the type that is designed to take paying passengers where they want to go, usually within a set area and often along a set route. Its forms include buses, subways, taxis, and commuter trains. When you use public transportation, you have to meet strict schedules. Also, sometimes you must have exact change for your fare.

For many people, ridesharing is a convenient form of transportation. **Ridesharing** is a transportation method in which people who live and work near each other share the driving and the driving expenses. If you do

Ridesharing might be the most economical way for you to get to work. What are some of its other advantages?

not have an automobile and cannot contribute to the driving, you may still be able to take part in ridesharing by paying a regular fee. As with public transportation, you must meet a schedule and allow yourself a little extra time to get where you are going. Many businesses and community groups sponsor programs to link commuters for ridesharing. In larger cities, you may see signs indicating telephone numbers to call for ridesharing information. Such signs are generally placed alongside major highways leading into the city's downtown area.

Considering Resource Conservation

A third point to consider when choosing a form of transportation is resource conservation. All forms of transportation require the use of resources. These resources may include your personal energy and time. They may also include resources in the environment, and also money. When choosing a way to travel, you may decide that it would be wise to conserve the resource that is in shortest supply.

Saving Personal Energy and Time

Different forms of transportation require different amounts of your personal time and energy. For example, driving an automobile takes much less time and energy than walking or bicycling. Therefore, you would probably choose to drive if your time or energy were in short supply. On the other hand, if you had the energy and time to spare, or if you wanted the exercise, you might decide to make short trips by walking or bicycling instead of by using an automobile.

Saving Environmental Resources

Many forms of transportation use up environmental resources. For example, automobiles, buses, and airplanes burn fuels made from petroleum. Many trains and subways run on electric power. That kind of power is made by burning coal or petroleum or from sunlight (solar power), the force of the wind (wind power), the flowing action of water (water power), or radioactive elements (nuclear power).

The world's supplies of sunlight, water power, and wind power will never be used

How often do you save environmental resources by walking or bicycling?

up. The supplies of petroleum and coal, however, are limited. In certain times and places, supplies of both have been short. As a result, many people try to conserve these resources. Some choose automobiles with small engines, which burn less fuel than automobiles with large engines. Others keep automobile use to a minimum and rely instead on bicycling, walking, or public transportation. Still others share rides whenever possible instead of driving alone.

Another environmental resource to be considered is the supply of clean air. Automobiles, buses, and other motor vehicles produce exhaust fumes that pollute the air with gases and tiny particles. Exhaust fumes are partly to blame for **smog**, a type of air pollution created when fog combines with smoke and chemical fumes. To protect the supply of clean air, many motor vehicles are now equipped with devices to control exhaust fumes. Some states regularly test motor vehicles to ensure that the exhaust they produce does not violate pollution control standards. Motor vehicles that fail the test can not be registered until the problem is corrected.

Saving Money

Different forms of transportation cost different amounts of money. Driving your own automobile is probably the most expensive form of transportation. Buying the automobile can be very costly. So can maintaining it and buying fuel and insurance for it. If you own an automobile, you may want to find ways to cut costs. For example, you can use public transportation instead of your automobile whenever possible. You can take advantage of a ridesharing program or, if necessary, organize one. You can learn to make some repairs yourself, and you can purchase gasoline for a lower price at self-service stations.

If you decide that automobile ownership is too expensive for you, you might instead choose to own a motorcycle, a motorized bike, or a bicycle. To learn more about these more affordable forms of transportation, see page 374. Remember that one form of transportation costs no money at all. When possible, consider walking.

Choosing to Buy an Automobile

After considering the various forms of transportation available to you, you may decide that it makes sense for you to buy an automobile. Your next step will be to take a closer look at the costs and responsibilities of owning this kind of vehicle.

Can you afford to buy an automobile? To find out, you need to understand the total cost of automobile ownership. This cost is much more than just the purchase price. Also, since that purchase price is likely to be more money than you have on hand, you may need to understand how to pay that price by getting a loan. Finally, you need to examine your current financial situation to make sure that the cost of automobile ownership fits comfortably into your budget. Only then will you know what kind of automobile, if any, you can afford. You can then begin shopping for an automobile. You will be choosing the exact make and model you want. You will also be deciding whether to buy a new automobile or a used one. If you decide to buy a new one, you will need to make sure that it includes all the equipment you want. If you are buying a used automobile, you will need to inspect it closely for quality. Then, you can settle on a price with the seller and, if necessary, arrange for financing.

Understanding the Total Cost

The first step in buying an automobile is understanding the total cost of automobile ownership. This cost includes both the purchase cost—which is usually paid for with a loan—and the upkeep costs. There is also a third type of cost called depreciation. The purchase cost, if paid for with a loan, is usually divided into monthly payments. For con-

P.S. What About a Motorcycle, Motorized Bike, or Bicycle?

If the cost of automobile ownership is more than you wish to spend, you may choose instead to buy a motorcycle, motorized bike, or bicycle. Like automobiles, these vehicles are available in several makes and models—new or used. As with automobiles, you will have maintenance costs and possible driving-related expenses. You will also need to obey traffic laws and ride with safety in mind.

If you choose to buy a motorcycle, you will have over thirty models from which to select. Most states require registration and an operator's license. Helmets provide important protection for motorcycle riders, and most states require them. Other protective equipment, such as gloves, leather boots, and reflective clothing, is often recommended.

If you want a vehicle that will travel up to 120 miles (190 km) on a single gallon of gasoline, consider a motorized bike. Most motorized bikes can reach a speed of 30 miles (48 km) per hour. For safety, they are equipped with a headlight, taillight, brakelight, and side and rear reflectors. If used on a main road, a motorized bike should also have a mirror, a horn, and a muffler. The driver should wear a safety helmet. Because motorized bike engines are simple, many owners handle minor repairs themselves. Most states require a valid operator's license. Some also require registration of the bike and require the owner to pass a written test to obtain a license.

If you want a vehicle that requires no gasoline, you might consider a bicycle. Bicycles can be found for various prices at bicycle shops, garage sales, and public auctions. Bicycle styles include the high-rise, the single-speed middleweight, and the multi-speed lightweight. Minor repairs are often done by bicycle owners themselves. In some states, bicyclists must pay license and registration fees. Additional expenses may include a bicycle lock, a helmet, and reflective clothing.

What information about the cost of buying and owning a particular model can you find in consumer magazines?

venience, therefore, the other costs are usually figured on a monthly basis as well. Note that some of those other costs are fixed costs, and others are variable costs. The fixed costs do not change no matter how much or how little you drive the automobile. The variable costs change depending on the amount of automobile use.

Paying the Purchase Cost

The most important fixed cost involved in automobile ownership is typically the purchase cost. Since this cost is usually high, few people can afford to pay it all at once with their own money. Instead, most people pay only a down payment and pay the rest with a loan, usually from a bank, a credit union, or the automobile dealer. Then they pay back the loan, with interest, in monthly installments. The amount of each payment is determined by the size of the loan, the interest rate, and the period, or term, of the loan. Different lenders offer different interest rates and different payment arrangements. Therefore, it pays to do comparison shopping for an automobile loan.

To figure a typical monthly installment payment, visit an automobile dealer to find out the purchase price of an automobile that you might consider buying. From that price, subtract the amount you could afford as a down payment. The remainder will be the amount you would need to borrow. Next, ask at a bank or credit union about the interest rate and repayment period for a typical automobile loan. Figure out the installment payments on the amount you would borrow as shown in the example on page 376.

In that example, a buyer plans to borrow $4,000 for two years at 11 percent interest. The monthly payment is figured in five steps. In Steps 1 and 2, the loan amount is multiplied by the yearly interest rate and by the number of years in the loan. The result, however, does not yet give the actual total interest charge. The reason is that with every monthly payment, the amount still on loan gets smaller. As a result, you do not have to pay interest on the full amount for the entire term of the loan. What then is the actual total interest charge? Lenders find out by checking special charts. However, for a rough estimate of the total, you can divide the result of Step 2 in half, as shown in Step 3. In Step 4, that total is added to the amount borrowed to show the total amount to be paid. In Step

Choosing to Buy an Automobile **375**

Estimating Monthly Payments on an Automobile Loan

Loan: $4,000
Yearly Interest Rate: 11%
Term of Loan: 2 years

Step 1
$4,000 (loan)
× .11 (11% yearly interest rate)
$ 440

Step 2
$440
× 2 (years in term of loan)
$880

Step 3
$880 ÷ 2 = $440 (estimated total interest charge)

Step 4
$4,000 + $440 = $4,440 (total to be paid)

Step 5
$4,440 ÷ 24 (months in term of loan)
= $185 (estimated monthly payment)

---

and variable costs to your figure for the monthly installment payment.

One final cost to consider is depreciation. **Depreciation** is the amount of value an item purchased loses over time because of use. The amount of depreciation on an automobile determines how much of the purchase price you can get back if you resell the automobile. You can figure depreciation by checking used automobile prices. For example, if a two-year-old automobile costs $2,000 less than the current model, the depreciation in those two years was $2,000. You may not want to figure depreciation as a monthly cost. However, you will want to be aware that your vehicle is likely to lose value over time.

Figuring How Much You Can Spend

Your next step in buying an automobile is figuring how much you can spend. If, as is likely, you pay for your purchase with a loan, you will need cash on hand for the down payment. You must also have enough money each month for the installment payments and upkeep costs.

Examine your financial resources to decide what you can spare for the down pay-

---

5, this total is divided by the number of months in the term of the loan. The result is the estimated monthly installment payment.

Considering Upkeep and Depreciation Costs

Upkeep costs involved in automobile ownership can be both fixed and variable. Fixed upkeep costs include the costs of insurance, license, registration, taxes, and parking. Variable upkeep costs include the costs of fuel, maintenance, and repairs. These costs too are part of the full cost of automobile ownership.

To include these costs in your total estimate, first figure monthly totals for the fixed costs. If any of these costs is paid just once a year, divide it by 12 to get a monthly total. Next, estimate monthly totals for the variable costs. Finally, add the monthly fixed

The costs of keeping up an automobile include both fixed and variable costs. Which kind of auto expense is this driver paying?

ment. Then calculate your monthly income after taxes. From that amount, subtract your total monthly expenses, including your rent or mortgage, utility bills, food and clothing costs, and so forth. Then subtract the amount you plan to set aside monthly as savings. The remainder will be the amount you can spare each month for the installment payment and for other expenses related to the costs of automobile ownership.

Deciding What You Can Afford

Once you have finished your calculations, compare the full cost of automobile ownership with the amount you can spend. Can you afford the kind of automobile you may have been considering? If not, you may need to change your plans. Figure the costs of different automobile makes and models until you find ones you can afford. Remember to figure the costs of used automobiles as well as new ones.

If you still find that you cannot afford an automobile, try reducing your other expenses so that you will have more money to spend. Also, try finding out if some change in your automobile loan arrangements could reduce the size of your monthly payments. If these steps are not enough, you may have to postpone buying an automobile and use other forms of transportation instead. You might also check into the cost of renting or leasing an automobile. For tips about renting or leasing, see the righthand column.

Selecting a Make and Model

Once you know which types of automobiles you can afford, you can begin selecting the exact make and model that you want. The best place to start may be the library, not the dealer's showroom. In the library you will find *Consumer Reports* and various automobile magazines that publish comparisons of different automobiles. These comparisons rate many different models in terms of safety, performance, comfort, repair record, and resale value.

Another good way to learn about makes and models is to talk to family members or

---

Tips
Renting or Leasing an Automobile

For business and other reasons, some people rent or lease their automobiles instead of buying them. Most renting is just for a few days or weeks. Most leasing is for several months or years. Here are some tips on renting or leasing an automobile.

- Most rental plans charge a fixed sum per day. That sum may include a charge for a set number of miles that you may drive. Otherwise, you will be charged for mileage separately on a per-mile basis.

- You always pay the fuel costs for a rented automobile.

- Some rental plans allow you to pick up or drop off a rented automobile in another city.

- A long-term lease may allow you to swap your automobile each year for a new model.

---

friends about the automobiles they drive. You might also visit an automobile repair shop to ask which makes and models need repairs most frequently. Try to get a range of opinions. That way you will not have to rely only on what you are told by the dealer.

When you begin examining particular makes and models, there are many points to keep in mind. Think carefully about how you will use the automobile. Will you be using it to carry many people or just yourself? Will you be using it for long trips or just on local roads? Will you be driving it in city traffic? What can you afford to pay for fuel costs?

Keep these questions in mind as you decide which of the following general automobile sizes you prefer:

- *Subcompacts* are the smallest type of automobile. They seat two adults in front and small children in back. However, they may be uncomfortable on long trips. Also, they may not perform as well as larger automobiles because their engines are usually small. Nevertheless, their fuel costs are low.
- *Compacts* are larger than subcompacts and will seat four adults comfortably on short trips. Compacts are easy to handle, and their fuel costs are low.
- *Intermediates* provide still more space and comfort. They perform well both in city traffic and on the highway. However, their fuel costs and upkeep expenses tend to be higher than those of smaller cars.
- *Full-size* or *standard* automobiles are the largest kind and include luxury models. They are the most comfortable for long trips. However, they may be expensive to own. They may also be difficult to manage in city traffic.

In addition to these four sizes of cars, there are trucks and vans, which also come in different sizes. Asking the questions listed above will also help you decide on a make and a model if a truck or a van is the type of vehicle you prefer to buy.

Would this car style be right for you? Why?

Here are some additional questions to ask yourself as you try to decide which of the different automobile makes and models you prefer.

- *Which body style would best meet your needs?* Would you like a sports car, or might your occupation make a different body style necessary? Will you often carry bulky objects such as furniture or suitcases? If you do, perhaps you should consider a truck, a van, a station wagon, or an automobile with a hatchback, a hinged rear window opening into a large storage area. Will you often have small children as passengers? If so, perhaps you need a two-door model with no rear doors that could open accidentally and endanger the children.
- *How much protection will make you feel safe?* Larger, heavier models are often considered to provide more protection in case of an accident. They may also be safer on wet or icy roads because their weight makes them less likely to slide.
- *What gas mileage seems adequate?* An automobile's **gas mileage,** or number of miles the automobile can travel on a gallon of gas or diesel fuel, will determine your fuel costs. For new automobiles, the gas mileage is printed on the price sticker. However, that mileage is an estimate based on ideal driving conditions. The actual gas mileage that drivers get may vary depending on driving habits, road conditions, and the like.
- *Which options do you want?* Do you want your automobile to have air conditioning, automatic transmission, a radio, and other extras? Adding them may decrease your gas mileage and increase the automobile's purchase price.

Deciding Between a New and Used Automobile

Another choice to make is whether to buy a new automobile or a used one. This decision may be based on the amount of money you can spend. It may also depend on how you plan to use the automobile. The chart on

Comparing New and Used Automobiles

New Automobile	Used Automobile
Advantages	
• usually has a better warranty • may be easier to buy on credit because of the warranty • may have a higher resale value • may require fewer repairs • usually is in good overall condition • usually offers a wide choice of styles, colors and options	• usually has a lower purchase price • may include options that you could not afford on a new automobile
Disadvantages	
• usually has a higher purchase price • may have a waiting period before delivery	• may have a very limited warranty or no warranty • may require more repairs • may be in poorer overall condition • usually offers a limited choice or no choice of styles, colors, and options • may have a lower resale value

this page will help you compare the advantages and disadvantages of new and used automobiles.

Deciding Where to Buy

Once you have chosen the type of automobile you want, you will need to find a respected and reliable dealer. Ask family members or friends to recommend dealers. Find out if those dealers provide good service not just at the time of purchase, but also later, for maintenance and repairs. Also, try to find a dealer who is located near where you live or work. A convenient location will make it easier to have your automobile serviced.

New automobiles are normally bought from new-automobile dealers. Used automobiles, however, can be bought from individuals, new-automobile dealers, and used-automobile dealers.

An individual who is selling a used automobile may be someone you know or someone who has placed a classified advertisement in the newspaper. By buying from an individual, you may get a lower price than a dealer would offer. However, an individual seller probably will not provide a warranty. If you buy an automobile from an individual, make sure that it has not been stolen or is not about to be repossessed, or taken back by a bank or finance company. Always check the automobile **title,** the legal document that shows ownership. The seller must sign the back of the title and fill in the mileage information. Also, do not think that if you buy from an individual, you can avoid paying sales tax. The tax is charged when you register the automobile.

New-automobile dealers sell used automobiles that have been received as trade-ins. These automobiles were traded in by their owners to cover part of the purchase price of a new car. A new-automobile dealer's price is usually higher than an individual's, but the dealer usually offers a warranty on the automobile.

Some dealers handle only used automobiles. These dealers usually offer reasonable prices and sometimes help with financing. However, they do not always offer the *best* price or financing plan. Also, they may give only limited warranties.

Choosing to Buy an Automobile **379**

Inspecting for Quality

When you examine any new automobile, check first to see that it meets your needs in terms of appearance, comfort, roominess, performance, and cost. Then, take the vehicle for a test drive. Try it out on a highway and on city streets. See how well it gains speed and climbs hills. See how easy it is to maneuver and to park. These are all qualities that are built into the model itself and cannot be changed or repaired.

When you examine a used automobile, you need to check very thoroughly for defects caused by wear. Check the following quality points:

- *Outside:* Are there signs of accident damage? Is there rust or broken glass? Is any fluid leaking from beneath? Are the shock absorbers worn?
- *Inside:* Are the doors tight? Is the upholstery torn? Do the lights, radio, heater, and air conditioner work?
- *Under the hood:* Are there signs of wear on the engine? Are the hoses frayed? Has routine maintenance been followed on all engine parts?
- *On the road:* Take the automobile for a test drive. Does it have the power to climb hills and to pass other vehicles? Do the gears shift smoothly? Does the engine make unusual noises? Are the brakes tight? Does the automobile pull to the left or right during braking?

To be certain that you are aware of any defects, ask a mechanic that you know and trust to check any used automobile that you are considering buying. Even if this service costs a small fee, you may still find it worthwhile to make sure there are no problems.

Getting a Good Price

Once you are satisfied with the quality of the automobile you have selected, you and the seller can begin discussing its price. At this point, the most important thing to remember is that for automobiles, there is no such thing as a fixed retail price. Instead, the price will vary according to the circumstances of the sale. These circumstances include the extras that you want on the automobile, the condition of the automobile if it is a used one, the amount the seller will give you for a vehicle that you trade in, and so forth. Based on these factors, you and the seller will try to settle on a price by bargaining.

A new automobile will have a sticker on one window listing a price. This **sticker price** is the suggested retail price for that particular automobile. It includes all the extras built into that automobile. The sticker price will be higher than the **base price,** which is the price of the automobile with standard equipment only. The sticker price will be your starting point for bargaining with the dealer. To make a sale, the dealer will usually make you a better offer. Some consumer guides provide estimates of the lowest offer you can reasonably expect.

Used automobiles have standard prices. The standard price, or **book value,** for a used car can be found in the *National Automobile Dealers Association Used Car Guide* or the *Kelly Blue Book.* Both books are available in libraries. Newspaper classified advertisements also offer a general range of current prices. When you are bargaining for a used automobile, it pays to be aware of the book value. Remember, however, that the condi-

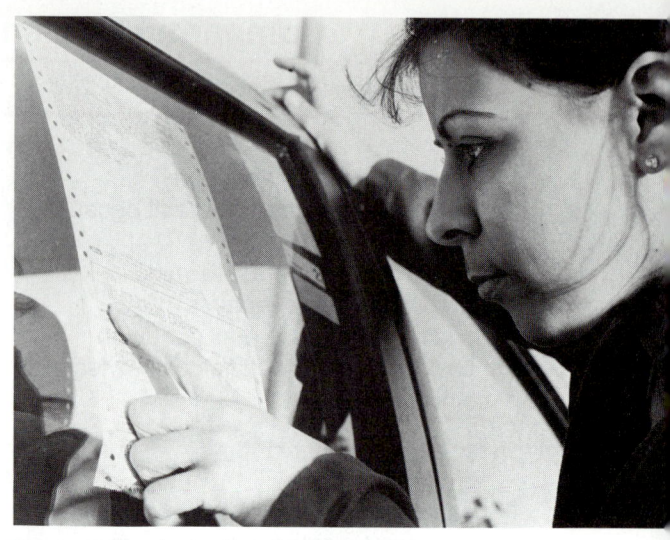

This customer is reading the sticker price on an automobile. Is it possible for a customer to pay less than the sticker price? Why?

tion of the automobile and its mileage can raise or lower the price.

For both new and used automobiles, remember that the price does not include the sales tax. Depending on the tax rate charged by your state, this tax can add a sizable amount to the purchase price. Remember to allow for this tax when you are making plans to purchase an automobile.

Arranging for an Automobile Loan

If you need a loan to pay for your automobile, you may have a variety of sources to choose from. Among these sources may be your credit union, a bank, a savings and loan association, the automobile dealer, or a finance company.

Generally, a credit union offers the lowest interest rates. If you do not belong to a credit union, try a bank or savings and loan association for the next-lowest rates. Always try more than one of these institutions. For example, a big bank downtown may charge a higher interest rate than a small bank in the suburbs. If a loan from a credit union, bank, or savings and loan institution is not available to you, try your dealer or a finance company. By checking with several institutions, you can learn which offers the best rates.

Owning an Automobile

Once you own an automobile, you have certain responsibilities. You must register it, and to drive it you must have a driver's license. You must also have automobile insurance. In addition, you will need to have routine maintenance work done on your automobile, and you will need to pay for any special repairs. Finally, you have the very important responsibility to drive your automobile safely and courteously.

Registering Your Automobile

By law, every automobile must be registered with the state department of motor vehicles. The registration must be renewed every year. For each registration and renewal, you will be charged a fee. Your automobile may also have to meet certain inspection requirements before it can be registered. These often include certification that your automobile meets pollution control standards. In addition, in some states you must have a minimum amount of automobile insurance. When you register an automobile, you are given a certificate of registration. You should carry this important document with you when you drive the automobile.

Obtaining Your Driver's License

To drive your automobile, you must have a driver's license issued by the state in which you live. To obtain this license, you must meet the state's requirements. These usually include a minimum age requirement, a test of your sight, a written test of the state's road regulations, and a road test of your driving skill. Like your registration certificate, your driver's license should be carried with you whenever you drive your automobile.

Your driver's license must be renewed periodically. There is a fee for each renewal. Check with your state's department of motor vehicles for any other requirements.

Buying Automobile Insurance

Automobile insurance protects you from financial loss if you are involved in an automobile accident. Automobile insurance is required by law in most, but not all, states. There are six basic types of automobile insurance. To learn about each type, see the chart on pages 382–383. These types may be combined in different ways to provide the coverage you need, want, and can afford.

(continued on page 384)

The standard system of automobile liability insurance depends on determining who was at fault in a given accident. Here is how the system works:

- *If you were at fault*, persons who were harmed or whose property was harmed may claim damage payments from you. Any successful claims will be repaid by your insurance company up to the limit of your policy.
- *If another driver was at fault*, and if you or your property was harmed, you can claim damage payments from that other driver. That driver's insurance company will repay successful claims up to the limit of the policy.

In some states, this system has been replaced by the use of no-fault insurance. **No-fault insurance** is a type of insurance that permits drivers to claim damages from their own insurance companies no matter which driver caused the accident. This system was developed to cut out the lengthy and expensive legal process of determining who was at fault in an accident. However, even under this system, drivers can sue others for damages under certain conditions.

Before you decide on a policy, discuss the advantages of each type of coverage with an insurance agent. Find out about discounts you may be eligible for. Discounts may be offered, for example, if you have a good driving record or if you have taken a driver education course. There are also discounts that depend on the number of automobiles you own and on their age, make, and model.

Shop around for the best coverage at the lowest price. There is often a great difference in policy costs from one company to another. Get several offers before you buy.

Maintaining and Repairing Your Automobile

Every automobile requires regular maintenance to keep it running reliably and smoothly. Regular maintenance is also needed to protect the resale value. The maintenance schedule varies with the make and model of your automobile. To learn what is proper for your automobile, check your owner's manual. Here are the most important elements in a maintenance schedule:

- *fluid check.* Check the levels of the brake fluid, transmission fluid, engine oil, power steering fluid, and antifreeze. Add more fluid as needed.
- *oil change.* Change the engine oil and replace the oil filter.
- *tune-up.* Replace the spark plugs, points, condenser if applicable, air filter, fuel filter, and PCV valve. Check the engine timing and adjust the carburetor. You may also replace the spark plug cables, distributor cap, and rotor.
- *brake check.* Inspect and, if necessary, replace the brake pads.
- *radiator check.* Flush the radiator and replace the coolant.
- *tire check.* Rotate the tires as recommended by your mechanic. Check to see that the tires are inflated to the proper pressure. This pressure is listed in your owner's manual or on a sticker located on the door jamb on the driver's side.

You can save on labor charges if you do some of the maintenance yourself. You can save on parts and supplies if you buy them at discount stores. Your owner's manual will provide instructions for maintenance tasks.

Repairs are another responsibility of automobile ownership. You do not have to be an expert mechanic. However, in an emergency, you should know how to change a tire and install a new fan belt. For safety, your automobile should always carry some basic repair equipment such as pliers, a screwdriver, a jack, a flashlight, and a tire gauge. You should also always have a first-aid kit.

More complicated maintenance tasks and repairs take greater care and usually require a specialist. For example, you will probably want to hire a mechanic for brake maintenance, wheel alignment, and repairs to the exhaust system. For information on how computers are used today to identify automobile repair needs, see page 385.

How Computers Can Help You

A Computer in Your Automobile

Besides the driver and the people in the other seats, more and more of today's automobiles carry another passenger—a computer! Now included on many automobile makes and models, an on-board computer can greatly improve safety and reliability. The computer can watch over many of the automobile's functions to make sure that everything is running smoothly. Also, if anything goes wrong, the computer can diagnose the problem and help indicate a solution. Some computers even have a "voice" that will alert the driver to safety problems.

One of the most important monitoring functions of an on-board computer is to check the exhaust for pollution control. Another is to check the mix of gasoline and air in the fuel supply and make adjustments as needed. Some computers can even check the brakes to ensure stopping ability.

Many of today's on-board automobile computers can be connected directly to computers in automobile repair shops. That way, data from the on-board computer can be analyzed to diagnose problems. This diagnosis tells the mechanic exactly what repairs to make.

In the future, on-board computers in automobiles may also provide many other convenience features. One feature might be computer-controlled road maps. These maps would appear on small display screens on the dashboard. They would show the automobile's position against a series of map "backgrounds" of the area through which the automobile was traveling. The maps would be transmitted from satellites in orbit above the earth. Perhaps someday almost all automobile functions will be controlled by on-board computers.

Belonging to an Auto Club

To be sure you can find help when your automobile needs repairs, you might want to belong to an auto club. Auto clubs offer their members services such as free towing, jump starts for dead batteries, and tire change and repair. Members can usually obtain these services at any time just by making a telephone call. Some clubs also offer other benefits, such as insurance, travel agency services, and discounts at selected hotels and restaurants.

There are many auto clubs to choose from. Decide which services you want and need. Then, look for a club that offers those services at the best price. Most clubs offer yearly memberships at reasonable rates.

Points to Remember

- The form of transportation you choose should always be safe. If possible, it should also be convenient and help you conserve resources.
- The full cost of automobile ownership includes the purchase price, upkeep costs, and depreciation.
- If you need an automobile for only a short time, you may choose to rent one. If you need it for a longer time, you might want to lease one.
- How you will use an automobile determines the size, style, and options you will need.
- Whether you buy a new or used automobile depends on your financial resources and intended use.
- Before buying an automobile, inspect it inside and out and take it for a test drive.
- Owning an automobile means that you must keep your registration, license, and insurance up to date.
- You have a better chance of keeping your automobile in good condition if you follow the maintenance schedule in your owner's manual.

Test Your Skills

DECISION MAKING

Imagine yourself in the situation described below. In this situation, a decision is needed. As you read, think about how to make good decisions. Then, answer the questions that follow. When you make decisions in the future, remember to ask yourself these questions.

Situation

To get to and from your job, you ride the bus. The weekly fare is $10. However, the bus is very slow. There are frequent delays that make you late for work. Also, in winter, waiting at the bus stop is very unpleasant. You are thinking about finding a different form of transportation.

You could probably afford to buy a used automobile. Counting all the costs—monthly payments, upkeep costs, and so on—owning even a used automobile would be much more expensive than taking the bus. However, with an automobile you could easily get to and from a second job, so perhaps you could earn more income.

Charlie's Used Cars is selling a used sports car that you would enjoy owning. However, no matter what the financing plan, the payments would be very high. With all the upkeep costs, you might have to spend every spare dollar of your present income. Perhaps instead you should consider one of Charlie's less attractive, lower-priced models. A third alternative is the used automobile your cousin is selling. Its price is the lowest of all, but it is very old and may need frequent repairs.

Questions

1. What is the problem?

2. What information do you need to help you make a decision?

3. Which of your values, goals, and resources may affect your decision?

4. List three decisions you could make. What are their possible consequences?

5. What is the best decision you could make? Why is it the best for you? What is the next best decision?

Terms

On a separate sheet of paper, write a definition for each of the underlined terms below. Base your definition on the clues you find in the statement(s).

1. Lesli likes the idea of ridesharing. By riding to work with a neighbor and sharing the driving expenses, she gets to and from work and saves money as well.

2. Where Joe lives, fog sometimes combines with smoke and chemical fumes from cars and other sources. On those days, the smog that results blocks the sun.

3. Meredith did not realize that the new car she wanted to buy would lose value as soon as she started driving it. Now, she knows that the value of most products drops as they are used and as they get older. She understands what depreciation means.

4. Sergio's car gets 20 miles (32 km) per gallon of fuel when Sergio drives around town. Sergio thinks his car's gas mileage is reasonable for the type of stop-and-go driving he has to do.

5. DeeAnn keeps in a safe place the title that proves she owns her motorcycle.

6. Lane wants a truck with lots of extras. Unfortunately, the sticker price for new trucks with the features Lane wants is higher than he can afford. Lane hopes to find a dealer who will sell him his first choice for less than the sticker price.

7. Stacie is interested in a new car with no extras, just standard equipment. She plans to tell a dealer that she will only pay the base price for a car and does not want a model that is loaded with extra features.

8. Ross purchased a used van for its book value. He looked up the van's standard price in the *National Automobile Dealers Association Used Car Guide*.

9. Hoa lives in a state that has no-fault insurance. If she is in an automobile accident, she can claim damages from her own insurance company. She can do this, no matter which driver caused the accident.

Questions

1. Name two ways to conserve environmental resources when traveling from one place to another.

2. Why is it important to understand the effect of depreciation?

3. What are four of the questions you should ask yourself when selecting an automobile make and model?
4. Name three places you can shop for used automobiles.
5. List four factors to check when you are taking an automobile for a test drive.
6. Why are automobiles not sold on the basis of a fixed retail price?
7. What factors cause used-automobile prices to vary?
8. If you need a loan to pay for an automobile, what are three of the types of financial institutions you can check with?
9. How often must an automobile be registered with the state department of vehicles?
10. Briefly describe the six types of automobile insurance and the reason or purpose for each.
11. Identify the most important elements in a regular maintenance program for an automobile.

Activities

1. Explore the different ways to get around in your community. Decide which form of transportation is best for you and why in each of the following situations: going to school, to a part-time job, to buy groceries, to buy shoes, to the post office, and to visit friends or relatives. To help you decide which form is best and why, consider safety, convenience, and resource conservation.
2. Go shopping for a new automobile. Make a cost chart that includes the sticker price, options, freight charges, sales tax, and other costs.
3. Think of a new automobile that you might like to buy. Check to see if *Consumer Reports* rates that make and model. If so, report any new information you learn from the article. How might this information influence your decision to buy that particular make and model?
4. Pretend that you are selling a used automobile. The automobile could be yours, your family's, or a friend's. Write an ad that includes the price, important features, and an indication of quality. Check the book value of your make and model to help you set a fair price.
5. Estimate the yearly costs for automobile registration, insurance, gasoline, and oil changes for your own, your family's, or a friend's automobile. What can you conclude about these costs of automobile ownership?

Appendixes   392

Glossary   416

Index   426

Appendix 1

Maslow's Hierarchy of Needs

One of the best-known theories about human behavior is the "hierarchy of needs" described by the psychologist Abraham Maslow (1908–1970). (A *hierarchy* is a ranking system.) This theory lists a number of different kinds of needs that Maslow believed influence people's behavior. Maslow's theory is illustrated in the following diagram.

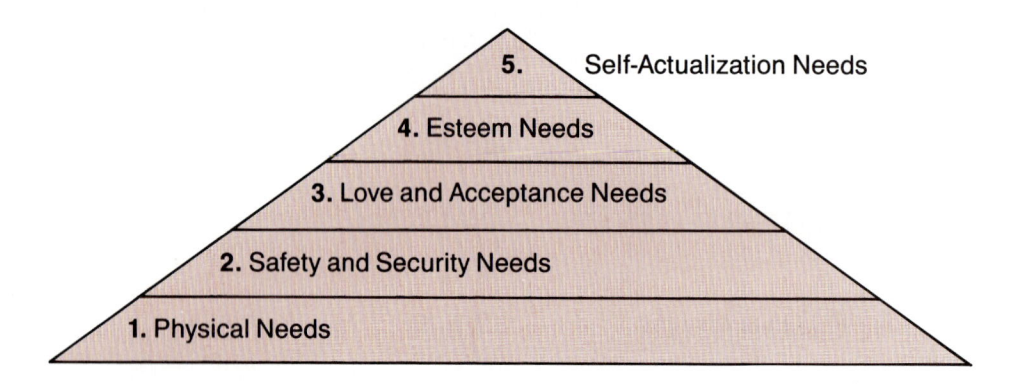

```
                    5.    Self-Actualization Needs
                 4. Esteem Needs
            3. Love and Acceptance Needs
         2. Safety and Security Needs
    1. Physical Needs
```

Each level in this "pyramid" represents a different category of human need. Level 1 represents the basic physical needs that must be met for the body to survive. These include the need to eat, the need to breathe, the need to rest, and the like. Level 2 represents the need to feel safe, now and in the future. Level 3 represents the need for loving relationships with other people and for the feeling of belonging in a social group. Level 4 represents the need to feel self-respect and to be recognized by others as a worthwhile person. Level 5, the topmost level, represents the need for self-actualization. This is the need to develop new skills and abilities, to be creative, and to find fulfillment in helping others.

Maslow arranged these needs in the order shown because he believed that people can "grow" psychologically from one level to the next. That is, when people succeed in meeting the needs of one level, they can move on to satisfying needs on the next-highest level. For example, according to the theory, when people meet their needs for food, rest, and the like, they can begin concentrating on meeting their need for safety. Of course, the theory also implies that people must satisfy each level before they can progress to the next one. For example, a person will not be able to concentrate fully on esteem needs until the need for love and acceptance has been met.

According to Maslow, the higher a person progresses through these levels of needs, the greater that person's happiness and sense of well-being. Those who have reached the top level are the happiest of all. They are free to concentrate on realizing their full potential as human beings.

Appendix 2

Practical Manners

Good manners has been called the art of helping other people feel comfortable. More than a set of rules, good manners makes you more pleasant and fun to be with. It helps you enjoy yourself more, too. Here are a few basic rules of manners that you should know.

When Sending and Receiving Invitations

- When planning a party, call or send invitations a week in advance. Be sure to include the time, date, and place.

- When you receive an invitation that includes the letters "R.S.V.P.," respond promptly.

- A formal invitation, such as to a wedding, calls for a neatly written reply on good paper.

At a Dinner Party

- At a small dinner party, do not eat until all are served. At a larger party, follow the lead of your host or hostess.

- Rather than lean across the table, ask the nearest person to pass you a dish you want.

- Never groom your hair or apply makeup at the table.

When You Are a House Guest

- Follow the customs of your hosts as to wakeup and bedtime hours, mealtimes, and activities.

- Make your bed, tidy up your room, and offer to help your host or hostess in the kitchen.

- Write a thank-you note to your host or hostess within a day of your visit.

When Giving or Receiving Gifts

- Choose a gift that is not too showy and that is appropriate for the recipient.

- When opening gifts, express thanks for each one, even if you like some more than others.

- Send a thank-you note promptly for any gift you receive in the mail.

At a Wedding

- If part of the wedding party, you have special duties. For example, the best man safeguards the wedding ring for the groom and proposes the first toast at the reception.

- At a wedding ceremony, sit where the ushers direct you. Some seats will be reserved.

- It is customary to wish the bride happiness and to congratulate the groom.

When Someone Has Died

- Express your sympathy to family members in simple terms. "I am so sorry" or "We will all miss her" are appropriate remarks.

- Do not ask about the illness or manner of death, and do not try to make light of the loss.

- A note of sympathy will be appreciated. Keep it brief and sincere.

Rules for Tipping

- In a restaurant, tip the person who serves you. It is appropriate to tip 15 percent of the bill—more if the service is especially thoughtful.

- Tip a hair stylist 15 percent of the total charge. If the owner of the shop styles your hair, it is usually customary not to tip.

- In many places, building superintendents and others are tipped yearly. Ask a neighbor what the custom is.

On the Telephone

- When calling, always let the telephone ring at least six times. When someone answers, give your name immediately: "Hello, this is Peter. Is Maria there?"

- At work, answer the telephone with the company name ("ABC Toys") or the name of the person whose line is ringing ("Mr. Kim's office"). Ask who is calling and offer to take a message.

- Speak clearly when using the telephone. Use your normal tone of voice.

When Addressing Public Officials

- When writing to a mayor, a governor, or a member of Congress, address the letter to, for example, "The Honorable Barbara Jones," followed by the correct office name and address. The letter should begin, "Dear Sir" or "Dear Madam."

- When speaking with a public official, use the proper title. For example, a mayor may be called "Mayor Smith," "Mr. Mayor," or "Madam Mayor."

When Traveling Abroad

- Learn some of the customs of the country you are visiting, as well as a few words of the language—especially "please" and "thank you."

- Sample unfamiliar dishes, and show your appreciation of the ones you enjoy.

- Do not stare at local people, and ask permission before taking photographs.

Practical Manners 395

Appendix 3

How to Read Employment Ads

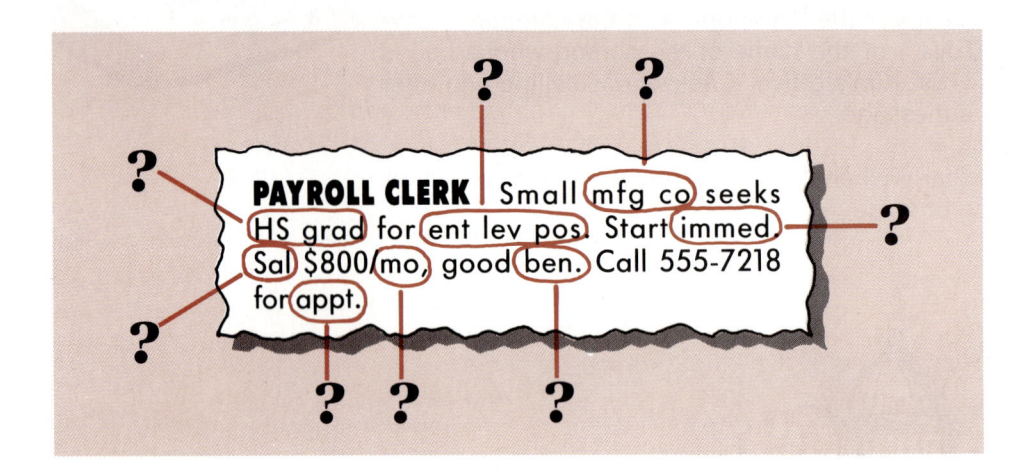

PAYROLL CLERK Small mfg co seeks HS grad for ent lev pos. Start immed. Sal $800/mo, good ben. Call 555-7218 for appt.

The employment ads that you see in newspapers often consist almost entirely of abbreviations. This style is used to save space because newspapers generally charge advertisers by the line. If the abbreviations are unfamiliar to you, the ads can be very confusing. Here is a list of the abbreviations most commonly used in employment ads.

Common Abbreviations in Employment Ads

What It Says	What It Means	What It Says	What It Means	What It Says	What It Means
admin	administrative	FT	full-time	pos	position
appl	apply	HS grad	high school graduate	pref	preferred
appt	appointment			PT	part-time
asst	assistant	immed	immediately	req	required
ben	benefits	incl	included	sal	salary
co	company	knowl	knowledge	secy	secretary
cust	customer	mfg	manufacturing	serv	service
EOE	equal opportunity employer	mgmt	management	supv	supervisor
		min	minimum	w	with
exc	excellent	mktg	marketing	wk	week
ent lev	entry-level	mo	month	wpm	words per minute
exp	experience	oppty	opportunity		

Appendix 4

Wills

What happens to your belongings when you die? If you have no will, the state decides. If you have a will, you decide.

A will is a legal document that tells who should receive your property after your death. A will can make sure that your wishes are carried out. It can also save your family and friends worry, arguments, and hard feelings. As a responsible adult, you should have a will, no matter how much property you have or how long you expect to live.

A simple will is quick and inexpensive to prepare. However, it is recommended that you have a lawyer prepare or review it. Clear and proper wording will ensure that the instructions in your will can be carried out.

A simple will, such as the one below, names an *executor*. This is a responsible person who will make sure that your will is carried out. It directs that your debts and funeral expenses be paid out of your estate promptly. Then, it tells to whom the remainder of your estate should be given.

At the end of the will must appear your signature and the signatures of at least two witnesses not named in the will. The witnesses are testifying that they know you and that you signed the will in their presence.

A will must be stored carefully. You and your lawyer should each keep a copy in a safe place. Check your will each year and make changes, with your lawyer's help, as needed. When you make a change, make sure that every copy of the old will is destroyed.

Another legal document that you may want to prepare is a *living will*. It tells your doctors to withdraw or withhold life support systems if you cannot survive without such aid. If you decide you want a living will, it is recommended that you have a lawyer prepare or review it. Give copies to your doctors and family members. Keep the original in your files. If you decide you no longer want a living will, make sure that every copy is destroyed.

I, Sarah Halpern, presently living at 1140 Bellevue Avenue in Oak Falls, New York, hereby make my last will and testament.

I appoint my sister, Rachael Halpern, to be executor of this will.

I direct my executor to pay my debts and funeral expenses out of my estate as soon as possible after my death.

I give the rest of my estate to my sister Rachael and my brother Michael, to be divided equally between them.

I have signed and sealed this will in the presence of witnesses on the 10th day of March, 198–.

_____
(Signed)

_____ _____
(Witness)   (Witness)

Appendix 6

Resisting Impulse Buying

When you shop, do you sometimes come home with many more items than you had planned—and with a lot less money? If so, you may be a victim of *impulse buying*—buying without thinking. This kind of buying is a sure way to break your budget.

Stores try to boost sales by encouraging impulse buying. Here are some facts to keep in mind as you shop. Being aware of them will help you resist the urge to "buy first, think later."

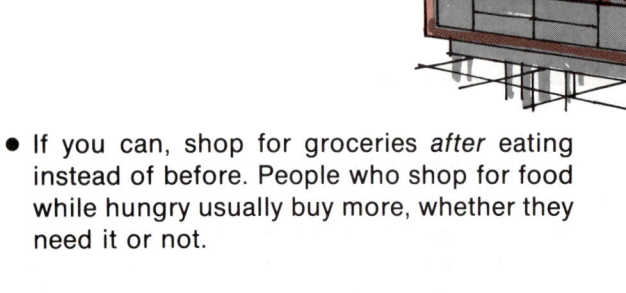

- If you can, shop for groceries *after* eating instead of before. People who shop for food while hungry usually buy more, whether they need it or not.

- Store layouts encourage sales of high-profit items. Shoppers usually buy more during their first few minutes in a store. Therefore, tempting, high-profit items are often put in the outside aisles, where people shop first.

- Giveaways and in-store demonstrations are used to sell new products. Sample the item if you like, but do not buy more unless you really need it.

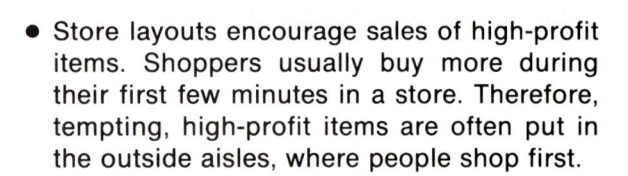

- Items are often placed in stacks or attractive displays at the end of an aisle. Do not assume that such items are lower-priced. They may not be! Compare prices before you buy.

- When an item is marked "Special Purchase" or "Our Low Price," do not assume that its price is any lower than usual. Unless it is marked "On Sale" or "Reduced," you cannot be sure, so compare first.

- To get the best buy on an item, you should probably not buy the smallest package. The largest package may not be the best buy, either. Check the *unit price* displayed by the store. For each size, it tells you how much the item costs per ounce or other unit of measure.

Resisting Impulse Buying **401**

- Cents-off coupons *can* save you money. But be sure that the item is one that you would buy anyway. Also, compare the reduced price with the prices of competing brands. A regular-priced brand may still cost you less.

- Shoppers are more likely to buy items stacked at eye level. As a result, stores sometimes put high-priced brands and packages at eye level, while placing low-priced ones close to the floor. Bending may bring you bargains!

- Displays near checkout lanes are designed to encourage impulse buying. Shoppers choose candy and other high-profit items while waiting in line. Before you buy, ask yourself if you really need the item.

Appendix 7

Agencies That Help Consumers

The following trade and professional organizations will help resolve complaints about specific types of businesses:

Major Appliance Consumer Action Panel
20 North Wacker Drive
Chicago, IL 60606
(800) 621-0477 *(toll-free)*

Automotive Consumer Action Program
 (AUTOCAP)
8400 Westpark Drive
McLean, VA 22102

Furniture Industry Consumer Advisory
 Panel
P.O. Box 951
High Point, NC 27261

American Medical Association
535 North Dearborn Street
Chicago, IL 60610

Direct Marketing Association
Mail Order Action Line
6 East 43rd Street
New York, NY 10017

The following federal government agencies offer advice and assistance to consumers:

Consumer Product Safety Commission
Washington, DC 20207
202-492-6800 *(in the District of Columbia)*
(800) 638-2772 *(toll-free elsewhere)*

Food and Drug Administration
Department of Health and Human Services
5600 Fishers Lane, HFE 88
Rockville, MD 20857
(deals with safety of food, drugs, cosmetics)

National Health Information Clearinghouse
P.O. Box 1133
Washington, DC 20013-1133
(703) 522-2590 *(in the District of Columbia)*
(800) 336-4797 *(toll-free elsewhere)*

Occupational Safety and Health
 Administration
Department of Labor
200 Constitution Avenue, N.W.
Washington, DC 20210
(deals with complaints about on-the-job safety)

Auto Safety Hotline
Department of Transportation
Washington, DC 20590
(202) 426-0123 *(in the District of Columbia)*
(800) 424-9393 *(toll-free elsewhere)*

National Credit Union Administration
1776 G Street, N.W.
Washington, DC 20456

U.S. Postal Service
Office of the Chief Postal Inspector
Washington, DC 20260
(deals with complaints of mail-order fraud)

Federal Trade Commission
Bureau of Consumer Protection
Washington, DC 20580

U.S. Department of Agriculture
Superintendent of Documents
U.S. Government Printing Office
Washington, DC 20402

Appendix 8
Nutritive Values of Foods

Adapted from *Nutritive Value of Foods,* Home and Garden Bulletin by the United States Department of Agriculture—Agricultural Research Service.

Food	Portion	Food Energy (Calories)	Protein (Grams)	Fat Total (Grams)	Fat Saturated (Grams)
Dairy Products (Cheese, Cream, Imitation Cream, Milk); Related Products					
Cheddar cheese	1 oz	115	7	9	6.1
Cottage cheese, low fat (2%)	1 cup	205	31	4	2.8
Mozzarella cheese, whole milk	1 oz	90	6	7	4.4
Mozzarella cheese, part skim milk	1 oz	80	8	5	3.1
Parmesan cheese	1 tbsp	25	2	2	1.0
American cheese, processed	1 oz	105	6	9	5.6
Swiss cheese, processed	1 oz	95	7	7	4.5
Half-and-half (cream and milk)	1 cup	315	7	28	17.3
Whipping cream, heavy	1 cup	820	5	88	54.8
Sour cream	1 cup	495	7	48	30.0
Whole milk (3.3% fat)	1 cup	150	8	8	5.1
Low-fat milk (2% fat)	1 cup	120	8	5	2.9
Nonfat milk (skim)	1 cup	85	8	Trace	.3
Chocolate milk	1 cup	210	8	8	5.3
Chocolate milk shake, thick	1 container (10.6 oz)	355	9	8	5.0
Ice cream, hardened (about 11% fat)	1 cup	270	5	14	8.9
Ice cream, soft serve	1 cup	375	7	23	13.5
Baked custard	1 cup	305	14	15	6.8
Chocolate pudding from mix, cooked	1 cup	320	9	8	4.3
Yogurt, fruit-flavored	1 8-oz container	230	10	3	1.8
Yogurt, plain	1 8-oz container	145	12	4	2.3
Eggs					
Cooked, fried in butter	1 egg	85	5	6	2.4
Cooked, scrambled	1 egg	95	6	7	2.8
Fats, Oils; Related Products					
Butter	1 tbsp	100	Trace	12	7.2
Margarine	1 tbsp	100	Trace	12	2.1
Corn oil	1 tbsp	120	0	14	1.7
French dressing	1 tbsp	65	Trace	6	1.1
Italian dressing	1 tbsp	85	Trace	9	1.6
Mayonnaise	1 tbsp	100	Trace	11	2.0

Carbo-hydrate	Calcium	Phos-phorus	Iron	Vitamin A	Thiamine	Ribo-flavin	Niacin	Ascorbic Acid
Grams	Milli-grams	Milli-grams	Milli-grams	Inter-nat'l units	Milli-grams	Milli-grams	Milli-grams	Milli-grams
Trace	204	145	.2	300	.01	.11	Trace	0
8	155	340	.4	160	.05	.42	.3	Trace
1	163	117	.1	260	Trace	.08	Trace	0
1	207	149	.1	180	.01	.10	Trace	0
Trace	69	40	Trace	40	Trace	.02	Trace	0
Trace	174	211	.1	340	.01	.10	Trace	0
1	219	216	.2	230	Trace	.08	Trace	0
10	254	230	.2	260	.08	.36	.2	2
7	154	149	.1	3,500	.05	.26	.1	1
10	268	195	.1	1,820	.08	.34	.2	2
11	291	228	.1	310	.09	.40	.2	2
12	297	232	.1	500	.10	.40	.2	2
12	302	247	.1	500	.09	.37	.2	2
26	280	251	.6	300	.09	.41	.3	2
63	396	378	.9	260	.14	.67	.4	0
32	176	134	.1	540	.05	.33	.1	1
38	236	199	.4	790	.08	.45	.2	1
29	297	310	1.1	930	.11	.50	.3	1
59	265	247	.8	340	.05	.39	.3	2
42	343	269	.2	120	.08	.40	.2	1
16	415	326	.2	150	.10	.49	.3	2
1	26	80	.9	290	.03	.13	Trace	0
1	47	97	.9	310	.04	.16	Trace	0
Trace	3	3	Trace	430	Trace	Trace	Trace	0
Trace	3	3	Trace	470	Trace	Trace	Trace	0
0	0	0	0	—	0	0	0	0
3	2	2	.1	—	—	—	—	—
1	2	1	Trace	Trace	Trace	Trace	Trace	—
Trace	3	4	.1	40	Trace	.01	Trace	—

Nutritive Values of Foods

Food	Portion	Food Energy	Protein	Fat Total	Fat Saturated
		Calories	Grams	Grams	Grams
Fish, Shellfish, Meat, Poultry; Related Products					
Fish sticks, breaded, frozen	1 fish stick	50	5	3	—
Salmon, canned	3 oz	120	17	5	.9
Tuna, canned in oil, drained	3 oz	170	24	7	1.7
Tuna salad	1 cup	350	30	22	4.3
Bacon, broiled or fried, crisp	2 slices	85	4	8	2.5
Ground beef, lean with 10% fat	3 oz	185	23	10	4.0
Ground beef, lean with 21% fat	2.9 oz	235	20	17	7.0
Roast beef, lean and fat	3 oz	165	25	7	2.8
Sirloin steak, lean and fat	3 oz	330	20	27	11.3
Beef and vegetable stew	1 cup	220	16	11	4.9
Chili con carne with beans, canned	1 cup	340	19	16	7.5
Lamb chop, lean and fat	3.1 oz	360	18	32	14.8
Beef liver, fried	3 oz	195	22	9	2.5
Ham, light cure, lean and fat, roasted	3 oz	245	18	19	6.8
Boiled ham	1 slice	65	5	5	1.7
Pork chop, broiled, lean and fat	2.7 oz	305	19	25	8.9
Brown and serve sausage	1 link	70	3	6	2.3
Bologna	1 slice	85	3	8	3.0
Frankfurter	1 frank	170	7	15	5.6
Salami	1 slice	90	5	7	3.1
Chicken breast, fried	2.8 oz	160	26	5	1.4
Chicken drumstick, fried	1.3 oz	90	12	4	1.1
Chicken half, broiled	6.2 oz	240	42	7	2.2
Chicken chow mein, canned	1 cup	95	7	Trace	—
Turkey, roasted	3 slices	160	27	5	1.5
Fruits and Fruit Products					
Apples, raw, unpeeled	1 apple	80	Trace	1	—
Apple juice, bottled or canned	1 cup	120	Trace	Trace	—
Banana	1 banana	100	1	Trace	—
Fruit cocktail, canned, in heavy syrup	1 cup	195	1	Trace	—
Grapefruit, raw	½ grapefruit	50	1	Trace	—
Grapes	10 grapes	35	Trace	Trace	—
Grape drink, canned	1 cup	135	Trace	Trace	—
Cantaloupe	½ melon	80	2	Trace	—
Lemonade, concentrate, frozen; diluted	1 cup	105	Trace	Trace	—
Oranges, raw	1 orange	65	1	Trace	—
Orange juice, frozen	1 cup	120	2	Trace	—

Carbo-hydrate	Calcium	Phos-phorus	Iron	Vitamin A	Thiamine	Ribo-flavin	Niacin	Ascorbic Acid
Grams	Milli-grams	Milli-grams	Milli-grams	Inter-nat'l units	Milli-grams	Milli-grams	Milli-grams	Milli-grams
2	3	47	.1	0	.01	.02	.5	—
0	167	243	.7	60	.03	.16	6.8	—
0	7	199	1.6	70	.04	.10	10.1	—
7	41	291	2.7	590	.08	.23	10.3	2
Trace	2	34	.5	0	.08	.05	.8	—
0	10	196	3.0	20	.08	.20	5.1	—
0	9	159	2.6	30	.07	.17	4.4	—
0	11	208	3.2	10	.06	.19	4.5	—
0	9	162	2.5	50	.05	.15	4.0	—
15	29	184	2.9	2,400	.15	.17	4.7	17
31	82	321	4.3	150	.08	.18	3.3	—
0	8	139	1.0	—	.11	.19	4.1	—
5	9	405	7.5	45,390	.22	3.56	14.0	23
0	8	146	2.2	0	.40	.15	3.1	—
0	3	47	.8	0	.12	.04	.7	—
0	9	209	2.7	0	.75	.22	4.5	—
Trace	—	—	—	—	—	—	—	—
Trace	2	36	.5	—	.05	.06	.7	—
1	3	57	.8	—	.08	.11	1.4	—
Trace	3	57	.7	—	.07	.07	1.2	—
1	9	218	1.3	70	.04	.17	11.6	—
Trace	6	89	.9	50	.03	.15	2.7	—
0	16	355	3.0	160	.09	.34	15.5	—
18	45	85	1.3	150	.05	.10	1.0	13
0	7	213	1.5	—	.04	.15	6.5	—
20	10	14	.4	120	.04	.03	.1	6
30	15	22	1.5	—	.02	.05	.2	2
26	10	31	.8	230	.06	.07	.8	12
50	23	31	1.0	360	.05	.03	1.0	5
13	20	20	.5	540	.05	.02	.2	44
9	6	10	.2	50	.03	.02	.2	2
35	8	10	.3	—	.03	.03	.3	Trace
20	38	44	1.1	9,240	.11	.08	1.6	90
28	2	3	.1	10	.01	.02	.2	17
16	54	26	.5	260	.13	.05	.5	66
29	25	42	.2	540	.23	.03	.9	120

Nutritive Values of Foods

Food	Portion	Food Energy	Protein	Fat Total	Fat Saturated
		Calories	Grams	Grams	Grams
Fruits and Fruit Products (continued)					
Peaches, raw	1 peach	40	1	Trace	—
Peaches, canned, water packed	1 cup	75	1	Trace	—
Pears, raw	1 pear	100	1	1	—
Pineapple, canned, heavy syrup	1 cup	190	1	Trace	—
Raisins, seedless	1½ oz packet	40	Trace	Trace	—
Strawberries, raw	1 cup	55	1	1	—
Strawberries, frozen	1 container	310	1	1	—
Watermelon	1 wedge	110	2	1	—
Grain Products					
Bagel	1 bagel	165	6	2	0.5
Biscuits, from a mix	1 biscuit	90	2	3	.6
Italian bread, slice	1 slice	85	3	Trace	Trace
White bread, enriched	1 slice	70	2	1	.2
Whole-wheat bread	1 slice	60	3	1	.1
Grits or hominy	1 cup	125	3	Trace	Trace
Oatmeal	1 cup	130	5	2	.4
Cornflakes	1 cup	95	2	Trace	—
Puffed rice	1 cup	60	1	Trace	—
Wheat flakes	1 cup	105	3	Trace	—
Angelfood cake	1 piece	135	3	Trace	—
Cupcakes with chocolate icing	1 cupcake	130	2	5	2.0
Devil's food cake with chocolate icing	1 piece	235	3	8	3.1
Pound cake	1 slice	160	2	10	2.5
Brownies with nuts, from home recipe	1 brownie	95	1	6	1.5
Chocolate chip cookies, from home recipe	4 cookies	205	2	12	3.5
Oatmeal and raisin cookies	4 cookies	235	3	8	2.0
Crackers, rye wafers	2 wafers	45	2	Trace	—
Doughnuts, yeast-leavened, glazed	1 doughnut	205	3	11	3.3
Macaroni and cheese, from home recipe	1 cup	430	17	22	8.9
Corn muffins	1 muffin	125	3	4	1.2
Egg noodles	1 cup	200	7	2	—
Noodles, chow mein, canned	1 cup	220	6	11	—
Pancakes, made from mix	1 pancake	60	2	2	.7
Pie, apple	1/7 of pie	345	3	15	3.9
Pie, pumpkin	1/7 of pie	275	5	15	5.4
Pizza, cheese	1 sector	145	6	4	1.7

Carbo-hydrate	Calcium	Phos-phorus	Iron	Vitamin A	Thiamine	Ribo-flavin	Niacin	Ascorbic Acid
Grams	Milli-grams	Milli-grams	Milli-grams	Inter-nat'l units	Milli-grams	Milli-grams	Milli-grams	Milli-grams
10	9	19	.5	1,330	.02	.05	1.0	7
20	10	32	.7	1,100	.02	.07	1.5	7
25	13	18	.5	30	.03	.07	.2	7
49	28	13	.8	130	.20	.05	.5	18
11	9	14	.5	Trace	.02	.01	.1	Trace
13	31	31	1.5	90	.04	.10	.9	88
79	40	48	2.0	90	.06	.17	1.4	151
27	30	43	2.1	2,510	.13	.13	.9	30
28	9	43	1.2	30	.14	.10	1.2	0
15	19	65	.6	Trace	.09	.08	.8	Trace
17	5	23	.7	0	.12	.07	1.0	0
13	21	24	.6	Trace	.10	.06	.8	Trace
12	25	57	.8	Trace	.06	.03	.7	Trace
27	2	25	.7	Trace	.10	.07	1.0	0
23	22	137	1.4	0	.19	.05	.2	0
21	Trace	9	.6	1,180	.29	.35	2.9	9
13	3	14	.3	0	.07	.01	.7	0
24	12	83	Trace	1,410	.35	.42	3.5	11
32	50	63	.2	0	.03	.08	.3	0
21	47	71	.4	60	.05	.06	.4	Trace
40	41	72	1.0	100	.07	.10	.6	Trace
16	6	24	.5	80	.05	.06	.4	0
10	8	30	.4	40	.04	.03	.2	Trace
24	14	40	.8	40	.06	.06	.5	Trace
38	11	53	1.4	30	.15	.10	1.0	Trace
10	7	50	.5	0	.04	.03	.2	0
22	16	33	.6	25	.10	.10	.8	0
40	362	322	1.8	860	.20	.40	1.8	Trace
19	42	68	.7	120	.10	.10	.7	Trace
37	16	94	1.4	110	.22	.13	1.9	0
26	—	—	—	—	—	—	—	—
9	58	70	.3	70	.04	.06	.2	Trace
51	11	30	.9	40	.15	.11	1.3	2
32	66	90	1.0	3,210	.11	.18	1.0	Trace
22	86	89	1.1	230	.16	.18	1.6	4

Nutritive Values of Foods

Food	Portion	Food Energy	Protein	Fat Total	Fat Saturated
		Calories	Grams	Grams	Grams
Grain Products (continued)					
Popcorn, plain	1 cup	25	1	Trace	Trace
Rice, instant	1 cup	180	4	Trace	Trace
Rolls, brown-and-serve	1 roll	85	2	2	.4
Rolls, frankfurter and hamburger	1 roll	120	3	2	.5
Rolls, hoagie or submarine	1 roll	390	12	4	.9
Spaghetti with meatballs and tomato sauce	1 cup	330	19	12	3.3
Waffles, from mix	1 waffle	205	7	8	2.8
Legumes (Dry), Nuts, Seeds; Related Products					
White beans with pork and tomato sauce	1 cup	310	16	7	2.4
Black-eyed peas, cooked	1 cup	190	13	1	—
Peanuts, roasted	1 cup	840	37	72	13.7
Peanut butter	1 tbsp	95	4	8	1.5
Sunflower seeds, dry	1 cup	810	35	69	8.2
Sugars and Sweets					
Jams and preserves	1 tbsp	55	Trace	Trace	—
Jellies	1 tbsp	50	Trace	Trace	—
Granulated sugar	1 tbsp	45	0	0	0
Milk chocolate candy, plain	1 oz	145	2	9	5.5
Syrups, table blend	1 tbsp	60	0	0	0
Vegetables and Vegetable Products					
Broccoli, cooked	1 cup	40	5	Trace	—
Cabbage, coarsely shredded or sliced	1 cup	15	1	Trace	—
Carrots, raw	1 carrot	30	1	Trace	—
Cauliflower, raw	1 cup	31	3	Trace	—
Celery, raw	1 stalk	5	Trace	Trace	—
Collards, cooked	1 cup	65	7	1	—
Corn, whole kernel, canned	1 cup	175	5	1	—
Cucumber slices	6 lg. (⅛" thick)	5	Trace	Trace	—
Green beans	1 cup	30	2	Trace	—
Lettuce	1 cup	5	Trace	Trace	—
Mustard greens, cooked	1 cup	30	3	1	—
Peas, green, frozen	1 cup	110	8	Trace	—
Potatoes, baked	1 potato	145	4	Trace	—

Carbo-hydrate	Calcium	Phos-phorus	Iron	Vitamin A	Thiamine	Ribo-flavin	Niacin	Ascorbic Acid
Grams	Milli-grams	Milli-grams	Milli-grams	Inter-nat'l units	Milli-grams	Milli-grams	Milli-grams	Milli-grams
5	1	17	.2	—	—	.01	.1	0
40	5	31	1.3	0	.21	Trace	1.7	0
14	20	23	.5	Trace	.10	.06	.9	Trace
21	30	34	.8	Trace	.16	.10	1.3	Trace
75	58	115	3.0	Trace	.54	.32	4.5	Trace
39	124	236	3.7	1,590	.25	.30	4.0	22
27	179	257	1.0	170	.14	.22	.9	Trace
48	138	235	4.6	330	.20	.08	1.5	5
35	43	238	3.3	30	.40	.10	1.0	—
27	107	577	3.0	—	.46	.19	24.8	0
3	9	61	.3	—	.02	.02	2.4	0
29	174	1,214	10.3	70	2.84	.33	7.8	—
14	4	2	.2	Trace	Trace	.01	Trace	Trace
13	4	1	.3	Trace	Trace	.01	Trace	1
12	0	0	Trace	0	0	0	0	0
16	65	65	.3	80	.02	.10	.1	Trace
15	9	3	.8	0	0	0	0	0
7	136	96	1.2	3,880	.14	.31	1.2	140
4	34	20	.3	90	.04	.04	.02	33
7	27	26	.5	7,930	.04	.04	.4	6
6	29	64	1.3	70	.13	.12	.8	90
2	16	11	.1	110	.01	.01	.1	4
10	357	99	1.5	498	.21	.38	2.3	144
43	6	153	1.1	740	.06	.13	2.3	11
1	7	8	.3	70	.01	.01	.1	3
7	63	46	.8	680	.09	.11	.6	15
2	11	12	.3	180	.03	.03	.2	3
6	193	45	2.5	8,120	.11	.20	.8	67
19	30	138	3.0	216	.43	.14	2.7	21
33	14	101	1.1	Trace	.15	.07	2.7	31

Nutritive Values of Foods

Food	Portion	Food Energy	Protein	Fat Total	Fat Saturated
		Calories	Grams	Grams	Grams
Vegetables and Vegetable Products (continued)					
Potatoes, french-fried	10 strips	135	2	7	1.7
Potatoes, mashed, prepared from raw with milk and butter	1 cup	195	4	9	5.6
Potato chips	10 chips	115	1	8	2.1
Potato salad with cooked salad dressing	1 cup	250	7	7	2.0
Sweet potatoes, canned	1 piece	45	1	Trace	—
Tomatoes	1 tomato	25	1	Trace	—
Tomato catsup	1 tbsp	15	Trace	Trace	—
Vegetables, mixed, frozen	1 cup	115	6	1	—
Mustard, prepared, yellow	1 tsp	5	Trace	Trace	—
Miscellaneous Items					
Sweetened, nonalcoholic beverages					
Carbonated water	12 fl oz	115	0	0	0
Cola-type beverages	12 fl oz	145	0	0	0
Fruit-flavored sodas	12 fl oz	170	0	0	0
Ginger ale	12 fl oz	115	0	0	0
Root beer	12 fl oz	150	0	0	0
Gelatin dessert	1 cup	140	4	0	0
Soup, chicken noodle	1 cup	55	2	1	—
Soup, tomato	1 cup	90	2	3	.5
Soup, vegetable beef	1 cup	80	5	2	—

Carbo-hydrate	Calcium	Phos-phorus	Iron	Vitamin A	Thiamine	Ribo-flavin	Niacin	Ascorbic Acid
Grams	Milli-grams	Milli-grams	Milli-grams	Inter-nat'l units	Milli-grams	Milli-grams	Milli-grams	Milli-grams
18	8	56	.7	Trace	.07	.04	1.6	11
26	50	101	0.8	360	.17	.11	2.1	19
10	8	28	.4	Trace	.04	.01	1.0	3
41	80	160	1.5	350	.20	.18	2.8	28
10	10	16	.3	3,120	.02	.02	.2	6
6	16	33	.6	1,110	.07	.05	.9	28
4	3	8	.1	210	.01	.01	.2	2
24	46	115	2.4	9,010	.22	.13	2.0	15
Trace	4	4	.1	7	—	—	—	—
29	—	—	—	—	0	0	0	0
37	—	—	—	—	0	0	0	0
45	—	—	—	—	0	0	0	0
29	—	—	—	—	0	0	0	0
39	—	—	—	—	0	0	0	0
34	—	—	—	—	—	—	—	—
8	7	19	.2	50	.07	.05	.5	Trace
16	15	34	.7	1,000	.05	.05	1.2	12
10	12	49	.7	2,700	.05	.05	1.0	—

Nutritive Values of Foods

Appendix 9

Food Additives

Additive	Why It Is Used	Some Foods in Which It Is Used
Artificial Colors (red no. 40, blue no. 1 or 2, yellow no. 5 or 6, green no. 3)	to add color	candy desserts sausages soft drinks
Artificial Flavors	to add flavor	breakfast cereals candy desserts most processed foods soft drinks
Ascorbic Acid	to add vitamin C and to help preserve food	breakfast cereals soft drinks
Aspartame	to add sweetness	chewing gum cold breakfast cereals cold-drink mixes gelatin pudding
BHA or BHT	to preserve food	baking mixes breakfast cereals chewing gum instant potatoes
Carrageenan	to emulsify ingredients	chocolate milk ice cream infant formula
EDTA	to emulsify ingredients	margarine salad dressing soft drinks
Hydrolyzed Vegetable Protein	to add flavor	instant soups sauce mixes
Mannitol or Sorbitol	to add sweetness without adding many calories	candy chewing gum low-calorie foods
Monoglycerides or Diglycerides	to emulsify ingredients	baked products candy peanut butter
Monosodium Glutamate	to enhance flavor	cheese many processed foods seafood soup

Additive	Why It Is Used	Some Foods in Which It Is Used
Natural Colors Beta carotene	to add yellow coloring	baked products cheese
Caramel	to add tan or brown coloring	root beer syrup
Polysorbate 60	to emulsify ingredients	imitation dairy products
Propyl Gallate	to preserve food	meat products potato snack chips vegetable oils
Propylene Glycol	to emulsify ingredients	candy cheese ice cream salad dressing
Saccharin	to add sweetness	diet foods and drinks
Salt	to add flavor	many processed foods
Sodium Benzoate	to preserve food	many processed foods
Sodium Nitrate	to preserve food	frankfurters ham luncheon meat
Sorbitan Monosterate	to emulsify ingredients	cakes frozen puddings icings
Sugar	to add flavor	sweetened foods
Vanillin	to add flavor	baked goods candy ice cream

GLOSSARY

abrasive cleaner a cleaner that contains fine particles that help scour heavy soil

alcoholism a psychological and physical dependence on alcohol

alterationist a person, usually a clothing store employee, who changes the fit of clothing

annual percentage rate (APR) the rate of interest paid for the yearly use of credit

annual percentage yield (APY) the rate at which money will actually earn interest in a given savings plan in one year

annuity a plan by which a life insurance company agrees to provide the purchaser with a certain cash income

anorexia nervosa (an•o•REK•see•uh ner•VO•sah) a health problem experienced by people of normal weight or less who constantly see themselves as overweight and who therefore severely limit the amount of food they eat

apprenticeship program a job opportunity designed to teach a profession, trade, or craft through structured, practical experiences

aptitude a natural ability or talent

automatic overdraft a service that allows a person to write a check for an amount greater than the amount in the person's account

bait-and-switch advertising a deceptive sales practice in which stores deny customers the opportunity to buy the product or service advertised and, instead, offer another item that is higher in price or lower in quality

bankruptcy a procedure that forces a person who is deeply in debt to allow most of his or her assets to be sold at public auction

bartering the exchange of one person's skills, energy, time, or materials for someone else's

basal metabolism the amount of energy needed by the body when it is at rest

base price the price of an automobile with standard equipment only, before any extra features are added

basic food group a group of foods that supply many of the same nutrients

beneficiary a person who has been named by a policyholder to receive the benefits of the policyholder's insurance policy

benefit the dollar amount an insurance company pays for covered charges

bleach a whitening agent

body image how people appear physically to themselves and to others

body language the combination of posture, body movements and gestures, eye contact, and facial expressions that people use as they talk or use sign language

bond a loan to a company or government agency, normally repaid with interest and typically made for the purpose of investment

book value the standard price of a used automobile, based on the year, make, and model

budget a plan for using income to meet specific goals

build a person's combination of bone structure, muscle development, height, weight, and proportions

bulimia (byu•LIM•ee•uh) a health problem experienced by people who are obsessed with the fear of becoming overweight and yet crave food, and who therefore binge-eat and then induce vomiting and abuse laxatives

calorie a measure of the energy a person gets from food

cardiopulmonary resuscitation (CPR) a set of procedures to help a respiratory failure victim breathe and keep blood circulating

cardiovascular fitness having a strong heart and blood vessels that are able to circulate blood easily

care label in a garment, a sewn-in tag describing the care the garment will need

cash loan an amount of money borrowed for a specific purpose

cashier's check a check written on a financial institution's own account and signed by one of its officers

checking account statement a report of all checks, deposits, withdrawals, and charges made on a checking account during a given time

citizen a person who has the full rights and protection of a nation

civic duty what a person *must* do to contribute to the welfare of the nation

civic responsibility what a person *should* do to contribute to the welfare of the nation

claim in insurance terms, a policyholder's written notice to his or her insurance company that benefits are due

co-insurance clause a statement that requires a policyholder to pay a certain part of a covered charge

collateral property pledged as security in the event that payments are not made as was agreed

color scavenger a fiber that has a tendency to pick up soil and loose dyes from the wash water

coloring a person's combination of eye color, hair color, and skin color

commission a percentage of the dollar amount of products or services sold by an employee

communication the two-way process of sending and receiving messages

comparison shopping using several different sources of information before deciding which of several products or services to buy

compounding a method of calculating interest whereby at the end of each interest period, the interest earned during that period is added to the account total on which interest is figured for the next interest period

conditional sales contract a type of installment credit that requires a buyer to completely pay for a product before receiving legal ownership of it

consolidation loan a combination of many existing debts into *one* total debt

continuous-cleaning oven an oven in which regular cooking heat interacts with a special coating on the interior to prevent burned-on food splatters

cosigner a person who agrees to repay a loan if the borrower does not repay it

cost-of-living raise a pay increase equal to the percentage that prices of products and services have risen during the previous year

covered charge an expense that an insurance company agrees to help pay

credit an agreement to pay for current purchases some time in the future

credit bureau a company that gathers credit information on consumers and shares that information with creditors and other credit bureaus

credit insurance a type of insurance that pays credit obligations if a borrower dies or is disabled

credit rating a history of a person's credit accounts

crime watch program a cooperative effort by neighbors to stay alert to and report any suspicious activities occurring within their neighborhood

dead-end job a job that offers no possibilities for growth in either job duties or pay

debt the amount of money owed to a creditor

decision making choosing from among several alternatives

deductible the dollar amount a policyholder must pay for some covered charges before an insurance company begins paying any benefits

default failure to make payments when they are due

depreciation the amount of value an item purchased loses over time because of use

depression a condition characterized by feelings of deep sadness and hopelessness

diagnosis an identification of a disorder based on an analysis of symptoms

disability income insurance a risk-sharing plan that provides an employee some income during a long illness or while injured and unable to work

dividend a portion of company profits paid to a stockholder

dry-heat cooking a cooking method that uses no additional liquid to tenderize or flavor a food

drying cycle a temperature and time setting designed to dry certain types of fabrics

ease room for free and easy movement inside a garment

elements of design line, color, texture, and shape

eligibility a set of conditions that a person must meet to become a policyholder

emotional appeal an attempt to get a consumer to buy primarily on the basis of feelings

empathy a willingness to see and feel things from another person's point of view

emphasis accenting one part of a whole

employment ad a classified ad in which an employer or employment agency announces a job opening

employment agency an organization that offers professional assistance in locating a job

emulsifier a type of food additive that helps maintain or improve the texture and consistency of foods

endorsing signing the back of a check

evicted legally forced by the landlord to move from a housing unit

exchange policy a seller's policy that allows a customer to return an unwanted item and get either a replacement or an item that costs the same

excise tax a tax added to the purchase price of certain products and services

exclusion an expense that an insurance company does *not* agree to help pay

fabric finish any treatment of a fabric that either changes its appearance or improves its performance

fabric softener a laundry product that reduces static and helps fabrics feel soft, smell nice, and remain wrinkle-free

federal income tax the amount of money each wage earner must pay to help support the federal government

finance charge total amount of money paid for a purchase made on credit

financial priority the relative degree of importance a person gives to any one of his or her financial goals

fixed expense a payment made at set times and for about the same amount each time

flexible expense a payment that varies in amount each time it is made or that does not have to be made according to a schedule

floor plan an outline of a room or rooms that shows the location of walls, doors, windows, hallways, closets, and electrical outlets

food additive a natural or synthetic substance that is added to a food and that affects a particular characteristic of the food

food poisoning a physical condition that can occur in a person who eats food that has molded or is otherwise contaminated

fraud trickery or dishonesty used to get someone else's money or other resources

full warranty a guarantee that the warrantor, or backer of the warranty, will fix a defective product or part at no cost to the buyer

furnished rental a rental housing unit that is equipped with many basic home furnishings

furniture template a two-dimensional form that shows the amount of floor space a particular piece of furniture will occupy

gas mileage the number of miles an automobile can travel on a gallon of gas or diesel fuel

generic product a product that is generally sold in a plain package with no advertising

goal what a person sets in order to accomplish or get something he or she wants

government grade mark a symbol, established by a U.S. government agency, that indicates a specific level of taste, texture, and appearance for certain kinds of foods

government inspection stamp a symbol, established by a U.S. government agency, that indicates a food is wholesome and safe to eat

gratuity a tip

gross pay the amount of money earned by an employee—the pay before taxes and other deductions are made

hang tag on a garment, a removable label that may provide information concerning the manufacturer, fiber content, care, and other characteristics of the garment

harmony blending a variety of parts into a unified whole

health insurance a risk-sharing plan that helps pay medical or dental expenses

Heimlich maneuver a set of procedures used to force air out of a choking victim's windpipe in order to push out the material that is blocking the flow of air

heredity the combination of characteristics a person gets from parents and earlier ancestors

immersible capable of being placed under water; used in referring to certain electrical appliances

immunization a treatment for protection against a particular disease

implied warranty an unwritten guarantee that the item being purchased is in working order and can perform the task for which it was sold

impulse buying deciding to purchase an item on the spot just because the item suddenly seems appealing

Glossary **419**

pension plan an employment benefit whereby an employer regularly pays employees a set sum after they retire

perishable a food that can be stored for only a few weeks or less and must be refrigerated

personal data sheet or **résumé (REHZ • uh • may)** a one-page summary of a person's employment qualifications

personnel department the section of a large organization that handles hiring of new employees and other matters such as employee records and benefits

place setting the set of basic items used by a person for eating

policyholder a person who buys an insurance policy

prescription drug a drug that can be obtained only with a prescription

preservative a type of food additive that helps protect a food from browning, mold, or other damage from oxygen or bacteria

press cloth a piece of fabric, placed on top of a garment, to keep the iron from directly touching the garment

pressure point a point on the body where an artery passes over a bone

pretreating applying a cleaning agent directly to a heavily soiled or stained area before washing the item

pretreatment product a laundry aid that is sold separately as a spray or a liquid to work on spots, stains, and heavily soiled areas

primary colors red, yellow, and blue

principles of design proportion, rhythm, balance, emphasis, and harmony

priority the relative weight a person gives to a need, value, want, or goal

produce fresh fruits and vegetables

product label a piece of paper or cloth that carries a written identification or description of the product to which it is attached

professional attitude a concern for doing a job in a way that makes both the employee and employer proud

profit the amount of money a business has left after covering all of its expenses

promissory note a written promise to repay a loan under the conditions specified

promotion an increase in an employee's responsibility within an organization

promotional material the combination of messages that a business uses to interest consumers in its products or services

proportion the relationship among the parts of something and between each part and the whole, based on the way space is divided

provider a business from which a policyholder gets services related to an insurance policy

public transportation the type of transportation that is designed to take paying passengers where they want to go, usually within a set area and often along a set route

rain check a record from a store that shows a customer tried to buy during a sale but could not because the store ran out of the sale item; it allows the customer to buy the item at the sale price when the store gets in a new shipment

ready-to-wear apparel clothes and accessories that are mass-produced

real estate property—either vacant land, land with buildings on it, or buildings only

Recommended Dietary Allowances (RDAs) scientifically reached estimates of the highest amounts of basic nutrients that a healthy person might need each day

redress a remedy or solution to a problem

reference a person who can vouch for someone's character and ability

refund policy a seller's policy that allows a customer to return an unwanted item and get money back

regular charge account a credit account that requires full payment within thirty days for charge purchases

regular checking account an account that requires a minimum balance but usually no monthly service charge as long as the minimum balance is maintained

resource whatever it takes for a person to achieve a goal

resource management what people do to get the resources they need and then to use those resources to meet their goals

resource sharing a combining of resources by two or more people

resource substitution a person's use of one of his or her resources in place of another

resource trade an exchange of resources between two people

respiratory failure stopped breathing

return for credit policy a seller's policy that allows a customer to return an unwanted item and either get credit for future purchases or have the charge removed from the customer's charge account

revolving charge account a credit account that allows partial payments on charge purchases but charges interest on the unpaid balances

rhythm repetition of an image to create a flow

ridesharing a transportation method in which people who live and work near each other share the driving and the driving expenses involved in getting to and from work

safe-deposit box a metal container kept locked in a commercial bank or other financial institution and rented out to individuals for safe storage of important documents and other valuables

salary a fixed amount of money paid to an employee at fixed intervals throughout a year

sales tax a tax added to the purchase price of a wide variety of different items

savings account a savings plan that may not require a minimum deposit and does not specify a deposit period

savings certificate a savings plan that requires a specified amount and deposit period

savings plan a method that allows a person to deposit money with a financial institution, earn interest on it, and withdraw it in a fairly short period of time

seal of approval a symbol that indicates the product is endorsed by an independent agency

secondary colors those colors made by mixing two primary colors

security deposit the money a person pays to guarantee that he or she will take care of property and pay bills promptly

self-cleaning oven an oven in which a special cycle seals the oven shut, heats the interior to a very high temperature, and so burns off any food splatters

self-concept set of ideas a person has about himself or herself

self-esteem a sense of worth

severance pay the money a few employers give their employees to help cover expenses between jobs

shape the outline of an object

shock a condition in which the victim's body processes are severely depressed

shoplifting stealing merchandise from a store during business hours

side effect an unwanted and harmful reaction that a person may have to a given drug

small-claims court a court that handles minor legal disputes

solvent a substance capable of dissolving other substances

special checking account an account that requires a monthly service charge but no minimum balance

spending record a written statement of an individual's or family's expenses for a certain period

standard of living the combination of necessities, comforts, and luxuries a person can afford

starter set usually the set of items that four persons will use when eating

state income tax the amount of money each wage earner in a state must pay to help support the state government

sticker price the suggested retail price for a particular automobile

stock a share in the ownership of a company, usually acquired for the purpose of investment

stockbroker a person who buys and sells stock for others for a fee

stockholder a person who owns stock in a company and participates in the company's profits and losses

store-brand product a product that is processed for a specific store and sold under a label associated with that store

stress any force or influence that upsets a person or makes that person's body work harder than usual

sublet clause a part of some leases that allows a tenant to rent his or her rental unit to another person

substance abuse using any drug (including alcohol and tobacco) in heavy, repeated amounts that may damage health and also cause other problems; using any illegal drug

symptoms signals that the body gives to indicate a disorder

tax exemption or **tax allowance** an amount of income the Internal Revenue Service (IRS) says does not need to be taxed

tax-deferred annuity an annuity for which the buyer may avoid paying taxes on the purchase money until the annuity payments begin

taxes the source of money for all services provided by the government

tenant a person who pays rent and lives in a housing unit

texture an object's surface characteristic

title the legal document that shows ownership—for example, of an automobile

trade and professional organizations groups of trade or professional people who spend time, energy, and money promoting their industry or profession

traffic flow the pattern that people follow as they walk through and between rooms

traveler's check a check with a set denomination printed on it

underweight weighing more than 10 percent below one's desirable weight.

unemployment compensation the money a state offers for a limited number of weeks to persons who have lost their job and are looking for other work

unfurnished rental a rental housing unit that is equipped with a range and refrigerator but no other furnishings or equipment

unit pricing a system of marking items to show how much they cost according to a particular measurement, such as an ounce or a pound

Universal Product Code (UPC) the set of vertical lines and numbers that appears on product labels and that identifies the product's name and price when passed over an electronic scanner

value in general terms, an idea, belief, or quality that a person holds dear; in design terms, the lightness or darkness of a hue

verbal message a message expressed in words, whether spoken or written

vested eligible for pension benefits

wage the amount of money paid to an employee per hour or day, or for each piece of work completed

wage-earner plan a procedure that permits a debtor to repay debts over an extended period, usually three years

want something a person selects to meet a need

wardrobe classic a style of clothing and clothing accessories that has been popular for many years and changes only slightly from season to season

wardrobe fad a style of clothes and accessories that is popular for only a few weeks or months

wash cycle a series of cleaning actions used to clean a single load of laundry

water softener a chemical that ties up the minerals in hard water and allows soaps to work and detergents to work more efficiently

work cooperative program a job opportunity that allows students to gain paid work experience while completing their schooling

work policy a rule or procedure set by an employer to ensure that work is accomplished safely and efficiently

work-style preference the way a person likes to perform a job duty, in terms of work methods, work conditions, and the like

worker's compensation insurance a type of insurance that most employers buy to cover the cost of their employees' job-related illnesses and injuries

written warranty a statement in writing of what the seller, the manufacturer, or an independent agency guarantees about a product or service

W-2 form a statement of an employee's gross pay during a year and of the amounts withheld for income taxes and contributed to Social Security during that year

W-4 form the paperwork that authorizes an employer to deduct a certain amount of federal income tax from an employee's paycheck each pay period

INDEX

Abrasive cleaner, 237–38
Abuse
  physical, 354–55
  substance, 347–52
Accessories
  clothing. See Clothing; Wardrobe
  housing, 194, 230–32, 234–35
Accidents
  automobile, 348, 356, 370
  taking precautions against, 355–56, 370, 374
  treatments for, 362–64
Additives, food, 322–23, 414–15
Adulthood, 2–5, 8
Advertising, 149, 151, 400–402
  accuracy of, 145–46, 148–49, 151
  employment, 53, 396
  housing, 197, 198
Alcohol, 347–50
  and driving, 348, 370
Alcoholism, 348–49
Alterationist, 259
American Red Cross, 361, 362, 363
American Sign Language, 26, 28
Amino acids, 294–95
Annual percentage rate. See APR
Annual percentage yield. See APY
Annuities, 108
Anorexia nervosa, 344
Apartments, 200–201
Apparel, 248. See also Clothing; Wardrobe
Appliances, grooming, 288
Appliances, kitchen, 334, 336–37
  cleaning of, 238–40
  dishwasher, 336–37
  for preparing food, 191–92
Apprenticeship programs, 55, 57
APR (annual percentage rate), 129, 398–99
Aptitude, 50
APY (annual percentage yield), 106
Armed forces, 55
Ascorbic acid, 297, 299, 404–13, 414
Auto clubs, 386
Automated teller machines, 123
Automatic overdraft, 136

Automobiles, 373–86
  base price of, 380
  book value of, 380–81
  maintenance, 384, 385
  and other forms of transportation, 370–73, 374
  ownership costs, 373, 375–77
  responsibilities of owning, 381–86
  and safety, 348, 370
  selecting, 377–81
  sticker price of, 380

Bait-and-switch advertising, 146
Bakeware, 190–91
Balance, as a design principle, 220, 221–22, 223
Banking, electronic, 123
Banking and savings institutions, 105–6
  credit cards from, 132
  finance charges of, 128–29, 398–99
  investment plans from, 109
  loans from, 135–36, 381
  savings plans from, 104–5
Bankruptcy, 138
Bartering, 17
Basal metabolism, 305
Basic food group, 302–3
Bathroom
  fixtures, cleaning, 237–38
  supplies, organizing, 234
Beds, 189
Benefits
  insurance, 75
  job, 48, 72
Better Business Bureau (BBB), 146, 156–57, 170, 177–78
Bicycles, 374
Bleach, 272
Bleeding, 363
Blend, fabric, 254
Blinds (window), 193, 231
Blood alcohol levels, 348
Blood donor, 361
Blood pressure, 344–45, 353
Body image, 344
Body language, 28–30
Bonds, 109
Braille, 26, 28
Breads, 302–3, 326–29
Breast self-examination, 353–54
Budgeting, 94–103, 318

Build, of person, 251
Bulimia, 344
Burglar alarms, 203
Burns, 363–64
Buying. See also Shopping
  automobiles, 373–81
  impulse, 171, 400–402
  insurance, 75, 381–84
Buying clubs, 170

Calcium, 297–98, 299, 404–13
Calories, 304–5, 404–13
Cancer
  breast self-examination for, 353–54
  and tobacco, 350
  warning signs of, 354
Carbohydrates, 295, 307, 404–13
Cardiopulmonary resuscitation. See CPR
Cardiovascular fitness, 345
Care labels, on clothes, 256, 268
Career counseling, 50, 51
Carpets, 193–94, 230, 237
Cashier's check, 126–27
Cereals, 302–3, 328–29
Certificate of deposit, 104–5
Chairs, 189–90
Charge accounts, 131–33
Checking accounts, 120–26
Checks, types of, 120, 126–27
Cheese. See Dairy products
Chicken. See Poultry
Choices. See also Decisions
  adult, 4–5
  of products and services, 34–36, 146–47
Choking, 362–63
Cholesterol, 295, 296
Cigarettes, 350–51
Citizen, 36–37
Civic duties, 38–40
Civic responsibilities, 37–38
Cleaning
  of clothing, 256, 268–75
  household, 194, 235–40
  kitchen appliances for, 336–37
  storage of equipment and supplies for, 234–36
Clients, working with, 84, 85
Clinic, medical, 358
Clothing. See also Wardrobe
  cleaning, 256, 268–75
  ironing, 283–85

426 Index

mending, 275–82
packing, 284
selecting, 249–62
storing, 235, 283
Collateral, 130, 133, 134–35, 136
Collectibles, 110
Color, as a design element, 208, 212–17, 223
Coloring, personal, 251, 252
Color scavenger, fiber as, 269
Color schemes, 214–17
Color wheel, 212–13
Commission, as job payment, 47–48
Communication, 26–27. *See also* Messages
  styles of, 31
Community
  environment, influence of, 9–10
  and values, 12–13
Comparison shopping, 165–66
Complaint, letters of, 176, 177
Computers
  in automobiles, 385
  budgeting by, 103
  for checkout systems, 318–19
  for clothing designs, 260
  consumer information about, 150
  to detect medical problems, 359
  and electronic banking, 123
  furniture arranging by, 228
  and home safety systems, 203
  for job and career counseling, 51
  nutritional analysis by, 301
  for recipes and shopping lists, 320
  as a resource, 18
  in sewing machines, 276
  shopping by, 167, 170
  for starting a business, 87
  and telecommunications, 27
Conditional sales contracts, 133–34
Conservation, and transportation, 372–73
Consolidation loan, 136
Consumer cooperatives, 168–69
Consumer Product Safety Commission (CPSC), 145, 403
Consumers
  agencies helping, list of, 403
  credit counseling for, 137
  information for, 145–46, 148–58

rights and responsibilities of, 144–48
Consumer's Bill of Rights, 144–45
Convenience foods, 311, 326–27
Cooking
  appliances for, 334, 336
  kitchen center for, 233
  methods of, 327–31
  with recipes, 331–33
Cookware, 190
Cooling, 199–200
Cosigning, for loan, 130, 134
Costs
  automobile, 373, 375–77
  housing, 186–87
  opportunity, 17, 164–65
Couches, 189–90
Counseling
  career, 50, 51
  credit, 137
  for emotional problems, 354, 360
County extension service, 158
Coupons, 172, 318, 402
Coworkers, working with, 83–85
CPR (cardiopulmonary resuscitation), 363
Credit, 127–38
  applying for, 129–31
  cash loans, 134–36
  charge accounts, 131–33
  conditional sales contracts, 133–34
  counseling about, 137
  problems with, 136–38
Credit bureau, 130
Credit cards, 131–33, 398–99
Credit insurance, 128–29
Credit rating, 130–31
Credit unions, 104, 106
  loans from, 135–36, 381
Crime-watch program, 199
Curtains, 193–94, 231, 237
Customers, working with, 84, 85

Dairy products, 302–3
  nutritive value of, 404–5
  preparing, 329
  storing, 326
Debt, 136
Decisions. *See also* Choices
  influences on, 5–11
  making, 17–20
Decorating, home, 229–32
Deductions, for taxes, 73–74, 80, 112
Default, on debt, 136
Democratic society, 36–40

Dental care, 287–88, 360
Dental insurance, 75, 77
Dentists, 360
Dependence, on drugs, 348, 351
Deposits, security, 186, 202
Depreciation costs, of automobile, 376
Depression, 354, 360
Design
  elements of, 208–19, 223, 229, 250
  principles of, 220–23, 229, 250
Detergents, 270–72
Development stages, of individuals and families, 7–9
Diabetes, 345
Diagnosis, of illness, 353
Diets, 306–8
Dinnerware, 192
Disability income insurance, 75, 77–78
Dishwasher, 336–37
Displays, product, 151
Dividends, stock, 109
Doctors, medical, 353, 358, 359
Door-to-door salespeople, 133, 170
Draperies, 193–94, 231, 237
Dress codes, 249
Driving
  and alcohol, 348
  safe, 356, 370
Drug abuse, 347–52
Drug labels, 357–58
Drugs, over-the-counter, 353
Drugs, prescription, 351, 357–58
Dry-cleaning, 256, 268
Dry-heat cooking, 327–28
Drying clothes, 274–75

Efficiency apartment, 197, 201
Eggs
  grading, 324
  nutritive value of, 404–5
  preparing, 329
  quality of, 325
  storing, 326
Electrical maintenance, 240
Electric shock, 355–56
Electronic banking, 123
Electronic mail, 27
Elements of design, 208–19, 223, 229, 250
Emergencies, 360–64
Emotional appeal, in ads, 149, 151
Emotional health, 347
Emotional problems, 354–55, 360

Index **427**

Empathy, 32
Emphasis, as a design principle, 220, 222, 223
Employment. *See* Job
Employment ads, 53, 396
Employment agencies, 53–55, 56
Endorsement, check, 122, 124
Energy. *See* Resources
Energy, and nutrients. *See* Food
Enriched food, 322–23
Environment, effect of transportation on, 372–73
Equal Credit Opportunity Act, 129, 131
Eviction, 202
Exchange policy, 176
Exchanging, clothes, 259
Excise tax, 40
Exercising, 345–46
Expenses
    and budgeting, 94–103
    household, 187
    types of, 94–95
Eye color, 251, 252

Fabrics
    clothing, 253–56
    dry-cleaning, 256, 268
    drying, 274–75
    for home sewing, 261–62
    household, 192–94
    sorting, for cleaning, 268–69
    texture of, 218–19
    washing, 269–74
Fabric softener, 272
Factory outlets, 166, 168–69
Fair Credit Billing Act, 131
Fair Credit Reporting Act, 131
Fair Debt Collection Practices Act, 136
Family
    environment, influence of, 6–9, 12
    relationships, 4
    responsibilities, 3–4
    roles, 4–5
    and values, 12
Fasteners, sewing on, 281–82
Fats, 295, 307, 344
    cooking with, 328
    in foods, 404–13
    saturated, reducing, 296
Fat-soluble vitamins, 296–97
Fatty acids, 295
FDA (Food and Drug Administration), 145, 323, 403
Federal Deposit Insurance Corporation, 106

Federal Savings and Loan Insurance Corporation, 106
Federal Trade Commission, 146
Fiber, in food, 295
Fibers, in clothing, 253–56
FICA (Federal Insurance Contribution Act), 79–80
Finance charges, 128–29, 398–99
Finance companies, 135–36, 381
Financial priorities, 96–97, 102
Fire prevention, 356
First aid, 362–64
Fish, 302–3
    nutritive value of, 406–7
    preparing, 329
    quality of, 325
    storing, 326
Fit, of clothing, 251, 253
Fitness, 344–46
Flatware, 192, 309
Flea markets, 166, 168–69
Floor coverings, 193–94, 230, 237
Floor plan, 227–29
Floors, cleaning, 237
Food
    additives, 322–23, 414–15
    basic groups, 302–3
    basic ingredients, 311
    energy, and nutrients, 294, 295, 305
    and fitness, 344–45
    grading, 324
    inspection, 324
    labels, 296, 300, 322–24
    nutritive values of, 404–13
    poisoning, 326–27
    preparation of, 326–38
    shopping for, 318–26
    storage and preparation center, 233
Food and Drug Administration. *See* FDA
Fortified food, 323
Fractures, 364
Fraud, 145
Freedoms
    adult, 4
    economic, 34
Free enterprise system, 34–36
Friends, 9–10, 52–53
Fruits, 302–3, 319, 324
    nutritive value of, 406–9
    preparing, 327–28
    storing, 326
Furnished rentals, 197
Furniture, 187–90
    arranging, 226–29
    cleaning, 237
    as a housing expense, 187, 197

Furniture template, 227, 229
Fuses, electrical, 240

Garage sale, 166
Garbage disposal, 337
Gas mileage, 378
Generic products, 152
Glassware, 192
Goals, 13–15
    and emotional health, 347
    financial, 96–97, 102
    and resources, 16
Government
    and consumer problems, 157–58, 178, 180, 403
    jobs in, 54–55
    participating in, 38
Government grade mark, 324
Government inspection stamp, 324
Grains, 408–11
Gratuity, 310, 394
Guarantees, 153–55
Gums and teeth, care of, 287–88, 360

Hair
    care products, 287
    color, 251, 252
    dryer, 288
Harmony, as a design principle, 220, 223
Health
    emergencies, 360–64
    insurance, 75, 76–77
    products and services, 356–60
Health maintenance organization. *See* HMO
Healthy lifestyle, 344–56
Heart
    and diet, 295, 344–45
    and exercise, 345–46
Heating, 199–201
Height, and weight, chart, 306
Heimlich maneuver, 362–63
Hems, 256, 257, 277, 280, 281, 282
Heredity, influence of, 6
HMO (health maintenance organization), 77
Home
    accident prevention, 355–56
    living arrangements, 195, 196
    security, computerized, 203
Homemaker, 2
Hospitals, 358–60

Housing
    accessories, 194, 230–32, 234–35
    costs of, 186–87
    furnishings for, 187–94
    renting, 197–204
Hue, 212–13
Hypervitaminosis, 297

Immunization, 358
Implied warranty, 153
Impulse buying, 171, 400–402
Income, and budget, 99–102
Income tax, 39, 111–12
    deductions for, 73–74, 80, 112
Individual retirement account. *See* IRA
Inflections, voice, 28, 29
Installment credit, 133–34, 375–76, 398–99
Insufficient funds, in checking account, 126
Insurance
    automobile, 381–84
    credit, 128–29
    dental, 75, 77
    for depositors, 106
    disability income, 75, 77–78
    group plans, 74–78
    household, 187
    life, 75, 78
    medical, 75, 76–77
    terminology, defined, 74–75
    worker's compensation, 77–78
Intensity, color, 213, 251
Interest (financial), 104
    on checking accounts, 121
    as finance charge, 128–29, 136, 398–99
    as income, 112
    and savings plans, 104–7
Interest-bearing checking account, 104
Interests (personal), 50
Internal Revenue Service. *See* IRS
Interview, job, 61–64
Investments, 108–11
Invitations, 393
Iodine, 297–98
IRA (individual retirement account), 108
Iron, in foods, 297–98, 299, 404–13
Ironing, 283, 285
IRS (Internal Revenue Service), 74, 111–12

Job
    advancement, 48, 82
    applying for a, 57–60
    availability, 48–50
    beginning a, 70–74
    benefits, 48, 72
    changing, 85–88
    computers for finding a, 51
    duties, 46–47
    finding a, 52–57
    interviews, 61–64
    orientation, 71
    pay, 47–48, 78–79
    performance evaluation, 72–73
    promotion, 48
    safety, 356
    security, 48
    setting, 47
Jury duty, 39

Keogh plan, 108
Kitchen appliances, 334, 336–37
    cleaning, 238–40
Kitchen equipment, 190–92
    cooking with, 332–34, 336
    storage of, 232–34
Kitchen work centers, 232–34
Kosher foods, 318

Labels
    care, on clothes, 256, 268
    drug, 357–58
    food, 296, 300, 322–24
    product, 151–52
Laundry, 235–36, 268–75
Leasing
    automobiles, 377
    housing, 202
Legal aid society, 179
Leisure, clothes for, 248–49
Letters
    of complaint, 176, 177
    job application, 58, 60
License, driver's, 381
Life insurance, 75, 78
Lifestyle
    decisions about, 5
    healthy and safe, 344–56
Lighting, 199–200
Line, as a design element, 208, 210–11, 223
Linens, bed and bath, 193, 234–35
Listening, 30, 32–33
Living arrangements, 195, 196
Living room, 234–35
Living wills, 397

Loans, 134–36
    for automobiles, 373, 375–76, 381
    and finance charges, 398–99
Lobbying, 38
Loss leader, 172

Magazines
    computer, 150
    consumer, 150, 155–56
    decorating, 229–32
Magnesium, 297–98
Mail fraud, 146
Mail-order houses, 168–69, 170
Maintenance
    automobile, 384, 385
    household, 194, 235–36, 240–42
Manners, 309–10, 393–95
Markets, food, 318–19
Mass media, 155–56
Mattresses, 189
Maturity, bond, 109
Meals, planning, 302–4, 308–12
Meal service, 308–9
Measurement
    of food ingredients, 332, 333
    of nutrients, 298–301, 305
Meats, 302–3
    grading, 324
    inspection, 324
    preparing, 329
    quality of, 325
    storing, 326
Medical insurance, 75, 76–77
Medical services and products, 356–60
Medicine
    over-the-counter, 353
    prescription, 351, 357–58
Menus, 308, 309, 337
Messages. *See also* Communication
    receiving, 30, 32–34
    sending, 28–31
    types of, 28
Microwave oven, 238, 334, 336
Military service, 40, 55
Milk. *See* Dairy products
Minerals, 297–98
Mobile home, 197, 200
Moist-heat cooking, 327–28
Money. *See* Resources
Money management, 94
Money market account, 109
Money market fund, 109
Money order, 126
Monopoly, 146
Motorcycles, 374
Motorized bike, 374

Index   **429**

Moving, 202, 204
Mutual fund, 109
Mutual savings banks, 106, 135–36

National-brand product, 152
Natural fibers, 253–55
Needs, 12
    hierarchy of, 392
    and shopping, 164
Neighborhoods, evaluating, 199
Niacin, 297, 299, 404–13
Nicotine, 350
No-fault insurance, 384
Noise levels, 201–2, 227
Nonprofit organization, 156–57
NOW account, 121
Nutrient density, 305
Nutrients
    amounts of, 298–301
    and calories, 304–5
    types of, 294–98
Nutrient supplement, 296
Nutrition
    and additives, 322–23
    and fitness, 344–45
    labels, 296, 300
    values of foods, 404–13

Obesity, 305
Office of Consumer Affairs, 157
On-the-job training, 55–57, 82
Open dates, on foods, 323
Open stock (dinnerware, flatware, glassware), 192
Opportunity costs, 17, 164–65
Optical illusion, 208
Organ donor, 361
Ovens, 238, 239, 334, 336
Overdose, drug, 351
Over-the-counter medicine, 353
Overweight, 305

Packing
    clothes, for trip, 284
    to move, 202, 204
Painting, household, 230, 231
Patterns, sewing, 261
Pawnbroker, 135–36
Pay, 47–48
    deductions from, 79–80, 112
    period, 78–79
    severance, 86
Pension plans, 108
Perishables, 311
Personal care products, 285–88
Personal data sheet, 58, 59, 61

Personnel
    departments, 63
    government, offices, 54
Pest control, 241–42
Pets, and rentals, 186, 199
Phosphorous, 297–98, 299, 404–13
Physical abuse, 354–55
Physicians, 353, 358–60
Pictures, for decoration, 230, 231
Pillows, 193
Place setting (dinnerware or flatware), 192, 309
Plants, decorating with, 231–32
Plumbing maintenance, 241
Poisoning
    first aid for, 364
    food, 326–27
    preventing, 355
Pork. *See* Meats
Poultry
    grading, 324
    preparing, 329
    quality of, 325
    storing, 326
Prepared foods, 311, 326–27
Prescription drugs, 351, 357–58
Preservative, 322
Pretreating, before washing, 269, 272
Prices. *See also* Costs; Expenses
    automobile, 380–81
    food, 318, 319, 321
Principles of design, 220–23, 229, 250
Priorities, 15, 96–97, 102
Produce, 319. *See also* Fruits; Vegetables
Product labels, 151–52. *See also* Care labels; Drug labels; Food labels
Profit, 36
Promissory notes, 134
Promotional material, 149–51
Proportion, as a design principle, 220, 223
Proteins, 294–95, 299, 307, 404–13
Public transportation, 371
Pulse, 353, 363
Purchases, 171–73. *See also* Shopping

Rain check, 172
Raises, pay, 48
Range, 238, 239, 334
RDA (Recommended Dietary Allowance), 298–300, 301
Reading, 33–34
Ready-to-wear clothes, 257–59

Real estate, 109
Real estate agencies, 197
Recipes, 311, 320, 331–32
Recommended Dietary Allowance. *See* RDA
Recordkeeping, financial, 112–14
Recycling, clothes, 259–61
Redress, 147–48, 173–74, 176–80
References, personal, 58, 59
Refrigerator, 238–40, 334
Refund policy, 176
Relationships
    adult, 3–4
    at work, 47, 83–85
Renting
    automobiles, 377
    housing, 186–87, 197–202
Repairs
    automobile, 384, 385
    household, 240–41
Repossession, 138
Resources
    computers as, 18
    of family, and decisions, 7
    and forms of transportation, 372–73
    managing, 15–17, 81
    and shopping, 164–65
Resource sharing, 17
Resource substitution, 16
Resource trade, 16–17
Respiratory failure, 363
Responsibilities
    adult, 3
    civic, 37–40
    consumer, 144–48
    job, 72–73
    shopping, 173
Restaurants, 308–10
Resting, for fitness, 346
Résumé. *See* Personal data sheet
Retirement, 107–8
Return for credit policy, 176
Revolving charge account, 131
Rhythm, as a design principle, 220, 221, 223
Riboflavin, 297, 299, 404–13
Ridesharing, 371–72
Roles, adult, 2–3
Room, for rent, 201
Roommates, 195, 196
Rugs, 193–94, 230, 237

Safe-deposit box, 114
Safety
    driving, 348, 356, 370
    and forms of transportation, 370

to prevent accidents, 355–56, 370, 374
of products and services, 145
Salary, 47
Sales, 172–73, 175
Sales personnel, 133, 151, 170
Sales tax, 39–40, 379–81
Salt, 344–45, 415
Saturated fats, 295, 296, 344, 404–13
Savings, 102–7
accounts, 104
Savings and loan associations, 106, 135–36, 381
bonds, 109
certificates, 104–5
Seals of approval, 152–53
Seams, 256, 257, 277, 280
Secondhand stores, 166, 168–69
Security deposits, 186, 202
Self-concept, 10, 347
Self-esteem, 11, 347
Service contract, 154
Services, shopping for, 170
Sewing, 261–62, 275–82
Sewing machine, 261, 276, 277–80
Shades, window, 193, 231
Shampooing
carpeting, 237
hair, 287
Shape, as a design element, 208, 219, 223
Share account, 104
Share certificate account, 104
Sheets, 193
Shelves, 230, 232, 234
Shock, 364
Shoes, 254
Shoplifting, 173
Shopping
by computer, 167
decisions about, 164–66
for food, 318–26
impulse buying, 171, 400–402
places for, 166, 168–70
planning for, 171–72
problems with, 173–74, 176–80
responsibilities, 173
for services, 170
Sign language, 26, 28
Skin care, 286–87
Skin coloring, 251, 252
Small-claims court, 180
Smog, 373
Smoke alarms, 203, 240
Soap, 270–72
Social health, 347
Social Security
benefits, 107

card, 57–58, 70
deductions, 79-80
Solvent, cleaning, 272
Specialty shops, 168–69
Spending record, 97–99
Standard of living, 4–5
Starter set (dinnerware), 192
Stocks, 109
Storage, 190, 199
of clothes, 235, 283
of financial records, 112–14
of food, 192, 326–27
of household belongings, 232–36
Store-brand product, 152
Stress, 352–53
Studio apartment, 197, 201
Sublet, of rental, 202
Substance abuse, 347
Suffocation, 356
Sugars, 295, 345
as food additive, 415
nutritive value of, 410–11
Suicide, 354, 360
Supermarkets, 318–19
Supervisors, working with, 72–73, 83, 84
Supply and demand, 36
Synthetic fibers, 253–55

Tables, 190
Talking or speaking, 28, 29
Tax allowance, 74
Tax-deferred annuity, 108
Taxes, 39–40
income, 39, 73–74, 80, 111–12
sales, on automobiles, 379–81
Tax exemption, 74
Teeth and gums, care of, 287–88, 360
Telephone
manners, 395
sales, 170
and telecommunications, 27
use, for applying for a job, 58
Telephone "hotlines"
for emotional problems, 354, 360
for physically abused, 355
Temporary employment agencies, 56
Textiles, household, 192–94, 234, 237. See also Fabrics
Texture, as a design element, 208, 218–19, 223
Thiamine, 297, 299, 404–13
Time. See Resources

Time schedule, for meals, 337–38
Tipping, 310, 394
Title, automobile, 379
Tobacco, 350–51
Tolerance, alcohol, 348
Towels, 193, 234
Trade and professional organizations, 155, 176, 403
Traffic flow, in home, 226–27
Transportation, 370–73, 374. See also Automobiles
Trash compactor, 337
Traveler's check, 127
Trends
in fashion, 250
and goals, 14
Truth in Lending Act, 129

UL (Underwriters' Laboratories), 152, 192, 194
Underweight, 305
Underwriters' Laboratories. See UL
Unemployment compensation, 86
Unfurnished rentals, 197
Uniforms, job, 249
Unit pricing, 321, 401
Universal Product Code, 318–19
Unsaturated fats, 295
U.S. Cooperative Extension Service, 158
USDA (U.S. Department of Agriculture), food grading, 324
Used automobiles, 378–81
Used clothing, 259
U.S. Postal Service, 146, 403
U.S. RDAs, 300
Utensils, kitchen, 187, 190
Utilities, 187

Vacuum cleaners, 194, 236–37
Value, color, 212, 251
Values, personal, 12–13, 164
Vegetables, 302–3, 319, 324
nutritive values of, 410–13
preparing, 327–28
storing, 326
Vegetarians, 318
Vitamin A, 297, 299, 404–13
Vitamin C. See Ascorbic acid
Vitamins, 295–97, 299–300, 301, 307
added to foods, 322–23
in foods, 404–13
Vocational testing, 50
Voting, 37–38

Index **431**

Wage, 47
Wage earner, 2, 34, 39
Wage-earner plan, 138
Wage garnishment, 134, 136–38
Wallpaper, 230, 231
Walls, decorating, 230, 231
Wants, 13
Wardrobe, 248–49. *See also* Clothing
    classics, 250
    fads, 250
Warranties, 153–55
Washing, clothes, 256, 268–75

Water, 298
Water softener, 272
Water-soluble vitamins, 296–97
Weight, body, 304–8, 344, 345
Wills, 397
Window coverings, 193–94, 230–31
Withdrawal sickness, 351
Work. *See* Job
Work cooperative programs, 57
Worker's compensation insurance, 77–78
Work experience, 52

Work policies, 72
Work record, 80–86, 88
Work-style preferences, 50, 51, 52
Writing, 30
Written warranty, 153
W-2 form, 112
W-4 form, 73

Yard maintenance, 242

Zinc, 297–98